One Foot in Heaven

Woman and Gender

The Middle East and the Islamic World

Editors

Margot Badran
Valentine Moghadam

VOLUME 5

One Foot in Heaven

Narratives on Gender and Islam in Darfur, West-Sudan

By

Karin Willemse

BRILL

LEIDEN • BOSTON
2007

This book is printed on acid-free paper.

Library of Congress Cataloging-in-Publication data

A C.I.P. record for this book is available from the Library of Congress.

ISSN 1570-7628
ISBN 978 90 04 15011 9

PRINTED IN THE NETHERLANDS

Heaven is under the feet of mothers

(*Hadith*)

There are three places for a woman: in her father's house, in her husband's house or in her grave

(*Hadith*)

To the women of Darfur, in particular those of Kebkabiya,
whose grace, courage, and resilience inspired me,
that they, and their families, may persevere, and survive this war;

To Leen Vroegindeweij who died too young, too soon.

CONTENTS

PART TWO

SETTLING

BIOGRAPHIC NARRATIVES AS TEXTS-IN-CONTEXT

ACKNOWLEDGEMENTS

To acknowledge those who contributed to the genesis of this book brings back memories, happy and sad, of a journey past. Mapping memories is like arranging snapshots; it means to recollect experiences coherently, while in fact they are patchy and lack chronology. So if I have forgotten to mention anyone here, please blame it on a lapse in my memory, not because I feel the less indebted.

In the first place I want to thank the women of Kebkabiya, some of whom will become known to you in the course of this book. I can never thank them enough for their hospitality, protection, joy, trust, care, warmth, and generosity. I want to thank in particular Hauwaya Tamba Shai, Fauwzia Khatir, Zeinab Abbas, Munira, Mahalla and Sikina Adam Rujaal, Helima Nur, Nawal Hassan Osman. Thanks are due also to Umm Selema and her daughters Aliya, Adola and Hikma, all the market women on the main market of Kebkabiya, especially Sikina, Rhogheiya, Hanan, Iqbal and Nawal. With fond memories I remember the *sittaat* Fatna, Farduz, Al-Watif, Hauwa, Zeinab, Khalthoum. I also think of all the other female teachers of the Intermediary School for Girls as well as those teaching at the Primary Schools for girls in Kebkabiya with gratitude.

I also can not thank enough Joke Schrijvers and Peter Geschiere. They were both enthusiastic and inspiring guides on my academic path, and became friends along the way. At last I can officially express my feelings of heartfelt gratitude for their encouraging and stimulating supervision, for setting an example and for their faith in me. I also thank Lidwien Kapteijns, fellow 'Darfur' scholar, for her critical and stimulating comments, and her friendship. Anke van der Kwaak and Tine Davids, apart from best friends you were enthusiastic, critical and caring colleagues all the way.

I thank the Netherlands Foundation for the Advancement of Tropical Research (WOTRO), the CNWS Research School of African, Asian and Latin-American Studies (formerly the Centre of Non-Western Studies) for their generous financial and infra-structural support for the research in the 1990s. The Faculty of History and Arts of the Erasmus

University Rotterdam I thank for facilitating a sabbatical. I am grateful to the Netherlands Institute for Advanced Study in the Humanities and Social Sciences (of the Royal Netherlands Academy of the Sciences) for making me a fellow-in-residence (2005–2006), which allowed me 'space to think'—and write: especially Eline van der Ploeg, Anne Simpson, Petry Kievit and Kathy van Vliet for all their help and support in turning my Ph. D. into this book.

In Sudan, I owe Dr. Paul Wani, Dr. Zeinab B. Bakri, and more in particular Dr. Salah es-Sahazali, Tamadur Ahmed Khalid and Cor Hacking of the Development Studies and Research Centre at the university of Khartoum; Dr. Ali Karrar at the National Records Office; Dr. Balghis Badri and Dr. Someiya of the Ahfad University for Women, Umdurman; and Salah Nour el-Huda for the personal and academic help they extended to me. The Oxfam project members in Darfur at that time are owed my deep gratitude, and I thank you for your friendship, especially Karin de Jonge, Malik Adam Idris, Saleh Abdel Majid, Farrah Omar Bello, Yussuf At-Tayeb, and Dr. Adam. Thanks also to the support of the staff of the Documentation Centre of the Africa Studies Centre, Leiden University (The Netherlands); Jane Hogan of the Sudan Library of Durham University (England); my colleagues at the CNWS; my fellow Africanists, especially José van Santen, of the Africa Ph. D. seminar of Prof. dr. P.L. Geschiere of the Department of Cultural Anthropology; and my colleagues at the Department of History, Erasmus University Rotterdam, in particular Alex van Stipriaan, Gijsbert Oonk, Henk Schulte-Nordholt, Joep á Campo, and Wieke Vink.

My manuscript would never have evolved into this book if not for the help of Henk S. Wijma of Henk Wijma Grafisch Design for drawing Hajja's maps; Johan de Smedt for his photographs; Marla Seidell for the language editing; and Trudy Kamperveen at Brill Publishers for her professional advice and her patience.

Gert Willemse, Riny Willemse, Yoke Zandbergen, Marleen de Smedt, Anke van der Kwaak, Tine Davids, Lilian Bezemer, Judith Vroom, thanks for everything. And in memoriam Leen Vroegindeweij, my love, my home base and eternal support, who suddenly died in May 2006 when this book was about ready to go to press. Arend Nour and I will remember you, us, always.

Karin Willemse
Leiden, June 2007

PREFACE

The research on which this book is based was finished before 9/11 and before the Darfur War reached the level of violence it has suffered since 2002. Although every day brings bad tidings and horrible news, and although it will give no solace to the families who have fallen victim to the massacres and other violent attacks, I know that the women who figure in this book are still alive. One of the reasons is that Kebkabiya, the town where I lived in 1990–1995 for about one and a half years altogether, is a garrison town. Even though Misteriya, the *Janjawiid* control center and stronghold of one of its warlords, Musa Hilal, is located in Kebkabiya district; and even when many of the attacks on villages took place in precisely this area, people living inside the town have so far been relatively safe.

To this function as a garrison town Kebkabiya allegedly owes its name. Gustav Nachtigal, the German traveler who visited Darfur in 1874, credited the founding of the town to 'King Bokkor' who ruled from approximately 1700 to 1720. He fought King, or Sultan, Arus from the neighbouring Wadai Sultanate in a battle near the place that was to become Kebkabiya, as Nachtigal states: "He was victorious in this battle, in which the Wadai warriors threw their shields away (Qabqabiya means 'they threw their shields away')".[1] Alternatively, this founding myth is ascribed to the son of this Sultan Bokkor (or Bukr), Sultan Tayrab (ruling 1752–1785). He brought the Sultanic court from Turra in the mountains of Jebel Marra to Shoba, some five kilometers from the Wadi where his garrison camped at present-day Kebkabiya: in this version Tayrab's soldiers 'lay down their shields' after a battle was called off. Whatever version is correct, Kebkabiya has retained its importance as a protected town to this day. Also its importance as a trading post dates back centuries as it was located on several of the trading routes from West-Africa to the Maghreb, Mecca, and on one

[1] Gustav Nachtigal, (1879–1889). *Sahara and Sudan*, Volume IV 'Wadai and Darfur', [368]: Translated and annotated by Allan and Humphrey Fisher, (1971: 281), Hurst: London.

of the most famous caravan routes, the *darb al-arba'iin* or forty-days road, up to Cairo.[2] Al-Tunisi, who traveled in 1799 with the caravan of his father from Cairo to Darfur, described Kebkabiya in 1803: "The environs of which reminded me of the country places in Egypt; but the town is better built, richer, and more lively. Many foreigners are seen there. The natives are, for the most part, wealthy merchants, having a great number of slaves, with which they trade".[3]

In this town, about two hundred years later, I conducted the anthropological research that forms the basis for this book. It is about a society that has always been in the process of change and transformation, but whose survival has become threatened by the recent events in this region. It is not my place to foretell if the lifestyle and culture that I represent in the following pages have become extinct in the process. I do, however, want to express the hope that Kebkabiya may live up to its name: that the people of Darfur, from whatever background, and in particular the leaders who are waging the current war, will find the courage to make peace and the wisdom to keep it: and will have a government that will sustain it.

Originally this book was written as a Ph.D. Thesis with the same title. My goal was to have the empirical research process guide the theoretical insights needed to understand local dynamics. The current publication has been updated. Moreover, I have added introductions to each of the three parts in which the book is divided. The introductions of the parts contextualise the concepts I used while looking for meanings and alternative understandings of local events and narratives. In addition, Chapter 8 contains an epilogue in which I reflect on the war in Darfur since 2003.

I dedicate this book to the women of Darfur, for it is women who are most important in the processes of reconciliation and survival. I think in particular of those incredible women in Kebkabiya who hosted me and made me feel at home and whom I have come to admire for their beauty and strength, articulateness and determination, hospitality and sense of humor. They trusted me to take their narratives across borders so their views would be known and they have encouraged and inspired me to write this book.

---

[2] Apart from Nachtigal, see also for example O'Fahey (1980: 130–133).

[3] Quoted in Alex de Waal (1989: 67), ref., el Tunisi, M. (1854). *Travels of an Arab merchant in Soudan.* Abridged and trans. B. St. John, (London: Chapman and Hall).

GLOSSARY

Notes on transliteration and translation of non-English words

This book is based on oral sources. Turning narratives into texts presents huge problems with regard to the spelling of names and phrases in local language. Moreover, the pronunciation of the colloquial Sudanese Arabic differs in some instances considerably from the standard Arabic. My intention is to stay as close as possible to the original context in which the narratives were told and listened to. Therefore my transcription does not correspond to the rules required for writing in the Arabic language. I follow the policy of the International Institute for the Study of Islam in the Modern World, Leiden University, to give priority to easy pronunciation for the English-speaking lay public.

For some Arabic words, which appear often in Arabic transcription, such as *shari'a* or *Qur'an*, I opt for an orthodox transcription. For names and places, I use the spelling as found in most maps or again closest to the local pronunciation. Therefore 'Kebkabiya' and 'Sinin' instead of the long vowels with which these are written in Arabic documents: but also *Janjawiid* and *darb al-arba'iin* as this is how these names appeared in most publications. For names of places where different kinds of transcriptions exist, such as for example El-Geneina or Al-Junaynah, I opt for the use of Al- and the most often used transcription, in this case Al-Geneina. For names of persons, which start with 'al' I also use a capital in order to indicate that the prefix belongs to the surname, as in Al-Bashir, or Al-Turabi. For plurals of Arabic or colloquial words, I add an 's' to the singular to make the text accessible for non-Arabists. Only when a person gives such a plural in a narrative, I give the plural with a reference in a note or in the main text. In general I refer to the meaning of a local or Arabic word or phrase as soon as it appears in the text. In the glossary those words are to be found which are mentioned in more than one place and in the analyses.

Abu/Abba	father. Also used in indicating a married man: the name of the eldest child (son) is added.
Agit	the signing of the marriage contract in the presence of an *imam*
Ahl	group of people. In this case members of an extended family (patrilineal and/or matrilineal)
Ajina	lumpy drink consisting of milk, sorghum, sugar
Ajr	religious merit
Al-umma al-islamiya	the righteous Islamic community
Ansar	'assistants' after those people of Medina who converted and helped the prophet Mohammed in spreading Islam. In the context of the Sudan: the followers of al-Mahdi. Nowadays the members of the UMMA, political party
Aragi	a knee long shirt worn by men over a wide pantaloon (Fur local dress)
Asida	thick sticky porridge daily made of sorghum or millet
Baksheesh	a tip or free gift in money or kind
Beni	my son. Also used for indicating an ethnic group
Dakwa	peanut butter used in salads and sauces
Darb el-arba'iin	forty days road. Trade route between West Africa and Egypt, which runs through North Darfur.
Dilka	local scrub made of sorghum, scents and oil
Faqih	a religious teacher. Also used for healers and diviners (*fuqara* pl)
Fitna	sexual promiscuity, chaos, social disruption. Also 'femme fatale'
Funjaal	a porcelain cup for drinking coffee. The coffee grains are read for fortune telling
Gabila	tribe
Gubba	burial mound of an important person, mostly a saint
Gusl	the ritual washing by women to purify themselves before praying, especially after menstruation, sex or giving birth
Gutiya	circular built wattle-and-daub room
Hadith	a saying referring to (the time of) the prophet Mohammed or about events during his life. There are thousands of these sayings
Hajj	pilgrimage to Mecca. One of the 'pillars' or religious duties of every Muslim
Hajja/Hajj	an honorary title given to a woman/man who has fulfilled the obligation of the pilgrimage to Mecca. Also used as a polite way to address an elderly woman or man
Halaal	advisable or preferable on religious grounds

Hanafi	one of the two law schools which are applied in the Sudan
Haraam	forbidden on religious grounds.
Hijab	amulet, head veil
Ilm	knowledge
Jahanna	hell
Janna	paradise
Jellaba	a worker and a trader from the Nile Valley. In Darfur also more generally used for people from the Nile Valley
Jihad	the holy war of Muslims against the unlawful. Also effort to keep to the right religious path to God
Jir	fine powdery millet
Karama	alms. Also used for a ritual meal
Khalwa	a Qur'anic school
Khawadya	foreigners (from the west). *khawadiya* (f) / *khawadyaat* (pl)
Kisra	thin sour pancakes
Kom	a pile often used as unity for selling fruits or vegetables
Kufar	unbeliever
Ledgna sha'abiya	popular committee(s)
Madrassa	school
Maliki	one of the two law schools which are applied in the Sudan
Merissa	a local beer made of sorghum or millet
Mutabakh	a matted food cover
Naas	to 'belong' to your compound (people of),
Qadi	the judge of the *shari'a* court
Rakuba	a shelter built of wood, millet stalks and/or burlap
Sala(t)	prayer, five times a day
Sanduq	box. Also used for a rotating credit association
Semaya	name giving ceremony for a baby seven days after giving birth
Semen	clarified butter
Shahada	vow of belief
Shanta	bag or suitcase. Also used to indicate the bride price which comes in a suitcase
Shari'a	the Islamic law
Shi'a	the smaller of the two main divisions of Muslim believers. Split over the issue of the succession of prophet Mohammed
Sunna	a practice prescribed on religious grounds (mostly the *Qur'an*)
Sunni	the largest group of the two main divisions of Muslims
Sura	chapter from the *Qur'an*

Talaaq	divorce. This term or a variation based on the same root (t, l, q) used by the husband for renouncing a marriage
Tobe	the typical Sudanese outer garment (or veil) for women. It consists of a six to nine meter cloth, which is often made of a colourful and thin fabric that women wrap loosely around themselves, over their dresses or trousers (also spelled as *tawb*)
Umm	mother. Also used for indicating a married woman: the name of her eldest child is then added
Umma	the community of righteous believers. Based on the followers of prophet Mohammed. Also: the UMMA party (Sudanese political party)
Ummahaat/Ummayaat	motherhood
Usra	a core family (persons sharing a household)
Wa'iz	a religious advisor, often wandering around the countryside to give religious speeches
Wadi	a dry riverbed, which carries water in the rainy season
Zaka(t)	taxation, often about ten percent of the income. A religious duty or 'pillar' for the upkeep of poor Muslims

LIST OF MAPS AND ILLUSTRATIONS

Sudan Maps

Illustrations (courtesy of Henk S. Wijma of Henk Wijma Graphic Design)

Photographs (courtesy of Johan de Smedt: photographs no. 1, 2, 5, 6, 10, 11)*

* Fold-out maps and photographs can be found between pages 38 and 39.

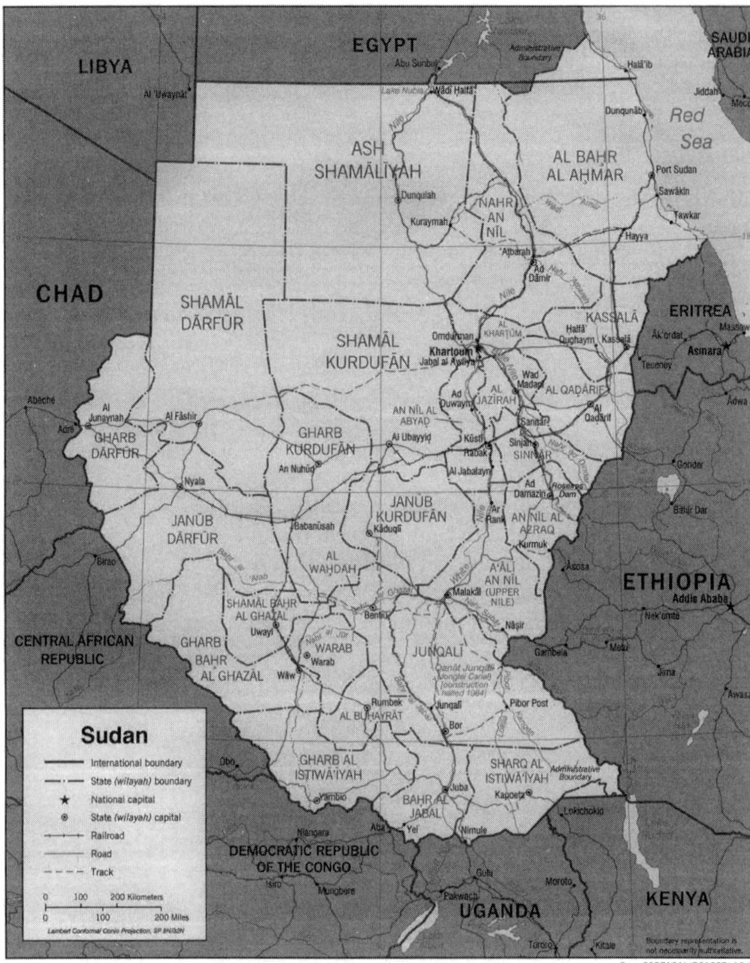

Sudan Map 1: Sudan (Political), 2000.
Source: U.S. Central Intelligence Agency.

SETTING OUT FOR RESEARCH

> *Bismillahi ar-Rahman, ar-Rahim*, In the name of God, the Compassionate, the Merciful... Ever since this government has come into existence, it has been very aware of the importance of religious issues. It has created many new offices in the Ministry of Religious Affairs in order to supervise religious issues. It also founded *ad-da'wa al-islamiya*, the Islamic Call. Allah told us to call everyone to Islam everyday, and He told some of us to be responsible to advise others on Islam...[1]

This introduction by a local *faqih*, a religious teacher, is the opening of a series of religious speeches delivered by a so-called *ledgna sha'abiya*, or popular committee, in Kebkabiya town, Darfur, West-Sudan, on December 10, 1991. As the dry season in Darfur—which lasts from September to May—is a suitable period for travel, the five members of the popular committee had come down from Kutum, the district capital. Their assignment was to inform the population of Kebkabiya about proper conduct according to Islamic principles, based on the viewpoint of the new Islamist regime that had come to power in June 1989. These types of speeches delivered by popular committees and government institutions and officials were prevalent throughout the duration of my two fieldwork periods in Kebkabiya, from October 1990 until June 1992.

That afternoon, there was an announcement on the market that the popular committee from Kutum would deliver several speeches. I was chatting with Hajja, my host, at her spot on the market place, when members of the local popular committee used loudspeakers to call Kebkabiya's population to join the meeting. I decided to postpone my planned trip to Al-Fasher and attend the meeting. That evening at eight o'clock, I joined the small crowd of women huddled together near the northern mud wall of the main mosque together with Nura, Hajja's daughter. Although the meeting was held on a market day when many people from outside Kebkabiya had come into town as well, the crowd

[1] The speeches, which I recorded, were delivered in Arabic and translated into English by Sa'adiya, my local interpreter. I have chosen some excerpts that seem most important for introducing the context of my research. See further chapter 1.

was quite small. While I was walking over to where most of the women had found a place to sit, the amplifier was adjusted and we listened to the following speech:

> Greetings to the people of Kebkabiya Town, I greet you, and the greetings I use are Islamic. We are losing them in favour of those that came from our enemies, the first enemies of Islam. *Sabah al-kher*, good morning, *masah al-kher*, good evening, *ahlaan*, welcome; these greetings are not Islamic: the Jews used them in the past in Al-Medina. We copied them. They don't want Islam to grow. From now on everybody should greet with Islamic greetings, like *salaam alaikum*, peace be upon you. Allah told us that if somebody greets you with an Islamic greeting, you should reply or use an even better one. If you reply *alaikum salaam*, and peace be upon you, you have ten credit points, if you add *ar-rahmatu*, mercy, you get twenty points and adding again *barakatu*, blessing, gives you thirty.[2] If you greet fifty people like this, it will give you fifty times these points. This is a present from Allah: so don't lose it. It is your duty to use these greetings and to teach your children, your wives and your families the right greetings. If we follow this principle we will become *al-umma al-islamiya*, the righteous Islamic community…

At first the problematisation of greetings sounded preposterous to me. When, on subsequent visits, other popular committees addressed this issue as well, I realised it served as a way of discussing the correct behaviour of Muslims in general. By referring to the 'beginning of Islam', the focus is simultaneously on the main political goal of the current Islamist, or 'fundamentalist' government: to cleanse the country of impure and improper habits like using un-Islamic greetings. These only divert the minds and hearts of the people from the one and only 'right' way as laid down by the teachings of the prophet Mohammed: the Islamic way or *shari'a*. This media offensive formed part of the 'Islamic Call', *ad-da'wa al-islamiya*, or 'Mission' as quoted above. The main goal of this Mission, or what I call the 're-Islamization Project' was not only to change state politics but also to transform the Sudanese society at large into a righteous Islamic community, or *al-umma al-islamiya*.

This political project was instigated by the junta, which had come to power via a coup on June 30, 1989 and was led by the paratroop officer Mohammed Omar Al-Beshir. However, the man in control was said to be Hassan Al-Turabi, the leader of the National Islamic Front (NIF),

---

[2] The complete reply is "wa alaikum as-salam wa rahmatu (Allahi) wa barakatu", meaning "may the peace, mercy, and blessing of Allah be upon you".

which had only been founded in April 1985. The influence of Al-Turabi on Sudanese politics had a longer history, however. The NIF is in fact an offshoot of the Muslim Brotherhood[3] in which Hassan Al-Turabi has been actively involved since 1965[4] when he was rallying for votes during the elections under the name of the Islamic Charter Front (El-Affendi 1991: 89). He attained the post of attorney general and Minister of Justice in 1979 under the military rule of Nimeiri (1969–1985). In this capacity he prepared the so-called *hudud*, or punishments of criminal acts based on an Islamist interpretation of the *shari'a*, or Islamic law, which were implemented in 1983 (Salih 1991: 62, El-Affendi 1991: 112–114, Woodward 1990: 167, 184).[5] Al-Turabi retained his position even when Nimeiri was ousted in 1985.[6] Therefore the implementation of the *shari'a* on the first of January 1991, over a year after the new Islamist government came to power, did not come as a surprise.[7]

On March 22nd 1991, all newly established federal states (except for the southern state) accepted the *shari'a* as the basis for lawmaking and lawkeeping practices. Moreover, as the government considered that the Sudan was not properly Islamized everywhere, it instigated what it called *al-mashru'al-hadari*, or the Islamist Civilization Project in order to 'purify' Islamic beliefs and practices in the Sudan (Al-Ahmadi

[3] Called *Ikhwan*, later *Ikhwam al-Muslimoon*, the Muslim Brotherhood in the Sudan was founded in 1948, modeled after the Muslim Brotherhood founded in 1928 by Hassan al-Banna in Egypt and the *Jamaat al-Islami* set up by Abu Al-Ala Al-Maududi in India in 1941. The influence of the Muslim Brothers dwindled when the socialist Nimeiri came to power through a military coup in 1969. In 1984 Al-Turabi founded the National Islamic Front, which is basically an offshoot of the Muslim Brotherhood (Simone, 1994: 68–69).

[4] Turabi had been member of several bodies within the *Ikhwan* from the beginning, but could not actively participate due to his attendance at London University for an M.A. and later the Sorbonne in Paris for a Ph.D. He joined the Muslim Brothers openly during demonstrations against the military junta in 1964. His higher education turned out to be an asset in gaining a prominent position in the movement, which became evident only in 1969 (Al-Ahmadi 2003: 89; El-Affendi, 1991: 65–76, 131–145).

[5] The Islamic laws proved to be the major stumbling block to settle the dispute in the south by the democratic regime in 1985 (El-Affendi 1991: 131; Sharif 1991: 50–73).

[6] Al-Turabi himself was ousted as speaker of parliament by president Omar al-Bashir in December 1999; after a power struggle between the two, his political offices closed down in May 2000. I will return to this issue in the conclusion.

[7] The *shari'a*, the Islamic law, was officially introduced as the Civil and Penal Code on the first of February 1991, and implemented on the 22nd of March 1991, except for in the three southern states (Harir et.al. 1994: 272). However, the Penal Code was applied since 1983, the so-called *hudud* or September laws, under Nimeiri.

2003: 28). The speeches the popular committee delivered at Kebkabiya formed part of this Civilization, or rather re-Islamization, Project.

During the course of my research I began to realise that these speeches offer a key to understanding both the moral discourse of the current Islamist government in the Sudan and the alternatives open to the population of Darfur to act upon that discourse. The different messages put forward by these speeches exposed the new government's perspectives on moral issues and on policy directions, all of which were based on a particular interpretation of the *Qur'an* and other Islamic principles. At the same time these messages, in a local context, proved open to multiple interpretations, leaving room for alternative perspectives for the population of Kebkabiya to reflect and act upon. It is precisely this combination of establishing political viability and the legitimisation of power relations on the one hand and, on the other hand, the ambivalence of the same messages as to how to relate to these power relations, which intrigued me.

The new moral discourse had a profound influence on local power relationships, on the narratives of those people I engaged in my research and on my own position during the course of my research. Therefore, the speeches delivered on that windy night in early December 1991 are important in order to understand these reflections and actions and thus the direction of my research.

For me, the most interesting was the influence of this discourse on the narratives of working women, whom I wanted to focus on in my research. Before I turn to these speeches in Chapter 1, however, I want to elaborate on the focus and goal of my research. I will begin by reflecting on some events that took place during my first fieldwork period as they profoundly influenced the choices I eventually made over the course of my research. The theoretical, methodological and representational nature of these choices is thereby considered.

The First Fieldwork Period: Perspectives of Working Women

I set out for Kebkabiya for my first fieldwork period in October 1990 with Johan, my life partner, and with Yasmin, a woman I had met previously when working as a consultant in another area of Darfur. Johan also used our stay to finish writing up his research on environmental problems in Tanzania. Yasmin accompanied me in order to assist me with my research and to undertake some of her own. I divided my fieldwork into two periods, both taking place during the dry season from September to May (1990–1991 and 1991–1992). This was related to my intention to work with seasonal migrant women who came from the surrounding plains to the mountains to hire themselves out as agricultural labourers during those months, after their own rain-fed crops were harvested. I had witnessed this phenomenon during earlier fieldwork in Jebel Marra, a volcanic mountain where the people had both rain-fed staple agriculture and irrigated cash-crop agriculture (cf. Willemse 1991).

As it turned out, we never left Kebkabiya. At first the Head of Security proclaimed the area around Kebkabiya 'insecure' because Chadian guerrilla fighters allegedly camped there, and had mined some of the area. "They might take you for a French spy", he explained, referring to the punitive expeditions into Darfur by the Chadian army of the then-president Habré. One of Habré's officers, Idris Debi had defected from the government army and had sought refuge in Darfur among his 'fellow' Zaghawa, a semi-nomadic group of camel owners that wanders in the area which stretches across the boundaries of Northern Darfur and Northern Chad and Southern Libya (Harir 1994; Prunier 2005: 63, 69; Tubiana & Tubiana: 1977). In December 1990, after Debi took over the government in Chad, the Chadian presence in Darfur slowly decreased, but we still did not receive permission to leave Kebkabiya and we could only guess as to the reasons. For example, the many incidents allegedly related to 'ethnic conflicts' and highway robberies, which increased with the onset of the famine; or the implementation of *shari'a* law on the first of January 1991, which drew many demonstrations, both pro-government and anti-foreigner, in many places, including Kebkabiya.

Furthermore, with the build-up of the Gulf War since August 1990 during which Sudan sided with Iraq, Johan and I were seen as potentially 'hostile' subjects, which further diminished our chances to follow the migrating women: in January the threshing season in the lowlands would be over, and migration to the fertile mountain range would begin. I also wondered whether the women would be migrating that year at all in such an unstable and insecure area. As January wore on, and the chances to venture out of the town did not improve, Yasmin and I decided to investigate other possible research subjects within Kebkabiya itself, although our focus remained on 'working women'. Neither of us had experienced working in a town. In order to get a better idea of the composition of the population and of themes relevant to working women we decided to do a survey, albeit reluctantly. My former experiences of conducting a survey had taught me that working with structured questionnaires generally renders the research situation more hierarchical than necessary. There is far less space for dialogue and interaction, aspects which I think have major importance in research with and for women. Moreover, the results of the survey I did conduct during my former research had proved unreliable, precisely due to the formal context that was evoked by my direct questioning, the use of pen and paper, and the de-contextualized nature of the information asked.

However, our accommodation was located far from the centre of town in a newly built ward. Frequent trips through the sandy streets of Kebkabiya in the blistering heat did little to alleviate our confusion over the composition of the wards, even though Kebkabiya is a relatively small town of about 10,000 inhabitants.[8] In addition, the reluctance of government officers to allow us to draw from their material made a survey one of the few alternatives to understand more about the build-up of the town, if only to allay our insecurity about how to go about our research.

We drew up a list of 220 randomly chosen households, which constituted approximately 10 percent of households in each of the ten wards. We used a register of names from the Department of Co-operations, recently updated due to a change in the distribution system. This system works with ration cards for allotting subsidised goods like sugar, tea, soap, etc. to each officially registered family and tends to be quite accurate. With the help of the female teachers who were living with their families in different wards, we conducted the survey. On one occasion, a female teacher named Maryoma and I were in a quarter of the town situated at the outskirts of Kebkabiya across the *wadi*, or riverbed, where many of the poorer families lived. On request, the *sheikh* of that ward had notified the women on the list, but on arrival it seemed as if all the women of the ward had turned out. We learned that the women of the quarter presumed we were representing the *zakat*—obligatory religious tax—office, a recently established 'alms-giving' governmental organisation. Afraid to miss their share of the *zakat*, as had happened on a previous occasion, almost all the women had decided to await our arrival.

---

[8] The figures I received from different sources differ with respect to the number of

Most of the women appeared less well off than other women I had met so far; their faces were worn-out and tired. I felt embarrassed that I had not come to give them money or work, but 'just' to interview them. It made me aware of the futility of my research. As a result I was rather upset as I asked Maryoma to explain to the women that I had come to Kebkabiya to ask them about their lives and that I hoped to write a book. At this point I was prepared to leave it at that and to give up on the survey. To my surprise some of the women who stood nearest us said:

> Oh, you write a book! Well, that is fine: Tell the world how we suffer, tell them how hard we work, every day again, without the help of our men or of the government.

These women started to explain to those standing out of earshot what our visit was about. Some of these women nodded their heads, shouting things like: "*Ya khawadyia*, foreign woman, take us, we have something to tell you!" Or: "Take my story with you in your airplane!" Others simply walked off. Maryoma and I decided to pursue the survey with the women on our list and to compensate them financially for their loss of time. These talks were even more remarkable. We anticipated their references to the hardship of daily survival, but their recurrent criticism of the new government, which was more often than not blamed for their living conditions, was revealing.

Ultimately, the survey provided us with information on several issues; for example the predominance of female-headed households, the ethnic composition of each ward and population data on aspects such as age, marital status and educational backgrounds of the women and children in the households.[9] However, my most beneficial insight was of a different nature. Until that point I had been quite at a loss as to a new focus for my research. The politically volatile situation, due to ethnic conflicts, security problems and the Islamization policy of the government, in combination with increasing proof that a famine was imminent made me seriously question the salience of pursuing academic research in such an unstable environment. The need to change both the direction and location of the research made me feel dispirited. I had hoped, in collaboration with Yasmin, to share the results of our research with the

---

inhabitants, both of Kebkabiya town and district. In Chapter 2 I will elaborate on these figures.

[9] See annex for some of the results of the survey.

women involved for the possible betterment of their economic situation. With no experience in urban settings, neither Yasmin nor I could easily see a way to refocus our research, especially within a town where our movements were so tightly controlled.

However, the women in that under-privileged ward of Kebkabiya reminded me of the Fur women from my former research in Jebel Marra (cf. Willemse 1991). The Kebkabiya women had a similar oppositional attitude towards the government. In Jebel Marra, the women would ask me if I was going to 'my country' whenever I went for a short visit to the plains surrounding the mountain. When I explained that my country was overseas and that Sudan was supposed to be their country, they would laugh at my naivety. What had the Sudanese government ever done for them, but take things from them? Government officials would come for taxes on everything they owned and take their young men who would migrate to their towns. The few educated sons and daughters would eventually remain in the Sudan and would be lost to them as well. No, in their view Sudan was not their country.

The conception of Sudan as an 'other', a hostile, country has a historical foundation as Darfur had become part of the Sudan only since 1916, when the British declared an end to the Fur Sultanate and added it as a province to the Sudan. Since then Darfur has been virtually neglected in terms of investments in political, economic and social development, a situation that continued after Independence in 1956 (Grawert 1998: 167–205; Harir 1994: 155). The Fur women of Jebel Marra were summarising a century-old experience of domination and opposition to a government that nominally counted them as its citizens but had done little to improve their living conditions.

I was surprised that the women I interviewed reflected on their government in a similar vein, while living in a town such as Kebkabiya, which had a high-profile governmental presence; which had a hospital, several primary schools and two intermediary schools, one for boys and one for girls, a thriving market place and some established development projects. I was intrigued by the basic oppositional stance the Kebkabiya women had toward that same government that seemed to provide them with these services. A government which, despite waging a one-million-dollar war with its own citizens in the Southern part of Sudan, would put such an effort into effectuating an ideal, of the righteous Islamic community, the *umma*, via regulating, in particular, the conduct of its female citizens. The amount of money and energy required to maintain this control was disconcerting considering Sudan's bankrupt economy (Harir 1994: 15; Lake 1990: 181).[10] Why would the Sudanese government do this?

The memories of those boisterous, strong and independent women I had come to know and cherish in Jebel Marra triggered another memory. The somewhat bewildered looks of people 'back home' when I informed them that I was intending to do research in the Sudan. Their mental image of 'Sudan' was one generated by the western media; an African country stricken by famine and war and simultaneously an Islamic state with its supposed oppression particularly of women who were depicted as powerless and submissive. Without wanting to deny the plight of the majority of Sudanese people, this image did not do justice to the strong, independent manner of most Sudanese women. Darfurian women, especially, who are renowned for their energetic demeanour and independent attitude concerning economic and social affairs, did not fit into this image at all. Those were the women I had come to admire and love for their humour, inventiveness and intelligence (cf. Willemse, 1991). The women I met in Kebkabiya radiated this same strong, almost proud attitude. My fascination and determination to try and adjust images of the 'submissive Islamic woman' or the 'downtrodden African woman' was reactivated.

I realised that if I were to pursue my research within Kebkabiya I would not understand the condition of the apparently underprivileged working women without consideration of their daily lives, hopes and perspectives *in relation to* the moral discourse and policies of the current government. No matter how precarious my own position was due to international politics and the local government's suspicion about my intentions, I decided that I could not be neutral. Furthermore I realised that although I might not be able to help the women in changing their circumstances, I could attempt to put their views into writing, even though this at first seemed trivial when compared to the enormous problems the women confronted. I decided to write about the women's views because they might never otherwise have an opportunity to articulate their perspectives or wishes. With no literacy skills, I assumed they could not enter into discussions or find ways into public opinion to formulate their views and so defend their rights. Those women whose lives were so visibly touched by the effects of

[10] Africa Confidential gave the double amount (31 July 1992) not counting the damage to livestock, agriculture lands and assets and human losses.

the re-Islamization project should have a major part in my research. I wanted to present them as actors in their own right who actively reflect on the political, economic and social processes influencing their chances for daily survival and not just as victims of fate. By giving space to their opinions and hopes, I wanted to try and gain an understanding into the ways in which power and resistance works in this particular situation.

The focus on the experiences of women in relation to the local power structures does not have an extensive tradition in studies that have been done so far on Darfur. Highly interesting are the travel accounts, particularly of Al-Tunisi (1845, 1851); Browne (1806); Burckhardt (1922); Nachtigal (1971). Most work is on political history, state formation and intellectual and religious facets (cf. Beck 1998: 254–280) of well-known regimes of Darfur: such as the Keira or Fur Sultanate in particular by O'Fahey (1971, 1980a), (see also Fadl Hassan & Doornbos 1977); the *Turkiyya* under Zubayr Pasha (cf. O'Fahey 1980 a & b); and the *Mahdiyya* (O'Fahey and Abu Salim 1970; Holt 1958; Ibrahim 1979, 1980, 2004; Kapteijns 1985a; Theobald 1959, 1965). Most of these studies are based on archival material from both the pre-colonial period and colonial period, such as Fur documents from the Archives in Al-Fasher or the Mahdist Archive and National Records Office in Khartoum; documents from rulers like title deeds, letters and contracts (Kapteijns and Spaulding 1988; LaRue 1984, 1986; O'Fahey and Abu Salim 1983, 1994); as well as administrative reports of the diverse administrative councils and courts. While archaeological and ethnographic research has been conducted by colonial officers like Arkell, Beaton, Lampen, MacMichael, Holt and Theobald,[11] there is hardly any work on social history. Even within the contemporary period, the ethnographic work is scarce. Barth, an anthropologist, wrote one of his most well known articles, 'Economic Groups and Boundaries' (1969) based on his fieldwork in Jebel Marra. Haaland, a colleague of Barth, and who is still remembered in Kebkabiya, did write on the fluidity of ethnic identity (1969, 1972, 1982). Apart from the work of these anthropologists, the most important work for me is that of Paul Doornbos (1983, 1984 a & b, 1986) who did anthropological research in the border town of Foro Boranga. Other works based on anthropological research in Dar-

[11] See for some selected works that have been published by these authors the list of references.

fur are from Holy (1974, 1989) on the Berti and from Tully (1988) on Dar Masalit, while Alex de Waal has written an insightful work on the nature of famine in Darfur (1989). More recently books have been published on the backgrounds to the current war in Darfur by Flint and de Waal and Prunier both published in 2005. In addition, there is a lot of unpublished material, 'grey' literature, and published works with a limited circulation.[12] Although this overview is not exhaustive, ethnographies on Darfur are rare.[13]

The record is even less impressive on women specifically. Kapteijns (1985b) has written interesting historical pieces on gender relations. Grawert (1992, 1998) wrote on women and agriculture in Kutum.[14] These studies aside, I did not have much to build on in relation to the particular direction my research took. I therefore relied mostly on works from a diverse range of feminist scholars on contemporary Islam and women's issues as well as feminist theoretical and methodological issues, for the framework of my research. This work can therefore be located at the crossroads of critical feminist studies and ethnographic research on Darfur.

The communication with in particular the poor women I met during the survey led Yasmin and I to decide to focus on working women, who seemed the least powerful. Furthermore, the survey led us to the insight that the category of 'working' did little to differentiate between the women of Kebkabiya: virtually all Kebkabiya women deserved that title. It took another event to realise that other differences were relevant with respect to the groups of working women.

[12] Other work is either on language (Beaton, 1969; Von Funck 1986) or development issues (Adam et al.: 1983; Ahmed 1977, 1989; Van der Wel & Ahmed 1984; Doornbos 1984) like agriculture and nomadism (Rünger 1987; Tubiana & Tubiana 1977; Umbadda & Abdul Jalil 1984) or disasters like drought and desertification (Ibrahim 1980, 1982; de Waal 1989). There are numerous smaller articles and reports of consultancies and development programs, most of them shallow concerning the analysis of social relations and power structures, with notable exceptions like Doornbos (1983, 1984, 1986); Duffield (1979); Martin (1985).

[13] See also Cunnison (1966) on the Baggara, predominantly in neigbouring Kordofan: there is also some unpublished work like the Ph.d. Thesis of Adelberger on the Fur of Jebel Marra (1988).

[14] My M.A. thesis on women in Jebel Marra was published in Dutch (1991).

The Government Elite's View on Working Women

The following event took place during my first fieldwork period, towards the end of Ramadan, the holy month of fasting, in April 1991. Johan, Yasmin and I were living near the girls' intermediary school and the houses of government officials. As a result we had regular contact with teachers and members of the government elite. One evening Johan and I were walking home when at the corner of a street we saw a group of government officials seated on carpets. They had just finished eating their *fatuur*, the meal which breaks the day's fast. Eating out in the street enables as many men as possible, including strangers, to break the fast together, a religious virtue in which the women could not participate. The host, Ar-Rahman, was one of the most senior Kebkabiya officials and he invited us to join them. He had become a regular visitor at our house and he obviously considered me to have the intermediate status of an 'honorary male'. During Ramadan it would be extremely discourteous to decline food or drinks from a *fatuur*. We took our places at the edge of the carpet and accepted a cup of strong, sweetened tea. Once used to the darkness I recognised most of the men as government officials, some of whom we had come to know quite well. After the usual elaborate greetings and other formalities the discussion turned to the *shari'a* implemented last January.

Johan and I were asked what we thought of the Islamic laws. We were both hesitant, careful not to be too critical, even though we had previously had some relatively open discussions with some of the senior officials present. I commented that it was difficult to make any concrete statements, as first we needed to understand its implications for people in Kebkabiya. Johan gave the example that there were rumours that girls might be forbidden to work on the market, which had raised concern among the market women. I added that the girls' income was often quite important for their families in order to survive. Ar-Rahman, answered:

> It is better for the girls themselves to be removed, because after nine months she will have an extra mouth to feed.

A senior officer, whose nickname was Imam because of his extensive knowledge of the *Qur'an* pointed out that it was not the daughters' task but the mothers' to work at the market. The daughter would be better employed taking care of her brothers and sisters inside their compound.

There was further talk. The idea was proposed that the girls' lack of education was the cause of their undisciplined behaviour. Our conversation drifted to the virtues of education and Ar-Rais, a junior administrator suggested that these girls should follow the example of female teachers, who 'know how to behave'. Due to the 'grading system' for promoting teachers and in order to counteract nepotism, young unmarried female teachers, in particular, were posted away from home and their families every two or three years, often to far off locations, so I asked boldly:

> What if young female teachers are posted far away from their homes in little villages, without their *waali*?

My question made our hosts shake their heads as if they were sorry that I did not understand. They agreed teaching was a religious duty and that if there is a need for teachers, women should take it as their responsibility, regardless of the consequences. Al-Rahman added:

> The difference is that an educated woman is aware of her behaviour and knows she should take every precaution to act according to the rules. But girls in the market are uneducated, aren't they, Miss Catharina, and therefore their behaviour is irresponsible and only bad things can come from it, right?

The question was rhetorical. Ar-Rahman continued:

> If a girl sits in the market selling vegetables but especially when serving tea, men will surround her and there will be attraction between the two. Many of these girls will get children illegally. Women cause *fitna*, sexual promiscuity.

In the silence that followed Johan suggested that this should not be blamed on the women, as there are two persons involved. Ar-Rahman teasingly replied:

> But you do know, Mister Johan, Miss Catharina, that men are the weak sex and women are the ones who like to seduce them.

In the laughter these remarks drew I once more risked turning their logic upside down. I proposed that the government could appoint official *waali*s, or guardians. *Waali*s could protect the market girls by warning men who were hanging around the women for too long, rather than removing the women. It was not an original idea. It had been a suggestion from one of the 'informal' gatherings of the Tadaman women's organization which, like all kinds of organizations, had been banned ever since the current government came to power. Everyone became serious again and consecutive speakers were adamant it was better to keep women at home. Imam concluded:

> The first task of the woman is and remains being a mother and a wife and thus to be in her home.

At that moment Ar-Rahman's son appeared to collect the teacups and the talk turned to the *Eed*, the festival at the end of Ramadan. Visits to family and friends were planned and anyone required to be on duty was pitied. As the evening progressed the temperature dropped and after finishing a second cup of tea, Johan and I felt we could depart.

Rumours about the consequences for women had abounded ever since *shari'a* was implemented at federal state level the previous month. Most women wondered whether they would be compelled to wear the 'Iranian veil' (the new Islamic dress, which was allegedly imported from Iran) or whether they would only be required to wear the *sharp*, a short shawl worn knotted around the head. Women teachers variously discussed whether they would really be prevented from travelling on their own and if the wearing of perfume would be banned. The threat to the jobs of tea and market women was also discussed. However, nobody seemed to take these threats seriously and until I left in June 1991 nothing untoward took place.

Nevertheless, the rumours became a reality. By the time I returned to the Sudan in October 1991, there had been many changes in public life. The government policy based on the Islamist Civilization Project in order to 'purify' Islamic beliefs and practices in the Sudan and the Islamist moral discourse which justified it, focused on the conduct of women in the public arena and proved to have concrete consequences for all women who entered public life for professional reasons (Al-Ahmadi 2003: 28). For example, almost immediately after accepting *shari'a* in 1991 the Khartoum State Public Order Act (KSPOA) was implemented in the Central State of the Sudan. Its aim was to attain the segregation of men and women in public by developing 'the legal power of establishing total discipline in all aspects of life to [sic] the regions of Sudan including Khartoum' (Sudan Human Rights Voice 1994: 2; cited in Malik 1995: 41).

The act led to the so-called *kasha* politics,[15] or street cleaning campaigns, which were justified as a 'religious obligation' and which targeted women from different class backgrounds differently. Women's paid work could only be justified if there was an explicit economic need. The women were required to obtain a permit, which invariably cost more than they could afford; most street vendors could just survive on what they earned. In order to control the activities in the 'non-formal' sector of large towns the Act regulated the working hours of street vendors in article seventeen of the KSPOA, which stipulated that women were strictly forbidden to sell food and drinks between five o'clock in the evening and five o'clock in the morning. These are actually the peak hours for street vendors, of which poor migrant women constituted a majority.

Urban professional women, mostly from middle- or high-class backgrounds, were also abused in public, either verbally or physically by often self-acclaimed vigilantes. In some cases women were brought to a police station for appearing in public in 'un-Islamic' attire: western clothes, too short, colourful or tight local Sudanese *tobe*s,[16] too heavily perfumed, or wearing too much jewellery or makeup (Al-Ahmadi, 1994, 2003: 53–55; Hale, 1997: 197–200; El-Malik, 1995: 36–42).[17] Female university colleagues started to wear their heads covered at least in public, even if they had never done so before. At Khartoum University violent clashes had taken place between pro- and contra- NIF students, such that parts of the university had to be closed.[18]

---

[15] These *kasha* politics also entailed displacements of migrants particularly from the South and from Darfur. Simone (1994) therefore states that the government thus exposed its intent to 'enforce a strict ethnic and cultural, as opposed to religious, territorialization of the country—since Western Muslim groups are as much an object of displacement as are Southerners...' (Simone 1994: 68).

[16] The current fabric was introduced under Turco-Egyptian rule (1823–1882) and made in India, which was a British colony at that time (Spaulding 1985: 193). The new fabric caused a different way of wearing, as compared to the local veil, which was made of homespun coarse cotton or even of leather. Nowadays the *tobe* is typically a four to six meter long cloth of about a meter width, which is loosely wrapped over the 'indoor' clothes, often a skirt and a blouse, a dress or even trousers.

[17] Sudan Human Rights Voice (1994: 2) cited in Malik (1995: 41). Also female students were targeted. For example, the police kept a close watch on Ahfad College, an all women's university. There have been several cases of girls who have been taken from the private buses to report to the police station because of 'indecent' dress. The girls received a punishment of 15 strokes with a wooden stick and had to sign a declaration that they would dress according to Islamic rules in the future. However, so far it seems that these are incidents rather than daily practice (see for example Seuren 1998).

[18] Khartoum University was partly closed, but some master courses were still run-

Initially, these decrees took effect only in Khartoum, the seat of the government. Governors of other States soon followed this example. In July 1991 all tea women at Kebkabiya market were removed and their licenses withdrawn. The government officials gave as their reason that the women's occupation was 'particularly' noxious implying that the women had too many opportunities for attracting and seducing men.

In Kebkabiya, the new Islamist policy had diverse consequences for different groups of working women. It had been clear from the earlier discussion with the government officials, that selling at the market in general was considered morally corrupting especially when girls were involved. Within this classification, however, government officials saw tea women as potentially the women most dangerous to the public order. Their job would bring them into close and regular contact with *ajnabi*, strange men or rather, non-relatives. The apparent susceptibility to sexual promiscuity of tea women would cause *fitna*, sexually induced chaos, in society: tea women were explicitly equated with prostitutes. At the same time they were seen as the opposites of female teachers. A female teacher was given as an example of the proper, respectful woman although many were unmarried women working away from their legal and moral guardians, their families.

For their part, female government officials, such as secretaries and female teachers working in Kebkabiya received circulars stating that they should adhere to an appropriate Islamic dress code. The government propagated black synthetic dresses, the 'Iranian' veils, especially for women working in the government service.[19] Although the female teachers did not adopt this alternative veil which would only leave the eyes uncovered, many of them did dress more strictly than before, for example by putting on a scarf and longer skirts under their white *tobe*s.

Both groups of working women were directly confronted with the effects of the new moral discourse. The combination of removing the tea women from the market and the insistence on a more sober and strict 'Islamic' dress code for female teachers was central to the attempt

---

ning and affiliated institutions carried on with their courses. Other universities, like Cairo University Khartoum Branch, Juba and Umdurman were still running. The women's private university, Ahfad, remained open.

[19] This project was called the 'Project of veiling the working woman' and instigated by the Sudanese Women General Union, the women's wing of the NIF. Al-Ahmadi (2003) states that the Islamic dress the government subsidized, was to be considered a government invention which became a 'political uniform' that distinguished those who 'belonged' from the alien 'other' (Al-Ahmadi 2003: 99, 105).

of the new government to 're-Islamise' public life as part of the application of the moral discourse on gender. As this moral discourse was also the basis of the distinction between female teachers and market women, I will focus on these two different groups of working women in the remainder of this book. A distinction that is based on the male educated elite classification of working women as respectable and disreputable. My analyses will be on the diverse ways in which these two groups of working women perceive, negotiate and devise strategies to cope with the moral discourse in order to defend their own interests, in order to be economically active, while being regarded as proper Muslim women and on their possibilities to transform that same discourse in the process.

Discourses and Narratives in a Local Context

In October 1991, I returned to Kebkabiya alone. Johan was occupied with a project elsewhere and Yasmin had returned to her work at a local non-governmental organisation. This time I chose to stay at the compound of Hajja, a widow who lived with her two daughters and three grandchildren in the middle of town, near the market place. I was eager to begin working with the tea and market women, although I also wanted to continue my discussions with the female teachers whom I had met during the first fieldwork period. Soon after my return I visited the market, which was held every Monday and Thursday. Immediately I missed the *gahawi*, the small coffee and tea places of the *sittaat as-chai*, the tea women. I had never believed the law would be so fiercely enforced; the tea women were often the most vulnerable and poorest women who sold tea and coffee for want of other sources of income. I decided to try and trace some of these missing ('removed') tea women and set out to find Helima. Johan and I had often taken our cup of tea or coffee at her place when visiting the market during my first stay. It was some time before I located her. I visited her on several occasions to talk over many issues, but mostly we talked about what had happened since I had left four months previously.

I learned from talking to Helima and the other market women that the government had removed the tea women shortly after I had left. It had begun with a meeting between the E.C. (the Executive Commissioner of the Area Council), the *shartai* (the paramount chief of the Fur and head of the local 'tribal court'), and the *qadi* (the judge of the *shari'a* court). These high officials called for a meeting with all other government officials, army and police officers and they discussed the way the Islamist policy of the new government was to be implemented. The results of this meeting had been announced and justified in public addresses and on the local radio. After this, orders were given by the E.C. to the police and the court to execute the new decrees while the *shartai* informed the rural authorities outside Kebkabiya town, which in turn disseminated the information to their villages. In addition to these officials, public committees were also called on to enforce the new policies. The officials were told that they particularly had to stop young girls from 'disturbing' the public order. The tea-making utensils were taken from the tea women and those who persisted in going to the market had their pots broken. Some time later when a group of elderly tea women went back to the market they were rounded up and taken to the police station. The police informed the women that if they were caught on a subsequent occasion, they would be taken to prison and either whipped or fined. There appeared to be no logical reason why the married and elderly tea women were removed as well as the young girls, but no one had tried to come back to sell tea since then. After several visits to Helima, I asked her if she would mind if together with Sa'adiya, who was to be my assistant during my second stay, we could audiotape some further conversations particularly on her life. Helima agreed to my request.

Sa'adiya was an English language teacher at the local girls' intermediary school who was approaching the end of her maternity leave during my second fieldwork period.[20] Sa'adiya visited me on one of my first days back in town and offered to work with me: in this way she could earn some additional income and practise her English at the same time. I was overjoyed that she was willing to assist me, for as a teacher who had grown up in Kebkabiya, Sa'adiya belonged to the educated elite and was well known by local families as well.

As arranged, Sa'adiya and I returned to Helima's and made an hour-long audiotape of her narrative. It had been a first session for all three of us and at first I felt that the somewhat awkward silences

[20] Women obtained the right to 'maternity leave for eight weeks' according to art. 25 (1) of the Individual Labour Relations Act of 1981; and the right to apply for one year of unpaid leave for lactation purposes and in addition leave of at least one hour from work for the purpose of lactation (art.30 Public Service Regulations of 1975, cited in Hale 1997: 138–139).

and at times subdued attitude of Helima was due to our insecurity and inexperience. Only when reflecting on the context of our session, I had mixed feelings. Although I had earlier experienced that a research situation is never devoid of hierarchical relations I felt more ill at ease than I expected to be. As if I had been trying to snatch a story from Helima she might not be prepared to give me. And for which I could not do or give much in return.

The experience with Helima resulted in my adoption of a new approach. It proved difficult to trace other tea women, as they were no longer visible as such. I would not be able to witness the daily lives of tea women and their dealing with 'strange' customers and government interference. Following my chosen route would result in reliance on hearsay, on 'second-hand' reflections of the tea women and those living in their vicinity. More important, however, was the realisation that my uneasiness over our talk had not so much to do with the particularities of my session with Helima, but with the moral discourse which had changed the context in which all tea women operated, as well as their fates, almost overnight. Regardless of the circumstances or Helima's disposition, I should not have been surprised that Helima could not be very open in her reflections let alone be outspoken: this political context would have had an effect on any tea woman's narrative.

So instead I decided to work with the market women who were still able to work. I took this decision partly because of the predicament of the tea women, but I realised I was simultaneously complying with a classification of high and low ranking working women as defined by a powerful, male Islamist government elite. In my decision to follow up on what was seen as important and as accepted locally with respect to categories of working women, I had in fact stepped into the same discourse, which I wanted to examine critically.

Unwillingly and unwittingly, my research had thus become not only a tool to analyse a given situation at a given period of time but also it had become part of that particular historical context. With hindsight I realise that I had participated in a 'key shift' in history (Foucault in Mills 1997: 26). My research was part of rapidly changing relations of power and the discourse imposed by the new government. The dynamics between the new moral discourse of the government both in word and deed on the one hand, and its material and immaterial effects on the Kebkabiya people (myself included) on the other, were apparent in everyone's reflections even when they considered the past. The dominant moral discourse was an important part of every day life in Kebkabiya, not merely influencing it, but trying to constitute a new morality as 'normal', as common sense (Billig 1991: 26). The converse also proved to be true; the daily practices and reflections of Kebkabiya people affected the discourse, adjusting and transforming it during the course of events.

During the same period I had frequent contact with market women and female teachers and I was quite surprised by their outspoken, direct and frequently critical attitude. Particularly when the women were with each other, they would ridicule men, including government officials and their 'duties'. However, when I asked the women directly for their opinions on events in public life they were more often than not as hesitant and evasive as Helima. I felt challenged by the dilemma. How to understand the submissive demeanour in some of the women's reflections? If I took the deferential attitude of these working women at face value, it might suggest that the government's moral discourse was all encompassing, all-powerful and influential. This approach would deny the women agency, an aspect I had wanted to bring out by focusing on their narratives and experiences in the first instance. Moreover, how was I to analyse the narratives of the working women without suggesting that they are confined and contained within the subject positions the Islamist moral discourse seemed to impose on them? How could I understand the women's negotiating power if their words were not always as defiant and resistant as I would have hoped or even expected them to be? And, how was I to represent these women's narratives about themselves without stereotyping women as either victims or heroines and give depth to their narratives on gender, Islam and morality? In order to address all of these issues I turned to recent feminist academic writings that have in common a perception of doing research, which hereafter I will refer to as research 'against the grain'.

Against the Grain: Positions of Listening, Reading and Writing

In understanding the working women's narratives in relation to the Sudanese government's moral discourse, the concept 'against the grain' offers an enticing guide in the search for alternative subject positions within that discourse. In addition, it facilitates an escape from an over-simplified dichotomization of powerful/powerless, oppressors/oppressed; a way of thinking that has been particularly criticized by feminist scholars. 'Against the grain' is particularly helpful because in relation to the issue of 'women and Islam' certain discourses loom large. The images of women in Muslim societies as victims is still a feature of many current popular and academic writing, despite the efforts of feminist scholars to argue for a different perspective and alternative methods of analysis.[21] I have no illusion that I can easily avoid this imagery simply by a conscious wish: as Amina Mama has pointed out, 'intentionality is not enough'.[22] Therefore, 'against the grain' is also a device to prevent an easy slip into the dichotomies of oppressed and oppressors when it comes to understand the working women's reflections. I also use it as a tool to keep me alert for the different messages, both submissive and critical, which can be contained at one and the same time in seemingly self-evident utterances and reflections. Thus, it can help me to try and abstain from simple stereotyping into victims or heroines. Further, I want to regard these narratives as a possibility for 'discovering' alternative subject positions which working women can attain in the context of the dominant moral discourse. This book therefore centres on these narratives. Although the narratives of working women are central, I will also look into the narratives produced by the government and its representatives.

My use of the concept 'against the grain'[23] is inspired by writings of feminist scholars, of a critical, post-colonial and subaltern signature.[24] Some of these critical feminist scholars have referred more or less extensively to the concept of 'against the grain'. In particular, the term has been used by those feminist scholars who claim for themselves the label of 'third world feminist', or 'feminist of colour' within an academic setting that they regard as white-dominated and socio-political. These scholars use the concept of 'against the grain' in order

---

[21] See for some of these critical studies: Badran (1995); Jansen (1989); Joseph (1999, 2000) Lazreq (1988); Moors (1991: 114–122); Sabbagh (2002).

[22] In a lecture delivered at a postgraduate seminar organized by Lorraine Nencel (VENA/CNWS), Leiden, 11–15, December 1989.

[23] Meijer (1996: 78) refers to Judith Fetterley who developed the term 'resistant reading' (1978). Resistant reading is comparable to reading against the grain. However, I use the concept in a broader sense of the term, which I will explain below.

[24] In my thinking I am indebted to many feminist thinkers amongst whom some of the most important are: Abu-Lughod (1993); Braidotti (1991, 1994, 2001, 2002); Harrison (1993); hooks (1981, 1984, 1990); Mohanty (1991: 1–47, 2003); Schrijvers (1991, 1993, 1995, 1997, 1999); Spivak (1988 a & b, 1995); Trinh Min-ha (1989, 1992); see also Alsop et. al. (2003: 187–196). I also owe much to the discussions with Joke Schrijvers, Tine Davids, Anke van der Kwaak, Lorraine Nencel, Rosemarie Buikema, and Rajni Palriwala.

to come to terms with their own position and that of their research within academia. They emphasize the search for alternative voices and perspectives, and especially ways of reflecting on dominant ideas of history, knowledge, and identity within the parameters of academic discourses. The claim by these scholars that their analyses are based on their own experiences makes their writing not only theoretically innovative, but also profoundly personal and therefore political. For example, in the different works of these feminist scholars the notion of multiple identities, as a political strategy is illuminating. It points at a way of dealing with their position as the 'minorities', as 'others', within dominant discourses, both political and academic, by interpreting 'identity' as a political notion, instead of an inherent characteristic of a person (Anzaldúa 1987, 2002; hooks 1981, 1984; Lorde 1981; Mohanty 1991: 34).

The desire to relate the personal and the political to the theoretical and thus to transform theories of knowledge and what can be known has become part of the feminist thinking of the last decennia (Braidotti 1994: 146–213; Butler 1999: 3–9, 181–190; De Lauretis 1986: 1–19; Fox-Keller 1983; Harding 1986: 1–19, 1987: 90; Lloyd 1985; Moore 1994: 1–14; Schrijvers 1991, 1995: 19–29, 1997: 62–83). The recognition of the importance of embodied knowledge is thereby an important aspect that feminist thinkers and post-colonial and subaltern studies share. The 'politics of locations' gives room for acknowledging the multiplicity of intersecting identities such as gender, race, class, sex, nationality, etc., as situated in certain contexts: it depends on this context what identities get prioritized over others (Anzaldúa 1987, 2002; Braidotti 1994: 17, 2001: 13; Butler 1997: 1–41; De Lauretis 1986: 9–14; Moore 1994: 1–14; see also Alsop et. al. 2003).

However, whilst providing me with a potential route for my analysis of the identity constructions and the strategies used by the working women if they wanted to be economically active, 'against the grain' also presented me with a problem. None of the scholars to whom I refer for my perspective on doing research 'against the grain' give a clear indication as to how to go about doing research or reading or writing whilst using this method: How to understand this multiplicity and prioritizing in identity constructions of and by women? Therefore, I transformed the concept into a set of tools, which I could then use for my research. I call these tools: listening, reading, and writing against the grain.

Listening Against the Grain: Biographic Narratives

As my first talk with Helima did not work out as I hoped it would, I owe much to the discussions with and work of feminist scholars for not despairing. I am particularly inspired by Schrijvers, who has written and argued extensively with great sensitivity and awareness on the power-infested research situation.[25] As I indicated above, I had become acutely aware of feeling as if I tricked Helima into telling me her story without offering much in return. At the same time I realized that the hierarchy in the research situation between myself and those women I engaged in my research could never be completely resolved because of the sheer differences in class and economic power (Borland 1991; Stacey 1991: 11–121; Patai 1991: 137–155). In respect to this dilemma Schrijvers (1991) has articulated the ideal of a dialogical research situation in which 'ego' and 'alter' share some of the interest of the research. Apart from the fact that I presented women with culturally prescribed gifts of sugar, tea, sweets or dates, there were also non-material exchanges like 'experiences, points of view and types of knowledge (1991: 177)' which might have alleviated the power gap to some extent. However, I discovered it was not always up to me to decide upon the nature of the exchanges, no matter how much I tried to establish egalitarian contacts and dialogues in which both the women involved and I could ask questions and propose directions of research. The women involved could decide not only what to tell and how, but also what to withhold and when to be silent (cf. Kloos 1988; Nencel 1997, 2001: 15–26). Some women may even have decided not to be involved at all.

I realized that listening against the grain was not just about hearing words. It required an active stance to become aware of power differences. Then I could begin to discover how the differences influenced the narratives and attitudes of the women. It meant not trying to fill all the silences and hesitations as I considered them, when talking with Helima, but taking these as part of a woman's reflection and positioning in relation to the dominant discourses. Listening against the grain meant that I was trying to also hear implicit messages and

[25] See for example: Schrijvers (1985; 1993; 1995: 19–29; 1997: 62–83). See also Harding (1986: 1–19; 1987: 9).

hidden scripts, in short to understand subtexts (Fairclough 1992: 100–110).

The consequence was that I was intimately involved in the narratives the women offered me. That I audiotaped the women's words with Yasmin or Sa'adiya present must have had an undeniable influence on the reflections of the speakers. I was positioned, though differently, in the same moral discourse as they were, and I therefore became part of the same power relations, which pervaded their lives. My perception of listening against the grain is thus closely related to the view on knowledge as formulated by Schrijvers (1993: 156):

> Knowledge produced is seen as an outcome of dialogues, of inter- and intra- subjective communications, and of the confrontations of differing images of reality. Knowledge, in this view, is a temporary construct, determined historically, locally, and personally...

Listening against the grain is thus based on an epistemology, which sees knowledge as the result of social relations and interaction, in this case between the women involved in the research and myself. This production of meaning has consequences for the construction of identities, as Moore (1994: 3) points out:

> Inter-subjectivity and dialogue involve situations where bodies marked through by the social, that is, by difference (race, gender, ethnicity and so on), are presented as part of identities. The uses of the body, the particular circumstances of interaction and the readings made by others are all involved in the taking up of a position or positions that form the basis for the enunciation of experience.

The embodied nature of knowledge production thus has consequences for notions of self and self-awareness, which are constituted performatively and discursively (cf. Braidotti 1994: 36,183; Butler 1990: 16–17; Harding 1998: 105–165; De Lauretis 1986: 12; Smith 1990a; see also Kloos 1988: 228; Scholte 1974).

In connection to this view, the need to change my research plans actually turned out to be somewhat of an asset. With a still incomplete direction to my research, I was able to focus more on the nature of communication than on presupposed meanings and expected outcomes. The political situation had provided some of the direction and made me sensitive to local power structures with its almost imperceptible workings. I depended on the people I met, and particularly on the working women I tried to engage in my research during its course. All anthropologists 'feel' their way in the local setting and I was no exception: nor did I engage in this non-preconceived research as a *tabula rasa.*

Nevertheless, without a fixed goal I felt I depended to a larger extent than I had expected on the dialectics of local events and on the space the women would give me to engage in a dialogue in order to be able to do research at all.

Considering knowledge production to be inter-subjective and embodied meant that in order to listen against the grain, I had to be able to understand narratives as part of the multiple contexts in which they acquired meaning and, in turn, in what way these narratives constituted these contexts. I needed to understand the narrative of each woman in the context of her surroundings, her world as she understood it. I could only do so by participating in the rut and routine of the women's daily lives.

I had been able to establish a relationship with many of the female teachers during my first fieldwork period in October 1990—May 1991. I visited them after work, helped with some teaching, and even assisted at official events and meetings. Therefore, I had become part of their surroundings. In their capacity as teachers, both Yasmin and Sa'adiya had been part of these gatherings as well. With the market women, I still had to build up relationships when I returned for a second stay in October 1991. My host Hajja was a market woman, which facilitated my entrance to the market place. In the course of those first weeks of my second fieldwork period, I would make acquaintances with the market women at their spot on the market. Later I would visit some of these women at home. Only when I had been frequenting her home for some time would I ask her if she was willing to tell me her story. Only then did I introduce Sa'adiya, who was well known with most of the women I discovered along the way. As I wanted to be as non-direct as possible with the women, Sa'adiya and I had decided to ask the women to tell us about their lives and then see what they chose to tell us. In a way, we were asking the women to reflect on their past, hoping that this would lead them to reflect on the current moral discourse in their own way and on their own terms as well.

However, the use of biographic narratives in research in non-western contexts is not the prerogative of feminist scholars, nor is the method uncontested. Jean and John Comaroff (1992: 25–27, 238), for example, disqualify the biography for understanding non-western notions of selfhood. They consider the biography to be tied to the Cartesian 'I', the image of a self-conscious being, and to the rise of bourgeois personhood in the eighteenth century. In other words, the 'biographical illusion' is a western modernist fantasy 'about society and selfhood according to which everyone is potentially in control of his or her destiny in a world made by the actions of autonomous "agents"'.[26]

Although the use of biographic narratives is not the sole prerogative of feminist scholars,[27] in feminist research it has become an important way to understand women in their own words (Behar 1993: 1–23; Gluck and Patai 1991: 1–4; Mohanty 1991: 34). However, criticism also comes from within feminist studies. Abu-Lughod (1993: 30–32) points out that the conventions for telling about one's 'life' forces local ways of narrating into a western straightjacket that might alter the original narrative beyond recognition. She also objects to the genre because it focuses on the individual as isolated, separated, and thus alien from the lived day-to-day situation in which the life-historian is situated. Other feminists have pointed out that the method in the West reflects a male prerogative, a 'Great Man tradition'. It speaks of individual linear progress and power, of a hero who struggles and survives, which does not relate to the ways in which women experience the world.[28]

In short, the method has been criticized both from within and outside feminist studies for being too western, individualistic, modernist and viricentric[29] and therefore unfit to understand self-representations by women in non-western societies or to write alternative histories 'from below'.[30] Though I take these critiques and cautions seriously, I do not think that the failure to represent women well should lead to abandoning the attempt altogether.

My choice for trying to engage women in telling about their lives was strategic as I hoped it would allow me to understand the way they positioned themselves in relation to the dominant moral discourse, without me directing the conversation too much. Even though the label 'life-history' might trigger expectations about format, style, and

---

[26] Comaroff and Comaroff (1992: 26) after Bourdieu (1987); see for a critical discussion of the Comaroff's view: Geschiere (2001: 31–39).

[27] A well-known example of early use of the method in anthropology is the biography of Sam Blowsnake by Paul Radin (1962). For an overview of the use of 'life-histories': Langness and Frank (1981); both quoted in Aalten 1990: 54–58).

[28] For example, Okely points out that Saint Augustine's work, *Confessions*, is often referred to as the origin of the form, with Rousseau and J.S. Mills as other major examples of defining 'what constitutes a meaningful life'. (Okely 1992: 4–5).

[29] Viricentrism, coined by Schrijvers (see for example Joke Schrijvers, 1979: 97–117; 1985) is similar to androcentrism, referring to male bias.

[30] Biographies and autobiographies by elite women have been a popular genre in the Arab world for some time (cf. Abu-Lughod, 1998: 3–33; Ahmed 1988: 154–175).

chronology, I do not see this as sufficient reason to abandon the method altogether. I will therefore use the notion of 'biographic narratives' for referring to different forms of narratives on the self, which allows for the possibility of referring more loosely to narratives which reflect on only certain parts of a woman's life, both past and present, without necessarily being chronological (Okely 1992: 4–9).

I think that the failure to represent women well should not keep us from trying to find modes of representation, which do allow for a proper understanding of the 'original' narratives of selves. It is precisely this challenge that I take up in this book. The positioning by women in their narratives and the representation of these narratives by the researcher should lead us to understand to what extent women are allowed space, as well as take that space, to construct alternative subject-positions. It should therefore not be presumed that women do not present themselves as individuals, just as their belonging to a collectivity should not be taken for granted. A biographic narrative certainly does not give an easy and self-evident access to understanding the narrative as commentary on the dominant discourses. As Mohanty (1991) warns us:

> Thus, the existence of third world women's narratives in itself is not evidence of de-centering hegemonic histories and subjectivities. It is *the way* in which they are read, understood, and located institutionally which is of paramount importance. After all, the point is not just 'to record' one's history or struggle, or consciousness, but *how* they are recorded; *the way* we read, receive, and disseminate such imaginative records is immensely significant (1991: 34 [*emphasis added by author*]).

As Mohanty points out here, women position themselves in relation to hegemonic, or dominant discourses that define their room to maneuver and the scope for claiming subjectivity. The negotiation of such dominant discourses is therefore not always openly or clearly articulated, and hence not easily detected. It is therefore, not so much the form of the biographic narrative which is problematic, but how to 'listen well' in order to prevent easy generalising which might result in depicting 'third world women as passive, subservient, and lacking in creativity' (Behar 1993: 272). Mohanty's citation indicates the different ways that narratives should be read in order to decide upon their de-centring, or 'subversive' character. Although she does not give a directive as to how to do this, in my opinion one way is to acknowledge the multiple ways in which women as agents construct themselves by looking for the layered-ness of narratives of self. To do justice to the subaltern nature of texts, I tried to resolve this by developing ways to 'read' biographic narratives 'against the grain'.

Reading Against the Grain: Texts and Contexts

Reading against the grain is closely related to listening against the grain. The main difference is that in reading and re-reading, the transcribed and translated narrative of a woman becomes a 'text'. In order to clarify the multiple readings and interpretations this procedure gives rise to, I am making an analytical distinction between a narrative as a text and its context. I want to emphasize that this differentiation between a text and its context is an analytical device for reading against the grain. Official speeches and gossiping, daily routine and rituals, narratives and jokes, non-verbal communication and landscape markers are all, indistinguishable, text and context. These texts-in-context are again part and parcel of discourses. As Meijer (1996) asserts:

> Thus the question of how 'reality' relates to 'text' becomes the wrong question: They cannot be divided into two separate realms... [The question is] How texts produce subject- and object-positions, and how these positions are distributed along the lines of gender and race... how a text produces 'naturalness' (Meijer 1993: 368–369).

I aim at reading the narratives of working women as 'texts in contexts' for knowing how these produce subject- and object positions. I will read these texts against the grain in order to understand how the different classes of working women in Kebkabiya negotiate these positions while constructing their identities. From the diverse narrating positions I hope to get an insight into the alternative subject-positions these women thus construct, as both victims and actors, both compliant and resistant, both overt and covert, as well as to what extent they make strategic use of these constructions. People continuously reflect upon dominant discourses even when referring to common sense knowledge, whereby these discourses are not only acknowledged, but often negotiated and even adjusted (Billig 1991: 2, 26; Butler 1993: 1128, 226, 1997a: 20; McNay 2000: 57). This view allows me to take the narratives of working women in Kebkabiya as a way of understanding how they position themselves relative to the dominant discourse in daily life. I therefore perceive texts, all 'texts', whether written, oral, visual or corporeal, as argumentative and directed at the dominant discourses of which they are part.

The question, again, is: How to do this reading of a text against the grain as a practice? As I opt for reading against the grain as an alternative to the way texts are usually read (Mills 1997: 131–159), I cannot produce a blueprint of established methods to read a text-in-context. In addition to looking at *what* and *how* something is said, I have assembled some tools, for which I refer to the work of Davis (1996),[31] Meijer (1993, 1996) and Fairclough (1992, 1995).

For my goal of understanding the narratives of women as part of their context, the concept of inter-textuality is important. Inter-textuality is a term introduced by Kristeva who used it in relation to the work of Bakhtin in the late 1960s.[32] Kristeva (1986) stated that inter-textuality implies:

> The insertion of history (society) into a text and of this text into history ... (1986: 39, quoted in Fairclough, 1992: 101)

I use inter-textuality in its broadest sense as 'the sum of knowledge that makes it possible for texts to have meaning' (Meijer 1996: 23, cf. Fairclough 1992: 103–105). These meanings are never straightforward. Analysing a text relative to the context is a way to understand the complex ways in which people deal with power relations and related subject positions in diverse social settings. In principle, the number of readings of a text are multiple, potentially infinite, depending on the other texts relevant in the same context. This means there is always an ambiguity as to the 'real' meaning of a text. Thus ambivalence should be part of the analysis and should not be 'reasoned' away (cf. Fairclough 1992: 102). With respect to the narratives of working women in Kebkabiya, this implies that hesitations, silences, and interruptions are to be read as meaningful parts of the text.

As I deal with texts which have been translated from the Arabic into English, I will not be able to take into account aspects like wording, grammar, style et cetera as important indications of positioning of

---

31 In 1993, I took a course of 'text-analysis' led by the feminist scholars Kathy Davis and Lena Inowlocki (see for example 1993 :139–153) in which we considered the reading of texts in relation to dominant discourses.

32 Different dates are given for the same reference to a paper later published as 'Word, Dialogue and Novel'. Fairclough (1992: 101) gives 1966 for Kristeva's paper and refers to *The Kristeva* Reader by T. Moi (ed.) published in 1986. Meijer (1996: 20) gives 1969 as date of the introduction in and refers to *Desire in Language*, edited by Leon S. Roudiez, New York: Columbia University Press, (1980: 64–92). Both agree on the fact that Kristeva introduced the term in relation to her work on Bakhtin.

women with respect to the dominant discourse (cf. Fairclough 1992). Instead, I will concentrate on the positioning of narrator and reader in the focalization and textual representation in the narrative, by the use of pronouns, genitives, and generalizations. This will lead me to relate a narrative to historical, cultural and personal aspects of the narrator's context. Moreover, by reading a text-in-context I will look into the effect of and the argumentation in a text with respect to the dominant moral discourse of the government. This way of locating texts as parts of context, I will refer to as *con/text-analysis*.

In practising con/text-analysis the reader becomes paramount in deciding on and even creating the meaning, or rather meanings, of a narrative. Readings are therefore never unbiased, but are inevitably related to political, social, cultural and economic interests. This calls for self-reflexivity by the reader as interpreter as well as analyst (Fairclough 1992: 103–106; Ghorashi 2003; Meijer 1996: 22–24, 34–35; Nencel 1997, 2001; Schrijvers 1995: 19–29, 1997: 62–83; 1991; cf. Davids and Willemse 1993). As reader, recipient and interpreter of the narratives I am situated: my readings 'against the grain' are thus related to my positioning in the local context as well as in the contexts in which I will consider the narratives to be meaningful. In other words, my positioning in the moral discourse of the Sudanese government as temporary inhabitant of Kebkabiya, as well as my interest as a feminist researcher from the West will be reflected in those choices (cf. Schrijvers 1993: 156). In order to articulate my readings as dialectic and self-reflexive, the text I produce on these pages, my 'narrative', should leave room for a plurality of perspectives. This brings me to a third aspect of my method: 'writing against the grain'.

Writing Against the Grain: From Theory to Practice

Writing is the core business of an anthropologist's metier (Behar 1993). At the same time, this writing is not transparent, innocent, or self-evident. In the last decennia feminist and post-colonial theorists have tried to deal with the bias of their academic enterprise. As Harrison (1993: 409) asserts:

> The core of anthropological discourse has been historically constituted as a Western, white male domain, where the language of objectivity and value neutrality has served to mask and obscure mechanisms of silencing, alienating and subjugating the voices and subjectivities of white women,

> and the female and male descendants of the colonially conquered people denied history and access to anthropological authority.

In other words, writing in an academic mode as if the representation of narratives of women is unproblematic is making these women into objects, speaking for or past them instead of with them. As a result of this unmasking of academia's neutrality there has been a lot of debating over the possibility of writing a feminist ethnography (cf. Abu-Lughod 1988; Harding 1987: 1–15; Mohanty 1991: 31–41; Stacey 1991; Patai 1991; Trinh 1989: 85). I share Schrijvers' (1993: 144) conclusion:

> What puzzles me is the gap between (feminist) theorising and the actual praxis of experimenting with alternative approaches. In my view, one of the challenges of a dialectical conception of knowledge is to find ways of deconstructing the established dichotomy between 'the personal' and 'the professional' not only epistemologically and methodologically, but also in the practice of academic writing: no easy task...

My writing against the grain is related to this finding of alternative ways of representation. It is a representation that reflects the narratives as told by women in their specific location, as well as the positions and positioning of me as the researcher: a representation which is guided by my readings of these narratives. What I call the self-reflective mode is a way of overcoming the objectifying, neutralising and homogenising mode of anthropological academic writing: I also maintain that it leads to better, because 'situated' understandings of lived realities (Braidotti 1991, 1994; Davids and Willemse 1993: 3–14; Ghorashi 2003; Nencel 1997, 2001; Schrijvers 1993). But then, how to represent narratives and its narrators without objectifying them, without making women a footnote to their own stories? Moreover, in relation to my own position in this process of knowledge production: How can I write myself into this academic text and not fall into the trap of solipsism?

A first requirement of writing against the grain is to make room for multiple narrating positions and constructed identities in the narratives of the working women. To be able to 'read against the grain' I intend to represent the narratives as completely as possible. Although I can never reproduce the narratives on these pages exactly as they were told, because of the translations and thereby the editing which was involved, the twists and turns in the narratives represented in this book reflect the context in which the research took place, and my role in these, as much as possible. It is only in this way that I can leave the texts relatively open to multiple readings. However, the space available in this book does not allow for more than two or three of these extended narratives. I have chosen to represent two narratives in depth. The consequences of this choice will become clear in the course of my con/text-analyses of the narratives.

Although it took me some time to realize that the number of narratives that could be placed in my book would be limited, it was not hard to decide whose narratives would be well portrayed here. One in particular was that of Umm Khalthoum, a female teacher at the kindergarten who took on the name of the renowned Egyptian singer I teasingly had given her because she could sing so beautifully.[33] She was married, with eight children, she had lived in Kebkabiya for about four years, and liking each other, we felt close in spirit and character. Closer to home was Hajja on whose compound I stayed throughout my second stay. She had enchanted me with her narratives in the first place. Having been on *haj* early in her life, financed by her own savings, she carried its honorary address, *hajja*, with pride. Both Umm Khalthoum's and Hajja's narratives are largely based on several audio taped sessions. However, these sessions were part of an ongoing communication I had with Hajja and Umm Khalthoum, but also with other women: informal chatting, discussions, joking, non-verbal communication, and reflections on and by others. This 'ongoing communication' between the women and myself is part of the inter-subjective knowledge production as well as part of the dialectical process, which together form an aspect of 'listening against the grain'. At the same time this process is the context against which the narratives will be 'read against the grain'. Self-reflexivity is necessary for understanding my role in the process, both as part of the narratives and its contexts. I now realise that the choice for Hajja and Umm Khalthoum might have been mutual, as increasingly we became part of each other's lives. Therefore, my representations of biographic narratives of both women are to some extent autobiographical.

The focus on the process of knowledge production rather than only on its outcomes, on dynamics, contexts and sub-texts rather than facts does not allow for an orthodox representation. Consequently the format of this book is not a chronological sequence, nor one of hypotheses

[33] I use pseudonyms to make the women less easy to trace. Especially for historians, this fact is problematic as it makes the 'historical source of information' unverifiable and thus the information unreliable. As I think that knowledge is the result of a process, of interaction, and related to a specific context I contest the implicit suggestion, that a colleague, however close to me and my background, would be able to receive the same kind of narratives from these women. Therefore, this 'problem' is futile.

linked to theory followed by empirical proof. By analogy with the way my research developed, I will structure my argument as a process of evolving and 'becoming'. Thereby it is imperative to distinguish my views and reflections from those of the women involved: to distinguish my readings from the diverse interpretations that the narratives offered, and to tell my pre-occupations apart from those of the narrators. This means, that I do not present here a preconceived analytical framework, to which the narratives constitute mere illustrations, examples chosen to fit the theory. I aim at a process of theoretical discovery grounded in every-day experiences by working women in Kebkabiya, whereby the narratives of the women represent the embodied, situated soil from which springs the theoretical reflection.

While writing, I felt that the process resembled the peeling of an onion. It turned out to be a teary job of many layers and multiple (cutting) edges. As I peeled, I came upon different layers giving new insights into the recurrent themes in the narratives of the women, new meanings to events I had witnessed and experienced during my stay in Kebkabiya and new perspectives on the moral discourse of the government. One frequently recommended method for representing narratives is the use of chronology. The method involves readjusting events and understandings gained in the local 'context of discovery' in the final text to fit the analysis so that the author's representation forms a neat, closed and objectified picture, which thus constitutes the 'context of justification' (Kloos 1987). Given my approach, chronology does not have a place in this thesis. In other words, events which took place early during my stay in Kebkabiya might come up in later chapters as part of the process of dialectics in which seemingly meaningless events might get meaning in a context of importance at a later date. Both Yasmin and Johan might appear and then disappear from my narratives as they might or might not be part of the contexts, which are important in order to understand a narrative.

The messiness of 'peeling an onion', in the sense of understanding the process of inter-subjective knowledge production as a dialectic process, is a point of departure for 'writing against the grain'. In my attempt at representing the narratives as part of their contexts, and vice versa, this resulted in a rather unorthodox way of writing up, in particular when representing the diverse narratives, those of the women involved and of myself. My desire to 'write against the grain' has therefore consequences for the format of this book.

Of Discourses, Texts and Contexts: The Format of the Book

The title of my book, *One Foot in Heaven*, refers to two *hadith*, religiously inspired sayings, based on religious texts and stories about the life of Mohammed. These *hadith* proved to be representative of the ambiguity in dominant moral discourses on the 'good Muslim woman'. An ambiguity that was displayed in the narratives of the government on the correct role of women, as well as in the negotiations of these discourses by different groups of working women. These *hadith* therefore constituted the hinges around which the diverse narratives and intersecting identities revolved. In order to understand these movements, the book consists of three parts, each focusing on a different dimension of the process of the inter-subjective knowledge process, on different narratives and subjects. Although the representation follows the process of inter-subjective knowledge production 'bottom-up', this is not done in a void. Therefore each part is introduced by a brief and thus specific theoretical and analytical history of the most important concepts and theoretical perspectives, which are articulated in the chapters in that part. They represent a history that constitutes a part of my narrative coming of age as an anthropologist.

Part One—Settings: Discourses and Contexts, focuses on those discourses that constitute the most important context in which I will 'read' the biographic narratives as well as diverse events in Kebkabiya against the grain. This part therefore contextualizes the choices I made for the kinds of readings of the narratives I will represent in this book and deals mainly with the concepts of discourse, contexts, and agency. It exemplifies the main contexts of my 'listening against the grain': both the academic context of the insights and presuppositions I brought with me and the context of Kebkabiya, the local setting in which I performed my research. In Chapter 1, I will try to understand the terms of the discourse of the Islamist government in contemporary Sudan, which determined the positions that were allotted to diverse subjects. For this reason I will contextualize the speeches of the visiting popular committee introduced at the beginning of this chapter. I will relate the diverse themes addressed in these speeches to different historical contexts, as well as to discourses on women and Islam in two different locations, the West and the Sudan. Although these seemingly falsify and contradict, undermine and negate each other, the discourses are quite similar in the way women are objectified. This encourages me to consider some feminist perspectives on the issue of

'Women and Islam' in order to position myself in relation to both discourses.

In Chapter 2, I introduce the local setting of Kebkabiya, the provincial town in Darfur where I conducted my fieldwork in the two periods mentioned. I will recount events and experiences in a self-reflective mode not as a goal as such, but to provide insights into local and national power relations that I otherwise would not have been able to grasp. This serves to better understand how the local situation intersected with the Islamist moral discourse on gender. This, in turn gives another context to the ways in which working women in Kebkabiya and myself were positioned. After the 'what, who and where' of my research, I will end Part One by considering the 'how'. Here I will indicate on what textual and discursive aspects I will focus in the analyses of the biographic narratives of the working women I met.

In *Part Two—Settling: Biographic Narratives as Texts-in-context*, I will represent the narratives of two women: Hajja, a market woman, in Chapter 3 and Umm Khalthoum, a teacher, in Chapter 4. The biographic narrative as research method, as analytical means, and as a mode of representation and the idea of performing identities are the concepts, which I relate to each other. In my contextualisations, I focus on the way each woman reflected on the discourse and to what end. This 'reading against the grain' of the narratives of both women, is related to diverse contexts, which connect to the diverse layers in the 'texts' these narratives constitute. In order to distinguish the biographic narratives of Hajja and Umm Khalthoum and the narratives of contextualization and analysis, which I construct around those narratives, as well as my self-reflexive account, I will use distinct paragraph headings and section indicators, which I explain in the introduction to Part Two.

The reading of the biographic narratives as 'texts-in-contexts' is focused on understanding the ways in which each woman constructed multiple identities. Therefore, in Chapter 5, I look for similarities and differences in the narratives of Hajja and Umm Khalthoum by doing a rather unorthodox comparison: I will relate both narratives to each other and to structural differences between the classes to which both women belong. This search aids my understanding of the commonalities in the negotiations of the moral discourse by both women, which was a result of their identities *as women*. The differences in interpretation of the moral discourse and the diversity in negotiations by both women as reflected in the narratives will be related to their different socio-economic backgrounds, based on aspects like locality and class.

In *Part Three—Unsettled: In the Border Zone*, I will take another look at the insights gained from the analyses in Parts One and Two. The flexibility and permeability of boundaries and the contingency and flux of constructed identities, in particular of gendered identities, are the focus of this last Part. Therefore, I will try to come up with a more dynamic perspective on power relations and related discourses, strategies and identities, which appeared quite self-evident in the first two parts. The main concepts I use for gearing this process are deconstruction, border-zone, and difference. In Chapter 6, I will deconstruct the self-evidence of the differences between 'the' market woman and 'the' female teacher as put forward by the dominant discourse of the government. In looking at the narratives of some colleagues of Hajja and Umm Khalthoum, it becomes clear that aspects such as education and generation resulted in varying constructions of identities among the market women and among the female teachers. The unmarried status was for young working women from both classes an issue which they took into account when reflecting on their positions in relation to the dominant discourse. However, the options open for young single market woman to construct alternative subject positions differed from the ways single female teachers could negotiate their position as single working Muslim women. In relation to the 'marriage problem' as the Sudanese government put it, in Chapter 7 I will relate the moral discourse on femininity to constructions of masculinity. Female teachers, who were members of the same class as government officials, proved to be able to claim more space for negotiating an alternative subject position than the discourse seemed to allow for. Educated elite women therefore turned out to be most successful in articulating an alternative subject position in reference to the construction of masculinity by educated elite men.

My representation of the research as a process does not lead to a conclusive and authoritative end. As a result, Chapter 8, *Boundaries Con/Text-analysed: Gender Identities and Resistance* is to be read as a way of rounding off my narrative as an anthropologist rather than as a set conclusion. In this narrative, I will discuss the different perspectives with which I have listened, read and written the narratives of working women in Kebkabiya against the grain. These are the rhetoric, the argumentative and the strategic perspective. They bring out the relations in the narratives between the subject positions, gender identifications and strategies of narration by both classes of working women. With respect to the strategic perspective, I will consider the possibility of taking the narrated identities as forms of resistance. This will lead me to consider again the relation between femininity and masculinity in the Sudanese context, this time with respect to national and ethnic identities. In the Epilogue of Chapter 8, I will briefly reflect on the war in Darfur. Although I have no first-hand information about the conflict, my research in the 1990s and my preliminary research in Khartoum among Darfur migrants in 1999–2000, led me to denounce the idea that this is an ethnic conflict, or ethnic-religious conflict between Sudanese Arab Muslims and Black African farmers, as some politicians, academics and the media would have it. I will, rather, argue for considering the war as a problem of citizenship.

1 A typical street in Kebkabiya (courtesy of Johan de Smedt)

2 The main market day in Kebkabiya (courtesy of Johan de Smedt)

3 Hajja's sister taking care of Hajja's place at the onion market

4 Young married market women and their children at Kebkabiya market

5 Young single market woman selling fruits at Kebkabiya market (courtesy of Johan de Smedt)

6 Umm Khalthoum dressed in a white *tobe* during a school activity (courtesy of Johan de Smedt)

7 A classroom at the Intermediary School for Girls at Kebkabiya

8 Umm Khalthoum with five of her children

9 Hajja in her white *tobe* with her (grand-)children and her co-wife's children

10 Female teachers and author at a picknick
(courtesy of Johan de Smedt)

11 The Fur *shartai* Ahmedaii, local leaders and project members at a *karama* (courtesy of Johan de Smedt)

12 Local women from Hajja's neighbourhood and author at a coffee party

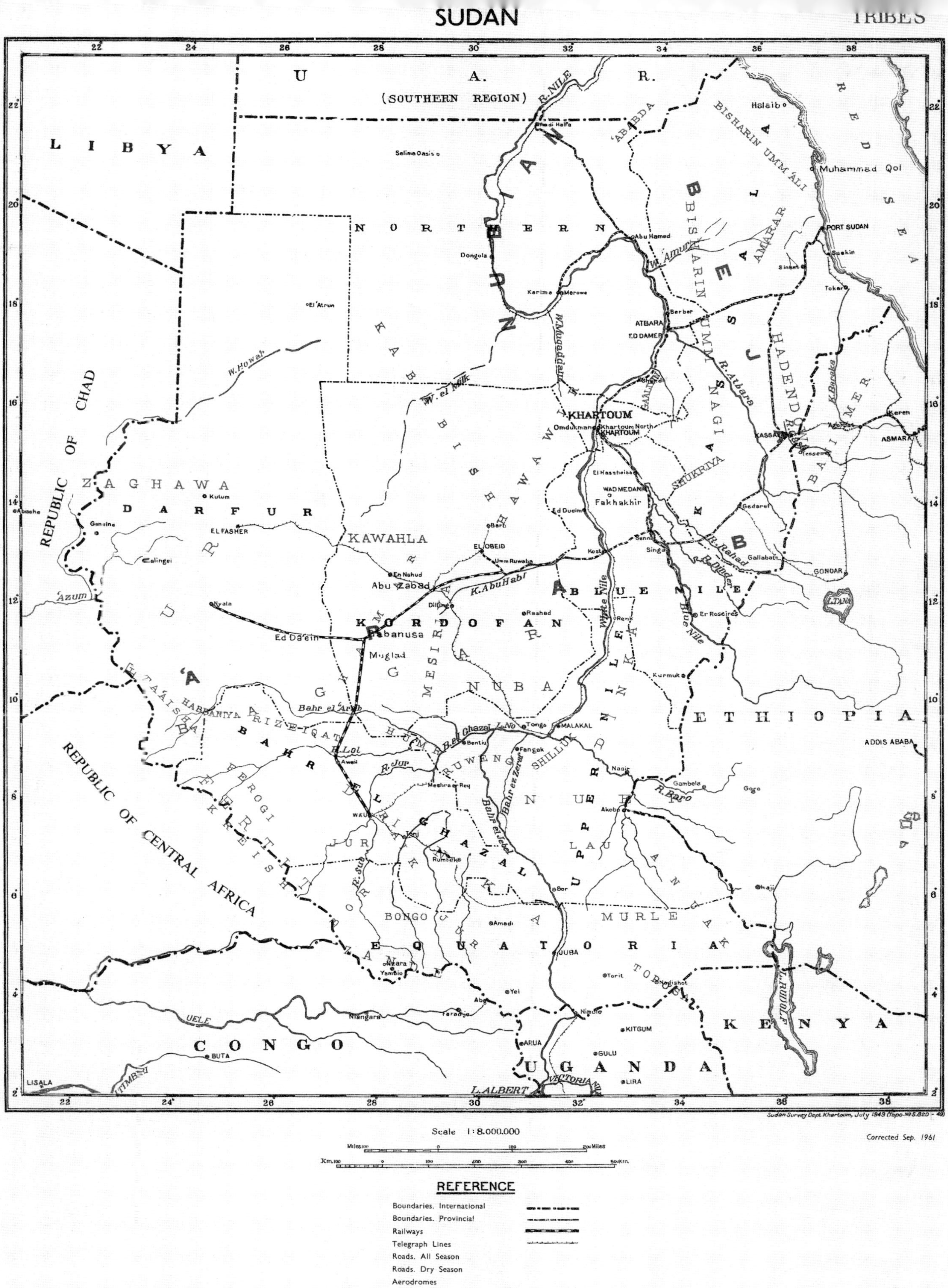

Sudan map 2: Sudan (Tribes) 1961 [1949]. Source: Sudan Survey Department Khartoum.
Note: no mention of Arab camel nomads in Northern Darfur.

Sudan map 3: Sudan (Political, in Arabic) 1961 [1952]. Source: Sudan Survey Department Khartoum.
Note: On this map Kebkabiya is given - between Al-Fasher and Al-Geneina.

PART ONE

SETTINGS
DISCOURSES AND CONTEXTS

[Thesaurus]

Setting: *Fixed Contours, Location, Site, Backdrop, Scenery*
Surroundings: *The surroundings or environment in which something exists*
Set for Performance: *The set, including props and scenery, where actors perform a film or play*
Period or Place of Story: *The period in time or the place in which the events of a story take place*

When writing about the narratives of working women in Kebkabiya, I do not deal with words only.[1] Along come sounds and smells. I remember the sounds coming from the clusters of compounds, which bordered the wide sandy streets along which I plodded ever so often. These mingled with the sounds of the desert wind tearing at the *hosh*, the compound walls of millet stalks; with those of donkey charts driven by boys who would click their tongues to fasten the speed of their overburdened donkeys; with the crowing of roosters from somewhere in the quarter; and always there would be voices, of men, women, children. Different voices, which, especially on a market day, would blend with all other sounds into the convivial noise of social gathering. I also remember the smells of 'coming home', however temporarily Kebkabiya was my home; of the cattle in the pin, or the musky scrub, *dilka*, used for smoothing and scenting the skin which Hajja used regularly, or of *asida*, the thick sorghum porridge, we ate almost daily, its taste and texture smoothened by the rich gravy that goes with it, and which at first I had difficulties to swallow. Now I sometimes wake up in the morning yearning for its taste: but more so for the people who in my experience, belong to preparing and sharing this local staple. Despite the moments of loneliness and of longing for my loved ones 'back home', of the lack

[1] In each of the introductions of a Part, I will use notes also to refer to literature: as these introductions serve as a guide to my research and representation thereof, I sometimes refer to a considerable number of sources, which might render the text otherwise difficult to read.

of privacy especially when ill, or of the fear of 'bandits' roaming around the country side, at those moments I long to be in Kebkabiya again. Not only because of the pace of life, the desert landscape, or the intense colours of people moving with ease and grace. It is also who I would become when I was addressed with '*Sitt* Catharina', the honorary term of 'Misstress or Madame' extended to educated women who work for the government. A title I shared with the female teachers, my one time neighbours when Johan, Yasmin and I lived in a stone-build house—with-corrugated-roof adjacent to the intermediary school for girls. Or my feeling of pride and protection when I was genealogically located with '*naas*' Hajja, 'belonging to the people' of Hajja, and situated at her compound in the middle of town, next to the market place.

Part One constitutes the first step in my search for the ways in which working women in Kebkabiya constructed gendered identities in the context of the dominant Islamist discourse of the Sudanese government. For me, writing about working women in Kebkabiya is writing about a specific place. It is about particular 'Settings', a term which refers not only to a *scenery* or the *fixed contours* that constitute the *backdrop* of events, although I might represent the context as such, in order to be able to read the biographic narratives 'against the grain'. 'Settings' is taken to refer more specifically to *surroundings in which something exists* as well as the *period in time or the place in which the events of a story take place*; in other words the *site* where the subjects *perform.* 'Settings' thus refers to both set places and spaces of action.

The term 'settings' is important in order to qualify the notion of 'context'. I will read the biographic narratives of working women against the grain by applying what I call a 'con/text-analysis'. The slash refers to the intertwining of texts with the particular contexts in which these carry meaning: it also indicates that the distinction between text and context is an analytical device. 'Text' refers to a wide array of 'readable' signs whether written, oral, visual, corporeal, virtual, imaginary, or any other sensory mediation. This reading of texts as signs takes place in certain contexts. 'Context' is thus a discursive *site*, a space in which texts are allotted meaning and thus are constituted by, and in turn constituting, discourses. 'Discourse' is 'that by which reality becomes ordered' and 'the means by which differences, for example between people, become produced'. Discourses therefore can be 'anything that carries meaning' as well as those 'things we do'.[2] By relating

[2] Foucault (1972: 80). The quotations between brackets all come from Alsop et. al.

discourses to specific settings, these meanings become tied to particular spaces and places, in a set period of time. Discourses are made up of both texts and contexts, with material and immaterial effects that permeate both the 'inside' and the 'outside' world. This importance of location, of a specified context for understanding the meaning of texts, relates 'settings' to the notion of *intertextuality*.

In the introduction I pointed out that the notion of *intertextuality* allows for texts to have a multiplicity of meaning and thus it creates conceptual room for ambiguity with respect to 'the' meaning of a text.[3] I consider this term helpful as it stimulates me in looking for other meanings of the narratives of working women than only the obvious. At the same time the suggestion that *intertextuality* can, in principle, give rise to countless interpretations is also problematic. In daily practice the reading of a text is bound to the particular context in which the process of constructing meaning takes place. Like Fairclough, I assume that *intertextuality* (i.e. the 'productivity of texts') 'is not in practice available to people as a limitless space for textual innovation and play: it is socially limited and constrained, and conditional upon relations of power'.[4] The relation between *intertextuality* and power is important as it points at specific discourses which may restrict the number of readings of a text in a specific context.

The notion of 'settings' therefore qualifies the more general notion of context to a more particular, in time and space defined context of Kebkabiya. My use of 'settings' allows me as the narrator of this book, to anchor events, and their representation in narratives, to a particular location in a specified period of time. A setting in which, at the time of my research, certain discourses dominated and gave precedence to certain textual meanings over others. Dominant discourses can thus determine which meanings are represented and reproduced as the 'truth'.[5]

In understanding why in Kebkabiya society some discourses dominate more than others means I have to look for 'key-shifts' in Sudanese history which gives an insight into the 'working' of current discursive

(2003: 81–82) discussing Foucault's view of discourse and which I reproduce here. See also Mills (1999: 6).

[3] Fairclough (1992: 105); Mills (1997: 148–159).

[4] Fairclough (1992: 103), quoted also in Mills 1997: 154).

[5] Foucault (1981: 70).

structures.[6] The same is true for discourses on Islamic societies in the West. Part One therefore focuses on those discourses that are relevant in the two main settings of my research: the local context of Kebkabiya in which I conducted my research as well as the academic context in which this research was given meaning and turned into a scientific text. The main dominant discourse the narratives of the women and men of Kebkabiya negotiated with was the Islamist moral discourse of the new military government of the Sudan. This government came to power in 1989, only a little over a year before I arrived in Kebkabiya. It claimed legitimacy on the basis of its Islamist project for a 'new' Sudanese state that would thus throw off the shackles of its (post)colonial history. To achieve this, the government constructed a specific interpretation of Sudan's political history that emphasized specific *intertextual* readings of its political goals, moral discourses and practical interventions. In this way the Islamist dominant discourse of the Sudanese government can also be seen as a 'key-shift' in that it produced a new 'regime of truth'. In order to understand what this shift has meant for the local people, I look in Chapter 1 closely at the speeches delivered by government officials of the popular committee addressing the townspeople of Kebkabiya in December 1991, the same speeches I referred to in the Introduction. In these speeches Darfur men, women and foreigners were are all allotted particular subject positions by the Islamist moral discourse. The close reading of some parts of these speeches points at the subject positions which the Islamist government in Sudan ideally allotted to men and women.

The notion of 'Islamism' is sometimes referred to as 'Islamic fundamentalism',[7] a term that has triggered heated debates in the West. In these debates a particular imagery is projected onto the Islamic world. No 'postcolonial'[8] account can ignore Said's work '*Orientalism*' (1978) in which he reflects critically on this imagery which points at a particular relation between the West and what he calls the 'Orient'. Said shows how the western body of knowledge based on travel accounts, poetry, eye-witness reports, and novels of mainly white European males, pro-

[6] Foucault calls this way of historical research 'archeology of knowledge (Foucault 1972)'.

[7] As the term is often used in a denigrating and pejorative way, I prefer Islamism. See Chapter 1 for an elaboration on this issue.

[8] 'The notion 'postcolony' identifies specifically a given historical trajectory—that of societies recently emerging from the experience of colonization and the violence which the colonial relationship involves (Mbembe 2001: 102)'.

duced a collective western image of the 'Orient' rather than reflecting any 'real' society or culture. The Orient was construed as the 'Other' and was cast in negative terms that denigrated it and contrasted it with the civilised, and thus superior, notion of the West. Scholars working on Islamic societies were often beguiled by this regime of 'truth' and also (re-)produced this 'knowledge' so becoming complicit in the 'Western style of dominating, restructuring, and having authority over the Orient'.[9] In this sense, Said's work itself constituted a key-shift in the academic history of thinking and writing on the relation between 'West' and 'East'. In Chapter 1, I position myself and my research in terms of this Orientalist discourse by tackling the topic of 'Women and Islam', an issue which has aroused much debate both in the 'West' and the 'East'. In Chapter 2, I go on to look at how men and women in the local context of Kebkabiya town reflected on the positioning of women in relation to the 'new' Islamist moral discourse as well as on the way I was positioned by it.

The notion of 'Settings' thus provides a focus of analysis to explore which discourses are most forceful and thus dominant or hegemonic in restricting the number of meanings of a text in a particular context, in a certain location at a given moment in time. My 'reading against the grain' is a way of understanding the biographic narratives of women as part of this setting. It does not refer to just a 'reading between the lines'. Rather it is part of 'resisting reading', which requires the reader to take a different reading position than the one offered by the discourse that directs the meaning of the text.[10] In my 'reading against the grain' this resisting reading is a means with which I will try to deconstruct a text in its context in search for its multiple meanings. I will also thus try to understand alternative identities working women construct in relation to that dominant discourse. This brings me to the issue of how to view 'subject' and 'identity', as Said, like Foucault, did not take into account the possibility of people negotiating their position within discourses. I turn to post-colonial, subaltern, gender and feminist studies in order to

[9] Said 1978: 4; see also Mills 1997: 106–108; Moors 1991: 114–115.

[10] See Meijer (1996: 78) refers to Judith Fetterley who developed the term 'resistant reading' in 1978 in: "The resistant reader: A feminist approach to American fiction". Resistant reading is comparable to reading against the grain in order to find positive, and potentially empowering female subject positions which are often not provided by the text. See also Spivak (for example 1999: 266–311;) for a similar strategy in order to understand the perspective of the 'colonized subject' or 'subaltern' on its own history of domination.

understand the way 'subjects' construct 'identities' as actors who are actively involved in the (re)production of (colonial and postcolonial) knowledge, domination and subversion as well as in resistance. This view of the relation between texts-in-context and identities of subjects brings into view the notion of *intersectionality* and *intersubjectivity*. Analogous to *intertextuality, intersectionality* and *intersubjectivity* refer to the possibility that subjects who share the same context, do not necessarily relate in a similar way to the subject position they are allotted by the dominant discourse. The different evaluations and experiences subjects may have of the discourse and its effect, despite the fact that they are positioned similarly, points at the possibility that subjects construct their identities differently: this is indicated by the term *intersectionality*. It also allows for understanding the agency of subjects, however restricted their subject positions may seem: this is indicated by the notion of *intersubjectivity*.

In Part One *intertextuality* is the main focus of analysis as it looks at those dominant discourses that restrict and determine the context in which I will read the biographic narratives of women as texts. As *intersectionality*, which will be the focus of Part Two, and *intersubjectivity*, which is the main theme of Part Three, are related to *intertextuality*, I will here briefly give a background to the way I perceive these terms and the way they are connected.

Intertextuality and identities

As with the notion of *intertextuality*, the identities of a person in a particular social context are restricted and limited by normative dominant discourses.[11] Dominant discourses define and articulate certain identities for certain people. In my research I will focus in particular on how the Islamist discourse defined certain gendered identities for women, thus allotting women, and men, certain circumscribed subject positions. Thereby there is a restricted number of identities which are allowed for; for example in the case of the Islamist discourse in Sudan women are cast in particular as wives and mothers. What is interesting for me is to understand how different classes of women in their daily lives are able to construct multiplicity and diversity in their identities while adhering to these restricted identities of mothers and wives.

[11] The notion of normative discourses relates to Foucault's thesis about disciplining the body and the connection to power (1979), see for example Alsop et. al. (2003: 82–83).

The notion of identity is highly contested as it suggests fixity, closure and unification, while I consider identities to be fragmented, fluid and transformative. Still, I opt for 'identity' rather than 'identification'[12]as I think that people construct their notions of self *as if* these are fixed, stable and unified as it is the only way people can make sense of and deal with the processes of change and transformation that they are part of. In short, what people do by constructing identities is to 'fix the flux'[13] whereby an identity is not an 'essence' but a 'positioning' within a discourse. The illusion of identities as closed, unified and stable are the result of a process of marking difference and excluding what is 'other' in order to arrive at a constructed, and thus temporary closure.[14] I do not want to do away with the notion of identity, but rather, re-define it as a process of 'becoming'.

In order to explore this process of becoming, I connect *intertextuality* to *intersectionality*. People do not have identities, they perform them whereby I do not consider the performance to refer to an 'interior essence' that exists prior to the social influences which form our identities. On the contrary, it is through our performances and those of others that we create ourselves as subjects, where the performance 'passes as(*sic*) the real'.[15] Thereby gender intersects with identities based on class, ethnicity, race, age, sexuality etc.[16] Although these intersecting identities can not be separated, for reasons of analysis I will try to understand how, in a particular context, the particular intersection of certain identities is prioritised by women in order to negotiate restricted 'dominant' gendered subject positions. For me *intersectionality* refers precisely to the multiplicity of these identity constructions, and of the variability of the way some identities are prioritised over others depending on the context. Thus, *intersectionality* also refers to the (variable) ways that people construct identities to fix the flux in particular contexts, in particular periods of time.

---

[12] See for example Hall (1996: 4) who also deals with both concepts and issues of fixity and fluidity.

[13] This expression I borrow from Meyer and Geschiere (1999) who use it in the context of globalization and the construction of local, communal identities (1–14); see also Gayatri Spivak (1988).

[14] Hall (1990: 226 and 1996: 4–5).

[15] Butler (1990a: viii). See also: Alsop et. al. (2003: 99–101); it should be read as 'passes for the real'.

[16] Among feminist scholars this intersectionality has become common place. See for example Braidotti (2001: 16); Butler (1990a: 3); Moore (1994).

This prioritising is, however, not (always) conscious, voluntary, or at will, nor is it pre-determined or defined. Again there is a dynamic between the way the context is constituted by—and in turn constitutes—a multiplicity of (normative) discourses and the way in which people are positioned. This process creates a contingency of meaning, both of the text-in-context and the related subject positions. In a similar way that the notion of 'settings' helps me to focus on a specific context for understanding, in principle, infinite possible meanings that texts may have, it helps to restrict the possible intersecting identities that are performed in narrating about one's self.

My endeavour to read the biographic narratives of working women for intersecting identities in relation to intertextuality calls for a spatial conceptualisation of identity as 'the spaces in which we are called on "to identify" ourselves, the locations in which we are asked to declare our identities... This requires a spatial discourse in which the body shifting between different spaces/sites, serves itself as the site of different forms of subjectification'.[17] A spatial notion of identity allows for an understanding of the positioning of subjects in certain locations taking up certain identities as different from others, in other locations. 'Settings' thereby not only refers to this compounded view of subjects as located in time and place, but also to the space allowed to persons to negotiate the terms of their daily life.

My understanding of how persons negotiate identities in a certain setting, will thereby be a 'mapping, not tracing'[18] of identities, as 'the map has to do with performance',[19] while tracing suggests linearity, the self-assured connection from a starting-point to an end station, a point of arrival. As I want to discover how the negotiations of the dominant discourse on gender might lead to the construction of alternative subject positions, mapping forms a means to create the open mind this requires as 'mapping is experimental and future oriented, seeking to imagine what has not yet come into being'.[20] Thereby the reference to

---

[17] Rose (1996: 140–142; quoted in Silberstein 2000: 10–11).

[18] This is the title of Silberstein's introduction 'Mapping not tracing' of the edited volume *Mapping Jewish Identities*. See also Pile and Thrift 1995 (47–49) who relate the map to the subject in order to think power, knowledge and meaning in spatial terms (see also Silberstein 2000: 5). A different kind of 'tracing' is dealt with by De Certeau in his notion of 'tour' (1988: 115–130). I will return to this notion in the introduction to Part Two.

[19] Silberstein (2000: 6) refers here to Deleuze and Guattri (1989: 12–13).

[20] Silberstein (2000: 6–8).

the 'body shifting between different space/sites' brings me to the notion of *intersubjectivity* which articulates both the embodied nature of subjectivity and the relationality of identity constructions.

Arriving at a bend in the road: Intersubjectivity and the issue of agency

I consider the narratives of working women in Kebkabiya to be not just 'texts'. They constitute the ways women position themselves in a text within a particular context and the meanings constructed in relation to both. In telling their narratives women are subjected to the same discourses which endowed them with subjectivity.[21] While engaging in this process of subjectification the ambiguity of the meaning of narratives creates room for the narrators to negotiate those restricted and often restrictive subject-positions which are allotted to women. While the notion of *intersectionality* makes it possible to understand the multiplicity of constructions of self within women's narratives, and the negotiation of subject-positions in a certain context, it leaves open the question how alternative identities are thereby constructed.

The notion of *intersubjectivity* refers to the process whereby a person can only 'become one's self' in relation to other individuals who thereby become part of this 'self'.[22] The contingency of meaning of text-in-context has its bearing on the multiplicity of identities. If the meaning of a text can not be completely controlled, then narrating about one's self might also create ambiguity about the meaning of that self. This may lead to the construction of alternative subject positions, and in the process discourses may be transformed, which leads me to the concept of agency.[23] 'Agency' is thereby not an attribute or a property of a person, but refers to the 'ongoing reconfigurings of the

---

[21] The question of the relation between subjection and subjectivity is highly debated. I take my lead from discussions of the work of Butler (for example 1993, 1994, 1995a&b, 1997; see also for example in: Alsop et. al. 2003: 99) in relation to Foucault (see for example Alsop et.al. 2003: 80–85, 94–114; Mills 1997: 103). For a discussion on 'ex-centring' the subject by Kristeva see for example "The critique of the sign" in Coward and Ellis (1977: 122–159).

[22] Lacan has referred to the acknowledgement of this 'becoming' by the ego, in psycho-analytical terms, as the 'mirror-stage' whereby 'the ego is not self-contained and autonomous, but is intersubjective and depends on its relations with the other' (Lacan 1977, discussed in Moore 1994: 42–43).

[23] See also: Alsop (2003: 81–84).

world'.[24] In these 'reconfigurings' the body is 'ones primary location in the world, one's primary situation in reality'.[25] The body becomes an interface between the material and the discursive, which renders our knowledge of 'the world' embodied and situated and thus partial, subjective and located. Thereby 'experience' is an important way of acquiring knowledge of and in the world.[26]

At the same time, an individual is not autonomously engaged in this process: becoming a subject means that one is positioned relative to others. This connects agency to *intersubjectivity*; to the space between subjects. *Intersubjectivity* together with *intertextuality* and *intersectionality*, provide me with the analytical tools to view people as capable of critical reflection of the same discourses that seem to determine their actions, thoughts and desires *in relation to others*. This is true as much for the women narrating their narratives as for the anthropologist. As I myself became a part of the local configurations of power, discursive struggles and narrated identities, I also became a subject in these *intersubjective* processes of knowledge production. Thereby I brought also part of my identities from another context, that of my 'home', into the intersected identities I constructed in that context. In order to 'critically reflect' on the discourses that position me and direct my own actions, thoughts and desires, I have to engage in an ongoing process of self-reflexivity.

In doing so, I want to take you, as reader, by the hand and *show* rather than *tell* about this process of understanding. This is not just an issue of choosing a format nor a mode of representation: it constitutes the core of doing research 'against the grain'. A West-African saying goes: '*l'étranger ne vois que se qu' il sais*', 'the stranger sees only what s/he knows'. By taking one careful analytical step at the time, I hope to learn how to see more than I know. However, representing this process of seeing differently, following its meandering course, is never innocent, nor transparent and it does not reflect the actual chronology of discovery. What you will read is, like all anthropological representations, a 're-reconstruction'. In other words, this book represents my reflections on modes of listening, reading and writing 'against the grain' with the benefit of hindsight and the privilege of the pen.

---

[24] Barad (2003: 818).

[25] Braidotti (1991: 219).

[26] An insightful historical account of experience is given by Joan W. Scott in her article 'The evidence of experience (1991)'. See also the introduction to Part Two.

CHAPTER I

FOREIGNERS, FEMALES AND DISCOURSES ON ISLAM

> Greetings to the prophet Mohammed, may peace be upon him and on ʿAli and their companions until the Day of days. *Salaam ala ahbaab ar-rasuul*, Greetings to the beloved of the prophet.

After the opening lines of the local *faqih* I quoted in the Introduction,[1] it is the popular committee's turn to take the stage. The first of the five members, who is also a *faqih* begins, as is the custom at every sermon, with elaborate blessings related to the prophet Mohammed and other illustrious religious persons, using a microphone. The other four members are seated on a makeshift elevation, all of them bathed in generator-driven neon light, a rarity in a town such as Kebkabiya, which has no electricity.

During the speeches I sit with the other women behind a parked Land Rover, out of sight of the stage as if we do not really belong to the audience. It is probably just as well, for I have my tape recorder with me to record the speeches. Some teenage boys have gathered around some of the black sturdy bicycles. They joke and jest just out of hearing distance from the main audience. The men, who are slightly more numerous than the women, sit in the illuminated area in front of the stage, near the central entrance to the mosque. I will start this chapter by relating the subjects discussed in the speeches to the local context, as I understood it at the moment of recording, whilst listening to the addresses. Next, I will focus on the main subjects of these speeches, in particular on the way these were formulated and argued. In this way I want to gain an insight into the goal of the moral discourse. Moreover, these considerations will lead me to position my research and the biographic narratives of the women within its academic and political context.

---

[1] I pick up the speeches after the address of the *faqih* whom I quoted in the introduction when he was discussing greeting habits. These are the opening lines of the speech of the first speaker of the popular committee from Kutum.

The *faqih* has finished his speech on the correct Islamic greetings and now his colleague takes his place behind the microphone. His speech addresses the audience directly:

> …Now the government has declared *shari'a* and where are we? Did the country declare it or we? The government will control with fixed punishments, but what about our souls, what about our behaviour? This depends on us; we have to raise our consciousness, in order to correct our behaviour, and that of our children, our families. This is what Mohammed our prophet told us. When a Muslim knows wine is *haraam*, forbidden on religious grounds, it means *shari'a*. When he knows that adultery is *haraam*, he knows that it is *shari'a* too. And if most people know these things, then only a few left will be punished, if the government catches them. If we follow the right and give up the bad, we will be the right nation, *al-umma al-islamiya*… And if we do not, that means our belief is still weak… This is a test for us, to see who are better in their deeds and lives. And we will know after we die. Did God create us and life and death for play? No! He created these as examinations for us. And if our lives are as bad as they are now, why don't we obey God honestly? Why don't we obey him wholeheartedly?
>
> If we want to live like this, in a worldly way, not bothering about life and death, we can disobey Allah and be worldly, like the Europeans. If you believe in worldly things, not in death, and aspire to a life like that of the *khawadyaat* (the western foreigners), then after death you will go to hell. But in your worldly life you will be happy and have a high standard of life. If you don't want to go to hell, then follow the right way of Allah. Give up disobedience of God and follow His way correctly so. He will give us the good things in the world and we will go to heaven as well…
>
> If we don't believe and obey but follow the western foreigners because we see they make aeroplanes and bombing equipment and we return from their countries, saying 'They are very happy in their countries, they have a high standard of life', we will become preoccupied with their things. Our hearts might follow their lifestyle but we will not gain from it. Only if we believe and obey, we will be given as he gives them… But the happiness of life means little for in the life hereafter one day equals a thousand days in this life: if you live a hundred years, it means in the life hereafter, you will live two hours and 24 minutes…

I hear women around me snorting in disagreement; others giggle a bit while the speaker is comparing their standard of life with that of the foreigners from the West. Some women start talking to each other while others are bending over their babies, trying to feed them under their *tobes*, the typical Sudanese veil of a six to nine meter cloth about a meter in width, which women wrap loosely around themselves over their dresses.[2] The *tobes* now protect them from the biting desert wind.

The speaker urges his audience to take responsibility for their souls by taking heed of the Islamic rules about the correct conduct: to act *halaal* as opposite to *haraam*.[3] If people would only follow the *shari'a*, the path of Allah, and become better believers instead of 'craving for' the western goods and lifestyle then they would be rewarded in the afterlife. In this part foreigners are perceived of having a bad influence on the Sudanese due to their lifestyle but the speaker also suggest that they are to be perceived as enemies. The 'aeroplanes and bombing equipment' clearly refers to the Gulf War, which was waged earlier that year. I now also see a connection with the Jews being the 'first enemies of Islam' as indicated by the first speaker: Israel had been a target of Iraqi bombing during the Gulf War. Clearly the beginning of Islam and the current political situation of the Sudan are somehow related. This is also reflected in the greetings at the beginning in which he explicitly refers to 'Ali, the cousin and son-in-law of the prophet Mohammed, who formed the fourth successor, or *khalif*, to the *Sunni* Muslims, but the first "righteous" successor in *Shi'a* perspective: though this issue of succession was a bone of contention for ages, 'Ali constituted the first *khalif* or *Imam* who was acknowledged by both the *Sunni* and *Shi'a* Muslims. This might refer to recent political changes as Iran has since the founding of an Islamic state figured as an example and an ally for the current Islamist regime of Sudan (cf. Warburg 2003: 209).

The main issue in this section, however, is to get people back to the right path. To convince his audience, the speaker uses apparently complicated mathematics to indicate the quantitative nature of suffering in the life hereafter. Towards the end, the argument gets a peculiar twist when the speaker points out that through the effort of abstinence, Muslim believers might be able to enjoy the same standard of life as western foreigners already do in this life. This statement gets another dimension in the next part of his speech:

> If we would be *kufar*, infidels, Allah would open his good things for us like for the Americans. They do as they like. But we are not infidels;

---

[2] The *tobe*, also spelled as *tawb* or *tob*, in its current form was adopted by bourgeois women under the Turco-Egyptian rule (1823–1882) when a new fabric produced in India, which was a British colony at that time, was introduced. The new fabric caused a different way of wearing, as compared to the local veil which was made of home spun course cotton or even of leather (Spaulding 1985: 193).

[3] Prescribed on religious ground as opposite to forbidden on religious grounds.

> there is belief in our hearts. Nevertheless, we are not honest believers. If our hearts would be clear, Allah would open all good things for us as well, like for the infidels. But we are with ill hearts. Would God let the ill of heart go? No, he will punish them! This punishment we can feel now: you work, the mother works, your children work and even then the income is not enough. You can compare 1950 with today. In the past, the employee was comfortable and happy and his salary was enough to provide for his family. And now it is not. We say because that was the time of the British, but this is not true: they destroyed our works. This is because we don't follow the right way of Allah. Our lives are very difficult and hard, we work and work and it is not enough for us. We can't fill our stomachs. This is our life today... And now, are we also dressed with the dress of hunger and fear? Yes, we are and we ask the foreigners for relief and we beg them... They give us relief but it is so little, it hardly fills our stomachs. Because they are our enemies! They don't like you until you follow their religion. They give you money and deceive you: they want you to be with them. All Muslims return to God's way! This dress of hunger and fear is not going to be taken away until we follow the right way and only if we part behave better. There is also no end to the armed robberies even if Omar Al-Beshir[4] brought planes and heavy guns to fight them. Understand this well and keep in mind that this is from Allah because we left His way. This is His punishment. Who can take this dress from us? Only Allah. Hunger, even if we plant all the ground with crops it will not satisfy us. Until we return to Allah, and believe in Him honestly...
>
> This community is a bad community. You can find many children here without fathers: more than twenty in one quarter. And we ask God for pity? And we say that we are Muslims and we kill among ourselves? Did God create us to fight and harm each other? He created a lot of tribes and nations for us, to get to know one another and to understand each other, not to fight... Now we have become divided amongst ourselves: Arabs, Fur, Tunjur, Zaghawa, Gimr, all tribes on their own, killing each other...

In this section, foreigners are again cast as enemies, this time due to their history with the Sudan: as former colonisers and as donors of, predominantly, food-aid. Although the foreigners are given the blame, they are not the ones who are punished. Punishment is the fate of the 'ill of heart' in Darfur, who are struck thrice: with economic hardship, ethnic clashes, and immoral sexual practices. The economic crisis affected the whole of Sudan, but in particular employees who are referred to in the first sentences. Most employees live in towns, depending on a

[4] The captain who led the military coup at the 30th of June 1989 and who became self-acclaimed president of the Sudan of the military junta.

salary that makes the effects of inflation and rising prices for them more obvious. Further, at the moment of speaking Darfur was once more dealing with a famine, the previous one having only occurred in 1983–1984. The relatively short period since this last drought had left little opportunity for people to recover, especially since the harvests in the intermediate period (1985–1989) were not particularly good either.[5] Finally, the speaker refers to religious texts in order to condemn the ethnic fighting which had recurred since this drought period. In Darfur these so called 'tribal' clashes took place mainly between the nomadic groups, the Arab and Zaghawa, and sedentary farmers, the Fur, Tunjur and Gimr, who quarreled over access to resources such as water and grazing/agricultural fields.

The economic crisis, famine, and ethnic conflicts are related to the bad conduct and disbelief of the Darfur population. As the local population evaluates the former foreign, colonial and non-Muslim, government of the British positively and now praises and relies on foreign, Christian, food-aid that are both effect and cause of their current dire circumstances.

The vice the speaker mentions next is not related to these disasters, but concerns illegitimate, or (so-called) fatherless, children within Kebkabiya town. When he continues it is clear that this forms a bridge to the last part of his address:

> You will teach your children and all women the *Qur'an*, because women are the foundation of the community. If the community is educated and understands the *Qur'an* well, it is due to its women. If it is uneducated, it also comes from them; they are the ones who raise our children. So teach your women the *Qur'an* and they will raise the children of the future generation to be a *Qur'a*nic generation… The government declares *shari'a*, but we are the basis, the beginning…
>
> Now I want to address the subject of mass-weddings… Allah created Adam from mud. And from Adam's left side he created Hauwa. Hauwa alone was not complete and Adam alone was not complete: Hauwa is part of Adam and Adam is part of Hauwa. He created from them many people and he created marriage to live in. How to live in marriage? It means that we have to marry and the husband and wife should be together so that their hearts are quiet and at peace in their home. Now we know the demands of Allah and how to obey. But how does our belief relate to relatives? It tells us to love our relatives and to keep in touch with them. This is the right social relation between people. And we know

[5] Oxfam seasonal crop assessment Darfur (1986–1992).

> that a woman alone is incomplete and a man alone is incomplete. If we leave our youngsters like this, to ask them to save a lot of money in order to be able to marry, we ask you: "Do you want your children to stay like this?" For there is no money. Our prophet Mohammed said: "You can marry the poor and you will get rich". This richness is from Allah. With marriage, you can keep your family and your religion... Bad people are those who are not married, this is what prophet Mohammed told us. Do we leave these bad people as they are? It is important to solve this problem. If you can get government-subsidised sugar, will anybody forgo that sugar? If the government brings you millet, will you decline it? I don't want to talk too long because there are other colleagues who want to speak tonight. I ask Allah for us all to make us good Muslims and to follow the correct way. Maʾasalama, goodbye...

In this part, the speaker switches to a completely different subject: the relationship between men and women. Women are portrayed predominately as mothers; they would become better mothers if they gained more knowledge of the *Qur'an*.

Next, the speaker turns to the issue of marriage. He points out that marriage is an obligation the prophet Mohammed has ordained, but also refers to the financial costs related to marriage which makes it difficult for 'youngsters' to marry and which makes them 'bad people'. The youngsters are not the only ones who are blamed, because their relatives arrange the marriages. The relatives should change their demands with respect to the level of the bride price and elaborate wedding parties: the government has even suggested a token bride price of one Dinar as prescribed in the *Qur'an*. Alternatively, just as sugar and millet is subsidised, families should make use of the state-sponsored mass-weddings. The speaker suggests that all of these serve the religious duty for people to 'live in marriage'.

In discussing the complementary nature of marriage he suggests the 'incompleteness' of both Adam and Eve without a spouse. This becomes clearer when the next speaker Sitt Miriam, representative of the Women's Committee takes over. She starts by saying that she will speak about the importance of women in establishing a Muslim society:

> ...I want to explain women's activities under this government. How was the position of women before Islam came, before our prophet Mohammed? At that time, the community considered a woman of little value and she had no voice in community matters. Men looked down upon women and they buried their daughters alive until Islam came. After the coming of Islam, in the time of our prophet Mohammed, it changed the life of women and it gave women their freedom and changed the ideas of men. Women shared in the *jihad*, the holy war of Muslims against

> the unlawful. In addition, they got educated just like men. Many women joined their men while they were fighting the infidels. Take our Lady Aïsha, for example. Some men even came to Ashia to learn from her about Mohammed's talks... This means that women got an opportunity to be important in the community...

Sitt Miriam starts her speech by referring to the time of prophet Mohammed. As in many discussions with educated elite men and women, Islam is championed for having elevated the status of women compared with the position they had before that time. Aïsha, locally pronounced as Ashia, the most beloved of Mohammed's wives, is brought on stage. She figures prominently in many *hadith*, which report on how Mohammed passes a religious problem on to Aïsha to answer, thus displaying his trust in her intelligence and devoutness.[6] This and her participation in holy wars make her a role model for the good Muslim woman. No wonder that Sitt Miriam continues by discussing women's issues in contemporary Sudan:

> ...How to make a good Muslim woman and to educate her, to make her a polite woman? It requires her to believe in Allah honestly. Nowadays women have left the right path, *shari'a*. She runs after other, more worldly things. She imitates western countries. This means that girls like to join boys at parties and in other places and they are leaving the houses of their families without permission. The *Qur'an* says that women have to cover their bodies and to veil themselves. They should not uncover unless their father or husband or husband's father are the only ones present. And to brothers and sisters and their sons and daughters, one can uncover. And old men and women who are not interested in the private parts of women. Prophet Mohammed said that a woman has to cover all of her body except for her head and her hands. You all know very well that Allah created us to fulfill our duties. He ordered us to fast and to pray, to give alms and to go on *haj*. He ordered women to be veiled. If we compare the prescriptions in Islam with people's behaviour, we have to conclude that women have left the right path. It is a big waste that fathers and mothers tire themselves to save all for their daughters who follow the behaviour of western countries, in their fashion and makeup. For example, fathers buy a *tobe* for £S 7.000[7] and a dress for £S 3.000

---

[6] Aïsha bint Abu Bakr, locally pronounced as Ashia, is seen as the source of 1200 *hadith*. Her fame is not only tied to her status as most beloved of the prophet's wives, or because she was educated and intelligent, daughter of the first *khalif* or successor of Mohammed, but for her disputed behaviour. Apart from allegations of adultery, of which she has been cleared, the *Shi'a* hold her in contempt because of her resistance to 'Ali as successor of her husband (Raven 1997: 34).

[7] On the 3rd of February 1992, the Sudanese Pound was floated and *de facto* devaluated from 1 U$ = 15.15 to £S 90 (Harir et. al. 1994: 273). However, on the

> and it is not even a dress fit for Muslim women. It is better not to spend a lot of money on useless things. Islamic dress is not as expensive as these clothes. Moreover, you burden your father with wanting such an expensive dress that even does not fit the Islamic prescription? If women dress themselves in an Islamic way, it is preferable because Allah ordered them to dress like that.

Sitt Miriam moves from an example of a perfect Muslim woman, Ashia, to the sinful behaviour of local Darfurian women, especially the teenage girls. Like the previous speaker, Sitt Miriam describes the imitation of the West as 'running' after worldly things and its effects are illustrated with examples of the disrespectful way girls especially behave. By talking about veiling in conjunction with the five 'pillars' or basic duties of every Muslim, the duty of a woman to veil herself gains religious importance. In Darfur, the veiling of women is not a new phenomenon, but the fact that the *tobe*, the original 'Sudanese' dress is seen, as 'not fit for Muslim women' is new. Every year, around *Eed*, the current government calls on women to abide by the correct dressing code. In newspapers and magazines, the issue is debated and the government has even started to subsidize the so-called Iranian veils, black tent-like garments which are cheaper, more uniform and less 'exposing' than the colourful, transparent, and expensive, *tobes*.[8] Sitt Miriam continues:

> ...It is our duty to inform women because they are the foundation of our community. If a woman wears long dresses and covers all of her body and she walks all around town, no boy will comment on her or talk to her. And even when they talk to her they will talk decently and won't say bad things. Some girls wear short dresses with their hair uncovered and they walk in the street in order to attract boys, which is a bad habit in this community. Sometimes you can find girls at night in the market. What are they buying? They spend all day doing what? And then they have to go out shopping at night? Why? They also sit in the market, little girls selling at the market! I also blame mothers, fathers, brothers and uncles. They should prevent their girls from selling at the market. I ask you to do your Islamic duties. Wearing long dresses is like praying, for it is obeying an order of Allah... Allah said that you have to wear

---

unofficial market the rate of the Sudanese pound to the dollar was already high in December 1991 to fluctuate strongly after the release of the Pound from the official £S 90 to 150 S£ to skyrocket to 800 £S.

[8] Also in television broadcasts, which are more numerous around Ramadan to divert the attention off the fasting, I have watched this issue been debated over and over again. However, these channels cannot be seen in Darfur and in Kebkabiya televisions are not even available.

> a long dress and a veil to cover your head, not the *tobe* or dresses like that… And the important thing for women is to be taught the *Qur'an*: many bad habits may be the result of being uneducated. The duty of the Sudanese Women's Committee is to have literacy classes so women will know how to deal with the problems of their families. We are going to raise the reputation of Darfur… It is better for us to behave and treat others according to the prescriptions as written in the Qur'an and I ask Allah to forgive you and me. *Salaam alaikum.*

Once more, Sitt Miriam addresses the girls. This time because they are buying and selling at night at the market. The relatives are also blamed for letting their daughters and nieces roam freely around town. However, the most important issue is once again the dress code: a girl can go out safely if she is properly dressed for 'there will be no boy commenting on her or talking to her'. Correct dressing is now quite explicitly referred to as a religious duty: 'wearing long dresses is like praying'. As in the first part of her speech, when she suggests that veiling is comparable to one of the pillars of Islam she implies that veiling is one of the basic duties, which it is not. This reveals Sitt Miriam's low opinion of her audience as they are not expected to know this since they are illiterate: this viewpoint makes her call to the female audience to follow the literacy classes organised by the Women's Committee a logical conclusion. The aim is a society in which women have an important role, comparable to that of the women in the society Mohammed built up (*umma*). Sitt Miriam has hardly returned to her seat when the next speaker, Sitt Huda, starts her speech:

> *Bismillahi ar-rahman ar-rahim*, I greet you in the name of God, the Compassionate, the Merciful. I am going to talk about obedience to the husband. Because mothers are looking after the children, the community will be good or bad according to the way she raises her children… Mohammed said: *Janna tahta al-rigleen al-ummayaat*,[9] heaven is under the feet of mothers. Heaven is very near for women, *al-nisa*, but our disobedience to our husbands, not respecting them, is the cause that takes us away from heaven. We can't sense heaven, unless we respect our husbands and obey them. Here are some of the duties of women: to pray, to fast, to obey their husbands, to keep their genitals from others, except from their husbands. Darfurian women especially are always looking down upon men. If her husband says: 'Don't go out of the house', she says: 'Ah, he is nothing, I will go without his permission'. A woman has three places: in her father's house, in her husband's house or in her grave

[9] Also *Janna tahta al-agdaam al-ummahaat*, paradise is under the legs of motherhood. *Janna* has the same roots as *jeneina*, garden, for heaven is often pictured as a garden.

> … A man is stronger than a woman in many things. He has to look after his wife and children by providing all the necessities in the house with his money and the woman; she has to look after her children and to take care of the house, to clean it. She has many duties in the house. But if she doesn't obey her husband, she will not go to heaven. If she prays but doesn't obey her husband, her prayer is useless… A man should marry a woman according to her religious behaviour. Our belief should not be a show for the outside when nothing comes from the inside… It is better to wash our hearts from hating others and from being spiteful and instead to obey our husbands. Saeedna Ashia, she was educated and a scientist and she knew about poetry as well. Behind every gentleman is a woman … The first person to believe that Mohammed was a real prophet was his wife, Saeedna Khadija bint Ghoilid… If we look at women nowadays and her husband would come home saying this ['I am the prophet'] she would run from her home. But Khadija was a nice and gentle woman … Even if we would do many good things, we will not be able to equal Fatima, prophet Mohammed's daughter… It is better to obey your husbands and not to look down upon men… For now, I want to say goodbye for it is midnight and you are going to sleep, *ma'asalama*, goodbye, go with peace.

In the same vein as her predecessor, Sitt Huda addresses women as the foundation of society first and foremost in their capacity of wives and then mothers, which is concurrent with the moral discourse of the government. These 'proper' roles are related and connected to well known *hadith*, and, again, to the five pillars, and is akin to a division of labour and responsibilities between the spouses. Men should provide for their families and women should take care of the children and the housework, and, above all, be obedient to their husbands. Consequently, women should not leave their houses without a reason or without permission from a male relative.

This perspective is also boosted by Sitt Huda's reference to the most renowned women related to the prophet Mohammed; Khadija, his first wife and the first Muslim;[10] Ashia, the most beloved, and Fatima, Mohammed's daughter who married Ali, the most loyal companion of Mohammed.[11] These women are important to Sitt Huda in order to

[10] Khadija bint Khuwalid was a rich widow who married the orphan Mohammed who worked for her organizing her trade-caravans. She supported him financially, morally and socially. During her life Mohammed stayed monogamous and she born most of his children, amongst them Fatima, and she is revered as 'mother of the believers' (Raven 1997: 34–35).

[11] Ali and Fatima begot two sons, Hassan and Husayn who constitute the rightful successors of Mohammed for the *Shi'a* Muslims, a position Hassan only got after the

reinforce her appeal to the women in the audience, as Sitt Miriam had done before her.

The women around me reply with the appropriate blessings when the names of these renowned women are mentioned, but they also scold the speakers under their breath when they find themselves accused collectively of disobedience to their husbands, leaving their houses unaccompanied and looking down upon them. It indeed sounds preposterous. Darfurian women are quite prominent in public life because they are performing economic tasks outside their homes, not because they 'wander around', as is the expression for those who are out to contact men for a sexual liaison.[12] The preponderance of women in economic affairs has even earned them the doubtful reputation that they 'work as hard as donkeys, but are cheaper'. In particular, non-Darfurians claim that Darfurian men are lazy and that they can easily marry four women because the women do all the work while all the man can do is lie on his bed and sleep. Therefore, the women's presence in public life in Darfur has an economic reason and not a sexual one, a fact that is widely acknowledged.

Now, it is already ten o'clock and the wind has become stronger and colder. Some women pull their *tobes* tighter around their shoulders and up to their eyes. Others gather their belongings and take their leave with extensive greetings, which earns fierce hushing from the male audience while the last speaker is introduced. It is Ahmed Yussuf, a representative of the provincial Department of Religious Affairs of the district capital. After the usual Islamic blessings, he addresses the audience:

> My family, *salaam alaikum*, I want to talk to you about the *hadith* and the *Qur'an* of our prophet Mohammed, peace be upon him. I'll talk to you, not with official talk, but in an ordinary way. We want to continue on the Islam and on Quranic behaviour. In January of this year the leader of the government held a meeting: he was Omar Al-Beshir and he declared *shari'a*. It was broadcast on television and appeared in newspapers and in many different magazines, in many countries. It was world news that Omar Al-Beshir declared *shari'a* in the Sudan. We have wanted *shari'a* since independence when the rules we were ruled with were based on British laws and government, until now. All the governments of the

---

first three successors. These *khalif* s were chosen by the first community of Muslims and referred to as the rightful successors for the *Sunni* Muslims (Raven 1997: 39–41).

12 See for example Altorki (1986) for a similar use of 'wandering around' in Saudi Arabia where she did research among the elite.

> Sudan wanted to change the rules, but they couldn't. Then this government came and wanted to rule with *shari'a*, the best rules because they come from the *Qur'an*, while people made the other rules. The *shari'a* rule will be complemented with rules made by this government. The government brought many changes. It gave us the popular committees and it changed the system of districts into one of states. The ruler is now a *waali*, a governor. *Waali* comes from Islam, but *haakim* is not.[13] In Nimeiri's time, they changed the system into *itihaad al-istraaki*, socialist unions. Now we changed that in *al-ledjna sha'abiya*, the popular committees. But the aims of Nimeiri in 1969 were different: at that time they had the people swear to protect and serve their government honestly. The popular committees, they swear to serve the state and country and to serve the community. It means to serve your family and your district. You are in Kebkabiya and that means you will protect Kebkabiya and you will serve the people here. However, you should not occupy yourself with other affairs, because these rules are from Allah. Allah is to advise you and to make you well if you are ill and to feed you. This rule is not the one of the British. Allah also causes you to be promoted in or to be fired from your job. This government takes care of *shari'a* more than anything else. It taught pupils in the schools to stop foreign customs and to say 'Allahu Akbar', God is great, if something is praiseworthy and not to clap hands. The duties of the popular committees are to collect the traditional habits and customs of the communities and to encourage those that follow Islam. To protect the community because you swear you will serve your family and community and if there is a need you can tell your government that this community needs this or that. You are to protect your community from wine and adultery and foreign habits ... Many bad things are still happening in the quarters. The religious efforts are not like the former ones. Now we have a new duty. In the past the Department of Religious Affairs used to advise people with talks and then leave them alone. Now we have permission from the government to report about bad customs and bad behaviour and to send it to the popular committees so they can decide on what to do about it quickly. The government, the Ministry of Religious affairs and the popular committees are all united to solve the problems of the community... We are not united for a bad cause, we only want to stimulate good behaviour and create good Muslims...

This time the speaker starts by referring to the audience collectively and compassionately with 'my family', signaling the apotheosis of the speeches: first addressing men, then women, and finally all of them together as related, as united for a just cause. An Islamic cause initiated

---

[13] *Haakim* is an originally Turkish term for a governor, stemming from the *Turkiya*, the Ottoman, or Turko-Egyptian rule under Mohammed 'Ali 1822–1880. *Waali* is an Arabic term for the same position (Fluehr-Lobban et. al. 1992).

at a national level, with international acknowledgement, and taking shape at a local level by people who swear to protect and serve their families, community and nation. This speaker summarises some of the issues addressed by the former speakers, and thereby promotes the popular committees and their special duty of collecting, reporting and correcting peoples' behaviour and customs, 'protecting' the community against bad practices. A duty he in fact bestows upon all of his listeners, thus claiming legitimacy in creating a common project.

At a conference in Khartoum from 29 April to 2 May 1991, it was decided that popular committees were to operate at all administrative levels, from villages and town quarters to states, in order to act as intermediaries between the local population and the government (Kevane 1996: 28). This conference was held specifically to come up with:

> New ways of organizing the political system in the Sudan... 'Popular committees' on (*sic*) local basis were proposed, on the lines of the Libyan model, as the 'Western-style, multi-party parliamentarism' was rejected as not suitable for Africa and the Sudan (Harir et. al. 1994: 272).

The different popular committees of the different levels would have contact regularly with each other through meetings and visits, such as, at the occasion of the speeches reported above.

The committees both facilitate dissemination and implementation of government decisions and are a means to control and report back to the government on the result of these policies at a local level. The committees thus are not only the heralds of religious messages, but guardians of the new Islamic order as well. In order to promote their version of the good Muslim citizen the government staged a media offensive. However, the media infrastructure in the Sudan is limited as only the large towns have electricity and receive newspapers.[14] So, in the 'outlying' areas, such as Darfur, the ideas, policies and demands of the government could only be conveyed orally, by way of speeches, such as the ones discussed here.

As I recorded these speeches, I was slightly concerned about their obvious messages: foreigners from the West and local women are not to be trusted. However, the reactions of those I met during the days

[14] After the coup the 15 member Command Council for the 'Revolution of National Salvation' banned all political parties, trade unions, strikes and all newspapers except for the army newspaper, meant to curb opposition (Harir et. al. 1994: 271). Other than via government controlled radio and television broadcasts and in these speeches people in Darfur had little possibilities to acquire news.

following the speeches did not give me any reason to feel further alarmed. On the contrary: if there was a discussion at all about the meeting, it concerned the messengers rather than the message. They were criticised for their myopic vision concerning the need of the people of Kebkabiya for food and other necessities in these times of drought and ethnic conflicts.

However, the speeches clearly put the blame for the problems in Darfur on western foreigners and Darfur women, both subjects figuring prominently in my research. The government's discourse on Islam proved to have a profound influence on both local power relations and on my research. The speeches can be seen as a kind of map to the new moral discourse of the Islamist government: to local power structures, their intended direction of processes of change, and the construction of 'new' identities. This map needs more contours than I have been giving here. Therefore, in the remainder of this chapter, I will return to the speeches and connect them to the diverse discourses to which they refer.

The Speeches: Constructing a New Image of Muslimhood

In the popular committee's speeches quoted above, the Sudanese government is cast as truly Islamic and the Darfur population as bad Muslims, but nevertheless, citizens whose conduct can be redeemed. This redemption is in the speech closely related to the attitude of the Darfur population to foreigners and females. Except for their potentially corrupting effect on the Muslim society, foreigners and females, in this case Darfur women, do not seem to have much in common. However, the rhetoric used and solutions given match each other: foreigners seem to act well, handing out grain, but their intentions are bad, because they want to undermine Islam. Darfur women seem to act badly; they have incorrect attitudes about proper attire and are disobedient to their husbands. Although their intentions may be good, the fallacies might be the result of the women's lack of religious knowledge, something appropriate education can redress.

The government has different, but related perspectives on the avenues to salvation of its citizens: less influence of foreigners on Sudanese society and greater influence of Muslims on the behaviour of women. The structural positions of both subjects are thus comparable: both foreigners and women by way of contrasting help clarify the boundaries of the Muslim self. I call this casting of foreigners and females the construction of a significant 'other', after Caplan (1984). He states that fundamentalist groups use the significant 'other' in order to define themselves. In this way this 'other' offers a way to delineate and represent the boundaries between themselves and other groups in society (Caplan 1984: 21). The speeches should thus be considered a carefully orchestrated message, an endeavour to create both the self and the other, good and bad, true and false, in other words, a coherent and clear regime of truth as a device with which the Sudanese government claims legitimacy. (Caplan 1984: 21; Foucault 1980: 131; Silberstein 1991: 8–11).

The first 'other' against whom the good Muslim self is given contours and a homogeneous content are the 'enemies' of Islam, the followers of other religions of the Book,[15] Jews and Christians. The first speaker discusses greeting habits. The seemingly innocent custom is referred to as a crime because it originally came from the 'first enemies' of Islam, the Jews. By referring to the 'beginning of Islam', the time of Mohammed and the source of the unerring texts like the *Qur'an* and *hadith*, the first speaker claims a firm religious basis. In this way he constructs a common point of reference for the discussion on what is 'real' Islamic, both for his audience and for the speakers who follow him.[16]

However, Jews are not only perceived as enemies in a far off past, but also in relationship to more recent politics. Ever since the Six-Day-War in 1967 the relationship between Israel and most Arab countries, including the Sudan, has been strained.[17] This more contemporary political aspect of the relationship with Jews seems even more proba-

[15] *Din al-kitab*, or religion of the book, refers in the history of Islam to the Jewish and Christian religions since they all refer to a Holy Book and to one god with connected traditions. The followers of these religions constituted the *ahl al-dhimma*, payers of a tax, the *jizya*, in exchange for 'protection', *dhimma*. They were not considered subjects for conversion (Raven, 1997: 224).

[16] See for the importance of holy unerring scripts for fundamentalist movements for example Caplan (1984: 14); Hunter (1993); Hawley and Proudfoot (1994: 10–14).

[17] The Six-Day War meant the defeat of armies of the Arab countries surrounding Israel that had been perceived as a threat ever since its founding in 1948. This defeat has had a major impact on the self-perception of the Arab world and has lead to animosities between Israel and the Arab World since. When having a visa or entry stamp of Israel in one's passport entry into the Sudan was and still is forbidden. The Camp David negotiations between the Egyptian president Saddat, the Israelis and as main 'outsider' the Americans led to strong rifts among the Arabs. Sudan never acknowledged the agreements and this aggravated the negative feelings between Egypt and the Sudan. For further details see for example Esposito (1992).

ble when directly after the Jews, the next enemies are discussed: the *khawadyaat*, a generic term for 'foreigners' from the West. Europeans are referred to as the 'allied forces', which used high-tech air-fighters and 'precision' bombing during Operation Desert Storm (1991) in which Sudan, apart from Mauritania, supported Iraq. Throughout the Gulf War, Saddam Hussein, the leader of Iraq, in his speeches linked western allies to Israel. Thus the two enemies, the two religions of the book, Jews and Christian *khawadyaat* both constitute the eternal enemy to the Islam, on religious and political grounds.

Although the *khawadyaat*, are referred to collectively, in the remainder of this speech the British and Americans are singled out. The commonality of these western countries lies in the political, economic, military and donor relations with the Sudan. Further, both countries have been consistent in voicing their opposition to Islamic states and pan-Islamic political alliances throughout the Middle East and Africa. The British, under Margaret Thatcher's premiership, were the first European allies to support the US in its intention to bomb Iraq without premonition. In the Sudan, this resulted in diminished diplomatic ties and reduced aid, both financial and practical from both the United Kingdom and the United States of America.[18]

The British were the colonial power in the Sudan until 1956. They had governed the country as an occupying foreign power and as such constituted the earliest political enemy for the Sudan as a modern nation-state. The British are therefore described, not just as foreign donors, but as a non-Muslim government with links to the previous colonial time which ruled by different and by implication wrong mores.

The speakers obviously presume their audience to have a positive image of the British colonial government. They falsify this image by pointing out that the British are the source of the difficulties that the Darfurian people now face: 'they destroyed our works'. Immediately before this statement, the problems of economic decline were pointed out while the speaker then continues with references to the drought and famine. The British are thus indirectly connected to the destruction of the economy and of food crops. This is elaborated upon in the next few lines where there is mention of 'the dress of hunger and fear' and of the

---

[18] IMF declared the Sudan 'non-cooperative' in September 1990. The Saudi government voted against the Sudan in the IMF council Harir et. al (1991: 271–272). See for example Copson (1994: 141–146); Johnson (1994: 126–113); Wohlmut (1991: 204–247); Brown (1990 a & b).

fact that the British donations of food can never satisfy the Darfurians 'because they (the British and Americans) are our enemies'! Further, not only are British intentions bad, but malicious because the British as a nation are trying to lure the Sudanese people towards the Christian faith. Politics and religion are thus presented as one and portrayed in terms of local prosperity or disasters.

The relationship between America and the Sudan came into the fore after the Sudan gained independence in 1956. The Americans, fearful as they were about the spread of communist influence, supported the Sudan military and economically; Sudan was perceived as an island in the middle of socialist and communist states as Libya under Khadafi, Egypt under Nasser, Ethiopia under Mengistu and Somalia under Barre[19] (Woodward 1990: 169–172).

In Darfur, the Americans are particularly known as aid-donors, especially food aid. Due to the number of sacks of grain with USA printed on them, the drought of 1984–1985 even gained the name of *Sanat Reagan*, the year of Reagan, the—then—president of the U.S. Moreover, although Nimeiri had socialist sympathies and Sudanese gained scholarships in communist and socialist countries such as Russia, Poland and Czechoslovakia particularly during the 1970s, the main destination for young men were the oil countries and the West (Bakri and Khameir, 1985: 53–67). Both the free donations of grains and the stories from migrant workers and in the media have created an imagery of America and Europe as wealthy, prosperous places to which one would want to go.

After the fall of the Berlin Wall and the 'thaw' at the end of the Cold War, American investment in Africa as a whole was reduced. The Sudanese government was forced to look elsewhere for sources of support. The Gulf Crisis accelerated the change in allegiances by the new Islamist government from former allies like America, England and Saudi Arabia, to 'Arab' nations like Libya and Iraq. In October 1990, the Sudan signed a treaty with Libya to (Harir 1994b: 149, 271–272). In 1991, after the Gulf War ended, Iran sent military help to the Sudanese Islamic government in support of the internal war with Southern Sudan. Further agreements between Sudan and both Libya and Iran (and possibly with Iraq) were signed to facilitate the sending

[19] The Nile is, moreover, very important for the agriculture of Egypt. Egypt being both a bridge and buffer between Africa and the Middle East, its security also meant relative political security in the whole area I (Woodward 1991: 117–118, 131).

of grain, sesame oil, and meat in exchange for petrol, military and infrastructural aid (Harir et. al. 1991: 272). Moreover, Turabi established the PAIC (Popular Arab and Islamic Conference) which sprang off the Iraqi-funded Popular Islamic Conference and which figured as an alternative to the Arab League and the Organisation of Islamic Countries (De Waal 2004a: 190–193).

Therefore, westerners, in particular the Americans and British, serve as a point of reference for the speakers as both are part of not only the national and local history but serve to constitute a collective and shared memory. Sudan's history with foreigners is consequently one of political, military, economic, and technical dependence. Even now, after the change of government and the Gulf War which resulted in a pull-out of western donors, there is still considerable pressure by western countries on the Sudanese government to comply with the demands of the West concerning economic, political and human rights issues (Wohlmut 1994). The dependence is often cast in terms of inferiority-superiority in which Sudan is portrayed as 'behind' in all aspects of the development of life. However, in the perception of the Kebkabiya population, the British and Americans carry different meanings, and it is precisely a discussion with these local perceptions that the speakers engage themselves with. Therefore, in this respect, the reference to foreigners as enemies is not only a way of claiming national political legitimization, it is also used in legitimising its policy at a local level. One example is the policy to the civil war detailed in the following *fatwa* issued in April 1993 by a conference of 'ulama':

> The rebels in Southern Kordofan or in Southern Sudan have rebelled against the state and have waged war against Muslims, with the prime objective being the killing and massacring of Muslims, the destruction of mosques, the burning of copies the Quran, the violating the honour and dignity of Muslims, while the rebels are being driven and instigated *by the enemies of Islam from amongst the zionists, the Christian Crusaders, and the forces of arrogance*, who have been supplying them with food and arms Therefore the rebels who are Muslims and are fighting against the state are hereby declared apostates from Islam, and the non-Muslims are hereby declared Kaffirs [infidels] who have been standing up against the efforts of preaching, proselytization, and the spreading of Islam into Africa. However, Islam has justified the fighting and the killing of both categories without any hesitation whatsoever. (As quoted in Kevane and Stiansen 1998: 19 [*emphasis author*]).[20]

[20] Issued by the Islamic Religious Conference on 27 April 1993 at Al-Obeid and

In this *fatwa*, referring to the 'enemies of Islam', the same foreigners who figured in the speeches legitimise the *jihad*, even against Muslims.[21] The speeches are thus both a legitimisation of the political course the current government takes by claiming a complete break with the past and a justification of its policies, even when it concerns the killing of its own citizens. The 'other', in the guise of foreigners and their history with the Sudan, thus serves as a means to construct the image of a new Muslim self on both the local, national and international level. It is surprising in this respect that the speeches do not make more use of a period in which the Islam was also used as a means to assemble diverse ethnic and sectarian groups under the banner of the one true Islam, the Mahdiyya (1885–1899).[22]

The Mahdiyya was the Islamic state founded by Muhammed Ahmad Al-Mahdi who ousted the ruling Turko-Egyptian government or *Turkiyya* (1821–1881) from what is now called the Sudan. The Mahdi refers to *al-Mahdi al-Muntazar*, the Expected Guide or Rightly Guided. The idea of the Mahdi is based on an eschatology, which claims that a saviour will reveal himself in times of severe crisis and social upheaval.[23] When Muhammed Ahmed ibn Abd 'Allah claimed to be the Mahdi', he rapidly gained a following, at first predominantly from the West, Kordofan and Darfur, where he was essentially in hiding whilst collecting his followers. His proclaimed goal was the purification of Islamic practices and the unification of Muslims then dispersed over the diverse Sufi-orders. After a series of battles Muhammed Ahmed ibn Abd 'Allah succeeded in overthrowing the 'foreign regime' and established the first Islamic State in the Sudan which lasted until 1899 when the British reclaimed the state back as an Anglo-Egyptian Condominium (Holt 1970, Theobald 1949; 43–44; Beck 1998: 262).

Shortly after the establishment of the *Mahdiyya*, Mohammed al-Mahdi died of illness and was replaced by the Khalifa Abdullahi. He was

distributed on the Internet on 16 August 1995 via the Sudan-List. A copy of the original Arabic text proved impossible to obtain (*cf.* Kevane and Stiansen 1998: 19 n. 41).

[21] See for a different transcription of this *fatwa*: De Waal (2003: 72–73).

[22] Nimeiri, the leader of the former military regime (1969–1985), for example, does glorify Mohammed Al-Mahdi, Mahdism and even the Ansar and their political leader, who was in fact his opponent, in his first book on Islamism 'The Islamic path why (*Al-nahj al-islami limadha*.)?' (Cairo, 1980, see: Warburg 2003: 152).

[23] In *Sunni* belief the Mahdi would precede the Second Coming of Christ. In this version he would first have to fight *al-Masih al-Dajjal* or anti-Christ who had reeked havoc and caused chaos, before the prophet 'Isa' or Jezus, might re-appear. In other versions he would be the herald of the end of the world or the religious and political

a Ta'isha, one of the Baggara nomadic cattle groups from Kordofan and Darfur, which formed the main body of his army. After the defeat of the Khalifa and the establishment of the Anglo-Egyptian Condominium in Sudan in 1889, uprisings led by men who claimed to be the Mahdi recurred, particularly in Darfur where the Nyala Revolt of 1921 cost the government many casualties in defeat. These so-called neo-Mahdists claimed that the British were the real *Dajjal*, devil, and that these foreigners had to be driven out before the second coming of Christ could be effected (Duffield 1979; Harir 1994a: 23–24; Holt 1970; Ibrahim 1979: 440, 2004: 88–113; Kapteijns 1985: 239–243; Theobald 1949: 32–33, 38).

Apart from trying to oust foreigners, the Mahdi's Islamic reform was directed at the lifestyle of the population that called for a social transformation. The Mahdi issued wide-ranging legislation on land ownership, trading and also family and social life. The latter included strict dress codes for women who were expected to avoid public spaces under the threat of a beating. Women were prohibited from greeting and talking to strange men and emotional outbursts of either joy or sorrow at weddings or funerals were denounced as inconsistent with Islam (Beck 1998: 262; Holt 1958: Ch. 5).

The similarities in the moral discourses of the Mahdi and the current Islamist regime which both made legitimate their policies with reference to 'general' Islamic principles, is striking. The fact that both of them point at foreigners as the culprits and focus on the conduct of women raises the question as to why the speakers did not make use of this fact when addressing Kebkabiya's population. The absence of this argument can be further queried because the history of both the Mahdi's and the Khalifa's building of power is so related to the history of Darfur: even when Darfur was never fully occupied by the Mahdist forces it even now boasts a large number of *ansar* (followers of the Mahdi).

The answer might be found in the address of the last speaker, Ahmed Yussuf, who takes Sudan's independence as the point of departure for his promise that this government will do things differently in that it will put a real effort in creating a real Muslim community. Thus, his

restorer of Islam (Holt 1958; Ibrahim 1979: 440; Theobald 1949: 32–33). Among the *Shi'a* the Mahdi is called the 'hidden Imam' who is basic to *Shi'a* belief about ascendancy (Theobald 1949: 32).

point of reference is post-colonial Sudanese politics, where two political parties, the DUP and the UMMA party dominated the political arena. The DUP, based on the Khatmiyya Sufi brotherhood, originated in the East of Sudan and was founded by the Mirghani family; over time the DUP attracted mainly traders.[24] The UMMA party was founded by the Mahdi's posthumous son and takes its constituency mainly from the *ansar*, the followers of the Mahdi, and of large landowning agriculturalists (Fluehr-Lobban et. al. 1992: 129–132, 141–143; Harir 1994b: 129–135; Woodward 1979: 124–135). Both parties were thus based on different religious brotherhoods, with a constituency mainly from groups of different occupational background and from different areas in the country. They were the main antagonists competing for power in the new political structure of parliamentary democracy since Independence. The DUP and the UMMA have dominated the political stage ever since. Moreover, it was an UMMA dominated democratic government, which the current military regime toppled with their coup of 1989. The coalition regime with As-Sadiq Al-Mahdi, the great-grandson of the Mahdi, as president had committed itself to implementing *shari'a* law, which proved a major impediment to solving the political crisis of Southern Sudan.

The current regime clearly distinguishes itself from these political parties, thereby claiming a discontinuation of the past in that its path will lead to success where their predecessors, particularly the UMMA party, failed (cf. Harir 1994a: 44–57). The new government, in order to not only clarify the boundaries of the new Muslim self, but also to find a new idiom with which to create a positive self image thereby reconstructs its past as a history 'gone awry' (Hunter 1993: 34). This history includes the *Mahdiyya*, also because of the relation of the UMMA with this first Islamic state of the Sudan. The current regime puts its effort in claiming discontinuity with the more recent political past and which at the same time suggests continuity with a more remote Islamic and *Qur'an*ic past of the real *umma*, the community of the Prophet Mohammed. This remote past is used as a common denominator for all Sudanese to overcome sectarianism, become 'real', modern, Muslims and thus transform Sudanese society into a righteous community of believers, the real *umma*.

---

[24] The party was first called the National Union Party. The main political difference between the two parties around Independence was that the NUP called for unity with Egypt while the UMMA wanted an independent Sudan (Woodward 1990: 134–140).

However, it is clear from the speeches that this new, good, Muslim is not to be found all over Sudan—yet. The speakers draw boundaries on the basis of locality between Sudanese who are good Muslims and those who are not: Darfur people are obviously not well Islamized and thus not good Muslims and they need special guidance to find and stay on the right path. Darfur has been Islamised since the 17th century, but not Arabised (Harir 1994b: 124–136; Hassan 1977: 201–204: O'Fahey 1980a: 8–13) and this is taken to be a sign of weak Islamisation. Local customs and local forms of Islamic practices and beliefs are equated with 'bad behaviour'.

The speeches and decrees such as the *fatwa* quoted above not only justify the actions of the government as being Islamic: in the process political differences are transformed into religious heresy. Text and action are thus part of the same moral discourse of the military government. The government attempts at constructing a new image of Muslimhood and the speeches offer a way to understand how the new government perceives the different subject positions of diverse groups of Sudanese. The differentiation of good Muslims from non-good Muslims in remote areas, for example Kordofan and the Red Sea province, but particularly Darfur is refined in the distinctions, which are constructed among men and between men and women. In order to gain insight into the way different groups of Muslims can claim authority and status within the new moral discourse of the Islamist government it is necessary to understand not only what is said in the addresses, but also the way these are formulated.

Foreigners and Females: Constructing a Modern Male Muslim Identity

Apart from foreigners, women are constituted in the speeches as the 'other'. They are pictured as a main problem the government and the local population have to deal with, in order to become a righteous community of Muslim believers. It is not unique for these speeches to address women specifically. Since the coup in 1989, the Sudanese Islamist government has been consistent in focusing on the conduct and demeanour of women in public life. The call on Darfur women to act 'properly' according to the standard set by the current government is in line with its discourse. It is in this case strategic that women deliver the speeches directed at the female audience as this is in accordance with the segregation policy. At the same time women can claim common ground with the female audience because of gender.

As I noted earlier, both female speakers refer to the so-called 'pillars of Islam' when discussing the basic religious duties of Muslim women, which serves to claim religious authority. This exposes a perception of the local female population as illiterate and non-acknowledgeable on religious subjects. That they are obviously taken to be easy to fool is a reason for giving the speeches in the first place. This is strategic in two ways. It is a rhetorical device as in her opening lines, in which Sitt Miriam refers to education as a means to make women better mothers and better Muslims, is also her conclusion: only educated mothers may help create a better Muslim society. Although she seems to echo the ideas of her male colleague before her, but with quite a different implication: it is not men who are called upon to teach 'their' women, but the Women's Committee, which already organizes literacy classes for female Muslims. This is another strategic issue related to the position of Sitt Miriam and Sitt Huda.

The speeches of the female speakers display ambivalence about the status of women in Darfur, as they are portrayed as both the strength and weakness of the righteous Islamic community. On the one hand they are conceptualised as its foundation and future, on the other hand they are cast as subversive, undermining society, all depending on their attitude as good or bad Muslim women. Despite the differences in focus and reference in their discussions, both Sitt Miriam and Sitt Huda tread on common ground. In their negative evaluations of the conduct of Darfur women, whether that of unmarried girls in the outer world or of married women inside their compounds, both implicitly refer to *fitna*. This concept indicates not just 'chaos' but rather the fear for 'uncontrolled' women who cause sexual disorder in public life and is therefore used in the sense of 'femme fatale' (Altorki 1986: 35, 168). In the speeches, women are held accountable for seducing men and thus causing chaos in public life, thereby disrupting the social order.

When it comes to transforming the negative attitude into a positive role for women, Sitt Miriam, the first speaker, sees it in correct dressing in cheap and sufficiently covering veils and in modest behaviour of women in the public sphere. In short, girls should not be seen as sexual beings, as this is incompatible with their future role as 'the foundation of the community': to be obedient wives and dutiful mothers within the walls of their compounds.

The second speaker, Sitt Huda, elaborates upon this foundational role of women. She constructs married women as belonging to the private world, inside their houses and hidden from sight: '… Our belief should not be a show for the outside when nothing comes from the inside…' Like Sitt Miriam, she addresses the freedom of movement of a woman outside the home, but this time it is evaluated as reprehensible instead of correctable, and constituted as an act of defiance of the authority of the husband or the father.

The two *hadith*s Sitt Huda quotes summarize the ambiguity inherent to the symbolic construction of Muslim women. Women are seen on the one hand as a key symbol of the right society, the 'golden age' (Caplan 1987: 56: Hawley 1994: 26), as mothers and wives who transfer 'tradition', the right moral values, on to the next generation. On the other hand women are seen 'not only as [being] symptomatic of cosmic dislocation but as [being] its cause (Hawley 1994: 27)'. Therefore, Darfur women could be the foundation of the community, if only they were educated: this solution for correcting the present, is thereby related to the religious past, to the elevated status of women around the Prophet Mohammed who were educated as well.

In the first instance, these two speeches on female conduct seem to be just a refining of the address directed at the male audience. Similar to the discussion on foreigners, women are seen as both the cause of the status of Darfur males as bad Muslims and as an object in redeeming this status. As the male speaker who introduced his female colleague asserted clearly: women are under the custody of men who have the obligation to 'teach your women and your children'.

Therefore, women seem at first to be predominantly the responsibility of Muslim men. This is also to be read from the way that the male speakers address their audience. All throughout the men's speeches, the structure of their addresses is similar. First, the presumed opinion or common sense notion of the audience is formulated, thus suggesting that the speaker can look into the hearts and heads of his audience as if they are his own. Then each speaker engages in an argument with these perceived notions, mostly centred on falsifying a positive notion of the 'enemy', whether through Jewish greetings or a western lifestyle. The speakers' use of pronouns is not at random but strategic, as in: "This depends on *us*. We have to raise *our* consciousness, in order to correct the behaviour of *ourselves*, *our* children, and *our* families".

By using 'we' and 'us' it is obvious that it not only concerns men talking to men, but that the speaker openly identifies himself with the male audience. Consequently, he can talk knowingly about their 'common' vices, which makes the sermon sound more like a confession than an accusation. Finally, the audience is given the 'right' solution to such common problems as banditry, ethnic clashes and famine: to become better Muslims. This is a solution in line with the current political course and thus serves not just as a piece of advice but as a way to convey what is 'politically correct' according to the current government. The last speaker is very clear that this political correctness is not just a view, but also gives direction to actions:

> Now we have a new duty. In the past, the Department of Religious Affairs used to advise people with talks and then leave them alone. Now we have permission from the government to report about bad customs and bad behaviour and to send it to the popular committees so they can decide what to do about it quickly.

In a manner similar to his colleagues, Ahmed Yussuf calls on the Sudanese to become better Muslims and thereby one of 'us', from the perspective of the current NIF government. Nevertheless, this 'us' is deceiving, for men are called upon to spy on others and to report each other to the popular committees. Men are invited to be competitors in engaging in 'better works'. Instead of calling for a harmonious *umma*, this is a disguised pledge for a divided community split by suspicion, in which particularly Darfur men are seen as the opposite of the good Sudanese Muslim man. Darfur needs a popular committee, such as the one in which the speakers preside, to keep men on the right track. Even though the boundaries between a good Sudanese Muslim as opposed to a bad local (Darfur) Muslim is contingent as redemption is close at hand, this view disqualifies the Darfur population itself to decide on the correctness of their behaviour. Even if it just takes to believe better to attain a better spiritual and material life, only the government is able to judge when people have become 'good enough' Muslims and have become full members of *al-umma al-islamiya*.

At the same time, the reference to the 'problem of women' creates a significant 'internal' other (Brown 1994: 175–201). This makes it possible for the speakers to create a common goal by calling for control over those who are close at hand for every man: their female kin whether daughters, nieces (Miriam), or wives/mothers (Huda) since it is their conduct which is decisive in making the community an *umma*. Like the foreigners who were used as objects in order to construct the contours of a good Muslim, women are thus objectified to create a common goal for the redemption of Darfur men and they shift from being a burden to becoming a boost to a 'good' male Muslim identity.

It is surprising that although the new Sudanese government has a million-dollar-per-day civil war with southern Sudan at its hands it invests in subsidized veils, separate buses, and government sponsored mass-weddings (Harir 1994a: 15). The moral discourse is obviously one of the foundations of the policy of the Sudanese government. This discourse therefore constitutes an important context for my research on women and work in Kebkabiya. However, it is not the only context of importance for my research. Sitt Miriam and Sitt Huda disseminate images of the good Muslim woman which, interestingly enough, match the presuppositions in the West about the fate of women in Islamic societies: confined to the private sphere, banned from public life, under custody of their male relatives without freedom of movement and always strictly veiled. This conjunction of the moral discourse of the Sudanese government on gender and the imagery in western society of women and Islam therefore merits a closer look.

Studying Islamism / Islamic Fundamentalism: Discourses on Women and Islam

The rhetoric used by the Sudanese government to adhere to the only 'true' Islam and to 'purify' the country of wrong believers, and its establishment of an Islamic state has earned the NIF military regime the label 'Islamic fundamentalist'. Islamic fundamentalism has been a topical subject in the media and in academic works since the founding of the Iranian Islamic state by Khomeini in 1979 (Zubaida 1989: 3–11 Sayyid 1997: 88–90). Since the Gulf War at the beginning of the nineties, an academic controversy on the relation between Islam and the term fundamentalism has evolved.

The objections against the term 'Islamic fundamentalist' stem from the fact that it has American-Christian roots, that it homogenises different strands of (Islamic) beliefs, practices and movements and that it is almost never used in self-labelling. In short, it is an objectifying term, which 'constructs binary oppositions between political projects related to Islam and those in the West, between 'exceptions' and 'normalcy' (Sayyid 1997: 15). I share the perspective of those academics, which argue against the use of the term 'fundamentalism' however cautious those authors are who do use the term (cf. Caplan 1987, Hunter 1991; Marty and Appleby 1993).[25] The most important problem I see is, however, as Talal Asad puts it:

> …[T]here cannot be a universal definition of religion, not only because its constituent elements and relationships are historically specific, but also because the definition is itself the historical product of discursive processes (1993: 29).

Sayyid (1997) who also refers to Asad, adds that the main problem of the concept of fundamentalism is that it does not rely on its internal coherence but, rather, on a

> 'shared' assumption regarding the role of politics, truth and religion… As such… [it] can only produce a particular cultural understanding of fundamentalism (1997: 15).

Thus, the concept fundamentalism as used in the West attempts to give characteristics of phenomena of which 'we' already have decided that these are fundamentalist. This makes it a descriptive rather than an analytical concept, with moral overtones as it is tainted with western prejudice about the viability and legitimacy of an Islamic political project.

In their critiques, Asad (1993) and Sayyid (1997) therefore reflect on the diverse conceptualizations of fundamentalism in terms of power, truth and religion, which relates it to the notion of discourse as formulated by Foucault (1979: 46). In this perspective, truths about fundamentalism are produced rather than an inherent quality of certain statements: there are no 'true' and 'false' opinions or viewpoints. Different statements about the term 'fundamentalism' are only different ways of structuring the areas of knowledge. These are related to different social practices of in- and exclusion (Mills, 1997: 67) and to constructions of notions of true and false knowledge: in other words to the establishing of a 'regime of truth (Foucault 1980: 131)'. This means that discourses generate, legitimate, support and empower certain kinds of meanings, questions, debates, and conversations while suppressing, de-legitimating, and dis-empowering others (Silberstein 1991: 9–10). It is precisely a process of exclusion and dis-empowering which takes place in the West in relation to understanding 'fundamentalism': it is

[25] Martin E. Marty and R. Scott Appleby's multi-volume 'Fundamentalism Project' (1991).

for this reason that diverse authors disqualify the term fundamentalism in favour of Islamism.

An alternative is to use the term Islamism to refer to political Islam in specific contexts. The term explicates the fact that the Islam, by reference to the *shari' a*, *Qur'an* and *hadith*, is at once a (political) means and an end. This does not mean 'political' only in the sense of party politics or the control of the state as explicit or main goal. It can be used for any group or movement which takes Islam as an ideology, a total mode of life, as well as the basis of a (perceived) socio-political order and which has some form of Islamisation of people and government as its aim (Karam 1998: 15–16; Rosander 1997: 4–5). In this perspective an Islamist is:

> ...Someone who places her or his Muslim identity at the centre of her or his political practices. That is, Islamists are people who use the language of Islamic metaphors to think through their political destinies, those who see in Islam their political future (Sayyid 1997: 17).

A perspective, which is attractive as it proposes to analyse the way in which Islam is used as a reference for daily conduct and for politics and not taking this for granted. Part of the Islamist movement's appeal stems from its association with modernity, urbanity, and material success. However, in western debates, both popular and academic, the cosmopolitan and modernizing aspect of Islamism is ignored and obscured by picturing the movement as a reaction to the West, meaning a rejection of modernity (Rosander 1997: 10; cf. Caplan 1987: 1–24; Silberstein 1991: 1–14; for Sudan: Bernal 1997).

I will use here the term Islamism in relation to the specific context of the current Sudanese NIF government. However, I do not disqualify the term 'fundamentalism' altogether. Using 'Islamism' does not counter the vices that cling to the term fundamentalism. It still refers to Islam as the 'problem' since we do not use terms like Christianism, Judaism, and Hinduism in a comparable way. Nor does the term prevent the negative connotations of the phenomena thus labelled. It therefore might even lead to reifying the essentialist approach it tries to counter as it might suggest that Islamism is not comparable to any other political project that draws its base from religious 'foundations'. I consider 'Islamism' a more appropriate, therefore more specific, label but using it does not automatically lead to better analysis. Therefore, I feel that it is no use to discard one term in favour of another, suggesting as if that is a more 'true' concept. It is more interesting to try to understand the discursive representations of fundamentalisms and Islamisms, both by its adherents and its analysts (Harding 1991).

Thus, my focus of analysis is the interests and ideologies of the groups who construct and are constructed by these terms. Thereby scholars and adherents, those from 'the West' and 'the Rest', 'us' and 'them', and in the context of this book 'I' and 'you' from whatever perspective, all become subjects of the same discursive and analytical plane. On this plane discourses do not simply express struggles or systems of domination, but are that for which and by which one struggles (Mills 1997: 12–14; Silberstein 1991: 10–13). In the diverse reflections on fundamentalism and Islamism, the struggle seems to be predominantly about political legitimacy and the construction of a national identity while coping with the post-colonial condition, competing on an equal footing with other, so called western modern worldviews and political projects. Or, as Sayyid asserts:

> ...The Islamist project is an attempt to make Islam a master signifier of the political order. It is the struggle to establish which signifiers will constitute the unity and identity of a discursive universe ... (1997: 48).

The controversy over the terms Islamism/Islamic fundamentalism thus not only refers to phenomena in Islamic communities, but also to a western project of producing truth in order to claim power: this is the western 'democratic' political project of the nation/state based on the division between state and religion. The Islamist/Islamic fundamentalist project and its adherents are thereby cast in western discourses on 'modernity' as the 'other'. Academics involved in analysing Islamist political projects are therefore, however unwillingly and unwittingly, involved in producing discourses on its legitimacy as well. The debate over definitions is thus a discursive practice related to our situatedness in discourses on Islam in our own societies.[26]

However, what then constitutes this unity and (common) identity of this 'discursive universe'? In my analysis of the speeches above it turned out that women constituted a means to assemble diverse groups of Muslim men, in this case Sudanese, and make them all potentially belong to the category of the 'good' if responsible Muslim. It seems to me that the controversy around the labelling of the phenomena indicated with political Islam, Islamism or Islamic fundamentalism involves

[26] I refer to modernity as an 'emic' concept in the West and try to think of the possibility of an 'Islamic modernity' based on the case of the Sudan (Willemse 2005).

another controversy: the importance of gender issues. Like Hawley (1994), I am surprised that:

> ...[T]he matter of gender ideology had received so little attention in the nascent literature on comparative fundamentalism (25).

This is particularly curious because in debates, both popular and academic, on political Islam the 'issue of the veil' looms large. Moreover, there are excellent studies available on the relationship between women and the state in Muslim societies (cf. Afshar 1993, 1994; Kandiyoti 1991; Karam, 1998; Moghaddam, 1994). However, in the works of scholars I have been discussing, women seem to have gone completely out of sight, while at the same time they are continuously implied. For example, Sayyid (1997), one of the fiercest criticisers of the term fundamentalism, denounces the issue of women as an analytical category by rejecting one by one the characteristics which Sahgal and Yuval-Davis have formulated as aspects of fundamentalism (Sayyid 1997: 8–18). I do not want to consider the detail of Sayyid's argument, but point at the intriguing fact that though it is not discussed explicitly, gender does come into the discussion when Sayyid positions himself as a scholar on Islamism rather than fundamentalism.

To start with, Sayyid selects from the numerous scholars who have been writing on fundamentalism one work, *Refusing Holy Orders* (1992) edited by his female colleagues Gita Sahgal and Nira Yuval-Davis.[27] He proceeds by dissecting piece-by-piece three aspects which Sahgal and Yuval-Davis see as constitutive of the concept of fundamentalism: it aims to exercise control over women's bodies... its adherent's understanding of religion is correct... it conflates politics with religion (1997: 8–14). Sayyid falsifies each aspect as if these are separate arguments: as if he is dissecting a frog and with every limb claims that it does not represent the frog as a phenomenon. Finally, and for me the most telling, is his discussion with the assertion of Sahgal and Yuval-Davis, that fundamentalist projects aim to control women's bodies. Sayyid states that this is beside the point as 'exercising control over bodies is the function of governmentality itself (1997: 10)' and as such an aspect of all kinds of regimes. Sayyid is right in pointing out that

[27] Sayyid himself legitimates this choice in a note stating: 'The reason for selecting these writers is not because they are necessarily representative of attempts to theorize fundamentalism... nor because I think their account is paradigmatic, but rather because their work makes clear the conditions of its discursive possibility (1997: 27, n. 6)'.

control over the (female) body is not necessarily only true for Islamic fundamentalist politics. However, although Sayyid explicitly states he does not want to suggest that 'governance is gender blind (1997: 11)', he does not give an idea as to why the issue, not just of gender, but specifically of the conduct of women in public life has such a centrality in moral discourses such as that of the Sudanese government, and also of other political projects in diverse parts of the world.[28]

In my opinion, Sahgal and Yuval-Davis (1994), although not intending to be a reply to Sayyid, put forward a view in a later article that I think is relevant enough here to quote at length:

> Retaining the general term 'fundamentalism' has proven to be very important for WAF[29] speakers who have found that women from diverse backgrounds can relate to the phenomena we are describing. This sense of common experience is fundamental for political mobilisation and creates links across religious and cultural specifics. As it does not deny difference in context and circumstances, it is a very different response to earlier homogenising and ethnocentric 'sisterhood is powerful' feminism (1994: 9).

In this sense fundamentalism is not reserved for specific religious movements, but can be used for all kinds of ideologies and political or 'cultural' movements that refer to fundamental 'religious and cultural' features as a prescription of the way women are positioned. The term 'fundamentalisms' in the plural is therefore helpful when comparing experiences of women as subjects involved in 'political mobilisation' (cf. Van Santen and Willemse f.c.).

In other words, in the discursive struggle over 'Islamism/Islamic fundamentalism' women seem to be an, albeit contested, 'other', even when not explicitly articulated as such. This contested role of women as boundary markers is not just a matter of analysis or theoretical viewpoint. Just as in the case of the controversy over the term fundamentalism, the issue of women in Islamic societies has a history in western thinking as well. The fact that I, as a citizen of the 'western' nation-state

---

[28] See for example Charlton, Everett, and Staudt (1989) for colonial states; Wilford (1998: 5–6) referring more generally to gender and national identity.

[29] WAF stands for Women Against Fundamentalism, a group of women making a stand against all kinds of fundamentalisms who also edited a journal with the same name which published diverse articles on fundamentalism, both pro and contra, amongst which the article of which this quotation is taken. See also for example Nederveen-Pietersen (1994: 2–6), who wrote the article to which Sahgal and Yuval-Davis reacted.

of the Netherlands and as an anthropologist in the Sudan, am situated in these diverse discursive fields of struggle over meaning merits a closer look at discourses on Islam, Islamism and women.

Discourses on the Islamic Other: Orientalism and the Image of Women

> In the last two and a half years, we have seen remarkable and hopeful development (*sic*) in world history... [F]or twenty-five million women and girls, liberation has a special significance. Some of these girls are attending school for the first time. It's hard for people in America to imagine... The advance of freedom in the greater Middle East has given new rights and new hopes to women. And America will do its part to continue the spread of liberty...Three years ago, the nation of Afghanistan was the primary training ground for al Qaeda... The Taliban were incredibly barbaric. It's hard for the American mind to understand 'barbaric' ...Women were forbidden from appearing in public unescorted. That's barbaric. Women were prohibited from holding jobs. It's impossible for young girls to get an education. That's barbaric. It's not right...
>
> These are extraordinary times, historic times. We've seen the fall of brutal tyrants. We're seeing the rise of democracy in the Middle East. We're seeing women take their rightful place in societies that were once incredibly oppressive and closed. We're seeing the power and appeal of liberty in every single culture. And we're proud once again—this nation is proud—to advance the cause of human rights and human freedom. I want to thank you all for serving the cause. The cause is just, the cause is right, and the cause is good. May God Bless [you]. (*Applause*).
>
> (Address of President G.W. Bush at the White House – 12 March 2004)[30]

Bush has been championing the cause of women in the Middle East since the attack on the twin towers on 9/11 2001. From the quotations above it is clear that the Bush administration is trying to justify its intervention of US troop in Afghanistan and Iraq as a 'just cause' by intersecting the 'war against terrorism', in particular against the 'barbaric' Taliban and Al-Qaeda, with the protection of women and their rights: to education, to work, to human rights, to freedom. The issue I want to address here is not whether Bush is fighting a just

[30] Bush's address is entitled 'President, Mrs. Bush mark progress in global women's human rights. Remarks by the First Lady and the President on efforts to globally promote women's human rights' (The East Room, March 12, 2004, 2,34 p.m. – 3.08 p.m. EST; http:/www.whitehouse.gov/news/releases/2004/03/20040312-5.html) accessed 12-04-2006.

cause or not: I picked out the above sentences in particular from his half-hour address,[31] because of their familiarity. About ten years earlier, in the same period that the Islamist government implemented *shari'a* law in the Sudan in 1991, several Dutch newspapers featured numerous articles on the Islamist 'threat'.[32] For example, an article by Frits Bolkestein, the conservative right-wing Dutch politician who held several positions, which caused his opinion to be of great influenced in the Netherlands as well as other European states during the 1990s.[33] His address at a meeting of the Right Wing International in Luzern on 9 December 1990, was published in two national Dutch newspapers and is formulated in terms comparable to those used by Bush:

> ...After a long history with a range of black pages, rationalism, humanism and Christianity have brought forth several fundamental political principles, such as: the division between state and church; freedom of speech; tolerance, and non-discrimination... And how does Islam deal with these values? ... Non-discrimination? The way women are treated in the world of Islam tarnishes the reputation of this civilisation. (Bolkestein in *De Volkskrant*, 21-9-1991 [*translated into English by author*]).

Pim Fortuyn (1997: 58–77), who once was a co-party member of Bolkestein[34] before he founded his own party, articulated similar ideas on Islam, women and civilization. The current debate on Islamism and the 'terrorist threat' in the Netherlands, in particular after the murder of Theo van Gogh (2 November 2004), is waged in exactly the same terms. The argument consists of two lines of reasoning. In the

---

[31] These lines resemble similar statements in other addresses Bush gave at diverse occasions since 2001 (cf. Viner 2002).

[32] This speech triggered all together 250 reactions in the two main national newspapers, *De Volkskrant* en *NRC Handelsblad* between September 1991 and 1992. Members of the Muslim community in the Netherlands have taken parts of his speech and comments as offending. Two citizens of Zeist and Utrecht sued Bolkestein on grounds of "offending a group of people on religious grounds or convictions about life and inciting hate". The public prosecutor has declared the complaint without cause (De Volkskrant 12-9-1991, p. 19). Also national newspapers of other European countries and the United States were featuring articles and columns on the perceived Islamic threat and Islamic fundamentalism.

[33] Bolkestein had been Secretary of State of Economic Affairs (1982–1986) and Minster of Defence (1988–1989) before he became leader of the conservative 'liberal' party (VVD) from 1990–1998. The party has been member of consecutive coalition governments since 1994. Since 1996 he has been chairperson of the Liberal International. He was member of the European Parliament in the period (1999–2004).

[34] Before Fortuyn founded his own party (List Pim Fortuyn) in 2002, he has been member of the Socialist Party (PvdA, till 1986) and later of the Conservative Right Wing Party (VVD).

first place, in all of these cases the superiority of western culture in general is argued by constructing Islamic societies as inferior: as uncivilized, undemocratic or even barbaric. This view exposes the orientalist discourse whereby the Orient is described in negative, oppositional terms so as to construct a positive self-image of the West (Said 1978). The Islam is here cast almost as a personified force, which acts on its own right thus fitting enemy images which serve to legitimate power relations of a political, socio-economic and cultural nature. For example, after the thaw in the Cold War the then seated secretary general Willy Claes pointed at the 'Islamic treat' as the new challenge for NATO. Similarly Bush, like Blair, Balkenende and numerous other European (and Russian) politicians, use this notion of Islamic 'threat' in terms of terrorism and militantism for justifying the waging of wars in Afghanistan and Iraq and within their own borders: 'the' Islam has become an obsession for the West (Said, 1981).

In discourses on 'the Islam' the reference to the reprehensible treatment of women constitutes the second line of reasoning. Women are pictured as subordinate to their male relatives, victims of a misogynist Islamic society. They are seen as doomed to suppress their potentials because of a patriarchal system with compulsory veiling[35] as the ultimate marker of this submission.[36] This relatively widespread western discourse has resonance in colonial times. Leila Ahmed (1992) for example refers to Lord Cromer, the British Consul General and Minister Plenipotentiary in Egypt (1883–1907) who reflected quite explicitly on the differences between the British colonisers and the Egyptians, as Ahmed as well as Viner point out, each referring to Cromer:

> 'Whereas Christianity teaches respect for women, and European men 'elevated' women because of the teachings of their religion, Islam degraded them'. (Cromer quoted in Ahmed 1992: 153).[37]

[35] Between 1989 and 1994 Netherlands national newspapers ran 99 articles on the veil (de hoofddoekjes-kwestie) (*Contrast* in Lutz 1996: 128). At the same time, some of the journal and weeklies featured pictures of veiled women while these did not address the issue of women at all, but were used simply as an icon (Willemse, 'From eastern fairy tale to western myth', unpublished paper based on an address to the JOVD, the youth organization of Bolkestein's VVD, 1997).

[36] See for a critical discussion of this view in western popular and academic works on the 'discourse on the veil': Ahmed (1992); Abu-Lughod (1998: 3–33); Al-Guindi (1999); Jansen (1989: 290–293); Lazreq (1988); MacLeod; Moors (1991: 116); Yegenoglu (1998).

[37] Ahmed quotes from; Earl of Cromer, *Modern Egypt, 2 vols*. (New York: MacMillan, 1908: 146–155; 538–539).

> It was Islam's degradation of women, its insistence on veiling and seclusion, which was the 'fatal obstacle' to the Egyptian's 'attainment of that elevation of thought and character which should accompany the introduction of Western civilisation...' The Egyptians should be 'persuaded or forced' to become 'civilised' by disposing of the veil (Cromer quoted in Viner, 2002, Cromer's words are between quotation marks).

As the Sudan was part of the Anglo-Egyptian Condominium, it was officially ruled from Egypt. Cromer's perspective therefore reflected the attitude of colonial rulers towards Sudanese society, which was considered even less civilised because of its 'black' population.[38] His view was not unique to the foreign British elite in Egypt, however. In 1899 Qasim Amin, an Egyptian lawyer, published 'The liberation of women' and in 1900 'The new woman', works which are generally seen as marking the beginning of feminism in the Arab world. He endorsed the view that the veiling of women and their low educational status was an impediment to civilizing Egyptian society, thereby inherently declaring the western civilization as superior. (Abu-Lughod 1998: 11; Ahmed 144–168). The positioning of women[39] thereby:

> ...Has become intertwined with another position, that of traditional (and passive) versus modern (and active), with the Orient associated with the first and the West with the second term. The Orient [was] is seen as lacking something, and progress is deemed to be only possible through Western intervention (Moors 1991: 116).

However, neither Cromer or Amin, nor Bush or Bolkestein for that matter, had the rights of women high on their political agenda, on the contrary. Amin was 'not among those who demand equality in education' but he promoted primary education in order for women to fulfil a 'wife's duty to plan the household budget... to supervise the servants ... to make her home attractive to her husband...—and... her first and most important duty—to raise the children... (Amin quoted in Ahmed 1992: 159)' Cromer, who passed as the 'champion of the unveiling of Egyptian women' was, in England, the founding member and

---

[38] See for example Francis Deng (1989) and Leek Mawut (personal communication 1991) for a historical account of this racist perspective.

[39] Kabbani states that 'Oriental' women are either 'erotic victims or scheming witches who spent their lives in sexual preparation and in sexual intrigue' or 'pious, passive and passionless' reflecting the Victorian values on womanhood. She refers to the *Arabian Nights*, which were written down only in 1704 by the Frenchman Galland, and to colonial images of Islamic women (1991: 26–27). As it is the image of the veiled woman that is prevalent in discourses on Islam in the last decennia, I will only reflect on this image. See also Lazreq (1988); Moors (1991: 114–122).

sometime president of the Men's League for Opposing Women's Suffrage (Ahmed 1992: 153). Bush cut off funding of international family-planning organisations which offer abortion services, while he has converted 22 January, the anniversary of the law suit Roe vs. Wade which made abortion available on demand, into the 'National Sanctity of Human Life Day'; at the same time he is comparing abortion to terrorism (Viner 2002).[40] Bolkestein also used feminist rhetoric to claim the allegiance of Dutch women for his viewpoint on Islam, while his right-wing political party generally holds quite conservative views of equality and women rights: "I guess many of the Dutch women share my opinion, because the way women are treated in the Islamic world are a stain on their reputation".[41]

In all these cases feminist ideas are hijacked by western, or western oriented, politicians: by finding fault with the treatment of women Islamic civilisation is denigrated and at the same time colonial rule or post-colonial western domination is legitimated. Ahmed (1997: 155) even calls feminists the other 'handmaid of colonialism' (apart from anthropology). The images used in western politicians' references to women and veiling serve not only to depict an essential difference, but also to 'render morally justifiable its project of undermining or eradication the cultures of colonised peoples (Ahmed, 1992: 151)' and, I would add, of current day post-colonial Islamic nation-states and (trans-)national communities as well.

The discourses of the Sudanese government and of Bolkestein and Cromer on women in Islamic societies seem to reinforce each other as they all focus on women and the issue of the veil. However, in most Western discourses the veiling *of* women marks women's submission and docility, and is taken to be a sign of the backwardness of the Islamic society as a whole (Kabbani 1991: 56; Lutz 1996). The debate is not one between men and women, but one between men *over* the (veiled) heads of women. It is not so much the fate, rights and happiness of women in Islamic societies that is central here, but the capacity of men with different cultural backgrounds to rule. In this respect women's veiling becomes not only a marker of their own subjugation, but of

---

[40] Viner's article in *The Guardian* (21-9-2002) entitled 'Bush is not the first empire-builder to wage war in the name of women'.

[41] See Lutz (1996: 133–134) for analyzing this quotation as a way to attract female voters. Not only Bolkestein, but also other authorities in the Netherlands and elsewhere use feminist arguments in order to legitimate their negative attitude for example on the issue of veiling on schools (cf. Lutz 1996: 133–134).

the inferiority of their society as well: a sign that Muslims were not able to rule themselves, at least not yet.

In contrast, in the discourse of the Sudanese government the right veiling *by* women symbolises virtue and progress, a sign of the elevated status of its Islamic society modelled after an idealised image of a society located in the past, the *umma*. Veiling by women therefore represents the control of society by Muslim men as well as their political viability. This symbolic value of women is not a feature unique to the Islamist discourse, but according to Hawley (1994) an aspect to be found in other forms of fundamentalism as well:

> ...For men, the motifs of otherness and nostalgia, both prominent features of fundamentalist consciousness, reinforce each other and meet in a conservative ideology of gender that reconstructs an idealized past and attempts to reshape a present along the same lines. (1994: 32)

Hawley states that otherness and nostalgia produce a kind of 'religious machismo', the sense of the 'necessity for maleness to reassert itself in the in the face of manifest threat' which at the same time requires women (and children) who are to be defended against such threats (1994: 32–33).

In other words, both in the 'West' and the 'East' the forceful imagery of the Islamic Woman proves quite resilient.[42] In both discourses, veiled women are seen as symbols reflecting the state that their Islamic society is in: the inferiority and backwardness in the West, the progress and elevated status in the East. Despite the different goals of the usage of this imagery, women are in both cases treated as an icon, a fossilised image symbolising an either outdated or golden, past.

This former image of the Muslim woman also looms large in academic works on Islamic societies.[43] While most academic works on 'non-western' societies have neglected women for most of the twentieth century, this is clearly not the case with works on Islamic societies,

---

[42] Jansen (1989) states that the emphasis on the correct conduct of women is due to the fact that the personal status laws concern mainly family matters and issues related to the personal sphere, both seen as the prerogative of women. These laws are based on Islamic texts, and constitute a corpus of texts which is written down. See also Mernissi (1991).

[43] Especially the last decennia several critical assessments of this imagery in academic works have appeared, notably in feminist studies in particular from those written by female scholars from an Islamic society. See for example: Abu-Lughod (1989); Ahmed (1992: 164–168); Jansen (1987, 1989); Joseph (1986); Lazreq (1994); Moors (1992, 1999); Sayigh (1981); Suad (1986).

which even show a 'female bias (Jansen 1989: 297)' and a 'woman-complex (Sayyigh 1981: 258)'. In these viricentric works women are constructed as objects completely defined by their Muslim identity and as a homogeneous and static category, an unchanging and unchangeable part of an a-historic 'Islamic' society. Also in this case it has become a discussion *over* Muslim women, not *by* or *with* them. Islamic women in all these cases are being talked for and over and silenced in the process.[44] What is at stake, then, is not the absence of women in public and in academic discourses on Islam, but their representation (Abu-Lughod 1989: 267–306; Jansen 1989: 289–306; Lazreq 1988: 81–107; Moors 1991: 115; Kabbani 1986).

Interestingly, and painfully, enough on some occasions, western feminists have taken a perspective on the issue of veiling comparable to these conservative political and academic viewpoints. One of the reasons for this is, that not too long ago women in the West have done away with restrictive dressing codes as a way of claiming freedom of movement and feminist rights. The veil is perceived as a comparable sign of enclosure, submission and segregation (Lutz 1996: 132–134; Moors 1991: 114–122; Yegenoglu 1998: 97–99). This view was based on the main viewpoint of feminist scholars in the 1970s and 1980s that women all over the world were in a structurally similar position as subordinate and oppressed as women. It is precisely the attribution of similar experiences to seemingly comparable features and situations, which is problematic (Moore 1994: 11).

Although in the speeches quoted above, women are constructed as the other 'within', the female speakers Sitt Miriam and Sitt Huda do take a speaking position addressing other women in an authoritative way. The women's speeches addressed to women is consistent with an Islamic rationale of segregation and I could take their message at face value and see these female speakers as ventriloquist of the government's viewpoint, calling for their own subjugation. However, this would construct these women as mere cultural dopes or dupes, without critical awareness, and more as victims of the moral discourse than their male colleagues. However, although they are only addressing a female audi-

[44] In the last decennia especially feminist scholars have produces excellent works in which the historical and local context and the experiences of women did get a place. That there are too many to name them all is an indication of this new way of analysis. See for example Jansen (1987, 1989, 1994); Karam (1998); Lazreq (1988, 1994); Macleod (1991); Moors (1992, 1999); van Santen (1993).

ence, as women they are allowed to take the stage and speak in a mixed company to a mixed audience. Therefore, the question the speeches pose is: to what extent do these women use their speeches to construct an alternative female subjectivity? Moreover, to what extent does this possible alternative subjectivity relate to their anonymous, presumed illiterate female audience? More specifically this begs the question as to how both classes of working women in Kebkabiya negotiate the Islamist discourse for their own strategies in order to attain their own interests? The speeches of the female speakers therefore merit a closer look, in line with the analysis of the words of the male speakers, to see what they say and more particularly, how they say it.

Back to the Speeches: Difference and Defiance

If the speeches delivered by the female speakers, Miriam and Huda, seem ambivalent with respect to the evaluation of the status of Darfur women, the aim of the speeches is quite straightforward. Comparable to their male colleagues, they address their female audience as moral subjects in order to make them more unified, to create from them 'good' Muslim women by advising them on the right conduct. There are, however some remarkable differences.

In their speeches, the female speakers come to the same conclusion as the male speakers with respect to the fact that Darfur women need guidance in order to become better Muslims. The solution to educate women in order to make them better Muslims as suggested by Miriam neatly corresponds with the introduction by her male colleague: women should be educated in order to become better Muslims. However, instead of seeing men as those who have to teach their wives and children, Sitt Miriam insists that the Sudanese Women's Committee, the sub-section of the regional popular committee of which both female speakers are the representatives, should take up this task.

Moreover, the female speakers use a different rhetorical strategy compared to their male colleagues. When discussing the vices of women, Miriam and Huda address the women choosing more often 'she', 'you' and 'them' than 'we' as their male colleagues did. This is especially true for Miriam addressing the girls, and to a lesser extent for Huda who does use 'us' when talking about the obedience to 'our' husbands. It is clear that they consider their female audience more as the 'other' than 'us'.

The reason for this is to be found in the different subject positions men and women are allocated in the moral discourse of the Sudanese government. In her speech, Sitt Miriam relates the 'bad habits' of Kebkabiya women to the fact that they are uneducated; therefore it is the educated women who are indispensable in providing literacy classes, which will 'raise the reputation of Darfur'. This sets both Miriam and Huda apart as educated women, as those 'who know how to deal with problems of their families', how to behave and to treat others according to the prescriptions in the *Qur'an*. Obviously, their educated status gives them the authority to speak to the female audience. Therefore the labels both women apply to their female audience, namely uneducated and illiterate, not only suffices to portray the local women as 'bad' Muslims, but also serves to differentiate the speakers from their female audience. This is exemplified by the first sentence of Miriam's address, when she states that women should have greater faith in order to become better Muslim women and to become educated. In most arguments it is the other way around, to acquire education leads to better Muslims. In other words, Miriam sees 'being educated' as a goal, not just as a means, and as concomitant to being a good Muslim.

The fact that the female speakers need to be differentiated from their female audience more strictly and more obviously than their male colleagues is understandable, given the ambiguity on women's position in the moral discourse which constructs women as the main point of reference for both the 'good' and 'bad' Islamic society (cf. Hawley 1994: 27). The status of a good Muslim woman is constituted by prescribed acts and materiality, which is detectable for all to see: in dress codes, behaviour and general demeanour, in trying not to cause *fitna*. Men's attitude towards becoming better Muslims is less detectable and more a matter of intention. This puts the female speakers in a different position than their male colleagues: they have to prove their 'different-ness' from 'bad' women in clearly detectable ways in order to prevent allegations of corrupting Sudanese society because of speaking in public as women. This is particularly important as the speakers themselves call on the women to be obedient and modest within the walls of the compounds of their male relatives. In their speeches the position offered to the faceless and nameless audience, the unidentified and unidentifiable mass of women, seems to be uni-dimensional based on a negation: *non*-educated, *non*- (proper) Islamic, *non*-elite women unified by a location, Darfur. Thus, the fact that we know these two female speakers by their first names with the addition of the honorary title of 'Sitt', lady or mistress used in particular for female government employees, sets them apart from their anonymous audience. At the same time, the lack of their surnames, which would refer to their fathers, constructs these women as exemplary women outside the realm of kinship relations: as generalized symbols of female Muslim virtue.

The difference in position and esteem between these visible, speaking women and their nameless, silent audience is not only merited by the fact that they are on stage addressing the anonymous audience as subjects. It is also given materiality by their white *tob*e: the white veil which marks women wearing them as educated and working for the government, which not only makes them 'white veil' workers, as in 'white collar' workers. While the ordinary *tobe* is denounced by Sitt Miriam for being 'un-Islamic', the white *tobe* protects their reputation as virtuous women: they signal the fact that they work for the government, even when they move in public without male chaperones. So, while each of them is a named subject and speaks from a position of high profile and public visibility, this exaggeration of their exposure is, being clad in white *tobe*s part of their circumscribed position and status as 'Sitt'. They are at one and the same time acting out their virtue as Muslim women while checking their reputation as elite women and at the same time securing their relative anonymity. This difference in dress therefore marks opposing categories of women, of educated elite women opposed to non-elite 'local' women and constructs a hierarchy among women. This hierarchy means also a difference in positioning with reference to the discourse on the Sudanese Muslim woman.[45]

The discourse on the right role of women as constructed with and in the speech lends space to different kinds of female subjectivity, of educated and non-educated women, which deconstructs the image of a homogeneous, unified Muslim Woman while it is being constructed. In this respect, it is for example interesting that the male colleague who introduces Sitt Miriam emphasizes the need to marry in the government-subsidised mass-weddings. Sitt Miriam does not even hint at this phenomenon in her address although she does underline the plight of parents in relation to wedding their daughters. Sitt Huda focuses on already married women and mothers. In her speech, the

[45] This image is officially only valid for the northern part of the Sudan, as the South voted against *shari'a* law and is exempted from the Islamization project. Unofficially, however, also Southern women are seen as targets of this moral discourse, particularly when having migrated to the North (Simone 1994: 185–187).

replacement of the concept of 'mothers', *al-ummayaat*, in the saying 'Heaven is under the feet of mothers' with 'women', *al-nisa*, is curious, as motherhood is such an important aspect of female Muslimhood. Is it a slip of the tongue? Should I read this as a sub-text? My main aim is, as I stipulated in the Introduction, to understand the ways *both* classes of working women (female teachers and market women) negotiate, stretch, negate and, possibly, transform the boundaries imposed on them as part of the discourse. I am particularly interested in the ways that both classes of women thus create space for their own wishes, needs, desires and interests. Do the female speakers as educated elite women indeed occupy a speaking position, which makes a difference to the discourse? What alternative subject positions does the discourse offer the working women in Kebkabiya, both to female teachers and market women? Before looking for an answer in their own reflections, I will first turn to the local context in which these speeches were expected to carry meaning: this was also the context in which (for the duration of my research) both classes of women, in addition to Yasmin, Johan and myself, lived together.

CHAPTER 2

THE SETTING: RELATIONS OF RULING IN KEBKABIYA

Discourses and power relations are constitutive of people and places, but are also constituted by these and as such are part of everyday life. Consequently, as an anthropologist I became part of the discursive dynamics while taking part in Kebkabiya daily life and while I was positioned in these discourses I, similar to the other working women, had to come to terms with that subject position in turn. In this chapter I will clarify to what extent the position of the 'other' of the foreigner and the female came together during the research period in Kebkabiya town; and how Johan, but predominantly Yasmin, and I became part of that local context and negotiated our positioning during the course of our stay.

Getting Settled in the Town of Kebkabiya

Johan and I fly from Khartoum to the capital of Northern Darfur, Al-Fasher[1]at the beginning of November 1991. From there, Yasmin arranges a lift with a Land Rover of one of the local development organisations. We drive through the dry, stony landscape, interspersed with trees bordering the banks of dry rivers, and mighty mountain ridges simmering in the late afternoon heat. For decades, traders, slaves, armies and pilgrims took the trans-African trade route from West Africa, either bending off here in North-Darfur to the northeast to Egypt, following the *darb al-arba'iin*, the forty-days road,[2] or going straight

[1] The name of the town is taken from *al-fashir*, the encampment of the Fur sultan whenever he went on a tour or military campaign. It developed into a more fixed location and became the indication for the permanent royal court at Lake Tendelti, which now is the town of Al-Fasher (O'Fahey 1980: 24–26).

[2] The place where the *darb al-arba'iin*, the forty-day road to Cairo started was called Kobbei. It was located near current Al-Fasher. It functioned as a boarding place as well as the main administrative and trading post where the Sultan could exert his monopoly on trading the rare items of the caravans against cloth, salt, wheat and other local

east, via Suakin, to Mecca, and vice versa: there were also those who stayed. Lorries and Land Rovers have for the most part replaced the camels and horses of the caravans since colonial times. Ever since Italian donors built an all-weather road in 1989, even a bus service has been set up which connects the market and administrative centre Kebkabiya to Al-Fasher, shortening the trip of about twelve to only six hours.

The green we detected from afar comes from trees growing along the *wadi*, the dry riverbed along which Kebkabiya stretches. The town itself is not so green and extends over an enormous area with sandy streets, walled compounds and low, one-story wattle-and-daub and mud brick houses with an occasional acacia tree. As soon as we are well into town, the driver tells us that we have been lucky: one week ago bandits stopped a bus at one of the dry river crossings on the way. Two people were killed in the ambush; all the others were robbed.

It proves difficult to find a place to live. The stationing of a large army division in Kebkabiya one month before our arrival, in order to halt the so-called 'tribal' clashes in Darfur has taken up all vacant rooms in government buildings. There is also a constant stream of people who migrate to Kebkabiya because of these conflicts and because the drought of 1990, the second in a row. In the area around Kebkabiya, ethnic clashes aggravate the effects of the drought, which prevents people from growing their food at places outside the boundaries of their villages. The newly arrived hope to find work, food, safety, or at least help from their relatives and they have taken up most of the cheaper places in town. There are even two small sections to the northwest of Kebkabiya called '*jimjabá*' and '*kalashjabá*', 'we came because of the jims/kalashnikovs', both referring to automatic guns used in the ethnic conflicts (cf. Flint and De Waal 2005: 54).[3]

After one month, we find ourselves a newly built house in 'the new extension', one of the recently established segments of Kebkabiya town. It is located near the girls' intermediary school and the houses of the government officials and teachers. The rent is outrageous, even for a stone built house. Also, it is quite a distance from the centre of town where the older quarters are built around the central mosque, hospital

---

products. Many of these caravans also visited Kebkabiya itself (see preface). See for more details Hassan (1977); La Rue (1984); Nachtigal (1879–1889); O'Fahey (1980: 139).

[3] Flint and De Waal give a similar account for displaced who settled around Nyala, who were called *jimjabuu* 'the rifle brought them'.

and market place. I am not happy with living in a fancy house erected in stone, in a newly established ward at the outskirts of town. Most families seem well off and have moved to this quarter only recently. There is hardly any social network, which I, as an anthropologist, can 'step into'. I face the dilemma of how to build up relations with the longer established, and mostly less well off, families and socialise with them while living so far from the centre of town. So for our first impression, Yasmin and I rely on the results of the survey, however general and shallow, and information gained from notables, project members and stories from the few people we do come to know in those first weeks.

Darfur, like the other regions bordering the Sahara, is an ecological transition zone and is located at the western boundary of the Sudan.[4] In the north lies the desert, then going southwards are the arid savannah grass- and woodlands leading to the more wet grasslands and finally the tropical rain forests in South Darfur (see map). The population varies markedly both in terms of means of survival and ethnic or 'tribal' groupings. In North Darfur, the area in which Kebkabiya is located there are mainly camel nomads and some cattle nomads, apart from the sedentary farmers. Camel nomads, who live mainly in the northern desert that stretches into neighbouring Libya and Chad, are labelled 'Arab' referring in fact to 'Bedouin'. The Baggara[5] are cattle nomads and they are interchangeably seen as part of these Arabs and as a separate ethnic group, since they wander with cows in the middle and more southern zones of Darfur. The droughts of the last decades have forced many cattle nomads to trek with their cattle in the region south of Kebkabiya. Arab camel nomads come with their camels more often, earlier and ever more deeply into the southern edges of their nomadic routes than before.[6] Agriculturists, who increasingly have difficulties to harvest enough to survive on, inhabit these areas (De Waal 1989: 50–54; Ibrahim 1982; Tubiana & Tubiana 1977).

[4] With an area of approximately 160,000 square miles it borders Libya, Chad, Central Africa and Uganda. Though Darfur has been part of the Sudan since the first of January 1917, the Chadian border agreement between the French and the British was signed on 10 Jaunuary 1924 (Harir 1994: 150–151; Theobald 1956: 225).

[5] Baggara means 'cows' and is correctly spelled as 'baqqara'. As in Darfur the 'q' is pronounced as a 'g', I use this transcription.

[6] For an early study of desertification of Northern Darfur, see Fouad Ibrahim (1980). He points out that the recurrent droughts and growing human use of the arid zones along the Sahara, together have led to the desertification of this vulnerable area.

Kebkabiya is a provincial town, located at the northern foothills of Jebel Marra, in an area that straddles the transition zone of desert and savannah grass- and woodlands.[7] The *Fur*, *Tama*, and *Zaghawa* form the majority of the inhabitants of Kebkabiya.[8] The *Fur* is the major ethnic group in this area while the *Tama* migrated here from Chad at the end of the nineteenth century: both are sedentary agriculturists. The *Zaghawa*, a semi-nomadic group wandering across the border of Chad and Northern Darfur have, like the *Arab* who form a minority in town, settled here only recently. Being located near the road, which connects the capital Al-Fasher to Al-Geneina at the border with Chad, Kebkabiya provides possibilities for young men to find work. However, due to the absence of significant industrialisation, it is only government services, agriculture, and the market, which offer most of the permanent opportunities for work. Recently, opportunities in brick making, construction work and household services have become available to labourers.

The influence of periods of drought, which occurred more frequently and more severely since the 1970s, has resulted in a steady stream of migrants settling in Kebkabiya, mainly from the rural areas surrounding Kebkabiya. While in 1985 the Town Council recorded some 10,000 inhabitants for the town, in 1991 this number had risen to over 15,000.[9] Each ethnic group in Kebkabiya is said to have settled in that part of town, which is situated in the direction from where they came. The different quarters of the town therefore have, apart from their official name, the name of the ethnic group that is presumed to have founded that part of town, where the ethnic leader is also living. However, some of the recent settlers, predominantly Arab and Zaghawa, and the recently arrived Fur have found a place to live in the older established quarters near the centre of town as well. Therefore the supposedly ethnic homogeneity of the wards did not hold due to the new

[7] Many of the figures in this part are based on the survey Yasmin and I conducted during our fieldwork, unless indicated otherwise. See the annex for a selection of tables with figures.

[8] In the survey these groups constituted respectively 23,5 %, 20,6 % and 17,2 % of the women interviewed, as related to the ethnic background of the father.

[9] These numbers are estimations and should be referred to with caution. For example Adrienne Martin, who conducted a study for Oxfam into farming systems in Kebkabiya area in 1985 produced different figures (Martin 1985). Moreover, migrants are only registered as inhabitants after a four-month waiting period, and only after they have paid a registration fee. This is something the poorest households will not be able to do.

inhabitants and because of intermarriage. In the rainy season, from May to September, there is less trade since the roads are less accessible and most traders and market women have to cultivate their land, if it rains at all. These are also the months that some members of nomadic groups, mostly women, children and elderly people, forage for wild food and small hunt, or work on a piece of land to grow the staple, sorghum. Near Kebkabiya there are several seasonal camps where, in normal times, nomads would stay for a short period when migrating down south or back north.[10] The droughts forced the more unfortunate nomads to sell their camels and find another way of living, mostly by settling down. Before that would happen, the family group that formerly travelled together would split. The elderly, women, and little children settled in one of the places they would know from their migration route. Meanwhile, the men, especially the younger ones, travel with a smaller herd up to the arid areas far to the north (Grawert 1992; Martin 1985; Tubiana & Tubiana 1977). One of these camps has recently turned into a quarter of Kebkabiya since it has become permanently settled with increasing numbers of ex-nomadic peoples.

Outsiders can, when in need, also ask local landholders either to rent some of their land, to cultivate it on a sharecrop basis, or to exchange the temporary usufruct rights (ownership rights) for animal products. Everybody is entitled to take rain-fed land that is not in use to grow food crops on. If someone wants to use such a plot, he or she must first consult the local leader, in the case of Kebkabiya the *shartai* of the Fur who is also head of the local court. He has the right to allocate land-use rights in Kebkabiya. If the land is used by someone, the *shartai* might act as intermediary. This is reminiscent of the *hakura* system, which was operated under the Fur sultanate. The sultan would allot areas or plots of land to a collective, such as Muslim migrants, through a title-holder who represented the sovereign. The owner of the title deed had the power to divide usufruct rights among his followers and to ask rent if he wanted so. The land itself was communal and inalienable through sale, reverting to the sovereign when in disuse. Thus authority over land also meant political and administrative authority over those who lived

[10] *Dar Zaghawa*, is an area, which was allotted to the ethnic groups of Zaghawa, who are semi-nomadic, in the colonial era. The Arab nomads did not receive a *dar* as they were considered to be moving around continuously. Both groups were located in the far north of Darfur, which has now become a difficult area to survive in, due to drought and desertification. I will return to the problems of the *dars*.

on it or used it, in particular the 'founder' or *sid al-fahas* (master of the axe) who was entitled to tax its inhabitants and represent them in political decision making (Barth 1982: 6; La Rue 1984; O'Fahey 1980; Harir 1994: 178).

Interestingly, although Kebkabiya is a town, most households engage in food production themselves. Mainly women cultivate the rain-fed crops: the growing of the staple, *durra* or sorghum,[11] on rain-fed land is a predominantly female business.[12] However, the usufruct rights of women to rain fed land does not strengthen their economic position per se. Moreover, with the failing rains of the last few decades, land is lucrative only when irrigated by pumps in order to grow cash crops and this is something in which the women are not involved.

Men dominate irrigated agriculture. It has gained ground, in a literal and figurative sense, in Kebkabiya since the beginning of the 1980s. Before that time people used to irrigate with a *shadoof*, a wooden devise to pull up water, which could irrigate only small plots of land. In the 1980s, the first motorised pumps were brought in from Gezira, the agricultural scheme in Central Sudan dominated by the family and followers of the Mahdi. With these, large tracts of land could be watered, which caused irrigated agriculture to become more popular. As pumps required investments, technical know-how and social contacts most small farmers did not have, this kind of agriculture was successful mainly when operated by wealthy farmers, traders and even government officials.

Irrigated agriculture is employed along the *wadi*, the dry riverbed that carries water during the rainy season and which is easy to dig for water during the dry season. If irrigated, these fertile plots of clay soil (*tin*), even when access to them is on a communal basis, are in continuous use.

Especially when trees, which are perceived as private property, are planted on the plots, the land in the course of time becomes considered as the property of the cultivator. This land can now be bought and sold, and other kinds of contracts like sharecropping are in use as well. Thus, a difference has developed between communal, sandy soil (*qoz*)

---

[11] On some higher altitudes also *dukhn* or bullrush millet is grown, which is seen as producing better grain providing finer flour making a better *asida*, the porridge daily prepared as breakfast and sometimes even lunch.

[12] Eighty percent of the households own usufruct rights to land, mainly to rain-fed land. In almost 80 percent of the cases, women owned the land herself and of them 74 percent, cultivated rain-fed crops (tables 6 and 7 annex 1).

of rain-fed land used for growing the staple mainly by women, and the irrigated plots which have come into the private hands of men who grow there predominantly cash-crops.

From the survey, we learned that many non-educated women are *de facto* heads of their houschold. Migrants, i.e. husbands, uncles or sons, are often not able to send goods or money to their families regularly. If men send money at all, it arrives erratically and many women have to earn their own income. Divorce and polygamy are closely related, as there is a trend among men who migrate to marry another woman in the place where they find a job. Sometimes he divorces the earlier wife or wives, but more often, he neglects his duties of sending money to the family that stayed behind. In both cases, women are forced to fend for themselves.[13] Unable to grow their own food because of drought or to work in order to earn money, many women feel forced to sell at the market particularly in the dry season, which runs from about September till May. This favoured option for most poor women to earn money has resulted in a growing number of women who sell predominantly food, fruits, vegetables, or drinks at the market. Even when the head of the household is around, women often need to find extra sources of income in order to meet the high costs of living. Drought has resulted in shortages and transportation prices add to the ever-rising prices of goods. Most women therefore prefer to earn their own money. Not only, because they do not want to be dependent, but also because they do not want to be a burden to the families of their relatives.

This is particularly true for market women who want to sell produce from their farm or those of others. The income of market women is highly instable. For these women the income is highly reliant on the dry season and the safety of the area for travelling. Moreover, the income of market and tea women fluctuates per week and is therefore never reliable and most often the money earned is hardly enough to survive on.

Helima, one of the tea women I visited often during my first stay told me she earned ten to forty Sudanese pounds a day in the dry season when marketing is favoured.[14] This means that she gets a return of £S10 for every pound of sugar she buys. In a good week she earns about £S200 to £S250 from which she still has to deduct the money

[13] This neglect is a legitimate reason for women to file for a divorce. From the survey it appeared that co-wives are relatively more common among women who had little or no education.

[14] At that time the official rate was 1U$ = 12 Sudanese Pounds (£S).

from which she buys her tea, coffee, sugar, spices and charcoal. Still, it is a reasonably good income if one considers that a junior teacher earns for a start between £S400 and £S600 per month.[15] The only investment women have to make, apart from the tea making utensils, which every woman has in her kitchen, and some cloth, plastic or burlap for displaying wares for sale, is a license of £S100, which should be obtained from the Ministry of Health.[16] This accounts for the popularity of making tea among poorer women. Paradoxically, the popularity among women of making tea and selling food products has reduced its profits. In slack periods the income from selling at the market is little anyway so the prospects of earning a good living from selling tea, or other products has become less favourable.

This insecurity over the means of survival is what marks women out as poor. However, I discovered with time that poverty is not only measured in money, since the 'normal' economy is not completely monetary. In years of sufficient rain, one's status is highly dependent on self-sufficiency where it concerns the staple and other crops that are used for daily use. In our survey, most people indicated that 'poverty' meant to them that they had to reduce the number of meals, and that they had fewer possibilities to engage in an exchange relation using their crops. De Waal (1989) in his work on famine in Darfur comes up with the same idea on poverty. Famine and poverty are closely related in a self-sufficient economy. 'Destitute' people themselves did not evaluate the lack of means of material survival *per se* as the main factor of their poverty, but the lack or breaking down of social networks which can support one in daily survival. De Waal's conclusion is therefore, that destitution is not so much related to little income, or material wealth, but to the idea of not being able to lead a fulfilling life in the sense of not being able to eat the highly valued staple, *asida*, millet porridge, not 'belonging', and the loss of autonomy in making productive decisions. This last aspect also makes wage labour in the eyes of the local population shameful (de Waal 1989: 57–58).[17]

Among the elite, status and money are related, but also to a limited extent, however. Wealthy traders and the salaried white-collar workers,

---

[15] See Hale (1990) for the salaries of white-collar workers according to grades.

[16] The Ministry of Health is responsible for the market's hygienic conditions. Women selling food and drinks are therefore medically checked and pay for their license to the Ministry of Health.

[17] This was particularly the case in Jebel Marra (see Barth 1974; Willemse 1991).

employed by the government or by development projects and the bank depend on money for maintaining their elite lifestyle and marking their elevated position.[18] The traders, together with the local leaders belong to the local elite who is revered by the local population. The educated elite distinguishes itself from the traders and the local tribal elite by their occupational and educational background and is seen as the 'government elite'. Although the government provides its employees with subsidised goods and free lodging, salaries hardly keep pace with the rate of inflation. Nevertheless, the educated elite constitutes the most powerful force when it comes to the implementation of government decrees and their influence on the moral discourse. As I would learn in the course of my research, it is precisely the boundaries between classes and the way these are established and maintained which are central to the ways elite and non-elite groups perceive and deal with each other. Therefore this internal differentiation of the elite has obvious consequences for the way Kebkabiya is administered.

Setting the Stage: Local Elites and Ruling Relations

In order to get acquainted with our neighbours and to introduce ourselves to the notables in Kebkabiya society, Yasmin suggests having a *fatuur*, as the Sudanese breakfast is called, as a *karama*, a ritual meal, in this case a kind of 'housewarming party'. She proposes we hold it on Christmas day. I am hesitant. I do not like the idea of showing off and that on such an inauspicious day. Yasmin is adamant. She thinks this day is perfect, as Christmas is a holiday in Sudan as well so most of the government officials will have a day off then. She proves to be right. The reactions are enthusiastic and we learn that the Head of the Rural Council has even postponed an official rally in support of the implementation of the *shari'a*, the Islamic law, planned for that day. When the rally is held the next day, he speaks of tolerance towards 'our Christian friends'. Even commenting that they, meaning us, are after all 'fellow' believers of the Book.

We prepare the *fatuur* with the help of neighbours, who cook and provide us with the cutlery, china, cups, bowls, carpets, taken from a local cooperative, and all the other necessities for such an enormous

[18] As there is hardly any private enterprise in Darfur, this branch offers no job opportunities to educated people.

gathering of about a hundred guests: neighbours, teachers, government officials, like administrators, police and army officers, local leaders of all ranks arrive together with the paramount leader of the Fur, the *shartai*. Most of the officials come with their wives.

When the men have been served the large round aluminium trays, which feed up to ten people, with *kisra*, the sour pancakes, bread and about eight bowls with food, covered with the brightly coloured food covers so specific to Darfur, the women may eat in what is temporarily the 'female' part of our house, near the outside kitchen. It is interesting to see that each tray is occupied selectively: neighbours, government officials' wives, the young unmarried girls, and female teachers each share a separate tray. From Johan I gather that also among the men there seems to be a seating arrangement. The *shartai*, and his entourage shared some trays with project members; the higher government officials shared some amongst them, with the neighbours together sharing another tray. The relationships among these men seemed cordial enough. However, the seating arrangement at our party charted the political and social relations of men belonging to the two parallel operating administrative elites active in the town of Kebkabiya: the so-called government elite or employees and the local 'tribal'[19] elite.

Because of the widely spaced quarters, the town extends over a large area. It takes us weeks to find our way around town and even longer to realise that the layout of the town and the offices says a great deal about the way the administration is structured. On the outskirts, at the far western boundary of the town are the main government offices hosting the offices of the District or Area Council of which there are six in North Darfur. The Distict Council of Kebkabiya is again divided into three Rural Councils: Kebkabiya, Sereif, and Seraf Umra.[20] The government offices administer services like education, labour, health, finance, the co-operatives, and are accountable to their Head Quarters in Al-Fasher. Situated halfway between these offices and the central market place inside Kebkabiya are the offices of the Rural Council. This council is accountable to the District Council and responsible for

[19] The use of 'tribe' has become highly problematic and the term 'ethnic group' is used instead. I retain here this term but because it was used in these particular cases by the *shartai* and other leaders of ethnic groups themselves, as well as taken to be the most correct translation of 'gabila' (see also Stiansen and Kevane 1996: 8). I use quotation marks to indicate my reservations about the term.

[20] By the end of my stay in 1991 Kutum had taken the place of Kebkabiya as District Head Quarters.

the 141 Village Councils some of which now have become quarters of Kebkabiya town.[21]

Inside the town, near the smaller of the two mosques the office of the so-called 'tribal' administration and 'native or tribal' court is located. The office lies at the far end of an enormous empty space in between the government offices and the houses of the government officials. The normal opening hours are on market days when people from outside come for their shopping, so they may come with their complaints to Kebkabiya. The court is presided over by the *shartai*, Ahmed Ahmeddai, paramount leader of the Fur, the largest ethnic group in the area.[22] During those first weeks, Yasmin and I had some talks with the *shartai*. In one discussion, he explains that in case there is a conflict between Fur and other tribes in the area, it is the *shartai*, who will try to negotiate peace at the local, 'tribal' court when the conflict is still in an early stage. In these dispute settlements he is assisted by other members of this court amongst them two other paramount leaders, *maliks*, one of the Zaghawa and one of the *Arabs*, and seven sub-heads, or *omda*s, of which four are Fur, and Tama, Arab, Gimr one each. They act as intermediaries at dispute-settlements in which their ethnic groups are involved, or as arbiters in conflicts in which they do not have a stake. If the conflict has already escalated the *shartai* informs the government representatives in Kebkabiya and a peace conference might be called for. The *shartai* is assisted by his brother for local affairs and management and at court by the leader of the Gimr, who was put forward by the *shartai* because this ethnic group is not involved in the tribal problems in the area.[23]

People nominated Ahmed to his position in 1964 after his father died. His position in the administration changed, however, when Nimeiri came to power in 1969. Nimeiri, like his predecessors, was confronted with the problem of governing an enormous area with a diverse population. He reduced the power of native administration by replacing 'tribal' leaders with a more democratic institution of chosen vil-

---

[21] See also A. Martin's report to Oxfam U.K (1985).

[22] The father of Ahmed was Ahmed Ahmedai Mohammed, who died in 1964. At the time, he was deputizing for his eldest brother who was *shartai*, but died in 1962.

[23] The ethnic leaders in Kebkabiya District have chosen both deputies. Eight *omda*s and 270 *sheikh*s chose the brother of the *shartai* unanimously while the leader of the Gimr was chosen, by majority vote during a secret ballot by the members of the 'tribal' court. This should prevent the person elected from being biased against those who opposed him.

lage committees[24] and a new system of geographic divisions.[25] In 1972, after he was elected President in a staged national referendum, he founded the Sudanese Socialist Union (SSU) as the single legal party, which functioned as the primary political apparatus of his regime. The socialist ideology claimed a break with the past under the slogan 'Unity in Diversity' with equality for the masses. Youth and women's unions were formed by the SSU and numerous SSU councils at village and town level were established in order to engage in community services and self-help projects, like the building of hospitals and schools (Fleuhr-Lobban et. al. 1992: 137–138, 155–156, 210; Woodward 1990: 125–130).

Nevertheless most local leaders and their 'tribal' dynasties kept their importance alongside, and increasingly interrelated with, the local governmental administration (Stiansen and Kevane 1998: 28; Al-Shahi 1991: 148–159; Woodward 1979: 8–10,12; 1990: 146–156). So, when the Fur *shartai* Ahmedai was re-installed in office in 1986 because of the recurrent 'tribal conflicts', this in fact formalised an already existing situation.[26] The 'National Salvation Committee' that heads the current junta vowed after the coup in 1989 to re-structure the local administration promised under former governments.[27] Not only in order to make government interference and control of the lowest levels more efficient, but also in an attempt to stop nepotism. The newly founded 'popular committees' (*al-ledgna al-sha'abiya*), however, are organised on the same

[24] As Woodward comments, 'Down with native administration' was in fact one of the slogans of the 'revolution' and was soon given serious consideration by the new and radically inclined government (1990: 122).

[25] Before that time Kebkabiya fell under the authority of Kutum District. At the end of my stay the old division has been restored and Kutum is again the district capital of Kebkabiya.

[26] During the democratic regime, the issue of the local government was again discussed and the *shartai* regained his power in November 1990. Both dates were given by *shartai* Ahmedai himself, although he referred to the 'Nimeiri regime', which was toppled in 1985. As it is the case, the re-formalisation of a local administration was started under Nimeiri, but formalised under the transitional interim regime of Suwar Al-Dahab (Head Transitional Military Council) and Dafalla Al-Gizouli, Prime Minister in 1986 (Fleuhr-Lobhan 1992: 400) and then finalized by the current government. This indicates the general agreement of the need for local intermediaries for the ethnic conflicts.

[27] More often than not, support depended on rewards in kind or on ethnic and family affiliations. Therefore, after Nimeiri was ousted and the elected democratic regime was installed in 1986, there have been attempts at reviewing the system of Village Councils.

basis as the village committees under the Nimeiri regime before them: also, their task is to organise mass involvement in governmental issues.[28]

However, in Darfur the recurrent ethnic clashes have occurred since the 1970s, but with more intensity during the 1980s and early 1990s when droughts became more frequent meant a larger role of the local 'tribal' authorities in peace negotiations. This has led to the existence of two parallel administrations: a local 'tribal' and a national governmental administration. The relationship is an uneasy one. Though each seems to have its own sphere of power; based on different ruling rationales, they frequently fall out with each other as they have jurisdiction for the same area. The government officials see the 'tribal' conflicts as a nuisance, a problem of local magnitude, related to drought, backwardness, and tradition. 'Tribal' leaders are mistrusted because of their potential to sabotage agreements and their unreliability, being allies one day, and enemies the next. More importantly, the 'help' of the 'tribal' leaders is perceived by the government officials as a sign of their own failure to solve local problems and a devaluation of their capacity as administrators.

The duplication of involvement creates a fuzzy situation as to where the responsibility for arbitrage and decision-making lies. On the one hand, the use of local leaders suggests that the 'tribal' conflict be seen as an indigenous local affair. On the other hand, the presence of the army and the involvement of both local and regional government officials make the 'tribal' conflicts a national issue as well. The awkward relationship between the two elites is detectable in the way solutions to ethnic problems are put forward and implemented. A frequent solution for these conflicts is that the *shartai* or government orders 'tribal' leaders to disarm their followers and collect the arms in Kebkabiya. As no one ever completely complies with these instructions, if at all, the army is trying to 'solve' the conflicts directly using force and coercion, sometimes even before the peace talks are concluded.

The ultimate resolution of the Fur-Arab conflict, one of the dominant ethnic clashes in the Kebkabiya area illustrates the ambiguity well. The major eruptions of the conflict occurred between 1987 and 1989. The so-called 'tribal reconciliation conference' for the Fur-Arab conflicts (1987–1989) at Al-Fasher took place between 29 May and 8

[28] Adrienne Martin visited Kebkabiya in 1985 as a consultant for Oxfam and registered accounts about nepotism. During my own research, these newly established popular committees were also alleged to be susceptible to nepotism.

July 1989. It was presided over by the military Governor of Dar Fur. However, it only took place after a committee of mediators comprising mostly of the Darfurian tribal leaders had visited all the different ethnic groups and established a peace plan between February and May 1989 (Harir 1994: 172–173).[29] The big question was, who and how the terms of the agreement, which were decided upon during the conference would be implemented: by government interference or by the tribal authorities?[30]

The seating arrangement at our housewarming party among the women also formed an indication of relationships and networks, although in a different way than among the men.

Single Female Teachers and Suitable Living Arrangements: The Boarding House

During the first weeks of our stay there is one group of neighbours who visits us regularly: the single female teachers living at the boarding house 'next door'. As one of them, Fadjur, got a lift from Al-Fasher from the same Land Rover we came on, we have been in contact with them ever since we arrived in Kebkabiya.

The boarding house lodges five single female teachers who all teach at the only intermediary school for girls in Kebkabiya. This school is the highest level of education for girls inside the town of Kebkabiya and has been established in 1979.[31] For secondary education girls have to travel to larger towns in Darfur, like Al-Fasher, Al-Geneina or Nyala. Most of the women teaching at the intermediary school have a secondary high school education and are therefore assigned to Kebkabiya

[29] At the meetings of the conference 110 Arab and Fur representatives and twenty-one mediators of the government were present. Casualties and losses were decided upon, respectively for Fur and Arabs: 2,500 against five hundred died; 40,000 against 3,000 head of life stock lost; 400 Fur villages containing approximately 10,000 residents against seven hundred Arab tents and residences were burned out of existence.

[30] The reverse is true for the Chad-Libya conflict fought on Darfur soil. In principle international conflict has been marked as an ethnic conflict, of Zaghawa looking for help from their 'relatives' in Darfur. In this case 'tribal' and government authorities also had to combine forces.

[31] Primary schools have six grades and are the same as elementary schools. Intermediary schools have three grades and are the same as lower-secondary schools. The secondary high schools have four grades preparing pupils for university or college (cf. V.L. Griffiths 1975: 5).

from outside. Kebkabiya is considered to be a 'hardship' post, because of its remoteness, lack of electricity and running water, but also because it is considered 'backward'. This makes running a household in combination with teaching a tedious affair. As a result mainly young single teachers are assigned to such remote places as Kebkabiya for short assignments of about two years. As there is always a shortage of qualified teachers in remote areas like Darfur, married female teachers are allowed to teach at the place where her family lives. Now even some high school leavers resident in Kebkabiya have been hired in order to teach in the lower classes of the intermediary school, even before they are properly trained at a Teachers' Training Institute.[32] As a result those single teachers who live at the boarding house are better qualified than the resident teachers and, like us, outsiders to the town.

After some weeks Yasmin starts to frequent the boarding house more often, at first only in the evenings. Slowly she spends more and more time at 'the other side' and sometimes she even does not return home for the night. At first I consider it fortunate that Yasmin has an opportunity to spend her leisure time since there is not much to do in Kebkabiya, and I accompany her often. But I feel increasingly uneasy with this ever more frequent visiting. Yasmin is entitled to deal with her spare time the way she wants. At the same time we had agreed that she would translate for me while living at the same house, and the few visitors we do have those weeks, mostly come during the evenings. I feel I need her for translation as long as I do not master the colloquial well enough to understand conversations on my own.

In the same period we set out to formulate new research questions. Perhaps that is when her enthusiasm dwindled. She and I did not have any research experience within a town. She was reluctant to visit the families in the neighbourhood, or the market, or the homes of some of the local women I had met in the street. When I brought the subject up she confessed she thought it was difficult to study people she had come to know so well, like the teachers, or who lead lives she could not feel much sympathy for, like the housewives in our neighbourhood: as for the poor, she felt powerless. She wanted action, felt useless and dispirited, and I understood her feelings, for to some extent they matched mine.

[32] This Institute, also referred to as College, was founded in 1934 by the British in the person of V.L. Griffiths, located in Bakht Al-Ruda (Griffiths 1975).

I felt the same incompetence and disappointment at not seeing ways to establish contacts and trust with women we could and wanted to work with. In the back of my mind was the hope to be able to do transformative research, to understand the daily lives and burdens of poor women and to find a way to transforming them, on the conditions of the women themselves[33] However, I had come to Darfur as a researcher while Yasmin's expertise had evolved around being active for poor women, trying to help them in food-aid programmes and consciousness raising programmes of a more structural nature. Moreover, it was her native Darfur we were working in. Doing 'just' research must have seemed so superficial when facing the problems of women migrating to Kebkabiya because of the drought. However, when I suggested we involve them in the research she was disinterested and hesitant, commenting we did not have 'anything concrete' to offer, which was true of course. In those same weeks the build-up of the Gulf-War reached its climax and there were fierce discussions among all educated elite members, male and female. Yasmin and I agreed on the foolishness and hard-headedness of both sides. Then, on 7 January, the Gulf War started.

Even in a remote town like Kebkabiya, it was a significant event. It turned out that almost every family had a relative working in the Middle East. A lot of 'Saddams' were born, a name formerly not used in the area. The war created a shortage of petrol and government offices were closed on both Fridays and Saturdays, instead of Friday only. The working days were longer. There was less transportation of goods to-and-from Kebkabiya, which meant shortages of many food items in the market.

The Sudanese government sided very openly with Iraq. When, on 1 January the Sudanese government announced its intention to declare *shari'a* in all but the South of Sudan, the atmosphere, particularly in Khartoum, got already more aggressive towards western foreigners, and this was only aggravated by the onset of the war. The declaration of Saddam Hussein, that the 'Mother of all Wars' had started and that it concerned in fact a *jihad*, a holy war, had its resonance in the Sudan. In

[33] The term transformative research comes from Schrijvers (for example 1991, 1992, 1995) and stems from her extensive experiences with what she calls 'participatory research' in Sri Lanka. Her perspective is related to viewpoints put forward by Mies (1982, 1983: 117–140), Huizer (1979: 3–41) and by the research group, which in 1976 founded the sub-department of feminist anthropology at Leiden University, VENO (Women and Development, later Women and Autonomy, VENA).

the Sudanese media, the western countries were accused of measuring by two standards: why was Iraq punished and Israel condoned? Now western foreigners, most of them working in development projects and food relief, were depicted as 'white devils' whose motives for giving aid should be distrusted. Most of the donors decided to evacuate their personnel for the duration of the war.

In Kebkabiya there were also fierce discussions about the fact that Arab countries had taken different sides in the war. But there was not a moment that Johan and I, as the only foreigners left in Northern Darfur, felt threatened. On the contrary, many of the Kebkabiya people we had come to know better, came to our house as usual and told us not to be afraid. We were 'good' people, as they put it, so no one would hold us responsible for the war acts of the western allies. Not all reactions in our surroundings were as soothing. There were people who saw the war not only as another power struggle between the North and the South, but also as one between oppressors and oppressed, between rich and poor, infidels and believers. Because my own research dealt with issues of Islam in relation to ideas on 'proper female conduct', I kept a low profile during these weeks, for fear of repercussions.

In this period Yasmin would listen to the radio whenever she was at home, to follow the developments of the war. Afterwards she would rush off, most often to one of the teacher's places or the boarding house. We hardly communicated anymore. At first I felt a bit awkward with this change of routine. When she started spending most nights at the boarding house, I had mixed feelings. Then she started to give evening English classes for the boarding house students in the afternoon. When I commented that we needed to spend more time on the research we quarrelled. It cleared the air and we found a compromise in that Yasmin moved back to our house while having a female teacher stay with her for the night in turns and occasional ventures into town during the day.

After some time, the Gulf War being over for weeks, we discussed what happened. Yasmin suggested our misunderstandings were related to cultural differences, while I thought they were of a more personal nature. Yasmin was adamant that it had to do with us being westerners who need more privacy than most Sudanese; she had learned so from working with foreigners. She had wanted to grant us some space to have our privacy. At that point I realised that it must have been difficult for Yasmin to deal with us as a couple, instead of only me, that she might have felt lonely and excluded and maybe even out of place.

During the weeks after the Gulf War was over we managed to focus on the research again. Yasmin concentrated on the female teachers and the local women's organisation *Tadaman*, Solidarity, which kept a low profile as it was, like all organisations banned by the government. Yasmin applied for funding for Tadaman at the Netherlands Embassy and established contacts with the women's organisation *Yid al-Marra*, Woman's Hand, in Nyala, of which she was one of the founders. Being able to engage in action clearly lifted her spirits. And so did mine. Nura, a local girl who had dropped out of intermediary school, cleaned and cooked for us, introduced me to her family living at the centre of town near the market place. I visited her family and neighbours frequently those last weeks, sometimes with Yasmin, more often on my own. Towards the end of our stay both Yasmin and I had found our way around town. This episode got another meaning, however, when I related it to another event.

Fadjur's Predicament: The Boarding House as Refuge

In my discussions with the single female teachers at the boarding house, one theme recurs repeatedly: their complaint about the persistent stream of gossip concerning their behaviour. The teachers feel that in general the people of Kebkabiya are distrustful and ignorant, especially women. One night, while drinking tea on a large carpet under a starry sky, the discussion emerges again: "They can't imagine that men and women can do things together that have nothing to do with sex", says Sitt Ashia, the headmistress bluntly. In particular, she singles out the market women:

> These women, they see us coming and are nice to you when you buy from them, but they say nasty things behind your back. These women have no sense. And besides, let them heed their own whereabouts: what are they doing there all day, when you only find customers at the market just before breakfast and just before lunch?

She is referring here to the stereotypical image of the market place as one of the central spots where most of the gossip is created or at least spread all over town. Fadjur adds another stereotype with respect to the market women: "They do not have anything else to do but gossip. Well … except maybe seeing men".

The female teachers all consider the gossip as a burden and an act of hostility towards strangers. It is especially single female teachers from outside who are the targets for the occasional verbal attacks. Some Kebkabiya residents obviously evaluate the relative freedom of these young single women negatively. They are scornful too of the frequent visits at the boarding house by other professional strangers to the town: young male government employees, such as teachers, army and police officers and administrators. The single female teachers are indignant about it because their reputation is important to the authority they may or may not have at school and towards their colleagues and other employees. This is particularly true of Sitt Ashia, who is the mistress of the intermediary school and has a high profile, as her job obliges her to attend meetings frequently in which she is more often than not the only woman. Everyone who lives at the boarding house feels watched and judged unfairly by people who should be grateful that the teachers are in fact trying to do their best to educate their children.

That Fadjur is fiercest during discussions on the local population's gossip is no coincidence. During our first stay, Fadjur was the main target of the gossip and slander by inhabitants of Kebkabiya. During one of our visits, the discussion ventures to the subject of the negative attitude of the Kebkabiya society again. Fadjur tells us how, in the former school year, she was living with the family of a school friend, Hannan who lived with her mother in the block with government's houses. Fadjur received visitors, amongst them some single unrelated male colleagues. The father of her friend works in Saudi Arabia and in a letter to him his brother complained about these visitors. Although the father, and the family of her friend, ignored the uncle's complaints and told her it was just the gossip of a silly old man, Fadjur decided to move to the boarding house.

A few days later we talk about her stay at the boarding house again. Fadjur explains that another reason for her move, despite the protests of Hannan and her mother, was simply the attraction of living in the boarding house: "I enjoy my stay at the boarding house very much. I feel free, more independent and less controlled". She hastens to add:

> O, there are strict rules, no male visitors at the compound, just in the office of the headmistress and only with a chaperone. And no men are allowed even in the office after nine o'clock

"So not much freedom after all", I retort, to which Fadjur reacts cheerfully:

> No, no, we are more free there. Look, at the boarding house we are amongst ourselves. We can decide what to cook, when to sleep, when to go out. No chores, except when you are on duty at the girls' boarding house or cooking. And because we have our own quarters, out of sight from the street, no one can easily tell lies about our behaviour, saying, 'I have seen her doing so and so, I have seen it myself', for no one can see anything. We are safe and our name is safe.

Fadjur evaluates living at the boarding house completely differently to how I had expected. These are young women who live removed from the protection of their parental homes, five of them cramped in one room without much privacy nor space to put their belongings. Adjoining the girls' boarding houses means that to some extent they are always 'on duty'. I expected them to see the boarding house as a necessary but unwelcome lodging. Apparently the discomfort does not outweigh the positive aspects as pointed out by Fadjur.

For me the importance of Fadjur's story is that it enabled me to understand Yasmin's predicament better. Yasmin was not from Kebkabiya either, and she was living with two foreigners, a woman and a man, in one of the recently built areas of the town. She was part of, for most inhabitants, a vague project, doing non-descript things, with a non-specific goal. Being relatively 'unprotected' in a house, which received many visitors, including single men, she might have felt wary of possible gossip and allegations because of this living arrangement, just like Fadjur did. I was not truly aware of the influence her living with us might mean to the way she was evaluated until she related to me an incident that occurred at the market place.

One day during Ramadan, Yasmin went to the market with two teachers of the boarding house to buy items for the beverages and special dishes so important for breaking the fast. Some of them are a rare treat and the ingredients are only available on the market during Ramadan and are quite expensive. Yasmin and the teachers had saved and pooled their money so they could buy the products in bulk to last at least the first two weeks. When Yasmin, who was keeping the money, was paying women the huge sums of money for their products, a woman called out to her: "Hey you, *khawadiya*, where do you come from? Can you buy from me as well?"

When Yasmin related this incident to me, she was quite light-hearted and chuckled about it. I was very surprised. I had been told repeatedly that *khawadya* for males and *khawadiya* for females was used only with reference to white people, to rich foreigners from America or Europe, and then only when not known by the speaker.[34] I could imagine the market woman might have referred to Yasmin as a foreigner when I was around, for dealing with a *khawadiya* and talking English with me might have reflected on her status as well. I had not been around, however, and had not visited the market with Yasmin for a while. If this was not the case, or if the woman did not know Yasmin to that extent, the label *khawadiya* might not only be reserved for foreign, white, western women, but for other 'non-local' or 'non-belonging' persons as well. In that case, the reference might have had to do with her behaviour rather than her identity. The fact that as an unmarried woman she was spending a lot of money and was able to buy in bulk, and was not 'known' locally, just like the other boarding house teachers, was 'strange'. In all cases the combination of being an outsider and one with wealth seemed crucial.

In any case, Yasmin was regarded as an outsider despite her Darfur roots, and notwithstanding the many years she had lived in Kebkabiya and the fact she had worked with and for so many families there.

Although the Gulf War might have aggravated whatever tensions there were, with hindsight I think that at the root was that Yasmin's identity was fuzzy, a status she could not afford as a single educated working woman. It explains the yearning of Yasmin to 'belong' in a way that suited her position best: although her situation was unique, she came closest to the position of the single female teachers. By making her link to the single female teachers more obvious, by staying at the boarding house, visiting colleagues with the female teachers, and even teaching English evening classes might have marked her as 'one of us' by the teachers and seen as belonging to 'one of them' by the Kebkabiya population. Therefore, like Fadjur, Yasmin might have considered her stay at the boarding house, among other single educated females, a necessity rather than a choice. Therefore, our misunderstandings and misreading of intentions might have been more about Yasmin's need to become a locally fitting social person and thus acquiring the 'right' class position and my failure to see this, rather than a difference based on culture or personalities, although these also might have been of influence.

[34] Foreigners from China for example would always be referred to as 'Siin' and Indians as 'Hind' and I am not sure if they would also be referred to as *khawadyaat*, but my guess would be that they would.

This also clarifies why Yasmin was not too keen to join me when I was trying to mingle with non-elite women inside Kebkabiya for 'informal' talks. In the perception of the female teachers, the non-elite population of Kebkabiya, and especially the market women, is constructed as the other, as the reason for their precarious position due to their gossiping. If she visited non-elite families, it would have been too overt but also too fuzzy in purpose, thus tainting her already fragile reputation as a single woman. At the same time it must have been difficult for Yasmin to articulate these feelings in front of me since she had prided herself in her experience with helping poor illiterate women, whom she had taught in the context of an official development programme.

For both Fadjur and Yasmin, the boarding house seemed to be a locus for the construction of a positive identity for single female teachers. It was not just the sense of solidarity, freedom, and friendship, which is an important incentive for living in an uncomfortable, cramped boarding house. It was predominantly the protection of their privacy against the public gaze and thus preserving their status and esteem, which made living in the boarding house enticing. The location constructed each of its inhabitants a social person who 'belongs'.

Interestingly, whenever I came across women and men from the 'non-elite' Kebkabiya population, including those I came to know better, they hardly discussed the single female teachers. Some of the market women noted that they were slow to settle their bills, but that concerned married female teachers. Moreover, female teachers were often referred to as role models with respect to their work and the way they knew how to run a household. Single female teachers seemed not important enough to discuss at length. What came up more often during those first acquaintances with the local population was my background.

Charity and Benign Rule: On Being British

During my ventures into the quarters, while joining the female teachers who assisted me in conducting a household survey I regularly met elderly Kebkabiya residents. Some were eager to relate the history of the town to me, others were proud to tell me the story of the arrival of their family or 'tribe' in the area. In many conversations, I was referred to as a member of the *gabila Britanniya*, extending to me a tribal affiliation with the British. At first, I considered this label a misjudgement due to my contacts with the local British NGOs taking into account that most of the aid agencies who have been operative in Darfur since the drought of '84-'85 were British. Moreover, as former colonisers, they were the first foreigners of whom most of the elderly had knowledge and therefore the most renowned. Older men and especially women of the local population often remembered the British era as a time of peace and plenty. Drought, banditry, and ethnic fighting hardly occurred under their 'reign'. As one woman put it, 'Even the grass was greener then and they [the British] brought the big white donkeys'.[35] They might have used the term British indiscriminately for all foreigners who 'did well' since especially elderly people might not be able tell the difference, or would they?

I became curious when during the same period Johan and I were regularly identified as 'Hollandiyiin' and not British. This was in reference to 'our' national football team, but more often in relation to the famine identified by several donor agencies in September 1990, directly after the second disastrous rainy season in a row. The Sudanese government did not acknowledge the advent of a famine (cf. Harir et. al. 1994: 272). Further, they were adamant that it concerned a 'food gap', 'like bubbles in a glass of coca cola', as a Sudanese official explained to me. Not the shortage of food, but inadequate distribution was the issue: the harvest had been bad in only a few areas and they could be provided by surplus from other areas in Sudan. The donor agencies were insisting that there was a widespread famine all over the Sudan. Negotiations on the organisation of relief aid had been going on for months, when the donor agencies pulled out their staff during the Gulf War. Hardly a month later when the war was over, the effects of the drought had become manifest inside the town of Kebkabiya. Migrants, who had left their homes due to the ethnic conflicts and the drought, had settled in Kebkabiya since September, and now their numbers grew. There was little to harvest around Kebkabiya either, but there was still food being brought onto the market from outside and from the irrigated gardens, although the prices were steadily rising. People started knocking at our door: not only asking for work or *karama*, alms, but also inquiring about food aid. On the radio, it had been announced that shipments of grain had arrived from the Nether-

[35] The speaker refers to a mule, which was a preferred means of transportation among some British administrators (personal information Dr. Breman, Head of the District Education Department in Kebkabiya).

lands in Port Sudan by mid-February, just after the Gulf War ended. People wondered what kept it so long. Some of them would refer to our compatriots, the doctors of Medicins Sans Frontières Holland (Doctors Without Borders) who had been based in Kebkabiya during the former drought. They had been handing out free medicine and food to babies at their feeding centres and had left only months before we arrived, due to a disagreement with and harassment by the authorities. Many expressed the hope that they would return to provide the same services again.

We knew MSF had no intention to return since the security in the area was not guaranteed. In addition, we knew about the slow progress in the negotiations between several western governments and the Sudanese, as the latter wanted the monopoly of the transportation of the relief grain to control its distribution. This was something with which the donors did not want to comply. However, to talk about this openly might bring us in a difficult position viz. a viz. the government. We told the inquirers we did not to know when it would come. Although this was true we felt uneasy and there was little we could helpfully offer. Doing research was a luxury in the face of the needs of these people. At the same time, this clear positioning of us as Netherlands nationals forced me to reconsider our suggested membership of the British tribe.

On several occasions during these weeks, I met elderly women who would urge me to 'just' say the *shahada*, the Islamic confession of faith, in order to gather *ajr*, or religious merit, since, as they would point out to me, this merit would secure a place in heaven. This is the ultimate goal of living according to Islamic principles laid down in what is referred to as the five pillars.[36] So I took these for well-intended and religiously inspired advice of pious old women, who by their advanced age were more occupied with death and the afterlife anyway.[37]

I realised that these local people were not just old raving men and women trying to convert foreigners to secure a good afterlife, when I had a curious conversation with one of these elderly women, Bitt Suleiman. When she, like so many others, first identified me as *Beni*

---

[36] These are: the *shahada* (vow of belief), the *salat* (prayer, five times a day), the *zakat* (taxation, between two and ten percent, to be used for the upkeep of poor Muslims), the *Ramadan* (Holy month of fasting) and the *haj* (pilgrimage to Mecca). Each of these gives different merit, which can also be 'lost'. I will return to this issue in Chapter 5.

[37] Converting someone to the Muslim faith means a certain entrance into heaven, so the concern of these women might not have been just me gaining religious merit.

Brittaniya[38] and next referred to the British as providers of order and abundance, I asked her why she thought the British would help people from Darfur at all. To my astonishment and Yasmin's astonishment, she answered:

> But don't you know that the mother of our prophet Mohammed was of the British tribe? Of course, they are good!

It sounded preposterous and the blasphemous nature of her remark made me wonder if the old woman was completely sane. For why would she risk making such a potentially dangerous remark in front of a stranger? When I realised that the religiously inspired 'advice' of the elderly people often coincided with reference to Johan and/or I being British I understood that another meaning was intended.

One aspect of most of the foreign aid, whether food aid, medicines, or roads, that amazed most of the people I met, was the fact that it was donated free.[39] In Kebkabiya the donations were likened to the giving of alms, *karama*, as a kind of *zakat*, the Islamic tax whereby rich people give two to ten percent of their wealth to be distributed to the poor: also a free donation. Therefore, the food donations were understood in such a way that the donors were conceived of as recipients of important religious merit.[40] By making the 'British' synonymous with 'good foreigners' and placing their deeds in a religious frame of reference, their goodness could be contextualised and understood by the local population. The same is true for their reputation of 'benign rule'. The *shari'a*, on which the Islamic law is based, is an institution to keep chaos or *fitna* at bay, and which has the *umma* or community of righteous believers as ultimate goal. Once the *umma* is attained, there is no need for *shari'a* anymore because one has internalised Islamic principles and every believer is therefore inherently 'good'.[41] This also requires

---

[38] *Beni* means 'my son' and is used in the sense of 'sons of' mostly used by subgroups from the *Baggara* and *Arab* cattle and camel nomads, to whom Bitt Jamilya probably traces her ancestry.

[39] In Jebel Marra, the free donations made the donated items suspicious and people would not care to receive these, unless they had to pay for it. This meant that traders would get hold of the free donated medicines and food and trade these at the market, often poured in smaller bottles, without directions how to use the drugs.

[40] De Waal (1989: 197–198) states: 'All Muslims, including strangers, are entitled to relief... One eighth of the Islamic tax *zaka* is to be given to travellers, including pilgrims'.

[41] In personal communication with high officers, this aspect was often emphasized. One of them even confided in me that according to him many of the western people working for donor agencies, and people like Johan and I did not need religion as

the extinguishing of poverty and need so that people will be allowed to devote most of their attention to religious contemplation. Keeping order and giving alms are not only seen as correct Islamic conduct but indispensable to establishing the community of righteous believers. It was these principles which the local, especially poorer, population depended on and which they apparently also connected to the conduct of the British in the past.

This might have been the reason why people wanted me to say the Islamic confession of faith, for then the acts of charity by members of my 'tribe of the British' would make sense from the Muslim perspective. I felt uneasy though. Food aid had not even arrived yet, and after all, it was the Dutch, not the British, who were known to be the first donators of food aid. Moreover, the British government had not been as unselfish and charitable as these stories seemed to make one believe, nor were the other western donor countries. Although most of the elderly men and women who vented these ideas were poor and illiterate, this celebration of the 'good foreigner' left a stale taste in my mouth. Foreigners are not inherently good and I was puzzled by the fact that the local population, in contrast to the government, tried so hard to convince me of the contrary. It did not correspond with my conviction that poor, uneducated people have a clear understanding of the power struggles of which they are part. During my second fieldwork period more than six months later, I had an experience with the local government. The episode made me realise that this issue of the 'Good Briton' had not so much to do with me personally, but rather with local conflicts and power struggles of which foreigners are only of slight importance.

Shari'a and Jihad: On Being American

At the end of October 1991, after the rainy season, I returned to Kebkabiya after an absence of four and a half months. At the end of my first stay, I had become increasingly interested in the position of market

we had internalised being good and being reasonable as a personal philosophy. This, he claimed, is what is meant by *umma*, religion was only a means to that end. For a similar kind of reasoning Mahmoud Mohammed Taha, founder and leader of the Republican Brothers, was hanged by Nimeiri on 18 January 1985 (Harir & Tvedt 1994: 267).

women. Now that I was back, I visited some of the market women I had met before, at the market place and later also at their homes. Six weeks after my second arrival the religious speeches discussed in Chapter 1 were delivered. The speeches were not the only public appeal the committee addressed to the population of Kebkabiya to instruct them on how to become 'proper' Muslims. The day following the delivery of the speeches the delegation toured the schools and organised meetings with local public committees as well. School children were told to stop clapping whenever a fellow student had performed well in class and to stand up and say *Allahu Akbar*, 'God is Great', instead. The women who had gathered at the meeting of the Women's Public Committee were told to teach their children *Qur'anic* verses instead of songs, dancing and playing. Women were instructed to take better care of setting the right example and therefore dress and behave properly, and study the *Qur'an* so they may assist their children. Moreover, they learned that some of the families in Kebkabiya had been visited by *khawadyas*, western foreigners, and this should be brought to an end, for these foreigners would have a bad influence on all household members. Curiously, and fortunately, none of the women present at the meetings seemed to be bothered by these instructions. Female teachers told me they thought it was nonsense to stop teaching children to sing, dance and clap: it would mean they had to stop teaching them the joys of life. And to stop having contact with foreigners: couldn't they decide for themselves who was to be trusted or not?

One afternoon in early February 1992 a police car stopped in front of Sa'adiya's house. Sa'adiya, a female teacher born and raised in Kebkabiya, had become my interpreter shortly after I arrived in Kebkabiya the second time. That day we had taped some stories of elderly people on the history of Kebkabiya. We were transcribing the tapes at Sa'adiya's house when a policeman came to fetch me. He had orders to bring me to a delegation of security officers that had arrived from Khartoum in order to 'evaluate' all projects foreigners were working on. Three men of the delegation started to ask me questions: why was I living at an old widow's compound; why did I want to research poor women? And, more personally: what was I doing here without my husband; and why did I not have any children? Then, all of a sudden the senior officer told them to stop interrogating me, recognizing his own signature in my passport. He apologized and gave me his card with the comment that whenever I needed help in Khartoum, he would be willing to assist me.

That day and the ones that followed many people visited me in order to hear what happened. People who had accompanied the delegation told me that the local public committee had suggested that I was an American spy. I was suspected of trying to get information that would undermine their society under the guise of doing academic research. Why had I first been living with my husband in a 'normal' house fit for foreigners among people of their standard and now chosen to return on my own, and to live with this old widow in a *gutiya*? Why did I visit poorer women, market women; what would I want from women who are ignorant and illiterate? After my 'interrogation' the head of the delegation had apparently gone to the public committee and had called them 'a bunch of gossiping sissies', a surprising comment given the circumstances. I was even more surprised, however, by reactions on the event from some of the poorer women from the neighbourhood.

Again, they accused the members of the public committee of being 'bad', as they had done after the religious speeches had been delivered. This time, however, their 'badness' was qualified. One of them was said to own a few cows, but to refuse his elderly mother even one glass of milk. Another was reported to visit a place outside town where beer was served. Whether true or not, the fierceness of the way these allegations were put forward astonished me. One of the women told me that she had been at one of the main government offices that morning. There, she had overheard a discussion of government officials with some of the members of the public committee, in which I was accused of being an American spy. She had gone inside the office and, according to her own words, hauled them over the coals, saying:

> Whose grain is it, that we eat, whose oil is it that we use? Why are your stomachs so big and round? You don't suffer, but we do! Where would we be if not for the Americans? And Karin does no harm; she is just doing research.

I was astounded. Whether she had done as she said or not, did not really matter: what on earth would she want to defend me for anyway, with the risk of being seen as a traitor? If she really had done as she said, would that not have repercussions, for her, her family or her work? And if not, why take the risk of being overheard just now, why risk anything at all for an outsider?

In the days following this incident, it became obvious that my position in the web of local power relations had changed overnight although I myself had done nothing to alter it. The incident had proven that I had to negotiate my position with local agents of power the same way as most 'non-elite' people in Kebkabiya had to. My identity as a foreigner and member of the elite did not provide me with immunity any longer. Perhaps my status as a 'woman without a husband' to some extent resembled the situation of many low-class women, which changed their evaluation of me as it had obviously made me more vulnerable as well. Whatever the exact reasons for this change in attitude, one of the consequences was that people in my neighbourhood now related differently to me than before. The people began to confide in me, especially when this concerned an intervention or decision taken by the government. Others must have taken this incident as proof of the danger I might represent to their own interests and they seemed to avoid me since that point, although I never knew for sure.

Obviously, the local popular committee experienced my research as a threat once I did not stay around the elite as I had done during the first fieldwork period. As I had 'crossed over' from the elite to the local population this had created dismay and distrust among members of the popular committee as to my intentions.

The construction of me as a British philanthropist on the one hand and an American spy on the other puts the speeches I represented in Chapter 1 in a different light. Contrary to the perspective of the government, the poorer, 'non-elite' inhabitants depicted foreigners, especially the British, as local heroes in times of need. It is for this reason that in the speeches the subsequent speakers of the popular committee engaged themselves in a unilateral argument with locally held opinions, and tried to negotiate a different view than that of the local population.

The divergence in opinions about me and about foreigners has diverse causes, all related to local power differences. Evidently, the difference in economic resources is important. The local population is in need of food and although there are food items available on the market, the prices have skyrocketed and many families cannot afford more than one meal a day. Therefore, it is in the direct interest of the local poor population that foreigners come with their food. Although the quality of the food aid is not very high, it feeds them when hungry.[42]

[42] This idea should be qualified since the experience of a famine is related to the shortage of the staple. Since food aid consists mostly of wheat and maze, this does not really relieve the experience of a famine. I will return to the issue of famine in Chapter 3.

This also has a social-psychological side, since the food aid means that poor people feel that someone is taking care of them. As an elderly woman told me:

> We don't care if we have to pay even a small sum for the grain. At least we know that our need is known. And you know, it scares the traders. As soon as relief food comes into town, even if it is just a little, they will lower the prices of their grain. They fear that when the rest of the free grain arrives they will not sell a single cup anymore!

In this quotation, as well as in the reaction of my neighbours to my clash with the local popular committee one can detect that the people of Kebkabiya feel that the elite, be it traders or government officials, do not care about the plight of the poor because they are not suffering themselves. In this power relationship, the foreigners are constructed as the only ones who are able to contest the power of the government elite, even by just being present.

It is therefore not surprising that older people especially from the local non-elite population hold the view that the foreigners are good people. This is not because people expect foreigners to really save them from economic hardship but as a way of expressing political criticism. For the stories about the 'good' Briton would always come up when the government or a government decision was discussed. Only rarely, the comparison was made openly: the British succeeded where the current government failed. In this respect, the comment of the old woman that the mother of Prophet Mohammed is British does not only serve to understand the 'generosity' of foreigners. It contains a political statement as well. The British are living up to Muslim moral standards of hospitality and alms-giving while their own Muslim government, which claims to hold on to the tenets of Islam more strictly than any of its forebears, fails to do so.

In other words, the local people I met had projected their own experiences with the current power relations and government decisions upon me. Not because I mattered all that much, but because I offered a means by which negative evaluations of the current politics could be released with reference to the past. In this way, the local population could vent its discontent without putting their grievances in squarely political terms. By referring to a distant past, to the 'time of the British' the present government was evaluated and dismissed, but always indirectly. It hardly ever occurred that the government policy was criticised as such: the so-called 'non-elite' population obviously felt it was not in the position to protest against the policy of the state for all decisions and decrees are put in religious terms. To criticise politics would mean criticising Islam, which would be seen as heresy. Although the government officials were criticised and ridiculed, it was always on social grounds: they were greedy, indifferent, or stupid. This attitude also clearly indicated the asymmetry in the power relations: the criticism had to be 'underground' because the ruling elite was in a position to react as representatives of the current government.

The mechanism of ridiculing and circumventing direct criticism is a 'weapon of the weak' as James Scott (1985) has phrased it. However, in the present political climate in the Sudan, groups, which did have power to speak up before and which did influence state policy, are silenced and forced 'underground'. Intellectuals and politicians all over Sudan and especially those from Darfur feel hard hit by the current government.[43] With the local population, they are of the opinion that Darfur has always been neglected by the state concerning resources and investments. Darfur is therefore seen as the most backward part of the Sudan after the South. The efforts to re-Islamise Darfur have to be seen in this light as well. The 'backwardness' of Darfur and the specific problems of ethnic conflict and famine is the consequence of lack of knowledge of and education in Islamic principles, according to the official view. Intellectuals from Darfur maintain that this view is not only problematic because it refers to Islamic principles instead of economic causes, but also due to the interpretation of those principles. They consider the version of Islam, which is now forced upon them, related to the arrogance of Central Sudanese, which is not necessarily the 'right' or the only possible interpretation. Like the 'non-educated non-elite' they have stopped speaking up and turned to ridiculing and referencing to a distant past to couch their criticism in.

I was considered to be suspicious by the popular committee only the second time that I stayed in Kebkabiya, living as I did on a 'local' compound near the market. Therefore, it is obvious that indeed my living arrangement was an issue. Earlier, we were living near the ward of the government houses and the intermediary school in a stone house. Apparently we were regarded as part of the elite and considered

---

[43] See for example Harir (1994: 144) and Kevane (1998: 37–40) for an elaboration of the attitudes and perspectives of the intelligentsia. In Chapter 8 I will return to this issue in relation to both local and national affairs.

'harmless' in the eyes of government officials. This, in turn, might have made us suspect, or at least marked, to the local population, to our neighbours who did not belong to the educated elite; this may have been the reason why we were considered 'off limits'. When I moved lodgings this second time, because I had come alone, the effect was reversed: local Kebkabiyans visited me often enough, but this time the elite treated me suspiciously. This was also apparent in the way the single female teachers of the boarding house, with whom I had socialised so often during my first stay, related to me during my second stay.

During that second stay, I had less contact with the single teachers. In the first place, I was aware of my own preoccupation with this infrequent contact. Since I started living with Hajja and working with Sa'adiya I became more acquainted with married teachers, as I wanted to understand their position in the light of the current moral discourse as well. They lived dispersed over Kebkabiya and visiting them at their houses simply left less time and opportunities to chat with the single teachers at the boarding house. Moreover, the married teachers invited me to visit them at the same hours during which the single teachers were at leisure. I suspected it also had to do with the fact that Hajja's compound was located near the market and that it did not offer enough 'protection' against the 'public gaze': not so much by the physical nature of the wall around her compound, but because Hajja was considered non-elite.

How close my guess is occurs to me only when on another occasion I am confronted directly with the dividing line between elite and non-elite women. One day, near the end of the school year, I am invited to come to the football ground in order to attend the parade of all schools in Kebkabiya. The public is seated at one of the long ends of the football square. I walk to the football grounds together with my neighbour Magda, who is pregnant. I offer the chair reserved for me at the front rows to Magda, which she declines. I want to offer her the chair again, aware of the habit of urging people several times before it is proper to accept what is being offered, when the female teachers Fadjur and Mirjam touch my arm and greet me enthusiastically. Still holding out the chair to Magda, I introduce them to each other but Fadjur and Mirjam do not seem to notice my attempt and ignore Magda completely. Before I am able to turn to Magda to offer her the chair again, she has walked over to a shady spot at the stone benches where other neighbours have found themselves a seat already. Fadjur and Mirjam drag me over to the front row of this 'VIP' area reserved for government officials, local leaders, teachers, project members and the occasional anthropologist. I feel embarrassed because of this rude incident, but do not know what to do.

The following week I happen to pass by the office of the headmistress, Sitt Ashia, and I am invited to have lunch together with her and the other single teachers. As I have no prearranged visits on this day, I gladly accept the offer. The teachers living in the boarding house have recently moved into the newly built rooms with whitewashed walls joined by a veranda where colourful flowers in pots give the place an almost picturesque outlook. The tables, chairs, and beds have beautiful covers, and the place looks like nothing like what I have seen at the homes of the women I have visited so far. The lunch is very good and tasty. After lunch, we chat a bit, lying with our heads against each other's legs. Sitt Ashia laments that she would love to go back to her parents in Al-Fasher as soon as the school year is over because she does not like the Kebkabiya people. Without thinking I say, "But Sitt Ashia, surely you won't say that all people of Kebkabiya are stupid"? Instead of answering my rhetorical question, Sitt Ashia says in a high-pitched, cracked voice, "Here is Hajja"! Imitating the local slang saying something, I hardly understand, adding quite vehemently:

> You surely wouldn't say you can discuss the subjects and talk about life with Hajja they way you do with us, do you, Karin?

Fadjur adds: "No education, no civilization". The others start laughing and joking, which allows me to avoid answering Sitt Ashia's rhetorical question. Nevertheless, she has hit a nerve. I know she is disappointed about the fact that I decided to stay at Hajja's place and declined her offer to stay at the boarding house. She feels abused in her hospitality and perhaps rightly so. However, there is more. She seems to criticise me, for 'betraying' not only her hospitality, but also the trust put in me as 'one of them', as a teacher of higher education, as an educated woman, who fits into their way of thinking, of talking about issues of work and personal life. Moreover, I feel I cannot explain again why I am doing this, as I tried on previous occasions. As before, she would wave away my claim that I wanted to live among those I was doing research with, saying: "You can research the market women and stay with us at night". I feel as if she takes my choice and my attempt to stand up for women such as Hajja almost as a personal affront. I keep silent.

Both the incident at the football grounds and this conversation with Sitt Ashia makes me feel uneasy. The uneasiness turns out to be a confrontation with the dividing line between the female teachers and local women. It is a fact that this division is felt as more important, more of an issue, than I had understood so far, which I find striking.

These events made me aware not only of an undercurrent of local power relations between government elite and non-elite Kebkabiyans. It illuminated another difference that was put forward in the speeches as well: between educated women and illiterate women. More specifically, it showed the difference between the female teachers with whom Yasmin and I socialised during my first stay and the market women with whom I lived during my second fieldwork period. Not only occupation, but also location marked this difference.

Working Women: The Danger of Strangers, The Virtue of Knowledge

Monday and Thursday are market days in Kebkabiya. People come, especially on Thursday from all over the district to town to sell produce and buy what they need. Lorry drivers arrive the night before, and spend the entire day unloading and loading, bringing and taking goods to wherever they can to make a profit. Kebkabiya provides mostly agricultural produce, such as onions, tomatoes, oranges, mangoes, grain, clover, and clarified butter. There are both edible and inedible wares from other parts of the Sudan, and imported goods from Chad, Libya, and West Africa, and a few from Europe, America, India, and the Arab countries.[44]

The core of the market consists of the Kebkabiya traders' stone- and iron-built shops and stores. Most of these shops are open all week. Here one can buy the luxury items such as soap, canned fruits and vegetables, sweets, sugar, tea, coffee, spices, batteries, and other non-edibles. In separate shops shoes, cloth, perfume, cutlery, kitchenware, and all other items needed for a household are for sale. In addition, there are service providers such as tailors, shoemakers and artisans. Finally, there are the petty traders who sell in small amounts the produce they buy in bulk thus making a small profit. The latter group deal mainly in

[44] The animal market is at another location just outside town and operates under strict supervision of the government, to check on stolen animals, tax paying, and veterinarian requirements.

dried produce like dried tomatoes, dried peppers, tamarind, *karkadea*,[45] *kauwwal*[46] dried garlic, and different kinds of beans and peas.

At the northwest side of the market are places where women from different ethnic backgrounds sell their specific wares on the twice-weekly market days. The Zaghawa and Arab come with milk, *roob* (a thick kind of buttermilk), and *semen*, clarified butter. The *hadadiin*[47] sell their different sizes of pots and other earthenware. The women from agricultural groups, mainly Fur, provide *zaaf*, the palm fibre in different colours used in making *mtabakh*, the food covers Darfur is famous for all over the Sudan. Most women at the market sell food, however, and most of them sell seasonal products such as tomatoes, salad, peanut butter, fruit, and dried berries or beans: those women who come from outside Kebkabiya sell these in smaller amounts, and from 'informal' places at the fringe of the market, under trees or in the shades of shop-walls, than the petty traders from inside town, who occupy two separate parts on the market. Other women sell home produced food products such as *kisra*, the sour thin pancakes used with every meal, also peanuts and peanut butter, or nutritious drinks of milk products and sorghum or millet. Those women who sell on a daily basis occupy stalls at the centre of the market and deal mainly in vegetables and fruits.

Near the meat market are the restaurants, all owned by men, which serve both meals and beverages. Before the removal of the tea woman from the market, most customers would take only their meal in the restaurant and would walk over to a coffee shop of one of the many teawomen to drink tea or coffee as a desert, because even if slightly dearer, the quality was superior.

During my second stay, Johan visits me for a few weeks. One market day, after Johan and I have taken lunch at a restaurant, Hassan, a clerk at one of the local government offices; and Mustafa, who works at the farmers' co-operative, join us. While we sip our tea Johan expresses his disappointment over the bad quality of the tea at the restaurant and

---

45 Dried hibiscus leaves.

46 *Cassia occidentalis* (L) fermented and dried leaves used in the sauce that goes with *asida*, the daily porridge.

47 These women are blacksmiths' wives, who are commonly known by this term meaning 'iron workers'. Blacksmiths, and their wives, have in all of Africa a separate status, but with different connotations. In some areas, they are seen as outcasts, or as 'untouchables', working as clients to patrons of a certain ethnic group, as is the case in North Darfur for example among the Zaghwawa semi-nomads. In other parts they are revered as the keepers of fire and bringers of life and therefore have a high status (for West Africa see for example: Conrad and Frank 1995).

laments the absence of the tea women. Hassan looks up with a slightly crooked smile and says that this is what the implementation of 'Islamic values' means. He agrees with it, but says it does little to redress the economic crisis:

> Men cannot provide for their own families so it forces women to try to find a job to provide their household with an income. Maybe you remember the tea woman who was sitting over there?

Hassan points at the spot where Johan and I used to take our tea with Helima. Her husband was in Libya, so she had to earn money to take care of her family. "He is still working elsewhere, so how can she cope?" He asks rhetorically. "So what do you think about these plans?" I ask. Because of Hassan's critical reflection on the plight of tea women, I expect him to be also critical of the recent policy to remove tea women from the market. Indeed, both Hassan and Mustafa agree that women who live in difficult circumstances, such as Helima, should be allowed to earn a living. Nevertheless, they both feel that this is only possible for women older than forty years of age and women in special circumstances such as widows and divorcees. For younger, unmarried and married women it is 'dangerous', they tell us. Johan asks why this is so and Mustafa answers that it is because non-related men can approach women easily and he points at the soldiers and other men who linger around young women selling vegetables and fruits. "Especially tea women cannot escape contact with their customers as they sit around her waiting and drinking tea", he explains. Johan jokingly asks if they think that Sudanese men are not to be trusted. Hassan replies in a serious tone: "Seriously, they can cause *fitna*, unrest in men's daily life, and chaos in public life if they are not controlled and restrained", he says, pointing to one of the quarters adjacent to the market:

> You know, the *merissa* places, where they brew the local beer, are the worst. Customers stay inside the huts even longer than at the tea stalls, and it is more hidden than drinking tea as we do now. These women serve food and drinks even at night when the lorries stop for a break. And God knows what happens then.

I look at him in surprise. "But that is something else than making tea in full view of all market visitors", I protest. Then Mustafa, while swinging his cup with the residue of the coffee grains, tells us without looking up:

> At the end of Nimeiri's regime, when he implemented *shari'a* law in 1983, fewer women were going outside. The men stayed near their wives and

> gave them money so they needn't take a job. And even men who were absent wrote letters to their male family members to provide for them. At that time women obeyed their husbands and their husband's male kin. But when Al-Mahdi came into power in 1986 the implementation was left to the regional governments and the number of illegitimate babies increased.

Mustafa seems convinced that this is a result of the fact that the women did not obey their male relatives anymore and took to the street again. He goes on:

> The new government does not want any discussion anymore about the question if a certain *shari'a* law is going to be implemented in a district or not. They state that if one is a true Muslim, one has to accept these laws as just without question and to obey them. Other crimes, such as theft and murder, will also be reduced when we have *shari'a*. Public committees, installed to implement decrees and decisions handed down by the national government will create this change.

Then he looks at his watch, and both Hassan and Mustafa rise while shaking our hands, and hurriedly take their leave in order to get back to their offices. Educated elite men would articulate the same ideas as articulated by Hassan and Mustafa. Interestingly enough, the conduct of women and the political signature of the ruling government are related quite un-problematically in these discussions. It may have been a kind of window dressing, as open criticism would be too risky. However, the way both men articulated their views on women, work, and Islam was reminiscent of the rhetoric used in the recent moral discourse of the government on gender and ideas vented by those government officials who were to implement the decrees of the government: like those who voiced their opinion in the Introduction. It became increasingly clear to me that the moral discourse of the government on gender, and specifically on women, was related to the structural differences that were perceived between female teachers and market women.

This difference was based on the notion of knowledge of a circumscribed nature. Education gives knowledge of worldly matters and of religious duties, and obligations. This is indicated by the notion of *ilm*, which refers to all knowledge, both worldly and religious.[48] The fact that the economic activities of female teachers are directly related to

[48] The duty to acquire *ilm* is stipulated for all Muslims in one of the first *suras* of the *Qur'an* after the opening *surat al-fatah*. The chronology of the chapters of the *Qur'an* does not follow the chronology of their reception by Mohammed, but is based on their importance.

dealing with *ilm* on a daily basis makes them not only knowledgeable about religious issues, but also leads them to know the right demeanour, speech, dress codes and etiquettes, in short, of the proper conduct of a good Muslim woman. As a consequence, female teachers enjoy a high status, although they are working outside their homes, and irrespective of being married or not: their relationship to 'ilm' even makes them stand out in relation to any other women, whether non-elite or elite, whether they are working outside their homes or not. Educated elite women are not only seen as setting an example as the female Muslim, who forms the basis of the formation of a 'good Islamic community': they are most often also the wives, sisters, or daughters of elite men and thus close to those who implement the decrees of the Islamist government. This means that their investment in the Islamist discourse is different from the non-elite women: because their activities as working women are revered and at the same time highly visible, and because their membership of the educated elite involves them personally in the daily business of government policy. It is precisely this relational aspect of the differences between market women and elite women that I will discuss in the last paragraph of this chapter.

Relations of Ruling and Female Subjectivity: Studying the Interface

As my research looks into the ways that working women in Kebkabiya negotiate the Islamist moral discourse on gender, I need to focus in particular on the interface between institutions, discourses, and subjects for understanding the dynamics of power relations in daily life. Institutions do not invent structures or discourses, but are constitutive of them, which means that, at the same time, discourses are part of institutions. While discourse theory sees the construction of 'selves' and of identities, as effects of discourses, whereby subjects are perceived as passive victims of oppressive ideologies, feminist theorists have tried to combine the notion of discourse with that of agency. Important thereby is the idea that one is not just subjected to discourses but that discourse is something one *does*; the adoption, rejection, negation, opposing, submission, transforming of subject positions which are available in dominant discourses is an *activity* in which women engage. The possibility of subjects to negotiate discourses means that they are actively involved in constructing identities in relation to those discourses (Mills 1997: 86–103; Smith 1990: 160–180).

From my experiences and the events I witnessed while living in Kebkabiya, I could understand the views behind the dominant discourse of the current government in that particular context. Market women and female teachers were locally seen as two different categories of working women as far as their social positions and moral virtues were concerned. Members of the government elite in particular saw the two classes of working women as opposites. Mobility and lack of education marked the position of market women. However, the discussions with the single female teachers living at the boarding house indicated that, despite the fact that they were engaged in handling *ilm*, their positioning as respected working women was contingent as well: they could not escape allegations of sexual promiscuity either. Although the single female teachers themselves referred to these allegations as silly gossiping and part of the backwardness of the local population, they were not completely unconcerned by these. Apparently education in itself was not a guarantee for a virtuous character or undisputed conduct and both groups of working women were scrutinized on their conduct.

This also reflected on my own status: as a female foreigner I was constituted by 'significant others' in this local context. As a foreigner and a female I was treated differently during the two periods I stayed in Kebkabiya. During my first stay I was positioned as an educated elite woman living in an appropriate location and in the company of my husband. Moreover, I was socialising mainly with other educated elite members. When I changed lodgings during my second stay, it changed my status and the positioning within the local power structure. Despite the fact that this time I was not marked as a potential enemy as the Gulf War had ended, I was considered more suspicious than during my first stay. As I indicated for Yasmin, apparently the location of my 'belonging' and the context of my daily life is what influenced the evaluation of my status as a respected or a distrusted woman.

Despite these ambivalences about the positioning of both classes of women, however, it is clear that women with different backgrounds have a different relation to those structures and institutions. As Mills (1997) maintains, 'Femininity does not have a single meaning, but depends on a wide range of contextual features, such as perceived power relations (88; cf. Moors 1994: 8–28, 49–71)'. Smith (1990) adds that: 'Femininity is addressed as a complex of actual relations vested in texts (163 quoted in Mills 1997: 88)'. In other words, differences among women in terms of discursive power are marked, by both their relations to others and their positioning within 'cultural' texts: written, oral and non-verbal. This means that femininity is thereby articulated and evaluated in precise formulated prescriptions about behaviour, demeanour, character etc. but apply differently to different 'kinds' of women based on class, ethnicity, age, marital status, etc, depending on the context. As a consequence these different 'kinds' women have differential access to discourses and thus different 'speaking positions' tied to relative power positions (Mills 1997: 97–99). The relative power position in relation to institutions and the moral discourse was for example clearly different for the female speakers, such as Sitt Miriam and Sitt Huda introduced in Chapter 1, relative to their female audience. However, even those in a position of relative power within an institution are not above the workings of discourses:

> Rather there is a combined force of institutional and cultural pressure, together with the intrinsic structure of discourse, which always exceeds the plans and desires of the institution or of those in power (Foucault in Mills 1997: 54).

In other words, female teachers who belong to a class that is constituted by the dominant discourse as the example of virtue and correct 'female Muslim conduct' are not above its workings, their position is neither undisputed nor undisputable. So both classes of working women have to continuously negotiate the dominant discourse in order to get the respect that goes with the subject position that is allotted to them. Therefore the idea of 'relations of ruling' as described by Dorothy Smith (1987) is helpful to understand these positions and processes of negotiation:

> 'Relations of ruling' is a concept that grasps power, organization, direction, and regulation as more pervasively structured than can be expressed in traditional concepts provided by the discourse of power... When I write of 'ruling' in this context I am identifying a complex of organized practices, including government, law, business and financial management, professional organization, and educational institutions as well as discourses in texts that interpenetrate the multiple sites of power (Smith 1987: 3).[49]

This definition is particularly interesting as it does not connect power to positions of persons, but to institutional, or 'organized', practices. These are taken to be part of power structures and dominant discourses and

---

[49] Also quoted in Mohanty (1991: 14) with respect to understanding the contexts in which women of colour are positioned.

vice versa, and once again are related to ruling which allots certain people positions of authority. In a later work Smith argues:

> When I speak here of governing or ruling I mean something more general than the notion of government as political organisation. I refer rather to that total complex of activities, differentiated into many spheres, by which our kind of society is ruled, managed, and administered. It includes... government and the activities of those who are selecting, training, and indoctrinating those who will be its governors. The last includes those who provide methods for accounting for how it is done—namely, the business schools, the sociologists, and the economists. These are the institutions through which we are ruled and through which we, and I emphasise this *we*, participate in ruling [*emphasis in original*] (1990: 14).

Although Smith is writing on western society, I find her perspective elucidating also for the Sudanese context as it takes ruling as a relational practice and part of a process.[50] This is a process in which the researcher (in this case myself) as an anthropologist has a place as well. By concentrating on relations, both the organisation of moral discourses and the ways women experience these in concrete historical and political contexts[51] can be analysed. This allows for an analysis of the differential positioning of women and the ways this positioning is both legitimated and used in enacting that difference, like in the case of Sitt Huda and Sitt Miriam relative to their audience in Chapter 1.

These differences are discursive and thus are not just 'textual' but also have relational and material consequences in 'daily life'. Discourses can then be seen as a means through which social relations between subjects are negotiated. This negotiation is an act of positioning oneself in relation to the norms dictated by the dominant discourse, as well as the (assumed) evaluation by others of ones positioning. Thereby the norm is almost never fully achieved (Butler 1990a: 70–90; Mills 1997: 91, 97; Smith 1990: 167, 204). Moreover, this positioning is to some

---

[50] This view comes close to the formulation by Foucault of 'discursive practices' as 'not purely and simply ways of producing discourse, they are embodied in technical processes, in institutions, in patterns for general behaviour, in forms for transmission and diffusion, and in pedagogical forms which, at once, impose and maintain them (1977: 200, in Silberstein, 1993: 9)'. I prefer relations of ruling as it emphasises the relational aspect, which takes women as agents. In addition, it takes ruling and governing as central in these relations, which is also central to the context in which women in my research chose their strategies.

[51] See for example Mohanty who also refers to Smith to do precisely that: looking for different contexts in which 'third world feminism' has developed (1991: 1–47).

extent also an act of citation, echoing previous usages and meanings of certain subject positions. This, what Butler calls 'iterability' is 'a repetition that is at once a re-enactment and re-experiencing of a set of meanings already socially established' (Butler 1990a: 140, quoted in Alsop et. al. 2003: 103). However, this repeatability causes these subject positions to be contingent as the enactments take place in different contexts and relations, which in the process transform its meaning and might even transform the discourse that it refers to (Alsop et. al. 2003: 103).

This perspective allows me to consider both the female teachers and the market women as agents who negotiate their positioning within the Islamist discourse. However, because members of each class have differential access to that dominant discourse they are allowed more or less space for negotiation and possible transformation of the meaning of that subject position, and ultimately for adjusting the discourse. Women from different classes are differently positioned also because of their differing relations with those who implement the decrees dealing with the moral discourse on gender. Bearing this in mind, I want to perceive agency, not as an individually constituted aspect of a person, or a voluntary negotiation of a discourse. Instead, I want to define it as part of relationships that women can, or cannot, build up, maintain, claim, or use to their advantage. I therefore propose the term 'relational agency' as an important aspect of the way women construct their identities and look for strategies to survive in relation to others and in relation to a specified context.[52] This relational agency constructs women not as separate from other persons or conditions of survival, but sees them as part of the context of their day-to-day dealings.

Therefore I will focus on the relational dimensions of women's agency in a day-to-day context. This means that in my representation I have to chart the multiple sites in which both classes of women are negotiating the dominant discourse, considering these to be enactments of power in relation to their allotted subject position. In my analyses of the reflections of the working women in Kebkabiya I want to stress in particular the need to describe actual circumstances and histories of individuals and to reconstruct their negotiations of discourses, in this case the moral discourse of the Islamist government (Abu-Lughod

---

52 See also Mohanty (1996: 12–14).

1993: 6–25; cf. Moore 1994). This analysis leads to alternative ways to reflect on the negotiations by female teachers and market women of the dominant moral discourse and the strategies these working women opt for in order to defend their interest. I will analyse these negotiations via one such 'enactment of agency', namely biographic narratives, narrated by members of both classes of working women. In Part Two, the biographic narratives of Hajja and Umm Khalthoum will therefore be the focus of my reading and writing against the grain.

PART TWO

SETTLING
BIOGRAPHIC NARRATIVES AS TEXTS-IN-CONTEXT

[Thesaurus]

Settling: Establish or become Established, *Resident in a place, occupation, way of life*
Make or Cause Somebody or Something to Become: *Clear, calm, stable, or comfortable in a particular position*
Put in Order: *Or into a desired arrangement*
Stop Floating: *Move downward, and spread over something*

In Part Two, the biographic narratives of two working women, Hajja, a market woman, and Umm Khalthoum, a female teacher, take centre stage. In the next chapter entitled *Intermezzo: Crossing the Road* I will introduce both narrators by relating how we met each other, and how we chose each other to engage in a project focused on understanding our lives. My use here of the notion of choice does not suggest, however, that we were equal in opting for participating, as the project was initiated by me as a researcher and is analysed and represented here by me as an author. It does suggest that, notwithstanding this power difference, Hajja and Umm Khalthoum did claim agency when narrating about their lives, not only in relation to the dominant discourse, but also within my project, by making it—partly—a project of their own.

Sa'adiya is included in this process since she acted as interpreter and sometime interlocutor during my second stay in Kebkabiya, when Yasmin had other duties to attend to. It was during this second period that Sa'adiya and I recorded the biographic narratives of and with Hajja and Umm Khalthoum. Before turning to their narratives, I want to reflect on some of the merits and problems of the biographic narrative as a method of research, means of analysis and mode of representation.

Although I had intended to 'make use' of the biographic narrative as a method, its centrality as the main method in my research was unintended and unforeseen: it was the result of a sudden change in local political circumstances. The biographic narrative offered one of the few spaces in which I could explore the views of working women on the events of that time and on their positioning in the new Islamist government's moral discourse. For all of us involved in the project the past proved to be a relatively safe way to reflect on the present.

At that time, in the early 1990s, the biographic narrative was receiving renewed attention,[1] especially by feminist anthropologists. From its onset feminist anthropology had taken the relation between 'self' and the 'other' into account, often based on the categorization *as* women being cast as the 'other' in many instances in their own societies. Feminist anthropologists thereby questioned the dichotomy between the personal and the academic, the personal and the political, the personal and the theoretical.[2] The message that the anthropologist not only reflects on power-relations, but is engaged in these as well, both in the locations where she performs 'research' as well as back home, was not lost on me.[3] In my research it was not only my relationship with women that became a matter of research but their representation as well.

The problematising of the writing of ethnographies was echoed in the post-modern critiques of ethnographic writing, which earned this literary turn in anthropology the title 'the ethnography-as-texts' school which became known by the simultaneous publication of two works: *Writing culture. The poetics and politics of ethnography* (1986) edited by James Clifford and George Marcus, and *Anthropology as cultural critique. An experimental moment in the human sciences*, by George Marcus and Michael Fischer (1986). This (white) male dominated 'school' of anthropology championed experimental writing of the power-laden ethnographic 'encounters' as their prerogative. This claim has been severely criticized by feminist anthropologists for 'glossing over the contributions made by feminist anthropologists on issues of representation, reflexivity, the politics of dominant positions and constructed notions of otherness, as well as ignoring women's experimental writing'.[4] Apart from being criticized

---

[1] One of the oldest anthropological biographic narratives that was used as method of research, analysis and representation is Paul Radin's '*Autobiography of a Winnebago Indian* (1963)' narrated by Sam Blowsnake which Radin translated and annoted.

[2] Braidotti (1991, 1994), Schrijvers (1993: 143–144). See also Nencel (1997), Davids and Willemse (1993: 3–14); Okely (1993: 1–14).

[3] This was also due to the happy circumstances that I had been able to take classes from Joke Schrijvers, one of the first feminist anthropologists who discussed power relations and engaged in self-reflexive writing. See for example Schrijvers (1985, 1991, 1993). See also Callaway (1992: 31).

[4] Callaway (1992: 44). Renowned examples are Laura Bohannan's *Return to laughter* (1954) *Never in anger* (1970) by Jean Briggs, of which the first was written under a pseudonym and is sometimes derogatory referred to as 'confession literature', while

for their neglect of experimental writing by female authors, feminist scholars expressed a distrust of the enthusiasm with which mainstream anthropologists embraced postmodernism with its assertion that 'truth and knowledge are contingent and multiple' as these 'may be seen to act as a truth claim itself, a claim that undermines the ontological status of the subject at the very time that women and non-western peoples had begun to claim themselves as subject'.[5] Writing is political.

When I set out to live in Kebkabiya the biographic narrative of Nisa in *Nisa. The words and life of a !Kung woman* (1981), inspired me because of the open and self-reflexive way in which Shostak as ethnographer represented the perspective of a !Kung woman, Nisa, as well as her own perspective,[6] leaving it to the reader to decide on the differences and commonalities in these different ways of understanding.[7] At that time it was also one of the few ethnographic accounts that related the representation of biographic narratives to writing in a self-reflexive mode.[8]

Once I returned to my desk to write, I discovered that in the meantime more feminist anthropologists had explored the method.[9] In my opinion the anthropological works that remain today as primary examples of ethnographies representing biographic narratives of 'other'

Briggs book was meant as a self-reflexive account of the way Inuit dealt with emotions. See for criticism on different aspects of the postmodernists' neglect of feminist contributions: Behar (1995: 1–33); Behar and Gordon: (1995: 429–443); Mascia-Lees et. al. (1989: 7–33); Okely and Callaway (1992), especially the two introductions; Stacey (1991: 111–121).

[5] Hartsock in Mascia-Lees et. al. (1989: 15).

[6] It was also Marjorie Shostak's book *Nisa. The life and words of a !Kung woman*, published in 1981 and 1983, to which Clifford referred as an example of reflexivity and polyvocality and as inventive and experimental anthropological writing (Clifford 1986: 104–109). Shostak wrote the book while accompanying her husband during his research among the !Kung San of the Kalahari desert.

[7] See for example Mascia-Lees et. al. (1989: 7–33); Behar (1995: 1–33); Okely (1992: 39–42).

[8] There were older biographic narratives which have been re-discovered but most of them were not self-reflexive nor very articulate on power relations between the biographer and biographed. See for example Okely (1992: 39–42) on *Baba of Karo* (1955) by M.G. Smith.

[9] These edited volumes were published in the 1980s and 1990s, of which, *Cartographies of Struggle* (1984) by Mohanty, *Life/Lines* (1988) by Brodszki and Schenck, *Women's words* (1991) by Gluck and Patai and the more self-reflexive, mainly anthropological *Anthropology and Autobiography* (1992) by Okely and Callaway; *Gendered fields* (1993) by Bell, Caplan and Karim, and *Women writing culture* (1995) by Behar and Gordon provided me with excellent insights into the possibilities and problematics of the (auto-)biographic narrative as recorded and represented by anthropologists.

women are *Translated woman. Crossing the border with Esperanza's story* of Ruth Behar and *Writing women's world. Bedouin stories* by Lila Abu-Lughod, both published in 1993. These works constituted two different ways of representing women's biographic narratives, but both try to escape from generalizations, which would cast women as a homogeneous category. They both wanted to emphasize the differences and particularities of the everyday lives of the women whose narratives they represented, with quite different ethnographies as a result.[10]

Each of these authors in their own way has inspired me to write against the grain: also to me the narratives of women are central and my main aim is to represent here the particularities and specificities of the narratives of Hajja and of Umm Khalthoum. I therefore represent the transcribed biographic narratives as close to the way Sa'adiya and I recorded these as far as possible[11] and thereby I try to keep them as 'open' as possible. I will distinguish between the words of Hajja and Umm Khalthoum and my own interruptions during the recording so that the reader might judge my influence in the process of narrating: but also the perseverance of both women to overcome the hindrances this *khawadiya*, this foreign women, put in their way by her questions and interventions, to be able to finish the project about their lives. However, I am approaching this task differently from earlier writers. In contrast to Abu-Lughod and to Behar I do want to make more generalizing claims and give an analytical reflection on the society at large both women inhibit on the basis of these personal biographic narratives. I will try to do so in sections marked with '*context*' and '*con/text*' in which I give different kinds of 'contextualizations' of the narratives of Hajja and Umm Khalthoum.

These contextualizations constitute my own academic narrative with my reflections and interpretations, both those when I was living in Kebkabiya (*context*), and those I constructed with hindsight (*con/text*). To understand my own role in these narrative processes I will, in the

---

[10] Behar represented the life of one 'Mexican Indian woman' with her own anthropological reflections clearly differentiated, written in a captivating and convincing self-reflexive mode. Abu-Lughod chose for 'crafting, reconfiguring, and juxtaposing these women's and men's stories, to make them speak particularly to my concerns and those of my audience' such as patrilineality, polygyny, honour and shame. I see my own endeavour as somewhere between these works.

[11] Translation and transcription allows for only a restricted claim of representing words 'as told' (see Introduction). Moreover, in the period that I was frequently checked at home by the security, I decided to erase some of the narratives from the tapes in order to protect the narrators.

Epilogues to each of the narratives, turn the analytical gaze around and look inwards. In this way I shall try to assess my positioning in the Islamist discourse, as well as in the discourses 'back home'. It is at the same time a way of trying to be sensitive to the problematics of the power relations between researcher and the 'other': an attempt at studying sideways, although I have no illusion that egalitarian relations within the research setting can ever be attained.[12] Before I introduce Hajja and Umm Khalthoum I will here first reflect on some themes that arise when women's biographic narratives are the central focus of an analysis: identity, memory, experience and agency.

Experience, memory and the construction of identities

My desire to connect biographic narratives and (gendered) identities is met by Stuart Hall's definition of identities as part of a 'production' of giving 'names to the different ways in which we are positioned by, and position ourselves within, the narratives of the past'.[13] Similar to the performance of identities which is not only constrained by normative discourses, but constitutes those discourses in the process,[14] 'narrative practice does not simply unfold within the interpretive boundaries of going concerns, but contributes to the definition of those boundaries in its own right'. This means that the biographic narrative is both actively constructive and locally constrained: it is a performance which in the process constitutes both a '*discursive practice*' and '*discourses-in-practice*'.[15]

Hajja and Umm Khalthoum—and their audience—engaged in *a discursive practice* when they narrated their biographic narratives making use of certain 'narrative forms'. Narrative forms is different from genre or model as it indicates the nature of a narrative 'as fluid rather than fixed in the variety of shapes that it can assume'.[16] It is a culturally constructed way of relating 'themes, and the structure, shape,

[12] The notions studying sideways, studying downwards and studying up I take from Schrijvers (1991: 162–180). See for other critical reflections on the relation between ethnographer and the 'other': Patai (1991 137–115); Stacey (1991: 111–121).

[13] Hall (1990: 225).

[14] Butler (1990a). See also Smith (1990: 161–162, 166, 204); cf. Mills, (1997: 85, 88, 91).

[15] Holstein and Gubrium (2000: 106–107, 109–110).

[16] Personal Narratives Group (1989: 99).

and expressive styles of narrating about one's self'.[17] I propose that there are differences in these narrative forms between Hajja and Umm Khalthoum. This means I will look at the performances of narrating itself as a means to understand the ways gender intersects with other identities such as class, age, ethnic identity etc. in the local context of Kebkabiya town. The issue of *how* Hajja and Umm Khalthoum narrate about their lives in different ways, and what this says about the differences in constructing a gendered identity, will be taken up in Chapter 5. But before I can compare the differences between the biographic narratives I need to have an idea of the *what* and the *why* of the 'themes, structure, shape and expressive styles' of each of the biographic narratives of Hajja and Umm Khalthoum separately.

In telling their narratives Hajja and Umm Khalthoum constructed certain identities in certain contexts, thereby putting *discourses in practice.* As indicated in Part One, identities are fluid and changeable, a continuous process of 'becoming'.[18] I consider narrating a biographic narrative as a way of 'Settling' this continuous process of becoming. It makes one temporarily *established,* for example in a way of life, in the occupations or positions one has held: as a resident of the place one is living in at the time, as well as in inhabiting the narrative. Narrating about one's life, anchors it by *putting it into an order* that makes one feel *comfortable,* less *floating,* more *stable.* However, this is not to say that this 'Settling' is permanent, or that it is a smooth and self-evident process. In a particular context there may be more discourses at work, which need to be negotiated, and often these discourses are in conflict with each other.[19]

My aim in the chapters of Part Two is twofold: to understand how Hajja and Umm Khalthoum constructed intersecting identities in and through telling their biographic narratives; and how at the same time, both women thereby negotiated the dominant discourse that made them prioritize those identities in the first place. How then, should I look into these biographic narratives in order to understand the interplay of intersectionality with intertextuality and intersubjectivity in the way working women negotiate a gendered identity? As I have indicated with respect to 'Settings' in the introduction to Part One, the narratives can be seen as sites which can be read 'against the grain' for

[17] Piscitelli (1996: 89).
[18] Hall (1990: 221). See also Hall (1996: 13).
[19] Mills (1997: 100).

layeredness and multiplicity of discourses as well as identities. In order to untangle the relation between a life and narrating about that life a spatial metaphor would help to avoid self-evident or linear notions of the biographic narratives. I also thus want to address the issue of the claim to academic authority that anthropologists make by writing ethnography through the *way* they write about 'the other'. I do not just attempt to experiment with 'writing differently' but with a way of trying to eventually understand power relations at all levels and coming to terms with its effect on the analysis as well. Whether or not I succeed in doing so is for the reader to judge.

Memory and experience: Relational agency from performance to representation

> "Where is the place that you move into the landscape and can see yourself?"
>
> — Carolyn Steedman[20]

When Hajja or Umm Khalthoum tells about her life each of them has to structure her narrative. However their differences influence this structuring, both women will relate what they remember to some notion of temporality, whether in the present, past or future.[21] This temporality, however, does not necessarily entail a chronology,[22] on the contrary: my choice for the notion of biographic narrative rather than life-history was precisely to get away from this idea of chronology.

Narratives of self are necessarily reflexive as the narrator and the central figure in the narrative are the same.[23] Narrating about self thereby connects not only memory to time, but to a notion of 'experience' as well. Diverse scholars problematize the notion of experience as the locus of authenticity or truth[24] as it might suggest a pre-discursive reality. As Scott argues in an article entitled "The evidence of experience":

[20] Carolyn Steedman (1986: 142) quoted as motto in Couldry (2000: 44).
[21] Fischer-Rosenthal (1995: 256–257).
[22] Fischer-Rosenthal (1995: 256–258); Ong (1982: 19).
[23] Bruner (1987: 1).
[24] Couldry (2000 :52–57); Scott (1991), De Lauretis (1984), Braidotti (1994), De Certeau (1987 :217–218); Alsop et. al. (2003: 56–57).

> 'Experience is at once always already an interpretation *and* something that needs to be interpreted. What counts as experience is neither self-evident nor straightforward; it is always contested, and always therefore political'.[25]

Thus, in narratives 'experience' is constructed as an important point of reference, of a means to anchor one's memory of self and is at the same time a construction of and in itself. Experiences are not accessed or remembered at random: experiences acquire certain meanings in the process of constructing particular identities, and vice versa. In other words, experience is produced 'by one's personal, subjective, engagements in the practices, discourses, and institutions that lend significance (value, meaning, and affect) to the events of the world'.[26] So if memories are related to experiences, discourses, interaction and the performing of narratives itself too transform these: by (re-)telling narratives the memory can even be altered.[27] I do not consider the memories and experiences of Hajja and Umm Khalthoum as a fixed basis, like cornerstones from the past, on which they build their present identities. Memories and experiences are continuously reshaped, and in turn reshaping parts of a remembered past. A past which each of the women re-assembles while constructing their identities for the time being.

I do not consider this subjectivity and relativity of the process of narrating as an impediment to understanding the ways women as narrators construct identities.[28] On the contrary. I take it that by narrating about the past women reflect on their present positioning and vice versa. I see the insertion of the past in the present and of the present in the past as a means of clarifying these identity constructions as part of the process of fixing of identities. Thus narratives of the past give insight into present negotiations of subject-positions, both for the narrator and for the audience. When Hajja and Umm Khalthoum performed their narratives, their experiences and memories became part of an embodied intersubjectivity.[29] This brings into view the notion of relational agency as I discussed in the Chapter 2. In other words,

25 Scott (1991: 797; cf. 767–777).
26 De Lauretis (1984: 159).
27 Zur (1999: 53).
28 See for a discussion of this issue for example Leydesdorff et. al. (1996).
29 Moore (1994: 2–3); see also Alsop et. al. (2003: 172–173).

Hajja and Umm Khalthoum perform identities *in relation to others* in a specific context, which brings us back to the notion of location and space.

Tracing identities, thinking maps: Narrated space

"and I am a room of my own body"
— Amira Hess[30]

As I pointed out in 'Settings' in Part One, the notion of 'mapping' appeals to me as it might help me to avoid considering the construction of identities as a linear process. The cartographic metaphor[31] to articulate the spatial aspect of the construction of identities has been used in particular by feminist thinkers, like bell hooks, Gloria Anzaldúa, Trinh Min-Ha, Chandra Mohanty.[32] Their personal experiences as 'women of colour'[33] with ways in which race, class, and gender intersect in particular spaces, formed the basis for criticizing the feminist agenda for being colour and class blind.[34] It was the articulation of the daily encounters with constricting, excluding and localized experiences by women of colour that led feminists to turn their gaze inwards and acknowledge differences among women, and among feminists. The result was an urge to understand *intersectionality* not just as a free mixing and mingling of identities, and never 'just' personal, but to acknowledge these experiences of *intersectionality* and their inscription in the body as socially, politically, culturally and economically constructed.[35]

---

[30] From her poem *I. Amira Hess* in: Smadar Lavie (1995: 412).

[31] Especially in feminist and other critical studies the notion of cartography is popular. For example 'Cartographies of struggle' by Mohanty.

[32] Gloria Anzaldúa (1987); Ruth Behar (1993; 320–342), bell hooks (1984), Chandra Mohanty (2003: 43–85); Moraga and Anzaldúa (1981); Trinh (1989).

[33] The notions 'black', 'Third World' women and 'women of colour' are used to mark the positionality of scholars who experience discrimination and exclusion on the basis of perceived skin colour and/or location.

[34] 'One change of direction that would be really interesting would be the production of a discourse on race that interrogates whiteness ... Race is always an issue of Otherness that is not white (hooks 1991: 54)'. See also Mohanty (1991: 1–30). See for a study on racism in the Netherlands: Essed (1991); see for a reflection of this debate also Davids and Willemse (1993).

[35] Important works are *A bridge called my back. Writings by radical women of colour* (1981) by Moraga and Anzaldúa, and *Borderlands/La Frontera* (1987) by Anzaldúa. I will come back to these in Part Three.

To gain an insight into both the facilitating and constricting aspects of the ways gender intersects with other identities in place and time, the notion of 'mapping' may facilitate to chart this contingent and dynamic process. While 'tracing entails seriality, continuity, and development, a map must be produced, constructed, and is always detachable, connectable, reversible, modifiable, and has multiple entryways and exits and its own lines of flight'.[36] However, the dichotomy that is thus constructed between tracing and mapping makes me feel uneasy. If a woman narrates an identity in a linear way does my insistence on 'mapping' not impose an analytical frame on the narrative? To get away from this dichotomy I want to relate mapping to tracing inspired on the notions of 'map' and 'tour' used by De Certeau.[37] He pointed out that even when people seem to describe a linear process, in other words narrate acts (a 'tour'), they take as point of reference, and at the same time produce, a 'map' as the context in which those acts have meaning. In other words, tracing and mapping suppose and thereby construct each other.

When I attempt to read narratives against the grain I will try to understand how identities are 'mapped', even when they are constructed as linear, and thus narratively 'traced'. When a woman constructs her identity, even if she is using a linear description (tracing) she reflects at the same time on the directive and guiding discursive context, in both its material and immaterial aspects, in which that identity makes sense (mapping). For me it is precisely an understanding of the reflexive boundaries that these maps represent that may point at the way that dominant discourses determine and thus confine the space women have to construct a gendered identity: in short what the subject-positions are which are allotted to women by the Islamist moral discourse. These boundaries, however, may not be articulated and only be 'virtually' projected onto the mental map of the narrator.

So, how then can I discover the mapping/context with boundaries, which constitute, and are constituted by, the possible tracings/identi-

[36] Deleuze and Guattari (1989: 22), quoted in Silberstein (2000: 7).

[37] De Certeau also sees a difference between both: whereby places are structured by signs and stability spaces are structured by movement and mobility, and they constitute each other: 'space is a practiced place' (1984: 117). See also Crang and Thrift (2000: 19–25).

ties-in-construction that a woman can narrate?[38] In 'Settings' I referred to Hall who stated that 'the illusion of identities as closed, unified and stable are the result of a process of marking difference and excluding what is 'other' in order to arrive at a constructed, and thus temporary closure'.[39] This definition points at two strategies with which a narrator can restrict her identity in a specified context: by marking difference and excluding what is 'other'. As I concluded in Chapter 2, narrating one's biography is an enactment of a relational agency, which means that both strategies concern other persons in particular.

When constructing intersecting identities, a narrator may construct a 'difference' with reference to a, specified or implied, 'other'. By claiming difference, a narrator constructs a difference 'from' someone else, which entails a process of exclusion. Alternatively, when a woman narrates about her self by tracing identities she creates a temporary suggestion of consistency and linearity. This means she has to constrict her identity to certain prioritised spaces, leaving others 'blank': automatically constructing the non-act, the left-out, in short: creating silences. So trying to find differences and silences in the biographic narratives 'as texts' can point the way in understanding how women construct shifting intersected gendered identities, which are linked to specific contexts. It also allows me to understand the way women negotiate subject-positions allotted by the dominant discourse on gender by the Islamist government. Thereby my own positioning in this intersubjective process of knowledge production is of importance as well.

At the intersection: Journeying with Hajja and Umm Khalthoum

In Part Two, I will attempt different contextualizations of the biographic narratives. I will do so by representing the biographic narratives as complete as possible and connect them to the context of daily life, also taking into consideration my own relations with both wom-

---

[38] My way of linking social space, embodiment and positionality seems to reflect Bourdieu's insight on 'habitus'. However, despite his reference to enactment and the dynamic nature of embodiment, his view of habitus is quite static and resembles structuralist ideas about the reproduction of society, mostly paying attention to gender and class (see for example Moore 1994: 76–80). I maintain that the linkages between space, embodied performances and the negotiation of subject positions are themselves dynamic and effect change.

[39] Hall (1990: 226) and (1996: 4–5).

en.[40] I will mark the different analyses in my representation by using certain section titles. First I will look closely to what is being narrated and how this connects to the daily context of both women's lives, acting as a kind of cultural interpreter. I mark this contextualization by using the notion of '*the present in the past*', when the focus of narration is a past experience which points, often implicitly, to a legitimatization of a woman's positioning in the present: to explain how one has become who one is. This is in fact a kind of tracing and may suggest linearity as the present identity is taken as a point of departure to make the past seem logic. The notion of '*the past in the present*' refers to how a certain prioritized identity that is of importance in the present context is, implicitly or explicitly, inserted into the reflections on the past in order to validate that identity positively in the present: who one is, or may be considered to be, if one's past experiences are constructed in a certain way. This is about negotiating a unified and respected identity in the context of a current dominant discourse and entails a form of mapping: the boundaries that are set by dominant discourses serve as a means with which the reflection on the past is guided. As may be clear, both ways of looking at the past are merged into one and the same narrative. They constitute analytical tools in order to look for layered-ness of the texts, to understand the negotiations of the dominant discourse, and to discover alternative subject positions. As Hajja and Umm Khalthoum used tracing and mapping differently while narrating about their lives, I have used slightly different titles in each narrative as the heuristic markers of my contextualizations, which indicate the differences in which each woman constructed her identities.

In Chapter 3 I represent the narrative of Hajja and I will use the title *Context of narration: The present in the past* for a first contextualization. I will use *Con/textualizing—The past in the present*, as a title to refer to the analysis of how Hajja constructs differences, and what identities are prioritized over others by which she creates silenced or muted identities. Only at the end of my analysis of her narrative, do I come to a *con/text-analysis* of her narrative and do I understand her construction of identity *as* a negotiation of the dominant discourse.

In Chapter 4, which represents Umm Khalthoum's narrative, the heuristic markers are somewhat different in order to indicate the dif-

[40] As I indicated in the introduction, the fact that these narratives have been transcribed and translated into English texts makes some techniques of narrative analysis hard to apply, such as wording, grammar, punctuation.

ferent way she narrated her biographic narrative. This is partly due to the different relationship Umm Khalthoum has with the town of Kebkabiya compared to Hajja, and thus with me as her audience. In the case of Hajja I physically participated in the context of her daily life, both it's exciting and it's mundane aspects. So Hajja's narrative was to me more of an ongoing interactive process and the titles in Hajja's narrative indicate this dynamic nature of the way she performed her narrative. I met Umm Khalthoum mostly after she had finished with her daily chores, when she felt she was 'ready' for me. The performance of her narrative was confined to the privacy of her home. Despite the fact that I had more in common with Umm Khalthoum as an educated outsider of similar age, than with Hajja, her narrative was more distanced and closed than Hajja's. Umm Khalthoum's narrative was already more of a reflection as she was physically removed from most of the life she was reflecting on. This more static and analytical nature of her narrative is evident from the titles I use in Chapter 4, respectively *Context of the narrative: The present in the past* and *Con/text-analysis: The past in the present.* The narratives of Hajja and Umm Khalthoum and my analyses constitute a context-bound reflection on this process. In the *Epilogues* to each biographic narrative I return to that process in a self-reflexive mode, trying to see what other views I could have taken on their narratives. In this way I try to establish how my view and the material and discursive context we shared have constrained and confined my academic narrative and the identities, both mine and theirs, I constructed in the process.

Finally, in Chapter 5 I will look closer to the differences in the use of narrative forms by Hajja and by Umm Khalthoum, and thus their engaging in the *discursive practice* of narrating about one's self. In this way I try to establish to what extent the differences in *how* each woman constructed gendered identities point at differences in the possible avenues each woman has for negotiating the dominant Islamist discourse and thus to construct an alternative subject position.

CROSSING THE ROAD: INTRODUCING HAJJA AND UMM KHALTHOUM

> In Omdurman, my friend and I assisted As-Sadiq's mother in giving birth to As-Sadiq Al-Mahdi. I bathed As-Sadiq and my friend looked after his mother. In Khartoum, they took care of midwives at that time, the fathers of the babies. The grandfather of As-Sadiq, Abderrahman Al-Mahdi, was present because the father was absent; he gave us many presents. After seven days, they made a *semaya*, to get the mother for the first time out of her bed. He then gave the elder midwife who was our trainer, a tin of oil, a tin of *semen*, and a tin of *karkar*. He also gave one sack of sugar, one sack of dates, a sack of flour, a box of soap, box of vermicelli. To the senior midwife they gave a box of sweets, a big box of matches, a box of bathing soap, one tobe, a piece of gold they tied it round her arm, and. …

"Sandal", says Sa'adiya. "Alah yedik al-baraka", Hajja exclaims and without pausing continues:

> All the kinds of scents like *suratiya, mahlabiya, sandaliya*. In the house of this midwife there is a barrel: they filled it wnith sandal and one barrel of *karkar*, hair oil, and one of *semen*, clarified butter, one of oil. She sold part of it in the market. But when we are here in Kebkabiya there is nothing given to us midwives.

This excerpt is from one of the first of Hajja's narratives that I taped. Hajja tells Sa'adiya and me about her training to become a medical midwife when she was young. After she received her diploma, she was elected to attend the birth of As-Sadiq Al-Mahdi, the great-grand son of the illustrious Al-Mahdi who founded the *Mahdiyya*. He is the same great-grandson who would become prime minister in two of the democratic post-colonial regimes of the Sudan 1966–1967 and 1986–1989 (Woodward 1990: 97–137; 201–239). She would recount this episode on several occasions in almost the same words, sometimes changing a detail or two. This was hardly surprising, as this fact connected her own life with that of one of the most famous political and religious families in the Sudan.

Hajja was a tall and sinewy elderly woman who radiated energy and will power. With her intelligent eyes and slightly protruding teeth, her face could rapidly change expression from, most of the time, friendly, to occasionally, stern, and back again. During my first fieldwork period, I would usually meet her on the market when I accompanied her daughter Nura who was taking care of our household then. For me, Hajja was therefore primarily a market woman. It was only when I returned for my second field stay, that I realised her situation was more complex. Although market trading was Hajja's regular business and she only occasionally attended at births, this did not make her necessarily a market woman.

During this first fieldwork period, I also met Umm Khalthoum but only briefly. She was one of the few married female teachers living in Kebkabiya. During that first stay, Yasmin and I generally socialised with the single female teachers living at the boarding house. I have a vague recollection of Umm Khalthoum at a *fatuur* during Ramadan; a joyful woman, amply built, with a pretty, open face and regular features, fixing me with her welcoming eyes. She made an impression on me because of her beautiful voice and her eloquence at reading a *funjaal*: a tiny coffee cup to which sides the coffee residue would stick after finishing drinking the sweet and strong coffee, and which were read for fortune telling.

Shortly after I arrived in Kebkabiya for my second stay, I met Umm Khalthoum again, this time at Sa'adiya's compound. Umm Khalthoum and her daughter Kaltouma visited Sa'adiya in order to congratulate her on the birth of her baby. During this visit Umm Khalthoum tells us about her problems with 'Kebkabiya people'.

In a manner similar to the single teachers, she feels that the Kebkabiya people are quarrelsome and like to gossip and speak ill of others without apparent reason. The issue is not even directly about her, but about a family living in Kebkabiya, which she and her husband have assisted in arranging the wedding of one of their daughters. The family of Haj az-Zein has a bad reputation: during a meeting of the local women's organisation a woman told those present that her *tobe* had been stolen. The woman claimed that she saw one of Hajj az-Zein's daughters wearing the same *tobe*, thus implying that someone from his family must have stolen it. I do not understand why this upset Umm Khalthoum. Then Umm Khalthoum goes on to tell us:

> I then said: "What do you mean by that, do you suggest I might have done it?" But they ignored me and continued to talk about the fact that sheets were stolen, and they also suggested that this was done by one of the sons of that family. Then I said: "I don't understand why you are making such problems by spreading these ungrounded rumours".

> I put my tea back on the tray untouched and left the house. Ever since, these women are not greeting me any more and they even do not greet my children when they meet them in the street. But the worst thing is that this made my sister-in-law also spread rumours about me. Once she called on me and she found me with two friends of the family, officers in the army, who were visiting me. Afterwards she told people that there were strange men in the house of her brother while he himself was not around, and that I was without tobe, and that we were all drinking coffee together on her brother's bed.[1] I made a big fuss over it and they called a meeting of all people involved to solve the problem. I told them I did not want Zeinab to come to my house any more if she only wants to come and gossip about me. Zeinab said: "If my brother puts a sign on his door 'nobody'[2] is to enter this house I will come and visit them, if not I will stay away". I then said: "If your brother is going to agree with this he can go and divorce me, I'll go to my mother, it is not important". Even people my husband meets in the street tell him he should not let his family go to Hajj ez-Zein's house because they are bad people. They want to create dissent between my husband and me. You know, Sa'adiya, Karin, this really makes me unhappy.

The events with which Hajja and Umm Khalthoum introduced themselves to me proved to be of major importance in understanding the narratives they were to tell me over the course of the months that followed. Their preoccupation with aspects of their lives which did not seem to be directly related to their work as a market woman or a female teacher nor to the moral discourse of the government made me hesitant at first about portraying their narratives here. Moreover, neither was a 'prototype' of the women of their category. Hajja sold predominantly onions, but not daily and not always from the same place as the full-time market women would, who catered their fruits and vegetables to regular customers at the centre of the market. Umm Khalthoum was the mistress of the local crèche and therefore not as qualified as her colleagues who were teaching at the intermediary school. However, I decided to represent their narratives on these pages for diverse reasons.

To Choose or Be Chosen, That is the Question

The position of Hajja and Umm Khalthoum among their colleagues was less extraordinary than my first acquaintances with them led me to

[1] Beds are often used as sofas on the veranda in daytime.
[2] 'Nobody' in the sense of no unrelated men.

believe. Hajja's part-time selling at the market she held in common with many women as it was an important coping strategy for most women who could not grow their food on the fields in times of drought and armed conflict. Umm Khalthoum came from Omdurman. Her speech and demeanour betrayed her elite upbringing. Her background and her activities in the local women's organization, which was temporarily banned by the Islamist government, along with other female teachers gave her esteem and standing within the group of female teachers which served to overcome her low status as a kindergarten mistress. Her warm and sociable personality, moreover, did much to make her a welcome guest among the single female teachers.

In due course, I realised that the 'typical' market woman or female teacher does not exist. In that respect, none of the colleagues of either Hajja or Umm Khalthoum could have been taken as an example of their category of working women. With hindsight I think that it may have been even an asset to read the narratives of two women who had quite complex relations with the work, which made them belong to the category of market women or female teachers. This positioning might highlight more clearly the ambivalences and contradictions in their reflections on the government moral discourse, than the narratives of some of their colleagues might have.

However, an important reason for me to read and write their narratives was that I knew the context in which each of the women lived. I was living at Hajja's compound and slowly I became part of her daily routine, sharing in some of the daily activities and problems of her family. This offered me an understanding of what Hajja was trying to convey to me. Specifically, that the midwife in her stories and the woman I saw selling the market to earn a living, were in fact different identities she used in coping with adverse circumstances, which fate had put on her path. I also visited Umm Khalthoum at her house regularly. I could understand much of her daily life and personal experiences because she had her own compound on which she could claim some privacy. Here she could talk more freely than the single female teachers I visited regularly at the boarding house. Moreover, at her home she acted out her other identities that proved of importance in her narrative.

Because Umm Khalthoum had a family and a husband to take care of, her work as a teacher was intersected with other responsibilities related to family life. This made it possible for me to compare her narrative with Hajja's. This allowed me to reflect on commonalties and differences in their strategies to cope with the current moral discourse on wife and motherhood.

Our regular contact and the sharing of a daily routine, resulted in a different kind of relationship than I could build up with the other women. My relationships with Hajja and Umm Khalthoum were themselves layered and multiple, which did much to help me understand the layered-ness in their narratives. I would not have been able to 'hear' the narratives of other women with the same amount of contextual knowledge, with not only the words, but also the silences given a place.

The question remains as to what extent the choice of women and their narratives was entirely mine. I feel I was chosen as much as I chose Hajja or Umm Khalthoum. Both women knew that I was taping their individual stories in order to write about them, this was something they both acknowledged and took pride in. Hajja clearly had her own project with me: to take her narrative to the world beyond her horizon, to a world she did not know, but of which she had heard and to some extent had taken part in, and which would become the receptor of the narrative I had asked her to give. That I understood her narrative well was important to her because the world that would receive her narrative was that of the westerners, who also figured prominently in her recollections.

Umm Khalthoum and I hit it off from the beginning. She seemed to like having me around and telling me her narrative. The fact that both Sa'adiya and I already knew about some of the problems she faced turned out to be important for understanding the way she reflected on her past and built up her narrative. She would sometimes reconsider or rephrase the issues she had told us on tape, often off the record, sometimes on tape. Talking about her life served as a way of assessing, contemplating and in a way 'revising' it, as if it offered an opportunity to come to terms with the complexity of her situation and her feelings by reflecting on them. These considerations bring into view the position Sa'adiya and I had in the narratives of Hajja and Sa'adiya.

Listening, Reading and Writing Against the Grain: Biographic Narratives Con/text-Analysed

When I began listening to the narratives, I had a preconceived idea of what a biographic narrative should look like. Therefore, listening proved simultaneously more fun and more trying than I expected, not in the least because at first I was not prepared to 'listen well' to the way each woman was telling me her narrative.

With Hajja, I waited for the magic rapport and sudden pull that would trigger a long and uninterrupted monologue in which Hajja would talk about her life from her youth up to the present. I wanted only *her* words, without interference from myself, or anyone else. It never happened that way. There were always interruptions. Her daughters or grandchildren would come to ask for advice, money, or attention. Neighbours came in to chat, to borrow or return something, and her sisters came inquiring about her health or lending her a hand. Visitors occasionally came to greet her while they were visiting the market or would come to warn her that the birth of so-and-so was shortly due. But not only that: even if we succeeded in talking at length in the *gutiya* that was my home, Hajja would expect me to be an active listener. She wanted me to give exclamations of approval or disagreement, whatever the circumstances required, and to ask questions to indicate I was listening. I had to prove I was still interested in what she was telling and that she was still being understood. In this respect, Sa'adiya was indispensable, not just as translator, but as an intermediary. This was brought to my attention, when, during a short stay in 1995, Hajja told me again about the period during which she was a midwife. My Arabic had greatly improved during the period I had been living on her compound. However, when I tried to persuade her to elaborate on this period she answered: "No, lets wait for Sa'adiya, I want my words to be understood correctly". Hajja would address Sa'adiya directly, often as "Shufti, ya ukhti Sa'adiya", (You see, my sister Sa'adiya,) rather than addressing me. Sa'adiya's fluency in the *rotana*, the local dialects, made her perhaps more important an audience than I was. I think the most important aspect was that, although I was to put her story into print, I was dependent on Sa'adiya as mediator, to tell me not just Hajja's words, but to convey to me the 'right' meaning of her narrative. I was an outsider who was interested in her narrative, but who could not acknowledge what she was telling me in ways that Sa'adiya could. Therefore, not only I, but also Sa'adiya became part of Hajja's narratives, in her capacity as a local Fur girl who had become a member of the educated elite.

Over the course of three long sessions, Umm Khalthoum told her narrative in a way, which I thought, came close to what a biographic narrative might be. However, in these sessions as well, Sa'adiya and I had a more active role than I had expected. At first I needed Sa'adiya for translating the nuances in the Omdurman version of the Sudanese Arabic. Later I did not require her as a translator, but Umm Khalthoum would always invite us together for another session. She apparently took Sa'adiya and me as separate and equal participants in her narrative, finding common ground with each of us individually. Sa'adiya was a married teacher with children and had to combine work and household cores as she did. Moreover, Sa'adiya had to cope with problems in her private life similar to those of Umm Khalthoum. As for me, the presence of Johan made me a working wife as well, but not with the same concerns: I was important to her because I was an educated woman 'out of town' and therefore a relative stranger, like her. She obviously looked for sympathy and solidarity in order to come to terms with the situation she found herself in and which she could not control. I was an outsider who provided Umm Khalthoum with a sounding board and an outlet with which she could discuss issues and vent ideas and emotions without concerning herself about direct social repercussions.

Biographic Narratives as Representation

In the Introduction I indicated that I had two tasks with respect to the narratives of Hajja and Umm Khalthoum. Apart from my own interest in reflecting on their subject positions in relation to the moral discourse of the government, I have the obligation to describe and explain unknown aspects in the narrative of each woman. The latter is due to the fact that they told me about their lives presuming some of the context known. There are many local expressions, events, and peoples to which and whom Hajja relates to as being self-evident as I was living with her. As such, I will be a translator of context, painting the surroundings in order to create a more complete picture. Umm Khalthoum's narrative was taped on three different occasions, but as I visited her regularly, we continued discussing issues afterwards and in between as well. In this way, I became increasingly involved in her life and current predicament, which I have to some extent explain.

For this reason, I have opted for a combination of both the taped narratives with the context in which they were told followed by a more analytical reflection on the narratives themselves. This intention is not entirely inspired by my own wishes. It has also been dictated by the way that Hajja and Umm Khalthoum related their individual narratives.

Hajja would 'recount' parts of her life when a specific event triggered her memories. I realised that the rhythm of Hajja's life followed those of the days of the week. Each day had its own meaning with its specific activities, responsibilities, memories and locations which structured the way in which Hajja told her narrative. I will therefore use the concept of 'mapping' to understand the context of her life as well as when reading her narrative for clues to understand her different identities Hajja constructed and performed in relation to each other.

The, at times, distancing tone with which Umm Khalthoum reflected on her life when the tape recorder was running, cajoled me into taking a more distant position when analysing her narrative. This is due, not only to Umm Khalthoum's demeanour, but also to the fact that her story was less tied to local places, rhythm and events than Hajja's narrative was. However, I also considered 'mapping' as a way of reading her story, in order to be able to compare her narrative with that of Hajja. The way I structure my analyses of Umm Khalthoum's narrative is different however, related to the different narrative structure Umm Khalthoum uses in narrating about her life. I will turn now first to Hajja's narrative, because of seniority, but also because by her reflections the history and recent changes in the town of Kebkabiya will come to the fore, which are also of importance to the narrative of Umm Khalthoum.

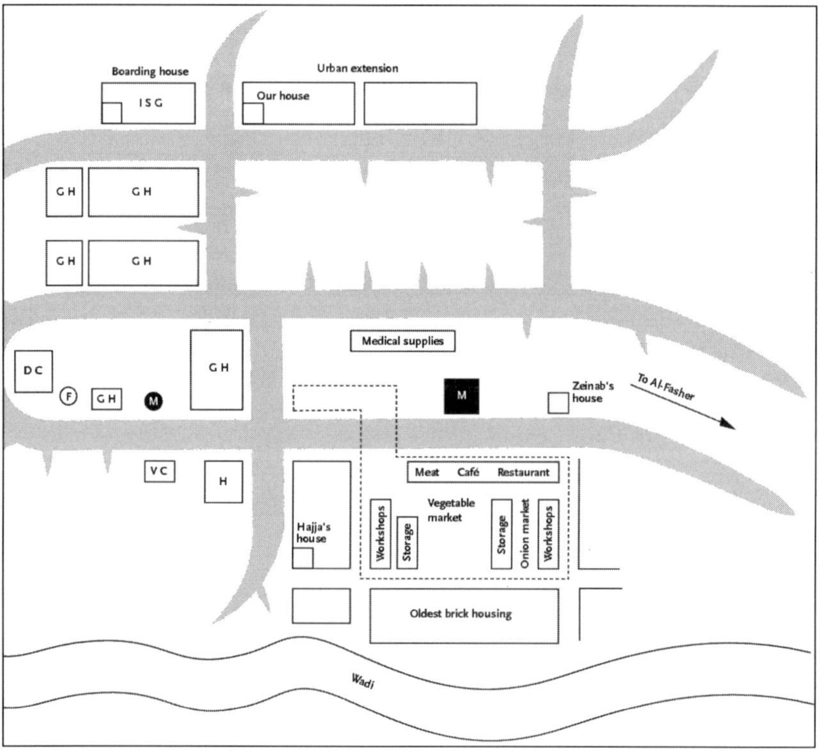

Legend to map of Hajja

ISG	Intermediary School for Girls	VC	Village Council
GH	Government Houses	TC	Tribal Council
H	Hospital	DC	District Council
M	Mosque	F	Faqih Sinin (burial mound)

CHAPTER 3

HAJJA'S WEEK: NARRATING HER LIFE IN TIMES OF CHANGE

Monday—The Minor Market Day

It is six o'clock in the morning and still dark. I get out of bed to go to the toilet. A faint light shines from the room where the family sleeps: Hajja has already risen to pray. When I return I meet Hajja on her way to milk her two cows in the kraal next to the compound. We greet each other with the habitual '*Sabah al-kher—sabah al-nur*', (Good morning). There is a biting cold wind. Hajja pulls her *tobe* closer around her, putting its tip between her teeth, while she crosses the yard. I go back to the warmth of my bed where I listen to the radio for half an hour. Hajja has barely finished milking when the first customer enters the courtyard to collect the fresh milk. Dressed in a sweater and jogging pants under a wide skirt I join Semira and Nura, Hajja's two daughters, in their room. The boiled milk is set in a large earthenware pot from where Nura, the youngest daughter ladles it into the buckets of one of the neighbours' daughters. The milk sells for £S10 per pint. Semira, the eldest and married daughter takes part of the milk and heats it in a pan on the stove. When it has boiled again Semira adds sugar to it. Then she divides the milk amongst the family: two plastic mugs for her three children and a glass each for herself, her sister, her mother and myself. Today is Monday, the 'minor' market day. Abdel Munim, one of the men who supply Hajja with onions, enters the compound with his donkeys carrying two huge sacks of them. He has collected the onions from the fields of his neighbours' and his own and has come to sell them to Hajja. The price has gone up. Two weeks ago Hajja bought a sack for £S1100.[1] Now they finally agree on the price of £S1250 per

[1] The exchange rate was approximately one dollar to twenty Sudanese pounds. It is hard to give exact rates due to the fluctuation of the money exchange market because of rumours about the possible fluctuation of the dollar, which took place some months later.

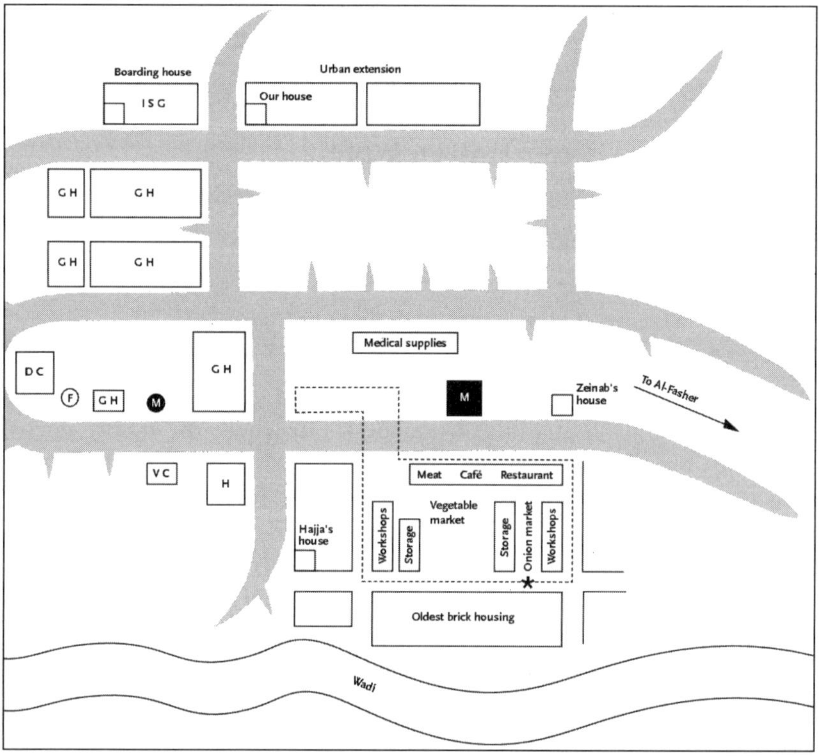

Map 1. Hajja at the Onion Market

sack. As Hajja has no money she promises Abdel Munim that she will pay at least part of the amount she owes him on Thursday afternoon, by the closing of the 'major' market day.

Nura has started to sort the onions according to size. She sets aside the small, dry onions. Nura removes the dry peels from the more juicy large onions and puts them in empty oil tins. Meanwhile, Semira has finished cleaning the courtyard with a bundle of reeds. Then she straps her baby to her back and goes to take the cows to the garden near the *wadi*, where they can graze on the stalks and small watermelons that remain there. She also takes a jerry can along so she can bring some water with her when she returns. It is getting busy on the road. Hajja takes one of the tins of sorted onions. She puts it on her head and walks to her place on the market. Nura goes as well in order to sell the remainder of the milk to one of the restaurants. I join them. With the money she collects from the milk, this time £S60, Nura wants to buy meat for lunch. Like the other days, no one has brought any meat to the market as the conflict between the butchers and the government about the meat tax is still unresolved. The only way to get meat now is by slaughtering animals clandestinely or by buying chicken inside the quarters. We have to make do with the *sharmot* (dried meat) still left from the goat I gave to Hajja a month ago.

Nura goes home to prepare breakfast. I look for Hajja who is in one of the sheds situated on the south eastern fringe of the market near the big traders' storage places. The sheds have only recently been put up in this part of the market and is reserved for market women selling onions, potatoes, and dried products like beans and home-grown spices, like Hajja, on the two official market days. Previously, Hajja sat near the butchers' hall at the north end of the market. As Hajja lives near the market she used to be among the first market women lucky enough to find a place there in the early morning. While customers queued for meat, they would buy their wares from these nearby located market women. Hajja would occasionally also sell oil, clarified butter, tomatoes, limes, and peanut butter. However, the government decided that the 'at random' seating of market women near the meat hall was an impediment to the traffic, which makes use of the road that runs alongside the butchers' hall. In order to structure the layout of the market the government set up separate places for women who were selling in this area: one on the far north western end of the market and the location where Hajja has her place. Both locations are less central than the butchers' place. Now she sells only onions because they are always in demand and easy to keep if she has not sold all of them on one day.

It is only nine o'clock and still early. The restaurants are preparing *fatuur*, the breakfast which most people usually take between ten and eleven o'clock. Onions are an important ingredient of the dishes they serve at breakfast and lunch. The cooks from the restaurants are Hajj's main customers at this early hour. After the first half-hour trade is low and at around eleven o'clock Hajja tells me to go and take breakfast at home. She asks her sister Tinja, who is selling onions next to her, to take care of possible customers.

Back home, we eat together from an enamel bowl the staple *asida*, a stiff porridge of sorghum or millet served with gravy. Hajja complains to her daughters about the slack market. This is unlike her. In fact, Hajja rarely talks about her trading activities. Whenever I ask her about her trading, Hajja gives short answers. Most of the time she refers to women, who work on the market daily, like Umm Wayma, her neighbour, or Zamzam, her co-wife's daughter. However, today is different. During breakfast, Hajja talks about the times when the market was still booming. I ask her how long she had worked as a market trader. Hajja answers:

I went to the market after my husband died, eight years ago now.

Nura interrupts her saying it is longer ago than that, more likely ten years. They agree that it was nonetheless before the last drought that started in 1984. I ask Hajja how she received her place in the market, what products she started selling then and why:

The first thing I sold was groundnuts. I started selling because I didn't have much money. I bought one sack of groundnuts, sold it, and had £S50 profit. I got my place from the government and paid money for my license. After I sold the one sack, I could buy other goods like onions, okra, and pepper. I am selling because I don't have enough money.

"What do you think are the best products to sell?" I ask her.

The best goods to sell are onions if the market is good. In the past if you bought three sacks of onions, the Zaghawa came to buy them to bring them to Dar Zaghawa: I would sell all the sacks in one day. Now the Zaghawa are not coming. I don't know what happened to them. They may be afraid of the armed robberies.

She clicks her tongue in disapproval. So I continue: "Do you have one fixed person, such as Abdel Munim, from whom you are buying or do you buy from anyone?"

Anyone, who brings onions to the market, I buy from them. First I had one person who brought me onions, Omr Saeedu, but he died. Even if, when entering the market, women on the road would ask him to sell them his onions he would say: 'No, these are Hajja's'. We were not relatives, but we had been neighbours. I take my oil from shops. When I sell all of it, the profit is one bottle of oil and an empty jerry can (£S150). Last year I sold turmus[2] *as well and dried okra, flour, and tomato-powder, limes. I used to pay women to powder it for me. In addition, for making*

[2] Yellow peas (*fasulia*) sold in small plastic bags. The boiled peas are a favourite snack during Ramadan.

jir, *the white powdery flour for making white* abrey,[3] *this would be done especially for Ramadan. I hired women. I gave my* jir *to my customer in Al-Fasher. He was also my neighbour here in Kebkabiya before. And now he works and lives in Fasher. I would sell two jerry cans of* jir *to him and I earned £S200, just from these two jerry cans.* Turmus *give a lot of profit. If you buy one* kora, *a bowl, with £S80, and you prepare them, you can find twice the amount as profit, £S160. But people eat it mostly in Ramadan. This year people did not even buy at Ramadan. Last year when I came with the bowl of* turmus *in the suq, I would make £S200 in one day. But this year the market is very bad, there is no profit.*

Abruptly Hajja gets up with the comment that she has to go back to her place. We walk back together each carrying another load of onions. Like most market women, Hajja sells onions per *koom*, a pile, which differs in the number of vegetables or fruits according to the kind. The women place the onions in piles of about five large ones priced at £S20 or ten small ones for £S15. Onions can also be sold per *safiha*, a rectangular oil tin, for £S270. While we sit in the shade of her shed, Hajja makes an account: one sack contains about 5.5 *safiha*. A sack gives between £S1485 and £S2200 income, a profit of between £S225 and £S950. However, Hajja never sells the whole of a sack. The bad onions are used for her own household and Hajja also gives onions away, as *bakshees*, a small gift, to regular customers, or as *karama*, alms, for those who need it or at a ritual meal.

As usual there are not many people from outside town at the Monday market. However, even for a minor market day it is very quiet. Hajja is not the only one who complains about this. One reason is that banditry and the ethnic conflict have extended to the vicinity of Kebkabiya town. Robbers attack even on the dirt roads between Kebkabiya and the surrounding villages. Now most people visit the market either on Thursdays, the major market day, seeking the security of travelling in relatively large groups, or not at all. Lorry drivers have also taken precautions and travel in *tov*, convoy. Groups of soldiers accompany them during the most dangerous part of the trip between Al-Fasher and Kebkabiya.

From Hajja's place, we have a good view of the storage places of the big traders. The traders buy beans, groundnuts, spices, etc., from

[3] *Abrey* is a drink prepared from crusty millet or sorghum flakes with sugar to which water is added. Red *abrey* is made of the more coarse sorghum flour and gives a brown drink, while white *abrey* is prepared from *jir*, which gives a translucent drink.

patrons who come from the surrounding villages. The traders repack the dry goods in large sacks of jute or plastic and send them to larger towns where the goods will fetch a good price. Alternatively, the goods are stored, awaiting better prices. While watching the hustle and bustle on the market, I ask Hajja if she ever has problems selling at the market:

I sometimes have problems with some customers who take some goods but don't pay.

She shrugs her shoulders and changes the subject:

In the past before their father died, I didn't go to the market. When I went to the market, my daughters were grown up. When I was working as a midwife and people called me to a lot of places, their father Abu Feisal[4] *would make breakfast for his children and for me as well. But now my daughters make food for me and for themselves. And when Nura went to Fasher to study, Semira stayed in the house.*

Hajja turns her attention to some customers. She sells two *koom* of large onions. She knows the customer well, she is a daughter of one of Hajja's former neighbours, and they talk for a while. Hajja gives her customer some extra onions. She often gives presents to her regular customers, but also she does this if someone buys a large amount of her goods. I am curious to know who helped Hajja to set up as a market woman. Therefore, I ask Hajja where she found the money in order to invest.

I had my own money, because women would give me some money when I assisted them in giving birth. I even went on haj *with my own money. With £S100, I went on pilgrimage. Ah, but that was in 1960 before I went to the market. Then money was worth more than it is now. Even the small coins we used to have like* tariifa, piaster, tarata, *they don't exist anymore. For* ya ukhti *[my sister], a hundred pounds means nothing these days.*

Hajja's tone gets increasingly bitter. She is about to say more but is prevented by a young woman who asks Hajja to check on the condition of her sister who is about to give birth. Without hurrying, Hajja gathers her belongings. One of the young boys hanging around her stall is sent to Nura in order to warn her that she has left for a consultation and

[4] As Hajja's husband was a very well-known figure in Northern Darfur I have lent him a pseudonym calling him the father of his eldest son Feisal, as is the custom.

that she needs her midwifery case. Then Hajja rearranges her *tobe*, asks her sister to take care of her wares, and joins the young woman. I decide to walk over to the other side of the market. Crossing the market is quite a trip through the hot, coarse sand in the blistering sun. Nevertheless, I enjoy the colours, smells and voices. When I pass by the so-called *suq al-khadaar*, the vegetable market, Hajja Atima sees me and calls me over. She gives me some lemons and bananas 'for my health'. I know she is trying to amend our 'customer-relationship'. I have reduced my shopping at Hajja Atima's stall because she charges more than the other women do. However, her fruit is excellent. I accept grudgingly. Not to do so would be offensive and I mumble something about 'maybe next time'. She laughs and tells me that she has the best fruit anyway and that she only gives me some just to remind me of that. Then I hear someone else calling my name from the opposite direction on the small sand road, where Rhoda, one of Hajja's nieces, has her stall. There are several young women with her, seated on boxes and *bambars*, the low wooden-and-rope stools. They are laughing loudly. "Ya Karin, come and join us", Rhoda calls. I find myself a place on a tin box and join in the joking and laughing of the group of women who collectively share a bowl of tomato salad with spring onions and peanut butter. I have a piece of bread stuffed in my hand and Selwa urges me: "Come on, eat Karin, you are much too thin to attract a nice man now that Johan is not here!" This bold comment causes the women to start laughing again. Accepting the challenge, I dip my bread in the peanut sauce and press some pieces of tomato between the edges of the bread saying: "How about you Selwa? You surely do not want to make us believe that those customers in their khaki trousers are so fond of vegetables that they have to come and buy them everyday". Now the others laugh while Selwa replies: "Hush, you big mouth, my brother is in the army and these men come to bring me letters and sometimes meat from him". Rhoda gets serious now, sighing: "All these men fighting in the South, when will this war be over, when will we be able to have our brothers, our cousins, and our sons here again?" The others nod silently. Zamzam comes along in a hurry to say she will come and give her share of the money she is due for the *sanduq*, or 'box', the next market day when Zamzam expects some of the traders to send her the money they owe her from selling her goods in Al-Fasher. She now needs her money to buy wooden boxes for sending her tomatoes back with those same lorry drivers to Al-Fasher. She quickly washes her right hand and takes a few bites of salad. Zamzam has also picked up on Rhoda's last words and says to me teasingly: "It also has its positive sides not to have your husband around all the time". Theatrically she takes hold of her belly for a brief moment. The jolly mood is back again. "Drink some tea with us, Zamzam", Selwa says. However, Zamzam has no time. She again washes her hands and rushes off, calling over her shoulder: "Karin, why don't you come and join me this Thursday and see how I deal with those drivers who handle my tomatoes?" This suggestion elicits some giggling from the women near me. It is five o'clock in the afternoon already. I stand up in order to go and see what is left of the lunch usually served between three and four o'clock. I long for a bath, which consists essentially of splashing water from a bucket over my head in the outdoor bathing place, before sunset when the wind gets stronger and colder.

Context of Narration—The Present in the Past
Hajja Selling at the Market

During the entire period I lived on her compound, Hajja was reluctant to talk about her work as a market woman. She would only discuss her work with me whilst at the market or when I asked her direct questions about it. Market trading is a necessity brought about by her husband's death some eight years before. 1982 clearly marks a watershed for her. Hajja's fate forced her to begin selling at the market; she needed the money.

Although Hajja began by selling groundnuts, nowadays she deals mainly in onions. Onions involve less risk than the more perishable fruit and vegetables, because they can be stored for a long time. However, they also give less profit. Like most women, she sells mainly on the official market days: Mondays and Thursdays. Occasionally Hajja sells on other days if she has products other than onions for sale. In this respect she differs from the market women who sell at what is called 'the vegetable market', which is located at the centre of the market. Here, the women have fixed places with displays that are shaded by a lean-to made of wood and burlap or corrugated iron and attached to large iron storage rooms. In these storage rooms measuring approximately a person's height, women can lock away their produce, chairs, and packing boxes during the night. Women who sell on a daily basis have this restricted area between the butchers, restaurants, and grocery shops reserved for them. They deal mainly in fresh fruit and vegetables. There are young and elderly women, married and unmarried, with or without children, and all of them are considered 'full time' market women. This label sets them apart from the occasional market women like Hajja who only sell on a market day and who trade in limited goods: those that keep for some time. This last group of women form row after row selling the same products at scarcely shaded spots with no displays.

Hajja's position as a low-ranking market woman might be the reason why she does not like to discuss her work. She might feel she compares badly with the market women on the central square. At the same time, Hajja's reluctance to talk about her trading activities might be due to the low returns she receives from her selling. This is what she emphasises at first: the slack market, a consequence of the lack of former customers like the Zaghawa. Possibly, her reluctance also relates to the moral discourse of the government on tea and market women. When I inquire about the problems Hajja has on the market, her abrupt assertion that she did not go to the market before her husband died can be taken as an argument with the government's moral discourse. Hajja is claiming that it is only now, being old and poor, that she has chosen to work on the market. Her assertion that in the past, when she worked as a midwife, her husband prepared breakfast for her children is related to her remark that her daughters were already adults and stayed at home when she went to the market. Implicitly she argues with the government's condemnation of working mothers who are cast as disobedient wives who by virtue of their absence from home while working cannot be 'good mothers'. Hajja emphasizes that the government allocated her a place on the market for which she bought a license. This statement must be considered in the same light: Hajja sells at the market legally. She performs her trading activities with the consent and the help of the same government that now seems to cast doubt on the market women's underlying intentions. Even my inquiry about her 'problems' with her customers is interpreted in the light of the current moral discourse: she considers them to be an euphemistic reference to 'indecent proposals'.

Throughout this part of our talk, Hajja asserts the importance of her job as a midwife. Firstly, when she talks about her investment capital, adding that she 'even' went on pilgrimage with that money. Hajja's career as a midwife not only set her up as a market woman to earn a living, but also enabled her to earn religious merit; pilgrimage is one of the five obligations of every Muslim. The fact that Hajja went on *haj* in 1960 is equally surprising not only because she paid for it herself, but also because she was relatively young when she went. Apart from the wealthy, most pilgrims are of an advanced age when they go, if they go at all. It is clear that Hajja thinks highly of her job as a midwife. Instead of reflecting on her work as a market woman, as I wanted her to do, she changes easily to speaking of her identity as a midwife. I saw this transition acted out when the young boy called Hajja to attend a birth. The woman was not in labour but Hajja felt her midwifery work was more important than her trading. Hajja's enjoyment of practising as a midwife became increasingly evident when we began to tape Hajja's story, some time later.

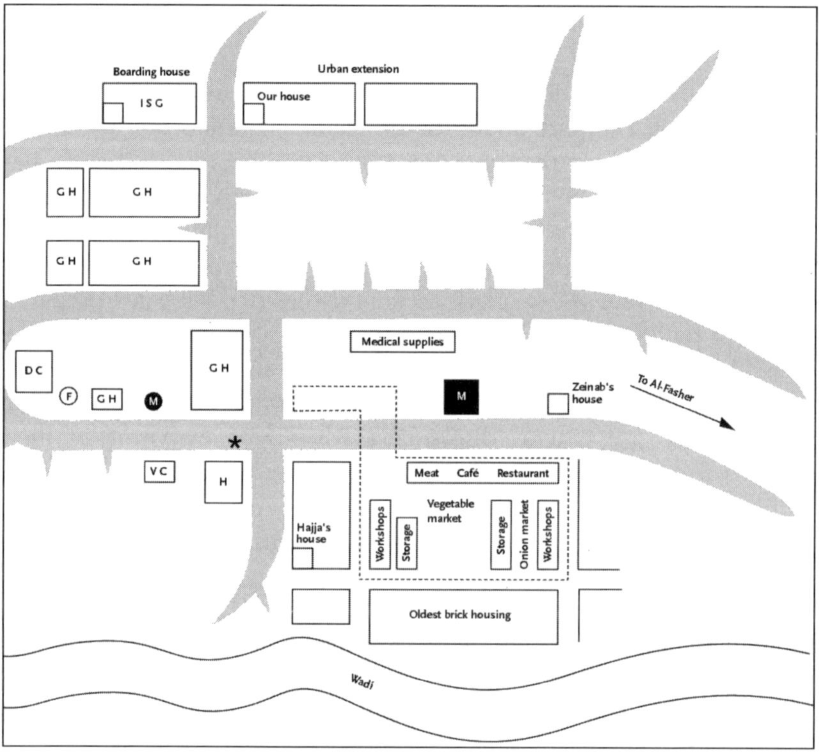

Map 2. Hajja located as midwife at the hospital

Tuesday—Hajja's Week: Just an Ordinary Day

It has been ten days since I last spoke to Hajja about her market work. I have asked her repeatedly to tell me more about her past. There is always something to be done. This morning Hajja is absent when I get up. She arrives when all the milk customers have gone, looking tired, but relieved. She was called to attend a birth and everything was fine. It is a boy and the family is well known and relatively wealthy. Hajja expects that on this occasion her reward will be better than usual.

After breakfast, Sa'adiya arrives. It is about eleven o'clock. We transcribe the tapes of stories about Kebkabiya's history. We have just settled ourselves in my *gutiya* when Hajja calls from outside: "Ya Karin, Sa'adiya, shall I tell you my story now?" I am surprised that now she offers her story so readily. She was not too keen to talk about her work on the market the other day. As she comes into my *gutiya*, she tells us she prefers to talk here, as we will be relatively undisturbed. Hajja sits on the uncomfortable modern chair nearest to the door while Sa'adiya and I sit on the double bed. Sa'adiya 'instructs' Hajja with the standard set of instructions; Hajja is to begin by stating her name and when and where she was born. While Sa'adiya presses the 'on'-button on the tape-recorder Hajja folds her leg under her and begins:

My name is Hajja Ishak. I was born in Kebkabiya. My mother was also born here and stayed until she was an old lady, who even drank during Ramadan.

"This is to say that she was demented", Sa'adiya explains.

She died when she was ninety-five years old. I was born after Sultan Ali Dinar, when the British came. I was born two years after the British started to rule in Darfur after Ali Dinar had died.

Sa'adiya and I count. The British killed the last Sultan of the Fur, Ali Dinar, in 1916 at Menawashi. Therefore, Hajja's date of birth must be around 1918. It makes Hajja approximately seventy years old, which seems too old for her constitution. *"Billahi" (Really)*? she says when I say she looks younger. She laughs. Sa'adiya suggests that the British might not have come to Kebkabiya in person directly after Sultan Ali Dinar's death in 1916 which might have confused the dates. Hajja replies that she is not sure and that I should check with some of her family members who are older than she is. I then ask her to continue her story on her youth:

My mother was born in Kebkabiya and was a Tama, my father was also born Tama. However, my father did not come from here, he was from Monjura, North

Geneina.[5] *By coincidence, my two sisters and I, we both married Tunjur who were cousins as well: they were Fur-Kunjura.*[6] *My father married two wives. His first wife died without children. He only lived with my mother. My father died and ten years after that, my mother. She died twenty-five years ago. My eldest sister, Hauwwa, was by another father. She was the daughter of Faqih Sinin.*

I would like to ask her about Faqih Sinin, but Hajja continues her own train of thought:

When I was a child I went to the khalwa.[7] *After I learned the* surat-al-Fatha,[8] *I left the* khalwa. *They stopped me from going to school. We had to work in the fields or tending cows. Boys could stay in order to learn more. They circumcised girls early and married them early.*

"Did boys and girls study together in the *khalwa*?" I ask when she looks at me expectantly.

I studied in Faqih Taj-ed-Din's khalwa *in Urra [a village near Kebkabiya, Sa'adiya whispers to me] and boys and girls were together in class. I lived in Urra and my father's fields were in Urra. We also had a field here near the town. Our field in Urra now belongs to my sister; she planted fruit trees, limes, and mangoes. At that time, there were no labourers and children had to help their parents. We would take* asida, ajiina, kisra, *and* medida tama[9] *with us to the fields. We had cows and we took milk from them, they had very big udders. One equals ten cows now, if you compare the milk they give. My mother was also farming. You*

---

[5] North Geneina was part of Dar Masalit until 1930. Dar Tama was a sultanate adjoining Dar Masalit (cf. Kapteijns 1985a: 12–20).

[6] According to O'Fahey (1974: 117–124) the names Tunjur and Kunjura could form a singular/plural pair in Fur. He suggests that the Keira clan, who came from the Kunjara section of the Fur people, ruled a kingdom in Jebel Marra, which formed part of the Tunjur Empire to which they were related by marriage. The Tunjur empire was located in Northern Darfur and nowadays the Tunjur are still located in that area, predominantly around Kutum (O'Fahey 1980b: 47–61)).

[7] A *khalwa* (pl. *khalawi*) is a religious school where children get *Qur'an* lessons. Before the introduction of the educational system by the British, these were the only established forms of education. Nowadays *khalawi* are still in use for *Qur'an* lessons. In Kebkabiya town lessons are only given in the evening, after the lessons at the government schools are over.

[8] This is the first *sura*, the opening chapter of the *Qur'an*.

[9] *Medida tama*, thick smooth drink of millet or sorghum, sugar and water, slightly fermented; *kisra*, thin sour pancakes made of millet or sorghum and water usually eaten at lunch or diner.

see, Sa'adiya, my mother, Hajja Shuluug,[10] *had six sons. She asked her grandsons Ahmed, Abderrahman, Idris, and Abdallah to come to her field to assist her. One of them said: 'Oh grandmother, your first husband was Faqih Sinin, and he was a sultan with his copper drum. Even then, you didn't stop farming. Now you are tiring us for this husband who is not a sultan. You don't want to stop working'. He meant that because she married a poor man, my mother wanted to work even more fields than before, when she had a rich husband.*

My mother and father had no separate land; the land belonged to my father. They worked on it together with us children. But at that time fields and houses belonged to men. If a woman cut her own trees the land was hers. If he divorced her, they could divide it in two, even when it belonged to the woman. If you had land with him, and he died, they will say it was his land, bass, and divide it amongst the children. My husband had three fields, and they put it in the inheritance. Shops, houses, animals, money, all were divided. This house was given to my daughters, and most of the gardens to Feisal. But we women were given one-eighth of the inheritance. Of course, we kept the cows, which were ours.

As usual, the subject of cows leads Hajja to ask me about Dutch cows. She is incredulous that there are cows, which can give so much more milk than the local ones like hers. However, most of the powdered milk one can buy in the shops is from 'Hollanda', with illustrious names like 'Dutch Baby'. This is evidence enough that 'my country' must indeed have a large surplus to be able to sell so much of it. I want to return to the subject of education and ask her: "At what age were you when you went to the *khalwa*?"

I was seven years when I went to the khalwa. *Girls and boys studied together, but boys would have two sessions: in the morning and the evening. In the morning, they wrote on the* loh, *the wooden slate that you can wash. In the evening they lit a fire and read. We brought wood, all the boys and girls, to the* khalwa *for the fire.*

"So you studied for three years at the *khalwa*?" I inquire.

Yes. They said: 'These girls are too big for the khalwa'. *Every girl who turned ten years old had to leave the* khalwa.

[10] *Shuluug* refers to the scars in her face. Especially in Northern Sudan, scarring is used as a means of beautification of women. Her mother's scars have another meaning, however. Hajja will tell us later about it.

"What did you learn at the *khalwa*?" I prompt her when she falls silent.

From the Qur'an, *the* sura's: Surat al-fatha, surat al-naas, al-falaq, al-ighlaas.[11] *They also told us how to pray. When I turned ten, my family taught me how to cook, how to make food covers, to grind. There was no mill at that time. We also brought wood from the forest and water: there were no servants around. My sister Tinya, and I went every afternoon to bring wood from the forest. But in the morning we would pound millet. It was very clean after that. Before we put it in a pot, my mother would clean it in a separate pot. Only after that, she'd put it in a pot for keeping. We prepared two sacks almost every day. Sometimes, when there was enough left, we didn't need to pound. Girls were married very early. My elder sister Tinya was married even before she was circumcised. They brought her* sheila[12] *when she still wasn't circumcised. Rich families also used to marry off their sons early: they would pay his bride price for him. Abdallah, my sister's son and his son are very near in age because he married so young.*

She nods, while contemplating this. When I want to ask her once more about the schools in Kebkabiya, she cuts me short. She turns to Sa'adiya, and says:

You know, ya Sa'adiya, there were no schools at that time, just khalaawi. *Every village had a* khalwa. *The most important in this town was Faqih Osman's. I didn't study in his because I was in Urra, Faqih Osman in Kebkabiya. Saleh Sinin, brother of Abdul Shaafi Sinin, had also a* khalwa, *here in* hei as-suq sabah. *That was after Faqih Sinin's death. Ali Dinar was defeated and the new government of the British asked the son of Sinin, Abdelshaafi to return. The British Government took the copper drum*[13] *of Faqih Sinin from Ali Dinar and returned it to his son Abdelshaafi. Faqih Sinin is buried in the* gubba[14] *and next to him is his daughter's grave. She killed seven men after they killed her father. Also men whom I knew were killed together with Faqih Sinin. Some of these men's children were killed as well. But their grandchildren live.*

---

[11] These are all chapters, or *surat*, from the *Qur'an*.

[12] The *sheila* is part of the bride-price with which the family of the bride prepares a wedding meal.

[13] The copper drum or *nahas* formed part of the royal regalia of sultans and other paramount leaders and was used to signal important meetings and decisions to his followers. Lower chiefs would use a wooden drum, or none at all (O'Fahey, 1980a: 86–87).

[14] A *gubba* is a burial mound, almost exclusively indicating the grave of an important figure. *Gubbas* are often taken as places of pilgrimage.

I ask her who Faqih Sinin is.

He founded Kebkabiya and he was my mother's first husband. I was not born yet. So you had better ask others about him. Let me see.

Hajja mentions the names of elderly women. Sa'adiya tells me she knows where they live. Sa'adiya asks Hajja to continue:

We all went to the khalwa. *But there is a difference between boys and girls in education. Girls hardly got any education, but boys went up to the fourth class of primary school and then they could become teachers right away. This was after they had studied in the* khalwa.[15] *For example, Jelat-ed-din became a teacher after the fourth class, and then he became an accountant at the government. He was a well-paid employee until he died. In the past, there were no schools, just* khalawi. *But when schools opened in Kebkabiya people brought their children. If there had been schools before, our district would have been better; it would have given us a better life. The schools in Kutum were established very early. Some people took their sons from here to Kutum, like Abu Halima's son, Mohammed Ahmeddai, Abu Kora Ahmeddai, Abu Mohammed, from Sultan Ishak. They carried them with their belongings on camels' backs and the fathers joined them on white donkeys and some went on horses. At that time there were no boarding houses, they had to live with their families. The first handing out of certificates, when they had finished their school, were to Abu Sésé and Abu Mohammed, Mohammed Ishak's son, Ahmed Yudjuk, Abu Halima's son, Abu Kora Ahmedai, Mohammed Ahmedai, both from the* shartai. *Five pupils. One girl studied in Kutum, Amuuna, you know, Umruwayba's mother. She was one of the first girls, but that was later. Many boys went to school. If they had put us girls in school, we would be comfortable now, not as it is now. When I was appointed for the training of midwives and had to go to Umdurman, I was afraid to go. But my father forced me. We were pounding millet, myself, my sister and another girl, Hauwa. I heard that there was an old cleaner in the hospital that they took to become a midwife. However, the medical assistant said she was too old. I said: 'O, I wished I was in the place of this woman', while we pounded the millet. The assistant heard me and directly he wrote my name down and sent the list to Khartoum. The reply came quickly and it stated that, 'the midwife aged seventeen has to report herself quickly'. The letter came to my father. At first, he was angry he said: 'You went to the hospital and talked to men, and registered?*

[15] Here Hajja refers to the so-called 'sub-grade' classes, where boys who studied at a *khalwa* could get their primary school certificate in four instead of six years.

You are not my daughter anymore!' I said: 'No I didn't go there'. After my father heard the real story, he said: 'In that case you will go at once'. I wept, but he told me I had to go. My father had white nurses' dresses made for me. My father told the medical assistant: 'You can take my daughter and escort her to Khartoum'. The government gave me a free ticket for travelling by road and I went. I spent nine months in Umdurman; I finished my training in time.

In my eagerness to know more about the history of education in Kebkabiya I do not react to her story. Instead, I pose a question that has no relation to what she has told us: "Do you remember when the first schools came to Kebkabiya?"

Ah, yes, I do know. The first school opened in the place of the fort: a school for boys. A teacher from outside, called Fadlala, was asked to teach the boys. His wife was called 'Sitt al-banaat'.[16] *He taught for two years and during the third year, they built madras Ad-Dauwrateen*[17] *for boys. Then came Al-Gharbiya*[18] *for girls. Then they brought Feisal Sennari from Fasher and Rhoda Mohammed Ahmed from Dar Sabah.*[19] *Another teacher with scars on her cheeks came as well.*

"How did people react the first time these schools were established?" I prompt her:

In Kutum, they didn't want to put the children to school at first. Nevertheless, when they started to build schools here, there were already educated people around. Here they could see that educated people became employees and could help their families. Only then did they start to bring their daughters to the schools. I didn't go to school at all, just the khalwa. *If I had been to school, I'd have been something bigger than a midwife. When I went to the school of midwifery, there were no schools in Kebkabiya yet; there was only the sub-grade in Kutum. After I finished the training and I had spent two years working, then they opened the first school. First I came from my training as a midwife with the wife of Fadlala, Sitt al-banaat; she stayed a long time without children. One day, I checked her in hospital and I said she was*

---

[16] *Sitt al-banaat* means literally 'lady of the girls', which might refer to her being a teacher, or a mother of only girls.

[17] *Ad-dauwrateen* refers to 'the school with two grades'.

[18] *Al-gharibiya* refers to 'the school in the west'.

[19] *Dar Sabah* means 'land of the morning, or area in the east'. In this case it refers to Central Sudan, the seat of the national government of both the British regime and successive Sudanese governments, which is located to the east of Darfur.

expecting a baby. But the others, the medical assistants and nurses, said this was not true. But I said it was. After nine months, Fadlala's wife gave birth and they gave me a present for seeing it well.

"Did you encounter any problems when you were midwife?" I inquire, trying to get Hajja talk on possible resistance to her employment and to travelling. However, she interprets it completely differently:

You know, ya ukhti *Sa'adiya, all my family, my sisters, and my mother wept and didn't want me to go, but my father insisted: 'Even if she dies on the road', he said. And I spent three days weeping. And at school I also spent five days weeping: I didn't want to learn. And an old woman-trainer, she named me Kebkabiya, she said: 'Kebkabiya we don't want to let you go, even when you weep your eyes out. So it is better to open your eyes and learn. You can go back to your family if you have your certificate'. After a few months, they gave me a model-woman that was pregnant. They asked me to assist her in giving birth. And I cut her vagina with scissors. I got fifteen exercises with the doll. Others had to do twenty-five before finishing. Then they took me to* the tarbiyat al-atfaal, *the, how do you say, eh…natural or illegitimate children's ward.*[20] *It was a nice place. It had cupboards, like this one, and it contained a lot of scents, sweets and dates, rice and flour and clarified butter and honey. Inside, the children without Islamic fathers and poor children, whose names were listed, they could come and have breakfast there. All these things came from the British. I stayed there for three months: they took me from the midwifery-school to the ward by car. No midwife had to walk. I had to cook for the children: rice, lentils, or soup. They would bring their own bread with them. I had beds ready in case a woman wanted to give birth. My* shanta,[21] *midwife case, was there too. One day, a woman came to me and told me she wanted to give birth. She wore a white* tobe[22] *like me. She came running, calling: 'Help me, help me'. When I opened her* tobe, *I saw the head of the baby coming out. I helped her give birth. I went to telephone after her baby had come, to telephone the people in the midwifery school, to ask them to come quickly and help me. I told them about the birth and asked them to come and fetch her. When I returned we found the woman had gone*

---

[20] An orphanage. See for more details on the history of the Midwifery Training Beasley (1992), Torsvik (1983).

[21] *Shanta* refers to box or suitcase, in this case the midwifery box with all medicaments a medical midwife uses: it therefore marks Hajja's status as an officially trained, rather than a traditional, midwife. A midwifery box from that period is on display at the Sudan Archive in Durham.

[22] A white *tobe* indicates the status of a woman working for the government. It thus 'legitimated' the women to appear on the streets on their own. See also Chapter 1.

but she had left the baby behind. The midwifery-school car brought the trainer and she could not find the woman either. They checked the toilet and bathroom, in the kitchen: we could not find any trace; it was as if she had flown away. She'd just gone. After six months the baby boy had grown and crawled around because they gave him good food. The government took care of the children very well. They ate and changed their clothes three times a day and washed the sheets daily. If Miss Diggins[23] *came and found little children weeping, or dirty or hungry, and it was your turn, she would be very angry.*

Something very strange happened to me at school. You see, ya Sa'adiya, ya Karin, it really was a very strange thing. I had a birth and I was with the woman and gave her an injection. She went to the toilet. When she went, she lost the baby and afterbirth all in one sack at once. I didn't find the doctor to check this and put the things in a glass bowl. If they would have had one of those big glass pots to keep body parts and other strange things in water in, I could have shown it at the hospital and they would have given me a present for dealing with such a strange thing.

Hajja relates some more of the cases with which she assisted. They are all more or less extraordinary cases, which she handled quite accurately. When she has given some very detailed accounts of her cases, I ask her: "Did you have other kinds of problems, such as personal ones?"

Only that I didn't want to go and was weeping a lot, and the woman telling me to study. It is better indeed to have opened my eyes, stay, and learn with them so I could go back to my family with my certificate. If I had a problem with a birth, which I could not solve, I would call the doctor, and I was always right. In the midwife school, they put two colleagues together. One would help the mother in giving birth and cutting the umbilical cord and the other would tend to the baby, to bathe it, etc. Some of my colleagues were very stupid; they needed twenty-four models to practice on before knowing how to assist with a birth. You know, ya Sa'adiya, I helped in giving birth to our raïs, as-sayeedna *As-Sadiq Al-Mahdi. My friend and I, we were elected to assist our teacher: I bathed As-Saadiq while my friend took care of his mother. Then, after the* semaya, *the name-giving party that takes place after seven days, it was the grandfather of As-Sadiq, who rewarded us with many presents because the father was absent. But our trainer, ya Sa'adiya, she really got a lot of presents.*

[23] Probably her name is Dickens (see for example Beasley 1922: 26, n. 7). As in Darfur the 'k' is pronounced as gaf as in 'digging' it seems logic that this name is thus pronounced.

Every time she tells this story, Hajja recalls all the presents that her trainer received as a reward. Her detailed descriptions still amaze me: the similarities in the versions, the numbers given, and the sequence of events. This part of her life obviously is very important to her. Like his great-grandfather, the famous Mahdi (1849–1885) As-Sadiq Al-Mahdi (1936–) not only became a prominent political leader,[24] but was seen by some as an important religious leader as well. Hajja mentions his grandfather, Abderrahman Al-Mahdi explicitly, for he was the one who gave lavish donations to the midwives. Abderrahman (1885–1959) was the post-humus son of Mohammed Al-Mahdi. He became very wealthy through agricultural schemes. The wealth allowed him to organise the former followers of his great-grandfather, the Ansar, into a political movement with modern aspirations (Fluehr-Lobban et.al. 1992: 139). Hajja finishes her recollections:

In Dar Sabah, they really knew how to treat a midwife then. But here in Kebkabiya nowadays there are no things given to us.

Sa'adiya suggests: "Because people here are poor". However, Hajja reacts vehemently:

No, no, in the past they used to give us gifts or money, but now they are very greedy. In the past they gave us a sheila[25] *full of millet and sometimes they gave us the white millet,* damirga, *after it was stamped in the* funduq. *For example, I assisted Sitt Mahbuba's mother with her eight children and she gave me eight* sheila *of millet, which is 480* ratul, *and eight bottles of* karkar, *one* kora *of sandal and one bowl of* dilka, *sugar and tea. And when they cut a sheep they gave me the front leg if it was a boy, a hind leg if it was a girl.*

Sa'adiya explains to me that a front leg is mainly bones and muscles, which is symbolic for boys because they work for their family and their hands are strong. The hind leg is meat and refers to girls because when they marry they bring in money for the family.

---

[24] As-Sadiq Al-Mahdi is the current political leader of the UMMA party to which was handed over the national government when the British left on the first of January 1956. He was leading the coalition government when the current junta took over in 1989. See Chapter 2 and 8 for more details.

[25] A *sheila* is 15 *kora* = 60 *ratul.* A *ratul* is 1 lb., approximately 500 g.

And the head, Hajja adds. *It was a lot, but now they give nothing.*

I ask her how many times someone has called her to assist with a birth recently.

In this month I have had three births: one of a soldier's wife from whom I got one bottle of oil and one bar of soap; one at a merchant's from whom I got £S20; and one from whom I have received nothing up till now. I get £S200 per month from the government, and £S100 'soap money'. This is far too little. Before we would get a white tobe, a dress, and shoes from the government. Now I am happy when the soap money is paid at all.

In fact, I remember Hajja going to the government offices several times during these last weeks in order to collect her midwifery salary, but it was to no avail. "So, why did you want to become a midwife?" I ask her.

Because I told my friends that: 'I want to go to Dar Sabah so I can bring you some customs from there. Like henna, so I can make henna for you and silk for plaiting into hair, to make it long, for you'. It was a joke, but the medical assistant heard it and took it seriously. When at last we finished the training, they collected us in the school on the last day: all the midwives were on one side and my friend and I sat on the other. I was very scared. The whole world turned black. The trainers brought a paper. And my friend told me: 'Oh, Kebkabiya, we are the last on the list of midwives that is why they set us apart like this, because we are the bottom of the class'. And it turned out she was the first of the nurses and I was the first of the midwives. After they called the headmistress of the midwives to announce the names, she said the first is Hajja Bint Ishak of the midwives, of the nurses is Mundamat Ibrahim Ishak. We embraced each other in joy, we were so happy to be the first. Then a car came to fetch us to bring us to the Governor-General.

Hajja's memories take her back to the presents in kind she received for a celebration meal and the medal she received and then lost a few years ago. I know Hajja cannot read, so I ask her how she recognises her drugs:

By taste and smell: sugar and salt by taste and medicine by smell and injections by shape and colour. Commetrin, one of the injections, I would give to a woman after she had given birth and the afterbirth had come. If the bleeding didn't stop, I had to telephone the nearest doctor in Umdurman. We know about injections from our training. We would give the first injection, Commetrin, in the upper arm. And an anaesthetic injection when we were cutting the vaginal opening and stitching at the spot itself. Our medicines were always present in our medical boxes. Twelve bottles were always ready. You can keep them without medicine as well just to tell the trainers what should be in them: one of salt, one of Commetrin and one of penicillin. I spent nine months in training school. After they were convinced I did well, they sent me back to my district. I was seventeen years old when I went to be trained and I came back when I was eighteen years old, after nine months.

When I returned, at first the people didn't want a medical midwife to help at births and no one came to fetch me. And the medical assistant had a disagreement with my husband. He didn't like me to work. The medical assistant took my box and sent it to Al-Fasher because I was not working, he said. When Miss Diggins came from Khartoum to Fasher and looked in the hospital cupboard she found the box and asked, 'whose is this?' They told her it was Kebkabiya's and she said: 'Why did you take it from her, was she the first in school?' She took the box and came directly to Kebkabiya, to our house, in the afternoon. She found me in the shadow of my fence, making food covers. When I heard the sound of a car, I thought that they were the guests of my husband, because he was the head of the traders. However, when I went to the door I met Miss Diggins and Sitt Hauwwa with her. I said: 'Welcome, welcome, come in'. And when she saw my food cover, she said: 'Oh, you are clever. Because they took your box, you are making local handicraft'. She asked me to come with her to go in the car to the hospital. There we found the medical assistant and she had an argument with him. She asked him why he had taken the box. He told her that for six months Kebkabiya didn't have any work. But Ms. Diggins said: 'Even if she hasn't worked for six years, you have no right to take it. You didn't forbid local, untrained midwives to work: is she going to have to assist hens and cows?' She then went to the shartai*'s house and he told her: 'Hajja is a very nice woman. Because all my wives are breastfeeding, I didn't call on her yet for they have not been pregnant but if anyone asks for a traditional midwife, who has no box, I will put them in prison. We have now a medical midwife and that is better'. This man,* shartai *Ahmeddai, was a very good and kind man. Miss Diggins said: 'Your district is very big and one midwife is too little to cover all. We want to ask you for two local midwives to assist her'. They brought Abderahim's mother and Abdelgadir Mahmoud's grandmother. I worked for twenty-five years in Kebkabiya and only after did the new midwives come: I worked in all the Fur villages, in the hills, in the flatlands: I went there by horse, by camel or by donkey. To every village I went two or three times. After that, they brought Umm Rashida. Then Dida, they took her to Mailo. Then many midwives came.*

"Was it a difficult job?" I ask her. Once more, I wanted to see if she would come up with moral issues or gender related problems. Again, her answer goes into a different direction:

Yes, it was, especially with the circumcision. We learned to cut in the right way, upwards. Nowadays they cut to the left, sideways, that is not good. Moreover, if you cut upwards, it grows back again even without sewing. However, if you cut sideways, it needs sewing otherwise it will stay as an open wound. Most of the women in Kebkabiya were not circumcised, and now the women in the villages are still like that. Outside Kebkabiya town, they are Fur mainly and they do not circumcise their daughters, only those near the town.

Hajja continues, she gives details about how she would assist with births for a severely circumcised woman she says:

O, the Zaghawa circumcision is very bad. I don't want my granddaughter to be circumcised like that. When they circumcised me, I was twelve years old, along with my sister Fatna and my neighbour's daughter. I am still unhappy about this. Because they put us on the chaff of millet when they cut us, so the blood was sucked into it, it also scratched our skin. And there is such a pain when you urinate and we cried. Nowadays people only cut the upper part of the clitoris. Last year ustaz[26] *Feisal had his daughters circumcised and they cut the upper parts only. However,* ustaz *Mohammed said, 'my daughters are not to be circumcised as long as I live and even when I die. If someone circumcises my daughters afterwards, I will meet the person on the Day of Justice', and he is Zaghawa.*

"Do you know when people started to circumcise girls?" I ask her, as I want her to say more on the subject.

A long time ago, it started in the Sudan. But in 1970, the government called all the midwives and told us we should stop all circumcisions of girls. I was called to Al-Fasher; the man came from Khartoum. This was in 1972. He told us it was forbidden. So now, the midwives circumcise the girls secretly. But it is not the girls who are important to circumcise: only for boys it is sunna[27] *to circumcise. The Fur people don't circumcise their girls and in the past Tama did not circumcise either.*

[26] This term is used to indicate a teacher, also used as honorary for an educated man.

[27] (Taken to be) prescribed by the prophet Mohammed.

In the town they do; this habit was brought from the east, from Dar Sabah. Only Zaghawa and Arab used to circumcise their daughters.

Her granddaughter, Ishraga comes in and asks Hajja where her mother is. Hajja's daughter has gone to buy some matches and soap from the market. Hajja tells her granddaughter to change her school uniform before going anywhere else. Hajja gets up, and says: "Next time I'll tell you more". She bows in order to step through the door as she leaves. Sa'adiya goes home as well.

Context of Narration—The Present in the Past
Becoming a Midwife

The fact that on this occasion Hajja offered to tell her story surprised me at first, because of her reluctance to tell about her life as a market woman. However, during the narrative I realised that this was the story she was and had prepared to tell. I had lived on her compound for some time now, and she consented, no, offered, to tell the narrative she had in mind. By recounting her youth, Hajja could put forward two identities that seemed good to remember. That is, the ones that she considered worthy of writing down for a larger public.

To start with, she connects the 'fact' of her age to an important historical event, the defeat and death of the last of the Fur sultans, Ali Dinar. Here Faqih Sinin enters her story as the father of her eldest sister Hauwwa. The anecdote Hajja then tells about her nephews who worked for her mother asserts that her mother was married to an important and rich man, before being married to her own, poorer, father. Thus, Hajja connects herself to, and indirectly even places her 'roots' with, an important man; a sultan, Faqih Sinin, the founder of Kebkabiya who fought against the renowned Ali Dinar and who met his death in a mythical way. Hajja is a Tama, in Darfur a numerically ethnic minority who have their *dar*, ethnic area, in modern day Chad. But as founders of the town they were in Kebkabiya a socio-political majority. Although most people in Kebkabiya shared this perspective it does not fit the historical records, which suggest that the Fur, the ethnic majority in the area and in town the second largest ethnic group after the Tama, were in fact the founders of the settlement, not Faqih Sinin:

> Tayrab had a complex of buildings erected at Shoba including his own palace, a palace for his *iiya baasi*, or royal sister, and a mosque, all built

> of burnt brick. Tayrab's palace is a square construction: a series of rooms around a central courtyard embedded in a maze of stonewalls (O'Fahey 1980a: 24).

The ruins of Shoba are some four kilometres south of Kebkabiya. The Fur Sultan Tayrab (1752–1785)[28] brought his court from the volcanic mountain of Jebel Marra to the plains and was the first to use square shaped buildings. At the other side of the *wadi* Kebkabiya appeared to have served as a garrison place for the sultan's troops.[29] However, this means that the place where Kebkabiya itself is now located was a moving camp. So what might Faqih Sinin's role be as 'founder', having lived at the end of the nineteenth century?

Hajja's contemplation does not give an answer to this question. She seems unsure about the historical facts of Sinin and refers me to others, mainly his family members. Either she really does not know much about Sinin's life, or there are other reasons to pretend to be ignorant. One reason why Hajja doesn't wish to discuss Faqih Sinin extensively might be her eagerness to talk about her time as a midwife. This focus on her work as a midwife is not only evident from the number of times she refers to her training as a 'medical midwife' but also in the way she inserts reminiscences of her life as a midwife or midwife-in-training into her answers, however misplaced they sometimes seem to me. Apparently Hajja has her own agenda.

Her reference to the ownership of fields leads her briefly to consider her current situation: both the property and inheritance rules are unfair for wives. Indirectly she makes clear that these rules are the cause of her current poverty as opposed to the elevated status she has because of her ancestry.

Right at the beginning of her narrative Hajja emphasizes that in her childhood there were only *khalawi*, or *Qur'an* schools where children could receive some education. Hajja states that "If there would have been schools before, our district would have been better, it would have given us a better life". Here she explicitly and directly relates the bad living conditions of her generation as a whole to the absence of schools in her youth. Next, Hajja makes claims of extra impediments

---

[28] O'Fahey mentions a possible other date 1763–1786 (1989: 16).

[29] There are several myths around the fact that Kebkabiya comes from the Fur '*kebi kabiya*', 'lay down the shields', after the sultan came to an agreement with his contester, in one story his son, in another his neighbouring sultan whom he had intended to attack (see Preface).

for women to gain access to education. She indicates that girls were at a disadvantage when compared to boys because the girls studied for fewer hours each day and completed the *khalwa* at an earlier age. Therefore, boys could make better use of the new British school system: even the first children sent to the British school in Kutum were boys, all sons of 'tribal' leaders, except for one. This fact also has its effects on her current situation: "If they had put us girls to school we would be comfortable, not like it is now" This is in fact the prelude to her story on becoming a midwife. In the next sentence, she changes from general references, like 'us' and 'our district' to 'I'. Although I press her to finish her story about the first schools in Kebkabiya, ignoring her story, Hajja points out that the lack of schools is the basis of her current misfortune. She comments: "If I had been to school I'd have been something bigger than a midwife". This assertion is strategic. She acknowledges that there are positions for women, which are considered 'better qualified' than a midwife. At the same time, Hajja suggests that she is clever enough to be a more educated woman, like Sa'adiya or even like me, if only there had not been such a lack of girls' education in her time.

Having thus established that the position of a medical midwife was the highest position open for women of her generation, she continues her narrative about her 'fate' as a midwife. This constitutes a second phase in her argument. In this section, she tells about her training as a midwife by the British, in the capital, Umdurman. The British set up a midwifery school in Umdurman in 1921 under the supervision of Miss M. Wolff a British nursing sister who was later joined by her sister Miss G. Wolf. At first, a four-month course was organised for midwives in central Sudan. In 1930, the course was extended to eight months in order to include infant welfare and hygiene, antenatal care and home visiting (Torsvik 1983; Bayoumi 1979: 147–148; Beasly 1992: 8 n. 27).[30]

There are three events, which stand out in Hajja's recollections of her time in Umdurman. First is her homesickness. Her wish to go to Umdurman was not a result of a strong desire to become a midwife, but because of a joke. Umdurman appealed to her because all the new things came from there, like 'henna and silk for plaiting hair'. Umdurman thus was a place of plenty, of government rule, education, but also of modernity. Next, Hajja makes clear that she did well as a midwife. She was a fast learner, who was to be the top student in

[30] Until 1948, it would be the only midwifery school. It had trained 544 midwives of which 404 were in practice (Bayoumi, 1979: 148).

her class. The most memorable is when Hajja assists her teacher in attending at *As-Sadiq Al-Mahdi's* birth. This was in 1936. The date settles the debate about her age: Hajja was indeed born in 1918 or 1919, two to three years after Darfur became part of the Sudan. This made her about seventy-one or -two when I lived with her.

Attending the birth of the later Prime Minister of the postcolonial state of the Sudan (1966–1967/1986–1989) must indeed have been a unique experience, which has gained meaning in retrospect: the baby she helped into the world was only recently the Prime Minister of the Sudan. This is perhaps the reason that Hajja remembers so many details about the presents she received at that auspicious birth. It is supportive of her assertion that at that time being a trained midwife gave her status. She tells us that 'no midwife had to walk' and refers to trips in a car, a novelty at that time; only reserved for the privileged classes. Hajja's complaint that her rewards nowadays are poor; is not just a reflection on the decreased financial reward of her job, but also on the decreased social-cultural esteem of her position. Her story is therefore not just a recollection of her past experiences as a midwife, but also a claim of a social position comparable to that of the educated elite women. This is obvious when she discusses her clothing. Hajja, like other women of the educated elite, works for a government service, and therefore wears a white *tobe*. Her recollection of the woman in a white *tobe* 'like me', who came to deliver her baby and then disappeared, serves to underscore her position. Firstly, she claims commonality with the elite woman because of her dress and secondly, she claims a higher, moral, status because the elite woman gave birth to an illegitimate child on her ward.

Hajja's training as a midwife connects her to the present day educated women in other ways as well. She received an official training from the British in far-off Umdurman, the government's seat. For example, Miss Mabel Wolff, who founded the midwifery service in the Sudan in 1920, wrote in 1937 about the staff of midwives:

> We treat them as ladies and expect them to be treated as such which greatly helps them to maintain their authority and position (Torsvik 1983: 8).[31]

Umdurman was not only the place where junior officers who later became the current educated elite were educated, but also where 'la-

[31] Sudan Archive Durham 580/2, quoted in Torsvik 1983: 8.

dies' were made. Hajja's stay in the capital and the contacts that she had with the British gave her special knowledge as well as a special status. The first of these was due to her midwife training. Once back in Kebkabiya, her training set her apart from the traditional birth attendants, or '*dayat al-habil*', midwives-of-the-rope,[32] and made her an 'educated' or 'medical' midwife, who received special attention from the Principal, Misses Diggins, when she toured Darfur.[33] Further, Hajja attended many births, including those of elite women. In that respect, Hajja is instrumental in something highly appreciated in her society by all women: having children. Further, Hajja's stay in Umdurman also gave her another kind of special knowledge, which set her apart from women of her generation. The knowledge included how to use a telephone, cupboards, being driven around in cars and contact with high British officials.

In the third part of her story, Hajja tells about the difficulties she had to overcome when trying to practice as a midwife. Firstly, there was the reluctance of the local population to approach her as a medical midwife. This reluctance was due largely to the medical assistant who would not allow her to practice. Ms. Diggins resolved Hajja's predicament by intervening, causing the *shartai* to offer his help. The second problem was related to the difficulties of helping circumcised women in childbirth. This occurred despite efforts by both the government and the educated elite men she mentions, to eradicate the practice. The discussion is a complex one. Laws forbade female circumcision in 1946, but the practice continues up to the present day. There are different kinds of female circumcision. The most severe form of circumcision is the Pharaonic type, which includes infibulation and cliterodectomy; it is also the most prevalent variety. There have been several campaigns, instigated by different governments with the help of religious leaders, to inform people about the illegality, also in religious terms, of the practice. However, it is one of the main sources of income for midwives and the continuation of its practice explicitly implicates midwives (cf. Dareer 1982; Slot et. al. 1983). These facts might explain the fierceness with which Hajja condemns the practice. She visited one of the meet-

---

[32] This refers to the local practice of using a rope hanging from the ceiling to which the woman in labour can find support and sometimes for pulling the baby down to the cervix.

[33] Ms. P.M. Dickens succeeded Miss. Hills-Young in 1943 as Principal of the Midwives Training School (Beasley 1992: 8 n. 27).

ings to ban the practice in 1982. She might have been well aware of the allegations directed at midwives. Hajja's vehemence was a way by which she could make sure that we knew her stance against it.

In her narrative, then, she gives the image of herself as a sensible and composed woman. Hajja received a good training and had a good mind to do her job in the best way possible, despite the barriers put in her way. This suggests that whatever impediments to practice midwifery she now encounters, and the economic problems she has to face because of that, they are not due to her own personal qualities, but to the short-sightedness and 'stinginess' of the people around her.

In telling her story, Hajja has to overcome another hurdle as well: my questions. I obstruct her occasionally by asking questions, which seem to display an indifference towards the story, which she is relating. Further, sometimes my questions are rude because they seem to doubt her qualities and respectability as a midwife. Firstly, when I inquire, again, if she encountered any problems while practising as a midwife. She almost ignores me by directing herself to Sa'adiya and repeating her initial resistance to going to Umdurman. The second time is when I ask her how she recognises her medicines if she cannot read. She ends her answer by stating: "I spent nine months in training school. After they were convinced I did well, they sent me back to my district". In other words only after her trainers thought she was trustworthy enough to operate as an independent midwife could she return to Kebkabiya and practice. So who am I to doubt her? The third time, when I ask if it was a difficult job and Hajja explains that it was, 'especially with the circumcision'. She has practiced for over twenty-five years so who am I to judge her capacities? However, as it turned out, her position as a midwife was not the only way in which she stood out.

Wednesday—Commemorating the Day of Faqih Sinin's Death

On a Wednesday, at the beginning of Ramadan, I walk with Hajja to the government offices. During Ramadan, some tea women have started to sell tea and food again. After sunset, together with food sellers, the women sit along the main road of town, in order to provide *fatuur* for fasting travellers and lorry drivers. Hajja had planned to go and sell food as well, but now the government has decided that women are not allowed to sell in the streets after dark. There has been a 'clean-

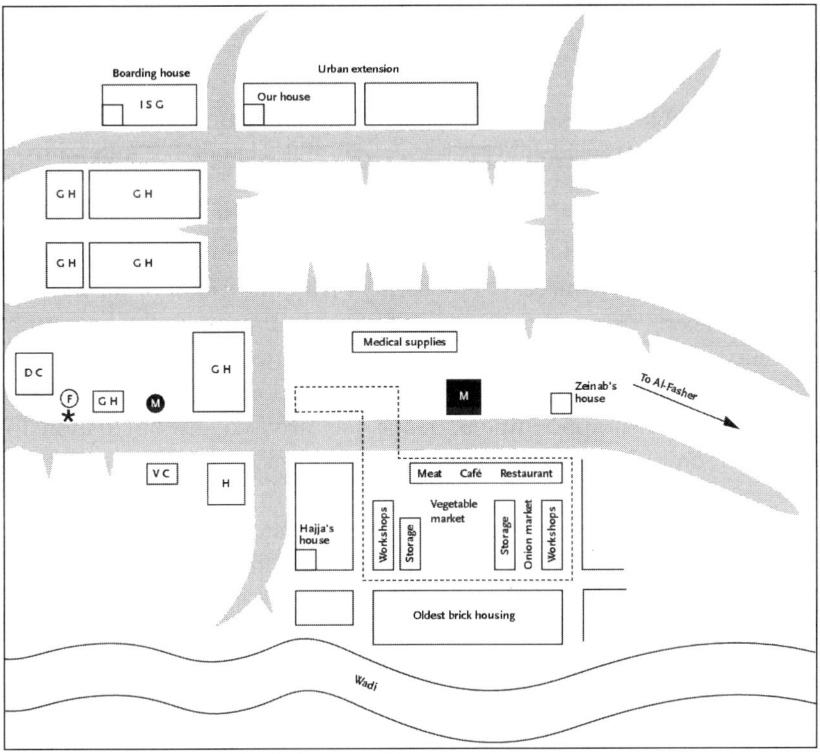

Map 3. Hajja at Faqih Sinin's burial mound

ing campaign'.[34] Soldiers and police rounded up the tea women from their location just outside town near the government offices, where most lorries stop for the night. Hajja goes to complain officially at the government offices. She argues that "As an old woman who has to take care of her household with two young women they should give me the benefit of the doubt". Ramadan supplies an extra source of income for women. They can sell food as well as the more expensive delicacies, which people only eat during Ramadan. Hajja mutters that an old woman like herself surely does not intend to be on the streets for any other reason than selling food. "Otherwise I will have to allow my daughters to work", she says as we approach the government offices. Just before we enter the southwest entrance of the *majlis*,

[34] Rounding up women is referred to with *kasha*, which has earned this policy the name of *kasha* politics (See Chapter 1).

the compound of the government offices, Hajja halts a moment with her hands raised as if she is reading the *Qur'an*; this is the habitual way of commemorating a deceased person. I ask her why she does this. Hajja indicates a place we have just passed; it lies about fifty meters east of the government offices. I look. All that I can see is a dead tree, which marks what looks like a pile of stones. A low wall of small rocks surrounds the mound. "Faqih Sinin's gubba" is all Hajja says, as we enter the courtyard of the offices.

The visit is not a success. The *mudir al-idari*, the Head of the District Council keeps us waiting for a considerable time. Finally, he simply announces that no women have permission to sell after dark. Our pleading is to no avail. We return home, disappointed and frustrated.

Despite our disappointment, Hajja has aroused my fascination by her mention of Faqih Sinin, who has made intermittent appearances in Hajja's conversations. Other elderly people have spoken of Faqih Sinin as well and at Hajja's suggestion I had consulted some of the people she recommended last time. However, I would like to know how Hajja herself feels about him. It is to no avail, Hajja evades my questions. Then, on a subsequent Wednesday morning, Hajja asks me whether I want to go with her to the *gubba* of Faqih Sinin as it is Wednesday today, the appropriate day of commemorating his death. She takes a small bag of dried dates and I add a bag of sweets. Using these as gifts, Hajja hands them out to everyone we meet on our way to the grave. When we reach the opening in the low wall, which surrounds the sandy area around the grave we remove our shoes. Barefoot, we slowly approach the mound of stones, while Hajja recites some prayers. Later she tells me she has asked for luck for my project and health for my family and the children to come. When we are near the grave, I see that a wall of only two rows of small stones surrounds it. On the rim of the wall Hajja places the remaining dates and then kneels to pray to Faqih Sinin and to his daughter Fatna, who lies buried next to him. Then she takes a hand full of sand. She places this in the empty date-bag and gives it to me: "It is for healing", Hajja whispers.

The visit at the *gubba* seems to have triggered Hajja's memories of her illustrious forebear. It is as if the physical experience of visiting Faqih Sinin's tomb has reminded Hajja of her identity as a remote descendant of this local saint. That same afternoon, Hajja has brought the dried millet stalks from her field to the compound from which she is going to erect a *rakuba*, a sun-and-windshield, for me. Having completed this task, she enters my *gutiya*, where Sa'adiya and I are chatting. Hajja asks me if I have my tape recorder ready. She sits once more in the modern chair. She composes herself, as if she is the queen mother. Without interference from Sa'adiya or me, she commences once more giving the formal information about herself, which lends her narrative an almost regal atmosphere:

My name is Hajja Ishak. I am from Tama tribe, and I think I am 61 years old. Both my grandmothers and grandfathers were born in Kebkabiya. My husband was Abu Feisal, he was born in Kutum and was Tunjurawi. He came with his family to Kebkabiya in the 1940s. I was his third wife. He married six times altogether and divorced three times. I had Nura and Semira with him, 19 and 25 years old now.

I was born in hei Urdi, the village just outside Kebkabiya: now it is hei as-suq januub. *All my family and all the relatives of Faqih Sinin are living in this quarter. This is the oldest segment in Kebkabiya. Then follows* hei as-shartai. *The* shartai *and his family and followers came from Ma'alaga about sixty years ago at the time of sultan Abdul Shaafi Sinin, son of Faqih Sinin.*

Before that time, Sultan Ali Dinar was in Fasher. The Khalifa[35] *sent Ali from Umdurman to Al-Fasher and Faqih Sinin to Kebkabiya. After seven years, Ali Dinar decided to fight Faqih Sinin. He told Sinin to give him his* nahaas, *his copper drum. Sinin refused saying, 'The Khalifa gave it to me'. Then the fight started. Up until that time Sinin and Ali had been friends. But Ali was jealous because all the tribes came to live with Faqih Sinin. First Ali sent some* khafirs.[36] *Then he sent Mahmoud, who was head of the army at that time, with many soldiers. Faqih Sinin conquered them and they fled back to Fasher. Twice after this, Ali Dinar sent armies. After many attempts, they shot Faqih Sinin inside Kebkabiya. Faqih Sinin had predicted his own death at* yoom al-arba, *(Wednesday). He prepared himself with a praying-mat, sword, and gun. Then he went to the place that would be his grave. He spread his mat and laid out his things and said: 'This will be my grave'. He waited for his assassins, there, at the place where now his* gubba, *burial mound, is.*

Hajja turns to Sa'adiya and asks her to explain this part of the history to me. Even though I assure both of them that I can follow most of it as the details have been subject to some of the written work on the history of Darfur, Sa'adiya stops the tape recorder. She explains to me

[35] 'Successor' or 'deputy' (Arab.), in Sudan more specifically used for Abdallah Al-Ta'ishi, the political successor of Al-Mahdi. Al-Mahdi died shortly after founding the *Mahdiyya*.

[36] *Khafir*, guard: in this case referring to the low status of the army.

that when Ali Dinar escaped from the hands of the Khalifa, the leader of the *Mahdiyya*, he returned from Umdurman to Al-Fasher, where he became sultan of Darfur. Faqih Sinin was still in charge of Kebkabiya for the Khalifa. Ali Dinar therefore considered Faqih Sinin an enemy and this is why Ali Dinar sent the famous army leader Mahmoud to defeat Sinin. I nod to show that also this is familiar to me. Hajja listens approvingly. I should get her narrative right she tells Sa'adiya. Sa'adiya puts the recorder on again and Hajja continues:

After they had killed Faqih Sinin, his assassins wanted to cut his throat so that they could take his head to Fasher. Fatna Sinin, Sinin's daughter, killed seven men trying to prevent them. Then the army took the family to Fasher's court. The family were presented to Ali and then he asked: 'Who is the woman that killed seven men?' He said to his women: 'Go and prepare this woman to be my wife, so I will have from her a son that will be as courageous as her'. Fatna answered: 'My father said that your army is one of women. How can I marry a woman?' Ali replied: 'Take Sinin's family and put scars on their cheeks'. My mother, grandfathers and grandmothers were all cut while they exclaimed: 'Dieng iyang shendi[37]' *[a very bad curse in Fur, Sa'adiya remarks]. Nevertheless, Ali didn't treat my family badly. He said: 'Faqih Sinin's family was not tired when their father was still alive and I don't want to give them hard work'. Ali arranged a separate place for them to live in. He gave them sugar, flour, oil, clarified butter, and honey. Every week he killed a sheep for them. He gave them okra as well. All things he gave freely. If someone was pregnant, he gave many perfumes to her husband. When my mother was pregnant, he gave my father many things. There was so much to carry that his brother had to assist him even to bring it to their house. With the sandalwood, he could assist in three births: my now dead brother, my sister and mine. He gave also* suratiya, mahlabiya, majmu', grunfur, mahlab *as well.*[38] *My mother told me that after Ali Dinar killed her husband, he married her to my father. He did not treat us badly. Ali Dinar also married people to each other.*[39]

After the British came and threatened Ali Dinar, he ran to Kalukitting with his army. Faqih Sinin's son, Abdul Shaafi Sinin said: 'I don't want to join the enemy of my father'. Therefore, he defected from Ali Dinar's army. The British killed Ali Dinar and then they returned to Fasher. They asked Abdul Shaafi: 'What is

---

[37] 'Your mothers genitals' (curse in Fur).

[38] Scents, oil and spices in order to prepare the local perfume, scrub and incense sticks, and henna indispensable at every major ritual such as circumcision, weddings, and births.

[39] Hajja refers here to the wedding payments (dowry, bride price, wedding party).

your name?' He told them and they asked him: 'Are you Faqih Sinin's son?' He replied: 'Yes'. The British opened Ali Dinar's house and gave Abdul Shaafi Sinin the nahas. *They asked him: 'You know your father's copper drum?' He said: 'Yes'. They returned it to him and gave him money as well, and he put it on camels to Kebkabiya. The British told him: 'You can stay in the place of your father'. After that, the* shartai *of the Fur,* shartai *Ahmeddai, the father of the current* shartai, *Adam Bosh, and the* shartai *of Tama, Ishak came to Kebkabiya. Ishak came from Chad alone with his family and about twenty-five servants.*

After that, they made one mahkama, *local court, in Kebkabiya. Shartai Ahmeddai became the head of the court. Abdelshaafi refused to become a member of the court. Shartai Ahmeddai said: 'You don't need to hit your copper drums here'. So Abdelshaafi answered: 'If I can't hit my drums here I'll go back to Al-Fasher'. Abdelshaafi was angry and went to Fasher. Since then, it is quiet here, because after this they did not fight any more. Now there is a family relation which made fighting difficult: shartai Ahmeddai married the sister of Abdelshaafi.*

The most important leaders at that time were from the different tribes, first of all there was shartai *Ahmeddai; then the Deputy, sultan Ishak of Tama; the third was melik Abdullai Ab Shook, of Fur; the fourth was* omda *Abdullai Rifa, also Fur. Now Adam Bosh, the* shartai *of Fur is still the first. Then follows Sultan Mohammed Ishak of Tama. These two are in charge of the local* mahkama-*office. The other tribes are members of the local court. From Gimr, Adam Ibrahiim Mansour is responsible for them. For Zaghawa, it is sheikh Hassan Shemassie. For the Korabaat, it is sheikh Abderrahim Yussuf and for the Tunjur, it is* faqih *Abakr Dugush, he is now the imam of the big mosque near the market, instead of faqih Atim, who is too old and blind now. The Arab Ereigat have* omda *Abdel Baagi and the Arab Mahariya sheikh Abdel Aziz to represent them. The people arranged this because the first tribes that settled in Kebkabiya town were Tama: in Kebkabiya district, most of the villages were Fur. In the town, after Tama came Fur, Zaghawa, Tunjur, and Korabaat. Arabs were moving all the time and they settled only recently in* hei ash-shaati. *The tribes settled in that part of Kebkabiya, from which direction they came.*

I am bemused again. There are so many names. However, it is clear to me that all of the ethnic groups that have settled in Kebkabiya since the fight between Faqih Sinin and Ali Dinar have a position according to the date of arrival. *Shartai* Adam Bosh is the son of the first *shartai* who was installed as head of the local administration. Mohammed Ishak is the son of the first Tama leader who settled in Kebkabiya after the death of Faqih Sinin, also a Tama. Mohammed Ishak is Deputy and this means that both the Fur and the Tama are still important local groups in Kebkabiya local administration. All the other 'tribes' only had representatives at the local court, which is the central institution for dealing with local administration. I ask Hajja whether this court was the first office in Kebkabiya. Hajja uses her fingers whilst counting them off:

The first office was Abdelshaafi's and shartai *Ahmeddai's. After Ahmeddai died his sons replaced him. And after the British, we went from About to Ashari, As-Saadiq, Nimeiri, Swahar ad-Dahab and Omar Al-Bashir who was the last.*[40] *All these governments made councils and offices here in Kebkabiya as well. The first office was in at-Tabiya,*[41] *the fort, where the big council is now. This was in About's time, in approximately 1957. The government would pay the salary to the government officials from there: someone came from Al-Fasher with the money. Now Omar Al-Bashir said that people must collect the money for the government officials in Kebkabiya, from the town and villages in their own district. The Rural Council is also new. They built new stores and offices inside Kebkabiya as well.*

"Do you remember anything about the first officers?" I ask Hajja.

The first employee was As-Sadiq As-Sennaari. First the people called the officers zabit, *like military officers, but now they are called* mudir al-idari, *District Commissioner.* Shartai *Ahmeddai had two guards. If someone caused problems, the guard would bring him to the* shartai. *Now nobody asks anything. The guards are lazy. You will be sent a paper if you caused a problem. It will ask you to go to the court without someone to force you to go.*

I feel it is a silly question, objectifying and distancing. However, Hajja is not disturbed. She knows all the names, the sequence of government offices that were opened and when, from prison to hospital, from bank to project offices. To Hajja it is simply an introduction to what she wants me to hear:

---

[40] These are the names of the consecutive national leaders after Independence, including the current military Islamist regime under Omar Al-Bashir. Some of these presidents were elected democratically; some came to power by a coup. See for example Harir, Sharif, Kjell Hødnebø and Terje Tvedt. (1994: 259–274); Woodward (1990). See also Chapter 1.

[41] Allegedly built by sultan Zubayr Pasha, sultan during the short-lived Turkiyya in Darfur (1874–1883). (Personal communication Shartai Ahmeddai, the head of the local 'tribal court' and paramount leader of the Fur in Kebkabiya area).

After the people came from Dar Sabah, so did a great many offices, also schools and other things. Life changed. Poor and rich are equals now: everybody can wear any dress they want. In the past only the rich wore expensive tobes *because of their prices. The rich were those who owned many cattle or camels or who had a shop or a big farm or garden. At that time, these people were rich. In the past people used to grow crops like millet, simple things. Oranges came only recently from Jebel Marra. Food customs have since changed—the dishes have changed. When Feisal was circumcised, his father slaughtered two bulls. We made meat and* asida *and* mullah, *all meals* asida *with* mullah *and sometimes* kisra. *Now you eat new dishes at parties. The new dishes are* warda, gimeh, *and* sijuk. *All of the things you could make, they came with the new products that came from the East.*

I am curious. Local dishes are therefore not local at all. So I ask her: "How did people get these new products?"

From the market, the traders brought the new products and foods. You could buy things in the market. Later they were available in the shops too. The first market was located in the area between the police station and north of hei as-shartai. *In Abdelshaafi's time when he quarrelled with* shartai *Ahmeddai, then the market was very big, but there were no shops at that time. Merchants sold using homemade shelters to protect themselves from the sun. They sold clarified butter, okra powder, milk, tomato powder, but there was no oil at that time. Everybody used the clarified butter from his or her cows. There was honey, but no sugar and no tea in Sinin's time. After Sultan Ali came, tea became available. Faqih Sinin drank coffee and he gave sugar to women if they came to visit him, to eat it with kisra. However, the shape of the sugar was different, and I found square sugar, the small cubes. It came from east and west, from* Abesher *and* Dar Sabah.[42]

In shartai Ahmeddai's time, the market moved from its first place to the big square, hei al-medaan, *which is now an empty square. The new place for the* suq *was during Mr. Moore's time. Moore planned the whole market himself. The British moved the market from the north side to its current place. The one who planned the market was called Mister Charles. The land for building on in this part of Kebkabiya was given by the British government. They said: 'Every merchant who has a shop, can have the land behind it'. My father was a merchant in the market. He even bought some of his land from other merchants.*

---

42 Abesher in nowadays Chad; Dar Sabah is the local term for the Nile Valley to the east.

The first people who opened a shop in Darfur were from the Fur tribe. That was Abu Feisal Mohammed and Abu Ashia.[43] *My husband, Abu Feisal was the first man to build a shop. Then Mohammed Ali Saleh, Mahmoud Ahmed, Mohammed Hassaballah, then Abdallah Hussein and my uncle, but he died a long time ago. Merchants sold* zaraag, firka, *and black crepe. Then* grunfur, mahlabiya, suratiya, *and* bitt as-Sudan.[44] *The first shop was built about fifty years ago with bricks of mud. My husband repaired it again when it became old. Mr. Moore planned the market and gave places to the people: if a man had money he would build a shop, if not a* 'kurnuk', *a building of mud and* ghassab, *millet stalks, or from zinc, corrugated iron. In Moore's time, the plots were free: those are the shops built west of the current market. The more recent shops are built on the eastern side of the market.*

The market started to grow when it moved to its current place. Some of the market planning was done in British time, some of it by the Sudanese government. Mr. Charles was the British engineer who planned the town for Mr. Moore. He laid down streets, the market, houses etc. The market grew because villagers, mainly Fur, sold their cows and came to buy a shop inside town. Some Arabs sold their camels and bought shops; and later Zaghawa with cows and camels sold some of them and bought shops. About fifteen years ago many of the new shops and kiosks were planned and sold by the Sudanese government. The price of one plot for a shop was £S55, which had to be paid to the government. Idris Juruf bought two of them. Abderrahman bought two, Hajj az-Zein three. The Sudanese government sold one plot of land for a shop for £S55 and you could build a zinci[45] *yourself.*

At that time, the rais as-suq, *the head of the market, was Abu Feisal, my husband. His task was to collect taxes from the other merchants for the government. There were taxes according to your income or property. The government told him that on fixed months they would come and collect the taxes, so he had to inform the merchants, and they would give their money to Abu Feisal. He prepared a list with names and taxes. He warned all the merchants about the time the government would come, took the list, and would gather the money from them. Sometimes the government would give him a small sum of money but he did not receive a formal salary. The* rais as-suq *was then Abu Feisal, but now it is Shumein and his assistant is Hassan Yunis. They also checked if people had their certificates to sell at*

---

[43] Abu Helima is the brother-in-law Hajja had spoken of earlier. She worked for her sister and sold *semen*, clarified butter, for him.

[44] *Zaraag* from *zarga*, blue, locally woven rough cotton cloth died blue, often used in local female dress; *firka*, special cloth for marriage and giving birth; *grunfur*, cloves; *mahlabiya* & *suratiya*, oils and liquids used for painting henna; *bitt as-Sudan*, lit. 'Daughter of the Sudan', a brand of eau de cologne.

[45] Shops with a roof of corrugated iron.

the market. They divided the subsidised goods amongst the merchants when it came from the government.

In the past there was not much money going round and we had the small coins like asharay *and* meliin. *Items were sold for these small pieces of money. There in the market the people weighed with ratul and half a* ratul, *not with kilos. They changed the coins into paper money not so long ago. This was in About's time. There were many markets outside Kebkabiya.*

Her reflection on the history of the town is intriguing. Nevertheless, I am eager to know more about her feelings on marketing. So I attempt a detour: "Were the markets at that time better than now?"

Life now is better, but before life was easy and cheap. The development now is good, but the past is the best. In the past, you would have one or two tobe*s and it was enough. Girls, if they had one or two dresses that was enough. Now they have six, seven and more pieces like skirts and blouses. In the past, in our country there were no skirts and blouses. The little girls had* zaraag *and leather aprons. Recently women have started to wear* tobe*s.*[46] *Twenty-five years ago, this fashion reached our area. I went to the midwifery school when I was seventeen years old. When I came back I was married to Abu Feisal and stayed with him for fifteen years. After that, the new* tobes *reached our area. The first man who brought* tobe*s from Al-Fasher was Abu Feisal, my husband. It was 'Bitt-al-Basha'*[47] *he took them from a British trader in Al-Fasher. We wore* tobe*s for the first time at Feisal's circumcision. The first woman who wore a* tobe *here in Kebkabiya was the District Commissioner's wife, the* zabit *of Kebkabiya. He came from Al-Fasher, sent by the government. The rich people bought the tobes. Other tobes were called* dawalib,[48] *people would say:* 'Al-gadir al-shilu, yashiilu, wa al ma gadir, yashiilu yighali fil dawalibu, (*if you can buy it wear it, if you can't, keep it in your cupboard*)'.

Eating habits changed too. Men and women did not eat together in the past; they didn't even drink tea together. You could not eat even with your husband, father, or brother. The first new food was addis, *then beans.* Addis, *lentils, came from the east, rice and white flour. The new goods, (the ones) we have now appeared in the market in Nimeiri's time. This is because people are free to trade on the market now. After the British left, our Head was About, but before him it was Ismael Al-Ashari. After About, Nimeiri took over power.*

---

46 The plural of *tobe* is *tawabih*, but I will use her an English plural for clarity.

47 'Daughter of the Pasha' (Egyptian officer) after the first elite women who wore this kind of veil in Darfur.

48 Plural of *dawla*, cupboard (Arab.).

In addition, the British government started to take taxes from people, from the farmers and the merchants. Now they take it from the people as well and divide it amongst the poor people. They said to the merchants: you can come and swear how much money you have, so you will tell the truth. They would take the zakat *after that and give it to the poor. They took the money and gave it first to the government. Now the government takes the tax from everything, even tomatoes per box, you have to pay. Millet, onions, everything is taxed. Houses are taxed every year. The government takes. They take per number of rooms or huts per compound. They take it from the head of the household. This is because the government wants to take their salary from this. The money is for the guards, midwives, and other employee's salaries.*

Hajja's detailed descriptions of these changes in lifestyle and the introduction of a money economy transfix me. I want her to continue so I ask her: "Did the government collect taxes from crops as well?"

Yes, they also took ardab[49] *from crops. They would measure the field and say: 'This field can have so many sacks'. If you did not get enough, you still had to pay them the estimated amounts. My father told me this. When I was growing up, they only took from shops; they did not take from fields anymore. In Mr. Moore's time, the government also took money. They started to take money for things in the British time. Shartai Ahmeddai was here before Mr. Moore.*

In the past the new things were bought first by the rich people only. There was gimeh, *wheat flour.*[50] *There were no mills, people ground wheat and millet with stones, by hand. Wheat became the common food for everyone when the people brought pumps and started to grow the food themselves locally. So it became plenty in the market, everybody can buy it. This started about fifteen years ago. In the past, the people used to eat* asida *for breakfast everyday. If you had guests you would make* asida *and* gurasa, ligemaat, *meat and make* madida jir *with milk from the Baggara and* ajiina zarga.[51] *This was if you were rich. The husband would divide the house into separate parts: for women, for men, and for guests. They built low walls between the sections. The first who built a brick house was my husband. After him came Mohammed Ali Salim, Mahmoud Ahmed, and Ibrahiim Azrag, Bolo. They were all traders. They wanted to build because they were rich traders*

---

[49] See for example Kapteijns (1985a: 228–229): it refers to the measure of grain that would be collected as tax. 1 *ardab* is about 190 kilos.

[50] Wheat was grown on the slopes of Jebel Marra as special food for the sultan and his court.

[51] *Gurasa,* thick pancakes; *ligemaat,* fried biscuits; *madida jir,* thick drink of fine white powdery millet with sugar and milk; *ajiina zarga, a* lumpy drink of milk, sugar and bits of sorghum.

and wanted to live nicely. The first man to make bricks was my husband, Abu Feisal. He was the first agent and built the boys intermediate school in Kebkabiya and the primary school in Berkaseira, paid for by the government.

I ask Hajja about the reason for the compound walls. I am expecting that she will discuss the protection of privacy, but she says:

What did you say, why do people first build walls? It keeps the animals outside, and if you have money you can build a good wall and you do not need to repair it as often as a wall made of stalks. There were wolves at that time and one of them once killed one of our bulls.

There were also women at the market selling salt, powdered okra, milk, and kisra. *They had everything: clarified butter, powdered tomatoes, food covers. They were mainly Korobaat. Men also sold powdered okra and spices, but this was from their shops. The most important tradeswoman was Hauwa Umm Shulugh.*[52] *She made cheese, powdered okra, powdered tomatoes, powdered peppers. She did not sit in the market: she sold from her own house. Now most of the women who are selling at the market and who are living near the market place are Tama. Most of the tribes are selling at the market, but most of them are Tama. Fur came on market day and would sell and then go back to their villages: only recently have they come to stay in town. The* shartai's *wives did not go to the market either to sell or buy. Because their husband was the* shartai *and he would not allow them to go. My father also forbade my family and me to go to the market. Even now there are women who still do not want to go to the market.*

"So you did not sell at the market before your marriage?" I ask Hajja. I want her to continue on this potentially moral issue without directing her thoughts too much:

No we didn't go to the market. Our father did not want us to go the market. When I went to help my sister in her house, I went to the market to buy semen, *clarified butter, for her husband, Abu Haliima. I bought clarified butter. If I filled five tins, he would give me five* piasters. *And sometimes I also prepared my own tins and gave it to Abu Ashia…*

"Yusuf Azrag?" Sa'adiya interrupts. Hajja nods and almost without a pause goes on:

---

[52] Later we learn that this is her eldest sister, the daughter of Faqih Sinin, and her mother.

...So he could sell it in Fasher. With the money he gave me, I bought my own clarified butter and sold it again. At every market day, I bought five tins of clarified butter for my brother-in-law. He gave me five piasters for it. Next market he gave it to me again and again. Until the time came when clarified butter was scarce in the market. Then I would come with mine and give it to my brother-in-law to sell it in Fasher. From that money, I bought gold for my daughters recently. I didn't like to go to the market and I didn't always go. I just wanted to help my brother-in-law. But most of the time I stayed at home to help my sister Hauwa in cooking, cleaning and helping her. She had many children and there were always a lot of guests as well. She had ten children. Seventeen months after every child she became pregnant again. Because women used to breastfeed twenty-four or even thirty months and did not become pregnant, people thought my sister was giving birth too quickly. After I had grown up, my father wanted to have me back in the house because he wanted to keep an eye on me himself. So he gave her my little sister to help her.

"So you were not among the first to sell at the market?" I was trying to manoeuvre Hajja back to the subject of the market women:

The first merchants in town were Jellaba...[53]

Hajja starts, but Sa'adiya interrupts her: "The first women, Karin means".

Aah, the first woman who sat in the market was Khadija Um Buluul. She sold zaf, *palm leaves, powdered pepper and tomatoes, spices. She was Korabaat. The second was my sister, Hauwa Umm Shulugh; she sold from her house. In her time there were no women making tea at the market, only men with café's. There were no restaurants in that time; they only recently started to make food in restaurants. Women sold* kisra *and curdled milk in the past, some still do now.*

Sa'adiya turns to me and explains that there were not many cars or buses at that time. Just the one which went up and down between Fasher and Geneina: "So there were not as many customers as there are now", she finishes and I ask Sa'adiya: "So women were not making tea then?" Hajja responds:

[53] *Jellaba* were small-scale private traders travelling around selling their ware. Originally the term was used for Arab merchants from the riverain groups like the Ja'aliyin and Danagla. In Darfur this term is used to denote all traders and businessmen who come from outside Darfur, mainly Central and East Sudan (Fluehr-Lobban et.al. 1992: 92–93; Kapteijns 1986: 41; 282; Kapteijns & Spaulding 1988: 175; O'Fahey 1980a).

Women started making tea seven or eight years ago. The first woman making tea was Hauwa Al-Fadl from the Birgid tribe. Then women from all the tribes started to make tea: Arab, Zaghawa, and Fur. Most of them now are Arab and Zaghawa. They were making tea, because they did not have money and they needed it badly, because of the drought. The first woman, who made tea, did so after her husband died. She stayed four months inside the house: nobody was looking after her so she started with making tea. Her husband died twenty years ago. First her brother-in-law and sons were looking after her, but when they grew up and had their own families to take care of they reduced their help to her. She made tea during three months and then other women followed her example. Zamzam, my co-wife's daughter, and her sister were not making tea at that time: their mother sold onions, dried okra, and tomatoes. Only later she did make tea. After the government stopped the women making tea, they went and complained to the leaders in the government: 'There is no family, money, people looking after us, what can we do', they said. But the men said, 'No, no, in Islam we have no room for this. You have to stop, so you stop'.

Hajja is very mild in her comments about women who make tea. She connects the predominance of Zaghawa and Arab women among the tea women to the drought and their resulting poverty. When I askher about this action of the government, I expect her to be as critical about them as when she went to the government offices to ask for a permit for selling during Ramadan. Instead she says:

It is good, wallahi, *because the* shari'a *said there is no need for the women to make tea. Some are now without work. They can go and make bricks near the* wadi.

Her answer surprises me. She had attempted to obtain a license to sell food during Ramadan herself. In addition, Zamzam, her co-wife's daughter who often visits her compound, was selling tea before the government forbade it. I had expected she would be quite critical of the government's view on women selling tea. Just to make sure I have understood her correctly I ask again: "Do you think it is shameful to sit in the market?"

Yes, in the past it was, but now everyone can sit in the market. Only the rich families would not go. Nowadays all people work: women work and men work in the offices, in the market, all the people are working together, mixed. Making tea is not good. Tea gives a lot of money, but the government has forbidden it.

"So why didn't people make tea in the past?" I urge her to continue on the subject:

Because tea is the 'mother of crime (Umm Kabayr)*': men come and sit around the women and that is not good in Islam. The girls' father or husband or brother does not agree with it.*

Not understanding if with 'the girls' she means girls in general or her own daughters, I ask her: "What about your daughters?"

No, no, no. I do not want my daughters to make tea in the market. Their uncles and I do not agree with this. Now I am selling things, others come and buy from me so I will have some profit. For example if I bought one pound of powdered okra and I want profit, and others come to buy it I will sell for £S22. Selling at the market is better than sitting in the house. If you sell onions and you have bought them, if you do not sell all of them, you can use the rest for yourself in your own house.

I remembered a comment made by one of the teachers to whom I spoke on the subject of women making tea. He had mentioned that only women from Kobé, a subdivision of the Zaghawa were making tea. To test this view I ask Hajja: "What about Kobé and making tea?"

Kobé and Bideiyat and Arabs do, but I don't know why.

In other words, although she does mention all recently arrived nomadic groups in one go, she does not see a relation between ethnic background and 'bad conduct' As I would like to know if Hajja sees a difference in the lifestyle of tea women and herself I ask her: "What do you think women do with the money?"

If they saved money, they will buy gold and the older women go on haj *with that money. But because men all migrated to Dar Sabah to get a job and they leave their women behind without money women needed to go to work outside the house. In the past, some of the men were not sending money or goods to their families until they returned home. Before, when a man wanted to live in Dar Sabah, he left a lot of millet and dried okra and tomatoes and some cows and goats for his family. If their clothes are old, they have to sell one bull or goat to clothe themselves. At that time, there were no lorries: they were travelling on foot to the Gezeira. They travelled for months.*

Hajja asks Sa'adiya if her husband, Ali, has already returned from his trading trip. Sa'adiya says she expects him any day: he should have been back two weeks ago. Suddenly Sa'adiya gets agitated. She has to go home because her children will be returning. Hajja also gets up from her chair. It is getting dark and she has to gather her cows from the cowboy who brings them from the *wadi* to their neighbourhood. 'Maybe we can finish it some other time', Hajja says to no one in particular while we walk towards the street, and we agree to find another moment next week to do so.

Context of Narration—The Present in the Past
A Local History of Changes in Culture and Class

We listened to Hajja's second narrative several weeks after the first one. In the intervening period Sa'adiya and I had followed up on Hajja's advice. We had found out more about the history of Kebkabiya, particularly the role of Faqih Sinin. Previously, Hajja was reluctant and had said she did not know much of Faqih Sinin. However, at the beginning of our second session, she refers to him quite extensively. It appeared that she felt the need to give her understanding of his fight with the last Sultan of Darfur, Ali Dinar. The fight, which made her mother both a widow and a captive of Ali Dinar.

Hajja's stepfather, Faqih Sinin, and his son Abdelshaafi belonged to the so-called sultanic elite of Kebkabiya. People saw him as a holy man and a just ruler. According to the records, Sinin was not a real sultan as he belonged to the military and administrative structure of the *Mahdiyya (1885–1898)*, the first Islamic State of the Sudan established by Mohammed Al-Mahdi. However, the community still revered him as both a sultan and a religious leader. It took Mohammed Al-Mahdi and his followers four years to recapture the Sudan from its occupiers, the Egyptians. During that period and after the Mahdi's death in 1885 his successor the *Khalifa* Abdullahi Al-Ta'aishi posted *Mahdist* followers, or *amirs*, at important places all over the captured area. In 1888 Faqih Sinin was appointed *amir* of Kebkabiya by Osman Jano the Mahdist army leader who organised a punitive expedition to Dar Tama,[54] which

[54] The 'Abu Gumeiza' uprising against the Khalifa was staged from Dar Tama, now in Chad. Faqih Sinin was preceded by another *amir*, or sub-governor, Adam Amer, who stood under the leadership of *amir* Zojal in Al-Fasher, both keeping Northern Darfur for

lies to the west of Kebkabiya. Sinin had been settled there for 10 years by 1898. This was the time when Ali Dinar escaped the *Khalifa's* hands. Once he was back in Al-Fasher, Ali Dinar proclaimed himself the new Fur sultan. The ensuing fight between Ali Dinar and Faqih Sinin therefore was not just a local squabble between old friends, but was instigated by more national political and military conflicts (Kapteijns 1982a: 175; Kapteijns and Spaulding 1988: 251–253; Theobald 1965: 36, 75–77).

The Mahdi preached both a purification and unification of Islamic practices and dogmas; therefore he demanded a pious attitude from his followers and particularly from his *amirs*. As a result, Faqih Sinin combined military, administrative and religious powers in one person. As Hajja had told us: the people in Kebkabiya perceived Faqih Sinin as a blessing, but the last sultan of the Fur, Ali Dinar saw him as a threat. To Ali Dinar, Faqih Sinin barred the way to the west, where the sultanates of Wadai and Masalit and the French colonists were located, in what is modern day Chad.[55] Ali Dinar had tried to defeat Faqih Sinin since 1902 but,

> ...it was not till the end of 1908 that this gallant old man's defences were broken down, and his head sent to the Sultan (Lampen, 1950: 34).

As Hajja told us, it took Dinar seven years[56] and considerable effort to achieve his aim of removing Faqih Sinin (Kapteijns 1985: 176; Kap-

the Mahdiyya (Lampen 1950: 22; Durham 731/2/25). Sinin was occasionally referred to as al-Mek, from *mellik*, literally king (Arab.), in Darfur also used to indicate the leader of nomadic groups, comparable to *shartai* (Durham 616/13/41; Kapteijns 1985a: 175–176; Lampen 1950: 22).

[55] In 1908, for example, the French claimed Dar Tama and Dar Masalit as part of Wadai, the part of nowadays Chad they occupied, and tried to build up friendly ties wit Dar Gimr, all Sultanates to the west of Darfur. In 1910 Ali Dinar in concert with Sultan Dud Murra of Wadai and Sultan Taj el-Din of the Masalit invaded Dar Gimr and Dar Tama, driving away the French allies and installing their own puppets. This again led to repercussions by the French, which ended only with the First World War. In 1909 the French occupied Abesher but in 1921 roughly half of the area, which had been in the French sphere of influence since 1909 came under British influence. In 1924 a border settlement was reached with some of the captured area returned to French Chad (Kapteijns 1985a: 394 and 1985b: 57; Lampen 1950: 40–50; Durham 731/2, 35–36; Durham 616/13/48).

[56] And he thereby withstood two of Ali Dinar's best generals, Abu Feisal and Mahmoud el-Dedingawi (Lampen 1950: 43; Durham 731/2/37). The record on Faqih Sinin is scarce, however, and mainly related to his political role. There are primary sources like letters and government reports, to be found for example in the Dar Fur Province Archives which were formerly in Al-Fasher (O'Fahey has registered the files, but during my stay in Darfur, I could not locate these); in National (formerly Central) Records Office in Khartoum; in the Sudan Archive in Durham at the School of

teijns and Spaulding 1988: 124). Interestingly, as Kebkabiya existed long before Faqih Sinin settled there, I at first thought that the construction of Faqih Sinin as the founder was a way of legitimating not only the numerical majority of the Tama in Kebkabiya, but also their dominance in local affairs. Especially because Hajja's way of talking about Faqih Sinin reminded me of the coming of the 'wise stranger' who founded the Fur sultanate, Al-Maq'ur. Its myth of origin tells about Ahmad Al-Ma'qur, an Arab from North-Africa who 'brought Islam' to the court of the then ruling Keira clan around the mid-seventeenth century AD (O'Fahey 1980a: 9–10, 122)[57] and married one of the royal women—in one version a daughter, in the other a sister of the sultan. They begot Suleiman Solondungo ('the Arab' in Fur) 'the first historical ruler of the Keira dynasty and may be dated with some confidence tot the mid-seventeenth century (O'Fahey 1980a: 9)'. However, Hajja's assertion of Faqih Sinin does not necessarily need to be a myth. After talking with several elderly people and consulting reports of British administrators and other archival material and secondary literature on this period, other reasons for this local history came to the fore.

From the quotation above and diverse other sources it appears that Kebkabiya was located strategically between Al-Fasher and the western borders of the Sultanate. The continuing warring factions had either taken hostage and enslaved the local population, or forced them to be conscripted to their army. This ongoing situation left the young and able bodied with the only other option; to flee the area to escape both. Conscription was prevalent under Zubeir Pasha's rule[58] and continued under the Mahdist forces and Ali Dinar all through the nineteenth and twentieth century (O'Fahey 1974: 124–183). This was especially the case when the Ta'aishi, a Baggara clan, were commanded to join their kinsman, the *Khalifa* in Umdurman after the death of Al-Mahdi in 1855, presumably of a contagious disease like measles (Holt 158: 117–120; Warburg 2003: 43–49). Anybody who remained was in danger of

Oriental Studies; and the Arkell Papers at the School of Oriental and African Studies. For descriptions of the kind of material to be found in these archives see O'Fahey (1980a: 185–188). Secondary references as far as related to other important political figures of his time, like Osman Jano and Ali Dinar in the literature mentioned above.

[57] The myth is more complicated: Ahmad Al-Ma'qur, who some suggest came from the Maghreb, was said to have introduced more civilized traditions, like table manners. Only later the 'bringing of Islam' has been added to his arrival.

[58] Zubeir Pasha was a slave raider and trader who first settled in South Darfur. Later he set himself up as a ruler of the Turkiyya (Holt 1958: 15–27; O'Fahey 1980a: 124).

contracting contagious diseases like measles, cholera, or smallpox. Abu Gemeiza, the leader of a revolt against the *Khalifa*, died near Kebkabiya in 1888. A similar fate had afflicted the force of Osman Jano (also Gano), the Mahdist army leader who posted Faqih Sinin at Kebkabiya in the first place. The entire force fell victim to an epidemic while in this area and Jano himself died while retreating to Fasher (Bayoumi 1979: 61; Holt 1952: 132–147; Kapteijns 1985a: 48–61; Lampen 1950: 25; Theobald 1965: 25). The diseases are reputedly linked to what is called the 'great famines', which afflicted all of current North, East and West Sudan (1888–1892) (Bayoumi 1979: 45–47). The people named the famine *sana sita*, 'year six', after the Islamic year 1306 when it began. In Darfur, the community also named it *sanat Jano*, 'year of Jano', which indicates either his part in the war or his death in that year. The title testifies to the fact that the population saw the fighting and forced migration as important causes of the famine apart from locusts and cattle disease which ravaged the area at that time as well (De Waal 1989: 71–73). Another name given to the 'great famines' of 1888–1892, was *Ab Jildai*, 'Father of the Skins'. This title refers to the fact that people had recourse to eat meat from 'impure' animals, as they were not slaughtered in the Muslim way (De Waal 1989: 74). However, this does not only indicate a real practice or refer to the total absence of food, for:

> All these names are powerfully symbolic of the breakdown of society, of being outcast, solitary, or dependent: all opposites to the ideals of belonging, community, and autonomy (De Waal 1989: 74).

In other words, the names may indicate the loss of sociability, of the sense of self as part of a community in which food and the sharing of food were important means of acting out belonging. Faqih Sinin settled in Kebkabiya, which indeed had been founded long before that time. In the period that he was posted there the area had become virtually depopulated. Disease and famine threatened the survival of people who felt displaced and destitute. Not only because of hunger and illness, but also because they lost a sense of belonging. If the elderly people in Kebkabiya I spoke with differed in their recollections about Faqih Sinin's ancestry or the direction from where he came, they all agreed that he was a pious and peace loving man, who 'even attracted lions and snakes to live in peace at his side' as one of them put it. Faqih Sinin obviously is seen as the person who rendered Kebkabiya a safe place again, a place to live and belong and to feel safe, and a place recaptured from the wild and made social again. The fact that some women pointed out to me that even wild animals lived peacefully with him seems a metaphor for precisely the 'cultured' aspect of living as the 'taming or domestication of the wild'. The local narrative about Faqih Sinin as founder of Kebkabiya might thus be a re-construction of a local social history as well as a construction to account for the prominence of his ancestors in current Kebkabiyan affairs.[59]

Hajja's shift to Faqih Sinin's son, and her stepbrother, Abdelshaafi Sinin marks a shift in the history of local administration and market practices. Hajja's personal history relates to both of these via her male relatives. She is related to the administration courtesy of her mother's first husband Faqih Sinin and his son Abdelshaafi and to the change in market place and practices because of her own father and her husband, Abu Feisal. In both areas, the British, the new powerful force in Darfur had a substantial influence. After gaining control of Darfur the British either transformed, or replaced the sultanic elite into a new administrative class. At the same time, they introduced new market places, taxes, and products (Kapteijns 1985a: 228–243; Doornbos 1984: 222).

Similar to his entire family, Abdelshaafi grew up in the court of Ali Dinar in a period when the British considered Dinar an ally. This was after Dinar 'escaped' from the hands of the *Khalifa*. When Ali Dinar revived the Fur sultanate, the British interpreted this as a form of indirect rule. However, Dinar renounced allegiance to the Anglo-Egyptian Condominium during World War I. When Dinar began to show allegiance to the French, he became regarded as a liability (Fluerh-Lobban et. al. 1992: 55–56; Kapteijns 1985a: 208–243; Theobald 1965: 142–145).

In 1916, Ali Dinar died in a battle with the British at Menawhashi and Darfur became part of the Sudan. When Abdelshaafi defected from Ali Dinar's army, he received his father's drum back from the British. The *nahas*, the copper kettledrum, is part of the regalia of the sultan that is a symbol of his position of power.[60] By handing over precisely this item and at the same time bringing the Fur *shartai* from his

[59] This positive evaluation of Faqih Sinin survives, despite the fact that the famine in Kebkabiya of 1900 was called 'Sinin' named after the war between Sinin and Ali Dinar (De Waal 1989: 71–73). This is probably due to the fact that Sinin is seen as the pious victim of Dinar.

[60] O'Fahey for example states: 'The granting (or withdrawal) of one or more *nahas* was a common way to regulate and regularize relations between sultan and tributary… [T]he tributary chiefs could be granted *nahas* either in recognition of their autonomy or to mark a shift of power within a tribe (1980a: 86)'.

stronghold Mu'alaga[61] to the district capital of Kebkabiya to administer the area, the British instigated, intended or not, the quarrel between Abdelshaafi and the *shartai*.[62]It might even have been a strategy to remove a potential pretender. Although the British gave Abdelshaafi the position of power in this part of Darfur comparable to his father, he was also a religiously inspired leader whom the British still feared because of various religiously inspired uprisings, which continued to take place in Darfur in the same period.[63] The British may have believed that another 'Faqih' in power posed a threat to political stability (Ibrahim 1979: 440–471; 1980; 214–239).

Regardless of the motive, the policy of 'indirect rule' gained a new impetus. Kebkabiya became a sub-*merkaz*, with British military officers as administrators at regional level,[64] and *nazirs* and *shartai*s who worked at district level.[65] Initially there were rewards for the local leaders' services in the form of the fines, taxes and local dues they collected.[66] However, after the application of the 'Sheikhs Ordinance Act' of 1928 they received salaries. In some areas, a Native Administration[67] budget was established as a payment for taking care of minor legal cases with the power to imprison in addition to fining convicts (Lampen, 1950:

---

[61] Kapteijns (1980a) states that the name referred to 'the place of customs (56)'. And might have been, not a fixed village, but the place where the *shartai* lived at that time.

[62] The British might have been acting on alleged knowledge of local power relations. Pembroke, Governor of Darfur 1925–1928, wrote in a report of 1922 that the Fur sultans were maintaining 'a system of decentralization with the proviso that the Fur ascendancy in public affairs was to be maintained at all costs (Pembroke cited in O'Fahey, 1980a: 86–87)'. Indirect rule would take in to account these 'local state of affairs'.

[63] These uprisings are also referred to as 'Neo-Mahdism' as they took place some forty years after the death of Al-Mahdi: one of the most well-known was the 'Nyala Revolt' in 1921 as this succeeded to attract quite some followers, nearly ousted the British, and led to a more strict curbing of Mahdist revolts (Ibrahim 2004: 50–61). See for detailed accounts Ibrahim (1979, 1980); Kapteijns (1980a).

[64] With notable exceptions like Gillan in Nyala in 1917 (Lampen 1950: 44; Durham 731/2/47).

[65] In Darfur, Pembroke (1925–1828) and Dupuis (1928–1936) tried to copy the policy of 'indirect rule' as applied in Nigeria. They re-created 'Emirates' out of the 'grouping of tribes under regional courts' in order to allow for administrative districts who could support a sound budget (Lampen 1950: 45; Durham 731/2/48).

[66] '…which, as military commanders and Mandubs no longer competed for them, were probably larger than under the Sultan'. (Lampen 1950: 44; Durham 731/2/47).

[67] See for example the edited volume *Kordofan invaded* edited by Endre Stiansen and Michale Kevane (1998) in which several contributions relate to the ideology, effects and failings of Native Administration.

44; Durham 731/2/47).[68] The Fur *shartai* Ahmedai became head of the local court by appointment by the British. In Kebkabiya district, he presided over the leaders of the majority ethnic groups.[69] If Abdelshaafi had not quarrelled, he might have become a member of the tribal court for the Tama. Sultan Ishak had come from Dar Tama solely in order to represent his ethnic group in an area where they had never settled before.

Hajja's reference to the guards of the *shartai*, who are not functioning anymore, also indicates a shift: from 'native administration' to government regulation, which took place under Nimeiri (1969–1985).[70] A change in taxation rules also marks the shift. Under the *shartai*, there were taxes on fields and animals. However, British rule, as represented by Mr. Moore,[71] saw the introduction of poll tax, a tax for persons, and the hut-tax, which taxed the number of *gutiya*'s and stone built rooms on a compound. These were the first taxes in a monetary form. Consequently, wide-reaching taxation, which would pay for government employees, such as herself, resulted in the need for money among the population at large.

In other words, Hajja has experienced several changes in government structure and ruling relations. Firstly, the government structure

[68] According to Lampen in Darfur local leaders 'had long been used to punish their subjects, but only as subsidiary authorities and the Sultan's *mandub* or *magdums*... [A] Mistaken policy which taught that their authority must be upheld by never reversing their decisions, led to an orgy of fining and imprisonment, often for the vague offence of disobedience of orders. Not only were appeals often rejected out of hand, but also the last refuges of the subject, voluntary exile or revolt against his chief, were sternly corrected and repressed when possible. From 1926 tot 1928 and later in some places, the most flagrant injustice, nepotism, and selling of posts were allowed under this mistaken policy. By 1930 more sensible councils had prevailed, and tyrannical chiefs were being punished and dismissed (1950 46; Durham 731/2/49)'.

[69] Lampen comments that in this way the 'tribal chief now has his traditional administrative functions... is now a legislator and administrator on the district council and an executive of the decisions of that body. He is also the judicial authority to decide on his own acts...Apart from the physical impossibility of combining all these functions, his opposition is getting anomalous (1950: 50; Durham 731/2/53)'.

[70] See Chapter 2 for an elaboration of this change.

[71] Moore served in Darfur from 1928–1946. Curiously enough, his name has disappeared from the list of the political service, although he is mentioned in the index. Also the files with data on his assignment in Darfur, his handing over notes and monthly reports could not be traced when I studied the Darfur Archive. The only reference I found is the one by Beasly (1992: 158, n. 162: 'In Khartoum early December one year Guy Moore announced with glee that he was setting off to Kuttum by camel all the way and that his next bath would be on Boxing Day; He used to fast in Ramadan as it was so hard on the servants') and in Wilfred Thesiger's autobiographic *The life of my choice*.

has changed from sultanic rule to governmental rule, at times democratic and at times dictatorial. Secondly, the economy has altered from a barter system to a market economy. Before, salaries had been in the form of a reward for the administrators and soldiers in kind or in *hakuras*, plots of land, which the receiver could freely use for growing crops or demanding produce from the inhabitants as a kind of tax. This tax constituted the salary as the title deeds exempted the owner from paying taxes to the sultan.[72] People were increasingly drawn into the money economy: the received their salaries in monetary form and were taxed in money based on wealth in fields, animals, houses, goods, and people; but also bride prices and bride wealth were increasingly paid in sums of money. Lastly, Hajja witnessed the change from a society divided into nobility, free commoners and slaves, to one based on classes related to value in money and occupation; both tied in with the change in governmental rule. This last change had not only stimulated the development of a local market economy, but in the course of the 20th century also:

> ...forced the inhabitants of the western Sudan into the national labour market and—since the market for agricultural goods and wage labour opportunities in the area were limited—into labour migration to the new cotton plantations of the Nile Valley. Thus the basis was laid for the political and economic marginalisation of the western Sudan that still paralyses the area today (Kapteijns 1985a: 394–395).

However, when I ask Hajja which time she feels was better she quite definitively states: "Life now is better, but before life was easy and cheap. The development now is good, but the past is the best". Hajja does not emphasise her plight at present, but rather her good life in the past.

Con/textualizing Hajja's Narrative—The Past in the Present
Belonging to the Local Elite

For Hajja the transition of the old sultanic elite to the new elite of traders and government officers did not carry very negative connotations because she was related to both. From the position of belonging to both groups of elite, she reflects on both periods in a positive way.

[72] See for the *hakura* system La Rue (1980); O'Fahey (1979). For a list of the diverse taxes, levies and communal obligations the Darfur population could be subjected to see O'Fahey (1980a: 103–104, 106–107).

For example, she recalls all the details of imported goods and change in life style, as well as the prominent people as if she was familiar with them. She refers proudly to her husband as an innovator, as a modern man who caught up with all the new developments and fashion, and gained wealth and influence in the process. From her perspective, it is understandable that Hajja prefers the past to the present. Because of her relation to Abu Feisal, she enjoyed the new lifestyle of the *nouveau riche*. Hajja's viewpoint is particularly clear from her evaluation of wearing a *tobe* which was a prerogative of the rich of her youth, of women like her,[73] but which now is a fashionable dress for everyone. Although the *tobe* is very expensive even now, women regard it as an indispensable item. Every woman *needs* to have at least several of them.

During this period, Hajja not only learned how to prepare and serve the new dishes, but also lived in the first stone house with separate parts for men and women. In other words, Hajja's own experience of changes in norms and values and the material conditions of her own life and status match the changes in Kebkabiya. However, Hajja's lifestyle and experience changed radically when Abu Feisal died ten years ago. Hajja reflects on this in the second part of her narrative.

The transition to the subsequent section comes with my question about the first women on the market. Sa'adiya had intervened before Hajja talks about the first and/or most prominent female traders. At this point, we enter her memories of a time when either her female relatives or she herself found themselves forced to sell at the market through need. One of them, is Hauwa Umm Shuluug[74] her half-sister and the only child of her mother by Faqih Sinin. Hajja emphasizes here the crucial difference that she sees between women who sell their wares from their houses and those who sell at the market. Her sister Hauwa Umm Shuluug was the most prominent tradeswoman, and she was amongst the first to begin trading, but it was always from her house. Hajja herself had bought clarified butter for her brother-in-law when she was younger and then sold it on for him, but she does not consider this to be 'selling at the market' either. By stating that the *shartai*'s wives

[73] As Hajja indicates elsewhere and as others told me on several occasions, most women wore several strips of the local coarse blue cloth or even skirts and chest-covers made from locally tarnished hides.

[74] Mostly *Umm*, mother, refers to the position of mother of the eldest child. In this case it means 'mother with/of scars' referring to the scars we know her mother received at the hands of Ali Dinar. Either her name refers to her mother, Hajja Shuluug, or it is a way of distinguishing her from her mother, while both wear the scars.

do not sell at the market and next adding that "My father also forbade my family and me to go to the market", Hajja establishes the elevated status of the family in which she grew up although "most of the women at the market nowadays are Tama". At that time her father, like the *shartai*, did not allow, but also did not need, his female relatives to sell at the market. Hajja justifies her own ventures in trading clarified butter by stating "I didn't like going to the market, I did it to help my brother-in-law". She thus prevents any suggestion that she or other Tama women might be on the market for other reasons than buying or selling out of need. In this manner, she legitimates not only her past endeavours, but also her current position. Hajja's family forbade women to sell at the market long before the government did. Thus reflecting on her past offers Hajja a means to justify her own position in the context of the current discourse of the Sudanese government on market women. She establishes her elevated social position, indicating that she was aware of the correct conduct for women when she was young, and abided by it, just as her father and sister did, when they could.

Hajja's argument with the current discourse is clear from the last part of her narrative when we talk about women selling tea at the market. She had been very mild in her comments up to that point, particularly when speaking about the plight of especially Arab and Zaghawa women who had to make tea to survive. Therefore, I was very surprised when she then so explicitly condemns tea women stating that 'tea is the mother of crime'. Hajja condemns tea making, but does not 'play the ethnic card'. In the same breath, however, she points out that for herself selling goods at the market is better than staying at home.

Hajja seems at the least ambivalent about her trading activities. I may have contributed to this response in the way I phrased my questions: by asking so explicitly her opinion on the action of the government, her reflections also take on a political connotation. If Hajja spoke openly against the government decrees it might jeopardise her own position as a market woman. Hajja knew from her own experience how fast words travel. Therefore, if she took a stand against the government, it might be dangerous and even lead to potential imprisonment. This gives me an idea of how Hajja uses her past to construct an identity in the context of the current moral discourse.

Therefore as I examine how Hajja constructs the last part of her narrative, I cannot justify labelling Hajja's changing perspective on selling at the market 'ambivalent'. She demonstrates that many women find themselves forced to sell at the market because their husbands have migrated to other parts of Sudan and do not send money or goods home. Hajja draws a parallel between herself, as a widow, and women with migrating men, all of who are female heads of their households. I understand this in relation to her explicit statement that her daughters must not even think about selling tea. She constructs a difference between selling tea and selling other goods at the market and then between being a married woman without a man, or young and single. Hajja's reference to husbands who migrate follows directly from when she comments that she does not know why Kobé and Arab women sell. I think we have to take these different sections as a single statement. Making tea causes crime when young girls like her daughters sell it at the market, but it is a completely different issue when it concerns female heads of households who need the income for her and her family to survive. Therefore, although Hajja states that the majority of the market women are Tama, she emphasises their plight as women who, like her, have to survive without a husband to provide for them. What Hajja stresses in creating a self-image is not the questioning of morals but economic need: she justifies her work as a market trader by age and marital status.

In addition, the time perspective is important here: women who sell tea are a recent phenomenon. As Hajja is an elderly woman now, she could never imagine doing anything so disreputable in her youth. In her youth when she might have attracted the attention of men, she could not have done so if only because there was no tea selling then. In this way, Hajja constructs herself as a virtuous woman, even in her youth. My next question is whether it is shameful to sit in the market. In the light of what Hajja has said, this is potentially insulting. Hajja overlooks my error in a sublime way when she discusses in more general terms the fact that 'nowadays all people work', implying that there is nothing special about selling at the market. Moreover, she compares her work with women working in offices: "…Women work and men work in the offices, in the market, all the people are working together, mixed". Hajja thereby suggests that the fact that women and men mix during work is not specific for women selling at the market. Here, she is criticising the double standard of the government. She implicitly argues that contact with men who are not kin should not be a reason for devaluating the work of women, any woman, selling at the market, when compared to educated women working in offices.

In other words, Hajja weaves her own life into that of a local history. She does this through her telling of experiences and the way she,

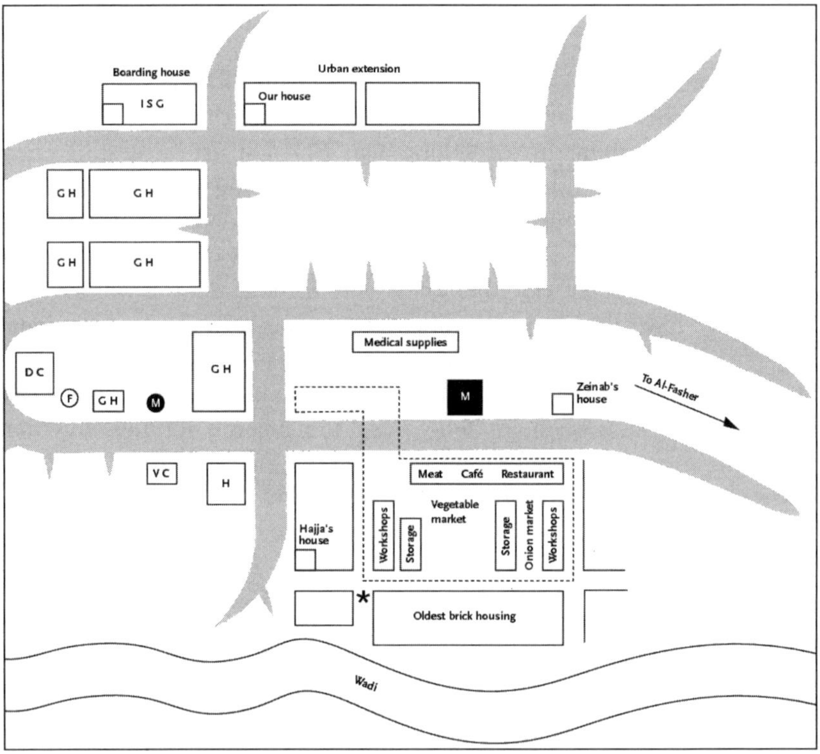

Map 4. Hajja's Family and Neighbourhood

uses both 'I' and references that are more general. All of these come together and construct the image of a woman of standing, well raised, sensible and wealthy, whose trading activities necessary to survive have now come under scrutiny of the government, unjustly so. Therefore Hajja is indignant about it and refers to the whole discussion on the—allegedly—disreputable actions of tea women, as if it has nothing to do with her. In her narrative Hajja therefore carefully reconstructs her life by building up an identity of an elite woman who, out of necessity, has to sell at the market. As she has known most of the local dignitaries all her life, Hajja tells her narrative in a composed, distancing way, taking the position of someone who has an overview and who is in control. So even when Hajja in this part does not talk about herself as 'I', but about others, about events and historical persons, it is through her 'eye' we evaluate that past.

Sunday—A Quiet Day

It is a relatively quiet day for Hajja. There is no mosque to attend for praying, there are no births to attend to, and it is not a market day either. The cows have been taken to the river. Even the fields are clear from the stalks and calabashes. They do not need any care until the rainy season in May. Hajja sits on a straw mat under her *rakuba* shelling groundnuts for making *dakwa*, peanut butter used in salads and sauces. Her eldest daughter, Semira is preparing to go to the market in order to buy more groundnuts. Recently, she has earned some money by selling the fruit from her part of her deceased father's orchard. Semira wants her mother to sell the peanut butter at the market for her. Hajja is not very happy about this but even so, she has started shelling them for her daughter. The women regard this as a task performed at leisure. Lately, whenever I visit women on their compounds, a basket with groundnuts is at hand ready for shelling. I sit down to help her. Hajja's sister Tinya, two of Hajja's neighbours and Sa'adiya come and join us for a while. Nura is busy heating sand mixed with salt in a *saj*, a large metal pan, on the fire to roast the peanuts in. After the visitors have left, Hajja, Sa'adiya and I talk for a while. I ask Hajja if she sold *dakwa* as well, after her husband died. She says that she did not. I tell Hajja that I really would like to know what life with Abu Feisal was like, how she felt about being married. Hajja nods and proposes that we tape her story right away while we are busy with the groundnuts.

In the beginning, I was married to a man from Zaghawa tribe. He was Ansar.[75] *He prayed well and fasted well and my father said: 'This man is a very religious man, he prays and I want to marry you to him'. I refused many times, but he gave me in marriage anyway. After the wedding day, my husband went to his village in Dar Zaghawa. He returned to Kebkabiya after seven months and after some time he told me: 'I want you to come with me to my family'. I had spent altogether three years with him. He wanted to take me to Dar Zaghawa. I refused. My father also said that he did not want his daughters to live far away from him. He said: 'I don't have any other children than my daughters, no sons, and I do not want my daughters to be far away from me. If you stay near Kebkabiya in one of the villages,*

[75] Followers of Al-Mahdi and his son, grand- and great-grandson after him, both religiously and politically.

you can take her with you. But not to Dar Zaghawa'. That man's name was Mohammed Ahmed. He was already married and had already children. He was not from my family, nor my tribe. And I had not chosen him, my father had, because he knew him well. So he divorced me. One month later, I went to the midwifery school.

The second husband, Abu Feisal sent somebody to tell that he wanted to marry me, and I agreed to marry him. This was because of the problem that had happened between him and me.

Sa'adiya and I look up at Hajja at the same time. It seems as if Hajja expects us to understand what she has just said. It is clear that neither of us have any idea. Hajja bends forward with a smile and goes on:

At first, he sent me Abu Hussein to ask me to marry him. I refused. I said he had two wives already and I did not want to marry him. Then one day he came himself to ask me to marry him. It was on the day that my uncle's wife had just given birth to a new baby and we had gone to offer our congratulations to him and his wife. Abu Feisal's wife Ashia and I had gone together to their simaya. *I went home with my friends. After we returned from the village, everybody went to their own houses. On our compound, we have small huts for my sister Fatna and for myself. Sometimes I slept with my little sister. At this moment, she is in Urra. She has no children. I lay down on my bed because I was very tired. My mother warmed water so that I could bathe. I bathed and oiled my skin and went to sleep. That day, I was sleeping in my hut alone. It was the hut where I kept my midwife box and I slept very deeply.*

At midnight, the moon was shining very brightly. I saw a man dressed in white inside the hut. I did not know it was Abu Feisal. So, I thought that one of the soldiers had seen me in the street near the army place. He would know that I have no husband so he has followed me to see me. I had not even finished wondering who he might be when I see it is Ashia holding a spear in her hand. At the same moment, Abu Feisal sees her and he grabs hold of the spear and takes it from her. So she started crying inside my hut. My mother woke up and heard the noise. She screamed, although she did not know exactly why: she thought something had happened to us. Many people gathered and they asked: 'What happened?' I said: 'Ask my mother, she is crying, so she must know the reason'. At that time, I knew the reason but I kept it a secret. I did not tell anyone. When they asked my mother, she said: 'Somebody came to kill my daughters'.

In the meantime, Ashia ran to her house and this man, Abu Feisal also went to his house. Now the man was afraid that the people would be thinking that he wanted to do bad things to me. So early in the morning, he rode on his horse and went to my uncle[76] *in his village and Abu Feisal brought him, my uncle, back with him. And Abu Feisal told my uncle that he wants to marry me. So my friends came and said to me: 'It is foolish if you don't marry this man. His wife came to kill you with a spear so now you have to marry him. To punish her'. Then my uncle came and he asked my father but he refused to marry me to Abu Feisal. 'This girl Ashia and Hajja grew up together so they are family. I don't want them to be co-wives'. Then the woman's father, Abu Ashia said: 'No, this man has to marry Hajja because my daughter wanted to kill her. So let him marry her and see if she can kill her'. My father still refused. He swore that even if Abu Feisal were the last man on earth he would not marry me to him. Next, Abu Feisal sent a man with his money to my uncle in the village and they agreed upon the marriage there. The co-wife's father and my uncle made the marriage, without my father's consent. My uncle came and told my father about the wedding and he said to me: 'If you don't like this marriage I will cut our connection at once'. So after they made the marriage in my uncle's house Abu Feisal asked some elderly wise men to go and talk to my father to ask him to agree and to forgive us. Abu Feisal brought other friends as well and organised a meeting that day to solve the problem. However, when I asked him, my father was still angry that I married Abu Feisal against his will and he told me to go away. So they took me to Abu Feisal's friend and we spent a day there. In one day, they built a* gutiya, *a house, a* kurnuk, *a kitchen, and a fence. It was at the place where the onion-market is now. Abu Feisal had a lot of money, and he hired many labourers to finish the job quickly. Then he bought a lot of utensils, pots, and furniture as well, because my mother would not prepare anything for me, as my father was still angry with me.*

After Ramadan on Eed-day, I asked a man called Iddu and Abu Ashia, my co-wife Ashia's father who is also my sister's husband, to go to my father again and to ask him to forgive me. Abu Ashia went and said to him: 'Hajja is a very good girl and she assisted us with raising our children. She didn't do anything bad except that she married. You know that to marry is not bad in Islam. And if it is about my daughter Ashia, I forgive her myself'. After Abu Ashia had asked my father to forgive me, my father forgave me.

The following year, the government announced that every trader had to live behind the place where he was trading from, so then we moved to this compound, behind his shop. At first, we had the plot behind a jellaba*'s shop and this place was the* jellaba*'s. He said that he wanted to change with us because we were behind his shop and he was behind ours. So, we arranged the exchange. The* jellaba *was very clever; he knew things because he came from Dar Sabah. Now his plot is the most*

---

[76] Helima tells me that although Hajja says 'Abba' (father), at that time it was used for father's brothers as well.

expensive one in town because it was a very suitable location to have a shop and houses.

Abu Feisal's first wife was Ashia; his second wife was called Ashia as well. After that, he married another wife named Ashia.[77] *At first when Abu Feisal went to marry her, her family refused. They said: 'This man married two wives and he did not have any children with them'. For his marriage, Abu Feisal brought two jerry cans of clarified butter, two of oil, one sack of sugar, two sacks of dates and two sacks of flour. In the end, the family consented to the marriage and he married the third Ashia. After two years of marriage, she had not given birth and Abu Feisal took her to South Darfur to a* faqih. *This* faqih *wrote to her from the* Qur'an *and after that she gave birth to her daughter, Amna. Then followed Sadiq, then Ashia. Then Abu Feisal married Umm Feisal who gave birth to Feisal and his three sisters but all the girls died. One of them was very beautiful; she had long hair. One day she went to her father's shop to buy soap. When she returned she collapsed at the entrance of the compound, with vomiting and shitting and she died. After Umm Feisal, he married me. And nine months after he married me he divorced Umm Feisal. At that time Abu Feisal had everything, millet, tea, and sugar. He divided it between us all even when he divorced her. He even did not take his blanket from her house; he left it there for Feisal. And his* hijabs, *his amulets, he left them as well to his son. But Feisal refused to live with his mother so he came and lived with me. I have two daughters because I did not give birth quickly. I spent twenty-five years without children. After I became pregnant with Semira, I said that if it is a girl I want to name her Atiaat, after the female doctor that helped me to get pregnant. I gave birth to Semira in Fasher Hospital, the normal way, without needing a caesarean section. However, in Umdurman they had cut my belly open in order to remove the meat.*[78] *When I gave birth to a girl her father cut seven sheep and Abu Ashia one sheep and the husband of my friend one sheep, they slaughtered nine sheep altogether. They invited all the people in Kebkabiya and in the surrounding villages. At the party, they made* kisra *of* jir *and* bread.[79] Fatira, *the nice biscuits, and rice with milk. At that time, Abu Feisal was a very good man with a lot of money. He killed deer and a lot of guinea fowl, which he brought to the house regularly, sometimes ten sometimes twenty and sometimes he himself would clean them. And when he cut a deer he made* marara, *the sauce made with intestines and would ask me to call the other co-wives, Zeinab, Ashia and my sister Hauwa and Abderrahman, one of*

---

[77] Boys and girls were usually named after the day and part of the day they were born. So even in one family, one could find the same name for different children and they were often distinguished by nicknames.

[78] A myoma.

[79] Bread was a novelty introduced in the colonial era.

our neighbours. We would roast the meat and eat it. We made sauce with the guinea fowl meat. We were able to get a great deal of sharmot, *dried meat, from it. When we were preparing Semira's* simaya, *you know, the name giving party, we had two oil tins full of* sharmot. *And a large quantity of clarified butter. Feisal used to take clarified butter from my house to the other wives' houses if it was their turn to make food for Abu Feisal. Abu Feisal said her name should be Semira. So it was.*

Hajja's story of her elopement puzzles me. She tells the story in such a distant tone as if it does not concern her own life. I want to try to identify some more of her feelings. I ask: "What were your expectations of marriage?"

No, there was not such a thing on my mind. I just trusted on my fortune, it depended on my luck. This husband I did not put him on my mind at all, I didn't like him at all. That is why at first I refused. It was only when his wife caused this problem that my uncle and the co-wife's father decided about my marriage. Meanwhile, I had a cousin; he was a policeman in Khartoum. He was my father's brother's son. We had agreed while I was in Umdurman, that he would come and ask me to marry him. Instead I lived with Abu Feisal for twenty-five years without children. After that, I went to have an operation in Khartoum to remove a piece of meat from my uterus. Directly, after nine months, I gave birth to Semira. I was still breast-feeding Semira and I didn't know I was pregnant again. I stopped breastfeeding Semira after seventeen months. Between Semira and Nura are twenty-six months.

I recognize an opportunity to turn to the subject of motherhood, a very central issue in the government's discourse on women. I ask a question although in fact I already know the answer: "So children are important?"

They are important, how can't they be? Hajja exclaims. Astma ukhti, *listen here my sister, look at my sister Hauwa. It has been three years now that she is just lying down. She cannot go outside. Her sons they bring her everything, not in pieces but in carton boxes. Some come from Idris in Nyala, some come from Abdalla in Fasher. Ahmed from the Jebel, if he is coming he brings with him two sacks of millet, one of flour and one of sugar, one tin of oil, and one of honey, a box of soap and bathing soap, and tea. And if she would have no children, where do all these things come from?*

Hajja is only referring to men. Therefore, I ask her if she thinks there is a difference between having boys and girls.

There is a big difference between boys and girls. You can see that from this example. Hauwa's daughters stay in the house, bathe her, and feed her from her own food. But my sister's sons are different from others' sons, they like their mother very much. Her son Abdalla, for example, when he comes from Al-Fasher every 1–2 months, and he stays with his mother and father one or two weeks, while he sleeps in his own room. He wakes up three times a night to look at them, to see how they are. To cover them if they are cold or to get them anything if they need it. He bought a warm jumper and blankets for them against the cold. If it is cold, he brings fire in a stove so they can warm themselves. He even warns them not to go too near the fire. And he comes back to be sure that they won't burn themselves.

As Hajja has indicated herself that her sister's sons are different, I try again, asking her whether she thinks that boys in general are better than girls are. To which question Hajja exclaims:

Boys are far better than girls!

Her vehemence surprises me. Sa'adiya looks up as well. I wonder if she would feel that her late motherhood and then only giving birth to girls were signs of misfortune. When Sa'adiya asks Hajja how she felt about married life, I add: "Did you have any problems?"

Married life was very nice. I did not have a great deal of work because Abu Feisal had two other wives who came before me. His half-brother, Abu Ashia, married my sister Hauwa and the men used to eat together. So we prepared food in turns: three days my sister, three days Ashia, Abu Feisal's first wife, and three days the second wife, Feisal's mother, so I had nine days of rest. In those days, I made food covers and did other handicrafts. I ground millet by hand as well, because we often had guests. I pounded a great many spices too. Many of the guests used to come from Kutum; they made us tired with their visits. We would need to make asida *in three pots for* fatuur, *and again for lunch, and again for supper. Abu Feisal had a gun and he killed a lot of game, to make sauce with meat of forest birds and gazelle: he used to hunt near here, at the place where the brick making is done now. I ground by hand and filled big earthenware pots with flour. I also prepared a lot of pounded millet. At that time, Allah made everything easy.*

When I celebrated the circumcision of Semira and Nura not so long ago, when they were about ten and eleven years old, I bought two pounds of sandalwood for only £S1. Someone brought it for me from Port Sudan. On the day of the circumcision, I had £S7. I bought one sack of sugar, half a pound of mahlab, gundaar, *cinnamon, cumin, black pepper, and one sack of onions. You can compare that with now: one tin of onions costs £S250.*

I want to ask her more about the birth of her daughters, but Hajja suddenly sits straight and points her finger at Sa'adiya saying:

I just remembered about the problems I had with Abu Feisal. One day, I was breastfeeding Nura. I had a donkey that could carry water and a labourer who sold water to the people for me. Abu Feisal told him to bring water to his two other wives' houses. My labourer brought them water every day, but Abu Feisal would not pay him. I noticed that the boy did not bring me any money for this service. I paid him a salary for his work. When Abu Feisal came I told him: 'If my labourer brings water to your wives' houses and you don't pay him I will quarrel with you or I will forbid him to bring any water again to you'. When I spoke to him like this, he punished me by hitting me in the face. I put my child down, stood up, caught him by his jellabiya, *and tore it to pieces. Our neighbour, the* jellaba *said to Abu Feisal: 'It is very shameful Abu Feisal, to hit your woman, she is near the grave now'. Because our custom is that if a woman gives birth and does not complete the forty days inside the house, her grave will be open. Only after forty days is her grave closed again. In these forty days she should be treated gently and not be punished and people should not quarrel with her.* 'Yagsal-leek, yagsal-leek' *he said to my husband. This means that it is not good that you loose your* ajr, *your religious points [Sa'adiya adds that* yagusara *means 'to loose your profit']. Abu Feisal answered: 'No, no, no, I did not hit her'. I replied: 'He hit me and he hit me. I am feeding my child and he hit me'. The* jellaba *said to Abu Feisal: 'You hit the grave, you want to make problems to yourself?' But, Abu Feisal always fought with his other wife Ashia. She was always crying and fighting and people would go to their houses to keep them apart. It was because she used to drink.*

I still wanted to know more about how Hajja felt firstly, about marrying a man who was not her first choice and secondly, when she was not his first choice. So I ask her: "Did you not want to be the first wife?"

I did, but it did not happen, this was my luck. Both my husbands, they were married before me. Many women do not like co-wives. We had our neighbour who was a jellaba *and his wife said that it was not good for women to have co-wives and she said that she hoped that Allah would harm co-wives. This was when women would come to her to ask how it was to have a co-wife. But I myself I do not hate co-wives. Some women hate them because they don't want their husband to divide things to them. This is because the days and goods were divided among co-wives. And women do not like co-wives because some men are not fair in how they divide things. Sometimes he spent three days in one house and five days in the other. And if he gave this wife three* ratul *sugar and the other five, which wife did he like more? However, Abu Feisal always divided goods and days equally between us.*

As I want to encourage Hajja to tell us more about her experience of married life, I take a detour asking her: "Did you think it was difficult to be married with a man who had more wives?"

I did not cause any problems to my co-wives. But I remember one day that Abu Feisal was in my house, it was my turn. And the cousin of my co-wife Ashia came to Abu Feisal in the evening and he told him: 'Your first wife is going to burn her house because you don't go to her house. She told me that if Abu Feisal does not come to my house today I would burn it'. But that day was mine, not hers. This man was Ashia's brother-in-law. At that time all the houses were built of straw: they were huts made of leaves and sticks, no bricks. So Abu Feisal got up and went to her house. When he arrived at her house, he found that people were holding her hands in which she had matches. As he arrived, he took a match out of his pocket and threw it to her. He said to the people standing there: 'Leave her, go to your houses, I gave her the match herself with which she can burn her house, I want her to burn it'. Then she felt ashamed, she went inside her hut, and slept deeply. She was extremely drunk. But I myself, I did not make any problems with any of them.

When Abu Feisal married Zeinab after me, I took all his things on my head to her house and Zeinab's mother told me that she did not know how to make jir, *because she was from an Arab tribe and they do not eat these dishes. She asked me to make* jir, khumra, karkar, *and* dilka.[80] *I made it all in my house and brought it to them. They were nomadic at that time, and Zeinab was staying at* farikh Al-Abas, *now* hei al-kubri. *Zeinab gave birth to ten children and I assisted her in all her births. I would wash her, make the soup and clean for her. Just me. So all her children they like me, because I didn't do them any harm. Everyday they, even now, are with me in my house. But their other aunt, Amma Ashia, the first wife of Abu Feisal, they don't like her.*

"So were you always treated fairly compared to the other wives?" I ask her.

---

[80] *Jir*—fine powdery millet; *khumra*—locally made perfume; *karkar*—hairoil; *dilka*—locally made scrub. These are all items given to and used by a young bride for beautification.

Abu Feisal treated me differently. Because I made a great many special things for him and I made a lot of it, whatever it was that he wanted. At that time, he also used to drink mashkuka. *It is an alcoholic drink made from red sorghum. I made it for him, but I never drank it myself. He brought his friends and they would drink. He brought me extra things, scents, sandal, and told me not to tell the other wives.*

I still wish to know if she thinks that her services to him are an obligation that comes with marriage, or whether Hajja sees it as her fate. However, when I ask her to explain to me the rights and duties of a husband and a wife, she begins to talk about the wedding ritual, which differed from the way it takes place now, especially in the kinds of payments which were exchanged between the family of the bride and bridegroom. Sa'adiya interrupts her, by asking her: "And after the wedding?"

When women are behaving badly, they can be divorced. Our husband did not divorce quickly. He said: 'If I divorce a woman I will not take her back, ever'. Men marry other women because some women like causing problems; they play around a lot and do not obey their husbands. The second reason is that if a man married a woman and after twelve years, she had not given birth so he may marry again to have children. The reason for Umm Feisal's divorce arose when Abu Feisal married me. We had cows and we milked them for ourselves. Then one day the servant milked Umm Feisal's cow at home, but she said she had milked it for me. When Abu Feisal came to her house, she asked him why the servants milked her cows for me. And she made a big fuss over it. After they fought, she told him: 'You are like a servant to me, you can put water for my bath in the bathroom'. So then he divorced her. Nine months after he married me he divorced her.

After me, he married Zeinab, this was before I had given birth to Semira. Her first children are older than mine are, and her daughter Hauwa is older than Semira. Zeinab was feeding Hanan at the time I went to Khartoum for an operation. After that she gave birth to Hauwa and then I was pregnant with Semira. I spent 24 years with Abu Feisal and then he married Zeinab in the twenty-fifth year. Between Feisal's mother and Ashia are fifteen years. I am not sure how long the other wives spent with him. Ashia's father married my sister Hauwa and she is my co-wife. Anyway, the one I liked most is Zeinab. We did everything together. But Ashia she is very quarrelsome, she doesn't like people. The things for Zeinab's marriage, I prepared it all myself, jir, dilka, khumra, baghuur. *I made all of them for her. Also I assisted her at the births of all her children. I washed, cleaned, and bathed her baby. My best friends who assisted me in giving birth and helped me after that, and visited me, are all dead now. Fatna Bulbul's co-wife was my friend. When I gave birth, she brought with her a glass pot of* dilka, *a bottle of* khumra, *a small bucket of biscuits and flour of millet, okra, tomato, and pepper powder. Her husband gave a sack of sugar and sweets and a sheep. Abu Feisal's wives did not work. They had small fields and he hired the labourers to work for them. Except for me, I was a midwife. After the harvest, he didn't ask from us to give him millet, we could keep it. Nowadays, they all work outside their houses. Zeinab in the market, Ashia as a cleaner in the hospital and she works in the market too. I was already a midwife before his death. He died before Sanat Reagan. How old was he? Nura was in the first class of high secondary school when her father died.*

Now, Semira has joined us. We are preparing *dakwa*, the peanut butter sauce used in the tomato salad. Semira counts aloud: "Nura was born in 1963, March 3rd. And I was born in 1961. Nura went to primary school and she did the examination in the sixth class twice. In intermediary school, she did her last examination three times. So it would be around 1982 that *abuna*, our father, died", Semira finishes. Sa'adiya adds that this was one year before the year of drought, which would lead to the famine of 1984–1985, *Sanat Reagan*, year of Reagan. Hajja nods and then continues:

When I was with my husband, he brought everything in the house, because my salary as midwife was so small. In autumn, we would bring food to the labourers who were working on the land and we would watch them working. After the harvest, every woman took her millet to her own house: whether it was a little or a lot, it was yours. And if the grain from that year's harvest was finished, Abu Feisal gave us from his own part. He would bring all kinds of spices like dried okra. In fact he would bring anything; powdered dried tomatoes, powdered red pepper, powdered dried meat, meat, and oil. At that time he had a hundred cows, I remember. At that time, Abu Feisal's women did not sell the milk: if there was milk left we made clarified butter of it. And your clarified butter is your own. If you want to sell it or make sauces with it, he did not interfere. And if it were finished he would give you more. He was a very kind man. All four of us had our own fields, and Abu Feisal had his own as well. He had three plots of land of his own and one was given to Feisal, Semira, and Nura together. They made a garden of it. He had already given Feisal another field before he died. He liked Feisal more than he liked his other children. The third piece of land is not yet divided between his children. It is lying fallow, just like that. I had my own fields: they were my father's. And Zeinab's fields were from Abu Feisal. She has now given them to her children. Ashia, the first wife, she planted her mothers' land at that time.

Hajja is referring to the division of Abu Feisal's property after his death. She leaves herself out of this description, so I ask her what she got out of the inheritance:

You know, Abu Feisal married many wives: he married six and divorced two. So he had many children and all of his property went into the inheritance. Feisal, the only son that Abu Feisal had with my elder co-wife Ashia—no, not the first Ashia but another Ashia—he received land with three mango trees and land on which he built a house and he has made a garden of it. My daughters received this house here and one quarter of a feddan of wadi *land with three mango trees, next to Feisal's, who was given most of the gardens. Zeinab, my younger co-wife, has many children: six girls and four boys. They allotted thirteen camels and land for farming and houses to them. To Zeinab's sons Ibrahim, Yasir, Al-Nur, Osman, they gave them land and four houses and one shop in the market. Abu Feisal had another wife with three daughters and one son. She received a shop and a house for the son. For his wives, there was very little, it all went to the children. We inherited some of the plots for growing grain. We only inherited one-eighth of his property. That is far too little to live on.*

I am surprised in the light of her recollections of his wealth there is so little left. I ask her: "But Hajja, where did the wealth go?" Hajja sighs, rearranges her *tobe* and says:

It was all stolen. All our sheep were stolen at one time. Our camels were stolen too. All the cows died of the cow's disease. One day I remember Abu Feisal gave somebody our cows, seventy-seven of them, to look after them. However, when the man returned them there were only seven left: they all died. From the nine, two were of someone else and seven ours. That happened in the drought of Abu Arba.[81] *And the camels, they came to tell us after some days that some were stolen, then that some had died and then again that they were stolen. And how the money was finished? I had £S 40 and I told Abu Feisal that I wanted to go with him to Fasher when he wanted to go there to buy a car. When we reached Al-Fasher, we went to the house of sister's son. He told his nephew that he wanted to buy a car, but his nephew said:*

[81] *Abu Arba*, 'Father Four' is the name of the drought of 1972–1973. De Waal (1989) writes: 'Famine names fall into distinct categories. One category consists of names referring to shortage of grain. Many of these refer to the small measurements of grain, those being the units whereby grain was sold in markets or distributed by community leaders from *zakat*, almsgiving, stores (72–73)'. *Abu Arba* refers to the size of the bowl used to measure one unit of grain, which was smaller than the bowl used for the same price before the famine.

'O uncle, you have cows and sheep and camels and shops and now you want to buy a car? Who is going to look after this all, your eldest son is still in school?' One of that nephew's friends told him: 'O my friend, we can buy goods with your money. I will take the goods to Birkaseira to sell them and we will gain a lot of money'. His name was Faqih Musa. He took all the goods to Birkaseira and did not return. When we asked him about it, he only brought small amounts. From that day on poverty came to us.

When Abu Feisal was ill he told his family that this man still owes him money. When the man came, he said, 'O, I lost my diary'. Abu Feisal said: 'I have my own in which I have written down our agreement'. And Abu Feisal's family blamed him asking him why he had given this man, who is not his uncle's brother, cousin nor son, so much money. And he answered that it is from God. The man said: 'I will go to Birkaseira and sell the goods and send you the money'. When he went, he escaped by taking a detour and in the end he went to Saudi Arabia on haj. *And when he returned from his pilgrimage he went via Kutum to Birkaseira and not via Kebkabiya. After that, another man heard that the man had taken from Abu Feisal and did not return him the money. The man had also taken from him. He ran away as quickly as he could from Fasher to Birkaseira and he took his goods back from this man. At that time, ya Sa'adiya, money was very important. I went with £S40 and bought 1,5 ounces of gold and a gold ring. This was all for £S40!*

Sa'adiya interrupts Hajja telling us that this is exactly what happened to Ali, her husband. Usually Sa'adiya does not say much about her husband, who is a trader. However, Hajja's memories trigger hers. Both the women lament the fact that men are not aware of the risks they pour on the heads of their families with these kinds of endeavours. Then Nura calls us from outside. It is four o'clock and lunch is ready. It is a simple meal of mashed vegetables with potatoes, some salad, scrambled eggs, and bread. Sa'adiya stays for lunch as well, because we are invited to a coffee party at around five o'clock at one of Hajja's neighbours, to welcome her son with his bride who have come from Saudi Arabia. Sa'adiya's son, Mohammed, sits in my lap and plays with my earrings while we eat quickly. At a quarter past five, we all get up to go to the place of the party. A large crowd has gathered at the party, we chat and drink coffee. There is a lot of laughter when the coffee dregs are read for future lovers, letters, or money or other pleasant surprises. It has become dark and lanterns are lit. The party continues far into the night.

Context of Narration—The Present in the Past
Remembering a Married Life

Sunday is a relatively quiet day for Hajja, unless there are people who need her as a midwife. Sunday is also a day when not much happens on the market: on Saturday, people from Jebel Marra and from Dar Zaghawa come to Kebkabiya, buying and selling potatoes and fruit and the next market day on which Hajja sells her onions is only on Monday. During her marriage with Abu Feisal, Sunday was probably one of the days she saw most of him, when he was not busy with the market or with visiting other men as what happens often on a Friday after prayers. Surprisingly enough Hajja tells us only now that she had been married for three years before she left for Umdurman for her midwife training. It was as if she has been considering whether to tell us or not. She must have been fourteen when her father married her to Mohammed. At the time of her divorce, she would have been seventeen.[82] Whether the marriage was ever consummated is not clear. However, it is clear that her father decided Hajja's fate concerning both her marriages and her divorce. Her father's reason for refusing to marry her to Abu Feisal seems to be that he was related to Hajja; his half-brother, Abu Ashia, is the husband of Hajja's sister Hauwa. More importantly, Hajja stayed as a young girl in their household to help out both her sister and brother-in-law which means that she virtually grew up with her niece, Ashia, one of Abu Feisal's wives.

Hajja's reasons for marrying Abu Feisal against her father's wishes remain unclear. Perhaps she felt this might be her only chance after her first failed marriage, or maybe she did consider Abu Feisal an attractive candidate with his wealth and social status and his connections to her family. It might even be the case that she feared a scandal if it became open knowledge that Abu Feisal had been caught in her *gutiya* at night. This would reduce her chances of marrying another man even more. The real reason, Hajja 'kept it a secret': not only from the people around her at the time, but also from us, her current audience.

In this narrative, her memories again centre on Abu Feisal. Apart from the wealthy lifestyle, with a remarkable eye for detail of goods and its prices, it is however not so much her position as a wife, but

[82] He left after the wedding day and returned after seven months after which they divorced. The three years of spending with her husband might refer to the lapse between her *agit* and the actual wedding, or the time they spent together after he returned from Dar Zaghawa.

that of a co-wife that she elaborates on. On several occasions, her reflections turn to her quarrelsome elder co-wives. Both women were called Ashia, their husband divorced them both and the reason was the same on both occasions; they were jealous of Hajja, the then youngest co-wife. However, when she discusses her own attitude as a co-wife, she emphasises her own abstinence of quarrelling and her care for and friendship with *her* younger co-wife. The quarrel with her husband that she does relate to us concerns the payment for the water carried by her donkey to the houses of her co-wives. While her fight with her husband might make her look jealous and quarrelsome herself, and thus contrary to what she wants to argue here Hajja legitimates her position by pointing at the quite divided obligations husbands and wives had to their households. She thus refers to her husband's obligation to be fair while in her narrative the *jellaba* who came to her defence functions as a witness to her right to demand this: in this case the fact that her neighbour is a *jellaba*, in other words an elite man, is important to 'prove' the correctness of his interpretation of an Islamic principle. Thus she could still keep up the image of herself as a good wife and co-wife: if her elder co-wives were jealous, unreasonably quarrelsome and vindictive, she emerges as a virtuous, just and admirable co-wife towards her husband and her other co-wives.

In a more indirect way, she also establishes her position as a good wife. She mentions the many guests she, her co-wives, and her sister attended to, and the work and care it took to keep the household running. At the same time that she emphasises Abu Feisal's fair and equal treatment of his co-wives because he stayed with them in turn, she also reveals herself as his favourite wife. Hajja seems to argue implicitly that his preference for her and her cooking was the reason why he stayed with her despite the fact that she did not bear children early in their marriage. He only married Zeinab some twenty-four years after Hajja so for a long time she had been the youngest wife, who is often also the most desired and sought after by husbands. Therefore, if he married her for saving her and his own honour, or for spiting his quarrelsome wife, he also married her for herself. Thus, her reference to him liking her food and drinks, his preference to 'eat' with her can also be interpreted as a preference for having sexual intercourse with her. In Darfur, 'eating' can also stand for enjoying sex.[83]

---

[83] De Waal states that this is common for other African languages where eating is used 'idiomatically to mean enjoy money, power, sex, and other good things (1989: 72–

It is not clear however, why she does not tell us this fact more directly. In fact, she remains unclear throughout her narrative about her emotions for Abu Feisal and the kind of relationship they had: she even seems to be contradictory at times, for example when she praises his generosity, while her quarrel with him was over what must have been to him little money he owed her over using her donkey. Although she had wanted to marry her cousin, a policeman from Umdurman, she does not seem to blame her husband for her more or less forced marriage. At the same time, there are only a few times when she refers to his character in a direct way when she calls him a 'very good man', describing the abundance with which he provided his wives on equal terms; and a 'very kind man' when towards the end of his life he loses his, and her, wealth because of his—misplaced—trust in people and in fate. However, at the beginning of her narrative she states explicitly that before her marriage she 'did not like him at all' and in general she refers to her marriage and her husband in a distant, objectifying way, even sometimes, referring to him as 'this man'. This could reflect her true feelings about him before their marriage and reflect her relationship with him, as they must have differed in age and she was only seeing him once every nine days and then often with many guests around. But it might also be a strategic remark to nip in the bud any suggestion that she desired, or even might have set up Abu Feisal's nightly visit that she enjoyed his company during their marriage. The strategy is not only related to establishing her moral virtue as a girl, but also to her current position as well.

Con/textualizing Hajja's Narrative—The Past in the Present
From Married with Co-wives to Widowed with Daughters

Hajja is now a mother of daughters, a fact that would prevent her from articulating such strong 'dangerous' emotions as passion and lust. This may be one of the reasons why she might not be very explicit about her emotions; her desires and (dis)likes in relation to Abu Feisal. It is seen as particularly appropriate for a woman of her status as an elderly woman and as a real *hajja*, to show restraint and piety. At the same time, by being neutral about Abu Feisal's character or conduct, Hajja in fact

73)'. Likewise, 'hunger' is used for all kinds of suffering. See also for example Bayart (1993); Mbembe (1992: 3–37) where these meanings of eating are related to political power.

creates credibility for what she is telling us about her own character and position in Abu Feisal's household. By playing down Abu Feisal's preference for her due to possible physical and emotional satisfaction, or whatever desire, she claims an exceptional position, which fits into the current discourse of the government on 'proper' behaviour for Muslim women. Considering her narrative in the context of her current life, being supportive of her other co-wives is also a claim to being a good wife. Hajja emphasizes her positive attitude towards her co-wives, and at the same time plays down her role as the favourite wife of her husband. With this manoeuvre, she simultaneously claims not sex but sociability as her hallmark, not her attractiveness to (a) man (men), but her care for her co-wives. She presents her attention to especially her younger co-wife, usually taken to be the greatest competitor to the elder co-wives, as her virtue. Hajja constructs her identity as a co-wife who overcomes socially inappropriate emotions like passion, jealousy, lust, and desire whilst at the same time displaying her virtue as a wife as well.

Hajja does not mention the importance of children in her life, nor does she elaborate on the miracle of having children after such a long time. This fact might relate to her depiction of herself as an admirable woman in her past life and in the context in which she currently lives. Her time of being without children is not important because this seems to be of no consequence for the course of her married life and her position as a (co)-wife. Apart from claiming respectable behaviour, she thus also 'detours' the issue of her working as a midwife, while married, and later, while having children. Also in this case her argument fits very well the current discourse on gender. Wives, and certainly mothers, are to stay at home, especially when her husband is so wealthy that he can easily afford it. Hajja, successfully, arrests any questions from us about how she combined midwifery and motherhood.

The relationship between Hajja's past life and her current position as a market woman comes to the fore when she states without hesitation that boys are better than girls. She points out her sister's sons, and completely neglects to speak of her own daughters. Hajja does not point out their virtues, the solace they offer, or their assistance with household tasks. She did not appear as a very warm or tender woman, despite the fact that she did care for her daughters, sought out their company, and liked to converse with them. Despite her actions, she related her explicitly stated preference for boys to their parents in their old age. She seems to hint at the fact that although she is also in her old age now; she still has to take care of her young girls instead of the other way around. It serves as a reference to her present adverse circumstances. While her daughters own land and her house and while she did not get a share of the inheritance, Hajja still has to take care of them. Young women need protection and therefore, her daughters force Hajja to sell on the market. Her current position as a working mother is therefore much more legitimate than when Abu Feisal was still alive. Her assertion that boys are better than girls is a way to underline the inescapable nature of her current life.

In her narrative, Hajja succeeds in reversing the evaluation of important aspects of her life according to common sense notions. The peculiar story of her marriage, which took place without the consent of her father or the dowry of her mother, even not being a choice of her own is turned into a tale of success, control and achievement. Hajja portrays herself as a good wife who never quarrelled with her other co-wives. She also presents herself as a third wife and co-wife who never made unreasonable demands based on jealousy or greed. Lastly, she was a co-wife who showed restraint as a wife and as a woman, even guiding and coaching her younger co-wife to become a good wife, like herself, virtuous, hard-working, caring and sociable.

Thursday—The Main Market Day

It is Thursday, the main market day, and Hajja has left for the market early. When I go to find her, she is busy arranging her onions, limes, and peanuts she is selling today. Every day it seems to get hot earlier and we each find a place in the shadow of the burlap cover over her stall. She asks me to take care of her pitch, while she delivers a tin full of onions to one of the restaurants in the middle of the market. Ever since the month of Ramadan started, business has improved and Hajja is much busier than before. When there is a lull in the trade, I ask Hajja about the goods that I do not recognize. Hajja explains that these are mostly wild products, which people relish in Ramadan for use in the special dishes. Hajja indicates the long brown strips with what looks like pods and explains:

There is tamarind, which makes nice juice and protects you against malaria. I want to sell turmus *myself; many people eat them during Ramadan. I hope I can find the raw ones and I will prepare them so people can eat them straight away.*

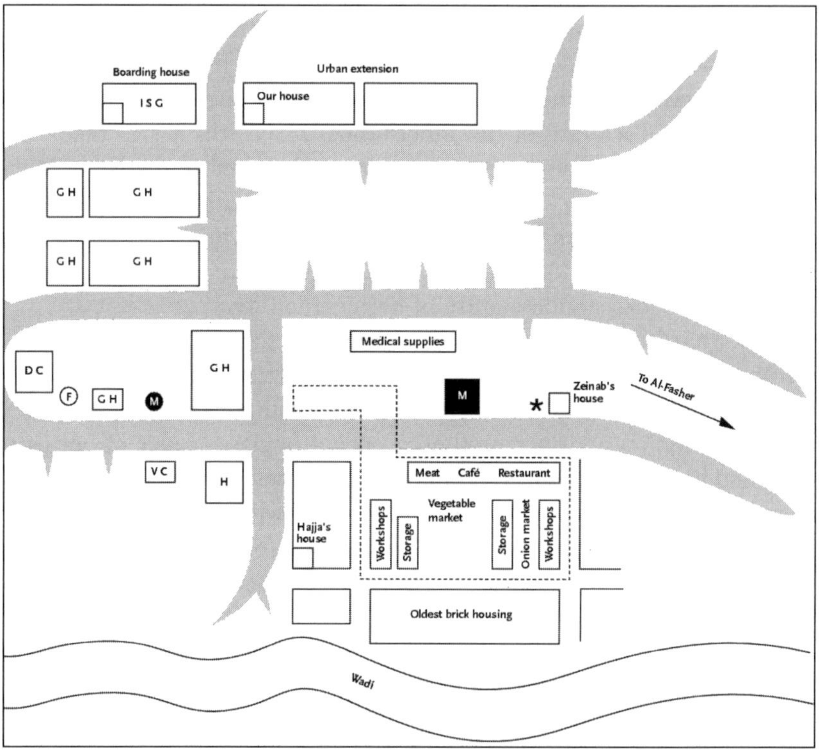

Map 5. Hajja and her co-wife

I know Hajja hopes to earn some money from the special dishes made for breaking the fast during Ramadan. At our compound, girls from outside Kebkabiya regularly come to pound kilos of millet. Hajja can then make the white powdery flour, *jir*, to make millet-flakes, the basis of a light, thirst quenching, drink. Recalling her story about her youth, I ask her why she does not make food covers anymore, as she did in the past?

I made food covers when I lived with my husband and I sold them as well. Now I can't because my eyes are not good anymore. When my husband was alive, he did not ask me about my own money, he gave us everything. So I went on haj *with my own money, the money of my food covers. I went on* haj *with £S100.*

I know Hajja has gone on pilgrimage to Mecca only once, and apparently she did not finance it only with her salary as a midwife. "So if your eyes were still good enough would you make food covers or sell at the market?" I ask her incredulous, for there are hardly any women selling them as most women are supposed to make them themselves as part of their dowry.

I would go to the market and make food covers at the same time. After I sold groundnuts, I sold onions and oil, balandora, *dried tomatoes, and limes.*

Hajja points at the limes that she has displayed in front of her in small mounds. At that moment, a young boy with a large palm leave basket buys two of them and a *kom* of onions as well. She gives him some small onions as present. Then Zamzam joins us. She asks Hajja if she can borrow some more money. The market is flooded with tomatoes now that the price is very low. Zamzam wants to take her chance and send her boxes with tomatoes to Fasher this time, as she fears the price there will get lower during the coming weeks. Hajja nods and in her turn inquires about her health and that of her mother. Zeinab, Zamzam's mother and Hajja's co-wife, had injured her leg, which prevented her from selling at the market for some weeks. Normally Zeinab sells onions, oil, and peanut butter at the other side of the market near her own compound. In the meantime, Zamzam's younger sister took care of her wares. Zamzam answers that Zeinab is well again and can leave her house again. Then Hajja says:

Good, come to us tomorrow, after prayer at the mosque, you and your mother and whoever wants to come, to taste the biscuits Mohammed, my cousin brought with him from Nyala. He came from his son's wedding in Nyala. He will give me the money from the jerry cans with semen *that he took with him to Nyala.*

Pointing at Zamzam, Hajja suggests that if I want to know more about the market trade and about selling to other towns I should ask Zamzam. Therefore, I walk with Zamzam over to an enormous *hedgli hedgli* tree, where row after row of pressed-wooden crates with aluminium rims is waiting, some with, others still without tomatoes. Zamzam walks over to a spot at the side where her daughter Selma is watching over her crates. While seated in the bit of shade that is available, I watch Zamzam buying crates and arranging sacks of tomatoes, which her brother brings to her by donkey.

When Zamzam has divided several sacks of tomatoes between about three quarters of the boxes she has assembled, she tells me to come and have some tea at Fatna's place, the daughter of the eldest co-wife of Zeinab and Hajja. When we arrive, we find Rhoda and Selwa having left their nearby stalls unoccupied for a moment. They discuss their *sanduq*, literally 'box', a type of rotating credit association. Women put a fixed amount of money together every week or fortnight, which is then handed over to one of the members so she can buy something expensive, such as utensils, clothes, a uniform for their school going children, or even goods in bulk for more profit on the market. "From my profit I will pay twice next time", Zamzam promises, and Rhoda sighs while saying she will arrange it just this once.

The next day, Friday, a day of prayer, leisure, and social visits, Zeinab, Zamzam and her two children arrive. Tea is made and the biscuits from Nyala are handed out. Nura, Zamzam, and Semira shell groundnuts, talking and giggling at one side of the *rakuba*, while Zeinab and Hajja talk quietly at the other side. Then Sa'adiya enters the courtyard. She has brought some goods for her sister, who is travelling to Fasher by lorry tonight and now stops by to greet us. As I will travel shortly after Ramadan, the talk turns to my immanent departure. Hajja almost orders me to bring the tape recorder. She then turns to me and asks me: "Tell me, what is left of your questions, I can talk about them now". I am a bit taken aback, but Sa'adiya puts on the recorder. Sa'adiya asks Hajja a question that we have used frequently to 'finish' a series of taping narratives: "As you look back now, is there anything you want to add to your story?"

Wallai, ya Sa'adiya, all my life have been full of happiness. No food problems, in the house: nor in my father's nor in my husband's. And no hardness I met upon, alhamdulillah. *Only after the death of my husband, life became hard. My father's name is Harnaan Ishak; he was a farmer from the Tama tribe. He was born in Kebkabiya. He met my mother in Al-Fasher after the fight of Faqih Sinin and Ali Dinar. Faqih Sinin's family and his neighbours were taken to Fasher. At that time, my father was a very respectable man, he was quiet, and Ali Dinar admired him. He therefore gave my mother, one of the wives of Faqih Sinin, to my father in marriage. He was Ali Dinar's guard at that time. He gave them many different scents. He made dry scents out of it three times. And after my mother gave birth to a son and a daughter, he named them Mustafa after his brother and Taja after his sister. My mother's first daughter was Hauwa, from my mother and Faqih Sinin and Taja from my father, then me, then Fatna, Tinya, then Fideen. They did not work for the government; they all worked at the market. Hauwa sold salt and cheese and* damirga, *cloth, from her house. She also sold tomatoes, okra and pepper-powder. She powdered many things as well and people would buy them from her. Tinya was also selling at the market: pepper, okra and tomato-powder and* jir *as well. Tinya came to the market as soon as she got married: directly after her wedding she went to the market. This was because Abu Feisal and her husband were half-brothers Abu Feisal gave his brother money to establish a shop but his brother lost all his money. So he became poor and his wife, my sister, went to the market twenty-five years ago. However, Fatna, she is a farmer. She has fields and gardens with mangoes. All our brothers died, so there were only girls left.*

Sa'adiya asks her if there were other men who took care of her sisters:

It is the man's duty to bring all the things for the house, and the woman's to cook, to clean and to wash etc. If the woman is an employee, she will bring in her share of the money. And if the woman is not an employee, the man has to bring everything to you. Powdered okra, meat, all the things you need in the house. The duties of men in the houses at that time, they took it differently: some are traders. Some of them are farmers. The farmers, after they harvested their crops they brought all their crops to the house. Millet or okra, or the cherry tomatoes, they gave it all to their women. But traders didn't want to give their wives a lot of oil or sugar; they were cruel. They would give one pound of sugar, half a pound of tea, half a bottle of oil, only little things, not like farmers did. However, our husband, if you emptied your plate or tin, he would fill it. Women's duties at that time were to cook, to wash, and to make food covers. Some other women at that time also brought water and wood themselves, but our husband bought it for us, and had it brought by others in all of his four houses. And they divided the days between us. My sister was with us in this too, because she was married to Abu Feisal's brother. The brothers would eat three days in each house and that would mean all their friends or guests as well as their servants would eat in one of these houses.

Zeinab adds that Abu Feisal has always been fair to her as well. That he also helped her brother in times of need, because he liked her brother, who also had been her *waali*, the person who represented her during the negotiations of her wedding. "Ah, it seems such a long time ago. Look at me, I am younger than Hajja here but my hair is much whiter than she". Hajja nods in agreement, saying:

My sister Hauwa is now eighty or eighty-five years old. I am sixty-six, I had forty-nine years of working and my age was eighteen when I started working. Tinya who came after me, is sixty-three. Medina is sixty. They named me Hajja. It was a joke. I was the youngest and it is a name given to elderly women. My name is Hauwaya, small Hauwa.

Context of Narration—The Present in the Past
Doing not Being: Constructing a Meaningful Life

In this last exposé, Hajja gives a summation of some of the aspects she elaborated upon in her former narratives. It is almost like an afterthought. Her age seems to have changed in this narrative to a younger one. I am not sure from where her sixty-six years of age comes from, but she relates her siblings to her younger age. Sa'adiya and I had decided on the basis of other dates mentioned in her narratives, that 1918 probably is her date of birth. It is as if she feels now, that indeed she cannot be seventy-six already. Curiously, she does not mention her work as midwife this time, although indirectly this identity is suggested, when she states that she worked for forty-nine years and started when she was eighteen years old. It might have to do with the presence of her co-wife Zeinab, who might trigger Hajja's memories specifically related to the life they shared. It might be even out of courtesy that Hajja does not want to spite Zeinab who is not only not 'trained' in any way, but she even had to learn from Hajja the basics of providing their husband with food and drinks. However, it is also possible that Hajja feels she has repeated her story of her life as a midwife so often now that she is convinced her message has been driven home to me. It is impossible for me to see her now as a market woman who was once a midwife. Hajja has succeeded through her narratives and her actions to construct the identity of a midwife who because of fate had to resort to occasionally selling at the market to sustain herself and her dependent daughters. A fate she shares with many of her contemporaries. Not only her sisters and co-wives who once were wealthy as well, but as she stated in one of her narratives, most market women are, like her, Tama, once the most powerful and economically viable ethnic group in Kebkabiya.

The implicit reference to fate has a strategic side and I need to read it in relation to Hajja's assertions of personal achievement and worth. The alternation of fate and achievement in her narrative matches Hajja's alteration in pronouns from we/us/them to I/me. The pronouns in their turn are related to generally accepted and expected behaviour on the basis of local mores on the one hand, and the celebration of Hajja as a special and worthy person on the other. This different positioning of herself as narrator is indicative of the way Hajja argues with the moral discourse. I want to take a last look at the alternations in Hajja's narratives and the way she constructs her identities differently. This exploration is meant to come up with an understanding of not only in what way she constructs her identities into a notion of self that fits the person she feels is, but also why she does this.

Con/text-Analysis—The Past in the Present
Respectability and Difference in Negotiating the Islamist Moral Discourse

The different identities Hajja has constructed while telling her narratives differ in the way in which she cherishes and enlarges them or disparages them and plays them down. Her claim on individual achievement matches her usage of pronouns and the tone in which she narrates her positions. The more frequent usage of 'I' when relating about her life as a midwife, and as a co-wife, emphasises her individual capabilities and qualities. This is moreover told with much gusto, in an animated and confident way: they were the only identities that she was prepared to talk about readily, without questions or direction from me.

Hajja does use 'us' and 'we' in these narratives with a more individual focus. Looking closer at those moments its strategic use becomes clear: she uses it mainly to establish the fact that some of the circumstances she grew up in could not be altered and were part of her 'fate'. Pointing out the bad educational situation in Kebkabiya when she was young and the inevitability of her betrothal to her first and second husband are ways to give the 'appropriate' context to 'read' her identities as midwife and co-wife. On the one hand, she is thus able to set off her identities as a trained midwife and as a caring and peace-loving co-wife as extraordinary achievements when measured against what was 'normal' in that period. On the other hand, the reference is important since it constitutes 'fate' in a more specific and circumscribed way. This fate should be evaluated in the context of the current government's discourse on moralities and the Good Muslim Woman. I will therefore analyse here the difference in attitude that comes with her differently constructed identities, as Hajja's way of dealing with negotiating the moral discourse of the current government.

Hajja's strongest claim to respectability is her identity as a medical midwife. Her training made her slightly more 'educated' than most of her contemporaries. It is precisely education, acquiring both religious and worldly knowledge, which deserves female teachers a high status although their work requires them to move in public life and 'mix with men'. It is just 'bad luck' that girls' educations reached Kebkabiya when

Hajja was already mature. She negotiates for a similarity with female teachers because she was clever enough but did not have those specific opportunities. Hajja's reflections on assisting educated women to give birth underline her superior knowledge at least in this area.

The other important status imposed by the government is to be a good wife and mother. Nevertheless, Hajja emphasises her co-wife status as if she feels that this makes her stand out more than raising 'just' two daughters only later in life. At times, she almost seems to be overdoing it in her efforts to prove herself to be a good wife. She even disclaims Abu Feisal all responsibility for her fate as co-wife and only refers to him in a positive vein. For example, in her last summary she evaluates his behaviour as a husband towards his wives positively in comparison to that of other traders. Hajja's co-wife Zeinab corroborates Abu Feisal's generosity.

The context of her negotiation with the moral discourse provides an explanation for her ambivalence towards Faqih Sinin. If we take Hajja's preoccupation with her identity as midwife as a starting point, it is Hajja's allegiance to the British for the diploma and possibilities they opened up for her personally that is at stake. It was the same British who brought in the Fur *shartai* putting an end to the political power of Sinin's son and thus of the Tama in the town of Kebkabiya. Moreover, Faqih Sinin also triggers the notion of a local form of Islam that the current government tries to reform. His burial mound still serves as a place of pilgrimage; his history ties him to the *Mahdiyya*. It is these kinds of practices and this politico-religious past of which Faqih Sinin is definitely an icon and which the current government wants to erase so as to purify the society from local 'wrong' Islamic practices and politics.

The most obvious reflection on this moral discourse in Hajja's self presentation can be read in the way she almost denies her identity as a market woman and emphasises its necessity because of her husband's death. She claims inevitability, the fact that she does not want to sell at the market, but needs to do so, when she ranks herself among all those women 'without a husband' who have to work at the market to earn a living. Thereby she makes strategic use of differences she claims between herself as a 'respectable' market woman, and others who might have ulterior motives for sitting in the market, especially tea women, whose behaviour she condemns. This difference she bases on age, marital status, an 'unblemished' youth, and the obligation to take care of her daughters, but also on the kind of products sold and that she sells with a permit acquired from the same government that now questions her right to sell at the market. At the same time she combines her argument based on these facts, with an assertion, in concordance with the government's view, that making tea is the 'mother of crime': this serves to underline her reluctance to sell at the market and her willingness to comply with the government's viewpoint.

Hajja's strategy throughout her biographic narrative is directed at constructing a status which comes closest to those respected by the new educated elite: an elite which is all powerful in the current government. On the one hand she includes herself in that elite by her repeated references to her profession of midwife, the right to wear a white *tobe*, in other words to claim the markers of an educated elite identity in her self-representation. On the other hand she denounces the right of 'other' women to sell at the market, and in particular to sell tea, in contrast with her own right to engage in marketing in order to provide for her fatherless daughters. In other words she creates a difference between herself and 'bad' market women: she thus distances herself from the negative imagery of market women as constructed in the dominant discourse, while creating space for constructing an elevated status: not just for my benefit, but in order to claim respectability by using the discursive possibilities and subject positions the current dominant moral discourse offers her.

Epilogue—Reflections on Hajja's Narrative

In December 1995, I went back to Kebkabiya for a short visit. There were many reasons for my return. Amongst them I wanted to understand Hajja's narrative better and to have some things explained. I also wanted to hear Hajjas opinion about the way that I had portrayed her and her narrative. I wanted her permission in a sense. I wanted a 'green light' so that I could go ahead with what I was doing with her words. However, Hajja was not to be persuaded. Sa'adiya explained to her that I wanted to translate my transcription for her so that she could comment on it. Hajja replied indignantly, 'All I told you was the truth. You may write down all of it'. My own attempts to present her with my analyses and reflections on our relationship were in vain. She would respond by retelling episodes from her life. She always started out by telling me about her experiences as a midwife. It was as if she wanted to make sure I understood her when she told me the first time.

I had started out doing research with the conviction that the knowledge process is a result of contact between people in a given context. During my research I was aware that self-reflexivity was a conscious mental strategy for understanding that process. However, it does not mean that during my research I could be totally aware of the exact routes and outcomes of its dynamics. It concerned the interconnectedness of the interaction between the women and their surroundings, and me, and with the knowledge that was constructed, produced, and consumed. Moreover, reflexivity proved to be a continuous process. After I had left Sudan, the process still involved Hajja, her narrative, and me as her houseguest and interlocutor. Back in Sudan, I wanted to use the opportunity to re-examine Hajja's narrative with her. I wanted to know how she felt about her narrative which she had told me some three years before. I also wanted to ascertain to what extent Hajjas emphases in her narrative were a reflection of our relationship. In other words, my task was to investigate anew in what respect the way we understood each other was a combination of our consecutive worlds and the joint one we shared together for a short period. Although Sa'adiya often took part in our conversations, I think I needed to delve into what *I* meant to Hajja. In this chapter my goal is to understand what Hajja wanted her narrative to mean to me, to my book, to my 'kind' of audience. Although Hajja can't reply on these pages, I do want to understand my involvement as part of the context of her narrative, our dialogue, however uneven and incomplete it may have been. Therefore, I will direct my reflections to you, Hajja, and see if your words, your narratives, talk back to me.

Self-reflection and Inter-subjective Knowledge

During my second stay in Kebkabiya, when I lived on your compound, the biggest impression you made on me had not so much to do with your past or your work, but with my own circumstances. I had been back in Kebkabiya less than a fortnight when you asked me to accompany you to Umm Bulbul's *karama*, a lunch prepared to commemorate her father who had died forty days before. In Islamic practice, this is the second occasion on which people can come to offer their condolences. The first is seven days after a person's death and burial. On this occasion, the relatives seemed less grief-stricken than I remembered from previous funerals; the deceased father had lived a 'good life' and died in old age. Both facts added to the relaxed atmosphere. When two weeks later I received my first letters from home, I was struck by their poignancy. My parents had written to tell me that my paternal grandmother had died some two weeks before. My grandmother was a proud, intelligent woman. Although widowed during her fifties, she actively continued her husband's business (with the help of my father). Although we had our disagreements, I greatly admired her. I was very upset by her sudden death. When I realized that her funeral would have been at about the time I attended the funeral meal with Hajja it consoled me.

Now, when I look back on that period, I think the coincidence made me link you to my grandmother more than I realized, Hajja. Like my grandmother, you are also an intelligent, active woman. You took care of your daughters and your grandchildren too. You loved them in the same way my grandmother would have done; your love was energetic and resolute, not pampering and tender. Your stories about your past soothed and comforted me. Your presence relieved me from some of the grief I felt over my grandmother's death.

The connection I felt between us had its bearing on the interpretation of your narrative. My grandfather had been a barber. He owned his own business and home in the Netherlands during the 1930s, a time of general unemployment and substantial economic crisis. Consequently, my grandparents were part of a middle-class of shopkeepers and executives who had an elevated status when compared to the majority of their fellow villagers. The status of 'local property owners' did not necessarily come with the certainty of wealth. Although my grandparents were not considered members of the local nobility they had a 'name' to keep up. Until my father took over the business in the 1960s, my grandmother had lived with a great deal of distress and material insecurity; the effects of the 1930s economic crisis, the Second World War and my grandfather's premature death in the 1950s were amongst them. Maybe I expected you, Hajja, to have the same fragility of status as my grandmother experienced. After some bouts of misfortune, with Abu Feisal's death as a major disaster, your status did not buy you the *kisra* you needed in order to survive. Therefore, I believe I understood the conflicting sentiments of belonging and not belonging to your class. However, I may have projected my grandmother's situation onto your own. If I interpreted your negative attitude towards market trading as a reluctance to be seen as part of a class, which received so much contempt by the new elite, it might just as well have reflected the attitude I knew from my own childhood.

Although I realized you were reflecting on the dominant discourse of the government when downplaying your job as a market woman, I thought you really did not like the trade. I reasoned that being a midwife was your favoured job and that in fact you detested being forced to sell at the market because it was the easiest way to survive. Now that I am back in Kebkabiya again, I realize that your reflections might have been more complex than I thought. You do prefer being a midwife. As soon as I asked you to tell me more about the elapsed years, you began by telling me once more about your training and work as a midwife. However, there have been changes in family life, which contrasted sharply with the daily routine I experienced when I lived in your compound in 1991–1992. To my great surprise, Nura has started running a restaurant in the evenings at the entrance of your compound. In addition, Semira wants to sell the peanut butter independently, whilst before she let you sell it at the market. And you, Hajja, you are still complaining about the small return the Kebkabiya market provides you with, and like last time you are blaming the 'weak market' for it. You tell me that it is worse than two years ago. However on this occasion there is no mention of the government, no sign of a negative attitude to trading from your side, no differences established between you and other, younger, market women. In fact there is no reference to the current moral discourse when I ask you about the trading activities of your daughters: no hesitance, no apology and neither a difference you make between your daughters and 'other', less scrupulous, young women on the market. You just comment that 'every bit helps' and it is good that your daughters are being kept occupied. You even planned to prepare locally prepared goods, like *dilka*, a strong scenting scrub, to take on your small *haj* (*haj al-umra*), to Sudanese migrants living in Saudi Arabia.[84] You almost relished the though of the possible profit it might bring you.

Perhaps you did not feel particularly negative about your market activities at that moment? Did your reluctance to reflect on your market activities during my previous stay relate to the way the educated government elite had talked about them? Although their opinion has not really altered, the fierceness of implementing the government's decrees has worn off. The government has loosened its ban on tea women. There were a few women operating openly again on the market. One

[84] A 'haj' is the pilgrimage to Mecca, constituting one of the five 'pillars' or obligations for all Muslims (the other pillars are: prayer, fasting, giving alms, and proclaiming the vows of Muslim faith).

of them is the daughter of your elder co-wife. Fatna Bint Ashia came from her marital home in Nyala, to Kebkabiya in order to take care of her mother. In Nyala the protest of the tea women had been successful; the tea women had never been completely removed from the market.

In retrospect, your reflections in your narrative might have been more strategic than I had thought, and thus more pragmatic and context-bound than I had realized. I had thought you had agreed with the view of the government because of your former elite status. Nevertheless, if that had been the case at that time, would you allow your daughters to cater to 'strange' men outside your compound, as you are now, even when in better economic circumstances? Last time, you referred to moral virtue when you discussed the negative aspects of market selling: was that more of a verbal acquiescence to a dominant 'public opinion'? However, I do not think you were 'just' window dressing. Perhaps the identities I analysed and thereby constructed, both for you and for myself, might have not been the only possible subject positions that could be negotiated by you in that context. I might reconsider the prioritizing of your identities as midwife and as a 'good' co-wife while downplaying others in looking more closely at the dynamics of our relationship, of the way our inter-subjective knowledge production might have other layers and allow for different placements than I have seen so far.

Hajja and 'Her' Khawadiya*: Belonging and Otherness*

When I reflect on our talks, whether Sa'adiya was present or not, it is clear that our relationship changed over the course of my stay with you. Nura had brought me to you for my second stay, undoubtedly, in part to compensate for the loss of income because she could no longer cook for our household: from visitor I became a paying guest. It was my gender that made it possible to live in your compound. We constituted a household of women, married and single, all without husbands. In time, you treated me increasingly with the distant care you showed for your daughters and grandchildren, openly referring to me as 'belonging' to your compound: as *naas*, 'people of', Hajja as you told those who inquired after me. When on my return visit I 'cared' in kind and not in money, buying you goods from the market instead of giving you money for services and goods, this gave me a different place, more kin-like, than before.

However, when you told me about your life, the fact that I was being treated like a family member was probably not that significant, if it mattered at all. You were aware that I was writing a book about Kebkabiya, which would include parts of your narrative. You would occasionally ask me in wonder if I was really writing a book and for whom I wrote it. I explained to you that the book was for a university degree and would be written in English so that people interested in Sudan would be able to read it. Without exception you exclaimed, "*Wallahi* (my God), a real book at a university you say? *Wallahi*, this is very good"! Nura was unfailingly exasperated by this and would say that you already knew this as you had asked 'a hundred times'.

Of course, the fact that your narrative would be in a book must have influenced your narrative and the images you presented of yourself. Nevertheless, I think the fact that it would be a book written in English might have made the biggest impression upon you. All *khawadiyas* and educated Sudanese converse in English. Notwithstanding differences in nationality, colour, gender, etc., English was, and still is the language of that group of people who by their education and job are part of the educated elite, a class of their own. Moreover, you had had contact with that class, with the British, before anyone else in Kebkabiya. The British had given you the education which made you not only the first medical midwife in the area, but also an acquaintance of some British officials, like Ms. Diggins, singling you out when she visited Kebkabiya, making you 'special'. You took pride in and gained esteem from the idea of having been part of the world of this new class. You not only had a diploma, but you also possessed knowledge of the unknown world of Dar Sabah, the East, of silk plaits and henna, but also about the capital Khartoum, even of the Mahdi family when delivering the later premier of Sudan. However, you did not learn their language or lifestyle although you had close connections with the British and an elevated status as a result. You did not read Arabic, let alone English. The command of these languages and lifestyle has recently become the main stake of the new elite class and you do not belong to that class.

It may not have been totally conscious, but in putting the present behind and making the past come to life may have been a way of connecting, of finding common ground between you and me (as a *khawadiya*). Revealing your long established relationship with their/my world might have been an attempt to increase your status in my eyes and at the same time decreasing the hierarchy between us.

However, in addition to bringing these connections to the surface, and the pride of being closer to my world than I had realized, there might have been another reason, which made you emphasize your excellence at being a midwife and play down your work as a market woman. It was a reason more directly relevant to your situation at that moment. What was at stake was not only gender, education or even ethnicity—being a *khawadiya*—but nationality as well.

The first foreigners you had met were British, but the more recent ones had been from the Netherlands. These foreigners had worked for Medecins Sans Frontières (MSF) Holland (Doctors Without Borders). Their compound was only a few doors down from yours. Everyone I met spoke with sympathy and even longing for the Dutch and their 'good works' as medical doctors. However, the MSF team had left because of security reasons, and most Kebkabiya people I met, especially those who had worked with them, expressed the hope that they might return. After the Gulf War ended in February 1991, there were rumors that the team's return might be imminent.

Moreover, you, Hajja, might have been hoping that on their return, the team would employ you for your knowledge about attending to circumcised women who were giving birth: a very specialized area of expertise which the Dutch doctors and midwives did not have. My book and your narrative in it may have helped. This is not such a strange thought. I had contact with many people involved in diverse projects in the area and had befriended some of them, both Sudanese and other nationals; one of them, a Dutch woman as well, had even become a good friend of mine. Although it was sheer coincidence, you might have felt it an omen that both consecutive heads of the Oxfam project were foreign women named 'Karin', like me. Therefore, I can understand that you thought you might have a chance. Towards the end of my stay, several people visited me to give me presents to take home, and mail to send. On separate occasions Ishak, the medical assistant, and Muna, one of your cousins asked me quite directly about the chances of MSF returning shortly. Both of them explicitly stated their wish to work for MSF. After both of these visits, you told me about the difficult births you attended, adding that the western doctors know a great deal, but not how to care for a circumcised woman giving birth. At that time, I took your comments at face value, for you talked often about your work and excellence at midwifery. Now I realize that you might have been giving me your curriculum vitae as well.

Market trading provided you with a more stable and reliable income, but to present yourself as a midwife was, amongst other things, a strategy, conscious or not, to keep the possibility of better employment open. I was, after all a *khawadiya*. However much you I might have felt part of your family, in your perception my network of friends and acquaintances (from the same ethnic, national and occupational background) might have provided my surplus value.

Such an analysis may make you seem more scheming than I intend. Alternatively, it might seem farfetched for an elderly woman working on the market. However, I do not want to exclude the possibility of socio-economic strategy, which induced you to tell me your narrative in the way you did. You were singled out, some fifty years ago, to take part in the exciting new knowledge on midwifery and on lifestyle in Umdurman. You became, therefore, if not a member, then at least part of that new upcoming elite class at that time. So now, in a different time, you might have a new chance to working amongst foreigners. Fate had brought you among the British. It might have been the same fate that had brought me to your compound as a possible connection to that other lineage of the 'British tribe', the Dutch.[85]

Another aspect of your self-presentation was the emphasis you placed on being a co-wife. You told me about the way that you married. It was a strange tale and I asked you about it again this time. I asked whether it was considered dishonorable, or at least strange, that Abu Feisal had appeared in your hut, with or without an axe. Moreover, what had Abu Feisal's intention been to come to you like that: why had he really wanted to marry you? Did people not frown upon your marriage when your father did not consent to it? "Abu Feisal repeatedly sent my uncle telling me he wanted to marry me", you gave me as an answer, "and because of what happened with his co-wife Ashia, because he was seen at my place, and because my uncle told me it was the best I could do I agreed". Then you started to retell the narrative. You were his favorite wife; he visited you often with his friends or trading partners to drink and to eat. In addition, the quarrel you had about the milk came back in your narrative.

[85] In Chapter 2, I have dwelt on the occurrence that I was at several instances taken to be a member of the 'tribe of the British'. This was due to a perceived similarity in attitude concerning relief in times of drought and crisis of the British towards the Darfurian people in the colonial period and the attitude of the Netherlands in the last decennia.

It may have been that because you had a 'good life' with him, both in material terms and as his preferred co-wife, you had erased the strange circumstances of your marriage from your memory. Certainly, no one else seemed to remember those circumstances anymore. On the other hand, maybe it was too shameful to talk about it whilst people knew I was living on your compound. Alternatively, maybe the fact that you had been married before made the case less alarming and dishonorable than I imagined. In any event, you yourself were not keen on talking at great length about your married life with Abu Feisal. Moreover, he appears to have been a difficult man, notwithstanding the wealth and status he had brought. He was demanding when it came to the care he expected from you and your co-wives, bringing many guests and customers to the house. Maybe it was his appetite for women, marrying six wives as he did, which made you reluctant to dwell on your relationship with him. On the other hand, his many wives and his activities in trading and construction probably kept him out of your compound most of the time and made him an absent husband more than anything else.

A possible reason for your self-representation might have been connected to my own background. You remarked that the wife of one of the traders from Central Sudan had told you that polygamous marriages meant trouble. At the same time, you were amazed that in the Netherlands we do not have polygamous marriages. Although I explained to you that both men and women might have (secret) lovers in addition to their spouse, and that the frequency of divorces in order to marry a next wife was relatively high, our monogamous lifestyle kept you occupied. Perhaps that is why you stood up for your own experience. You contrasted it with Netherlands customs and with the disaster the trader's wife had predicted, in order to demonstrate that your own life had not been of less value, less legitimacy, simply because you were not the first and only wife of your husband. It seemed as if you wanted to illustrate with your narrative that polygamy did not necessarily lead to the kind of distress it had caused Abu Feisal and his earlier wives, with quarrels and fights. I would take home a narrative of a life less ordinary and more satisfactory than could be judged based on the 'facts' of that life.

Moreover, in Islamic teaching a woman who displays restraint is highly valued: if nothing else, your conduct provided you with religious merit. In the context of discussions on the 'un-Islamic' behavior of market women, an emphasis on this demeanor should not be a surprise. Although I heard you talking about it only now, you might have been contemplating your own death all along. An emphasis on religious merit is a feature which many elderly people display towards the end of their lives: the more merit one has 'saved', the better the chance that person goes to heaven. Quarrelling, gossiping and telling lies are always quoted as ways in which one loses religious merit, especially for women. Abstention from this type of conduct increases one's religious merit.

In retrospect, we both constructed identities in order to 'fit into' each other's lives and expectations. You gave me a version of your life in which foreigners had a prominent position, as benefactors and bringers of new things, jobs and structures. Abu Feisal himself was someone who was an intermediary of these changes. You provided me with the means with which to 'hear' your life, to acknowledge the difference between your position now and in the past.

At the same time your positive evaluation of foreigners also reduced the possible tension brought about by the discourse of the government on foreigners, voiced by the local religious committee. It was not only you, as a market woman, who was in a precarious situation: so was I. My situation might have changed at any moment. The people of my 'tribe' brought aid, grain, gave medical help, were renowned for their wealth and services like education, and 'won' the Gulf War, but my power in local affairs was limited, as my interrogation by the security committee had proved. My helplessness in local affairs was even more marked when concerning specialized 'female tasks'. I could not prepare *kisra* or *asida*, or make the beautification products every woman needs for her adornment: nor could I recognize local herbs and seasonal fruits, important in times of drought, or find my way in the myriad of footpaths along the *wadi* leading to the fields on which women grew their grain in better times. After all I was similarly vulnerable to banditry and ethnic conflict when travelling outside town.

When I returned on my own in October 1991 for a second 'field-work' period, I did not just come to stay at your compound: I needed 'to belong'. During my first stay, my identity was quite straightforward, or so I thought, because Johan, Yasmin and I lived in a house of our own in the outskirts of town. I was seen as part of the newly arrived elite. In the second period, I acquired an identity that was derived from yours. I became '*naas*' Hajja (one of Hajja's people). Again, I was defined by residence. However, when you became both my social anchor and a very important subject in my research, I apparently needed a position that fit into my relation with you, from which I could listen 'appropriately'. My academic interest mingled with another feeling, one from my childhood, of listening with great interest to the stories of my grandmother. In this way I could not only listen to you with attention and ask you the questions of a stranger, but I could also act out the respectful demeanor of a minor. My submissive behaviour befitted your position and reduced the hierarchy between us. However, it concerned not only a listening position: I felt protected as well. My insecurity over what might happen when the political climate changed was eased by the sense of being part of a group of people who seemed to accept my presence without much hesitation.

Be that as it may, both you and I had to work with multiple identities in order to cope with the growing intensity of our relationship woven around the narrative of your past, and the everyday life in which other relationships were important as well. For me this resulted in an attitude towards you, which was both respectful and reflective, both with unabated admiration and with loving distance.

During this short visit, some four years after my last stay, the way you dealt, or refused to deal with my questions and the kind of life you lead now, have made things more complex and more confusing to me rather than clearer and more straightforward. After all, my need for your authorization was not only negated by your assertion that all you told me was true, it was rendered quite ridiculous. You could not read your narrative and you had to trust my 'good' intentions as well as Sa'adiya's capacity to translate your words for me, and vice versa. More importantly, you told me your story, which you were telling me again this time. You did not see what you could add to it, the 'true narrative' of your life. What I began to realize was that authorization of a narrative some years after it was constructed was beside the point: a narrative does not exist in itself, but only in the context in which it carried meaning. It had been 'our narrative', time and placebound. The narrative contained multiple layers and was open to multiple interpretations. The narrative could not be retrieved from the past of our interactions some four years before. All I could do was to try not to abuse your trust.

CHAPTER 4

UMM KHALTHOUM'S NARRATIVE OF HER LIFE

First Session—Early Memories: Youth and 'Coming of Age'

Two weeks after our acquaintance at Sa'adiya's house, Sa'adiya and I walk to Umm Khalthoum's house together. Surrounded by the same yellow plastered walls, which protect the privacy of all the government compounds in this quarter, Umm Khalthoum's house is hard to locate. It's around three o'clock and the streets are almost deserted, as it is lunchtime. Finally, a passing neighbour points her gate out to us. We have to push the somewhat tattered door of corrugated iron hard as its hinges have deformed and enter what once must have been a beautiful compound. The houses are rent-free for government officials and were built by the British. Now they have become weathered by years of occupation by various inhabitants: a brick wall just to the left of the gate closes off the left-hand side of the courtyard from view. The right-hand side of the house has two windows with blue shutters from which the paint is peeling off, the mosquito wire is torn and has given way at the edges. In front of the house, some flowerbeds have been dug, but the withered flowers prove how difficult it is to grow flowers in this climate.

Upon our call, '*naas al beet, salaam alaikum*', while clapping our hands, the door to the left of the windows is opened wide. Umm Khalthoum stands in the doorway of what appears to be a veranda and responds enthusiastically, '*wa alaikum salaam, ahlan wa sahlan ya Sa'adiya, ya Karin, itfaddallu giddam*'. While repeating '*giddam*'[1] to acknowledge her invitation, we walk up the two steps and enter the veranda that is used as the living room. The interior is remarkably neat and well kept. It contrasts

[1] '*People of the house, peace be upon you*', is (locally) a quite standard way of announcing one's entrance to a private courtyard. Because most courtyards do not have doors, clapping is more convenient than knocking. The answer by Umm Khalthoum as hostess, '*and peace be upon you, welcome you, Sa'adiya, and you, Karin, come and sit here (up front)*' is also standard. Repeating '*here (there) up front*' indicates that the visitor knows he or she can proceed, once her or his presence has been acknowledged.

sharply with the bad state of repair we saw on the outside of the house. Umm Khalthoum is dressed in a beautiful bright, pink *tobe*. She shakes our hands inquiring after our health and that of our families. 'Please, sit down', she says, while motioning to the two beds covered with colourful, clean sheets. As soon as we are seated, Umm Khalthoum's two eldest daughters, Kaltouma and Estma, enter with dates and lemon squash. They greet us softly, shyly shaking our hands and they hurry out of the room as soon as they have served us. First, as is the custom, we exchange news about our families. Sa'adiya's husband Jacub has not returned from his trade trip yet. Umm Khalthoum laments Saadiya's situation for being left to take care of her household alone. She inquires about the health of my father and mother and about news from Johan. Umm Khalthoum also asks about the well being of Hajja, Nura, and Semira. While sipping our lemon squash, we exchange small talk. Our conversation ranges over the banditry, the influx of migrants because of the drought and clashes outside town, the difficulty of finding girls to help with household chores, about school and the subsidies on sugar, tea, and soap. Then Kaltouma and Estma enter the room through the back door, carrying between them a large round serving plate. They remove the *mutabakh*, a matted food cover, which protects the dishes against flies and dust, thus uncovering several plates and bowls with different kinds of food. Umm Khalthoum has excelled herself with preparing special treats for us. There is pigeon soup, only prepared for people who are recovering from an illness or from giving birth, ribeye steaks, several meat dishes, like *shayya*, roasted pieces of meat, liver, mashed aubergines, chips and salad. Around the rim of the plate the habitual *kisra*, sour pancakes, and fresh white bread are draped to eat the food with. For dessert, there is sweetened vermicelli and *crema*, egg-and-milk pudding. The meal is delicious. It is all very relaxed and easy going. Umm Khalthoum's two daughters, Kaltouma and Estma, both friendly and beautiful, wait on us so that their mother, who has unwrapped her *tobe*, can stay seated and talk and eat with us.

Umm Khalthoum has eight children ranging from four to fifteen years old. The two younger girls and her youngest son are asleep in the bedroom adjoining the veranda. Both still sleepy, at one point they come and greet Sa'adiya and me; then Estma gathers them up to give them a bath. The other children, the eldest son and the two middle girls, are not at home: they took lunch early and went to their friends to play. After the lunch has been cleared away and we sip from very sweet tea, Umm Khalthoum asks us whether we are ready to tape her story.

It is quiet and cool on the veranda where we sit. Sa'adiya instructs Umm Khalthoum to give her full name, date and place of birth 'for the record'.

My name is Umm Khalthoum Rifii and I was born in Umdurman Banaat, thirty-four years ago. We lived there in a house of our own and my father was member of the Sudanese parliament. He was very wealthy, had a lot of money. Our house was built nicely with a lot of rooms and our life was of a high standard, with a lot of happiness. At that time, we were the five of us. I first went to the rhoda, *the kindergarten. It was co-educational, boys and girls mixed. It took three years and after that, I went to primary school. Then my father left the parliament and returned to his former job. He was storekeeper of 'ash-shagaal', the governmental supply store for public works. He was posted to Ed-Daein in Kordofan.*[2] *There he assisted in building the hospital and schools. We spent a year in Ed-Daein and then we moved to Al-Fasher. In Al-Fasher, he had two lorries and a small car, a 'Komer'. I was born in 1956. My father moved to Fasher in 1960.*

In 1962, I lived in Al-Fasher. We lived in Hei Al-Karaanik.[3] *My father bought a new house in* Suq Amm Dafasu, *in the middle of the town, he rebuilt that house, and we moved there. Life then was good and education at that time was good. I went to primary school in 1962. Learning was nice: we children, we liked going to school. The books were different from the books we use now: when the government changed the books, it changed the subjects as well. We had many subjects then, but now this is different. Nowadays, the educational system is not as good as before. There was no co-education in primary schools at that time. In girls-schools there were female teachers and in boys-schools male teachers. I felt comfortable. The lorries of my father brought goods from Zalingei to Fasher. Money was plentiful and we had no shortages.*

My father then moved to Zalingei in 1963: he came back and took us all to Zalingei. I was in the third class of the primary school. The schools in Zalingei were the same as in Fasher: the teachers were nice and the boys- and girls-schools were separate and taught by male and female teachers separately.

In 1965, I was in the fourth class; I sat for the examination in Al-Geneina because in Zalingei there was no intermediary school. A teacher called Umm

[2] Kordofan is the region, now state, bordering Darfur. Often these two states are referred to as Al-Gharb, 'The West' because of perceived similarities in ecological, climatological, economical and cultural traits from the perspective of the people living in Central Sudan.

[3] *Hei Al-Karaanik* is a well-known quarter in Al-Fasher near the hospital where mainly government officials lived. At that time it was the place where the 'well to do' lived.

Khalthoum Abal took all the girls in one lorry from Zalingei to Geneina to sit for the examination there. We had our examination and thirty of us passed. Fifteen failed. These fifteen returned to the fourth class of primary school. I passed and went to the intermediary school in Geneina where I lived in the boarding house. During holidays, we returned to our families. Intermediary school then was four years: in the fourth class, I had my examination. Unfortunately Nimeiri[4] *changed the educational system in the school year of 1969 to 1970: from four years primary and four years intermediary he changed it into six years primary and three years intermediary school. So I studied five years at the intermediary. After these five years, my father stopped me from going to high school. He arranged my marriage and said, 'this is enough. You know now how to pray, how to read the* Qur'an *and how to write a letter'. And he chose Abbas as my husband. At that time girls had no right to say, 'I want this or this, I want to work or study'. If you would say, 'I want this', they would say, 'you can leave us'. I told my father that I would like to go and study at the university, but he said, 'If you want to go to university, and not marry this man, you can go and never come back to my house'. So I agreed and stayed with Abbas.*

In the year that I was married, my friends at school went to secondary high school and I had my eldest daughter, Kaltouma. Properly it is Khalthoum, with a 'kha' and 'tha' and without an alif, but people here in Sudan pronounce it with a 'kaf', 'ta', and 'a'. When I married this man, he was working at the International Tobacco Company. After three years he left the Company and started to work as a teacher. Because the company had no future in Sudan, if they would make no profit any more, they would stop working here. And Abbas said, 'It is good to find a government job, they have good pension facilities'. When I had my second child, Abbas was a teacher. He took us from Zalingei to Fasher. When we came to Fasher, we found out that he had been transferred to Al-Geneina. Our life started to change. When he was in the company we had a lot of money and life was full of happiness. We had a station car at our gate and would go to the market easily or go on a picnic.

A woman comes in to pick up the bags she left with Umm Khalthoum while doing her shopping on the market. She is the neighbour of Umm Khalthoum's sister-in-law. After elaborate greetings, the woman leaves, even though Umm Khalthoum invites her to have a cup of tea several times. When she is out of hearing distance Umm Khalthoum whispers: '*al-hamdu lillah*', obviously relieved that the woman did not stay. "Where

[4] Nimeiri came to power by a military coup in 1969 and because of his alliance with the communists, later the socialists, he stated that children of all 'classes' should have access to education.

were we?" she asks but before Sa'adiya or I can say anything she continues:

You know, my father always wanted his girls to know a lot, but he did not want them to work in offices. For boys it was important to study so they would get jobs with the government. He had a lot of money; we had everything in the house so there was no need for us girls to work. But when I married, I left my father's house and my husband left the company for teaching. I found there was a big difference in life.

My father was taking care of us: he even didn't allow us to go on foot to school but would take us by car. He liked girls more than boys. He hired a teacher to teach us at home. In the afternoon, our father would pick us up again, although sometimes we would come with our friends, on foot. Then we grew up and men came to our father who told him: 'We want your daughter in marriage'. It gave him a headache. So he told me to stay inside the house and not to go to school any more. He wanted to marry me off directly.

Our father also gave us lessons about Islam. I didn't go to a khalwa. *I went to a* rhoda *in Umdurman but we were also taught religious subjects in the* rhoda: *some* sura*s and more of it in primary school: there we finished the rest of the* Qur'an.

The best part of my life was when I was at primary school and I lived with my father and mother, sister and brother: when there was a car in front of the house and we had a lot of money. There were no problems. At that time, my mother was the only wife of my father. But it became a very dark life after my father married another woman. He changed his ways and he decreased the money he gave to us. He became very rough and rude to us. He gave the other wives—at that time he had married two after my mother, one from Zalingei, one from Nyala, both living in Zalingei—a lot of things and treated them kindly. But when he came to our house, his face turned into anger, up until my mother asked him to divorce her. And he divorced her, because she was afraid that the other co-wives would make amal[5] *to her. In Zalingei there were a lot of bad* faqih*s, called* konjò, *don't you know Sa'adiya?*

Sa'adiya nods and says that these men are well know by this Fur term in the area of Zalingei, because there the Fur are a majority, but that in Kebkabiya most people call them *fekki*. Sa'adiya and Umm Khalthoum engage in a discussion about the question of whether these *konjò* are delivering only services that are evil, or if they can be consulted to

[5] *Amal* lit. 'to make' or 'works'. In this case it refers to possible 'works' of a *fekki*, from *faqih*, religious teacher, but in this sense it comes closer to diviner or someone engaging in witchcraft using potions, amulets or spells in order to bring misfortune upon someone else. *Konjò* is the Fur word for a diviner.

bring blessing as well. Sa'adiya claims the last, while Umm Khalthoum hesitates. She settles the discussion by saying:

Every woman who has co-wives, she will go to a konjò *in order to bring misfortune upon the other wives. We were eight children with our mother and she was still breastfeeding our youngest brother. She was a young woman; her hair was still black. My mother told my father: 'Why do I ask you to divorce me? I am afraid for myself. I am afraid your other women will harm me. You have already changed your behaviour towards us. When you enter our house you scold us'. And more of this, she said. 'But now I will live with my children until they've grown up and then I will leave them'. All of us stayed with my mother and my father did not ask her to leave the house. He was from Abu Zabbath. But my mother was from Umdurman. My father was a* jellaba,[6] *my mother was from Aswan, she came from Egypt. She was the first Egyptian in Zalingei and people would call her 'Masriya, Masriya'.*[7]

My father at that time treated her badly. He divorced her after she asked him to do so. She was divorced in 1964. After that, all the jellaba *in Zalingei came to my mother to ask her to be their wife. But my mother refused. She said: 'No, this is enough. I have had one experience that failed. I don't want to marry another time'. She had eight children and even with them they wanted to marry her, she was a beautiful woman.*

Her youngest daughter Hanan comments that she was 'as white as a *khawadiya*'. We laugh and Umm Khalthoum ushers her into the next room and tells her to go and play with her sisters. "But she refused them all", she adds, while closing the door behind her daughter.

Just before we went to intermediary school, my father left his work at the government and bought fifty cows, donkeys, goats and horses and moved from the town of Zalingei to a small place called Garsilla. He opened a big shop there. Our lorries brought goods from Umdurman to Garsilla. He took my mother to a farikh, *a kind of cattle camp. This was the first time for her to be in the west of the Sudan, then to the west of Darfur, then to Zalingei and then even to a village. There she lived with Arabs.*[8] *My father taught my mother how to milk cows and my brothers were cowboys, looking after the cows. They spent two years in the bush, my brothers, and*

---

[6] *Jellaba* is generally used for men who come from Central Sudan in order to trade in Darfur (See Chapter 5).

[7] From *Masr*, Egypt.

[8] Here she refers to the Baggara Arabs who travel around with cows, while higher up, in the vicinity of Kebkabiya, Arabs tend camels that survive better in the desert.

my mother, while I studied at school. I stayed with my grandmother in Zalingei. My mother became ill with malaria. During one of my holidays, I went to visit my mother in the bush and I found her in a bad condition: she had become dark-skinned and very tired. I asked my mother, 'How did you become like this?' My mother said: 'This is the life in the bush, you become ill and your body becomes weak and changes colour because of tiredness'. And my father was wearing aragi[9] *and long underpants, wearing a leather bag, the kind that Arabs have, on his back. He asked me to join him to the market. I begged him: 'Please father, wear your* jellabiya*'.*[10] *But he answered 'No, I am a man of the countryside; this is my way of life now. My tribe is Arab and I've become a real Arab'. So I followed him to the market and laughed at him until we reached the market of Garsilla. The farikh was called Sagerger. His shop was big, but he sold bad things: old, traditional stuff like* zaraag, damhuriya *and* aruusa, *old black plastic shoes and* zarifa, milleh, atrun *and only small bottles of scents.*[11] *I asked him: 'Why did you leave the government job and become like this?' He said: 'Life is like this, you can pass all kinds of life, simple and rich, happy and difficult, so you will learn a lesson in life'. He gave me a present, two pieces of cloth, but of a bad quality. We returned to the* farikh *and I spent nine days with them and found life there very difficult. And then, my mother became very tired and couldn't live there any more. So our lorry came and returned my mother to Zalingei and he lived with his other wife in the* farikh. *After he was left behind with this other wife, my father also found his life difficult. So he sold all his cows, returned to Zalingei and became an employee again, in the Jebel Marra Project. He saw that his children were tired, so he returned to his life of a government employee. But the wood had changed their language and their bodies. After that I went to intermediary school in Geneina and when I returned after four years, after I had finished school, my marriage was made.*

Umm Khalthoum is pensive for a moment. Sa'adiya and I both reach for our tea to take a sip and Umm Khalthoum calls for Estma in order to bring more tea. We tell her not to, that this is enough, but she says that she would like some more anyway. Estma enters in order to get

[9] *Aragi* refers to the knee long shirts worn by men over wide trousers. It is seen as the local dress for men in Darfur and considered 'underdressed' by elite standards.

[10] A *jellabiya* is a long, wide garment for men covering the whole body. It is mostly of white cotton and considered the Sudanese national dress for men, worn by all classes.

[11] *Zaraag* is coarse, locally woven and coloured blue cloth; *damhuriya* is local unbleached cotton; *aruusa* is a cloth used at weddings; *milleh*, salt; *atrun*, sodium chloride, salt given to animals. The sale of small bottles of scents, *zarifa*, is taken to be the prerogative of *gata'at*, petty traders who buy some goods in bulk from big traders and then sell in smaller amounts. The profit is relatively low.

some more sugar, which is locked away in a cupboard at the other side of the veranda. When she has left, Sa'adiya asks if she should turn the tape recorder off, but Umm Khalthoum says "No, let's continue". So I ask her if she can tell us a bit more about her time at the intermediary school and the boarding house in Geneina:

In the boarding house, the government took care of (the) students very well: they gave you a bed and two sheets and a blanket and a pillow as well. In the morning, the sheets in all the boarding-rooms were white. In the afternoon, we had to change the white for colourful ones. All the beds had white sheets and black blankets and it looked very nice.

In the boarding house, the room was divided into rows. Two teachers were responsible for looking after the cleanliness of the rooms and would report to the principal if someone was not clean. We would wake up early in the morning and we would clean the room and the floor and windows. After we cleaned the room and got dressed, the bell would ring and we'd go to the school area. After having had one or two lessons we would take breakfast: a good kind of brown beans, cheese, and big breads, also liver. The next day, we would eat beans and tahniya *and jam. For dinner a sheep would be slaughtered, so we would have a dish of fried meat, sauce with meat, and either pumpkin or macaroni with meat, or potatoes. The sauce would be very thick, nice, with a lot of oil. For supper we sometimes had rice and salad, mango, pineapple, or* coreris, *I don't know, it is a bit like jam.*[12] *I don't know, do you Sa'adiya?*

Sa'adiya describes to me something that resembles 'compote', but Umm Khalthoum cuts us short:

... and milk of cows. And if you wanted to eat the sauce from dinner, you could. If you didn't you could just drink your milk.

"When was this?" I ask her to be sure I am following her narrative correctly.

From 1965 to 1969. It was not necessary at that time for your family to give you food, as is the case now. They only gave you some pocket money for drinks or tea

[12] Liver is considered a delicacy eaten particularly at breakfast. *Tahniya* is a sweet, vast substance made of mashed sesame seed, sugar and oil; *mullah*, different kinds of filled gravy eaten with bread, *asida*, the sorghum or millet porridge, or *kisra*, thin sour pancakes.

at the school cafeteria, so you could treat your friends to a drink. The school gave us soap and dates and after dinner we had one hour of rest, to sleep or read, but you could not talk. After the rest period, the bell would ring and all would go to do sports: volleyball, basketball, or Ping-Pong. Also there was a library where you could sit and read. Sometimes we'd have a game between two rooms or boarding houses and teachers would come to watch. The one that won would get a present from the principal: either plastic flowers or money in an envelope. In the intermediary schools for girls, there were also men teaching. The principal was a man as well.

At the end of the year, the government prepared for every lorry that would take the students home, two sacks of bread, and one big tin of tahniya *and a big tin of cheese and two buckets of jam. One of the teachers would go with us and bring us to the houses of our families. And we would eat sandwiches on the way. Some girls would come weak from their families and return fat from their schools. But when I entered my married life I found it difficult, we had problems with money.*

As I would like her to elaborate on her period at school, I ask her: "Did you go to Geneina alone?"

Yes, I went, together with the other girls from my district in one and the same lorry to Geneina. At the beginning of the year, one's family would make kisra *and* karkar[13] *for rubbing in your hair. The* kisra *was dried and would be mixed with peanuts or sesame and sugar so you could take it and eat it with milk. If you went on holidays, food for the road was the responsibility of the school. As much food had to be taken with us so that even the last pupils on the lorry would have food when going on holidays: a teacher would go with us to supervise. Now this is not happening any more. In the past people were very responsible and principals were very gentle and caring. In the school, the principal would even taste the food and if it were bad, he would quarrel with the cooks. So at that time all the children liked schools: they were taken care of and all were happy. After this, I went to have my own house. The first years were good, and full of happiness.*

Umm Khalthoum has once more returned to the moment of transition to her married life. Curious to know what she felt herself about education, I ask her: "What did you want to be when you were young?"

I was bright at school and I wanted to become a teacher in intermediary school so as to know English, and to learn English and to teach English. And to go abroad and

[13] *Karkar*, oil or clarified butter cooked with spices for nice smell used to grease hair.

to have a Master's in English. Umm Khalthoum laughs and adds: *But my father stopped me.*

It is getting dark and while Estma serves us fresh hot tea scented with cloves, her eldest daughter Kaltouma brings in an oil lamp. I ask Umm Khalthoum if we can continue now or come back next time. Umm Khalthoum insists on 'finishing her story' as she puts it. Sa'adiya checks the tape recorder and Umm Khalthoum continues, changing gear as she does so:

When my husband left the company and became a teacher, my life changed. When my father married me to him, he was not drinking. But when he became a teacher he started to drink a lot of merissa.[14] *He left me in my father's house for six months. Then he returned without any money. At that time, my mother had left Zalingei for Umdurman. Abbas came to me and said: 'There is no way to solve the problem of money'. So we had to sell some of our household goods, like beds, sheets, pots and pans. Before, we had a full sitting room, a full bedroom, and a full dining room. We sold some of it and went to Al-Fasher, where he was posted as a teacher. We arrived in Fasher and found he was moved to a village in Al-Geneina.*[15] *At that time, I was nursing Emad, my second child.*

First we sold our furniture in Zalingei and in Fasher, we sold our cupboard of clothing and my first golden bracelet in order to travel to Geneina. In Geneina, we found that he was transferred again to a small village, Hassaheisa. He left us in Geneina and after some months, he was transferred again to Al-Hilla. We joined him there and we spent one year in Al-Hilla. Then we had holidays and wanted to visit our family, but there was no money to pay for the transport, food, etc. All of Abbas' salary went into drinking and he asked me to sell one of my other bracelets, so we could travel to Geneina. After we arrived in Geneina, we spent a few days so he could get his salary. He asked again for my gold, and I gave another bracelet: he sold it for ten pounds only: it weighed 0,5 ounces. When he returned he said again: 'Money is finished'. I asked why and he said: 'Just finished'. He drank it all, that is, he took merissa. *I had only two bracelets left.*

We travelled to Zalingei and spent our holidays with my father there. When the holidays were finished, again Abbas asked for gold to pay for the travel expenses, because his salary was in Geneina. This was the fourth bracelet I gave him. In Geneina, he got his salary and we travelled back to Al-Hilla. There, life is very cheap. Everything is cheap: millet, meat, and so on, but what harmed us was his

---

[14] *Merissa* is a local beer made of sorghum or millet.

[15] Al-Geneina is both a district and a town at the border between Darfur and Chad.

drinking. We spent another year in Al-Hilla and the next holidays came. I was pregnant with my third child, Mumtaz. I had to go and have my baby at my mothers' place, in Umdurman. So I sold my last bracelet of gold, to pay for the trip. All my gold was finished.

We travelled from Geneina to Zalingei and from Zalingei to Nyala by lorry. There we took the train to Khartoum. At that time, his salary was thirty-three pounds. In Khartoum, my mother collected me from the train and she asked me about my gold. I told her, 'We sold everything, all our furniture and utensils and my gold. We've lost everything'. So we started to build our life from zero, I spent my holidays with my mother, nine months. I had my baby girl and also stayed during my maternity leave. After that, teaching became difficult and very bad. When we returned to Darfur, we moved with only two beds and a humaar-malabis[16] *instead of cupboards. Teaching brings in little money and the life of teachers is like that of soldiers. But the life of soldiers is even better because they have a lot of money. And Abbas was still drinking a lot and all his salary was going into* merissa. *My life had changed. He drank wine and quarreled with me when he came home. And he divorced me twice. There remains only one* talaaq.[17]

I am quite surprised about these revelations. I knew she had problems with Abbas, she had even indicated that explicitly. However, I had not expected her to be so far into a divorce already. We decide to finish our session of today. Umm Khalthoum's eldest son Emad brings us sugarcane from which we peel the skin by pulling it with the front teeth. The pieces of fiber are sucked audibly and thrown on the floor. Umm Khalthoum now returns to the problems she has with Abbas. This concerns how he divorced her twice over minor things. First when she went to buy a *tobe* with his mother in Al-Fasher. The second time happened during last Ramadan after a quarrel over sugar. He started screaming at her in a loud voice, all the neighbours could overhear them. She is very embarrassed, she tells us, and feels very self-conscious when walking in the street. She feels the eyes of her neighbours on her back.

---

16 *Humaar*, donkey and *malabis*, clothes. It refers to a wooden construction to hang clothes over. It is used when one cannot afford a cupboard and therefore seen as a sign of temporary lodging or poverty.

17 *Talaaq* refers to divorce. A man can divorce his wife by uttering *talaaq*, divorce, or a related term *mutallaq*, you are divorced, or *talqana*, we are divorcing, on three different occasions. Umm Khalthoum's husband obviously has done so on two occasions already.

I am not happy any more, not like before. Before I did things with my heart and would say and do things as I thought them to be right. But now, Sa'adiya, what can I do? I am careful with every step I take, every word I speak. I am not myself any more. So I want to go home, to my mother's house. He can divorce me then. I have no need for men anymore. If he wants to divorce me, then he can, I have my children and I will go to my mother's house. One year ago everything was still fine, but now, having all kinds of problems with my neighbours and other people from Kebkabiya community, with on top of this the situation in which I find myself 'nearly divorced', I feel threatened, like an animal. Look Sa'adiya, Karin, I sleep badly or not at all at night. And now there is this man, he is a relative of my husband and he visits our house regularly and eats with us often. He courts me and he has proposed to me! He is a young man; I could be his mother!

Sa'adiya and I both exclaim "*La wallai, keef*?" (No, it is not true, how?) Umm Khalthoum laughs wholeheartedly, for the first time this afternoon. She blushes. For a moment, her troubled expression has gone and she looks like a young girl. It is a surprising change in her story, in both theme and tone. Then she adds:

Anyway, I have already born eight children and he hasn't even been married. What is the use of such a marriage? No, I don't want him, I don't want any man any more, I have had enough trouble. And, more serious now: *My life has come to a bad stage and for me marriage is a troublesome thing now.*

Her youngest daughter Eman rushes in and says that Jacub, Sa'adiya's husband is at the gate. He has just returned from his trade trip and has come to pick up Sa'adiya so they can go home together. Sa'adiya hurriedly takes her leave of us. We will meet again next day after breakfast. I stay a little while longer chatting with Umm Khalthoum. Umm Khalthoum continues: "I would have liked to go on studying so as to become a teacher, but my early marriage into which my father forced me, has prevented that". She states the hope that, when back in Umdurman, she can follow courses, especially in English, to enlarge her education and thus, her chances for work. "So next time I can talk with you on my own Karin", she says jokingly. We are both tired. Mumtaz enters with a *jebbena*[18] with strong, sweet coffee, this time flavoured with cardamom, which is served in small porcelain

[18] A bottle-formed can with a rounded bottom and a long neck, made of tin or baked clay, used especially for brewing and serving coffee.

cups. When it is my turn to read Umm Khalthoum's cup, I see her intense look in her eyes. I read Umm Khalthoum's as positive as I can feeling a bit awkward, but seeing Umm Khalthoum's grateful look after I finished I felt it was the least I could do to console her a bit.

Context of the Narrative—The Present in the Past
The Predicament of Being a Daughter and a Wife

Umm Khalthoum structures her narrative quite differently from the way that Hajja does. The days of the week have no bearing on her recollections, or on the themes that she discusses. However, the idea of 'mapping' can be applied to contextualising her narrative, if I take a larger map than I have done with Hajja: not only of Kebkabiya, but a map that includes Khartoum/Umdurman as the most eastern boundary and Zalingei as the most western boundary. Umm Khalthoum's life has evolved in the course of moving from Central Sudan to Darfur and vice versa and her emotions travelled along. In this respect, her major theme seemed be the contrast between the happy memories of her early youth and the worsening of her condition after her marriage. In her narrative, 'change' is directly connected to 'moving' in both senses of the word: to move and being moved. The changes in the conditions of her life instigated by the decisions made by her father and husband are connected to their 'moving' around because of their (decreasing) careers. This also 'moved' Umm Khalthoum with respect to her feeling of security and happiness as a result of these change of places.

Umm Khalthoum tells all of this in the context of changing historical conditions. At the beginning of her narrative Umm Khalthoum tells us how her father moved first from Ed-Daein in Kordofan to Al-Fasher and Zalingei in Darfur in the capacity as *jellaba*, one of the traders from Central Sudan Hajja referred to in her story. Like many of his temporaries he was a fortune seeker using his posting as government official, as an opportunity to trade products from Central Sudan in Kordofan and Darfur. Umm Khalthoum was from an elite family, with material wealth and an emphasis on education, also for girls, an important feature of their status.

The second historical event is Nimeiri's decision to change the educational system. One of Nimeiri's socialist ideals[19] concerned access to

[19] See Al-Shahi 1990; Woodward 1990.

education. He stipulated that every child, boy or girl, in towns and countryside, should be able to attend school. Therefore, extra schools were built, even in the smaller and more remote villages. By extending the period of intermediary school, Nimeiri stretched the period that the children could attend school near their parental homes. Most places like Kebkabiya would have both primary and intermediary schools, but only large towns had the secondary high schools. For most girls, this new system provided them with a chance to gain more education. However, for Umm Khalthoum this extension forced her to stay in intermediary school longer. In turn, this extra year prevented her from going on to secondary school before men came and asked for her hand in marriage.

The third historical event concerns the retreat of the Tobacco Company from Darfur. It supplied Peter Stuyvesant amongst others, and Abbas considered his job at the company insecure. He turned out to be right,[20] but his switch to teaching resulted in diminishing income and his drinking problems.

In other words, the historical events that Umm Khalthoum refers to are in all cases also causes of changes in her personal life, in each case a change for the worse. These changes concern her youth and her married life, which mark two different and opposed periods in her personal history tied to the careers and decisions of her father or husband. Both changes result in a change in Umm Khalthoum's status. Umm Khalthoum contrasts a happy, and un-cumbersome youth marked by abundance, education, and a caring father with a married life full of disappointments, hardships, and an irresponsible husband. In her viewpoint, her husband's proposal caused her to lose the opportunity to pursue education or, as Umm Khalthoum puts it, to learn English. When Umm Khalthoum tells us repeatedly that her marriage changed everything, she implies as well that her life changed for the worse; in fact her reflection on her marriage is one lament about the bad attitude of her husband and the bad state her life is in at present.

However, Umm Khalthoum's contrasting of the two periods in her life is not straightforward. Umm Khalthoum tells us that her youth was only happy in her early years when her mother was still the only wife of her father. At this time her father took care of her and stimulated

[20] *Tumbaq* is still grown as a cash crop, mainly for local use.

her to get educated. This period ended when he took another wife 'and changed his attitude towards us'. In contrast, at the beginning of her narrative when Umm Khalthoum refers to her marriage for the first time, she indicates that this period of her life also started well. She says: "When he was in the company, we had a lot of money and life was happiness. We had a station car at our gate and would go to the *suq* easily, or go on a picnic". This life changed when her husband switched jobs and started drinking. In other words, Umm Khalthoum consciously amplifies the good side of her youth, diminishing its sadder part, while emphasizing the bad side of her marriage, only touching upon the promising start. This constructing of a big contrast of her life before and after marriage is achieved by two episodes of her past that receive Umm Khalthoum's special attention: her father living in the bush and Umm Khalthoum's time at the boarding house.

Umm Khalthoum tells us about the divorce of her parents on two occasions. First she discusses the use of *amal* by her mother's co-wives, causing her father to be grumpy and foulmouthed when in their company, where he was kind and understanding before. Then she turns to her father's life in the 'bush' apparently with both her mother and his other wife. This episode seems an anomaly both in her life and in the structure of Umm Khalthoum's narrative. It is a 'bad' part of her youth but still told in much detail, though at first I have no idea what she wants to say with this part of her narrative. It might be that Umm Khalthoum feels this decision of her father is indeed an anomaly. She treats it as an intermezzo, which 'changed their lives', although Umm Khalthoum herself lived with her grandmother and later in the boarding house so she did not experience much of it.

This period of 'unhappiness' in fact sets off the 'normal' situation when her father was a government employee (to which he later returns) which to her was full of joy and when he was married only to her mother. I think that this is where her father's venture into the 'bush' fits in her argument about the way her life changed for the worse once she was married. Not so much the hardships of life in the bush might be at stake here, but a heeding of her father's character and the consequences of his actions for her life. Umm Khalthoum evaluates his demeanour, portraying him as oblivious to the needs of his wife and children. She depicts her father as headstrong, impertinent, extraordinary in his choices, and harsh to himself and his beloved. At the same time, it indicates his power to decide about his family's fate. Umm Khalthoum sees this as not only true in this particular case, but also when it comes to his decisions about her fate. His decision to marry her to Abbas must be evaluated against the same frame of reference: foolhardy and selfish and without considering her interest. Her early marriage was perhaps caused by a change in politics and bad luck, but certainly by a change in attitude by her father, which thus had nothing to do with her personally. Her father's time in the 'bush' is therefore a transitional period: her early marriage was just a consequence of the change in her father's attitude towards life and towards her future.

One of the few movements that are of her own accord is when she is in boarding school of the intermediary school in Al-Geneina. The boarding house period offered Umm Khalthoum education as well as leisure: the school taught her lessons as well as the right behaviour. By making her youth and her education part of the same period, the impression of a happy youth is what remains. School in a way was an extension of home.

In this way, Umm Khalthoum retains the difference between a happy youth, which includes her stay at the boarding house, and a difficult marriage, which was a result of her father's change of attitude after his stay in the 'bush'. The relation between both episodes is not only the fact that Umm Khalthoum actually lived at the boarding house while her father stayed in the 'bush', but also that both periods together mark a watershed in her status position.

Gaining an education was an elaboration of her elite position, as girls in that period were not usually able to follow an education, as Nimeiri was not in power yet. Therefore, Umm Khalthoum might feel the choice of her father to denounce his life of an employee might also be a negation and even diminishing of her status. This dilemma is exemplified in her reference to the *aragi* her father is adamant about wearing and her request to him to wear the male national dress, the *jellabiya*. Her father migrated from the capital to small towns in Kordofan and Darfur, and then to 'the bush'. These facts maybe a metaphor not only of the diminishing happiness and material security of Umm Khalthoum and her family, but also of the loss of their urban, governmental elite status. Her elaboration of her life at the boarding house should therefore be read as what has been lost by her marriage forced on her by her father.

A similar type of epic moving is related to her married life. Her financial security vanished when her husband took another job and started to drink, spending all the money. Her narration of the loss of her bracelets indicates that her material circumstances can also be read as a metaphor for her life as a whole. The golden jewelry a woman gets at her marriage, the *mahr* or dowry, is hers to dispose of.[21] Tradition states that the bride can sell the gold in times of need, mostly in the case of a divorce or the death of her husband. Although in Central Sudan the dowry is part of the bride price, and thus given by the family of the husband, in Darfur the mother of the bride is the donator of furniture, utensils, and sometimes even gold, to her daughter.[22] It is therefore not surprising that her mother notices her lack of bracelets. Umm Khalthoum's answer: "We lost everything", adding: "So we started to build our life from zero" therefore reflects the state her life is in. With the selling of every bracelet she not only lost wealth in gold, but also she became increasingly removed from her roots: the loss of her own wealth brought a definite end to her chances to (financial) independence and an elevated elite status. Loosing the wealth given by her mother meant loosing the promises of her youth and it changed her chance to happiness.

Con/text-Analysis—The Past in the Present
Father/Daughter, Husband/Wife

The main figures in her narrative are her father and her husband as the ones who decided Umm Khalthoum's fate. In her story Umm Khalthoum constructs positions and relations predominantly between herself and her father, and herself and her husband, which are important in order to understand her own subject position. Even though the two most important men in her life 'belong' to two different parts of her story, the positions she gives to them are structurally related in her narrative: in a serial, a parallel, and an oppositional way.

The serial relation is due to the chronology of her narrative: in her youth, the power to make decisions lay in her father's hands and on marriage, it was transferred to her husband. This serial position relates directly to norms and values of that period. Girls were supposed to marry as soon as they were considered mature enough. "It gave him a headache", euphemistically refers to the importance of a father

[21] In some cases, especially when the wealth of a family has diminished over the years, the *mahr* is seen as a premature inheritance, leaving the immovable property for her brothers.

[22] See for an elaborate and excellent study on the meaning of the *mahr* for women, in this case living in Palestine, Moors 1999.

guarding his daughter's virtue. Arranging her marriage released him of that obligation.

The positions of control of both her father and husband over Umm Khalthoum's life contain parallels in the way she talks about them. Their whims and shortcomings put a strain on the family life of both. Both caused distress and unhappiness for their families: in both cases, Umm Khalthoum is the recipient of their actions, the victim of their whims and inclinations. However, in her narrative the positions of her father and husband are not completely identical: it is her father whom she accuses of taking away her chances to a career; her husband 'just' made her life difficult.

This insight puts the construction of a happy youth and an unhappy marriage in a different perspective. Considering the two periods in her life together, her recollections of her youth proved a prelude for justifying the stage her life, her 'almost-divorced' stage, has reached now. It is therefore no coincidence that her reflection on this episode ends with a qualification of the immaterial side of her relation to Abbas: "My life changed. He drank wine and he quarreled with me when he came home. And he divorced me twice. There remains only one *talaaq*".

In other words, the seeds to her current predicament were planted during her youth and therefore she cannot be blamed for her failed marriage. In this narrative, Umm Khalthoum constructs her father and husband as the actors, a construction which makes her a victim. A victim of her male custodians, of fate: and at the end of our visit whilst we are chatting off the record she connects her current predicament in her personal life to the gossip and quarrels with people in Kebkabiya over her relation with Haj az-Zein's family, in which she also figures as a victim. She almost seems resigned to this role when she states: 'He can divorce me then. I have no need of men anymore'.

Umm Khalthoum's construction of herself as a victim should be read as a negotiation of the current moral discourse of the government. By disclaiming responsibility for the main decisions concerning her life, she cannot be blamed for her status as 'almost' divorced woman. She has obeyed her father, as a good daughter should, and she has tried to sustain her family with the bracelets, which are legally her own, as a good wife would. In this way she tries to salvage her status as a good Muslim woman.

The reference to the suitor is odd here. It is as if she wants to assert that she still has worth as a woman. Perhaps it is also to make her less of a victim than she has portrayed herself thus far in her narrative.

However, in the light of the current dominant discourse, I think it is an indirect claim of the acknowledged value of her as a good wife: to Abbas because she does not give in to the suitors passes, and in general as other men see her as a potentially good wife.

Interesting in this respect is the way that her mother figures in her narrative. When Umm Khalthoum is contemplating her current situation, her mother is apparently her only hope as the one who offers a possible refuge if her marriage fails: 'So I want to go home, to my mother's house'. However, while her father and husband as characters get depth, her mother, who Umm Khalthoum depicts as a sensible and strong woman, does not receive much attention. These aspects form part of her next narrative.

Second Session—After Marriage

Some time has passed since our last meeting. At the end of December Johan had come to visit me for several weeks. During this time, we live together in the *gutiya* on Hajja's compound. This means we have social obligations, guests to entertain, and social calls to make. It is the time of the *haboobs*; the cold desert winds that leave sand in every nook and cranny. The nights therefore are quite cold and dusty. Every morning we wake up covered with a layer of sand. As the 'bathroom' is located outside, next to the kitchen, bathing carries a high risk of catching a cold. So getting rid of the dust is only advisable once every four days when the family places a bathing tub in the kitchen. Even with this precaution, I acquire a backache. Whether it is the cold, the mattress, having carried something heavy, or the typing on the uncomfortable chairs, it is not clear, but the backache persists.

Although there is not much possibility of recording stories with the tape recorder because of the dust, I visit Umm Khalthoum regularly, with or without Johan, and occasionally with Sa'adiya as well. When I complain about my backache, Umm Khalthoum is sure I am under the spell of the evil eye. Umm Khalthoum insists I should see a renowned *faqih*, Abu Duggu in order to have him write a *hijab*, an amulet containing either herbs and roots or a *Qur'an* text, which will protect me against the destructive evil eye. I do as they advise and he gives me a potion of water mixed with the ink of a religious text that he has washed off from the wooden slate on which he had written it: I should both drink from and bathe in the potion. Abu Duggu also writes the text on paper, which I have to fold and carry round my neck as a *hijab* inside a specially made leather casket. Although I am sceptical, I follow his instructions for a few days. The backache disappears about a week later. Just to be sure, I keep the amulet under my pillow.

A few days later I meet Umm Khalthoum while I am plodding through one of the sandy streets near the market place. She asks me immediately when I will come to tape more of her story. She has already invited Sa'adiya herself and a few days later we sit again on her veranda drinking tea. This time, the tea is made from the sugar and tea I brought with me. Sa'adiya takes out the tape recorder and Umm Khalthoum asks where she had finished on the previous occasion. Sa'adiya says that she had been talking about her married life. Umm Khalthoum smiles and continues as if it has not been some weeks since our last talk.

Our first problem was in Ramadan. Abbas is very nervous and quickly irritated then. At simple things, he would say talqana.[23] *In Fasher, we had already had a problem and this concerned a simple issue as well. He gave me thirty pounds to buy a new* tobe *for myself. I went with his mother to buy one and spent all the money. After we returned, he asked me where the rest of the money was. He said: 'Why didn't you bring the rest of the money'? I told him: 'I went with your mother and the* tobe *cost thirty pounds'. When he became angry, I told the servant to take it back. The servant took it back and Abbas said: 'Why are you doing this'? Then he screamed*: talqana, talqana! *At that time, I was a young girl and I didn't know much about married life. After he divorced me, his family, his brother and his father, sat together and they returned me to him while I was still in Abbas' house. My family didn't hear about it. Then we moved to Kebkabiya in 1985. And then again in 1989 he brought home four* ratul *of sugar during Ramadan. We had many guests at that time. I used the four* ratul *in preparing the* fatuur[24] *for them and also in preparing food for the* sahuur[25] *at four o'clock in the morning. He said: 'Why did you use all the sugar?' Afterwards he said again*: talqana, talqana. *This was the second divorce. Other friends came, like Yusuf Jazzar, and they returned me to him. I didn't know much about divorce. But now I understand and I feel I didn't do anything wrong and that he hadn't any reason to divorce me. It is my father's fault, because he*

---

23 *talqana* (Arab.) 'We are divorced'.

24 In this case *fatuur* refers literally to 'breaking the fast', also '*iftar*' and refers to the first meal taken after sunset, the end of a day of fasting during Ramadan.

25 *Sahuur* is the last meal one can take just before sunrise, the start of a new day of fasting. The *sahuur* is thus meant to start the day with a full stomach but many forego this meal as it means waking up early while the last meal has hardly been digested.

gave me in marriage to Abbas when I was still a little girl: I wished he had left me to grow up and to know more about married life.

My life now changed from a soft one to hell and I hate him for it. I think that when I tried to build up my life, he destroyed it. Because I keep remembering that he divorced me twice without reason. This makes me even angrier. It is not an ordinary thing to divorce me: it is not as easy as eating or drinking. When this man, Yusuf Jazzar, returned me to Abbas, he said: 'You've a narrow mind, to give your wife such problems: it is not to be considered easy to divorce over such a simple thing, and you make life with your wife narrow and tense'. And every time I try to imagine how to create a happy life for my children, how to give them a luxury life and a nice house, I feel that, unfortunately, it is finished, because of these two divorces. And who is responsible for this? He is. And now I hate him even more, whenever he tries to be near me I look at him like a wild animal. And when he comes to me to have a chat, I remember the two wounds he gave me, what he did to me. And sometimes when we have a quarrel, ah, I become bored with him. I tell him, 'Now you can divorce me a third time so our relation will be cut forever. A third divorce and I'll go to my mother in Umdurman and you'll send money to my children so they'll grow up in a better way'.

This is the reason why I want to leave Kebkabiya. There is no hope of living with him forever. People say that Umm Khalthoum is very happy and very comfortable, but they don't know what I have inside. Because our last divorce was in Ramadan, he was fasting, and then he is quickly irritated, so my divorce may come soon. It was in Ramadan: if it had been before that time, I would have thought that he was drunk, but it was in Ramadan. I always live in pain now. And last year when he saw my pain, he stopped drinking.

If you have many children like I do, you have to prepare a good life for them. And if they see that their father and mother are sociable, they also will be comfortable in their life. I have decided to go to my family in Umdurman, so that even if my life will change when the third divorce comes, I will be near my mother.

Umm Khalthoum looks quite determined after this last exclamation. Both Sa'adiya and I are silent. Umm Khalthoum turns towards the door and calls Estma to bring us some more tea. After she has turned back to us she looks pensive for a moment and then continues:

In their life, my father and mother at first loved each other and we felt safe in our house, everything was available in sacks and tins. We didn't need to go and buy things with money from the market. We took it all from our fathers' shop. He brought biscuits in tins and sweets in buckets. And we had servants to go to the market and to the mill. He didn't want us to work. If we were bored sitting inside the house, he took us for a small journey, to see a park or to go to our garden. After he got married to other wives, my mother's problems with my father increased. This was because he was not fair to all of them and didn't treat them equally. And sometimes he stayed in the other house for seven days and in my mothers' house for only one day. Now I am comparing my life with my mothers' last years with my father: mine will be the same. My mother was the same age as I am and her hair was still black and she lived without a husband. She stayed in my father's house until she had seen us married and then she took my little sister and brother to Umdurman. And when she wanted to leave she asked my father to give her a kind of title deed of custody. It is a letter from the judge she could give to her brother so he would be her legal representative and responsible for the two youngest children, for everything, even for their marriage. My little brother died three years ago, while I was in Kebkabiya. He was shot in Iraq by bandits.

Sa'adiya and I both look up at her, as her remark is so out of the blue. Nevertheless, Umm Khalthoum continues:

My father at first treated us kindly, but at last he harmed us. Then, recently, he became ill. My mother was in Umdurman and her sons found land in Umdurman to build a new house on. When they returned from working abroad, they built a fashionable house for her. They took her on haj *to Mecca. They bought new furniture for her, for the kitchen, for all the rooms and even now, my brother in Saudi still sends her money. She has become rich. My father in Zalingei divorced his second wife and married another. The new wife has five children from my father. He became ill in his mind. We had all moved to Umdurman and left him with his new wife. So they sent him to us in Umdurman. We took him to Tijani's Hospital for nervous diseases, or, how do you say that, mental disorders. He lay there for forty-five days. When he became well, he said: 'I want to go back to my family in Zalingei', and he returned. After a few months, the illness recurred. At that time, I was in Fasher and they brought him to me. I asked Abbas' father to get* faqih*s in order to write for him from the Qur'an like* jawhara *or* majami'a. *I bought a sheep, slaughtered it, and prepared a meal for all* faqihs. *When they brought him here, he didn't remember anything: he could not pray, he didn't know what was happening to him. After that, he became well. A* jowharat-kamal, *if* faqih*s do it to you when you are ill, it can have two possible results. Either you die or you become well. The next day he said: 'Give me the* ibrik *and* muslayah'[26] *and he went to pray right away. He took off his old clothes and we bought new ones for him at the market. We fed him with*

[26] *Ibrik*, water container used for washing hands and feet before praying, but also used when going to the toilet. *Muslayah* is a prayer mat.

chicken and pigeon-soup: he spent a month with me. Then we bought a ticket for him from Fasher to Nyala and gave him money to return to Zalingei because his job was there. After he returned his wife refused him, saying: 'I don't want him because he is mad'. He remained single for years. In the tenth year, he got diarrhoea. They sent me a message saying my father is ill. While I was preparing to travel, another telegram arrived to say that he had died. I went to Zalingei to say ta'ziya[27] *I travelled with* ustaz *Breman's wife, Miriam. My sister was there to say* ta'ziya *as well. There, I found a letter written by my father three days before he died, addressed to my mother. It said: 'To Fayrouz. I ask you to forgive me, because I did you injustice. And if you would go to Mecca again on* haj, *can you ask Allah to forgive me'. At the end he wrote: 'I am sorry for my life. I feel sad going to die'.*

At that time, my mother was very comfortable. My brother changed her life for good. It was as if she became younger and if you saw her, you would say: 'That is not the Fayrouz we knew in Zalingei'.

Some men treat women badly and my mother, who had no money, became rich and went on haj. *She is happy now. And my father, he lost all his money, his cars all broke down and only the carcasses were left. His cows died, like his horses and other animals. His houses were sold. We had big schemes with a pump, which was bought by my eldest brother Ahmed, a son of my father by his first wife. He brought it for my mother but my father took it from her, saying 'he is my son, not yours'. Ahmed's mother was from Mowridaal-Abassiya*[28] *in Umdurman. My father married Ahmed's mother before mine. After she died, my father married my mother and brought Ahmed to my mothers' house. My mother treated him kindly. When he had grown up, he said: 'In the future I will give you a good present'. He got older and got a job. He said: 'You treated me well and didn't make a difference between me and your sons'. This is why he bought her the pump. Also, he bought land for her. He sent sixty pounds and he brought the pump from Uganda. But my father took it all. We learned many lessons in life. We passed through a farmer's life, an employee's life, a nomadic life and it coloured our life. Then we returned to an employee's life and our mother left for Umdurman and my father stayed in Zalingei until he died.*

After my father married the other women, they went to faqih*s and put spells on him. It is true. One day we opened the mattress of him in Al-Fasher and it was full of roots. His wives put it there so he would turn on us. Also there were a lot of* hijab*s. My mother had come from Zalingei to Fasher to spend her holidays with relatives and he stayed with them too. He went back to Zalingei early, and when our*

---

[27] *Ta'ziya*, literally 'consolation', is a prayer of condolences when paying one's respect to the deceased's family.

[28] Ethnic group coming from Egypt.

holidays were finished, he sent a lorry to pick us up, but he didn't come himself. After we came to Zalingei, they, his wives, brought a small jerry can with fruit juice with them, but we didn't drink it: we threw it all away. We asked our father to give us a house of our own because we didn't want to live with the other wives.

After two months our father hated us even more and didn't want to see us any more. When he came to our house he would scold us and curse badly. My mother also went to the faqih *and he told her that the other wives had made* 'chai', *a kind of tea with potion for their husband so he'd hate her and wouldn't want to live with her anymore. The* faqih *told my mother it would make my father hate her like blindness. She herself did not want to harm the other wives she even didn't try. She only asked the* faqih *to make a* hijab *to protect her so the other wives would not harm her. And now, in Umdurman, she still suffers from itching and headaches, this also was caused by them. She went to a doctor in Umdurman for it, but there is no cure for it. When my father divorced my mother, she told him: 'I don't want to go to my family in Umdurman right now, I will stay until my children here are grown up and married'. After that, she left.*

"Couldn't she go to a *faqih* in Umdurman in order to get rid of the headache and itching, or go to a *gubba* like people here would do?" I ask her.

Neither my mother nor me ever went to a gubba. *In Umdurman,*[29] *there are no such things like a* gubba *or a* faqih, *only in Darfur.*

Sa'adiya interrupts, saying: "I met Fellata,[30] men who gave women in Umdurman roots when I was there in order to keep their husbands from marrying other women". Umm Khalthoum looks surprised and says:

These men must have come recently. And they come from the West so they brought it with them.

She pauses for a moment and then continues:

Now, if I go to Umdurman, my life will change. I don't want another husband, I'll stay in my mother's house, just to help my children to grow up and do my job. People

---

[29] The tomb of Al-Mahdi, one of the most famous in Sudan, is located in Umdurman.

[30] *Fellata* is used for referring to people who come from West-Africa.

here do not know that I have been divorced twice. In the past, I didn't feel, but now I feel and wonder: why did Abbas harm me, divorcing me twice without any reason? I don't know, is it because I refused him in the past and my father ordered me to marry him? I told my father to let me be, to let me learn so my mind would grow and I could choose the right husband for myself. All my sisters and brothers were in school and they studied. My eldest sister went to a special school in Umdurman called irsaliyah, *where she studied English and Arabic. After moving into the fourth class he took her from school and we moved to Ed-Daein, he gave her away in marriage. Before we left for Ed-Daein, my grandfather asked my father to leave my sister in Bahri, in Khartoum. But my father refused and said: 'I don't want to leave my child behind'. Her husband was from Geneina and had lived in London. He was a teacher in a technical school: he spent ten years in London. My mother said: 'This girl is still young, you can leave her with me for a while'. But he said: 'No, I married her, so it means I married her'. Our family moved from Ed-Daein to Al-Fasher. In Fasher, they got married when she was sixteen years old, like me when I got married. My father couldn't leave his daughters unmarried when they were fifteen or sixteen years old. And we had another little sister, who was married to Abbas' brother when she was only fourteen years old. My eldest sister married in Fasher and they went to El-Obeid and then to the South. They had five children and he died in Umdurman, he was a diabetic, but he kept drinking. That is why he died. She moved to my mother's house and lived for eight years with my mother and her five children. She saw that life became expensive, so my eldest sister decided to work. She found a job in the army hospital in the medical service. Her job is to take care of the feeding of children. And when I went to Umdurman for the funeral of my brother from Iraq, I found her satisfied and comfortable and she looked even younger than I did. Between she and I are four children! She is more beautiful than a young girl is. She has four daughters and one son. She married off her first daughter, and the second is engaged to our cousin, the son of our father's brother. The bridegroom is an engineer at a TV satellite station. And still men come and ask her for marriage, but she refused them all. And I told to her: 'This place where you work is very susceptible and open for such proposals with all these men and soldiers seeing you without your* tobe.[31] *And you became beautiful and young and fat so it is better to marry another man: even I am admiring your beauty, what about men! For this reason you should marry'. She looks like my mother, just like an Egyptian woman. Two years ago I received the message that she married and I was very happy about it. My other sister, Feiza, was married to a man in Zalingei, Abbas' brother. He is an agricultural advisor. She has six children. And our little sister Selwa married in Umdurman and that is where*

[31] As she is working in an army hospital, she works in an army outfit of khaki coloured trousers and a knee long wide jacket, wearing a cap on her head.

she lives. Her husband has cars, his own house and he has a big chicken farm near Umdurman. He is still working with another company but saves his salary in order to build up the farm. It is four hundred feddan.[32] *All his money goes into it. This sister is the richest in our family. My brother, who comes after me, is working at the post-office in Umdurman. But he took his holidays and went to Saudi Arabia on a contract. Now he works at the Beni Sag-Company. Twelve years he is working there now. Mahadi, who is older than me as well, works in Saudi, in el-Taïf. And Ali is his own boss; he has a shop to repair audio-visual apparatus in Umdurman. He married a girl from a small village near Umdurman.*

In our time, our parents used to send their daughters to school. But when they reached maturity, they'd take them from school and marry them off. They couldn't complete their education. There were not a lot of women working at that time.

I look at her inquisitively and ask, "Why was it that one didn't allow girls to go to high school, to continue their education?"

They put their daughters in school just to have them learn but not in order to have jobs. At that time, life was easy and things were cheap and most families were comfortable. But after that, life changed and it became expensive. I myself didn't work and my husband became a teacher and I found that his money was not enough to live off, so I decided to work. I became a teacher of a crèche and now I assist him with this small amount of money, four hundred pounds per month, but it is better than nothing. Nowadays, all the girls want to become employees so they can help their families. Now female employees have become more numerous than before. In the past life was easy and cheap so families didn't need the girls' money. Even now, husband and wife work both only to survive. It is better to support each other, to bring up your children well. Life is difficult and everything is expensive. In the past life was cheap and we were not working then, but now life is very expensive and we need to work. All people need to work. And when my husband left the company and worked in education, I saw that his income is not enough to sustain our family so I also took my school certificates and asked for work. They employed me in the kindergarten, so now we complement each other with our salaries. It is better than nothing.

But nowadays all girls want to be employed, because life is expensive. Nowadays wife and husband can both work in order to assist each other. It is important that wife and husband work together in order to have their children grow up well. In the past when I was in my father's house, we had everything in buckets and we didn't need to go to the shop because everything is available in the house. If our neighbours

---

[32] A *feddan* is a measure of land: one feddan = 1.038 acres or 4200 square meters: 1 acre = 0.963 *feddan*.

asked for anything we would give it to them, but nowadays there is little money so we take things from the shop and we pay the merchants only after the salary has arrived. Everything in our house was in sacks, even beans and lentils, so even our hens laid their eggs on the sacks.[33]

But now we have nothing, we buy in pounds and ounces. Teachers have nothing, but merchants and traders; they are the ones that have plenty. Every teacher, if he wants to live with a family and to feed his children properly he has a second job, because the salary is too low. One needs to eat and dress. Everybody wants the other to work so he can be happy with his family and raise his children well. In the past, I wished to marry a wealthy man with a lot of money and to be happy and comfortable with him, I didn't mean to marry a teacher. The 'big' employee, the one with a high rank, would have been good as well. My father married his little daughter to Abbas' brother and I was married to Abbas and Abbas forgot all this, he is just mistreating me. On little problems he is saying: Talqana, talqana, *while all the neighbours can hear him. This hurts me very much. If you want to divorce your wife, you can do it quietly, so not everyone is overhearing you. Also in the* Qur'an *it is stated: 'If you want to live with a woman you can and treat her kindly. If you want to divorce her also do it smoothly*, bil ma'aruuf, *thoughtfully'. There is nobody to force me to stay all my life with Abbas, because he wounded me and now I am not comfortable with him. My children will grow up, even when I go to my family in Umdurman. They will grow up well, no problems will overcome them.*

In order to return to the subject of work that Umm Khalthoum had started with, I ask her: "So after you were married you started working as a crèche teacher. Was this your first job?"

In the past I was a homemaker and stayed in my house, I didn't have a job. After I married and became a homemaker, I needed to work and became a teacher in the rhoda, *the crèche. Because my husband left the company, and in the company there was a lot of money. So when he left it and started teaching, the money was too little so I had to work to help him in supporting us. I worked in the kindergarten because my certificate didn't allow me to work in another job. If my certificate had been better, I could have been a teacher in a primary or intermediary school. In the past, I wanted to be a teacher. But because my father refused and took me from school and married me to this man I didn't. In the past, I also choose this job because I could look after my little children. They could grow up near me. And I liked this job*

[33] When we transcribe the tape Sa'adiya explains that this means there were so many sacks standing around that even the hens feel comfortable to lay.

because it makes me a patient woman. Children cry and talk a lot and it makes me patient. And so I am able to listen to the crying and talking of eighty children and it gave me a good exercise to treat my children well in the house. But in the first years I suffered a lot because I had my own work in the house, to look after my children, to prepare food, to clean the house and I had my job. In the morning I had to make tea for the children, the oldest one had to go to school and the smallest ones I had to wash and dress so they could come with me. When I returned from the kindergarten, I had to prepare food for my family. My eldest daughter was in intermediary school and the headmaster forbade all pupils to go home for breakfast. After that, I had to go back to the crèche. Then again I hurried back home to prepare dinner and clean or wash some clothes or to do other things. But now I am comfortable because my daughters are grown up and I divide the work between them. One has to prepare dinner every day, the second has to wash clothes, and the third goes to the market to buy things and bathes the younger children. So I feel very comfortable with this. I only help with small things. When I come to have breakfast, everything is ready. I can sleep and take some rest before I go back to the crèche. After I come home, again I find my daughters working. If I want to, I help them, if I don't I can go to bed and tell them what to do. But I started working in Al-Fasher in 1984, and in 1986 they posted me in Kebkabiya. Two years ago the Ministry of Education sent me a letter stating that I was selected to go to Khartoum to attend a course so I can become a supervisor: someone who inspects the work and circumstances in other crèches. But I answered them in a letter saying that I want to apologise because I still have little children and I asked them for another chance the following year. Many problems came from Abbas: he didn't want me to work. He said: 'Don't work because you come from the crèche tired and you need a rest'. But I told him I want to contribute to our income because there is not enough money to sustain us and I want to work. My salary is very little but I used to have sanduq *with many people and I would get two thousand pounds after ten months. I told him that it is better than nothing; because when you stay at home your time is empty. After the* kisra *to eat the food with and the food itself is prepared, what is there to do? A person needs to work. When I came home from the crèche I started my housework: preparing food, cleaning the house, bathing the children so that I find that time is full. Staying at home is boring. It is better to change. If my husband had not left his first job, I would not have been able to work, because he doesn't like me to work. Even now, in the* Tadaman *women's association when I was asked to attend a meeting in Kutum on behalf of the association he was also opposed to me leaving and so I didn't go. He said: 'If you go, who is going to take care of your children and who are you going to stay with'? Also they asked me to go to Fasher, but again I apologized to them. He wants me to stay in the house, to have a rest, to prepare things for him and to look after my children. I work for money and I want to be able to look after my little children, as I do in the crèche. After the crèche they will go to primary school and Abbas is working there so in that case he can look after them.*

With a loud bang, the door of the courtyard is pushed open. Sheima, the one but youngest daughter of Umm Khalthoum rushes in yelling, '*Ya ummi, ummi,* mama, mama, you have to go to Hajj Musa's house. They need you for preparing the *baghuur* and *henna* and *riha*!' Umm Khalthoum looks up and tells her daughter to calm down. 'The marriage of Zeinab is taking place in a few weeks and they want me to prepare the perfumes for their daughter's *shanta,* bride wealth'. She smiles shyly: 'I am good at making those wedding things you know', and gets dimples in her cheeks. 'But there is no hurry, they only want me to give a list of ingredients I need'.

At home, I do not feel like eating very much. As usual, when a *haboob* is building I feel nauseous and light-headed. Soon the desert wind descends on us leaving a trail of dust and garbage in its wake.

Context of the Narrative—The Present in the Past
Mother's Past and/in Umm Khalthoum's Present

Umm Khalthoum begins the second narrative where she finished the last time. She discusses the same issues as during her first narrative. Yet at the same time she shifts the emphasis from her experiences during her youth to those during her married life which is concomitant with a shift from blaming her father to pointing at Abbas for her current state of misery: "*It is my father's fault, because he gave me in marriage to Abbas when I was still a young girl. I wished he had left me to grow up and to know more about married life*", to: "*My life now changed from a soft one to hell and I hate him for it. I think that when I tried to build op my life, he destroyed it. Because I keep remembering that he divorced me twice without reason*". This time she does describe those two earlier occasions and the 'minor' issues over which Abbas divorced her and this is indicative of her shift in focus and goal in her current narrative.

This shift is symbolized by Umm Khalthoum's description of her movements. The locations which figure in this narrative, are the same as in her first: Umdurman, Al-Fasher and Zalingei. This time Umm Khalthoum takes the initiative to travel from the capital of North Darfur, Al-Fasher, to the more remote Zalingei where her father is, at first ill, and later dying. Her intention to leave Kebkabiya for Umdurman: "... So that even if my life will change when the third divorce comes, I will be near my mother", this time has the connotation of a positive change in her current life. She reconsiders her parents' life after their divorce. This time, it is with a goal explicitly related to her own, current life: "Now I am comparing my life with my mother's last year with my father: mine will be the same". The comparison constitutes the main theme of her narrative.

In the discussion on her parents' lives after their divorce, she constructs an opposition between the fate of her mother and her father. The illness, poverty, and death of her father are all aggravated by the fact that in the end all his loved ones neglected him. He died alone and in regret of his life, especially of his mistreatment of Umm Khalthoum's mother. In contrast, her mother's life improved after she left for Umdurman. She became richer, happier, and looked younger than she actually was. On this occasion, her mother is the 'victor' in the dichotomy between her life (getting divorced, getting a better life) and her father's (divorcing, then worsening).

Further, in this case the dichotomy between her mother and father is related to the opposition between the rural and the urban, between being uncivilised and sophisticated, and to which she now adds a life of increasing misfortune and increasing satisfaction. Within this theme, one can understand Umm Khalthoum's recurring reflections on *faqihs* which might be triggered by my recent visit to one of them; in any case, the use of *faqihs* by her mother's co-wives were at the root of the change in fortune in her mother's marriage. Her insistence on the unavailability of *faqihs* and *gubbas* in Umdurman and the fact that she is quite adamant that her mother did not use the services of a *faqih* to harm others, only to protect herself are instrumental: Umdurman represents sophistication and education, and also, the wealth and even the class position which Umm Khalthoum enjoyed before her misery started. Her assertion that "Now if I go to Umdurman, my life will change" seems quite a sudden leap. However, it fits well into her endeavour to compare her mother's life after her divorce, with the future that might lie ahead for Umm Khalthoum. The dichotomy therefore also applies to the content of her life: from a difficult, unhappy marriage in 'backward' Darfur, to a satisfying, happier life at her mother's place back in 'sophisticated' Umdurman.

One can detect Umm Khalthoum's focus on the possible transitory stage of her life in the repeated accusations of both her father and

Abbas. After she has stated that her sisters were also married off at an early age, she also points out the difference: her sisters have done well in their life while she feels she has been left behind in every respect. Not only in her marriage, but also her chances of coping with her life: "If my certificate had been better I could have been a teacher in primary or intermediary school". She uses the discussion of the fate of her sisters to evaluate her own current situation. Umm Khalthoum is married to a man who not only prevented her from getting qualifications, but who also does not allow her to grab the few opportunities she has to get a better position with her current papers. She says of him, "A lot of problems came from Abbas, he didn't want me to work". In addition, she is quite explicit about the fact that all of her siblings, who are better off than she is, now live near Umdurman. Even her sister, who returned to her mother's house after the death of her own husband, has fared better than she has.

Umm Khalthoum accuses her father and husband for preventing her to study and work. So a 'return' to Umdurman, is a return to the happiness of her childhood, creating chances for a better life as both her mother and her sisters have proven. Thus, the goal of comparing her life with her female relatives serves to reduce the feelings of insecurity Umm Khalthoum feels due to the 'liminal' nature of her current situation. This brings me to consider the position Umm Khalthoum occupies in her narrative.

Con/text-Analysis—The Past in the Present
Reward and Redemption

If in her first narrative Umm Khalthoum relates herself mainly to her father and husband, in this part she shifts to also consider the relationship with other people: her mother and her siblings. Umm Khalthoum changes her focus in respect to the relations that she elaborates upon and she changes the tone of her narration. For example when she says, "I'll go back to Umdurman and you'll send money to my children so they'll grow up in a better way". She changes from a submissive tone, recounting what has overcome her, to a more assertive tone, of belligerence and determination. In addition, it is in this transition that she shifts her focus from the past to the future: from Darfur to Umdurman, from sadness to happiness and, from repression to redemption, from repercussions to rewards.

However, even though the tone of Umm Khalthoum's story telling has changed from uneasy, insecure to more decisive and determined, the way she talks about these problems still betrays a feeling of uncertainty and ambivalence. There is uncertainty in her feelings about a possible third divorce. She indicates this by the fact that in the first line of her story she states that her last divorce took place during Ramadan. Ramadan is a time when most people stop drinking alcohol even if they are usually drinking. Of her husband, Umm Khalthoum says: "He is very nervous and quickly irritated then". Towards the end of this first part she returns to this event, now stating: "It was in Ramadan: if it was before that time, I would have thought that he was drunk, but it was in Ramadan". This indicates ambivalence: the first reference to Ramadan indicates mitigating circumstances for Abbas' irritation, while the second reference is aggravating. She indicates this ambivaence about her situation in the next sentence when she points out that Abbas stopped drinking for her sake. She ends, however, with stating again that she would rather go to her mother instead of awaiting this last quarrel.

I have dwelt on this first part extensively because I think it is her ambivalence over her future, which is at stake in this narrative. It is the *hope* for redemption and reward that she seems to translate in a kind of security. Her mother is of major importance in this respect. She might offer a practical refuge once Umm Khalthoum would leave Abbas. Further Umm Khalthoum sees her mother's life as an example of what could happen to her own in the future. It is as if Umm Khalthoum implies that to do harm results in being harmed, and to do good is to get rewarded. However, Umm Khalthoum's mother does not get much depth again.

This time the shallowness of the character of her mother and the vagueness of their exact relationship is a consequence of the main issue which Umm Khalthoum has to deal with: to claim respect as a virtuous woman. I can only understand this issue by relating her narrative to the current moral discourse of the government. The emphasis in this discourse on the right conducts of women as wives and mothers influences the position Umm Khalthoum can claim. It is therefore imperative that she, first, disclaims any blame for the divorces, as she did in her first narrative. In this narrative she does this again, quite explicitly also in relation to Abbas. She comments: "I don't know, is it because I refused him in the past and my father ordered me to marry him?" Further, she adds: "I hate him for it. I think that when I tried to build up my life, he destroyed it. Because I keep remembering that he divorced me twice without reason". She does not go into the details of her mother's character and her own relationship with her. To do so, might have highlighted issues, which could have painted Umm Khalthoum in a light, which might question her attitude or character and give her a more active role in her divorce.

Second, Umm Khalthoum tries to prove her respectability by pointing out all that she has done to save her marriage. Umm Khalthoum makes a statement that she started working in order to add to the income of her household: "It is important that wife and husband work together in order to have their children grow up well". This is directly related to her assertion that her job made her a more patient and thus better mother. The relationship between her job and her role as mother constitutes the argument with the current dominant moral discourse

Her intentions make her a good wife, who even abstained from having a career by prioritizing the wishes of her husband. The fact that she has ended up in a divorce is to blame on her father and certainly her husband. She says: "And every time I try and imagine how to create a happy life for my children, how to give them a luxury life and a nice house, I feel that, unfortunately, it is finished, because of these two divorces". By going to her mother, or at least proclaiming to do so, she openly testifies that she will not allow Abbas, or any other man, to keep her from being a good mother. Umm Khalthoum states this quite explicitly when she refers to her suitor: "I don't want another husband, I'll stay in my mother's house, just to help my children to grow up and do my job". Her claim to respectability within the current dominant discourse therefore relates to her intention to: "create a happy life for my children".

Third Session—From Despair To Determination

It is February now, and Sa'adiya has been asked to return to school because of continuing staff shortages, even though she is on maternity leave. Not only are there not enough teachers; most are not sufficiently qualified. Now that examinations are approaching, Sa'adiya has been asked to do some teaching, especially in 'Islamiyya' and 'English', two subjects in which Sa'adiya excels. I visit Umm Khalthoum regularly. However, most of the time there are visitors, her children or her husband who want to chat either with Umm Khalthoum or with me, or both, and there is little time and space to talk 'in private'.

One day the lessons are postponed because of a visit of the Governor of Northern Darfur State, At-Tayib Sikha.[34] Cars with amplifiers, spitting out their message, notify the whole town. Everyone is required to attend the arrival ceremony at the large open square near the market place. The speeches and meetings concern banditry and ethnic conflicts in the area. Most of the discussions and meetings take place behind 'closed doors'. They involve the leaders of the main ethnic groups that are involved in the conflicts: the Fur, Zaghawa and Arab, and some of the smaller ethnic groups that serve as intermediaries. While attending the speeches Umm Khalthoum joins Sa'adiya and me, asking us to come over to her place afterwards to have some coffee and a 'chat'.

I bring some sugar and coffee and Sa'adiya brings some bread and tomatoes so that we can share our breakfast and so we won't feel uncomfortable about eating at Umm Khalthoum's home again. As soon as we are inside the compound, Umm Khalthoum sighs that all the speeches are the same:

Like the one at the women's committee. These speakers were ludicrous. They told us to take care that children do not waste time with dancing and singing but have to study the Qur'an. *How can you forbid young children to enjoy their time? How can a good mother force her children to stop playing and drag them to our Holy Book? This way they will never learn to love their religion!*

Sa'adiya agrees, adding that these committees want to show that they are changing the society as they promised, and that this is one of their ways of 'showing change'. Umm Khalthoum adds in a confiding manner:

You know, Karin, Sa'adiya, they even told us at the meeting that they had heard that some of us were visited regularly by khawadya*s and that this had to stop for a Westerner contaminates the household he or she enters. So they pointed out to us that children are very susceptible to influence from people from the West and that we had to deny them entry to our houses.*

---

[34] This is a nickname. I was told that *sikha* is a component of '*siqqa hadid*', railways. In Kebkabiya the governor, a former army commander and deputy and body guard of Bolad, has earned himself this name because he is renown for his severe and unstoppable actions and iron will. Flint and De Waal state that the name refers to the metal rods used for reinforcing concrete pillars with which he was wont to attack opponent during demonstrations (2005: 21).

Sa'adiya looks as puzzled as I do, so I conclude that it is also the first time that she has heard this. Umm Khalthoum concludes:

Don't worry, ya *Karin, we all know this is nonsense. We know you, we know Mr. Johan, we know the people from Oxfam and before that from MSF-Holland and we know you are intending no harm. We let them talk and afterwards all of us agreed that this was just to arouse feelings against foreigners and that we would not take any heed.*

The memories of my acquaintance with the security committee and the hostility of the local popular committee are still vivid. I am a bit confused and wonder to what extent this will influence my stay. In addition, I wonder to what extent it has already influenced my relationships with other people, and the narratives they told me. There is not much time to reflect on this however, because Sa'adiya pushes the button of the tape-recorder as a signal to continue our 'conversation'.

It is hotter now; the height of the dry season is clearly detectable. Once more, we sit in the living room. Flies are buzzing and from the street wafts of sounds, mixed with the pierced screams of playing children enter our space. The smell of sun-baked sand mingles with the metallic smell of the water that sits in the pots behind the screen at the other end of the room. Umm Khalthoum asks how my backache is and whether I still wear the amulet. I tell her it is under my pillow and that ever since I started 'using' it, the backache has not returned. She nods and says:

I want to have them made for my sister and aunt as well, in order to protect them. I also want to go to a Fur faqih. *The Fur is a very peaceful tribe and we lived with them in Zalingei, in our neighbourhood. They were very kind and we didn't have any problems with them. Not even after we moved to other places and my mother went to Umdurman. They don't like fighting or killing. It is true, they don't. This current tribal problem, it was in 1988 that the Arabs started it. As it is stated in the* Qur'an, *most of the Arabs are unbelievers. Because the Arab tribe the Qureish, of the prophet himself, was the tribe that liked fighting. They even fought Mohammed himself. They are very bad. Their daughters were buried alive after being born. And they were using bad spells, the evil eye, in order to harm others. So there is evilness and magic and illnesses, which cannot be treated by doctors. Like bone ache and backache, they are all the consequence of the 'eyes' of people. It is because people envy you, for example when you are rich or beautiful, and wish you harm.*

One day when I went to the market with Kaltouma, all the people were looking at me and not at Kaltouma. Kaltouma said: 'Why are they looking at you, I am younger than you are'! Some said to me: 'You've given birth to a lot of children and you still look young'.

"But you *are* beautiful!" I cannot help saying. To which Umm Khalthoum immediately replies:

Before I was more beautiful, when I was younger. But beauty is also a matter of the inside. Like your mother, Karin, from the pictures you showed me, you could see that she is still a beautiful woman. How old is she there?

"She is fifty-five in the picture", I answer, adding: "She was very young when she got me".

Your mother will be young even when she is eighty, because she is comfortable. But as for me, my spirits are down with Abbas. This will make me old soon.

"How can you become old, you are still so lively and attractive"? I ask her. Sa'adiya also tells her that her complexion and her roundness will stay with her, making her attractive even in old age. Umm Khalthoum then winks at us, saying: "But it is difficult to live without sex, to decide to not have sex any more. Some like it some don't". Sa'adiya animatedly adds that she knows more women who do not like to have sex than those who do "Because of the *tahur*, circumcision, it hurts". Then she rushes on: "But there are differences as well. I know a colleague who likes it, even though she has been circumcised. But for me, even though I am not cut, I do not like it at all". I look at her in amazement. I do remember the discussion we had once with the other female teachers around but I am still surprised she is so open about it. Before I can say anything Umm Khalthoum asks me if back home there is any circumcision. I answer 'no', knowing she already knows that. So I add: "But there are the same differences. Women who like it and those who don't, especially when getting older. If it runs in the family I guess I will be ok", I add a bit mischievously. "Oh, Karin", Umm Khalthoum giggles, "that is why Mister Johan's hair already turned grey", and we all laugh with her. "So do you think it has anything to do with each other, I mean, sex and circumcision", I ask Umm Khalthoum. She gets serious again, saying almost offhandedly:

No, I don't think so. I grew up with it. People told me it was sunna[35] *Mohammed, at least, this was said about the boys' circumcision. Because he started this, all Muslims have to follow Mohammed and to circumcise. If Mohammed hadn't done this, there may not have been circumcision. Nowadays, the doctors say it is very difficult for women especially in giving birth. Sudanese men like their women to be circumcised. They cut a part of the genitals, the upper part of the clitoris and the large lips*[36] *and sew these together. They leave only a small hole for urine and blood. On the wedding day, it is also difficult for women. A lot of women get wounded. There are two kinds of circumcision. One is the pharaonic one, it came from Egypt, and they cut all the flesh away and sew it tight. The other is not so severe; they don't take all the flesh. But nowadays in Egypt they only cut a small part, the upper part of the clitoris, and there is no sewing. Sudanese women, when they have to give birth, the doctor cuts with scissors on two sides, one to the left leg and up, in the direction of the navel. After giving birth, we are stitched up again. And the next birth, the same thing is done. Even when you give birth ten times, you will be sewn back again. But it is done with an injection, the sewing up after the birth, so you won't feel too much of it. Sudanese women, if they know that others are not well circumcised or sewn back, they will send her back to the midwife.*

I am a bit taken aback by the direct way she describes the operation and procedures but also the general way she does this. I, stupidly, ask her in the same general vein as she is discussing the procedures: "So what do women think of it?"

It is good for women, they like to have it, but it is also difficult for them. If a woman is not circumcised, men are not comfortable with the woman.

"So you think it is in the *Qur'an?*" I ask her, to get her to reflect on it personally, which of course does not work:

It is for boys. For girls it also is sunna. *Islam encourages it. But now some people want it to be forbidden for girls. This concerns the bad circumcision, the pharaonic one. Hajja also performed this circumcision a long time ago.*[37] *Girls had to stay in bed for forty days after the operation. After forty days, the skin has grown enough to cover the wound. They leave a very small hole, with a thorn from the tree or a small*

---

[35] 'Sunna' is used to indicate that a practice is prescribed by the prophet Mohammed.

[36] Labia majora.

[37] This points at the relevance of my role in Hajja's assertion that she does not engage in female circumcision in her narrative.

stick, so that the urine can come through only by drops. Sometimes, during the wedding, the couple would go to the doctor to open it. During labour, some women even died because of it. The doctor said circumcision brings a lot of diseases and pain when having the period, pain in the tubes as well. Because they cut an important part of the genitals so that the body lost a part that has a function for the body. Like the pain in the glands of your throat,[38] *they also say you have to take it out. But it is better not to, because its function is to catch diseases that come from your mouth. If you take this part out, your body will catch diseases more easily. For an uncircumcised woman it is easy to give birth: no cuts and no pain. But our grandmothers did the circumcision on us. Not all Arab countries have this practice, do they, Karin?*

The question is clearly a way for Umm Khalthoum to keep the more general discussion going. I remember a discussion with the female teachers during my first stay. Umm Khalthoum had voiced an opinion which many of the younger, single, teachers abhorred: that it is a part of culture and makes a woman more beautiful and, because of the pain, more human.[39] I do not want to make her feel self-conscious again, or criticised because of her 'backward' opinion as one of the teachers had said scornfully during an earlier discussion. Therefore, I answer carefully: "I don't know, some do and others don't", adding: "Also in non-Islamic countries you can find the practice, and I read that also in Europe at some stage it was a common practice, but I am not sure". Sa'adiya asks me if I knew about female circumcision before I came to the Sudan and what I think of it. I nod, and I cannot hold back. "I knew it was practiced, but I can hardly imagine how it must feel, I mean, the circumcision itself and then afterwards, the pain and the problems with menstruation and so on, I mean don't you..." Umm Khalthoum interrupts me:

...But here in Sudan, the men like it like that. The Qur'an *tells Muslim women that they have to obey their husbands. For example, in the past, all the women of the prophet bathed themselves at night and applied scents and* baghur.[40] *They would tell their husbands that if they want something of them, they are ready, if not, they will sleep.*

But now we are different from those women. We are not obeying in this way any more because I think that women don't want to lower themselves any more before

38 She refers to tonsillitis, a practice that has been applied locally even before the introduction of western medicine.

39 See Chapter 2 for a description of this discussion.

40 *Baghur*, a smoke bath with incense.

their men, like they did at that time. Yesterday I was with Abbas, but I refused him. He was very angry and was walking up and down. He wants it every day. In the past I would go with him regularly, not every day though. But now I refuse him completely. In my heart, I don't like this man any more. Can you help me with this problem, Karin, Sa'adiya?

I hesitate. I feel it is not easy to give advice in such a complicated situation. I do care about Umm Khalthoum and carefully I choose my words: "It really depends on what you want, Umm Khalthoum. I mean, you can separate for a few months and then you can come together with both your families and discuss it. In this way you might forgive him and start again. But if you feel like you really want to divorce him, well, then you have to think it over how and what. I guess it is best if you tell him everything that is in your heart and about what makes you angry, so he knows about your problems and anger". Sa'adiya adds: "It is difficult for children to grow without their father. After they have grown up, without a father, or with another man, they will give you problems again". Resolutely Umm Khalthoum reacts to Sa'adiya's remark:

My children don't like their father because he always scolds them. Yesterday Kaltouma went to Haj Ez-Zein's house and she returned late. He was very angry with her. That day we had a guest. He is a driver and has no family here. Abbas told him that he could spend the night with us. And they slept together in my room and I went to sleep with my children. Abbas was angry with this, because he wanted me. The guest was sleeping and Abbas was walking up and down all the time: Kaltouma did not return and he wanted me. I slept with my children and I was very glad that he was angry and frustrated while the guest was there. We always have this arrangement, if we have a male guest he sleeps with Abbas in our bedroom and I go and sleep in the room with my children. Now I discovered that Abbas has a secret in Hei As-Shati. He didn't like his daughter to stay with Haj Ez-Zein yesterday, but when he went to Hei As-Shati he was not angry. Kaltouma found out that her father has a relationship with the cleaner of his school, Fatna. He gave Fatna lesson books and exercise books for her children. He also helped her in getting her Sudanese nationality documents. I asked him: 'Why are you looking after her like this'? He answered that he did it because she is a very poor woman. I said: 'But she has a lot of relatives here from Beni Hussein[41] *who can help her'. He meets Fatna in the*

---

[41] *Beni Hussein*, sons of Hussein, indicating a sub-clan of an Arab nomadic group.

house of one of the cleaners at your school Sa'adiya, Miriam Mohammed. People told Kaltouma a lot about his escapades. Yesterday this Miriam came here to collect her certificates. He took my shoes and gave them to her, he said it was because she is very poor. All his women friends are cleaners. In Fasher he also had a cleaner as his friend.

You know, Karin, I feel that a co-wife in the right Islamic way is not wrong. But the way he is doing it is not right; he is just having mistresses. Within Sudanese custom, if somebody has a girl or boy friend without being married to her or him, it puts the life of the household under strain. There is no money, no furniture, because the money is spent on the other woman just like that. Islam forbids it. If you follow the rules of Islam, a man can marry the other. That is not a problem. But nowadays there is not enough money for him to marry another wife. And also one heart cannot hold two. If you like the one more than the other you will prefer that one. And there is no hope for the old one. He will love the new one, a new house, having a new life. He will start to change his ways in favour of the new wife.

Darfur men, if they see only one small hair turning grey they want another wife. Why? I am still young and I can still satisfy a man, if I want to! If men treat women like this, in the life hereafter they will be punished. I won't agree if he wants to marry another wife. If he marries again I will go to my family for once and for all. If he marries another wife, he will probably neglect my family and me. He will see me as his enemy. So then, it is better to have a divorce and go and live with my mother. It is his fault: he caused this by divorcing me twice, making a wound in my heart. If he divorces me for the third time, God is not going to punish me because I didn't start this bad thing.

Umm Khalthoum is all worked up again and I feel so sad for her. So I take her by the shoulders and hug her. Sa'adiya gets up to let her baby son, who until now has been sleeping in her lap, take a pie outside in the sand and I get up to take some water from the pot, for Umm Khalthoum and for myself. I ask Umm Khalthoum if she'd rather talk another time, but she seems genuinely surprised and says: "No, I am glad you have finally come again". So we sit down and Sa'adiya restarts the tape recorder. I want to take Umm Khalthoum's mind off her divorce. I ask her if she would allow her daughters to have an arranged marriage like the one she had. Specifically, I ask if there are differences between the marriage arrangements of now and then. Whether Umm Khalthoum misunderstands my question, or wants to tell her story, I don't know, but at once she starts to tell about her wedding:

I remember the shanta[42] *of my engagement. They brought a* shanta *for me, while I was in intermediary school.*

Umm Khalthoum's face develops a longing expression. She tells about the *agit* and the *aris*,[43] and the bridal *shanta* filled with scented sticks, henna, foreign 'spray' perfume, and scents, oils, spices and all the other ingredients needed for making the local perfume. She enlivens when she elaborately describes the numerous dresses, *tobe*s, shoes, five of each for her, but also for her mother and sisters. She goes on to describe the many dishes and the preparations of henna and perfumes. Then she touches upon a familiar subject:

After spending a year in my house with my new husband my father gave me al-Quwatta al-musallaha, *'the soldiers weapons', one big golden bracelet. Now it is called* 'Ahfaz malak', *'keep or save your money'. Abbas sold these all. They arranged my marriage and that of my younger sister on exactly the same day. She was married at thirteen, to Abbas' younger brother. After the* agit *I went back to school and finished my fourth year.*

She turns again to the elaborate wedding rituals, meals and beautification sessions, the enormous amounts of spices and perfumed oils, the animals slaughtered, and the meals offered. She really seems to enjoy the recollections. When she comes to the wedding day, she explains that she did the *gut ar-rahad.*[44]

I danced fifteen dances, outside in the compound in front of all the people. In the morning, they made a shelter of cloth like a tent and I danced the fifteen dances under it. The bridegroom has to wait and catch me when I suddenly fall down. If he

[42] *Shanta*, lit. bag also used for suitcase. In this context, it refers to part of the bride price delivered by the family of the groom to that of the bride.

[43] *Agit is* the signing of the marriage contract in the presence of an imam. It constitutes the formal wedding, but is generally seen as engagement only. *Aris* is a wedding. This refers to the actual wedding rituals and parties, which signify the social acknowledgement of the wedding. Only after these parties, the bride and bridegroom are considered to be 'really wedded' and only then, pregnancy is seen as legitimate.

[44] *'Gut ar-rahad'*, 'to put on the straw skirt' refers to the habit of dancing several bridal dances or '*argut al-hamaam*' pigeon dances. These are performed for a small circle of close family of bride and groom. Some two generations before the bride would only wear a straw skirt. Nowadays the bride is dressed in a sleeveless dress with a skirt above the knees, in some cases the bride even changes in dresses of different colours connected to the different dances and stages of the ritual.

doesn't catch me he will fail as a husband. After seven days the bride and bridegroom go with their friends outside to the riverside and the bridegroom has to cut a tree. We have dinner and after that, we go home again. Back home the bride has to stay forty days inside the house. She can go for a picnic though. After forty days, we again have to slaughter a sheep and prepare cake, tea, and drinks. The neighbours, family, and friends will come and plait the hair of the bride and prepare baghur *and put on scents.*

Her spirits have lifted, and Umm Khalthoum is pensive for a moment. She then continues:

It is different now. Before, if your father said you have to marry this man, you had to obey, old or young, nice or not. If you refused, he would tell you to leave. And it was shameful to leave your house; people would say this girl is a bad girl. If you obeyed your father, you were a good girl. But now, fathers ask girls, 'Do you like this man or not?' And also the shanta *now is very cheap, there are only a few dresses and tobes and scents, because everything is expensive. In my time, they brought me three* ratul *of sandal. These three* ratul *cost about 150* piasters*. But now one* ratul *costs two thousand pounds. So nowadays, the groom has to bring only half a* ratul *for five hundred pounds. And these days the bride doesn't stay in the house for forty days. One night and they go on honeymoon to Jebel Marra, Nyala, or Fasher to stay in a rest house. The wedding is different now. It is expensive these days. Only a few of the bridegrooms can buy a bull for the wedding day. And also the dishes prepared for the dinner are fewer. In our time, there were many kinds of dishes. The dinner of the wedding day is very fine, like* gimah, gunafa *all these things. For seven days the bride's mother has to make the choicest and most expensive food there is for the couple.*

Now she is silent for a moment, and I feel I can ask her what I wanted to ask her before: "And what about married life. If you compare now and then, which is better?"

Now it is better. Look at myself, I was ordered to marry Abbas; I didn't like him. My father said: 'If you don't like him you can leave my house'. When I had said 'Yes, I will marry him, but can you take care of me if there are problems'? He promised me he would. But he died before I had these problems. In my opinion it is better not to order girls to marry a man she doesn't like. If you love your husband, you can live with him forever. But if you don't you cannot. Abbas loves me a lot, but I don't love him. If he comes from outside, he will call me three times. And when he is eating he likes me to sit with him, he is comfortable like that. But my heart is not with him.

I am not sure what she means, and ask hesitantly: "What do you mean, do you mean sex?" Umm Khalthoum nods while she continues:

If men want it, they will ask women, but women will not ask men. Even if they want, they will not ask. Men do not like a woman who takes the initiative. This is my opinion. If people do it everyday, it is not good for their health. There is a difference between active and non-active women. It is better for women to keep to themselves because if men want it every day and they say yes, they can do it. If you don't want you can say, 'I am ill, I have fever or headache', so you can refuse him.

I can't help but laugh: this time it is my turn to nod in agreement while saying that the women I know might do the same.

Sudanese women are very modest. If she wants sex, she doesn't ask him and if she doesn't like sex, she also won't say so. Some people take seven, others ten or three days between having sex. She can refuse when she has her period. Some men want it every day. How is that with you, Karin?

"This is different for different women in the Netherlands as well", I reply hesitantly. "Some want it every day, others once a month or even never. But I am not sure how it was when I was younger, I mean, I think, I come from a small village and, I guess sex was a taboo. But I do know now that enjoying sex differs among my friends and among my female relatives, because we do sometimes discuss these matters". "Like we do now" Sa'adiya smiles. "And still no babies?" She inquires and I say: "Thanks to the pill". "Ah, so you use the pill?" Umm Khalthoum asks me. When I nod, she says:

Here in Sudan they say the pill is not good because it affects the health of the woman. But if she has problems she can use it. Like when she already has many children and she wants to space the births. I also used it myself. These years to have a lot of children is not good, it affects a woman's health. Four or three is enough. Then you can have a rest. Spacing between the children is good.

Kaltouma comes in and greets us. Umm Khalthoum asks her why she is so late and where she has come from. Kaltouma gives a vague answer and leaves to go and prepare lunch. "Difficult to have grown up daughters", she sighs. So I ask her: "What about Kaltoum's future?"

If she chooses her own husband, it is better for her. But it is still a headache to have young girls. These days boys and girls meet far away from the houses in cinemas and in the park. If he wants to, he will ask her to marry him, if not, he will just play around. And that is what the Islam doesn't want. Islam forbids girls and boys to sit together alone. Only when someone from the family is present they can. But we are not able to prevent them to meet each other or to decide they want to marry. If he is an honest man and really wants to marry, he will come to the girl's father and ask him if he can marry her. Still, it is different now; girls have more say in the choice of their husband.

"So, if you were young again, what would you do?" I ask her to get her back to considering her own life:

First, when I was young I didn't know about life, how it would be and what was going to happen. About giving birth and how to raise children, I didn't know about it. But now we start to know more about life. I am a mother and have become a wise woman. I am going to be a mother-in-law because I have daughters. If I would not become wise, people would say: 'She is an unwise mother-in-law'. It is better to look active and to take care of yourself well. My sister is older than I am, but if you look at her now, you would say she is younger. The duty of the mother in the house is to take care of raising her children and to be more cautious of the girls, more so than of the boys. To treat them honestly so they will grow up to be honest themselves. You can treat your daughters like your sisters. Laugh with them; tell them everything. If you treat your daughters like your sisters, they cannot hide anything from you. Teach them to take their responsibilities seriously from the beginning. So to divide the tasks in the house is a good thing. To have them performing these tasks after they return from school. If they grow up with servants who wash, cook, and clean for them, they think it is all right to lie in bed after they come home from school. If they can just wake up and have their lunch ready, they will become lazy children. And they won't care about their responsibilities. After the children turn twelve years old, or ten or fourteen, you don't have a need for servants, they can work themselves. And if the mother is educated she can check on their progress by looking at her children's exercise books to help them with their homework. This is because some children simply go to school and come back. They don't know anything and don't write. So if the mother is educated she can see how it goes. Some girls are not going to school straight away. They hide in a corner and wait until a boy comes and they will go with him to his house. If the mother is educated and her son comes and tells her: 'Today we had such and such lesson', then she can check the exercise book and see when they have their lessons. But it is also good not to be a serious mother all the time. It is better to be kind and to laugh and sing with them, when it is necessary. And to tell them stories. Sometimes you can be too serious, so they won't play with you. They should not make a dog out of you so they won't listen to your advice. To know the behaviour of your children is the important thing.

In the crèche we also teach children religious lessons. We give them seven suras. *And after they go to primary school they will get more lessons about religion. Sometimes I rehearse with them the religious lessons. I also give them the names of God, all ninety-nine names. In the first class of primary school, they teach them how to pray. After a child turns seven years old, it is important for mothers to ask their children to pray. So they get accustomed to it. The* Qur'an *says: 'If the child reaches the age of ten and doesn't pray, the father or mother should hit him or her'.*

When we grew up in our own house, we prayed together. We prayed, together with our father and mother. We obeyed our father and mother. But now, children don't. When our father came back from the office, we kept silent. We would not make noise. Everybody kept his mouth, and we would not make as much noise as these children would now. We stayed in our rooms and when the time for lunch came, we all came together and had our lunch. But now children are different. Even when you hit them, they don't obey you. To grow up in the past was better than now.

Her reference to the dangers that might befall her daughters prompts me to ask her: "Are your daughters going to the market to buy things for *Eed*?"

Nowadays it is very difficult to let your girls go to the market. They will meet boys and have dates. And no boy, even if he is a friend, is honest. So we are afraid for what might happen to these girls. Even their father tells me not to send the girls to the market. If their father is absent, I send two sisters together. But Abbas used to go to the market himself. Because at the market there are a lot of men: soldiers, teachers, and officers. They always look at girls and ask people 'who is this girl' until they know the place where she lives so they can contact her. Even I myself hate going to the market. If I could find a servant to go for me to the market, it would be better.

"And you, if you had enough money would you go out for work?" I urge her to continue on the subject:

Yes, even if I had money I would work, to fill the time and to meet friends. In my job I meet a lot of colleagues and visit them. And I like to teach little children. As they become older and have studied more they will meet me and say: 'This is Ummana, *our mother Khalthoum, in the past she taught us in the crèche'. Also I like to get to know other families via my work. I want to be remembered. I like the relationship between me and the children and their families. To make women active is a good thing. Sitting inside the house leads women to gossip, visiting each other, and creating problems for others. Also God will punish them. If you give the poor food or clothes or money or any gift, God writes your name and gives you credit,* ajr. *You will know this at Judgment Day. When you are gossiping and create problems for others you lose your credit, like fire eats leaves. And so because they have time to cause problems for other people, gossiping and quarrelling, and by hurting others they cause harm. Killing is better than creating these kinds of problems, because gossip is the cause of murder. So I am not working for money, because I tell myself to move, not to stay without work. I want to work in the country, to fulfill my duty to my country. If you stay without work, you will be lazy. Even on a Friday, we feel bored because we don't have work. Sometimes we go on a picnic for a change. I also want to work with women's organisations. If my husband were to stop me from working I would not obey him. Because men are suspicious, they have no trust. Even when he divorces me or something happens to me I can live on my salary. They have moved me to another grade and I can be a supervisor of the crèches.*

"Why is teaching such a good job?" I ask her:

Because teachers open the minds of the pupils and teach them about Islam and how to grow up with the right ideas. God will give you a reward for this, for teaching. And it is an easy job for women as well. Because if you have children yourself you can teach them and look after them. Teaching is better for women than for men. Because women are raising children in their houses, so it is easy for them to raise other children. But men are hardly looking after children. Schools are the best places for growing up because you can observe the behaviour of the children and you can correct wrong attitude and teach them proper conduct. I would also like my daughters to work. It is better than staying at home or selling at the market. If one works one is an important member of the community, people think. Working women, employees, are always following the right way of Islam, the shari'a.

"So what does the *shari'a* and *Qur'an* say about working women?" I push her logic:

Shari'a *does not prohibit women to work as long as you do not mingle with man. But there is no way this is possible. I used to wear long dresses and cover my hair and wear long socks. Because if men see women, they always comment on them, saying things like: 'This woman is beautiful', and those kind of things.*

"And your own work, do your think it is a good job?"

This work is my weapon. I can fight with it, to protect myself. If my husband dies or something happens to him, I can depend on myself, even though it is little money. In my opinion, work is important for women. Abbas earns £S900 and I £S360, plus Abbas' evening classes, £S700 per month. Together we have about £S2.000 per month.

This is not a very high income, especially with eight children and considering the inflation of the past months. At the same time, they seem to do relatively well. So I ask her a bit bluntly: "Do you have other properties that brings in money?"

I had a donkey but I sold it. That was because we wanted to leave for Khartoum, two months ago. He bought me a tobe *for £S7000. When he returned after a few days, he found that the price had gone up to £S20.000. He sold our land in Fasher and bought us things.* Tobe*s, gold, furniture, like armchairs and tables, curtains. He saved some of it and put it on the bank and from the other part, he bought these things. He saved 65.000£S. He bought dresses for the children and some gifts for his family in Fasher like for his sisters and his mother. We want to buy new land in Umdurman. We want to build a house there. After Eed we want to travel to Umdurman by airplane, we don't want to travel by road. Not since Ashari was killed by bandits when he returned to his family, it is too dangerous to travel by road. Abbas works in the army school and so they help him with buying his flight tickets. Some he can buy from the market.*

I am quite puzzled to hear about these plans. I know Umm Khalthoum wants to 'go back' to Umdurman, but I had the impression she wanted to go there on her own. So a bit hesitant I ask her: "But then what about the divorce?"

I didn't know about divorce before, but now I do. I did know about it before, but in Islam, we have three divorces. First you can come back to your husband and after the second as well, but after the third, khalas, *over, it becomes* haraam, *religiously forbidden, to come back. You can only marry another man after that. If I knew about divorce, that it would be as bad as this, I would not have returned to him. I could have returned to my family in Umdurman and marry again there. From the beginning, I did not like to marry him; I did it only because my father told me so. Now I am not comfortable any more with him. He went to Fasher and bought a fashionable* tobe *and gold for me. It is because he is nervous. One day he will say again* talaaq, *it is not far from him. In a house without love, there is no happiness.*

I get increasingly confused, so I try to check some of the things she said: "So do you have land of your own in Umdurman?"

It is my mother's land. My father had land, but he sold it. My mother is going on haj *again this year. Nowadays it costs £S100.000, very expensive compared to the last time she went.*

I try again with another question: "If you have your divorce and go to Umdurman you are going to marry again then, like your sister did?"

Men are afraid of a lot of children as I have. Because they need to eat and they make many problems. Cousins might say, 'O, she is young and we can marry her within the family'. But from outside the family it is not possible.

"So do you think that in this case it is better to live with your family or with your husband?" I continue.

If I would go to my mother and I am still as young as I am now, some people will not be able to control themselves and will try to do bad things. It is better to marry again.

I am really surprised and confused by this shift in perspective on her future, so quite out of the blue I ask her: "So did your brothers and sisters also go back to your mother?"

The eldest is Fathia, her husband died and she married again two years ago. Then Ali, married in Umdurman, he has two sons and a daughter. Then Mahadi in Saudi; Mahadi, he isn't married yet. After him, there were three miscarriages, and then she bore me. Then there is Mahmoud who is in Saudi as well. They took my mother to pilgrimage and built a house for her. They don't want to marry because, as they say, we want to improve the life of our families and then we can marry. Then came Feiza, she was married to Abbas' brother and is in Wadi Abbas near Zalingei. Then there is Suaad, who is married to a cousin. The last one was Mohammed, who was murdered in Iraq by bandits. They brought his body to Umdurman. But my father's children are in Zalingei. She was from the Arab tribe. All my sisters and brothers went to school. Some stopped at primary some at intermediary and some at secondary high school. I want to start again to learn. If I go to Umdurman my head is empty from problems.

Context of the Narrative—The Present in the Past
Being Desired and Determined

We taped the third part of Umm Khalthoum's story in the month before Ramadan. In it, Umm Khalthoum touches on quite different issues, and from a different narrating position than previously. Umm Khalthoum's reflections are influenced by the recent speeches of the religious committee. Their topic, during their tour of Darfur was teaching the population how to behave as 'proper Muslims'.[45] Umm Khalthoum discusses this at the beginning of our session. Moreover, it is now the month of *suaal*, the last month before *Ramadan*. In this month, many women and a few men keep the fast for a few days in a row, or on alternating days. Many women have to make up for the days when they could not or were not even allowed to fast during the last *Ramadan*. The omissions may have been because of menstruation or pregnancy, and for men, mostly because of long distance travel or illness. Everyone must account for these 'lost' days before the next *Ramadan*. Generally, this happens just before the next *Ramadan* starts. A small minority of (mainly elderly) women fast intermittently during this month because it will give them more religious merit (*ajr*). Elderly people, especially, are concerned about the amount of merit they might have gathered. The belief is that after death, the angel Gabriel guards the entrance to paradise. He will decide whether the person enters paradise (*janna*) or hell (*jahanna*) according to the merit gathered. The advent of *Ramadan* makes most Muslim people more aware of religious issues and discussions often centre on these. Therefore, it is not a coincidence that Umm Khalthoum uses religious references in her narrative as well.

Unlike in her former narratives, this time Umm Khalthoum hardly touches upon her own past to justify the situation in which she is in now. Instead, she relates to the remoter religious 'past' in order to discuss issues, which concern her present and possible future. If I consider the aspect of 'mapping' and 'moving' in her current narrative, Umm Khalthoum makes a connection in her recollections from the 'beginning of Islam' to her own possible future. The time of Prophet Mohammed, or the *umma*, is generally perceived as giving guidance for current and future issues that Islamic communities have to deal with. The wisdom comes in the form of the *hadith*, stories about the sayings

[45] This is the same committee that delivered the speeches presented in Chapter 1 of this dissertation.

and actions of Mohammed, and the *suras* the chapters in the *Qur'an*. In turn, these form the foundations of *sunna*: practices recommended by the Prophet. These historical guidelines enable Muslims to distinguish between *halaal* as opposite to *haraam*.[46] Umm Khalthoum's frequent references to these texts and to formal issues in her narrative might be related to the recent visit of the popular committee. The form of Umm Khalthoum's narrative of alternating 'public' common sense knowledge at times religiously inspired, and her personal convictions gives an oscillating structure to her narrative that is related both to the themes she discusses and her position she is negotiating in the process.

In the first half of this session of her narrative, Umm Khalthoum discusses herself alternately as having been written off by her husband and as an independent woman, who knows what she wants and what she has to offer. Further, she switches regularly between referring to 'official' opinions, based on common sense knowledge or perceived religious dogmas, and personal feelings and opinions. In these instances, Umm Khalthoum uses more general pronouns as a way of revealing how she herself thinks of these subjects. In some cases she switches from general opinions to her own life, couched in more personal pronouns, invariably related to her current precarious situation. In relation to the oscillating structure of Umm Khalthoum's story, the subjects of her story show an alteration as well. Taking the consecutive themes together, we see three major themes emerging. First, there is the discussion of 'women's issues', which relate to sexuality. Secondly, how she sees her role as a mother and her future role as a wise mother-in-law in answer to my inquiry after the future of her daughters. Lastly, how she understands the value of work and financial independence for women.

Women's issues constitute a theme in which this oscillation is most obvious. Circumcision,[47] beautification and sexual desire, and polygamy are all subjects that are to some extent a taboo to discuss in public. In referring to these subjects in a framework of formally acknowledged and condoned opinions, it serves as a way to legitimise her talking about it. In a way, the subjects prove to be related as well. In this case it

---

[46] Forbidden on religious grounds; debates on what is prescribed and what is forbidden on religious grounds are still waged within Islamic communities.

[47] Circumcision is considered only *sunna* for boys. It is in Sudan forbidden by law and also the Islamist regime is against the practice. It is continued however because of local notions of femininity, chastity, fertility, and beauty and seen as a religious duty. National and local campaigns have been waged since Independence to eradicate the practice.

is clear that circumcision is not of particular concern to her current situation, for she discusses it only in general terms. In Umm Khalthoum's argument, the issue of circumcision is connected to sex: 'Sudanese men like their women to be circumcised'. This subject gets her full attention in the next section where she goes from general to more personal reflections: 'But it is difficult to live without sex, to decide to not have sex any more. Some like it, some don't'. Then she reflects on the attitude of women in the time of the Prophet. Connecting the women around the prophet with using *baghur* is not just a reference to beautification, but to sexuality as well. She concludes with: 'But now we are different from those women. We are not obeying in this way any more because I think that women don't want to lower herself any more before their men, like they did at that time'. Her penultimate sentence: 'Yesterday I was with Abbas, but I refused him', is followed by her almost desperate: 'Can you help me with this problem, Karin, Saʾadiya?' Her route is sometimes the other way around: from personal to more general statements like in the case of polygamy: 'Darfur men, if they see only one hair turning grey they want another wife', continuing, 'Why? I am still young and I can still satisfy a man, if I want to'. Then she adds: 'If men treat women like this, in the life hereafter they will be punished'.

By tying her personal reflections to religious aspects, Umm Khalthoum gives herself an air of authority and self-assurance. This attitude is most evident when Umm Khalthoum denounces the women around the prophet as examples. Such an approach is highly unusual. The norm is to cite them as examples of virtue for both women and men to follow, as I have pointed out with reference to the speeches in Chapter 1. However, Umm Khalthoum uses them as an example of old times which are behind us. as an attitude that is not to be taken as exemplary anymore. At first, she took me in totally with her confident tone and certainty in what she was telling. However, the recurrent 'inconsistency' reflects her feelings of insecurity about the indeterminate state, which she now occupies. The tone of confidence does not so much reflect her current feelings as her hopes, a way of coming to terms with her ambivalent feelings over her future.

In the earlier narratives, Umm Khalthoum 'mapped' herself within the confines of the home, whether those of her father, her husband, or her mother and even within the boarding house. Whenever she discussed venturing outside the home, she emphasised the fact that she was accompanied, protected, and moving around in a proper manner, or for a proper goal. Whether it is her father driving her by car, the teachers delivering her at her home by lorry, going on a picnic with Abbas by car or travelling around in Darfur for his work. She found it important to let us know that she travelled in company, except for the illness and funeral of her father, but here it was the goal itself, which legitimates her moving at all. Her only ambivalence, as it turned out in the end, concerns her proposed move with only her children to her mother's home in Umdurman. It is her divorce and the consideration of her next 'move' that keeps her occupied throughout her narrative.

At the same time, this last narrative is like an apotheosis. In her memories Umm Khalthoum moved from the places she grew up in, where she went as wife and mother joining her husband, to end up in Kebkabiya, the place from which she recounts her story. In her narrative, Kebkabiya is a place 'in limbo' between her joyous past and insecure future, between her maturing in Darfur and her possible future 'back to her roots' in Umdurman. This travelling through the places of her past to her future leads to a literally 're-collecting' of memories which gave Umm Kharthoum clarity to reconsider her situation while it made all three of us see how things have become as they are now.

In this narrative, her relationship with Abbas and his actions are more central than they have been so far. Her reflections on her own beauty and sexuality in combination with her refusal of Abbas at first seem to be a self-assured assertion of her own worth. Then, quite candidly she discusses his affairs with 'cleaning women'. She seems quite light-hearted about it. However, she has previously commented that she will lose her beauty as she grows older, and more generally stated that in polygamous marriages the older woman would lose. These point to the fact that she might be worrying over this part of her marriage bearing her own divorce in mind. The background explains the last sentence of this part: "If he marries another wife he will probably neglect my family and me. He will see me as his enemy". The change from her discussion of *faqih*s to Abbas' mistress is understandable in this light. Her possible fear for becoming embroiled in the same misery as her own mother with her co-wives before her divorce might be the basis for discussing the workings of magic and spells.

Her confidences to us about Abbas' affairs come after her claim that her children hate Abbas. Thus, Abbas' irresponsible behaviour as a husband is also a reason for his disqualification as a father. In addition, in this case the comparison with the behaviour of her father after marrying another woman seems evident. Later in her narrative, Umm Khalthoum is for the first time quite explicit about her relationship with her children. When I ask her about her daughter, she elaborates on the problematic sides of raising daughters while at the same time displaying her fondness of them. Here, Umm Khalthoum emphasises her own worth, first as a mother, being caring and understanding and helpful to her children, and next as a wise (potential) mother-in-law. The opposition between Abbas as a bad husband, father and breadwinner who spends his salary on alcohol, and Umm Khalthoum as a good mother, wise mother-in-law, crèche teacher, and financially independent employee points at an implicit argument. She in fact sums up her qualities as a head of the household and as a qualified teacher in order to assess the possibility of being able to raise her children on her own once she is divorced.

The last part of Umm Khalthoum's narrative, in reaction to my question about other assets reveals the immanent departure, the final move, of Umm Khalthoum to Umdurman. Initially, it seemed to me a logical end to her narrative. I was therefore astounded when she announces she is intending to undertake this final move together with Abbas! Further, she does not present this as an action of Abbas', with which *she* has to comply. On the contrary, she seems to relish in Abbas' attention for her: him buying *tobes* and gold, and planning to build a house in Umm Khalthoum's beloved Umdurman. This shift in subject position is perhaps understandable in the light of the current dominant moral discourse of the government.

Con/text-Analysis—The Past in the Present
To Be Wise and Have a Future

In her diverse narratives, Umm Khalthoum mapped herself in the diverse households and in relationship to the persons who offered her protection in and by that same household. This is not only in a financial, physical, or social sense but also as a means of moral protection. The image she constructs along the way is of the dutiful daughter, obedient wife, good mother, and (potential) wise mother-in-law. First, Umm Khalthoum denounces responsibility for her current situation of an 'almost divorced woman'. She claims inevitability and therefore, disclaims responsibility. In her second narrative, she focuses mainly on the relationship between her father and mother. Her mother's life after the divorce of Umm Khalthoum's parents is a way of finding redemption and reward for Umm Khalthoum's correct behaviour, not only as daughter and as wife, but also as a mother. In this way, she is negotiating the current moral discourse. She has been a good Muslim daughter and wife all along so any mishap cannot be a result of misconduct. So how should I understand her subject position within the dominant moral discourse in this narrative?

In her previous narratives, Umm Khalthoum was the one who was depending on the whims of her husband and thus her move to Umdurman was an escape of the impending doom hanging over her head. Now the situation seems reversed. Abbas is the 'loser', and he now depends on her, wants her and waits for her: 'Abbas loves me a lot, but I don't love him'. At the same time, the moments when Umm Khalthoum displays her insecurity are the same moments when she reflects on her current problems with Abbas, such as the loss of sexual satisfaction and attraction, and the possibilities of a co-wife.

Umm Khalthoum is apparently still ambivalent about her fate and future, and therefore the subject is the same as in her first narrative. It seems that her movement from the present to the future takes her mind off the problems with Abbas, though they are there all the time. This is evident not only from the problems discussed, but also in her demeanour. However, her current reflection does in fact show a regained confidence in her strength. It is as if she has recovered from the shock of finding herself on the edge of being divorced. While shifting to the future, she also shifts her narrating position and displays not only increasing self-confidence, but also a degree of disdain for Abbas and his escapades. In the end, she can even talk about a possible next marriage. Her explicit statement in her first narrative that she '*does not need a man anymore*' when she discusses her suitor, is now replaced by her assertion that she wants to marry so men will not try to do 'bad things'. This shift in fact points at the negotiation by Umm Khalthoum of the current Islamist discourse, which is the hidden script in this part of her narrative.

In the dominant moral discourse, there is no place for divorced women, no matter how justified the divorce might be. Therefore, it is difficult for Umm Khalthoum to maintain a positioning as a good wife: what remains is her role of mother. The main theme that underlies her reflections is also this time the possibility of a divorce and the future that lies ahead. At the same time she now ventures into possibilities in the future connected to a re-assessment of her current position in relation to relatives other than her husband or her father. Her work is her 'weapon', a way of fighting for her own place. Umm Khalthoum thereby emphasizes her correct dressing as a Muslim woman, her virtue as a good colleague and, in the near future, her role as a wise mother-in-law. The care her mother received from unrelated men, especially from her stepson can be seen here as an indication of an assessment of the help Umm Khalthoum hopes to receive from her future sons-in-law. Her attempts at mapping herself consistently around her children and within the confines of a home, and in a respectable work environment make her a good mother, but not just any mother. She is an educated mother who can check her children's homework, advise her daughters on their conduct as well as control their behaviour and earn a living to literally take care of them. Her work itself makes her a better mother and a worthy person in society, both giving her social and religious merit. She thus can claim the status of the good Muslim woman in the context of the current Islamism discourse: she even allows herself to think of the possibility of becoming someone else's wife again, and thus restore herself also in that revered position. So if her future is still insecure, if Umm Khalthoum still feels ambivalent over a divorce from Abbas, in these narratives she at least has secured her status as a good Muslim elite woman.

Epilogue—December 1995: Umm Khalthoum's Quest

December 1995. As soon as I was back in Omdurman, I looked up your mother, Umm Khalthoum. It took me some time and effort but at last, I located her. I had a wonderful afternoon. I received presents as well as some to give to you in Kebkabiya. Your son, Yasser was there as well. He scolded Abbas under his breath so that your mother would not hear him. He told me that you were still in Kebkabiya, and still with Abbas. I must say I was very surprised. Not leaving Abbas is one thing, but not leaving Kebkabiya at all seems so far from what you were planning two years ago. After your narrative with all the sadness and finally the determination to change your fate, I was so sure you would go back to your mother. Even at that time you were preparing to go back to Umdurman, albeit together with Abbas. He had even sold furniture and land in order to cover the travel expenses of your trip. Why was the return cancelled?

It makes me reconsider your narrative. It was such a beautiful narrative, with layers going in circles and cycles, from a sad and bitter start ending in a victorious and almost elated happy end, in Umdurman. I had felt it was so much your narrative, without the frequent interruptions and interjections Hajja had expected from me, that it really reflected *your* struggle with your predicament. However, maybe it reflected our relationship as well. I must reconsider then, how I might have influenced your narrative and the way you related it?

Umm Khalthoum's Narrative Reconsidered

Staying with Hajja had probably made me more sensitive of my influence on her narrative as I obviously participated in her daily life, even if I did not know exactly how at the time. However, in your case, Umm Khalthoum, I was less aware of these possibilities. I was very keen on visiting you even when we were not taping your narrative. I became a regular visitor at your home. We chatted in your kitchen, played with the children in their bedroom, or had tea or coffee on the veranda, more often than not reading our coffee cups for signs of our future. Although our lives where quite different I felt we had much in common. Most of the time we talked about what happened around us, once in a while we discussed married life, love and hopes, work and colleagues, sex and the blessings of (future) motherhood or the need for contraception.

When I first met you, during my first stay together with Yasmin, we were often with the other female teachers. That must have been your first impression of me: although 'married' in the opinion of most, I fitted into the image of the single female teacher because of being childless and I did not have heavy household responsibilities. I could study and work without being bothered by children or a demanding husband, with Johan taking care of household chores after Nura had left for home.

As with Hajja our relationship developed while you told me your narrative. Consequently, I became increasingly involved in your daily life. Although I had met Abbas when he attended Johan's football matches, I did not have a clear impression of him. He was laughed at and called 'Yadeen', 'Two Hands', because when drunk he would fall and land on his knees and his two hands. While staying at your place taping your narrative, or just chatting, I also saw his other, more volatile side. Therefore, as your narrative centred on your problems with him, you had my sympathy. You used to compare your situation with mine saying: "Oh, you and Mr. Johan, you have such a wonderful marriage. We are all jealous of you". You were convinced that it was the envy of others that caused my backache to which only a *faqih* could find a remedy.

Despite my efforts to change the rosy picture you seemed to have, you and Sa'adiya were convinced that foreign men were nicer to their wives than Sudanese men. This was your joint conclusion from those who had visited Kebkabiya so far. You jokingly asked me if I had a brother to whom you could marry one of your daughters. You relished the stories I told you about how we lived in the Netherlands, with outings to movies or cafés with female friends or even on work-holidays. That I had lived in an apartment on my own instead of in a boarding house seemed both unthinkable and enticing to you. Sex and children were also favourite topics as we were about the same age. You inquired about contraceptives and some weeks later you asked me to find out if these were still available in Fasher.

There were also discussions together with other female teachers. In particular, I remember one of these discussions we had during a *fatuur* at Ramadan with women from the women's organisation. We were discussing circumcision[48] and it was a rather heated debate. Some were arguing in favour, maintaining that it increased the fertility of women and that the circumcision was, any way, ordained by the prophet Mohammed and therefore a religious duty. Others, like Yasmin, were strongly against, pleading for a ban on any type of female circumcision; because of the harm it does to both girls and women because of the adverse effects that circumcision might have, such as of infection of the tubes, causing infertility or incontinence, the agony of menstruation, sexual intercourse, and giving birth. Yasmin pointed out that already the British had forbidden it by law[49] and that even

[48] This might refer to infubilation, cliterodectomy, or both. El-Dareer gives five different kinds of circumcision to be found in Sudan, from *sunna* to pharaonic. The former refers to 'what is right according the sayings of prophet Mohammed or the *Qur'an*' and with respect to circumcision means a mild form of cliterodectomy, i.e. a slight cut in the skin of the clitoris. Pharaonic refers to the most severe form of cliterodectomy and infubilation: the whole of the clitoris, the *labia minora* and *labia majora* are removed and the wound rims are stitched together leaving only a small hole to let urine, blood and other vaginal liquids pass (el-Dareer 1982).

[49] This law was passed already in 1946. However, originally not much effort was put in erasing the practice. Under Nimeiri, especially since the 1970s there have been campaigns to make people aware of the fact it is not a religious practice and not mentioned in the *Qur'an*. Midwives have been especially targeted with local meetings where *sheikhs* and *shartai*'s, *faqih*'s and *imams* have vowed against it.

imams and *sheikhs* had agreed with that. When the discussion had gone on like this for some time, Sa'adiya asked me if our women were circumcised. I told her that they were not. I felt uncomfortable when I was further questioned, not knowing how to voice my opinion without embarrassing anyone. My feminist consciousness condemned the practice out of hand while I also saw that one could not expect women to do away with such an integral aspect of their femininity. I gave what felt like a rather lame answer, about how women bear the brunt of the pain and anguish and harmful effects. When pressed, I at last admitted that the idea of cutting any section of your private parts, or any part of your body for that matter, seemed horrible to me. Some women were nodding enthusiastically, whilst I spoke. Then you, Umm Khalthoum, interrupted, saying: "But it is part of our culture. It is beautiful, a woman's belly, when it is circumcised, smooth, white, and round like an ostrich egg. We give birth and we know it: would you like us to drop our children like goats?" It had been quiet for a moment, and then other women came in with their comments. One teacher remarked that Allah had made men and women perfect so why did we need to adjust his creation. Another teacher retorted that women are not only of service because of beauty, that giving birth without being circumcised is painful enough. The discussion then drifted to the possibility of having sexual pleasure or not when circumcised with much jesting and teasing as a result.

I disagreed completely with the implication of your comment that circumcision was good *because* it was part of culture, and *therefore* made you human, made you differ from animals. At the same time, though, I liked the way you stood up for who you were in this discussion, while you did not seem to be intimidated by the strong opinions of the women around you.

Less than half a year later, your opinion on Dutch men as well as on Abbas were unaltered, but your opinion on circumcision had changed. You now voiced the general opinion found among the female teachers that it was not right to circumcise. Of course, you might have changed your opinion by reflecting upon it yourself, but you might have been influenced by the opinion of others, and even by me. And for that matter: what else in your narrative was a reflection of our relation?

In retrospect, I know that our discussions during our taped and off-record talks, have had more influence than I realized when I looked for the meaning of your narrative. Of course, my gender, age, and married status were important. As all three of us were married women I think you could confide in Sa'adiya and me, understanding your predicament.

However, children were an important feature of your life, while I had none. During our conversations, you mostly downplayed this difference. You would stress the things we had in common, such as the fact that we were about the same age. Alternatively, that we had both been to school. Or even that your mother was called *khawadiya* because of her white skin, which made us share ethnic traits.[50] My position as an outsider meant that confiding in me would not have direct repercussions on your status or relationships with locals and colleagues. At the same time I suspect you relied to some extent on my opinion or that of Sa'adiya, at least for our approval and support, as you did not confide in anyone else about your marriage problems.

As our relationship developed, I told you more and more about my own life and we shared knowledge instead of just exchanging opinions. Therefore, my own desires and projections might have become part of your narrative. You expressed your wish to pursue education at university, something that had not been a strong wish at the beginning of our talks: you wanted to learn English so you could talk with my acquaintances and me. You said so jokingly, but I did feel a strong undercurrent of longing for a different life. However, that might have been as much a longing for an escape, for a life far from the hurt and the loneliness you felt living deserted by your husband in a strange town.

Therefore, throughout our discussions on issues other than divorce, such as polygamy or circumcision, I can imagine that you were looking for commonalties in order to create mutual understanding. You also wanted Sa'adiya's and my approval of and support for your side of the matter. I think you needed reassurance that, as your narrative highlighted, it was not your fault that Abbas had divorced you. In the course of you narrative you became a woman who decided about her own future now that her husband had betrayed her; who could stand up for herself and who could manage her own life (and that of her children), and in the process I more and more recognized in you the strong women 'back home' whom I had discussed with you. I was writing a book about your narrative and you wanted to be portrayed

[50] Skin colour and ethnic identity are closely related, also in the Sudanese context. I will come back to this in Chapter 8.

well in it. You wanted to appear as a sensible, intelligent, and virtuous, and educated woman. For this portrayal, you relied on Sa'adiya's and my evaluation of both your ideas and behaviour. Our discussions and talks might have made you more perceptive of my feminist ideal of a strong and self-assured woman than I realized. But then again, you *were* a strong and independent thinking woman, so our working together might just have allowed you to bring out that side of yourself.

This still begs the question to what extent I put into your narrative aspects that belonged to my perception rather than your conviction?

Back to Kebkabiya

I had only just arrived in Kebkabiya when I visited you at your home. You said you had been expecting me. Your welcome was warm and enthusiastic. It felt so good. You were fussing over me, saying I had grown too thin. We had coffee right away and exchanged some information about my parents and your children, when you asked how Mr. Johan was. That is when I told you that Johan and I had split up, or rather that Johan had left me. You took my hand and said you were so sorry, and we cried. I told you how sudden it had been, not only for me, but also for most of our friends and relatives. And that coming back to Kebkabiya was one way for me to come to terms with the divorce. Then you told me:

You know Karin, other have brought this upon you. Just as in my case, really. Zeinab, the sister of Yadeen, has put mihaya[51] *in the* zir, *the water container. She also sneaked under the windows and sprinkled the panes with it. This is why* ustaz[52] *started to behave so strange when I was around. It has been two years now that he divorced me. And nobody understands it. Everyone says: 'Umm Khalthoum is such a good woman, kind, sweet, sociable and hospitable. And she has given him so many children. Why would he want to divorce her'? Someone must have poisoned Johan to go against you as well. Someone has brought the bad in his heart by asking a* faqih. *The world is bad.*

[51] Liquid consisting of ink and water. The ink has been used by a *faqih* to write a *Qur'an* text on a wooden slate and with some formulas written and spoken while it was washed off the slate with water and put in a bottle. The *mihaya* might be benign or malign according to the wish of the customer who hires the *faqih*.

[52] Meaning 'sir' or 'master', in particular used to refer to male schoolteachers.

I wanted to believe you. I understood at that moment your wish, my wish, to be without blame, to feel that what had happened to me was illogical, unthinkable, and unjust. My own grief and sadness must have blurred my senses. At that moment I did not notice the 'Yadeen' and '*ustaz*' you used, more distancing references to Abbas than using his name, like you did before. Only when being back at my *gutiya* at Hajja's compound did I remember one sentence that puzzled me. You said: "It has been two years now that he divorced me". I thought you referred to your first two divorces, but I hesitated: might you have meant the third and final divorce? I also realized that you had said that you had become overseer of the kindergartens in the district. The next day I hurried to the government offices and found yours, which you shared with a male colleague. We chatted for a while drinking tea with your colleague Muna, at her office next door. Muna had been my neighbour when I lived on Hajja's compound and as soon as the door closed behind us, you started to giggle, and told us that your male colleague made passes at you. We had a good laugh when each of us in turn told about a similar situation. After finishing our tea, you asked me to come to your home in the afternoon with my camera. Your second daughter, Estma, and her new husband were married only recently, but the family from Umdurman could not come for the wedding. When I arrived, Estma had already dressed herself up in the wedding attire and I took a lot of pictures, to be sent to your family in Umdurman.

You had met Sa'adiya while getting back home and you had invited her to come over as well. Now, while we sip our tea I tell you, you look well, more comfortable and relaxed than last time. You nod in agreement saying:

Aye, because in the past, as I told you, I had a lot of problems. As I told you, ya *Karin,* sitt *Sa'adiya, two divorces had taken place without any fault from my side. So these divorces wounded my heart. Because I always thought: 'Why did this happen when it is not my fault'? And this made me even unhappier. He always made problems for me. He said: 'Why are you so sad about two divorces? I will declare the third one as well'! He would say this when he was angry. And he did not leave me in peace. So these problems were the reason that I lost my happiness.*

Sa'adiya starts to say something about the terrible insecurity one has to live with, but you want to go on. Therefore, you tell us with much detail how you prepared a lunch for your colleagues because the guard of the intermediary school had asked you to do so. His wife had been appointed to the school as cleaner, he wanted to prepare a meal as a sign of gratitude, but did not know how to prepare the dishes elite people eat. So he provided you with the food items and you prepared the supper. Then Abbas became angry with you:

We started quarrelling. He tried to hit me. At that time, we had a guest in our house, his friend. He caught Abbas' hand and prevented him from hitting me. That night I slept with my daughters to keep myself from being hit. In the morning he continued to quarrel. He asked me why I had left our room to sleep with my daughters. And I said: 'I don't want to stay in a room with problems and get scolded by you'. So for three days I did not return to my room. On the third day a visitor came, Yussuf. And he heard Abbas saying: 'I will divorce you, I will divorce you'. Yussuf, the visitor, told him to shut up and to come to his house, he and I, to solve the problem. We went and he asked Abbas to tell what his problem was. And he told him. He asked me also to tell my problem. And while I am telling him my narrative, Abbas cut me short, before I finished. He asked me to leave all things to him so he could divorce me. And I said, 'you have nothing you get from me and I do not want to leave my children with you. And I do not have any money that I have to pay to you, like sadaqa'.[53] *So he rolled up his sleeves and said: 'I divorce you' three times,* 'talaqta, talaqta, talaqta'. *This was in front of Yussuf who had called us to solve the problems. And Abbas said: 'Prepare yourself to leave my house tomorrow'. And I said: 'Oh, I do not want to go tomorrow, nor day after tomorrow, nor after, after tomorrow. I will stay with my children'.*

So now I feel more comfortable, I feel free now. Even if it is not good to get divorced while you have children, the pressure of problems I endured in the past makes me feel happy that I have been divorced. Even now, after he divorced me he quarrels with me. He even chased me out of his house. Sometimes I go to the house of the neighbours and stay with them until his anger resides. After he calms down, I go back to the house. Now there is no way of living together. He has been transferred to Nyala as a teacher and he agreed to take me to my family in Umdurman. It has been two years since we separated. Since the third of January 1994. It was on a Monday. I always store the dates of important events in my life in my memory.

Sa'adiya and I have not been saying much while you tell us about the aftermath of your divorce. Abbas' crying and trying his best to get you back: going to the court to plead 'temporary insanity', one of the possible reasons for declaring a divorce ungrounded. He asked his

[53] Payment of a woman to divorce from her husband, literally 'a free donation'.

colleagues to intervene on his behalf. He asked them to talk you into going back to him, to ignore the last divorce. He visited *sheikhs* to find a religious way around the divorce. Abbas even went to his father and to your brother to cajole you to return to him. However, you were not convinced:

If they find a religious way—Maliki *or* Hanafi[54]—*to get me back, I will be satisfied with him and we will marry again. If not, I do not want to come back to him. The sheikh from Girgo said: 'You are teachers, you are educated and you don't want to come back to your children'? I replied that there are a lot of educated women who have been divorced and who go back to their husbands if they don't complete the three divorces. But I have not, because he divorced me for the third time. These laws are from Allah and I fear Allah, not people. And after that Abbas went and told everyone in the street, in his house, in the whole community: 'Umm Khalthoum does not want to come back to me while there are ways to come back, but she refused'. So I said: 'You divorced me in front of your mother in Fasher. And the second time in front of my neighbours while quarrelling. You hit me. And the third time you also wanted to hit me but I brought myself into safety with my children. But we can live like brother and sister. And I can stay without marriage to look after our children. And we can put our salaries together in order to spend it on taking care of our children, to raise them well'.*

Apparently, Abbas was still not satisfied. First, he tried to appeal to the court, to undo the third divorce. When this also was to no avail, it would have been illegal (*haraam*) to live with each other after the third divorce, so he decided on another track:

Abbas said: 'I am a failed man. I wanted you to come back to me in whatever way, whether rightly or wrongly. Because the sheitan, *devil, whispered to me at that time'. And he asked me to stay. He told me: 'If a man comes he can marry you. After marriage, you can make problems to him or your children and he can divorce you. After that we can marry again'.*[55]

[54] *Maliki* and *Hanifi* refer to two law schools, which are used in the Sudan in *shari'a* court. When the last democratic regime was installed, the MP's voted which law school would be followed for the main rulings concerning issues of Personal or Family law. *Maliki* law is seen as more orthodox concerning interpretations of the *Qur'an*.

[55] In *Maliki* law it is stipulated that a man and a women who have been lawfully divorced (three times by the man or by court) can only marry again when the woman has had another marriage in between.

You seemed to imply that you did not like Abbas' last attempt to get you back. However, you seemed doubtful as well, especially because of your children. Abbas proposed you marry his friend who he initially accused of sleeping with you:

I want no one to marry you except for this man. He can go to Umdurman and marry you. After a short time, you can make a problem because he is not a real man and he can divorce you.

You do not seem too disturbed by this extraordinary 'scheme' of Abbas; on the contrary, your narrative developed an even more peculiar twist:

So even here in Kebkabiya some men asked me to marry them, but I declined. I told them I have a family, they are living far from here, I do not want to marry without their consent. So it is better to be near them, near my aunts and sisters and mother. Because I don't know what is going to happen after marriage. Like what has happened now in my life. Also my mother would not agree if I would marry again far away from them. But Abbas said, he decided, that this man would marry me. And we agreed that this man would come to Umdurman, marry me and divorce me. After that we will come back to our children and open a new page of our life. And even this friend of Abbas told some people: 'Yes I will go and marry her in order to solve their problem'. Now shortly we want to leave for Umdurman and we will see what is going to happen in the future. I am very afraid, Karin, sitt *Sa'adiya, I fear that the same thing will happen again next time. And sometimes I am feeling sorrow when I see women with henna and their babies. But when I remember the problems that I had I say: 'O, it is better to live without marriage'.*

You were adamant that you were going to pursue the divorce and in your last sentence, you confirm this feeling. In the light of your negative feelings about marriage and the problems that you had with Abbas, your consent to Abbas' plan sounds preposterous. Why would you go to such length in order to return to the strained situation from which you just seemed to have escaped? I guess you only told Sa'adiya and me about your divorce in so much detail because we both had the same experience. I was reluctant to respond at once, as I was not sure of how I felt about the last part of your narrative. However, Sa'adiya did. She agreed with you. She said she felt the same about this whole issue of divorce. That when she had left Jacub she did not want to return to him either, but that she had gone back because she wanted her children to have a good future. Umm Khalthoum's gaze turns to me and says:

Maybe you are lucky Karin, that you do not have children, which can make this divorce business a bigger problem than it already is.

I nod, considering your suggestion. I suppose it makes a huge a difference when there are children involved and I realise now that you have exposed my blind spot: I had never explicitly considered your role as a mother. You had not dwelt on it in your narrative or your chats with me for long. At the time, I did not realize that this might have been due to me not having children. Therefore, we had little in common on that subject. All that time I had not been aware that I was constructing a silence myself. Now I realize how important your children are, to your life as well as to your narratives. We have a joyous evening even though we talk a lot about each other's feelings of betrayal and disappointment, pain and sadness.

In the aeroplane, travelling back to Khartoum, enjoying the vistas of the desert, which are rare in their beauty, I keep thinking over what you told me. I realise your narrative of the last few days has a familiar ring to it. At the beginning of your narrative, you sounded so determined, strong, and self-assured about not going back to Abbas. All the loopholes in the law that he tried to find so you could ignore the last divorce were not taken as a rescue by you. Then at the end you relented and even seemed to agree in an intricate plan to go back to Abbas! Then again, you doubted that idea. This is exactly how your narrative developed two years ago.

Nevertheless, to be honest, I could now understand you better than I did that time, better than I wished I had. For when you said I was better off because I had no children, I felt unsure about my own feelings. Although it is hard to admit, at that moment I would have rather been in your place, despite the children, with an ex who tried so desperately to get me back. This thought shocked me, not only because I was wishing for a situation which would have been so much harder to cope with: it felt as if I betrayed my own feelings of anger and pride. This made me realize how extremely open and honest you have been about the multiple feelings, which I dared to label 'inconsistent' or 'incoherent'. I could now see my own ambivalence reflected in your assertion that you felt free and stronger now you were divorced and at the same time that you were planning to go back to Abbas. Keeping open the possibility of returning to Abbas probably had to do with self-esteem and social status ("You are teachers, you are educated and you don't want to come back to your children"?); with pride and practicalities ("And we can put our salaries together in order to spend it on taking care of our children, to raise them well"); but it also had to do with love. If not for the man in question, then at least for the young woman you once were ("And sometimes I am feeling sorrow when I see women with henna and their babies"). Like I once was, with hopes and dreams about a happy future, a happy end with the man you/I lived with for such a long time that he had become part of our own narrative, our own self.

As I had been part of your context and we produced the knowledge of your narrative in interaction, the way you perceived me must have been reflected in your narrative. You went from victim to victor, from subdued and unhappy to self-assured and confident about your future. Looking back, I suspect that the fact that these shifting subject positions might have been both what you wished yourself to be and what I projected on you. That the feminist stance I read in your narrative was as much my preoccupation as your reflection of that. My own experience with divorce and the insecurity it brought made me understand that what you narrated was not about 'inconsistency': it was in fact a quite eloquent articulation of your experience of freedom now you had, at last, your divorce and simultaneously the insecurity over what it might mean to lose not just a husband, but a way of life as well. A label that, I realise now, I gave to your narrative because at that time I could not understand your ambivalence behind your determination, but with which I could now sympathise.

CHAPTER 5

SPACES AND SILENCES: COMPARING BIOGRAPHIC NARRATIVES

Having the opportunity to talk about one's life, to give an account of it, to interpret it, is integral to leading that life rather than being led through it.

Lugones and Spelman(1983)[1]

The preceding pages gave ample room to the narratives of Hajja and Umm Khalthoum: narratives, which were both rich and multiple, testifying on pride and sadness, of happy memories and lost dreams, of past opportunities and future hopes.[2] By analyzing both narratives as part of their contexts I gained an insight into the construction of subject positions by each woman when telling her narrative, while Sa'adiya and I listened to them. However, I also want to say something about the social groups, the society, and the culture of which Hajja and Umm Khalthoum, and their narratives are part. My aim in this chapter is therefore to go from these personal perspectives to structural and discursive insights by comparing the narratives of Hajja and Umm Khalthoum. This will allow me to point out the similarities and differences in the ways the dominant discourse on gender is lived, experienced and acted out by different groups of working women in Kebkabiya

The question thereby is, to what extent the differences and commonalities of Umm Khalthoum's and Hajja's narratives offer a perspective on their negotiations of the Islamist moral discourse on gender, not as individuals but as members of their class. The commonalities might lead me to understand the ways in which those belonging to the category of working women negotiate the dominant moral discourse on gender *as* women living in a specific location and historical era. The differences are to be analyzed for the extent to which these might

---

[1] Lugones and Spelman(1983) quoted in Patai (1991: 148).

[2] Parts of chapter 5 and 6 appeared in "'One from the heart'. Family and friends in Al-Halla, West-Sudan", in: *Negotiation and social space. A gendered analysis of changing kin and security networks in South Asia an Sub-Saharan Africa*, edited by Carla Risseeuw and Kamala Ganesh. New Delhi: Sage. (1998), which I co-authored with Nawal H. Osman and Catrien Bijleveld.

be attributed to the intersection of gender and work with other localized identities, like class, but also marital status, generation, or occupation. These differences might also point at different avenues for agency, which I take to be constituted by the relations women maintain allowing for relational agency.

I will therefore first compare *how* Hajja and Umm Khalthoum narrate about themselves. This is not only an issue of focalization but also whether the *ways* they reflect on their lives as part of their surroundings say anything about the structural differences between both women and the way they construct their identities-in-context differently? At the same time, I will try to establish what the women are *not* saying by looking for the silences and gaps. By relating their narrative positions, negations, gaps, and silences to the historical and locational contexts in which they have meaning, I hope to determine whether the unsaid is to be intertextually understood as 'just' the unspoken, the common sense so ordinary that it required no comment—like a road so often traveled that it needed no indications of its course; or the unspeakable, the tabooed, the place where one feared to tread.[3]

Polyfocality/Polyvocality: How to Talk About One(s) Self?

In their narratives, Hajja and Umm Khalthoum make themselves the centre of their personal biographies; each woman is a heroine, struggling to overcome the barriers, which fate has put on her path. However, within the narratives this happens in quite different ways.

Although Hajja connected her reminiscences of her past to particular historical events, the narrative on her different identities was patchy, with many repentances, showing a shifting and fragmented structure, which made it seem incoherent and 'all over the place'. Although this might have been due to her background as an 'uneducated, local, poor, market woman', I felt uncomfortable as this view tied in too well with the government's perspective on market women. I decided to try and chart the contexts in which she related about her identities to see whether I could see an alternative structure in her narratives. Only

[3] See L. Nencel (1999) who elaborates on these different forms of silences in 'Ongezegd, onverteld, onuitgesproken. Gestalte geven aan gender in een veldwerkpraktijk (Unsaid, untold and unspoken. Embodying gender through fieldwork practice)'. See also Willemse f.c. 2006.

when reading her narrative as a 'text-in-context' I realized that her narrative was literally 'all over the place'. It showed me that while telling me about her life in the same context where that life acquired meaning, a context in which I also took part, Hajja had consistently mapped her narrative of herself. Her memories were triggered and certain identities were called upon when she, or we, visited certain places, or met certain people in the period that I taped her narrative. The bodily awareness of these 'defining' locations evoked her memories of that location and of the people connected to them. Hajja did not need to remember her life as a chronology as the landmarks of her narrative were tangibly laid out before her: her context of living constituted a map that gave her life and the narrative of that life a self-evident structure and coherence.

This 'map'[4] also structured my representation: certain physical markers of her identities were of particular importance on certain days of the week: she 'is' a market woman only when she sells at the market, on the specific market days, Mondays and Thursdays; she 'is' a descendant of Faqih Sinin only after we have visited his grave yard on a Wednesday, the special commemoration day of the founder of Kebkabiya. But she was a midwife every day of the week, practicing whenever she was needed. However, even those identities, which do not seem to have their roots in Kebkabiya, nor were connected to a specific day, and to which Hajja refers freely, still have a localized significance. She has become a medical midwife in Umdurman, but she 'is' one (and for a long time the only trained one) in Kebkabiya and its surroundings. An outsider made her a wife and a co-wife, but it is in Kebkabiya that she feels her positive self-esteem as a good wife and co-wife shaped and acknowledged.

The issue of constructing identities brings to the fore another discursive strategy that Hajja applies in her narrative. Hajja did not argue against the idea put forward by the government that market women are a potential threat to the moral order, on the contrary. While mapping her identities, she also established differences between herself and unspecified 'other' market women who, Hajja claimed, did have ulterior motives for sitting out in the open on the market. This strategy of

[4] Mapping and its counterpart 'cartography' are no new labels for referring to the construction of identities and struggles. See for example 'Cartographies of struggle' by Mohanty (1991). and 'Casting identities, gendered enclosures' by Nencel (1997). Listening to Hajja, it is the most helpful indication of what Hajja and I have been doing.

'the other' was also applied in her focalizations, using alternating I/we, me/us, and they/them, thereby prioritizing some of her identities while downplaying others. She thus created space for an alternative identity, without openly going against the government's view.

Hajja indeed becomes a heroine with special qualities, acted out in the identities as a clever, active and life-saving midwife and a caring, loving and non-jealous wife and co-wife which make her stand out as an individual. However, not as the 'lone achiever [who] has felt compelled to construct and represent her uniqueness, seemingly in defiance of historical conditions, but actually in tune with the dominant power structures which have rewarded her' (Okely 1992: 7). She is a consignee of an exceptional stroke of luck, who was overcome by major historical changes brought about by processes of 'modernity', which gave her chances in life. These chances enabled her to prove her unique capabilities and intelligence, as well as her awareness of what it means to be a 'proper' Muslim, but which did not alter the course of her life as a woman when it came to issues of power and her role as a mother and a wife.

She alternates from her individualistic notions of herself to her collective identities, told with different emphases and gusto. When I inquired about her relation to Faqih Sinin or marketing while not being in the specific location that 'belonged' to that identity, Hajja would direct me to people 'who know more about it'. In other words, those identities which she plays down, and from which she differentiates herself, are those for which she claims a shared, collective identity.[5] In this way she does not only denounce sole 'ownership' of that identity but she also claims a common fate and thus a shared responsibility. At the same time the individual and collective identities are not opposed or mutually exclusive. On the contrary, each identity constitutes and is constituted by each other and by Hajja's surroundings, her relationships, and her history. Hajja's 'landscape of memories' charts her life and the narrative of that life, lending it stability and coherence, integrating her seemingly fragmented identities.

Umm Khalthoum uses a quite different map in constructing her narrative. She relates to a larger map in respect to the geographic locations she narrates about and at the same time to a more restricted map with respect to her mobility in the context of her daily life. While

[5] See Mohanty (1991: 34–35).

Umm Khalthoum remembered her past, we were taken on a journey, from Umdurman where she was born, to several places in Darfur, between Al-Fasher in the east to Zalingei and El-Geneina in the far west, where she spent most of her youth and adult life. However, these places are not connected to her identities as they are in Hajja's narrative. She uses travelling as concomitant to the chronology of her life, which also structures her narrative as a biography from youth to the present. However, travelling itself is not an issue: it is a way of life, of her and her colleagues, as a consequence of the way the government service works.

It is therefore not difficult to understand why Umm Khalthoum's narrative seems much more self-centred, more integrated, and composed than Hajja's. This might be due to Umm Khalthoum's education as she might have an idea of what a biographic narrative might look like. Also in this case I have to beware of suiting the dominant discourse. For the relatively consistent narrative of her life almost hides the shifting locations and positions and the ambiguities she has experienced in her life as an elite woman. She comes with repeated themes and subject positions, from victim to victor, from daughter to a working mother (-in-law), from object to subject. She thus creates a circular, or even a spiral structure in her narrative as a whole, picking up on former constructions 'moving on', literally and figuratively, to another positioning. These progressive positionings constitute the core of her narrative and assist her in her claim to respectability as an elite woman. Although Umm Khalthoum seems to refer in a much more 'private' and personal way to her past than Hajja, the way she constructs her 'individual' identities as mother and wife is in itself public: most of her colleagues might recognize Umm Khalthoum's movements and pre-occupations as their own. If Hajja is secure in the stability of her local surroundings, Umm Khalthoum is secure in the notion that her colleagues have the same mobile lifestyle as she does.

As I gained from the narratives of other female teachers from outside Kebkabiya, as a consequence of this mobility, all educated elite women needed to assess and manage their identities in relation to their elite status in every day speech, contacts, and life-style. Narrating about one self, one's ideas and identities, is itself part of acting out an (female) elite identity and thus strategic in claiming a respectable and unblemished status.

This aspect of keeping up appearances is also prevalent in the more restricted mapping of Umm Khalthoum's narrative when she locates important events predominantly in the households of her relatives. Her emphasis on being a home-bound and obedient daughter and wife, who constructs her activities mainly within the confines of the consecutive homes, is part of a discursive strategy to construct herself as an elite woman with a proper life-style.

In Umm Khalthoum's narrative therefore, it is not the local geography in connection with people, which makes a difference to her identities. She does not refer to current collective identities with her colleagues, which would mean an emphasis on her identity as a working woman. Different from Hajja she focuses on a shared identity which is connected to remoter, 'remembered' relationships to her kin, like her mother and her sister. In this way Umm Khalthoum is claiming, comparable to Hajja, a shared fate and shared responsibility for a potentially negative status as a divorced woman. At the same time this tying of her identities to women of her family creates both closeness and distance. For although they are women who are close to Umm Khalthoum in spirit, relationship and a shared history, they do not share the day-to-day reality in a shared locality. Contrary to Hajja, Umm Khalthoum evokes a sense of disconnection between the construction of her self and her daily life. She thus manages to keep both identities, that of a relative who has ended up, like her female relatives, in a bad marriage, and that of a teacher-cum-mother (-in-law), separate. Umm Khalthoum's strategy of 'othering' therefore is not with respect to other women in a similar position, on the contrary: the differentiation in Umm Khalthoum's narrative is directed at contrasting the identities she in fact combines by differentiating them according to space and time: of the period before and after her father's marriage with a second wife, which is paralleled with the period in her marriage before and after Abbas became a teacher, both connected to the shifting of life in a town to that in a village, that of a happy and a miserable young woman, and finally, of a naïve wife and a wise mother, mother-in-law, and Mother of the kindergarten.

Both Hajja and Umm Khalthoum thus used a 'strategy of difference' to construct a narrative, a life, though the relation between the past and the present have in their narratives different goals. Hajja yearned for the past when life was better and did not talk about her future as if she felt, or feared, that her life would not give her many chances for improvement of her situation or that of her daughters. Umm Khalthoum used her past and those of her relatives, as a model for conceiving a better future, however uncertain that future might be.

These differences in using space/time locations for narrating one's life are not just a matter of different uses of geography, but the extent to which one 'belongs' to the local community: to the way Hajja and Umm Khalthoum maintain networks with the people involved in that locality. As I pointed out, Hajja immersed her narrative completely in her local surroundings, including networks of people, most of whom she has known all her life. Interestingly, when integrating all the maps of the diverse narrated sites, it appeared that Hajja is indeed literally situated centrally in the space of her networks. Peculiarly, this mapping made obvious that her close female relatives who occupied many of the fixed places on Hajja's map and who were thus all intrinsically part of the same experiential plane bearing the inscriptions of Hajja's identities, were hardly mentioned in her narrative: like the market women whom Hajja referred me to, and most of Hajja's family members living in *hei as-suq*, the area where Hajja's compound was located.

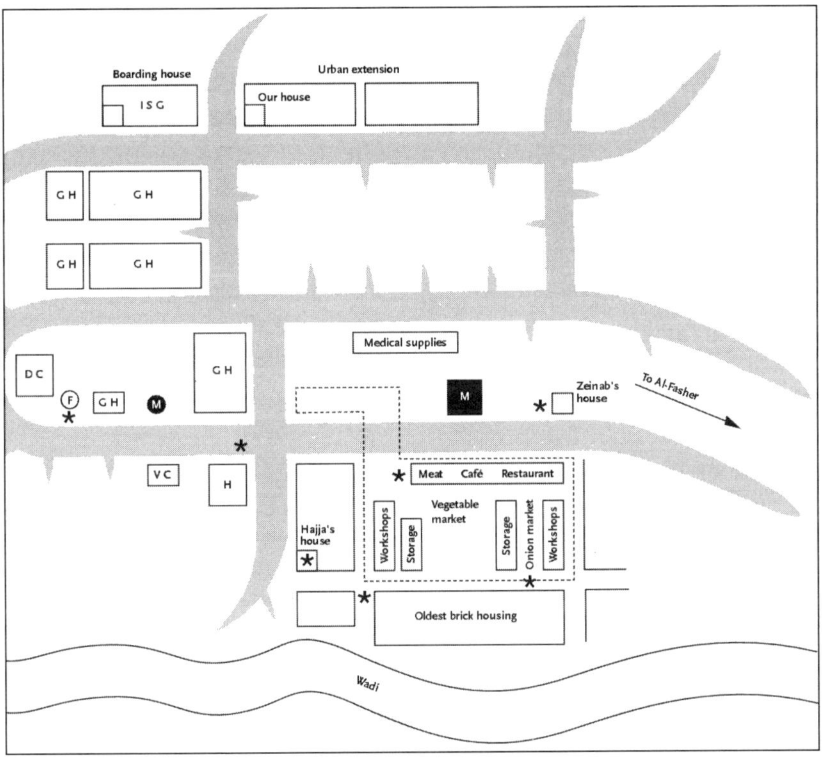

Map 6. Landscape of memories: Integrated Maps

This was also true for Umm Khalthoum, whose daily network was constituted by her colleagues. In her narrative Umm Khalthoum hardly referred to her daily surroundings as these were rather contingent; because of the inherent temporality of Kebkabiya as her 'home', but also in the light of her pending divorce. In the locality of her daily life her identity as a 'proper Muslim woman' was thereby also made contingent. Taking care of her nuclear family as a mother she could do anywhere, and this allowed her to claim a positive identity. However, Umm Khalthoum also evaluated her identity as a working woman positively, while she hardly referred to her colleagues whose status might boost her own and with whom she spent most of her time in Kebkabiya, in work and leisure. The differences and commonalities between both women thus can also be read from the silences in their narratives. But to what extent can these be read as discursive strategies?

Silences: Of Kith and Kin[6]

Listening to silences in relationship to my viewpoint that I want to take the words of women seriously might seem a contradiction. However, I think that in order to understand the lives of Umm Khalthoum and Hajja and their contemporaries better, their narratives have to be seen as part of their lives. Every utterance can be taken to be argumentative with respect to dominant discourses and common sense knowledge (Billig 1991).[7] Therefore, in narratives as well women are negotiating the 'norm/ality' of their lives. By continuously scrutinizing the context in which their narrative and their lives are structured they engage in a dialogue with the discourses which govern, invade, construct, and are constructed by, their lives.

Most of Hajja's family members have settled in the town in which she grew up. In her narrative though, Hajja hardly mentions the relatives and neighbours who are important in her daily life. This is peculiar. She deals with these people on a daily basis in order to perform her household chores and marketing activities.

Her daughters do most of the household work and her neighbours help her with larger chores, like building a *rakuba* or taking her grain from the fields. And what about Hajja's sisters Tinya and Fatna, her

---

[6] Large parts of this argument are elaborated upon in Willemse (1998).

[7] See for an elaboration of this viewpoint the Introduction.

aunt Umm Maryoma and several of her nieces who are all trading on the market and who even stand in for her whenever she is called away? They regularly come to lend Hajja a hand with whatever task needs doing. Further, they also regularly visit her during their leisure time. It is with them that Hajja shares a collective identity as a market woman and a relative. Let me take a closer look at the nature of the relationships Hajja has with the people she meets daily.

Hajja's household is an all women household and most of the visitors are women as well. When I once made a remark about this, Hajja told me that she was sad that her only brother had died and that she had no sons to take care of her. 'Daughters help you and will stay close, but sons can give you goods or money and they will arrange things for you with the government or the *rais as-suq*', she said. 'Look at Fatna, *ukhti shaygiga*[8] her son Mohammed is very kind. When Mohammed came back from a stay in Nyala he brought us a box with bars of soap, five pounds of sugar and five bottles of oil, and I am only his aunt (*khaaltu* mother's sister), not even his mother!' With no male household members around, unrelated men were unlikely to visit to socialize because Nura is not married and therefore had to be careful about receiving unrelated men. Only Farrah, the brother of the brother-in-law of Zamzam, Nura's half-sister, and their maternal cousin Yassir visited the compound of Hajja occasionally. They were both in the army stationed at Kebkabiya and most of the time they came to chat or iron their clothes bringing as a present: soap or matches, tea, sugar and sometimes clandestinely butchered meat. Referring to them consistently with a kinship term emphasized their 'not harmful', because kin, relationship.

Similar to Hajja's case, there were many households in Kebkabiya, which were headed by women. The situation arose because the male household head was absent while no brothers, sons, or other close male relatives were around. As Hajja mentioned in her narrative, apart from death, trading and out-migration were reasons for men to leave their families. With the drought and the deteriorating economic situation in Darfur many, especially the younger men have left for better places. One can interpret the migration of young men as a survival strategy. As it is women who take care of agricultural tasks, young men are only another mouth to feed: if they leave it releases some of the strain on

[8] *Ukhti shaygiga*, my full sister.

the household resources.[9] At the same time young men are in demand in the big towns, because of their supposed strength,[10] their flexibility concerning working hours and space, and their low wages.

Therefore, for Hajja, as for most female-headed households, it is indeed related women who constitute the more stable knots in each other's network important for daily survival. However, the emphasis on women in daily support networks of female heads of households is not just a 'fact of life', but is also related to structural aspects of the way people perceive different kin relations. I found this fact out almost by accident.

One night, when I ask Hajja what '*shaygiga*' means in *ukhti shaygiga*, which she uses when she talks about her sister Fatna, she looks a bit puzzled:

It means that she is my full sister, of course, from one father and mother. Ah, Karin, in your country all your brothers and sisters are of course shaygiga, kamil *(round, full)!*

I correct her saying that when a man or woman marries again after a divorce or being a widow, the children from the former and the new spouse are half-siblings as well. Nura, who has been shelling peanuts in silence so far, intervenes:

You see, Karin, here a lot of people have half-brothers or -sisters, akhwaan wa akhwaat bil-nus *but they do not belong to the same* usra, *family. Only if you are* shaygiga, *you belong to the same* usra, *your full brothers and sisters, father and mother and their parents. Your half-brothers and -sister don't belong to your* usra *but to your more extended family,* ahl. *Also the children of all your sisters and brothers and their children and the sisters and brothers of your father and mother and their children are* ahl.

Then Hajja takes over again:

---

[9] Grawert (1992), who did research in a district in North-Darfur, points out that if the drought or the economic crisis perseveres, older men will leave. Only when it is not possible to stay because of severe drought, women with the younger children will leave. See Grawert 1998 for figures of (out-)migration and economic returns.

[10] Women are considered strong workers as well and are employed in for example construction work or harvesting of sugar cane. However, because women often have children to take care of, towns are less popular for female workers.

My husband's ahl *belongs to his tribe. Everyone belongs to his own tribe. My tribe is Tama, but Semira and Nura are Fur, from their father. Also Feisal is from the Fur tribe because his father is Fur, while his mother is Berti, and he is* ahl, *not* usra *to us.*

Nura now stops shelling the peanuts and makes a dismissive movement with her arm saying:

When I was ill with malaria and I lay on my bed with fever, all the neighbours came within one day to visit me, but Feisal, wad abui, *my half-brother (literally 'my father's son'), only came to visit after five days. And when I really needed to go to the hospital in the next town, he did not want to give me his seat in one of the faster cars, so I had to go by lorry, which took the whole night. In the rainy season it was. Imagine, in the rainy season I travelled for two days in the open air until we reached the hospital. I nearly died.*

Semira, who just enters the *rakuba* adds that when Feisal returned from a trip to Khartoum he gave them as a present: "…Only a tea sieve, which lasted a week and gloves that were torn after hardly wearing them".

Nura spits in the sand with a face that leaves no doubt about what she thinks of him. Hajja hushes in an attempt to silence her, but Nura continues: '*Ahl al-umm min al-qalb, lekin ahl-abuk min ba'iid*': 'the family of the mother is from the heart, but your father's family comes from far'.

This talk with Hajja and Nura gives an insight into the expectations one has of 'close' kin. It is indicated by the saying '*min al-qalb*' the relationship children maintain with the kin of their mother is far more affectionate compared to those of their father. Women are those who stay 'at home', whilst men have become those who travel in order to earn a living. Even when men are not travelling, children virtually grow up with their maternal, especially female, family members who regularly help each other with household chores and other tasks, like the sisters and cousin of Hajja. These maternal female relatives, especially of your mother and your own sisters, are thus considered those from the heart and those from the hearth. As Nura later explained to me:

> *Those you have known since you were small are* 'gariib', *'close'. And however far they live when you are grown up, they will always stay 'close'. Like Mohammed, the son of Hajja's sister Fatna, who is still taking care also of Hajja, his mother's sister, with whom he grew up.*

Mohammed's assistance, however, is occasional. He is one of the matrilineal relatives with which Hajja maintains a relation of a more long-term nature. As these types of relationships are not part of ones daily support network, they belong to what I call a safety net, a network with people to ask for assistance in times of high need. Nevertheless, a (classificatory) kinship relation makes it possible for him, as well as for Yassir and Farrah to visit Hajja and her daughters without causing gossip. In the end, Hajja also referred to me as '*naas*' and occasionally even as sister or daughter, which made member of Hajja's daily support network as well.

Because Mohammed's help is so outstanding, Hajja remembers him in her narrative. The women in Hajja's daily support network are those with whom she shares tasks, time and responsibilities regularly (cf. Willemse et. al. 1998): mostly neighbours and relatives, not accidentally many of whom live in Hajja's vicinity and sell at the market as well.

The issue at stake here is that the silence on these relationships in Hajja's narrative is connected to the way Hajja deals with locality. Her relationships with her relatives are so self-evident, so common place, and so much part of the geography in which she lives that they are not an issue: they constitute Hajja's daily, collective, identity. It is thus not because they are not important to her, but these are relationships that have existed all her life. Hajja's biography is a narrative of what sets her apart from others, what makes her a 'heroine', and thus she emphasizes individual achievement instead of collective experience. However, even though this points at the silence as just the unspoken, there is a possibility of the unspeakable as well, as many of her female relatives sell at the market. Referring to them too openly in her narrative would be a liability to her attempt at constructing, not only a unique, but also a respectable self. This raises the question as to what silences are contained within Umm Khalthoum's self-presentation.

Umm Khalthoum's Disposition: Belonging to the New Elite Class

In Umm Khalthoum's narrative her relatives do constitute the main anchor in her narratives, serving as points of reference for constructing her identities rather than the locality she inhibits. While her relatives are, in turn, tied to the different locations between which she moved to-and-fro in her past Umm Khalthoum never mentions those who are close to her in daily locality: her colleagues. With them Umm

Khalthoum shares her identities as a teacher, a female elite member and as an 'outsider' and she spends most of her time outside her family life with them: at work, when organizing official and unofficial meetings, and most of her leisure time. So, why does Umm Khalthoum keep silent about her daily relationships with these women?

Due to the government policy of regular transferrals, the networks of female teachers will contain more colleagues than kin. As a consequence Umm Khalthoum has travelled all over Darfur because her husband was transferred so frequently. When he received his posting to Kebkabiya, Umm Khalthoum applied for a job there as well, so that she could add to their income. Therefore, in the case of Umm Khalthoum, similar to many other married elite women, her husband's profession—and her own for that matter—regulates the type of relationships that she can build up. Umm Khalthoum's frequent contacts with other educated women might be because there is no alternative.

However, there is another important aspect to consider as well. During a picnic with the female teachers, there was a discussion about the holidays after Ramadan. To my surprise Fadjur did not plan to go home as I thought she would, but had arranged to go with Yasmin to her parents' home in South Darfur. They were enthusiastically talking about the outings they would organize and the people they were going to meet, and they had even exchanged presents. One of the older teachers said to me, nodding with her head to both of them: '*Mukh wahed, qalb wahed*', 'one mind, one heart'.

I had not heard this said before, but the idea quite accurately phrased the way most teachers would relate to each other. Amongst them, being educated means being of the same mind, and being friends means sharing one's heart: both are seen as closely related. All teachers at one time or another had told me that education provided them with the opportunity to socialize with people of kindred spirit. With these people, they could discuss and exchange knowledge and ideas, share personal feelings, laugh and joke at one and the same time. Fadjur stated that this was one of the most satisfying aspects of her job: to meet those with whom one shares the same aspirations and 'outlook on life'.

Though teachers sharing lodgings at the boarding house take turns in preparing meals, married female teachers do not share any household tasks, and visits to each other's compounds only occur on invitation. However, based on shared work, responsibilities, knowledge horizon and lifestyle, they feel they share an identity as educated elite women. Although female elite members thus constitute each other's daily network due to the lack of relatives, paradoxically, female teachers emphasize their contentment to be able to choose those with whom one wants to socialize. Personal preference and achievement are emphasized not the lack of alternatives. Nevertheless, all teachers do have family and Umm Khalthoum emphasized in her narrative the collective identity with them, their shared fate and experiences in family life rather than individual achievement and the building of a network of colleagues. So what place do relatives have in the lives of female teachers?

Building a Network: The Nuclear Strategy

Sitt Khadija's ambivalence towards family members was displayed when she had just given birth to a baby. Though she had planned to give birth in her mother's house in Kutum, a town north of Kebkabiya as she had no relatives in town, her premature delivery of her baby forced her to stay in Kebkabiya. Her mother and a young niece had come down from Kutum, in order to assist her after she gave birth. One day, a few weeks after her baby boy was born, Sa'adiya and I were at her house. Sitt Khadija invited me so she could finish her narrative, which had been interrupted by the birth. I had just put the tape recorder on, when some guests came in. They were colleagues and after a short while they left again. Sa'adiya asked if her family had seen the boy already. Sitt Khadija then almost whispered that one of her colleagues had not turned up yet and that she thought it was a shame. She obviously felt very hurt and upset about it. She did not say anything about her family not arriving. Towards the end of our session, a woman from Kebkabiya appeared at the doorstep. On seeing us, she clearly felt uncomfortable and after quickly introducing herself briefly as Khadija's father's sister, she went on to the kitchen where Khadija's mother prepared lunch.

It puzzled me that Sitt Khadija took more offence at the fact that her colleague did not turn up than at the neglect of her family. And why did she say she had no relatives in Kebkabiya when she appeared to have at least one relative there? The only thing I could think of was, that maybe she did not like her family. Or she might have been glad not to be obliged to cater for them while being only with her mother after quite a heavy delivery. It turned out to be a combination of both.

When walking back one evening after a gathering of the female teachers from different schools, I ask Yasmin about their backgrounds. She shrugs saying: "They are from diverse families, rich and poor, and from different ethnicities, but we don't discuss those matters. It is the mind that matters, our thoughts and discussions, not our backgrounds", then reciting: 'One doesn't care about the one who is saying "my father is so-and-so" but about the one who is saying this is me'. The importance placed on education and an elite lifestyle in order to relate to each other on equal terms even results in a code of conduct. The code not only emphasizes the virtues of choice and achievement, but also condemns the idea of priding oneself on one's family background. This also concerned the ethnic and socio-economic backgrounds of the female teachers which, as Yasmin told me once, 'was of no concern to any one' in the sense that it is never alluded to nor discussed: the educational and occupational backgrounds were the most important determinants of one's status.

Therefore, in trying to read the silences in respect to relationships, a difference between Hajja and Umm Khalthoum becomes apparent. Hajja is situated squarely in a daily support network, which centres around kinship, real or classificatory, with an emphasis on women on the maternal side. Umm Khalthoum lacks kin relations and has to make do, even preferring the company of her colleagues in her daily life. This constitutes a network in which the reference to kin is not just silenced but even tabooed. Both silences reflect the way in which both women 'belong' in their daily lives as members of their social groups and the different emphases in each narrative. However, there are also similarities in their narratives. The question is how to understand these?

Umm Khalthoum Meets Hajja: The Differences in Similarities

Comparing both narratives, some of the themes which are referred to in detail by both women are strikingly similar: the way both reflect on their father, mother, their husband and the prominence of their elite membership as well as of education in their lives. The mothers remain shallow, secondary figures, although in the case of Umm Khalthoum she does constitute a role model and in the case of Hajja she is the main link to Faqih Sinin. However, as in the case with the women and men who figure in their daily networks, the meagre number of references to their mothers is not because mothers are not important in their lives, but because they are not important to the narrative at hand. The relationships between both women and the figures of their fathers, and of their husbands, are of a central meaning, of a constitutive force, but of what?

In both narratives, the father is depicted as the one who decides about their fate, not only concerning education, whether sending them to or taking them from school. He is also deciding on their subsequent marriage. One of the more self-evident reasons is that both Hajja and Umm Khalthoum are raised in a patrilineal society. Although the relationships of Hajja's daughters with their matrilineal relatives are experienced as close and emotionally secure, the patri-line is important in deciding on rights and duties.

Connected to the position of the father is that of the husband in both narratives. While Umm Khalthoum passionately evaluated her life with Abbas as one that turned out to be less comfortable and easy than she expected, Hajja's narrative refers in a quite distanced way to her husband in terms of wealth, generosity, fairness and his preference for her. Each woman, however, by connecting her fate as a woman 'coming of age' going from the hands of the father into those of the husband, implicitly refers to the first *hadith* as quoted by Sitt Miriam in her speech during the visit of the popular committee to Kebkabiya. However, due to the differences in background each woman reflects differently on that *hadith* in order to position herself in relation to the Islamist moral discourse.

Both women start their narratives with a reflection on the wealth they experienced in their youth and the decision-making power of their fathers. Both fathers were at some point traders and both women gave ample space in their narratives to the wealthy environment in which they used to live. This emphasis serves to express their belonging to a privileged group, an elite class, whether via the father or the husband. And it is precisely this commonality where the differences stand out. The difference is not only marked by the kind of food which is remembered, but also by the activities of both: like making huge diners for guests (Hajja) or having leisure time and going for a picnic (Umm Khalthoum); the parentage of the local founder with connections to the local leader (Hajja) or of a *jellaba*, a government worker and a trader from the East (Umm Khalthoum); and their social status as a married woman, a wife of a rich and influential trader with co-wives (Hajja) or the only wife of an educated man in a project or teaching position (Umm Khalthoum). In 'proving' their membership of an elite class, they expose their differences. I found out how important these differences are near the end of my second stay in Kebkabiya.

The Dividing Line: Education and Cultivation

It is the third week of Ramadan and although it is hot, most people I meet have acclimatized to the fast. This includes Umm Khalthoum, who tells me she has enough energy to talk with me about her life. During Ramadan, religious contemplation is almost tangible especially now day twenty-seven is approaching. As Umm Khalthoum explained, at the night of the twenty-seventh day of fasting Allah might send a message to some of his believers who could experience a miracle, a blessing of Allah himself.[11] When I ask her if women have the same chances to be rewarded as men, she says:

Yes, of course, all Muslims who have proven to be good believers, they all have the same chance. But some are better believers than others, and Allah knows this.

Without thinking, I ask her what differences there are which make you a better believer. She looks a bit taken aback and says:

Of course, there is a difference for example between the employed and unemployed women. The educated one respects people and takes an interest in others and respects her husband and takes care of her children better. The most important task of mothers is to look after them from rhoda *to primary school and to make sure they become good adults, which means to give enough attention to them and to be careful. Taking care of your children is easier in a town, to raise them well and healthy, for in town it is safe. Mothers are different. A mother in a town is more careful of her children than the mother in the village. The relationship between her and her neighbours is good as well. She also takes better care of her house than uneducated ones. The uneducated, only a few of them are good and look after their houses and children well. Most of them spend their time sitting in the market and going over to other women to chat.*

[11] *Laylat al-qadr*, night of decision or destiny (*Qur'an* 97), also called the 'the night of Power' when the *Qur'an* as a whole was sent to the lowest of the seven heavens and the angel Jibril (Gabriel) started his visits to Mohammed. Commemorated on the odd nights during the end of Ramadan, in particular on the 27th of Ramadan (Bartels 1997: 109). See for example Buitelaar (1991) for a reflection on the importance of this night in Morocco.

Or they go to the fields from morning until evening. The husband always finds her absent. But the educated one changes the design and furnishing of her house, to make it look nice. She also knows how to cook a greater variety of dishes and how to use different kinds of food. She knows how to cook alternative breakfasts today and tomorrow and after-tomorrow; she knows how to choose supper and to prepare for her husband the choicest kinds of food.

Uneducated wives are the opposite of this. Whether the husband eats well or not is not an issue to them. There is another big difference between employed and unemployed women. Every Eed[12] *they know what kinds of food to choose. For* Eed *educated women know how to make a lot of different kinds of biscuit. Also in their treatment of children they know that they have to wash their children every day and to change their dresses: their children are very clean, every day of the week. Some women, if they bath their children today they will not wash them again for three days. This is the result of education; it affects the habits of people.*

Although the differences Umm Khalthoum mentions do not surprise me, I am a bit taken aback by the fact that Umm Khalthoum seems to think that uneducated women 'do not care'. I am not sure what to say to this, so I nod, saying '*Billahi*', 'is it really?' Probably Umm Khalthoum feels that I might be doubtful, for she rushes on:

There is also a difference in marriage between educated and uneducated women. The educated ones, if the husband comes to marry her, most of them have good jobs and a lot of money. They always marry educated men, sensible men. In marriage, educated men bring nice shantas *with fine dresses,* tobes, *and a lot of nice things like good scents. Also he will build a nice house with furniture, a sitting room, a bedroom and a guestroom. Common people, if they choose a* shanta, *they choose the wrong colours together, those that do not match. Also the attitude towards their husbands is different. Educated women and their husbands, they eat together and walk together, they understand each other. They visit friends together and make journeys with other families. But the uneducated don't. They don't eat together with their husband. If they are asked to join they say 'no, no, no', and will cover up their faces. They will not eat with their bridegroom because they feel ashamed. They eat separately. The uneducated bride and her husband they share nothing together, they'll just sleep together, after they blow out the light they'll meet, they don't want to see each other. Also the brides are different. The educated ones put on henna, comb their hair, and*

[12] *Eed al-fitr*, also called the small Eed, marks the end of Ramadan and is celebrated with choices of good food, drinks, and sweets and with new dresses and little presents especially for children.

plait it well and they use khufra *and* dukhan[13] *to smell nice. They use the best scents. The villagers, they don't apply henna and they go without scents into their marriage. Even when they put the henna on, they don't make it black but keep it a very light orange.*[14] *There is not a good understanding between husband and wife and so sometimes their life together fails. But the good bridegroom asks right in the beginning if she agrees to marry him and they will be happy together and understand each other well. From the beginning they will love each other well and will have an engagement. Like this, they can have a good life. But in the village, brides don't see the bridegroom before their wedding day because their fathers make the marriage without their knowledge nor their consent. How can they live like this? It is not good. It is better to see each other face to face.*

At this point, I am a bit puzzled. Would she think of herself as a village girl, or does she consider herself to be a bride who has not been asked by her husband, as a woman who did not consent to her marriage, when she states: "If she agrees to marry him?" As if Umm Khalthoum can read my thoughts she adds, shyly smiling: "Abbas was not my choice and the other problem is that he drinks too much". As I am more eager to hear her opinion on the differences between classes of women, I ask her whether this difference has any consequences for the way they believe. She adjusts her *tobe* and then says:

Of course, there is a difference between educated and uneducated Muslims. The educated Muslim can open the Book herself, read, understand and explain to herself all there is to know about Islam. But uneducated ones they can only hear it from others like the wa'iz *from the mosque, if she goes at all. They will learn how to pray and how to wash after sex. Some still don't know how to wash themselves after sex.*[15] *The educated ones know. They also know how to pray. Uneducated women they don't know how to explain Islam or how to read or write. For example one day I was in the market with my daughter Kaltouma. A man wanted to explain a chapter of the* Qur'an *and he gave the* sura *the wrong meaning, he gave it the*

---

[13] *Khufra* refers to a smoke bath by squatting with ones skirt or *tobe* over a small pot with burning scented wood, scenting the dresses. *Dukhan* refers to a smoke bath taken in a hole in the ground with a heavy blanket or several *tobe*s over a bare body, of which the effect is comparable to a sauna, scenting the skin.

[14] Orange is the colour the skin turns into when pure henna is applied. In Sudan, the black henna painting is preferred as black patterns come out better on a dark skin. In order to get black henna, a natural or artificial black colouring is added to the henna, like *sibha,* or cadmium which is taken from old batteries.

[15] The ablution ritual washing or *gusl* is obligatory for women after having had sex, after menstruation and after the waiting period after giving birth.

opposite explanation. If he had been educated he would have known, but he wasn't so he didn't know the right roots to explain the meaning of the word. The Qur'an *is not easy to explain without knowing the right meaning of the roots.*[16] *There are differences between educated and uneducated people. It is not good to read the chapters of the* Qur'an *wrongly and to explain it wrongly. God will ask you after you die why you told people the wrong things. If somebody explains to you the right meaning, you can read the* suras *correctly because you understand the meaning of it. One man also wanted to explain a text from the* Qur'an *and he told the people that it meant: 'You should not try to earn a salary because it will cause you to burn in hell'. He completely misunderstood the lines because his knowledge of Arabic was not sufficient. Because in the past when they met someone of the family of an employee the person didn't want to take money from him because they believed they would then go to hell. They also said: 'The pupils in the* khalwa *go straight to heaven, but the children in the government school they will go to hell'. This was in the past.*

"You mean during the British time?" I ask. "Yes, in British time, but also afterwards. They had it from their grandfathers and mothers", Umm Khalthoum agrees. We talk further. We speak of the different implications of religion for men and women. We continue to talk of the children and of Abbas. However, the idea is clear: Umm Khalthoum sees a substantial difference between educated and non-educated women, or as she expressed it, employed and unemployed women. With this, she refers to the fact that female teachers and other women, who work for the government, have all had more than primary education and receive a salary paid by the government. However, from her argument it is clear that this is not the only difference. It is about lifestyle. It is also about the layout of houses with the right kind of furniture, about the right food and dress codes. It is about behaviour, especially towards your husband, and ways of speaking, about knowledge of the *Qur'an* and the right religious conduct. Knowledge is the key in her narrative. An educated woman is 'She [who] knows', whether it concerns how to prepare food, to take care of her children, to deal with her husband or to read the *Qur'an*.

It is not only Umm Khalthoum, but also Sitt Ashia and her colleagues who imply that 'good breeding' comes with education, with gaining knowledge. So all members of the educated elite whether male or female, consider Hajja to be part of the local, amorphous non-elite,

[16] The three consonants of each word constitute the root: related meanings can be made by adding suffix, prefix, etc.

because she is not educated and thus not 'civilized', but ignorant and backward. However, whilst Hajja is considered non-elite by these standards, locally she is seen as belonging to the town elite, or at least used to belong. So how has this difference come about? How it is that education has become the overriding element of being considered a member of the elite?

British Rule in Darfur: Education and the New Elite

The difference between Hajja and Umm Khalthoum based on their father's occupation is that Hajja belonged to the old, local 'sultanic' elite. As I discussed earlier, Faqih Sinin was serving in the military and administrative structure of the *Mahdiyya*[17] (1881–1898), the mission of Islamic reform proclaimed by Mohammed Ahmed Al-Mahdi, which resulted in the conquest of the *Turkiyya* (1823–1885), as the Sudan then was called. Umm Khalthoum's father was a government employee of the Sudanese government after Independence, in the 1960s. Originally, he served in a bureaucracy that was based on the administration introduced by the British and he therefore belonged to the new administrative elite, and so did Umm Khalthoum.

The historical process, which was instigated by the British occupation of Darfur is important in order to understand the distinction between these two kinds of elites, the local and governmental, and the positions Hajja and Umm Khalthoum can claim because of these differences. As I pointed out the British captured Darfur in 1916 and added the former sultanate as a province to the colonial state of Sudan in the years that followed (1916–1922).[18] Before that time the Darfur sultanate was the easternmost sultanate of the Sultanic belt and was used as an intermediate station for pilgrims and trading caravans from West Africa, where the sultanates of Wadai, Kanem and Bornu were located, to the east, in the direction of Mecca via the Nile Valley where the British resided; or to the north to Cairo via Kobbei, located near Kebkabiya, the famous starting point of the *Darb al-arba'in*, or forty-days

[17] In that period there was a wave of religious men claiming to be *the Mahdi*, the Rightly Guided or Saviour. The period of 1881 till 1885 was that between the proclaiming of the Mahdiyya and the final capture of the Sudan after killing 'China' Gordon, secretary general of the Turkiyya in Khartoum.

[18] See for example Kapteijns who elaborates on the process of 'pacification' in the former sultanates Dar Fur, Dar Masalit, and Dar Wadai (1985a: 171–244).

road. So in terms of trade, war, marriages, culture and religion Darfur had been a 'meeting ground of several African Islamic traditions (O'Fahey 1980a: 115–119)' and a zone of transition (Kapteijns 1985: 55).

After the British established their rule in Darfur, the ruling sultanic elite was replaced by, and in some cases transformed into, a new administrative class. The colonial government in fact created in Darfur a new urban middle class of civil servants, police and army officers, and teachers, which could help the British government to rule the vast area of Darfur. Most of these administrative officers originated from the Nile Valley. In their trail came the traders (Kapteijns 1985: 55; O'Fahey 1980: 46–115).

Umm Khalthoum's father was one of those who tried his luck in trade and services in the newly opened area in the West. Hajja's brother in law, Abu Helima, was one of these men, and her husband, Abu Feisal as well. The difference between them is the fact that Umm Khalthoum's father came originally from Umdurman as a government employee, and set himself up as a trader once posted in Darfur. This made him a *jellaba* in the eyes of the local community, used for every trader from the East, especially the Nile Valley. However, the differences between Hajja's family and Umm Khalthoum's family are not only the consequence of the differences in administrative structure: it is also related to the differences in the history of Islamization which had resulted in a particular Islamic code of conduct and lifestyle.[19]

In Darfur, Islamization had been a slow process. According to the myths of origin Suleiman Solong introduced Islam to the Keira Sultanate as a court cult, probably in the middle of the seventeenth century. He was the son of Ahmed al Ma'qur, an Arab Hilali from North Africa, who came to the Tunjur king and married one of the women of the royal clan, thereby converting the leaders of the Fur into Muslims and the Tunjur into the Keira Sultanate (O'Fahey 1980a: 9–10, 123: O'Fahey and Spaulding, 1974: 123–124).[20] In the centuries following this conversion, the sultans who were the heirs of this first Islamic

---

[19] Umm Khalthoum's narrative takes place in the 1960s. My overview is on the decades before that date and is therefore very brief and as a consequence does no justice to the historical record.

[20] The 'coming of the Wise Stranger who teaches a barbarous people civilized habits and marries the local chief's daughter (or sister), and founds a new dynasty' is a well known theme in founding myths of the states in the Sudanic Belt. In most versions this Wise Stranger was not Islamic. This identity might have been emphasized or even added to the narrative with hind sight (O'Fahey 1980a: 119–125).

ruler used the Islam and the knowledge of travelling *fuqara*, or wise Muslim men, to boost their image as divine rulers. These itinerant holy men came predominantly from West Africa, Abesher or Libya, on their way to Mecca, and the sultan attracted the most learned to his court. They were allotted *hakuras*, plots of land in exchange of their services at the court in writing down decrees, trade contracts and versions of royal history. Slowly, in the seventeenth and eighteenth century the Darfur population was introduced to Islamic principles by less learned Islamic teachers who wandered around the countryside (O'Fahey 1980: 115–130; O'Fahey and Spaulding 1974).

The *Turkiyya*, the Turco-Egyptian occupation by the Ottomans (1821–1881) at first had little effect on Darfur. A position that held until at least 1874 when Al-Zubeir Ragma Mansur defeated the Fur with his private army, which he had stationed in Southern Darfur for slave raids. He killed the Fur sultan Ibrahim Mohammed and took over his seat in Al-Fasher as the first Turkish governor or Pasha of Darfur.[21] On the third of August 1875, Zubeir Pasha defeated the newly elected Fur sultan Bosh near Kebkabiya. Zubeir allegedly built *at-tabiya*, the fort that now marks the place of the District Council offices in Kebkabiya (Holt and Daly 1988: 77–78; Lampen 1949). The *Turkiyya* lasted only eight years in Darfur and its emphasis on a more literal observation of Islam had less influence on social life here than in Central Sudan.

In the Nile Valley, Islamization spread more evenly across the population. In the sixteenth century, in the Funj Sultanate, the *fuqihs* were learned men who built schools and mosques. Under the Turco-Egyptian rule of Mohammed Ali,[22] traders and administrators re-organized the towns, which meant extensive contact with the local population. A new administrative structure that centred on the slave trade replaced the old sultanic regime of the Funj Sultanate in what is now Central Sudan. This transition from a sultanic to a mercantile rule stimulated the growth of a new powerful middle-class of administrators and

[21] He was of Ja'aliyin ancestry, coming from North Sudan and was never really trusted by the other governors (Holt and Daly 1988: 77–78).

[22] Officially, Muhammed Ali Pasha was acting in Egypt on behalf of the Ottoman sultan. In fact, he was an autonomous viceroy deciding independently upon the conquest of the Funj Sultanate in order to defeat the escaped Mameluks. These were the survivors of the military and governing elite whose leaders had been, in the previous century, the masters of Egypt and who, after the Ottoman conquest, had fled to Nuba in nowadays Northern Sudan (Holt and Daly, 1988: 47–48).

traders. (Holt and Daly 1988: 47–82; O'Fahey and Spaulding 1974).[23] The wealth and security this provided to the administrative and trade centres stimulated a growth of these towns causing the first urbanization in this part of the Sudan. Orthodox Islam provided the ideological justification for the new middle-class style of life in Central Sudan. This new Muslim identity was moreover tied to claims of Arab ancestry. Some even went to major centres of Islamic learning abroad. Because of this political process, the Islamic perspectives that became dominant in the Nile Valley were based on a combination of ideas from the Arabian Peninsula and Turkish-Ottoman culture. This influenced not only religious practices, but also daily life and cultural values (O'Fahey and Spaulding 1974: 80–81; Spaulding 1985: 150, 178–198, 238).

In Darfur, however, trade, in particularly in imported goods, had been virtually monopolized and restricted to controlled commercial centres by the sultan and outside traders.[24] Just as in the case of the influence of learned *faqihs*, the outside traders had little impact on the daily lives of most of the Darfur's inhabitants (Hasan 1977: 201–215; O'Fahey 1980: 115, 131–145; O'Fahey and Spaulding 1974: 160).

During the Anglo-Egyptian Condominium, the new colonial administrative elite that originated in the Nile-Valley, used these cultural and religious differences to distinguish themselves as a class from the local population. However, those Darfurians, notably from the former elite who aspired socio-economic mobility, slowly took over the social and religious codes of conduct of this new middle class. This attitude was soon followed by the lower classes which populated the towns in the decades following the imposition of colonial rule—as far as they could afford it (Kapteijns 1985b: 67; Khalid 1990: 54–115; Niblock 1987: 160–203; O'Fahey 1980a: 1–13).

The growing political and economic power of this new middle-class from the Nile Valley and their Islamic code of conduct had a profound influence on the position of women in Darfur. New dominant norms about beauty and chastity, such as dress codes and eating habits, housing and furniture, leisure and visiting habits were combined with new

---

[23] After Isma'il took over the reign of Muhammed 'Ali in 1863, the abolition of slavery called for in England led to an intensification of the struggle against slave-trade which took place predominantly in southern parts of the Sudan and Darfur. Therefore, increasingly European Christians were employed in the military and civil offices (Holt and Daly 1988: 74–75).

[24] Both *jellaba* from the Nile Valley and *khabirs*, large-scale operators controlling the trade from Kobbei to Cairo or Asyut in Egypt (O'Fahey 1980a: 132).

ideas on the rights and duties, tasks and desires, of women in the towns where the new elite settled. In the course of decennia these cultural markers were taken over as signs of social mobility. The Fur mothers, for example, in these towns started to circumcise their daughters. Not only was it seen as 'better' for Muslim girls, but it also gave access to upward mobility because it facilitated marriage into the new elite (Beasley 1992: 346–349; Bedri 1989: 68–69; Kapteijns 1985: 57; Khalid 1990: 54–115; Niblock 1987: 160–203).

Both Hajja and Umm Khalthoum refer to this *key-shift* in history. It is to these that Hajja referred to when she remembered the new dresses, goods, food, and food habits, which were brought to Kebkabiya. It is no wonder that the name the local population gave to the newly introduced *tobe*, or women's garment, was '*bitt al-basha*', daughter of the *Pasha*. The new elite women, who set the standard of this style of clothing, belonged to a new administrative elite that this time did not come from Egypt, but from the Nile Valley. However, to the local population they were still foreigners, with a code of conduct and life-style like the *Pasha's* of the *Turkiyya* before them. Indeed, Umm Khalthoum highlighted exactly these distinguishing cultural aspects, which were used to constitute class boundaries, when she discussed the 'differences' between the educated and non-educated women. Thus, the British colonial period brought more of a structural change than 'just' changing food items and clothing. Their intervention resulted in an administrative class, which existed next to the local elite of tribal leaders, traders, and agricultural entrepreneurs, and it set the standards of how to be a good Muslim person.

Moreover, under the British administration, education became one of the most important avenues of upward mobility. From 1916, at the beginning of the British rule until after independence in 1956, predominantly formal educated men were able to acquire a position in the Sudanese administration, ruling the country on behalf of the British. Formal, western education and most of the government positions were available mainly in the capital Khartoum and therefore offered opportunities especially for ambitious young men who had to migrate to the Nile Valley (Doornbos 1986: 12). Women could only belong to the new elite by marriage, or by parentage. So how does this relate to the access to education and government positions for women? To understand this development I will venture into a more recent history.

A History of the New Elite in Darfur

As I have already discussed, formal education was originally intended for men to be trained as junior administrators. Therefore, formal British education was for boys only.[25] The institutionalization of education for women took much more time and effort. In 1904 Babiker Bedri, the Controller of Education requested the Director of Education, Sir James Currie, to establish a girls' school. The Director refused to give him money, but stated that if Bedri wanted to start girls' education in his own house he did not have any objection (Starkey in Beasley 1992: 418; Griffiths 1975).

Therefore, Bedri added an 'unofficial' girls' department to the elementary school for boys at Rufa'a, where he lived. The first girl-pupils were his nine daughters and seven other local girls. He had campaigned among the local population by pointing out that:

> ...A modern educated young man would be attracted to an educated young woman for a wife; otherwise there would be a danger of loosing them to foreign wives. (Starkey in Beasley 1992: 416)

When the local population proved:

> ...Utterly opposed on this matter [H]e did not give up but sought out a woman to teach embroidery and needle work on the basis that once they had seen something work in practice, they would be in favor of it. This resulted in the appointment of Nafisa Bint Al-Makkawi, a local resident. (Starkey in Beasley 1992: 416)

In 1907, the school received a subsidy from the British government and was finally recognized officially three years later in 1910. At that time Khartoum and other big towns in Central Sudan, like Wad Medani were also requesting girls' schools to be opened (Starkey in Beasley 1992: 418). From this date, the number of elementary girls' schools increased steadily. For example in 1928, there were seventeen schools with an average attendance of 1000 girls. However, most of the schools were located in the vicinity of the capital. In Darfur, the first elementary schools were opened only in 1941, and in 1943, there were two schools running. These figures compare with thirteen in Northern Province, fourteen in Khartoum Province, and twenty-three in Blue Nile Province, all Nile Valley area. In the east, four were opened in

[25] See for example V.L. Griffiths (1975) for a description of the history of boys' education in the Sudan.

Kassala Province and in the west another seven in Kordofan. The schools had a total staff of 203 schoolmistresses with a deficit of thirteen (Starkey in Beasley 1992: 419).

In 1921, a Girls' Training College was established in Umdurman. At first, it seemed doubtful if the institute would be able to survive:

> The [Girls'] Training College had opened in 1921 with exactly five students and for this reason as well as doubts on its advisability progress of schools at first had been slow. The experiment, however, had been so successful that by 1939 the Umdurman schools were full to overflowing and disappointed parents and children had to be turned away every year. (Beasley 1992: 7)

However, Babiker Bedri's reason to lure parents into sending their daughters to school brought about the popularity of girls' education: it proved an asset in marriage. Girls' education was propagated as an aid to creating better mothers and wives, and educated girls were seen as most suitable partners for elite men. Apart from being an avenue for marrying educated daughters into elite families, fathers could ask higher bride prices for them.[26]

However, even as late as 1961, the *khalwa*, the Koranic schools, still catered for the majority of the youth and Sudanese receiving formal education in a western sense were still a minority (Beasley 1992: 7; Starkey in Beasley 1992: 419). In Darfur, there was originally great resistance against sending children, boys and girls, to the school of the 'devil', as the British schools were sometimes called. Both Hajja and Umm Khalthoum remember the negative attitude of the local population against British formal education. In Kebkabiya, Sitt Howeida, an elderly mistress who taught at the mixed primary school in Kebkabiya and who left just after my arrival, started her career because of the hostile attitude of the local population. Due to the hostility, too few pupils attended the newly established schools and therefore the British decided to establish a quota system. Every tribal leader had to send a minimum number of pupils to the new schools in their vicinity. As a result of the ruling, and because many tribal leaders did not have the power or the willingness to force parents to send their children, it was the chiefs' own offspring who had to help meet the British' demands. Sitt Howeida's father had been a Fur *shartai*. Neither the local population, nor her father, saw much point in the kind of education on offer. Therefore, there was not much resistance against sending her together

[26] See also Willemse (1998).

with some other young girls, who were not yet engaged in agricultural and household work, to these schools.

In this way sometimes a girl found herself in school simply to meet the quota. This is clear from Hajja's narrative when she points out who were the first to go to school in Kutum. They were all sons, and even one daughter, of tribal leaders. Sitt Howeida liked school so much that she decided to become a teacher, although her father resisted her choice for some time. Thus, she became one of the first qualified female teachers in Darfur. In addition to the children from the old sultanic elite, it was mainly wealthy families who could afford to send their children to school. These families could spare the labour force and pay for the uniforms, school fees, books etcetera, once formal education did become more popular. This meant that the already existing class boundaries were thus reinforced.

The situation changed when in 1969 Nimeiri came to power establishing a military government with socialist ideals He decreed that everyone, boys and girls, should be able to attend school (Khalid 1990: 341–349; Warburg 1978; Woodward 1990).[27] Education became free, new schools were planned in all provinces, even in the remoter villages. This meant a liberalization and democratization of the educational system.[28] The growth in both the numbers of schools and of attending children resulted in a high demand for both male and female teachers and offered an opportunity to educated women to teach. At the intermediate and secondary levels, separate boys' and girls' education was preferred. A government position became increasingly attractive to men and women. It not only gave access to a fixed salary, but also to other privileges such as housing, transport and subsidized goods provided by the government, apart from maternity and study leave, holidays and a pension (Bakriand Khalid n.d.: 150; Fluehr-Lobban et.al: 241–243; Hale 1996: 138–139).[29]

---

[27] This was stipulated in so-called five- and later ten-year plans, in line with the planning mechanism used in other socialist countries in Europe (Al-Shahi 1990; Hale 1996: 103–110).

[28] Although the plans were to cover all of Sudan with schools, hospitals, roads and socialist inspired organisations, the material and technological constraints in the Sudan of the seventies proved to obstruct this grand scheme. Capitals and accessible areas were more easily and thus more quickly catered for than the more remote areas, such as the South and Darfur (Al-Shahi 1990).

[29] This was instigated by the socialist ideology that the military leader Nimeiri claimed as his inspiration. Equality, for rural and urban areas, all classes and men

In Sudan, educated women employed by the government mainly work as female teachers[30] (Fluehr-Lobban et.al. 1992: 241; Hale 1996: 103–148). In Kebkabiya, the girls' primary schools were established in the 1970s and the girls' intermediary school at the beginning of the 1980s.[31] A large number of the female teaching staff posted in Kebkabiya was drafted in, complemented by teachers who came to Kebkabiya as the wives of government officials, like Umm Khalthoum and Sitt Khadija. A smaller number came from within Kebkabiya town itself. Thus, the teaching staff consisted of married and unmarried women, from both inside and outside Kebkabiya town.

Education became, rather than just a means of boosting one's class position, also an avenue for upward mobility.[32] However, the sheer fact of having an education was not enough to acquire an elite status position: only working for the government for a monthly salary makes one an employee, a member of the 'new' or government elite. In order to make this membership obvious, to act out one's status, a particular lifestyle is important. Apart from the privilege of wearing a white *tobe*, there are other aspects of elite identity, which mark a detectable 'difference' between elite and non-elite groups. Like her colleagues, Umm Khalthoum is very clear about the material differences and the maintenance of a *cordon sanitaire*[33] between her class and uneducated women.

The demands of living up to one's status results in spending a lot of money on utensils, clothing, housing, furniture, items for beautification,

---

and women were important backbones of this ideology. See for an elaboration (Hale 1996; Warburg 1978).

30 There are also some private companies operating, mainly in Khartoum, where its employees are also considered part of the new elite. The number of women working in these businesses is rising, but, just like women working as nurses and doctors, this number is relatively small compared to women working as female teachers.

31 In the town and district of Kebkabiya at the end of the 1970s and beginning of 1980s.

32 Many educated women were organised in the so-called Sudanese Women's Union, which was dominated by the Socialist Party of Nimeiri. Consequently, other women's organisations were founded, more often than not offshoots of other political parties. See for a history of women's organisations in the Sudan Bakri and Khalid n.d; Hale 1990, 1991.

33 Exemplified by the color white, not only of *tobes*, but also of the *tarha*, the white shawls worn by schoolgirls, and the white sheets used in boarding houses. As an elderly teacher, Sitt Yvonne, told me, this meant that women had to be careful in their movements and be aware of the locations where they went, and would keep bodily hygiene high as concomitant to mental and moral 'cleanliness'.

jewelry, and many of these items are imported from outside the Sudan. The upkeep of children requires even more money. Moreover, many of the ingredients for the elite's particular diet are bought as they are from either outside Darfur or even Sudan itself.

As the influence of the Central Sudanese culture is dominant in de educated elite life-style and Islamic principles this Nile Valley culture also influenced issues like partner-choice, settlement habits and the way kin relations are perceived. In order to understand the processes of change in marital and family arrangements among the educated elite in Darfur, I will therefore turn to recent work on Central Sudan.

When it comes to partner choice in most Central Sudanese societies, the marriage preference is a person who is considered *gariib*, 'close'. And as Boddy (1989) indicates:

> All kin, both consanguine and affinal, are deemed 'close' (*gariib*) to one or another degree. All, excluding full and half siblings, parents and their siblings, their spouses, and the siblings and children of parents' living spouses, are recognized as potential mates... Especially in the case of first marriages, people are tacitly encouraged to wed their closest available kin after these exceptions (77–78).

From this close kin the *awlad 'amm* (paternal uncle's children), patrilineal parallel cousin marriage, are preferred. In Darfur, the diverse ethnic groups had different preferences in relation to marriage partners. However, in towns patrilineal (parallel and cross-) cousin marriage has a preference, followed by matrilineal cousin marriage of both siblings of the mother. In Darfur as in Central Sudan:

> Ultimately, however, they [potential spouses K.W.] are not forced to seek such unions despite their alignment with official ideology; matrimonial strategies are practical, guided by self-interest or groups concerns having political, economic, and symbolic implications (Boddy, 1989: 78).[34]

The reference 'cousin' is used classificatory when extended to people who are no direct cousins, but who are from about the same generation and can be traced via grandparents and their siblings. However, the term is also used to stipulate kinship if the precise connection is forgotten in the sense that it can simply mean 'those who are married'. So, if two persons want to marry who are not related then the term also develops a figurative significance: the fact that spouses are close or will get closer as a result of their marriage, make them fall under the cate-

[34] Boddy refers here to Bourdieu (1977: 30ff.)

gory of *awlad 'amm*, (Boddy, 1989: 79). This principle is matched by the attitude towards paternal relations as we saw in the discussion of Hajja and her daughters about 'closeness': paternal ties are seen as less close and intimate, as opposed to maternal kin. In other words, paternal kin is considered as close as near strangers might be.

For the educated elite the change from living in extended patrilineal families to neolocal nuclear families is related to the practical aspects of job requirements. The frequent transfers to different parts of the country makes this type of families the most convenient. At the same time, the wish to live according to the elite norms and to reduce the demands from relatives the nuclear family has become, above all, an economic strategy to allow for an elite life-style. When two educated persons marry, they need many resources in order to be able to set up their elite household. As few families have enough resources to support the household of their married children, this money has, in most cases to come from the spouses themselves. A newly established household of an elite couple needs all the money they can spare to set up a 'proper' household (Bedri 1989: 68–69). Especially if one of them (or both) does not come from an elite family, it means that the couple has to try to avert demands from relatives that would put a too large strain on their resources. Resources which they need in order to maintain a life-style that makes them part of the educated elite and at the same time makes them seem 'rich' in the eyes of their non-elite relatives (Bannaga 1987: 99–101).

Moreover, apart from this 'practical' basis, the nuclear family also has been legitimated by the dominant discourse of gender-roles. Men are seen as the providers of the income with his wife as housekeeper and mother taking care of his offspring. This discourse thus creates a breadwinner-cum-housewife ideal, which can only be met by the establishment of a nuclear family: an ideal that forms the core of the Islamist moral discourse on gender.[35]

Sitt Khadija's reaction and Umm Khalthoum's narrative strategy thus become more intelligible. Sitt Khadija does not want her family around too badly; for finding their way to her home might also mean finding their way to her money. Moreover, the outward appearance of her aunt made clear that she is not a member of the elite. The fact that she is considered 'no family', might mean that Khadija does not

[35] This ideal is not specific for the Sudan. I will return to this issue at the end of this chapter.

consider her aunt suitable as a relative that extends her help to her *because* of her kin relationship in the location where she is first and foremost a member of the educated elite. The fact that she wanted to have her baby born at her mother's place was not only out of convenience. It was also because she wanted to keep her life as an elite woman, as female teacher and colleague literally separate from her family life. Apart from fear of having to share her limited income, the main reason would have been that some of her family members, like her aunt but also her mother, are not members of the elite and thus are not behaving 'up' to her standards.

Kinship is about rights and entitlements. Living in a nuclear family creates a different position for elite women and the positive or negative effects for women depend on the circumstances. Leaving the parental home also means that a woman tends to lose entitlement to family resources, not only to goods like land or assets, but also to labour, especially that of female relatives who can share in daily household tasks. This results in a heavier workload for elite women. At the same time, being the mistress of the household means that the wife after marriage has a different position vis-à-vis her husband. She therefore has more decision-making power concerning her own household and the household resources than she would have if she lived among her husband's kin. The absence of a mother-in-law makes her less inhibited and controlled by the relatives of her husband and, especially when she brings in money herself, her control over resources increases. For a woman like Umm Khalthoum also the negative aspects of her elite status have become obvious. On the one hand, her income makes her more independent from her husband, at least in her feelings towards him. At the same time, the absence of close kin, expressed in her longing to go back to Umdurman, makes her position more vulnerable during quarrels with her husband. In any case women would generally see their negotiating power within the household as an important reason to keep working even after the economic crisis had subsided. While their husbands maintained that now the income of the wife is badly needed but that they expected them to return to their compounds as soon as they could provide for their households themselves again (Khalid 1990: 312–324).

Among educated elite women, socializing with colleagues is obviously an ideal and therefore part of a discourse that makes one value highly the relationships with people of one's own standard. As a consequence of the upward mobility that acquiring education thus allows for, those acquaintances that are not educated are better not revealed to that same group of elite people—even though everyone knows about the fact that they are somewhere, as many are in a similar situation. The practical requirements of living as an elite family at the same time constitute a code of conduct. In this, the relevance of kin relationships are played down and even silenced as a strategy in order to keep up appearances as a member of the government elite, and at the same time as imperative to reproduce the ideal-typical image of the government elite.

As I indicated for both narratives, however, this silence is dealt with unevenly in relation to relatives. Men, especially the father and husband, but also an assisting stepbrother, such as Ahmed in Umm Khalthoum's case, or cousin, like Mohammed in Hajja's narratives, are constituted as actors, and powerful ones at that. Women, and particularly mothers, but also most sisters, are shallow figures. Umm Khalthoum refers to her mother as an example of how her own life might turn out. However, she does not give her mother much more character or agency, and in the end she still is the recipient of the actions of men, whether her husband, son or stepson. This silence on mothers might be connected to the *hadith* on motherhood, as quoted by Sitt Miriam in her address to the women of Kebkabiya. Perhaps the positioning of mothers by both Hajja and Umm Khalthoum becomes more intelligible if I look at their own position and positioning as mothers.

Heaven at Her Feet: Motherhood and Religious Merit

From their narratives and by participating in their daily lives I gathered that for female teachers, colleagues provide the major relationships in daily life. However, married teachers such as Umm Khalthoum and Sitt Khadija cannot count on, nor do they ask for their assistance in household cores. Sitt Khadija therefore needed her mother and her niece with her after her delivery, because she could not do her household chores on her own. If the children are grown up, like in the case of Umm Khalthoum, they can fend for themselves and daughters might even assist their mothers with household chores. Nevertheless, when the children are still young, female teachers have a lot of extra work, which they have to do on their own. In a town without electricity, running water, or gas, household chores are tedious and demanding especially with young children. Children not only need feeding and being taken care of, but the standard of the elite concerning hygiene and cleanliness is such that children need regular baths and changes of clothes. Many of these young mothers complained about their double burden and the fact that they could not get any paid help in the household. Sitt Khadija stated that the few girls she could find for doing some of the household chores were unreliable, in the sense that they might leave suddenly, without notice, to return only a few days later or not at all.[36] Some times women who pass by or migrate to the town would knock on the doors of especially the government houses to ask for work. However, this would occur only occasionally, mostly seasonally. And these women would be only hired for specific jobs for which they were deemed 'renowned'. So Fur women were hired for pounding grain and other products, Zaghawa women for mending fences, and women from other ethnic backgrounds for washing clothes or cleaning the courtyard. However, cooking is the prerogative of the wife. It is an all-consuming job in terms of time and energy: most households had to make do with the charcoal burners, and the lack of refrigerators makes a daily visit to the market almost indispensable. Further, in Kebkabiya the only place to socialize for educated elite women are on picnics and at the homes of the educated elite women. Such events require a lot of preparation and organization and it takes a great deal of energy to live up to expectations.

However, women also showed an obvious pride in mothering children. Children are highly valued and although most female teachers express a wish to have fewer children than their mothers did, all agreed that a life without them is unthinkable. To have children means to have value as a woman, and a security for old age.[37] Mothers value their daughters for their help with household cores, which makes life easier as soon as they are able to help out as Umm Khalthoum indicated

---

[36] Most available girls are from a Fur background, the ethnic majority in town and the surrounding villages. The Fur consider it shameful for a woman to have someone else do her household cores for money. In many Fur villages all exchange of labour for money is considered shameful while for women household chores and growing her own millet constitute her identity (see Barth 1974; Willemse 1991). So their 'unreliability' might be due to the fact that demands upon a girl's labour by family members are considered more important than that of an employer. In addition, teachers feel morally obliged to let the girls go to school and would easily let them go when the girl expressed a wish to do so.

[37] See Schrijvers (1985) and Den Uyl (1992) for a theoretical consideration of the paradox of mothering as the basis of vulnerability and powerlessness as well as empowerment of women.

quite explicitly. In addition, Hajja acknowledges the importance of girls when she refers to the parts of the sheep she would receive as a midwife when a baby girl was born: the hind legs that have a lot of meat. This symbolized the fact that at her marriage a girl brings in money as part of the bride price. However, it is not seen as a way of 'buying or selling' the girl, but an acknowledgment of the worth of her upbringing by her parents and of the loss of her labour in her parental home.

The value of boys is expressed in a peculiar manner: Hajja would receive for a baby boy the lean and meatless forelegs. These symbolize the fact that though boys in first instance are only 'another mouth to feed'; their assistance when they get older and work in the outside world is highly valued. This is due to the fact that boys can mediate between their mother and the outside world, especially with strange men. Moreover, in older age men are deemed to assist their parents in their upkeep. As an educated male friend of mine told me 'Sudanese men cannot disappoint their mother', indicating that a mother who lives on good terms with her son will have his support all her life.[38] Both Hajja when referring to her cousin Mohammed and Umm Khalthoum relating about her stepbrother Ahmed refer to this fact.

The pride in having children was expressed in a different way when during Ramadan. The daily fasting makes the evenings the right time for all kinds of social and religious events. The regular praying meetings, but also the daily reading and explanation of chapters of the *Qur'an* through the amplifiers of the mosque stimulates people to live the month in a contemplative, sacred atmosphere. Many see the fast and abstaining from worldly habits like drinking alcohol, sex and quarrelling even after the sun has set, as both a religious obligation and as a way to (re-)establish one's identity as a (good) Muslim.[39] As one of the teachers put it: "This is the only obligation, which one performs for Allah".

The contemplative mood and religious speeches influence the nature of all kinds of discussions, private or public. One day when I am visiting Umm Khalthoum, she tells me she feels complete again, after so many months of worrying and fretting over her problems. I ask her what she means by 'complete'. This time she does not venture into her own past in order to explain me her viewpoint, but takes the position of religious teacher, of a *wa'iz*:

---

[38] This relationship between mother and son can be found in many societies, especially in the Arab World. See chapter 8.

[39] See for example Buitelaar (1991).

The first thing for people in order to become a complete person in Islam is marriage. And after one becomes like me, a housekeeper, one has to pray well all five times a day. If you forget one prayer you can do it at another moment. The people are saying that the prayer, salaat, *is the pillar of Islam. If you neglect it, your building will fall down. Also, Ramadan is for all Muslims, women and men. If you would eat only one day without reason, you have to fast two months to repay for this one day. Islam allows breaking the fast if one is ill, or when a woman has her menstruation, or is breast-feeding and has no milk, one can eat. Or if a woman is pregnant and she throws up the food. It is better for them to eat and after Ramadan they can fast for the number of lost days. The third is that it is important to give poor people food,* zakaat. *The fourth is to treat your neighbour kindly and to say in the morning* sabah al-kher, *good morning, to those at the south,* sabah al-kher *to the east and to the west and to the north. And if a person falls ill, you have to go and visit that person in hospital even when the person is not a Muslim. A woman is a good Muslim if she gives food to her neighbours, the choicest food you have to give. If you are like this, your neighbour will be happy with you. Also, it is important to treat your neighbours' children well. The fifth is to visit the patients in the hospital. If you have sugar, you can make something for the patient, like tea, or* ajiina *or* nisha.[40] *If you have money, you can even make food for him. Some patients have no family here. Like one of the supervisors of the intermediary schools from Khartoum when he visited Kebkabiya, he was bitten by a snake, and had to go to the hospital. He has no family here. He knew Abbas, but when he was bitten he became unconscious and didn't know it was a snake that caused his state of mind. His foot was very swollen and he was very tired when they brought him in. He didn't know anyone, just Abbas. Abbas went to the hospital and took his clothes. I washed them and everyday we made drinks and food for him. Islam states 'every Muslim will help another Muslim'. A good woman is doing this without complaining. And the best Muslim woman is the one who, while tending to these tasks, walks in the streets in a respectable way. In a long dress keeping her body quiet, she is not to wave or gesticulate. Some make specific gestures in order to attract men. This is* haraam.[41] *It is better to behave very modest so men will not take notice of you. One has to wear long dresses with long sleeves and a good* tobe, *which covers all the body, because in Islam it is inappropriate for women not to cover their fine parts. So, women better cover their bodies, as Islam states. It is not good for women to go without* tobes, *because they'll attract men. These women walk around with bad intentions in their*

---

[40] Both sweet and nutritious drinks based on sorghum, *ajiina* with milk and *nisha* with water, and both slightly fermented.

[41] *Haraam* means forbidden on religious grounds. The opposite is *halaal,* which means advisable or preferable on religious grounds.

minds and their hearts. If a woman attracts men like this, she commits a crime. It is the duty of all Muslim women to be modest, and not to uncover their bodies unless in front of their fathers or mothers or brothers. It is impossible to uncover your body in front of strangers. But bad women are not behaving in this way, they are the opposite of this, not praying and not asking God to help them to be modest, and they even eat during Ramadan. They are not treating their neighbours well and this people live under the reign of the devil, they don't believe in Islam. They shut themselves off from praying, from their neighbours, and also from the need to visit their fellows in hospital. They don't wear the long dresses. After they die, they will go to hell. Because they did not follow the Islamic way.

Umm Khalthoum's answer is like a sermon, in wording and formality matching the religious explanations in and around the mosque. However, Umm Khalthoum's sermon is quite peculiar. The Islam acknowledges that there are five pillars which reflect the obligation every Muslim has. These pillars are *salaat*, praying, *sawm*, fasting during Ramadan, *zakaat*, alms giving, *haj*, pilgrimage to Mecca and the *shahada*,[42] the Muslim creed. It seems strange that she replaces two official religious pillars with her own view on things, which have a more topical influence on her local life. That she forgets the *shahada* is understandable, because she, like most Sudanese, is born a Muslim and will not be bothered with this first pillar as a way of becoming a Muslim.[43] That she forgets to name the *haj* seems a real omission. Especially because it has appeared in her own narrative when referring to her mother's happy life. However, the pillars Umm Khalthoum does give in her explanation are all virtues that belong to the Sudanese moral discourse. To be sociable and to treat strangers as your most valued guests are important foundations of what is called 'Sudanese' hospital-

---

42 The creed goes: 'There is no God but God and Mohammed is his prophet (*La illah il allah wa Mohammed rassul illah*)'. When pronounced and acknowledged as the one truth one is a Muslim. With reference to the Islamic Revolution in Iran, the term *shahaada* is also translated as martyrdom as the creed was used as a battle cry by fighters for the Islamic cause in for example the Iran-Iraq war: it makes the fighters martyrs who go directly to heaven when killed in this religious battle (*jihad*). See for example Taheri 1985: 317–320).

43 Al-Turabi, the leader of the National Islamic Front has put forward the view that this habit is not in accordance with Islamic teaching. He proposed to let people who are born in a Muslim family choose around the age of 18 whether they want to become Muslim or not. In this case the *shahada* would have its original meaning as pillar for all Muslims (interview Hassan Al-Turabi in *Achter de sluier*, TV documentary EO, 1998).

ity. I experienced this frequently, but also heard it said. A person would rather spend his/her last money, give away his/her last clothes, and give a visitor his/her own bed than be seen as stingy, inhospitable, and therefore un-Sudanese. Moreover, Umm Khalthoum thus formulates the Sudanese obligations of hospitality in terms of female practices and relates to them as religious pillars. Similarly, she connects the obligation for women to dress modestly to female moral behavior. So although her answer sounds formal and detached, Umm Khalthoum is in both cases obviously feminizing the pillars when referring to her own situation, and again, to her own 'good Muslim' behaviour in this respect. At the same time, her view ties into the discourse by the educated elite and by the government about the proper conduct of women. When I ask Umm Khalthoum what happens when Muslims do not abide by these obligations, she says: "Well, of course then you lose your *ajr*". When I show signs of not understanding immediately, Umm Khalthoum repeats: "You know, *ajr*, that which gives you access to heaven". I have heard of this but I am not sure how it works, I tell her. So she explains:

Well Karin, let me see. I told you about the pillars, didn't I? And these pillars, if you abide by them, it makes you a good Muslim and this is acknowledged in points you get allotted for your list. So when your time has come you stand in front of the angel Gibriel, Gabriel, who guards the gate to heaven. If your account adds up to a positive amount of ajr, *you can go through. If it is negative, you have to wait, and your fate will be decided upon: you will have to burn in hell until you can try again.*

"Points?" I ask again.

Yes points. Like for example for praying one receives one point every time. But for praying with a large group, one receives twenty-seven points.

Although the reference to *ajr* as points was also quoted in the speeches, I am still baffled. I realize that *ajr* refers to religious merit, but to look upon your good deeds as such a specific way of gaining points makes it sound like a game! "So in that case everyone should pray as much in company as one can", I go on. Now Umm Khalthoum looks a bit hesitant.

Well, yes, but you see Karin, men are better able to do that than women. But also your other deeds count. Most women don't drink wine, like men. Some men are not praying. And when men are drunk, even when they pray, their prayer is not well because their mind is wandering. Some are even drinking in Ramadan. This is the difference between them and good Muslims. The rightful Muslim wakes up very early in the morning and goes to the mosque. He takes his flashlight at three or four o'clock in the morning and goes to the mosque. But women can't. At that time women are still sleeping. They wake up late, because they are always busy with their children, some are crying, others are asking for things. But there are no such distractions, like children, which keeps men busy. Our prayers are always incomplete because while praying you watch if your children are not crying or falling from the bed. You will interrupt your prayer for them. The difference between men and women is that women's duties are never fulfilled, because they are busy with their children and men have nothing, which keep them busy at night, in the afternoon or in the morning. They can just go and tend to their Islamic duties.

I nod, a bit taken aback because my comment, which I gave without much thought, brings up such a gendered reflection on being a good Muslim. Moreover, Umm Khalthoum has not finished yet, for she continues:

There is also another difference between Islamic women and men, concerning their religious duties, like praying. Women cannot continue praying, they have to refrain from praying or fasting and from the religious duties during the pilgrimage if they have their period. After they wash their bodies and hair, they can start again to do the salaat. *Also after having given birth women are not allowed to pray or fast until she finishes the period of seclusion of forty days or sometimes even more, until the bleeding has stopped. After this period of time you have to perform the* gusl, *the ritual washing of your body and your hair and clothes, and then you can start your prayers again. In Ramadan, Islam allows some people to eat like people who are ill, pregnant women, old men and women that have their period. If you have your period you even are obliged to break your fast, you can not fast when bleeding, and you have to make up for the lost days after Ramadan, but in this case one day lost counts for one day of extra fasting. Men don't have any reason to eat in Ramadan or to stop the prayer or their obligations during* haj, *only women and patients. A woman has many reasons why she is not able to continue her Islamic duties like men. This is why men are more able to fulfil their Islamic duties then women because our duties cannot be fulfilled continuously. Islam is very large and it has a lot of possible explanations. If someone wants to know a lot about Islam, he needs to read and learn a lot.*

This last comment is added hastily and almost apologetically, and it seems to leave room for undermining the explanation she has just given. In order not to spite Umm Khalthoum, I decide to take a detour in understanding her own ideas about these dogmas. I ask her: "So men will go easier to heaven than women?" Umm Khalthoum wrinkles her nose and says:

Yes, if we consider it this way, a man gets more points than a woman, and more easily. But for women it is easy as well for 'janna tahta ar-rigleen al ummahaat', *'heaven is under the feet of mothers', our prophet Mohammed told us.*[44] *It means that women have all these problems of having to relinquish their duties due to their period and pregnancies and giving birth, because they are mothers who have to take care of babies. And we need these babies to become a strong and healthy and a good Muslim society. Maybe women do not get the points, but they raise the most important thing, which are new Muslims. So in reward, she has a place already near heaven. But like men can burn their points by drinking, women can easily lose their* ajr, *by not being nice to the neighbours or the needy, and by quarrelling and speaking badly about others. So it is difficult to know how near you are to heaven, for women they quarrel and gossip a lot.*

"So what does that mean for their *ajr* compared to men?" I ask her. "It means that women are closer, but can also get removed from heaven more quickly", Umm Khalthoum says in a definite tone.

In the period after talking with Umm Khalthoum, the relationship between motherhood and religious merit keeps me occupied. I considered myself lucky that the religious aspects of women's identity as mother came up. Motherhood seemed both a practice and a symbol of womanhood and as such ambivalent. In practice, to be a mother is considered difficult because there is a great deal of work with which it is associated. Further, it is difficult from a moral viewpoint because it makes it less easy for a woman to fulfill her duties as a Muslim. However, children can assist their mother, practically with household chores or financial help, and spiritually, by providing a woman with a privileged position when it comes to religious merit. Moreover, it is the only accepted social status a mature, married woman can attain.

However, the fact that this discussion came up so late during my research is also a matter for consideration. Why did Umm Khalthoum only talk about it now, while it would have been another good rea-

[44] It is considered a *hadith*, a narrative about the sayings from prophet Mohammed or about events during his life, which is also quoted in one of the speeches in Chapter 1.

son to boost her confidence about being respectable? Of course, she and other teachers discussed children, but I would have expected this aspect to have certainly deserved a place in her narrative so she could have claimed respectability on religious grounds. And not only Umm Khalthoum, but also other female teachers only came up with this *hadith* towards the end of my stay, during Ramadan.

I did not need to raise the issue of motherhood again myself. A few days later when I visited Umm Khalthoum late at night, after the breaking of the fast, she started the conversation herself.

You know, ya *Karin, this whole issue about motherhood, it is a very difficult thing for me as a teacher. For I want to do it right, to bring up my children well, but because of my work I cannot always be around when my sons or daughters need me. It is our dilemma: we cannot be good mothers, nor can we be good colleagues. We are always in between our duties as a mother and our duties as a teacher.*

It is a complaint I have heard often from other married female teachers as well. That there is never enough time to do one's job as a teacher and mother well enough. As I am still very intrigued by the connection between motherhood and religious merit, I ask her immediately: "So does this affect your *ajr?*" "I am not sure", Umm Khalthoum says hesitantly: "You know, we also earn points by teaching". "You mean because you combine motherhood with teaching?" I ask, not understanding quite what she means:

No, from teaching itself. I mean, in the Qur'an, *the first* sura *tells us that to acquire* ʿilm, *knowledge, is one of the most important obligations of all Muslims. And to give* ʿilm *is a very important religious duty; it gives a lot of merit.*

"So teaching in itself provides you with religious merit?"

Well, yes. Of course, the first kind of knowledge is about your religious duties. So religious teachers are even more important, because they clear your head, they point out the right way. But we also teach children, so they can read the Qur'an *themselves and to understand the proper meaning. But even teachers, who do not give Arabic language or* Islamiya, *even their subjects are important for children to learn about. Because all things in the world are from Allah. So we teach children to know all and to understand all that Allah has given the world. So if you learn about science, or history, you learn about what Allah has created, the world and its mysteries.*

I look at her and have to laugh because of the solemn expression on her face. "Did you realize that these last few days", I ask her teasingly. "No", Umm Khalthoum says, smiling: "But it destroys your *ajr* when you pride yourself in your good works, like talking about your merit too much or too often".

That the female teachers have not talked before about the fact that teaching gives them *ajr* might have to do with the fact that religious merit is a subject foremost in the mind during Ramadan, but less so in 'ordinary' times. Moreover, when I ask other teachers about motherhood and teaching, they do agree that their work gives religious merit. However, at the same time they emphasize the double burden and their feelings of failure, of not being able to meet expectations of their family at home nor their colleagues at work. One reason why Umm Khalthoum started talking about children in such a formal way is that it fits into the general way religious and 'daily' topics are discussed in this month. Nevertheless, this silence might be related to the fact that I have no children myself. As I did not have children of my own the mothers I met could not relate to me as a mother. If children were discussed in my company, then it was never as a common issue, as an experience we shared. The silence on children, also in a religious sense, thus could have had as much to do with my silencing, as with any thing else.

Still, Umm Khalthoum's elaboration during my last weeks in Kebkabiya made me realize that market women also had not discussed *ajr* and its relationship to motherhood: in fact none of them discussed motherhood at all. No complaining about double tasks, no reference to the problem of being a good mother because of working at the market, no reference to *ajr* or heaven for that matter either.

The Virtue of Silence: Discourses on Gender

At first, I do not know what to think of this and I do not dare to ask the market women I know straight away about their ideas on motherhood and *ajr*. Market women might feel ashamed as their long working hours and busy daily schedule leaves not much time for taking 'proper' care of the children within the walls of their compounds, and thus they might feel they fail to live up to the standard of 'good' mothers. Interestingly, Hajja did not refer in her narrative to motherhood as an important identity either. This is remarkable, because Hajja might have referred to the time of plenty when she raised her daughters at home, which would have supported her virtue as a mother. Whether this silence is due to the unspeakable or the unspoken, I do not want to abuse Hajja or any of the other market women by bluntly asking after their perceptions on motherhood.

In order to be able to analyse this theme, I decide to take a detour. One day when Sa'adiya is present I ask Hajja about *ajr* in order to see whether that triggers a discussion on motherhood as it did with Umm Khalthoum. When I ask her what she thinks about *ajr*, she promptly answers: "It is from God: if you do good things, he will reward you for it". Hajja looks at me expectantly. So I ask her: "How can you earn it?" And Hajja says without hesitation: "When you give to the poor or do your praying or your fast in Ramadan or if you fast outside of Ramadan". No reference to motherhood or working yet, so I try again: "Are there any possibilities to get *ajr* in normal life, for example by working?" Hajja replies promptly: "If you sit in the market and the things you sell are good and it is clear what you sell it gives *ajr* as well". I go on: "So does selling at the market give you *ajr*?"

It is ajr *because if one works, one can earn money to give to the poor or to give to others. But people who sit in their houses without work, they have no* ajr.

"But then, can you tell me, is there a difference in getting *ajr* for women and men?"

Men's ajr *is more than women's. If some people ask him (a man) for paying a new mosque, he will pay. And the poor ask him in the market, and if he gives them tea, or sugar or some dates, or if he gives the poor dresses, it all gives him* ajr.

Hajja's reflections do not touch upon mothering at all. Therefore, I try to have her consider the way she earns religious merit. "You are selling onions for food and upkeep of your family, so you do not have much left to give to the poor; how do you get *ajr*?"

I have other works [good deeds K.W.] with which to get ajr. *And I will also get* ajr *from these onions. Because when I give the poor two or three pieces, it will get* ajr. *But in buying and selling there is even* ajr, *if the seller is honest. It is* ajr *in selling when you are telling the truth. Like if you bought one sack for £S50, you can tell the other that you bought it for £S50 and that you want a profit of £S25.*

Not to deceive him with a higher price. Like some people, they bought things for £S5 but they say they bought it for £S20. This is haraam, *to say things like this.*[45] *Every work has* ajr. *Even of drivers. If he carries a lot of people in his lorry and he stops the lorry to go the restaurant to eat alone, he has no* ajr. *But if he gives food for all the passengers, he has* ajr. *And a* faqih *also has* ajr, *because teaches people. There is a lot of* ajr *in people who are teaching, such as schoolteachers and* faqih*s*.

I am glad to hear her last comment: apparently the idea of gaining merit with teaching is not something only teachers claim, but is more widely acknowledged. However, she remains silent on motherhood. I cannot hold back anymore and so at last, I recite to her the *hadith 'janna tahta ar-rigleen al ummahaat'*. And indeed, she knows the saying and she agrees that motherhood is a good reason for gaining *ajr*:

Because you have pain to get your children, and they soil you when they are small, so you cannot commit yourself to your prayers because you need to be clean for that. So, yani, *it is good*, wallai, *that mothers get their points from carrying this without complaining.*

She does not go into the issue whether she has been a good mother, or to what extent she feels that her work interferes with her being a mother. So I leave it at that: she might come back to it, like Umm Khalthoum did. But nothing happens. Until one day, I am seated with a group of young market women to share with them a bowl of tomato salad. Also Zamzam has joined them again, after an absence because of illness in which her sister has taken care of her place. Her infant son Amir is with her as usual, and while she suckles him Zamzam mockingly complains, pointing at Amir: "Look Karin, every time my husband has his leave from the army, I have another baby". All the women giggle and I jokingly tell her to hide next time he comes. "Oh no", Zamzam answers, "I like children, more than I like to be with him". Some of the married women now laugh aloud. Then I ask: "Don't you think that when the father is so far away that it is difficult to take care of your marketing and of your children?" Zamzam is again the first to react:

[45] Hajja refers to the Islamic prohibition on gaining a large profit from lending money (*riba*).

No not really, my son is always with me as long as he cannot walk, and my other children are with my mother or my sisters, no, they are well taken care of.

Zamzam frowns. Now I see my chance and try my luck. "What about the saying *Janna tahta ar-rigleen al ummahaat*?" Zamzam laughs, saying:

Ah, this is very true, mush kida, *isn't it*, ya *Karin. We work and we work and we work and we raise our children so they become strong and healthy and educated and then we can take a rest, at home or in heaven.*

Again, there is laughter at Zamzam's bold talk on this issue. After the laughter has calmed down a bit and Rhoda has ordered tea from Zamzam's half-sister down the road, I try again: "So you think it is alright to work on the market while your children are at home?" I feel a bit embarrassed, because I realize I imply that it might not be acceptable. But Rhoda takes the issue up now, asking me rhetorically:

Isn't it good that we work so our children can be fed and get ahead? Isn't it our task as mothers to see that they can get education and find a job with an organization or in the government? Aren't we good mothers, because we take care of our children's future?

The others nod, and so do I. Why didn't I think of it before? How could I be trapped in the elite view so easily? Like the Fur women among whom I did my earlier research, growing the staple is the main task of most women who live in Kebkabiya town. After good rains in May and June most women, and some men, grow millet and sorghum on the sandy land (*qoz*) further away from the river and in many cases also quite some distance from the town.[46] Men engage in agriculture as well, but need to grow much less because most of them are only required to provide food for themselves. Men provide children and wives with those things which cost money, like clothing, shoes, school fees, taxes and once a year large quantities of oil, meet, dried spices, soap. Men are thus required to provide those items, which cost money. They earn this by trading or performing paid labour, both activities taking place mainly during the dry season outside Kebkabiya. There are the newly introduced motorized pumps for dry season irrigation of the clay (*tin*)

[46] See Chapter 2 for reference to this division of land and labour, and appendix 1 for result of the survey, which supports this view. Also Willemse (1990).

soil that I discussed in Chapter 2. However, these are only an option for those men who can afford a pump, the diesel, and who can acquire a plot along the riverbed (cf. Grawert 1998).

In Kebkabiya for 'non-elite' female heads of households-without-men, motherhood is intertwined with both agricultural and marketing activities. A mother works in order to provide her children with the necessities and she is *therefore* a good mother. Marketing is not seen as disreputable by these women but as the logical consequence of failing agricultural returns. While elite women—and men—do feel a tension concerning working and mothering because of experiencing these as *oppositions*, market women in Kebkabiya see their work on the market as an *extension* of being a mother. Therefore market women do not 'hear' the dominant moral discourse, as the government elite would like them to; they see no inconsistency in working *and* being a good Muslim. I did not actually witness women perform any agricultural activities while I was in Kebkabiya. Therefore, I must have overlooked these local perceptions of gender roles. However, there is another reason for my neglect as well.

The elite's view on women fits the perception on motherhood and work prevalent in most capitalist societies with its conceptualization of labour as 'alienated' from the producer. This split between product and producer has also lead to a market economy which differentiates private from public activities, and which is at the root of a hierarchal valuation of salaried work and household work. This split leads to the modern elite gender ideology in Sudan which stipulates that the husband provides for the family while women are seen mainly housewives, taking care of household cores and children within the confines of her home. This process, referred to with 'housewifisation',[47] is thus related to a bread-winner-cum-housewife discourse that fitted the ideas about feminine and masculine roles in my own society so well.[48]

---

[47] This term comes from Mies (1981) writing on home industry in India. See also Schrijvers (1985), Den Uyl (1992) for an elaboration of this process in respectively Sri Lanka and India. Tully (1988) has described the articulation of the capitalist market economy with the local economy in Darfur and its consequences for the change in validating labour, land, technical items, based on gender, generational and (new) class differences.

[48] In Europe, the Netherlands ranges lowest concerning the childcare and other facilities enabling mothers to do salaried work outside their homes. In the 1970s and 1980s, children of mothers who did work outside the home were negatively referred to as 'latch-key-kids' after the keys they needed to get into their homes when mother would not be there 'waiting with a pot of tea'. See for example Morée (1992).

Therefore, educated elite women like Umm Khalthoum, who work outside the home, feel torn between their role as good mothers and good colleagues, because they have internalized 'modern' ideas on motherhood. In this perception, a good mother is a woman who takes care of her children and household within the private sphere, which is again related to the norm of the all-day round availability of the mother. That is why it has taken me some time to realize that the silence of the market women about their roles as mothers was not one of embarrassment. Instead, it was one of common sense ideas about being a proper mother: they refer to a different set of common sense ideas on gender than the elite does.

This difference between the elite and market women in their perception of the relation between motherhood, work and being a 'good' Muslim also carries a spatial aspect. The dominant discourse on gender of the educated elite implicitly refers to a gendered conceptualization of space. The men are providers and dominate the public space, with its economic and political institutions, while women are mothers and housewives *within* the walls of her compound, the emotional and personal space where family life takes place. Both Miriam and Huda, the female speakers of the speeches Chapter 1 emphasized this spatial nature of being a good female Muslim as well. However, for market women in Kebkabiya the space of family life is not confined to the walls of the compound. Taking care of children, feeding them et cetera, also takes place at the market place, or at someone else's compound, and in some cases by another woman other than the mother. This extension of 'private' life into the 'public' sphere is not the visual, negative, marker of the plight these women are in, but is consistent with a different perspective on what constitutes 'private' and 'public'. For market women, these are not so much opposed or clearly bounded spaces. Rather, they are relative notions bound to people who do and do not 'belong', to places one 'knows' and is 'known to', and thus to the history one has within the locality, in this case Kebkabiya.

Therefore, the fact that Zamzam's mother, sisters, and daughters assist her in taking care of her children point at a relationship between the practicalities and local notions of motherhood. Not only work, but also raising children is undertaken collectively, female relatives help when needed, in the spaces where mothers are able to be a good mother. The idea vented by Nura, that the family of the mother is nearer than that of the father is also related to this shared motherhood.

Thus, the sharing of tasks and responsibilities is not only a result of need, with so many female headed households around, but is also related to local norms and values about the proper roles for men and women. During my last visit, I ask Hajja if she thinks that tea women gain *ajr* as well. To my surprise, she answers:

They have ajr, *because they raise their children with the profit of their business. I also asked the government to allow me to sell tea. Because selling products at the market nowadays has no profit. But they refused to give me a permit. I told them that I am an old woman and I want to sell* asida *and* ajiina *and to take my things from the house with a cart to the place. Some of the* ledgna sha'abiya *said 'yes' and some said 'no'. There will be a meeting to solve this question. I don't want to run and hide like some women do. I want to sit and to stay. If they refuse, I will ask them to give me money, because I have children and not enough money to raise them. They give me LS200 per month from the hospital; it is not enough.*

Whether she succeeded in getting permission, I do not know. However, her intention shows that Hajja, apart from being a midwife and a market woman, even feels that to be a tea woman is legitimized by, in the end, her wish to be a good mother.

Silences, Gaps, Negations: Negotiating the Dominant Moral Discourse

In this chapter, I have compared the biographies of Hajja and Umm Khalthoum on narrative position and structure, on silences and gaps, on differences and similarities. The narratives proved both a reflection on and in a specific historical and localized discursive context, which provided chances and constraints, space and boundaries, promises and prohibitions. All of the above is applicable not only for Hajja and Umm Khalthoum, but for other women living in the same context as well. I have shown that the personal narratives of Hajja and Umm Khalthoum are not just individual reflections on problems in the present or private memories of the past. These narratives proved to be multi-layered and part and parcel of the construction of their current class positions in the specific location of the town of Kebkabiya. This was exemplified in the way each woman referred to herself in relation to Kebkabiya; its spaces and places, its inhabitants and her daily networks, and the current dominant discourse on gender; as well as in the way each of them referred to me.

The fact that Hajja and Umm Khalthoum narrated about comparable identities is a reflection of the importance of the current moral discourse of the government. The speeches of the female speakers as discussed in Chapter 1, problematized the relation between women, motherhood, the public sphere, and education. The ambivalence of the government on the subject positions that it allots to women was exemplified in the two *hadith*, which were quoted by Sitt Miriam: 'There are three places for a woman: in her father's house, in her husband's house or in her grave', and 'Heaven is under the feet of mothers'.

In Hajja's narrative, both *hadith* are referred to and argued with. She refers to them with the idea of a good and dutiful daughter becoming a good, caring and hard working wife within the walls of the compound of father or husband. However, she argues with them when she talks of how the ideal was jeopardized: by her marriage to Abu Feisal, which was contested by her father; and because her education and her work as a midwife took her venturing outside her home and even her town. At the same time, however, both new positions allowed her to claim a 'new, modern' elite identity. Her role as a mother, as referred to in the second *hadith* is not an issue that she elaborates upon. However, she does refer to her qualities as a caring and loving person when discussing her tending of her husband and her care for her co-wife Zeinab and her children. Moreover, her work on the market, has everything to do with being a, in the local community generally acknowledged good mother.

In Umm Khalthoum's narrative, the *hadith* on the right place of a woman was a theme prevalent in the first sessions of her narrative, when she discussed the control over her life by her father and subsequently her husband. Her status as a women-in-the-process-of-being-divorced did not sit with this *hadith*. Therefore, she shifted her emphasis to her role as a mother. First in relationship to her 'failed' wifehood, comparing her fate with her mother's. At last, she stretched the concept of motherhood, to include her future role as a mother-in-law and her virtue as a crèche mistress, Mama Khalthoum. In this way, she seemed to be able to justify her status as both a good mother and a good teacher, while in the process of getting divorced.

In their different discursive strategies, Hajja and Umm Khalthoum share a feature as well, however. Both claim respectability by pointing to the inevitability of their fate, whereby their fathers were instrumental also concerning their chances on educational background. Hajja constructs her father as the person who almost forced her to attend the midwifery course in Umdurman, although the lack of facilities in

Kebkabiya kept her 'un-educated'. Umm Khalthoum also points out that the lack of education is not her doing, but related to a change in the system as well as the decision of her father to force her into an early marriage: both women thus claims respectability and inevitability while disclaiming any responsibility for their current state.

However, the dilemma of the two *hadith* seems to be felt more clearly by Umm Khalthoum than by Hajja and in this chapter it has become clear why. The Islamist discourse on the proper gender roles is similar to the housewife-cum-breadwinner construction of educated elite family life. Hajja's position as a widow of a renowned local elite man is unambiguous and she can refer to the alternative local discourse on proper motherhood as a working woman. The fact that it concerns a sub-dominant discourse means she cannot articulate it within the dominant discourse, and this has created a silence. But as every discourse has its materiality and is to be found in relationships with others, it is prevalent in the way Hajja can rely on her kin for support of her role as mother. In this way motherhood becomes more a shared identity as well (cf. Schrijvers 1985, 1991). Umm Khalthoum has to keep her two identities as a mother and a working woman separate. So she claims on the one hand good mother and Muslim hood by referring to the culturally highly valued custom of hospitality, also to strangers as a religious virtue, even constructing it as a religious pillar. On the other hand she refers to teaching in the sense of extending knowledge, in terms of *ilm*, which is a religious duty as well. Umm Khalthoum attains closure, by connecting both identities, as her role as kindergarten teacher allows her to claim an extension of her motherhood identity at the same time. She thus acquires the status of a good Muslim woman, legitimating both identities in relation to each other.

Both Hajja and Umm Khalthoum negotiated the dominant discourse with reference to their multiple identities. They claimed a good Muslim identity by actively intersecting identities, prioritizing some, while down playing others. Thereby they constructed both individualized and collective identities relating themselves to other women, and men, in a strategic way. So in, by and through their narratives both women, within the boundaries of their contexts as members of their class, generations, location etc. they acted out a relational agency: an agency that got shaped by reference to their networks with other women and men, but also to their physical landscapes and remembered maps. Charting their reflections alongside their daily mobility or past movements, Hajja and Umm Khalthoum anchored their selves to spaces and places of belonging. By telling about themselves they embodied those space/time/locations in the past thereby acquiring a more or less unified, centered and fixed Self in the present, however temporary.

I can now also understand the shallowness of the characters of female relatives in both narratives. For both Hajja and Umm Khalthoum, their mothers were important as connections to the past, to a sultanic family tree or an example of rewarded motherhood after divorce, and, though less explicit, for love, care and emotional support. And at the same time they constituted no example, no role model when it came to the most important identities both women try to put forward with reference to the Islamist dominant discourse: of an educated, well-behaved working woman. The only female character Umm Khalthoum does elaborate on is her divorced sister who works at the army hospital. She is a still beautiful woman and mother, who is also divorced and, more importantly, a professional woman working for the government. No wonder Umm Khalthoum quite explicitly refers to her as an example.

This brings me to the silence in both narratives on the virtues and vices of motherhood. Interesting enough, although marriage is an important issue in the dominant discourse and in government policy, Hajja and Umm Khalthoum do not explicitly reflect on the issue of marriage with respect to their daughters. Both Hajja and Umm Khalthoum, however, expressed the hope that their daughters might be able to get more education than they had access to. Hajja even sold her gold in order to have Nura, her youngest, smartest, and still unmarried daughter, sit again for her examination of the intermediary school so she can go on to study at secondary high school. Umm Khalthoum is genuinely disappointed at the wish of her daughter to marry instead of studying. Though Umm Khalthoum is quite explicit about the right of her daughter to marry out of love, where Hajja is less articulate, the effort of both mothers has been for their daughters to acquire an education. It is precisely the dynamics between the hopes of the older generation of women, such as Hajja and even Umm Khalthoum, and the younger generation of their daughters that proved to be of importance for the positioning of this 'next generation'. This will be elaborated upon in Chapter 6.

PART THREE

UNSETTLED IN THE BORDER ZONE

[Thesaurus]

Changeable, Lacking Order or Stability: *changing often in a period of time*
Being in Motion, Moving about: *Not being in a state or position of rest, not regular or fixed*
Not Decided, Uncertain: *Not resolved, undetermined, full of doubt*

One of the reasons I had gone back to Kebkabiya was to see Hajja and Umm Khalthoum for solace to ease my personal distress. But it was not only that: I had also wanted the approval of Hajja and Umm Khalthoum for what I had done to their narratives, for my contextualisations and analyses. Returning from Kebkabiya I felt not reassured though. My trip had given another colour to my relationship with each woman, and my stay had comforted me but it had not given me the sense of release and relieve on a professional plane that I had hoped my return visit would give me. Sure, Hajja had started to retell her narrative, starting again with her time of glory as a midwife, which confirmed my idea that she prioritised that identity above all others. And Umm Khalthoum asked me to remove some parts of her narrative as these might expose too much of her hidden passions and silent wishes. While erasing these memories from her narrative, I realized that Umm Khalthoum's request boosted my analysis of her shifting positioning as well as her insecurity and ambivalence about her future, which I proposed she had enacted in her narrative. So why then, did I feel not more *confident*, did I not experience *determination* but, rather, *doubt* and discomfort? I felt *unsettled*, and I realized that the authorization I wanted so badly had probably more to do with my identity than Hajja's or Umm Khalthoum's. As Hajja had told me, if I would take her narrative 'by aeroplane all the way to the land of the British', she was confident that I would take care of the book that would come out of it. Indeed, it was my responsibility to scrutinize my academic narrative that reflected, and reflected on, theirs.[1]

[1] See Katherine Borland (1991: 63–75) and Marjorie Mbilinyi (1989: 201–204) for

My narrative so far has been intertwined with those of Hajja and Umm Khalthoum. In narrating their identities both Hajja and Umm Khalthoum had, each in their own way, simultaneously been negotiating the dominant Islamist discourse on gender. Not by openly contesting that discourse or the government *per se*, but by partly accommodating, each had claimed space to fit into as a good Muslim as well as a working woman. By reading the narratives of Hajja and Umm Khalthoum 'against the grain' I understood that each woman was, and each in a different way, negotiating the two *hadith*s which Sitt Miriam had eluded to in her speech in Chapter 1. In combination, these *hadith*s constructed the positions of 'wife' and 'mother', restricted to the space of their compounds, as central to Muslim femininity.

I also compared the different ways in which Hajja and Umm Khalthoum engaged in narrating as a discursive practice in order to try to understand how Hajja and Umm Khalthoum had mapped their identities in and on their 'Settings'. I realized that, in order to be able to attain subject positions as female working Muslims, each of them, in their own way, emphasized some, and played-down other identities while articulating and silencing diverse aspects of their lives in the process. By thus contextualising and comparing each biography I established in Chapter 5 that, in concordance with the dominant discourse on gender as articulated in the speeches, education connected to class were the most forceful constituting aspects of Hajja's and Umm Khalthoum's different negotiations of the moral discourse on gender.

At the same time both Hajja and Umm Khalthoum strategically constructed silences and differences with respect to some of the persons with whom they had a daily relationship. This silencing and differentiating constituted a strategy to enable them to construct a closed and unified self as 'in some situations, it may be even easier to decide who the other person is before deciding about one's own identity'.[2] In other words not only identities, but also the social relations of Umm Khalthoum and Hajja were 'narratively constructed': 'others' became indispensable 'anchors' of the identity construction process.[3] A process that at the same time produced relational agency: a process in which I, too, became one of these anchors.

---

very interesting insights gained from their attempt at 'feeding back' the narratives to the female narrators.

[2] Fischer-Rosenthal (1995: 253).

[3] Vila in Holstein and Grubium (2000: 105–106).

In comparing the biographic narratives of Hajja and Umm Khalthoum it appeared that there were two different discourses on femininity at work in Kebkabiya. There was a dominant and a silenced moral discourse as concomitant to the distinction between an 'elite' and a 'non-elite' class. A division which matched other differences, like work relations, household arrangements, the importance of kin relations and the perception of motherhood. It is precisely this neatness of this distinction, which *unsettle*s me. It matches the dichotomy between disreputable market women and respected female teachers as legitimized by the Islamist moral discourse almost too well. This gives reason for caution. The dominant discourse on female gender identities in relation to class is acknowledged and acted upon, which makes it after all a dominant moral discourse. However, it does not mean that working women, market women or female teachers, are cultural dopes or dupes who have completely internalised its common sense notions in their individual constructions of gendered self-identities. Rather, I take it that both dominant and sub-dominant moral discourses are providing possible options, more or less conscious, more or less effective, in different contexts of every day encounters that women from diverse backgrounds may opt for.

In order to allow myself here to break away from the discursive maps of both narrators I must again try to deconstruct my analysis of these narratives in order to *unsettle* the fixed and closed constructions of both women. I have to find the spaces, which Hajja and Umm Khalthoum left blank while 'tracing' certain identities in favour of others. That might allow me to discover other avenues that can lead me to an alternative view on the construction of Muslim femininity by working women. But how to go about deconstructing my own analysis?

My '*Epilogues*' to the narratives of Hajja and Umm Khalthoum were not just self-reflexive intermezzos to liven up the text but one of my attempts at deconstructing my own constructions. They were meant to turn my gaze inwards, to arrive at a different mode of understanding and of narrating in order to get away from my own fixed and closed identity of the researcher who contextualised these narratives. In Part Two, this 'self-reflexive mode'[4] created room for reviewing my own

---

[4] See Behar (1993), Ghorashi (2003), Nencel (1997), Schrijvers (1985, 1991, 1993). See also the special issue of the Dutch journal of gender studies (*Tijdschrift voor Genderstudies*) on this theme by Davids and Willemse (1993) which features articles (in Dutch) by these last five authors (excepting Behar).

academic narrative for what is was: as situated, partial, subjective and belonging to the context in which it was constructed, as Hajja's and Umm Khalthoum's narratives were. In this part I want to pursue this process of deconstruction in order to find alternative subject positions and decide to what extent these constitute avenues for change.

Deconstructing texts-in-context: Working women resisting the dominant discourse

Deconstruction means to be critical of accepted 'beliefs concerning truth, knowledge, power and self, and language that are taken for granted'[5] and to understand them as legitimisations of the status quo. Both postmodernist and feminist scholars have acknowledged the importance of understanding the constructed nature of 'truth'. From the onset feminist scholars have used deconstruction to scrutinize self-evident binary oppositions like ratio/emotion, political/personal, theory/practice, professional/personal, male/female: to take apart these self-evident pairs, to *unsettle* and expose the hierarchical ranking and power-relations which are constituted by and which constitute in turn these oppositions. Again, I will turn around and look back at the road that I have travelled with Hajja and Umm Khalthoum so far. I need another vantage point in order to see how Hajja and Umm Khalthoum, in attaining closure and fixedness, glossed over possible differences while constructing general and generalizing categories and dichotomies in their narratives. Constructions which I have taken as self-evident and re-constructed as such in my analysis.

Deconstruction is not directed at dichotomies only, however. It also requires me to look at the ways in which discourses determine, and as a result exclude subjects. To detect these silences in my analysis is not just a matter of professional ethics, but of politics as well.[6] It means to discover the views of those who are not heard, who do not have a clearly outlined place in the discourse.[7] The silences which are thus constructed in the process are to be mapped as well in order to understand those views that are thus suppressed and marginalized

---

[5] Flax (1987: 624).
[6] Spivak in Landry and Maclean (1996: 6–12).
[7] Mills (1999: 121).

by the dominant discourse. But where should I look for that what is supposed not to be there?

For tracing back my steps I turn again to the insights of feminist scholars who identify themselves as black or Third World women, or women of colour.[8] They have taken their own position as 'non fitting' as a starting point for theorizing the intersecting of identities as a continuously shifting experience, which depends on the spaces, and places where one is situated. They inspired me to accept the notion of mapping in Part Two: here they might lead me out of the quagmire of the seemingly solid grounds that my analyses so far were built on.

The work of these feminist scholars 'of colour' formed an important critique on the work of feminist thinkers who have emphasized the facilitating and potentially liberating aspect of the performed and fragmented nature of identities.[9] For bell hooks, for example, this fragmentation also yielded 'displacement, profound alienation and despair'.[10] Moore remarks that the 'reality of this experience is a series of complex crossings and recrossings'[11] which are inscribed in the body.[12]

From these personally inspired and inspiring reflections it has become clear that the same spaces and places in which certain identities are constructed and called for, may be differently experienced by those who are discursively allotted the same subject position. This occurred for example, in theorizing about the places where women of colour can take refuge from potentially discriminating and silencing contexts. hooks sees the 'homeplace' for black people as 'that space where we return for renewal and self-recovery, where we heal our wounds and become whole'.[13] Another important feminist thinker, Gloria Anzaldúa, states: 'I had to leave home so I could find myself'[14] as her choices were not accepted in the 'home' she was born into. Here it is obvious how

[8] These labels do not refer to any essential identity, nor to skin colour, but is a political term which these scholars take on to mark there positioning against a white dominated world. See for example Mohanty for a reflection on an 'imagined community' of Third World feminists' 'oppositional struggles' and 'communities of resistance' to emphasize this active positioning (1991: 1–10).

[9] This critique was in particular levied at Butler's notion of performing identities. She formulated her insights in particular with respect to sexuality, trying to 'unthink' the normality of heterosexuality.

[10] hooks (1990: 26, quoted in Alsop et. al 2003: 107).

[11] Moore (1994: 80–81).

[12] Moore (1994: 81), discussing hooks (1990).

[13] hooks quoted in Alsop et. al. (2003: 208–209).

[14] Anzaldua (1987: 16), quoted in Alsop et. al. (2003: 212).

different discourses compete over dominance in certain locations.[15] The acknowledgment of different experiences by women who are positioned similarly entails ambiguity and a lack of cohesiveness of subject positionings. It is this ambiguity which allows for agency: an agency which may be subversive as it is part of the intersubjective process of daily encounters and relationships that are locally constructed, reconstructed and transformed in the process.

Narrating one's biographic narrative is therefore not just about constructing identities and negotiating dominant discourses. It also constitutes a means for self-understanding, for realizing who one is as well as for 'understanding the world as it has happened'. It forms a way for 'creating shared worlds of meaning'[16] and thus it forms the basis for feminist struggles.[17] This is precisely why the agency that is produced in the process is relational: one can only exist and be acknowledged in a specific setting in relation to others. And who these 'others' are may shift, depending on the 'setting'.

In other words, the categorization of women as 'same' based on certain intersecting identities, such as gender and race, or in the case of Kebkabiya, gender, class, and location[18] does not mean that all women in one and the same 'gendered' category construct their identity in the same way. Neither does it mean that women who are similarly positioned experience this positioning in a similar way: none of them is typical nor a-typical for that category. The fact that narrating means an engagement in creating a 'shared world of meanings' indicates that this is not self-evident: that an effort is to be put in attaining that sharing.

So in order for me to understand diversity and the construction of alternative identities by women who formally belong the class-'categories' of Hajja and Umm Khalthoum, I have to find those women who are considered not to fit. To attain this goal I will in Part Three use the spatial notion of 'border zone' which I take from Abu-Lughod,[19] and turn it into an analytical space for trying to locate those women

---

[15] Dorothy Smith calls this the 'clash of discourses' (Smith in Mills 1997: 102).

[16] Fischer-Rosenthal (1995: 260–261).

[17] See for example Brah (1992, 1996); Lorde (1984: 112–113); Mohanty (1991: 1–47); Wekker (1996: 61).

[18] Since 2002, when Darfur became the stage of mounting violence, location has become constructed as ethnicity or even race. See chapter 8 for a reflection on this aspect of the war in Darfur.

[19] Abu-Lughod (1993: 12) refers to Renato Rosaldo (1989) for this concept. However, she does not elaborate on it, nor does she use it in analysis.

who do not fit the prescribed subject positions. For me this notion of 'border zone' refers both to the 'Borderlands' of Anzaldúa[20] and the 'contact zone' as conceptualised by Pratt. 'Borderlands' refers to a space of being in transit of being un-determined: to be able to 'explore notions of identity and subjectivity which reject concrete categorization'.[21] Escaping categorization constitutes for Anzaldúa the strength of the positioning of women of colour, or what she calls the 'new *mestiza*': she who 'copes by developing a tolerance for contradictions, a tolerance for ambiguity. She has a plural personality...not only does she sustain contradictions, she turns the ambivalence into something else'.[22] At the same time, escaping categorization is neither a smooth process, nor devoid of power differences or conflicts. Pratt's view of the 'contact zone' as 'social spaces where disparate cultures meet, clash and grapple with each other, often in highly asymmetrical relations of domination and subordination',[23] acknowledges this hierarchical aspect. In both views the spatial comes into view again as an important aspect of 'becoming' as Trinh Minh-ha points out, 'the question of identity is moving away from traditional queries into *who* am I' and 'progressively become questions of *when*, *where*, and *how* am I'.[24]

My goal for exploring the border zone is to understand to what extent women who are located in this conceptual space can be taken to resist the dominant discourse. This resistance does not need to be open or direct, but can be part of the ways in which women construct their identities and create alternative subject positions. It is precisely by contesting the homogeneity of the subject position allotted to women in the same 'category' that subverts that discourse. I feel that this view facilitates an understanding of multiple identifications by women, even when they share in one and the same space and formal subject position. At the same time that it allows for gaining an insight in how women enact agency, it might open up the closed analysis that I constructed in Part Two.

---

[20] See Vila in Holstein and Grubium (2000: 106) who also refers to 'borderlands' in the context of differentiation of racially grounded experiences.

[21] Alsop et. al. (2000: 213).

[22] Anzaldúa (1987: 79).

[23] Pratt (1992). Also quoted in Mills (2003: 121).

[24] Emphasis Trinh Minh-ha (1992: 157).

Coming to the end of this road: Border zone, liminality and alternative identities

In order to access the border zone, I need at least some indications for how to determine who 'belongs' there and who does not. As appeared from the biographic narratives of Hajja and Umm Khalthoum, the category of the good Muslim woman is always to some extent negotiated and moulded to fit the experiences and interests of the narrator. At the same time it became clear from Umm Khalthoum's reflections on the differences between educated and uneducated women, that there was a considerable overlap between the Islamist moral discourse on gender and the discourse of the educated elite on 'proper' gendered subject positions. Thus the educated elite had most stakes in preserving their privileged position in local society, and thus they might have invested most in assuring that the boundaries between both classes were obvious and self-evident to all. This means that I have to scrutinize the markers of difference as put forward by the ruling elite for its tenability for each class in order to find the women in the border zone.

At the same time the forcefulness of a discourse in regulating clearly demarcated subject positions may point at the fact that women are considered to be 'in need of' being directed, guided, and controlled: in other words, the assertion of dominance by certain discourses point at an acknowledgment of women's non-compliance or even resistance to those discourses. However, as long as the boundaries of the subject positions as put forward by a dominant discourse are not at stake, the status quo is not under attack. Women who are in the border zone are those who do potentially challenge the suggested norm/ality of the boundaries and presumed homogeneity of the subject positions allocated by the dominant discourse. However, not all women who thus construct an alternative subject position pose a challenge to the discourse on gender to a similar extent; some categories of women are more of a threat than others.

As a consequence, women who populate the border zone are in an ambiguous position in the sense that their alternative subject position may, or may not, prove to make difference to the dominance of the discourse. Women who do not fit are in fact in a 'liminal' position as long as their alternative identity can be considered to be in 'transition'. Although their positioning might question the tenability of the accepted boundaries, their subject position may be considered to be temporary. This means that these women from the vantage point of the dominant discourses and those groups in society that adhere to it, consider these women to not fit the accepted subject positions 'yet'; but they are expected to be 'fit in' in the future. Young girls, for example, are such a category in Sudan as the moral discourse of the government does not offer clear subject positions for young girls coming of age. These women are therefore presumed to become good female Sudanese, who will fulfil in the near future their prescribed roles as wives and mothers as part of their destiny.

However, when women in the border zone take up alternative subject positions of a more permanent nature their challenge to the 'taken for granted' borders between groups or between subject positions are more serious. These women expose the contingency of the moral foundations of the dominant discourse. Their positioning might call for a transformation of the same dominant discourse that is geared to the preservation of the status quo of the existing ruling relations. The distinction between women in the border zone, who do and who do not challenge the moral discourse is therefore not clear. Their different negotiations of alternative identities are part of a dynamic process with often-unforeseen effects, which might, or might not, alter the discourse and even induce societal change. In Part Three I will therefore look at 'other' women who were part of my local network and who narrated about their lives, in an effort to understand the dynamics of this process.

CHAPTER 6

IN THE BORDER ZONE: THE PREDICAMENT OF THE NEXT GENERATION

In this chapter, I will focus on the negotiations by market women and by female teachers of the class boundaries, as determined by the dominant discourse.[1] To begin with, I will attempt to deconstruct the tenability of the subject positions allotted by the dominant Islamist discourse, which depend on those boundaries. Marriage, motherhood, and work in relation to education constituted the most important aspects of class difference in Hajja's and Umm Khalthoum's narrative, as well as of the notion of proper female Muslimhood. Consequently, in this chapter, I will look for dissent, conflict and tension within each class while focusing on the relations between these aspects. Only after I have been able to assess who belongs to the 'border zone', may I understand what the effect of their alternative positioning is on relations of ruling. This will be further analyzed in Chapter 7.

Market Women in the Border Zone?

Although there were regular quarrels and tensions among the different classes of women, these could not self-evidently be considered negotiations of the dominant discourse. Also in this case the contexts in which to 'read against the grain' were of importance to understand the multiple meanings of these events. Towards the end of my stay, when I saw less of Sa'adiya because she had her responsibilities at school, I joined her after school hours, often in the evening at home or visiting some of her relatives or colleagues. Sa'adiya suggested we take the tape recorder with us, in case we might tape a narrative. One such occasion was during a visit with Sa'adiya's half-sister Hauwa, who lived with her mother Helima and two of her mother's co-wives on the compound of her

[1] Some of the material in Chapter 6 and 7 appeared as "'A room of one's own'. Single Female Teachers Negotiating Alternative Gender Roles", *Northeast African Studies Journal*, Special Issue 'Women in the Horn of Africa' VIII, no.3 (2006). Back issue 2001.

father, in an older quarter of town. When we arrived, Hauwa and her mother were shelling peanuts on a mat outside Hauwa's *gutiya.* After some chitchatting Sa'adiya took out the tape recorder, and while pressing the button, instructed Hauwa to start with telling her name, where she was born. Maybe Sa'adiya had been talking with Hauwa about my research, or it was because Sa'adiya and I were both seen as educated elite women, for after the formalities Hauwa immediately starts to talk about school:

My name is Hauwa Al-Amin Musa. My tribe is Fur. My mother is Gimr. I was in school and did my examination from intermediary school to high secondary school in 1979. I didn't succeed and I did that year again in evening classes. Then I succeeded but they didn't put me on the list with pupils for getting a place on one of the schools. My father went to the Ministry of Education to complain and they asked him to pay some money for the administration fee…

"All girls have to", Sa'adiya interrupts.

But he refused to give me money. To sit around without work is bad and I remember that it is better to sit in the market to earn money. I was born in a village south west of Kebkabiya, Jauwré, in 1963.

"There is a year between Hauwa and me", Sa'adiya comments. "We are from different mothers". Hauwa waits for Sa'adiya to say more. When she does not Hauwa continues:

Sitting in the market is for earning money. First I applied for several jobs such as a nurse, but when they held a lottery, I was always out. And to be a cleaner? No, it is better to sit in the market; there is more money in the market. At first, I sold kisra, *then millet and onions, oil, tomatoes. Now I am only selling one thing, millet. I like to sell millet because you can't lose your money. If it doesn't give you profit it still gives you the money you paid. It never gets less. Because it is dry, so you can keep it: if the price would become less you just don't sell. With tomatoes, you have to sell.*

"Did you have any problems while being on the market"? I ask her:

I had many problems from my family and from the government. At home, my mother and my sisters complained: 'If you go to the market, who is going to wash and to bathe your children'? Every day they complained. And when my husband came back he didn't allow me to go to the market, he forbade me to go. Neighbours did not give me any problems in sitting in the market. I went to sit in the market again when my husband returned to Iraq. Because he didn't send money to me. If he had given me enough money, I would not have gone to the market.

"And what about the government?" I ask her.

The government is now giving us a hard time. Because of the famine, they do not want us to sell millet to people from outside the district. It is not true we sell to other people for a higher price. But they did not forbid me to sell millet.

Hauwa is referring to the ban on transporting grain across district borders to areas where there is a food shortage as this might lead to food speculation with rising prices and to food shortages inside Kebkabiya itself. "Karin means the dress rules", Sa'adiya interrupts, adding: "Didn't you hear about the new dress codes for women"? Hauwa looks at us while saying:

I didn't hear about it.

"You did not hear the men from the popular committee when they talked about this with their amplifiers"? Sa'adiya asks again, incredulous.

I do not know, I did not know about new dress codes,

Hauwa answers again. To turn the discussion to another direction, I ask her: "If you would have enough money now, would you still go to the market"?

Yes, so as not to deplete it, I would try to gain profit from it. But if I had a husband who would give me enough money, I would not go to the market. And if I had enough money I would not start learning again, I would go to the market trying to raise my profit.

"And what about your husband, what did he think of it"? I ask her next.

I had my divorce from the judge. He divorced me because my husband is not staying with me and not sending me money. So I divorced. One day he went and spent six or seven years in Iraq. When he was in Iraq his friends wrote to him and told him that I was sitting in the market and selling. Maybe that is why he didn't send money to me. And I don't want my daughter to sell at the market, because education is better than to sit in the market. Because I have money. In the past my father did not want to give enough money to finish our school, not even to Sa'adiya. I hope she will be a doctor, if not then a teacher; that would be quite enough.

While Hauwa says this, she turns to Sa'adiya when Hauwa's mother, Helima enters the courtyard and joins us on the mat. She offers Sa'adiya and me some very sweet tea. While we sip the tea, Sa'adiya, Hauwa and her mother talk about the new wall of millet stalks around the compound. The way Hauwa talks about her trade reveals that she has a feeling and a taste for it. She started to trade at quite a young age, when she was still at school. And now she is in the millet trade, which is mainly a male affair since it involves going around the market and buying the small quantities of grain from farmers who come from outside. She stores the grain in sacks at her father's shop and sells when the prices rise though she cannot keep a hold on it as long as the big male traders can. However, she has done well as the grain trade keeps pace with the inflation and therefore she earns a regular and relatively high income. In this, she differs from most of the other market women who mainly sell the more perishable vegetables and fruits, which are only lucrative when sold on a daily basis and which are only available in season.

In her case, her assertions that market women can earn a lot of money have validity: even more than teachers. With the rising prices and continuing inflation, the salaries of the teachers lag behind. Lately many teachers have difficulties to pay the bills and towards the end of the month, many have to buy on credit. In the course of my second stay the government decided to raise the grades of teachers. However, their salaries were not paid for months in a row and in some places, strikes were organised.[5] On the other hand, in normal times the regular and fixed monthly income provides the teachers some security. Moreover, the teachers have access to subsidized housing, transportation, as well as food items such as lentils, oil, and beans, to soap and lamp oil and occasionally to cloth, matches, and other luxury products, which are quite expensive on the market.

The sudden turn in the last part of Hauwa's narrative is interesting. From discussing her divorce from her husband as a kind of legitimization to sell at the market, she suddenly turns to the issue of her daughter's future. Hauwa's insistence that she now can afford her daughter's education, something she herself lacked, is quite interesting and I wonder if there is more at hand than her daughter's future. So I ask her: "If your father had given enough money, would *you* have become a teacher"?

Yes, I would have gone again to school. Teaching is better than sitting in the market because you are sitting in offices and your work is limited by fixed working hours. Your dress is clean and your tobe. *But we, in the market we have to run to the market in order to buy from people from outside and to sell to others. Sometimes it is difficult to sell, because there are many women who want to buy from the people that come from outside. They call: 'Hey you, come here and sell to me', or: 'Hey you, come to me and buy from me'. At the meeting of the popular committee, they told us that women should sit inside their houses, not on the market. If they saved money for us, there would be no need for us to go to the market. But if you don't have anyone to support you, you have to go. Even if you have a husband, but he is not giving you enough money to support your family, you have to go to the market. If I had a husband who would give me enough money, I would stay inside the house. But I have no other family members working for the government, only Sa'adiya. But from our grandfathers family: aunts, uncles, nieces and nephews, all the boys became* faqih: *all of them went to the* khalwa.

"How did you start trading"? Sa'adiya goes on without a pause.

I started trading with three pounds. My brother gave me millet to sell at the market. I sold it, and with this money I bought other millet and profited again three pounds. This has been my capital and I trade with it until now. In 1978, I started to sell at the market during the school holidays: I made kisra *and my mother sold it on the market. I gave the money to my mother. I have been selling at the market for myself since 1981. I was eighteen years old then. But when I started to make* kisra *during the holidays, I was fifteen years old. Now I look after my family in the house: my mother, sisters, and brothers. I buy clothes for my children and things for the family.*

Then her mother interferes: "I always used to pay more for the household than they do. One bowl was at that time milled for five pounds and I paid for all the expenses". Hauwa nods and tells her mother she did so before, but that now it is different. Sa'adiya hushes them but when I say it does not matter Sa'adiya keeps the tape recorder running. I then remember what I wanted to ask her earlier about a comment she made. "How did you solve the problems between you and your sisters when you went to the market"?

We talked, and talked and talked a lot and we became tired of it. My mother said: 'No, I will solve this problem'.

Now she has been referred to in person, her mother obviously feels she can add her view again: "I told them: 'She is going to fetch things for you and you are sitting without work in the house so you can do the things in the house so she can go to the market'". Hauwa nods, and adds:

I came here after my husband went to Iraq. My brother collected me and brought me back to Kebkabiya for I had been living in his [her husband's] *village near Jebel Marra until that time. I came here and stayed with my mother again.*

"So why don't you want your daughters to go to the market, while you chose to do so after you returned"? I ask Hauwa again.

Because working in the market is hard work. It is hot in the sun all day and your kidneys hurt. And I wish for them to be educated and to have a good future.

Now her mother takes over again: "The good wife is to be educated, and to stay in the house and to clean and work in the house: this you can say". But Hauwa refuses to take the bait and shakes her head. She is silent for a moment, than turns to a, seemingly, completely different subject: "I would like to have just five children". To which her mother directly retorts: "Very few, you should ask for ten". Hauwa replies that five is enough because it is difficult to raise them. Then she turns to me: "We like children because if you become old they will look after you".

Both Sa'adiya and Helima nod in agreement and look at me expectantly. It is clear that my childlessness is referred to and confronted. It is not the first time this happens. I feel the need to explain myself in her terms: "Johan and I do want children". However, I hasten to add: "But we are still students so we did not find the opportunity to raise them yet. We hope we will earn enough money soon so we can afford a house to raise the child in". While I finish my sentence Helima adds a religious blessing: the 'asking' she uses when advising Hauwa to have ten children, refers to praying. Although it is not far from the truth, I feel the financial arguments are a lame excuse for not choosing to have children. Nevertheless, Hauwa seems to be satisfied, for she agrees by saying: "That is why I do not want too many children. I want to be able to raise them well". This comment resonates the elite view on having and raising children. I ask her if she wants to continue being a market woman. Before Hauwa can answer, her mother again interferes: "Trading in the market has more money than teaching". To this Hauwa answers vehemently:

Yes, more money, but also lots of work and a lot of tiredness! Also those educated women who work, they are clean, have nice clothes and no tiredness.

I look at Sa'adiya for a reaction, but she does not seem to mind that Hauwa thinks her job is an easy one. Hauwa continues:

Educated women know how to contact people in meetings. They have good grammar. But the uneducated are shy and don't know how to talk to people.

This obviously triggers something that bothers her mother who almost jumps up, saying: "Don't say we don't know anything; we understand anything"! Hauwa shrugs and as if to spite her mother she returns to her description of educated women:

There is a difference in making food and the kind of food they eat. Educated women can read from a cookbook and know how to make good food. Also in marriage, their houses are very clean and have nice furniture, it is arranged well. They choose good husbands.

Although Hauwa articulates the same opinion as her mother did on education and housekeeping, she looks mockingly at her mother, who, while going through her basket of shelled peanuts, snorts, but does not say anything. "Don't you wish to marry again"? I then ask Hauwa, to get her continue on her last subject:

Well, I would if it would be a very rich man, who would give me a lot of money and buy things for me. A good man is the one that has a lot of money that buys everything for you, so you will not become tired,

Hauwa says giggling. "Is that the most important thing for a husband, to be rich?" I press her to talk a bit more on the subject.

Well, he should be educated so he will understand everything. I don't like an uneducated one. He should have a redder colour than me so the children are not as black as I am. I would like to have red children.

At that moment, a neighbour appears at the opening of the courtyard. After elaborate greetings, she joins us. Sa'adiya shuts off the tape recorder and some ten minutes later we return home to our own compounds.

Although Hauwa's narrative was short, in terms of my attempt to deconstruct the category of 'the' market woman her disagreements with her mother are the most interesting, since both are or have been market women. The first moment when Hauwa's mother, Helima, interferes is to explain that it was she who, in the past, used to provide for her household, including for Hauwa's family. Helima is divorced and the absence of support from her husband forced her to work on the market. Next, she puts herself in the picture as the one who solved the quarrel between Hauwa and her sisters about household tasks. Helima's interferences construct the image of herself as someone who initiated marketing, and provided for her daughters and their future. She thus seemed to create a bond vis-à-vis Hauwa with respect to taking care of their shared households. At the same time, Helima obviously wanted acknowledgment for her efforts to raise her children in the past and not to have Hauwa take all the credits.

Therefore, although her mother seems supportive in her comments, the interferences during the interview also point at a conflict, or at least at differing opinions. The first moment when Hauwa and her mother disagree openly is when her mother suggests, "the good wife is to be educated, and to stay in the house and to clean and work in the house: this you can say". It seems as if Helima is articulating her objections against the fact that Hauwa sells at the market, despite her earlier assertion that she facilitated her daughter's trading activities. Hauwa seems to evade the issue by stating she would like to have just five children indicating that it is already hard to take care of her children as it is. It can be seen as an indirect rebuttal of her mother's definition of a good wife and mother. Hauwa has to take care of her children and cannot afford to be a housewife. At the same time, she uses arguments often used by the educated elite for not having too many children. This helps her in pointing out that she can raise them better than when she would by staying at home, but also shows her acknowledgment of the elite's view on family life.

The other moment of disagreement relates to Hauwa's wish that her own daughter, Helima's granddaughter, might receive education so she can get employment as an educated woman. Hauwa's positive evaluation of a white collar job as opposed to selling at the market might again be her way of showing that she is, like her mother, aware what a 'proper' life should be. In addition to the lucrative aspects of the job of a teacher, she also refers to 'reading from cook books', and 'knowing how to talk'. However, her mother reacts quite fiercely to the suggestion that female teachers are more acknowledgeable and articulate when she says, 'don't say we don't know anything, we understand anything'.

Both interferences by Hauwa's mother can be 'read against the grain' as arguments with the common sense notion that market women are uneducated and therefore ignorant, even immoral, making bad mothers and wives. The 'we' here might be read as 'we non-elite women', or even 'we market women' whereby a common identity between Hauwa and her mother is constructed, since that is the contrast sketched in Hauwa's discussion before her mother interfered. The disagreement is in this case related to how best to show me and Sa'adiya, their knowledge and acknowledgment of the dominant discourse. However, the intonation and body language of mother and daughter during the exchange of opinions do not suggest much solidarity between the two. On the contrary, they seem to belie the content of the words. The 'we' in 'don't say we don't know anything' therefore might also refer to a difference between Hauwa and Helima, despite the fact that they both belong to the category of market women. In order to understand the meaning of 'we' and how it negotiates the dominant discourse, I will turn to the colleagues of both Helima and Hauwa.

Elderly Market Women: Selling for the Future

Let me first consider Helima's positioning, who as an elderly market woman belongs to the same category of market women as Hajja. The first interference by Helima in the narrative of Hauwa concerned the fact that she herself had sold on the market to take care of her household, before Hauwa took over. Like most of the other elderly market women, Helima started to trade because she lost the support of her husband and she had to provide for their children herself.

Most market women evaluated their job as a mixed blessing. Like Hauwa, most of them thought it was hard work, physically trying and emotionally wearing because of the long days in the heat and dust, the irregular income and working hours. Most would emphasize the negative aspects, but everyone would also point out the positive sides. The access to money which one has at one's disposal, and the building up of a network of women other than relatives were aspects which all of the market women would refer to in one way or another. Colleagues from the market were always mentioned when I asked the market women whom they call on to help them in times of need or when organizing a party. The market place has become the centre of their social life.

One of the main differences, which became apparent, was that the full time market women were at least a generation younger than the part-timers. This difference had its bearing on the reason to sell at the market, the attitude towards marketing, and the attitude towards each other.[2]

The period when most of the elderly women started selling at the market was during the 1970s and early 1980s, when the recurrent droughts forced men to migrate and women into heading their households. In this period the attitude of most families towards education also changed. As I indicated before, Nimeiri's socialist policy meant in principle equal access to education for all, and many schools were opened. The generation of Sa'adiya and her sister Hauwa, and other women of their age therefore had the chance to attend a school in their vicinity. As these women were living in a town, where these services were most readily offered, and its attendance most easily controlled, they belonged to the first generation that as a rule attended primary education. The government provided the possibilities; the fathers, but frequently the mothers, the means by which the girls could follow up on this, like money for pencils, books, school uniforms, and fees. As the mothers lost the labour input of their daughters, they had to take care of the income and of the household tasks on their own.

---

[2] I became acquainted with both groups, about a dozen of each. I talked at length with five in each group, taping their narratives. Gradually, I learned that of the part-time elderly market women, two of the five had a relation with Hajja: her co-wife Zeinab, and her neighbour Umm Maryoma who was a daughter of Fekki Sinin's sister. Then there was Mahalla, who came only irregularly to the market, she was from the poorest quarter of town where she had hosted me when I held my (almost failed) survey there; there was Mastura, a former tea woman, allegedly one of the first to start the trade, who now sold vegetables; and finally, Umwayma Az-Zeit, an energetic elderly market women named after the oil she sold. The full time market women were all young women, all who will appear in the next section.

In all the narratives of the elderly market women, education came up in the same way as it did in Hajja's story: as a lost chance for themselves, as the hallmark of progress, and as a means to offer their children a better future. Schooling has even become part of a survival strategy where the spread of risks is the best way of dealing with the uncertainties of the Sudanese economy. It is remarkable that this is particularly true for daughters; apart from seeing this as an economic strategy, elderly market women obviously projected on to their daughters the hope for a life they never had themselves.

The younger generation of market women is therefore in a completely different situation compared to the elder generation of market women. Their mothers could look upon education as a kind of magic that would have done the trick and might have pulled a good life out of the hat. Moreover, as we saw in the case of Hajja, the goal to provide their children with a better future also legitimized their working on the market. However, many of the young market women were educated and still ended up on the market. Not all girls were as bright or as lucky as Sa'adiya and many of this first generation of schoolgirls shared the fate of Hauwa, for one reason or another. They returned to their homes to live again with their families without the qualifications to be able to apply for a white-collar job. Moreover, quite a few of them have taken over a place at the market from an elderly relative. The predicament of these young women is that they at least had the chance to get education and enter the government service, and failed.

That the young market women had different prospects from their mothers also meant that the young women had a different perspective towards marketing than the elderly women. For the latter group, it was a kind of last resort, a way of making ends meet when agricultural returns were insufficient, and thus to perform their identity as a good mother. The daughters had to live up to the expectations of their mothers and those created during their training at school. The wish to fulfil this promise made them look upon trading differently. However good they were at marketing and however much they liked the trade, being 'respectable' and leading a life of someone 'who knows' was obviously still enticing, as Hauwa seemed to indicate in her comparison of trading and teaching. This made them differ qualitatively from the elderly generation.

It is therefore not so remarkable that both Hauwa reflected on her trading activities as dirty, tiring and boundless in contrast with teaching, which is constructed as easy, performed in a clean and quiet environment within fixed working hours. Moreover, educated women were cast as those who could take better care of their husbands, their households, their children: as those who set an example for the right way of behaviour, of proper living.

So Hauwa's view, which matched those of other young market women, might be related to the fact that she attended school where education was geared towards formal subjects as well as acquiring the 'proper' elite behaviour. Helima formulated in similar terms the view on 'correct' female behaviour. The most interesting was that in both cases the image of 'the elite woman' was articulated quite uncritically in an almost rehearsed phrasing. It rather reflected an ideal typical description of elite behaviour and tied in neatly with the dominant discourse. As in the case of Hauwa and her mother, it seemed that the market women wanted to show that they were aware of what was generally considered to be 'right' even though their job and lifestyle did not fit the ideal. In the course of my research, negative evaluations of particular educated women were vented as well. Several female teachers had a name for being always late or even completely unreliable in the payments of their debts with market women at the end of the month when salaries are paid. Others were seen as 'pretenders', acting as the civilized, well-behaved and good-natured women in public, but distrusted for their 'real' thoughts and behaviour, especially when it came to moral issues. Nevertheless, in general reflections, the opinion on 'the educated woman', and particularly their job and lifestyle was favourable.

Despite the fact that this view was generally shared among the market women, the elderly market women were quite critical about the attitude of the younger market women, also phrased in general terms. The question is: "Why?"

The Difference Within: Market Women and their Expectations

The different ways in which the two generations of market women argue their right to be on the market is instructive. Umwayma Az-Zeit, an elderly market woman who did not have daughters of her own, stated for example:

I heard a lot of wa'iz, *religious advisors, who said it is not good for women to sit in the market. They said: 'It is good for women to wear long dresses with long sleeves and to have a sharp.*[3] *To sit in the market modestly, not to look at men to see where they are going, not to wave your hands too much, or to bend forward on your chair so people can see your buttocks* [while saying this she makes all kinds of sexy gestures and we laugh a lot about it]. *You have to sit politely. If a customer asks you for the price of a bottle of oil, you can tell him it costs £S80, and if it is a man, you cannot look at him directly. You just can tell him the price and he can take it or not'. I also agree with the advisors, it is not good to do like this, to do bad things in the market because if you make eye contact with a man, when a man sees a girl and they make a sign, it means they are going to do bad things. They came every year, the* wa'iz, *and one said: 'Trading itself is not* haraam; *it is only* haraam *if the women are uncovering their bodily parts. It is not* haraam *to sit in the market, but it is to sit there with short skirts'. The government stopped the tea women because a lot of men came and sat around them. And they wore short dresses. But also it is not good, because old women are widows and have small children and now they have no work any more since they have been stopped making tea. They don't know how to do another job, except making tea,* ajina, *or* asida…

Umwayma asserted that selling at the market is religiously legitimated. She thereby also shows that she is aware of how to do so in a proper way, as proposed by the government. However, like Hajja, she emphasizes that this is valid only for married elderly women, who sell out of need and who are always behaving modestly, which she exemplifies in her elaborations on proper dress and proper demeanour with respect to male clients. None of the elderly market women, who constructed this difference, ever named a particular young girl or referred to a particular event when this subject was discussed. This points at a discursive strategy whereby these elderly women used the Islamist moral discourse to claim the right to sell at the market and thereby at the same time they, willingly or not, positioned themselves squarely within the boundaries as set by that dominant moral discourse.

This meant that the position of the young, single market women was ambiguous to say the least. On the one hand they were good at their job, they liked to trade, were witty, and radiated an eagerness to sell. They put a lot of effort into making their stall look nice, frequently cleaning their fruit, which were displayed in attractive piles. The young women themselves suggested they were successful because of the quality of their fruit and vegetables and because their products were cheap.

[3] A *sharp* is a shawl covering the head, knotted at the nape of the neck.

Cajoling their many customers with extra fruit and vegetables, *bakshees*, it was self-evident to them that customers would come back when they felt they were treated justly. On the other hand, because of their success with the customers, their enjoyment of the trade, and especially their youth, the young women were accused of sitting in the market to create sexual liaisons. However, among the young market women there was again a difference in positioning between the single and married young market women.

The market women from this last category were, like Hauwa, quite successful in their marketing. Some were even pioneers as female traders, like Zamzam, the daughter of Hajja's co-wife. Zamzam was engaged in long-distance trade, selling tomatoes and other seasonal products via intermediaries and sometimes personally from Kebkabiya to large towns. Also Samiya traded long-distance in soap and oil in bulk via her father and his acquaintances. Due to the requirements of large sums of money, mobility and the reliance on trade networks outside town, these forms of trade are perceived as a male prerogative.[4] The long-distance trade is new to these women and it takes time, energy, money, and above all courage to be successful. Women like Hauwa, Samiya, and Zamzam are articulate and have a sharp sense of profit and demand, which makes them good at their work.

Interestingly, market women like Zamzam were also the most articulate with respect to the discourse of the government, and even articulated criticism, like Zamzam:

> *The right* shari'a *from which I hear is for husbands to keep their wives in the house: so they do not need to bring water, not to work in the fields and not to go to the mill. Even not to go to the market to buy things, but to stay in the house. But the ones that said this to the people, their wives go to the market, to parties; they go everywhere. If the* shari'a *would be implemented it is good for women so they can have their rest.*

Despite the fact that Zamzam seems to support the government's view on femininity, she also protested openly, being one of the few I heard doing so, at the prohibition to sell tea:

[4] Not all male traders are big traders. The small traders are called '*gata'at*', 'cutting', after the dividing of the goods bought in bulk into smaller amounts, which are then sold for a small profit.

Even they [the government] can take you to the court and you say that you haven't money to feed your family, they will let you go and allow you to sell at the market. And even if they want to stop all women from trading, we are not going to stop. We can stay in the market and they can come and put us in jail. And after they release us, we will go back again to the market. This will go on, and on. We will be coming back all the time. We are selling at the market, not stealing things from anyone. We are just waiting for our money.

Although their education is not the only reason why they are articulate and successful, it constitutes an important aspect. They have learned mathematics, they can read and write, and they have a grasp of the basic religious texts, norms, and values. In addition, they have learned to speak up for themselves. Their proficiency in Arabic also makes them more respected by the traders and lorry drivers on whom they often rely for sending their goods or returning their money. If education did not bring them a change in lifestyle, profession or status as their mothers had hoped they would, it did provide them with new avenues to trade and thus a transformation of the content of marketing for women.

At the same time, their venturing into this long-distance trading is looked upon with ambivalence. The trading trips take them out of sight of any of their family members and this gives them a precarious status. Even if they have to take care of their family because of their absent husbands, leaving the social control of the town while going to unknown and unprotected places and meeting strangers, marks the trade as obnoxious.

So in saying, 'don't say we don't know anything', Helima might indeed be positioning herself opposite Hauwa. Here the difference that is emphasized is not the right of Hauwa to sell at the market, but the right to refer to market women as stupid, or not understanding. Even Helima's assertion that a proper woman should stay at home might be a way of showing her resentment over the fact that Helima has been educated and not only knew about elite standards, but also has fared so much better in her trading activities than her mother did. At the same time Helima's reproach served as a way to expose her knowledge about the 'proper' norms of (elite) femininity. In this way she gave proof of the fact that she was not to be considered stupid or backward. Indeed, Helima has been negotiating her positioning within the dominant moral discourse in a similar way that Hajja (and other elderly market women) had: showing her acknowledgment and agreement of its terms, while at the same time suggesting that in her case as an elderly women fate decided differently.

However, an interesting part of the discussion is that although women like Hauwa, Zamzam, or Samiya were the most adventurous in their trading endeavours, and more outspoken and outgoing in their behaviour they were not singled out by elderly women as the most reprehensible market women. It was the young unmarried market women in their midst who bore the brunt of disapproval and scorn of the elder generation.

Young Single Market Women: The Predicament of the 'Lost Generation'

The single market women were aware of the discussions about their position. This became apparent when one of the girls who took her mother's place while she was in hospital, became pregnant. She was ostracized. Ighlas and Rana, who live close to her and had been friendly with her until that moment, even spat on her when she came to sit in the market anyway. When I asked them why they were so fierce, Ighlas told me:

People from the popular committee of our ward check on her: a police car is bringing her to the hospital and back home. They want to be sure she is pregnant and that she cannot get away with it. The stupid bitch, she has become pregnant while selling at the market and the popular committee will use that against us selling as well. Now they can prove that there are girls who make bad use of their contacts with customers. We need the money we earn and we do it in an honest way. There are enough possibilities to send a customer away when he is behaving badly or saying bad things to you. But she, she put a stain on our work. If we are going to be sent off the market, she is to blame. We want her gone.

The girl was replaced a week later by her elder sister.

So young market women scrutinized each other's behaviour in reflection of the dominant discourse on gender as well. At the same time, although all young market women alike scorned the pregnant girl, they also scolded the popular committee for infringing on their privacy. They maintained that it is not fair that they should be so closely controlled. I was therefore surprised by their reactions when I asked them about what they thought of the new dress codes that had been advertised by amplifier and public religious meetings by the public commitees.

All market women subscribed to the idea that women should dress modestly, in the sense that they should 'wear long'. Surprisingly enough, like Hauwa, most young women denied knowing about the new rules. Further, both young and elderly market women either claimed they dressed according to the code, which I could see they did not, or had their reasons for not complying with it. Mahalla, an elderly market woman who traded only occasionally told me that she had heard about the demand of the government to dress more strictly but as an illiterate market woman she had not yet heard anything officially. In addition, young market women all had their reasons why they could or should not to comply with the demands of the popular committee. As Zamzam did:

If you have money, you can buy the dresses, but if you don't you can't. I didn't buy long dresses and a sharp. *I become deaf and it makes my head itchy.*

Now even if it is true that the women did not hear about the new rule, the other answers, that it costs too much, is uncomfortable, and that it cannot be forced upon them, are defensive to say the least. What is interesting about these answers is that no one really contests the demand of the 'new veiling' itself: it is the negative effects that were resisted. Because of their education, with at least some knowledge of *Qur'anic* texts, I expected them to argue against the allegations of sexual promiscuity. However, this did not occur, even not indirectly.

That single young women do not protest too much against the discourse on the appropriate conduct of women might be related to their internalization of the elite ideas on gender and behaviour. Still, to leave it at this might give the impression that the socialization of these girls in the small period of time they stayed at school or even at a boarding house had been complete and perfect, and that they were in fact cultural dopes or dupes. As if the elite ideas had become part of the self-image and were not questioned any more and as if they might not have held opinions which differed from those of their age group. The silence with respect to the discourse on their behaviour was certainly partly due to the fact that these women might have subscribed in general terms to the ideal-typical imagery of femininity put forward by an elite for which they have been virtual apprentices while at school. However, in order to understand their aloofness the relation with their economic, social or other interests has to be established. In other words, what do they gain from keeping silent; to what extent is this silence strategic?

The silence among market women concerning the dominant discourse relates to the way the government discourse depicts them; that they are not educated and therefore do not know how to behave. As one of the high district officers commented when I asked him what his justification was for taking the tea women off the market:

You know, Miss Catharina, sometimes I envy these women. Religiously they are acting wrongly and it is up to us to teach them right. But if they die they still go to heaven, because they did not know so they cannot account for what they did. And we, even when I commit just the tiniest offence to my religion, I am going to be held responsible.

Therefore, the silence of the market women might be a strategic feigning of ignorance. By taking the position of the victim, both of fate and of the local popular committee, and not talking back in terms of the weapons with which they are attacked, namely religion, they protect themselves and their activities. As long as they pretend to be ignorant, they might be harassed, but also excused.

Even Zamzam and Hauwa, both highly articulate and smart market women, who attended primary school, professed to not know anything about the veiling issue and came up with a white lie. Their criticism of the government policy concerned the decrees related to their jobs, not those on their status as an Islamic woman. However, Zamzam did formulate views in which she also criticized the same elite class, albeit indirectly, while demanding the right to trade as long as there were no sufficient means to provide for their families otherwise. Interestingly, the young unmarried market women would, even though they told me they liked to trade, never pointed at Zamzam, or Hauwa or Samiya as possible role models when they talked about their future. Instead women such as Sa'adiya were referred to. So how does the silence of the single market women relate to the position of Sa'adiya?

As we saw with Hauwa, all of the young market women became acquainted with marketing as young girls by selling food at school, learning the trade from one of their female relatives. Although all young market women saw their trade as a job, to perform everyday and to try to be good at, the single young market women did not consider it as a job for life. Most of them still perceived their activities at the market as 'helping out'. Like Hauwa, all of them started selling because they replaced or assisted one of their elderly female relatives, who were ill, tired or too old to keep up with going to the market every day. Taking over from a relative meant that they did not need much money to invest and in this respect their coming to the market was a relatively easy affair. 'Being ill' more often than not meant that the elderly women were tired of the tedious work on the market and had their younger relatives represent them almost infinitively.

The aspirations of the young market women to become a member of the elite became apparent when I asked the young women how they perceived their future. In their narratives they all referred to elite membership as the most desirable future identity. One option was to become a member of the elite by virtue of acquiring (more) education:

I went to the intermediary school in Nyala for one year only. And my father sent me a message to come back to help him. I like to finish intermediary school still, if I have an opportunity I will. If only there would be a madrassa *for us big women. Education is useful for people; it helps them and enlarges their ideas. It can even help them in the house, with the housework and to teach their children.*

Ighlas and Rana, two sisters, had successfully finished high school and wished to pursue university education. This, they claimed, was even the only reason why they sold on the market and was for them thus a temporary activity.

Rhoda, Rana, and Ighlas were no isolated cases. Many girls who replaced a female relative on the market claimed they would continue their education as soon as they would have enough money. The other option was becoming a member of the elite through marriage, which was often discussed. Rhoda formulated it in a way many of her colleagues were thinking about this issue: "I want him to be a wise and educated man. He has to like and help people and he should not drink". As Hauwa emphasized in her narrative, most single market women put more emphasis on the kind of treatment they expected of a possible future 'educated' husband, than on his possible wealth. A different lifestyle appealed to them but more emphasize was put on the fact that an educated man knows 'how to treat a wife well'. In other words, most market women wanted a show of respect and politeness their fathers did not give their mothers, or their first husbands did not give them.

The fact that the single market women were selling at the market left their chances to marry an educated man rather small. The eagerness to get more education was seen both as a possibility to get a better job, as in the case of Rana and Ighlas, and as a means to get an educated husband, as in the case of Rhoda. These were the options open for them to live the life of an educated woman or at least to have an elite lifestyle and receive respect accordingly. These single young market women did not feel they really 'belonged' to the group in which they were placed by public opinion. They occupied the border zone in a state of 'liminality' in which nothing is worked out definitely yet as to their future social-economic status. It is this liminality, the fact that they felt they fit none of the subject-positions offered by the dominant discourse, which made them keep silent. The women did not feel they were defending their own rights *as* market women. They were active in trading not *being* traders, although they were indignant about the negative evaluation of their job and suggestions about their conduct as individuals. In the end, they wanted to become part of the same group that despised them.

Being too articulate; in other words, standing up against the elite to defend one's rights, might have made a girl too conspicuous. She might have become a target for the government since she was unmarried and they might have prevented her from selling at the market. At the same time this would jeopardize her chances to marry a member of that same elite at a future date. Although this might not have been as conscious as this analysis suggests, these girls were trained to comply with, and trying to attain, elite moral standards. Moreover, in terms of resistance and access to the discourse the odds were against the so-called 'local', 'non-educated' women anyway. These educated young women were the first to know that from experience: better to keep a low profile, to keep silent and bide your time.

However, education in itself is not enough to attain an elite status: a white collar, or white *tobe* job is necessary to make a woman a member of that class. Sa'adiya has reached that status, Hauwa, her sister, did not. All the young market women I spoke with had a sister or cousin who had made it into the government service, mostly as a teacher, who were predominantly teaching in another town or village in Darfur. Like Hauwa and Sa'adiya, they had had the same possibilities when they went to primary school and now their lives differed qualitatively. Whether due to capacities or (bad) luck, the result is that class boundaries run right through families. This meant that some of the young women might end up in the elite class as colleagues, whether directly after finishing school, like Sa'adiya or with a break to earn enough money on the market to allow for a continuation of education, as might be the case for Ighlas, Rana or Nura.

Therefore, the boundary between a disreputable girl and a respected woman might not only cut through families, but even through the lifetime of a single woman. The presence of educated women selling at the market deconstructs the category of the market woman as illiterate and thus non-acknowledgeable about religious issues. The centrality of education in constructing an elite status allows for upward mobility and inclusion of women from non-elite families into the elite class. As a consequence the liminal position of young educated women also problematizes the position of educated elite women. This means that some of these women do cross the boundaries, to arrive at border zone of the young female teachers.

The Boarding House as Border Zone: The Predicament of Single Female Teachers

The single female teachers who lived at the boarding house were another group of women whose presence challenged the boundaries between elite and non-elite women. As I concluded in Chapter 2, single female teachers who had the option to stay with family or friends preferred the boarding house. However, at the same time, this living arrangement of female teachers constituted a deviation from the expected and prescribed way of living from the perspective of the dominant moral discourse of the government as well as of the elite to which they belong. The two possible positions for women as put forward by the discourse were that of wife and mother. For single female teachers the *hadith*, 'There are three places for a woman: in her father's house, in her husbands house, or in her grave', gave them the possibility to stay single and live in their father's house, or by extension in the house of a relative. Single female teachers living removed from their families at a boarding house therefore seemed to embody the paradox of their class: girls needed to be taught how to be good Muslims and good women by other women. Yet Kebkabiya needed qualified female teachers from 'outside' because there was a shortage of them in the town itself. Due to the posting policy of the government, single female teachers were the most mobile as well as occupying lower grades which made them eligible for being assigned to an outpost. The boarding house, however, is in itself a space of liminality, as I pointed out in Chapter 2: a marked place by which young single women in an 'unmarked' position are safeguarded. This liminality means, though, that there is the expectation that these women will eventually leave the boarding house and move on to another life cycle, another identity with another lifestyle. To what extent is the boarding house indeed a spatial aspect of the border zone?

The way in which single female teachers living at the boarding house were evaluated varied among different groups. In my talks with young market women, the group of female teachers living at the boarding house were often referred to as an example of proper conduct for female Muslims and the future to which they aspired. This was especially true for single market women, like Rana and Ighlas, who were seriously planning, and had the skills, for a future as educated women. Even married female teachers would with longing point out how ideal the situation in the boarding house was; not bothered by demanding relatives, dependent children or degrading husbands, they were seen as best able to live the image of the self-contained and self-assured working elite woman. Unlike their married colleagues, they were seen as having the time and the ability to devote themselves with all their concentration and intensity to their work and their colleagues. At the same time the negative attitude of the local Kebkabiya population, in general referred to as 'non-educated' was evident in the complaints by the female teachers themselves. The most important allegations to the address of the single female teachers were that they were arrogant, and prone to amorous liaisons with one, or even more, of the 'available' single educated elite man, from the army, police, teachers or development projects, often also 'strangers' to the town.

In Kebkabiya there were intermittently four to five female teachers staying at the boarding house, their ages ranging from eighteen to thirty-eight years old. All were teaching at the intermediary school for girls. For the young female teachers the future still held the promise of a change of position from liminality to marriage and motherhood. However, for those of a more advanced age their living in limbo seemed much overdue. One good example was Sitt Ashia, the head mistress of the intermediary school for girls. She shared both the status and the future expectations of her colleagues at the boarding house. At the same time her person defied the notion of the boarding house as liminal space/time location, since she was well in her thirties, single and not even yet engaged. Moreover, her job brought her frequently into contact with men, without a chaperone. Because of her visibility and her age she bore the brunt of the disapproval of the local population of the unmarried teachers. It is therefore interesting to see how Sitt Ashia positioned herself with reference to the dominant discourse by the government. Again the issue is to what extent her negotiations made her, and other single female teachers, part of the border zone from the perspective of the educated elite class.

Who's Afraid of the Single Female Teacher?

From the moment I met Sitt Ashia at the beginning of my first stay I was fascinated by her. Although she was their 'boss', she shared quarters with the other female teachers on a fairly equal basis. She did not claim special treatment with respect to lodging and chores, sharing duties and leisure, as well as thoughts and doubts with her colleagues. I met her often at her office, at the boarding house, or at one of the outings or social meetings the school or one of the other colleagues organised. We had many conversations and much in common, although at the same time I felt she was keeping her distance.

During my first fieldwork period Yasmin and I shared much of our leisure time with the single female teachers, either at the boarding house, or at the house Yasmin, Johan and I shared. At first I was very taken by the harmonious and almost carefree way these women shared their chores, their thoughts and fun. However, after several months, this image of solidarity became tarnished. Fadjur and Karima, two of the single female teachers, had been very close. They often would go visiting together, fulfil duties together, such as overlooking the girls at the boarding house, and when one of the beds broke, they even shared one bed for a while. Fadjur came from Al-Fasher, while Karima came from Jebel Marra, the heartland of the Fur. Despite the fact that Karima's father was a Fur Shartai in Jebel Marra, she was regarded as a local girl.

Then, one day, I realized that Karima had moved out of the boarding house, apparently to live with her aunt and cousin at one of the wards at the outskirts of the town. When I inquired about what happened, I learned that they had quarrelled, although I could not get a straight reason. Yasmin told me that Karima was jealous of Fadjur, while Fadjur just shrugged and said it was a silly misunderstanding. Only Sitt Ashia was very clear about the reason for the split up: she told me that Karima was a 'country girl' and could not understand the ways of townswomen. According to her opinion the breaking up had only been a matter of time: rural and urban women differed too much to become really close. I was not so much surprised by Sitt Ashia's comment, I knew she held strong opinions, but the acceptance of her opinion by the other female teachers, even by Yasmin, was surprising.

Some time later I had a talk with a member of the popular committee, who also worked at the education department at the District Council. He told me that the female teachers were also under close scrutiny of the government as some of them, especially single, female teachers were not behaving up to standard. One of them had even been detected in the market dealing with drivers and traders in a way inappropriate for educated women. He was thinking of a punishment, not only to 'teach' this particular teacher, but also in order to make the other single female teachers aware of the right conduct.

I knew he was referring to Maryoma, who was a high school graduate from Kebkabiya now teaching at the intermediary school for girls. The demand for teachers had been consistently high for outlying districts like Kebkabiya. Therefore, young high school graduates like Maryoma, who came back to town, were asked to teach the lower classes of intermediary schools after a short course. In the years I was living in Kebkabiya there were about four to five of these local untrained teachers who taught at the intermediary school for girls. They would get their didactic training later, at courses they could attend during their assignment. In this way they could circumvent the four year course for teachers at Bakht Al-Rhuda,[5] which would have meant expenses for travel and boarding which her family could not have afforded.

Her mother was a widow and because of the inflation Maryoma decided to buy *berseem*, a kind of clover, and sell it in bulk at a higher price. As I found out later, the fact that she engaged in trade was not unique: Sa'adiya, Yasmin and even Sitt Fatna did the same. The problem was that she engaged in negotiations *herself* with 'strange men' in a public place, for all to see thereby openly challenging the difference between the market women and female members of the educated class. Maryoma's conduct rendered her a 'country girl' in the eyes of her colleagues.

The ousting of Karima from the boarding house therefore might have had to do with keeping up the idea of a safe and morally high

[5] The first Teachers' Training College was based there (Griffiths 1975).

standard of the place where civilized single educated women could live in order to be able to fulfil their duty. Sitt Ashia herself was in jeopardy if this image of the boarding house would be smudged. Karima was a rural girl, and what ever the allegation might have been, sending her away might have been pragmatic rather than just.

It was not just this incident in which the rural/urban difference was at stake. After this incident I became increasingly aware of jokes and little hints at this difference thought between the single female teachers: for example Sitt Ashia was frequently referred to as '*awlad ar-rif*' with hilarious laughter following. At first I could not grasp it: translated it meant 'people from the countryside', I was told.[6] I talked to Sitt Ashia often, seated in her office drinking tea, or at the boarding house after school hours. I taped several sessions with her during which I felt she was actively constructing an image of herself she wanted the 'world' to have of her. In our conversations, there were two aspects, which were predominant in her stories: to construct a difference with other women and the issue of marriage. As she brought up the issues together, she obviously felt they were related. To Sitt Ashia, education was presented not just as a personal feat, but also as part of her ancestry. She even sent me to her father in Al-Fasher because he was one 'of the first educated men in Darfur', implying that education ran in the family.

My father also studied at the intermediary school, which was then called 'wusta', *and he wanted to become a teacher, but he liked trading and he became a trader. And this made our life different from other families in Darfur: my father was an educated and very wise man. He understood things and was broadminded. He gave us our freedom. We grew up without knowing the difference between boys and girls: he treated us the same. So boys in our family can wash, clean, go to the market, mill and bring water… Most people forbade their daughters to go out in the street or to visit their friends, but this is not the case in our family. Like me, if I want to travel from here to London I am free, because my father and mother trust me. The whole family trusts me; it is not a problem.*

Here she subtly relates her father's educational background to the broadmindedness of her father towards gender difference, and thus the freedom she had as a girl. To what extent her reference to the 'equal' treatment of boys and girls is related to the ideas of Yasmin or me is

---

[6] 'Rif' might refer to the Rif-mountains in Morocco to where Sitt Ashia traced her genealogy.

not clear to me, but the point she wants to make the more so: she is different from other 'daughters', like Umm Khalthoum or Sa'adiya, for she is trusted and free to go wherever she wants due to the broadmindedness of her family. Apparently this issue is of great importance to her, for every time I talked to her she would refer to this 'fact':

And also my father has just one wife, my mother. It is therefore a good life without many difficulties or problems. There might be questions from you like why I am not yet married while I am already thirty-three years old. I didn't marry yet and I am the oldest in my family now unmarried. My eldest and younger brothers and sisters are all married except for my youngest brother and me. If I don't find a good man, the best possible husband, I still don't want to marry, even now. But if I find a good one I will marry. My mother as well: her parents did not interfere in her marriage choice. My mother is also very broadminded, she learned this from her family, Egyptian broadmindedness. Her father was at that time head of the army, pasha. *My father was not Egyptian; he came from Morocco. He came to Egypt with his family and* auwlad ar-rif *people are famous for their freedom, in all of Fasher. They did not control their daughters or make any problems, but even so, their daughters are very polite and modest and behave properly.*

In this part she brought up another of her 'themes', subtly putting a question into my mouth as to her single status. My positioning in her story made me realize that she was aware her narrative would become part of my academic project and thus she turned the tables: she controlled her narrative as a project she had with me. The way she structured her story and phrased her thoughts indicated that what I got to see from her was her social persona, a construction of herself as a headmistress, belonging to a class of high standards, a 'model family'. At the same time she had to deal with her single status, a possible flaw and potential liability, for someone who wanted to construct herself as a 'model' woman. But she tried to turn this flaw into an asset since she was raised in an exceptionally broadminded and educated family, whose daughters were nevertheless 'very polite and modest and behave properly'. And it also dawned on me, that *awlad ar-rif* does not refer to a rural identity, on the contrary, in this context it indicated her Egyptian/Fasher background, an indication of an elevated 'real' urban status.

In her narrative the suggested broadmindedness is at the basis of her seemingly relaxed attitude towards marriage. She is quite explicit about the fact that this situation is due to a combination of fate and choice.

And she can act like this because her family not only condones her, but also *supports* her in this. This means that she is behaving like a dutiful daughter according to the attitude of women in her family. She is not different in the sense that she is rebelling against her family, because she is just being 'like her mother'. She is different from her colleagues in the way she is treated by her family. As she told me on several occasions, the people of Kebkabiya cannot understand this:

But the community does not understand that as a headmistress it is part of your job to do these things. They think that even when a woman is a leader, she should talk to men in a restrained way. They think it is wrong to sit or to talk with men. This community is very backward and uneducated, especially Kebkabiyan women. Because they learned from their mothers that it is not polite to talk to men, except to your husband. They know I have reached this age while I didn't marry and I stop in the street to talk to this man and in the offices to another, and contact them for all kinds of matters and they think it is scandal. I didn't take it seriously; I did not feel offended. I treat them as if they do understand. If I am in a small community it means you have to know how to treat them and how to communicate with them. Kebkabiya has always been behind in education.

Here she creates an opposition between her broadminded family and the narrow-minded Kebkabiya population, which makes it almost an offence to even ask her about her single status. So if I had the intention to inquire about her single status in a negative way, she has already forestalled this by constructing a dichotomy, which puts her into a positive light. At the same time she displays her own broadmindedness with reference to the same people who scorn her. She even constructs this attitude as part of her position as a teacher at the same time putting words into my mouth, again controlling the conversation:

It is our duty to teach in every town in Sudan, in Fasher, Geneina, I even taught in Halfa. I came to Kebkabiya because of my new grade. So this might be the last year for me in Kebkabiya. It is also a nice and good place. But I have my family in Fasher, my father and my mother, and they are getting old and I want to look after them. And now you are going to ask me: 'If you marry what are you going to do?' This depends on the man I am going to marry. But I hope he will be from Fasher. And in Al-Fasher I even hope he will come from Auwlad ar-rif.

In this part she again is not so much a selective, unwilling bride-to-be but, rather, a dutiful and patient daughter who hopes her marriage will allow her to stay near her parents. She is all one might hope for in a daughter. Interestingly, she here puts her fate into the hands of her husband-to-be. I wonder about this resigned attitude and ask her how she feels about marriage:

These days I hope to marry, if I find a suitable and interesting man. And I will be a very lucky woman if I find a good and educated man who is not suspicious. I will be happy if I find one. This does not mean that I only like people who finished university or who have a high job, no. It is important to be educated and have knowledge, but it is not important what job he has, or if he is studying in university. The one I want has to have finished high secondary school. If he is working in the government it is not bad. He should be a model man, an example of someone to keep up a good married life. Because I am employee and working for the government I have a lot of friends and colleagues and they might visit me in the house and this needs a broadminded husband. Not to let people interfere in our life. I have my own ideas about marriage in my mind. I hope to find one with these qualities.

At the beginning of this reflection Sitt Ashia is still the dutiful daughter but she more and more has her demands of a good husband: suitable, meaning, well-enough educated and not-suspicious: he should be a model man. And that basically means that he also has to be broad-minded enough to have her have the life she has now. To have friends to visit her, without letting 'people interfere in our life', whoever those 'people' might be. Then she ends definitely in charge stating explicitly that she has her own ideas about marriage. By repeating the last sentence she emphasizes that such a man is not easily to be found, which makes her unmarried state legitimate. I ask her if she knows such a man and she surprisingly tells me about an engagement some ten years earlier:

First they chose a husband for me in 1979. They arranged the engagement, but I did not agree with it. He came to my father and my father also did not like him. But because his father was a gentleman, a noble man, and he was our neighbour, so my father agreed. We spent a lot of years engaged but then I broke off the engagement. Until now a lot of men come to me and ask me to marry them, but until now I did not find the right one. I don't want to love a man before marriage: only after marriage that can come. I want the well-educated man with a clear mind, who is civilized and broadminded. I don't want a man who says: 'Hey you, you can't go out of the house, you are a woman and you should stay in the house and not go out for work'. I like my freedom, to do as I decide. We should trust each other.

Also in this case she tries to balance her position as dutiful daughter against following her own wishes and having her own ideas of a suitable man which she quite explicitly states towards the end of this quote. She wants to work, freedom, decision making and taking power and this means he has to trust her. However, there is a curious reference to the issue of love in between these two parts. It is meaningful that it forms the bridge between the dutiful daughter and the working woman who has her ideas about marriage: it follows an almost imperceptible reference to the fact that she did have many suitors, in other words she is attractive enough as a marriage partner, but she just did not find the right one. Neither her choice nor her denouncing of the offers to marry is based on something fleeting like love; it is only related to the kind of man 'on offer' and to fulfil her duty to work, even after marriage.

During our first stay in Kebkabiya, our house, especially in those periods that Yasmin actually lived with us, became an often-frequented meeting place for the educated elite men and women. I realize now that it was the perfect middle ground and alibi to meet prospective marriage candidates in a more or less controlled, chaperoned environment. During that period Sitt Ashia got acquainted with a project member whom she liked and who also seemed interested in her while Fadjur got the attention of one of the higher army officers. For quite a while a kind of silent courtship took place, with amongst others Yasmin as go between, for she knew all of them quite well.

Eventually the engagement between Sitt Ashia and her suitor was not coming through. As the courting had taken place in all discretion, there were not many people involved and there was hardly any gossiping. Yasmin told me later that the couple had gone quite far in arranging meetings between their families, but that the mother of the bridegroom had objected to his choice: she rather had him marrying his cousin as had been arranged years before. In the end he consented. When I spoke to Sitt Ashia after this event about her ideas on marriage, she said the following:

If you are working, it is better to be married as well. Like me, when I came to Kebkabiya I wished that I was married. Then you can solve the problems of this courting and stop all these men who visit you and ask you to marry them. Many people came to me asking me to marry them and they differ in attitude: some are good, some are polite, and some are not satisfied quickly. If you are married they will treat you as if you are a different person. Because if a man comes to visit you he realizes that he is visiting a married woman. Like some men now sit on your chairs while you are behind your desk and they will talk for hours and waste your time, so you can't work.

Although this is the first time Sitt Ashia indicates that she would have liked to be married, the reason is pragmatic and, again, related to her work. Yet, while Sitt Ashia discussed her broken-off engagement she seemed quite resigned to the ending of her relationship, even somewhat relieved.

Other single female teachers shared Sitt Ashia's reflections on the 'right' man. The issue of a prospective husband came up during many of the discussions the female teachers had about their future and about marriage. Even the local women's organization problematized the fact that many single women had troubles to marry. In their view the high bride prices were the reason. The local women's organization 'Tadaman'[7] decided that as soon as the ban on organizations would be lifted they would campaign for lower bride prices especially for educated women in order to facilitate their marriages. However, in the discussions this was not mentioned as the main obstacle to marriage. Rather the female teachers discussed the issue of love of which they proved ambiguous. All at one time expressed the hope for a marriage out of love while acknowledging it would be difficult to find someone in this way. When I inquired about this 'love business' as it was referred to, it turned out that they were set to find a respectful, educated and 'broadminded' man, just like Sitt Ashia had stated, who would rather not be a relative.

Apparently, the single female teachers, but also Yasmin, have been successful in resisting the pressure to marry, even though they were far into their twenties and even their thirties. Their negotiations of their single status were similar to those of Sitt Ashia. They said they were more than willing to marry, if and when the 'right' husband would come along. The similarity in wording and ways of arguing their single status in the reference to the 'good' husband who 'has not yet been found' might be part of a discursive strategy. This made it possible to act different from the way that was expected within the dominant discourse while referring to a cause legitimated by or within that same dominant discourse.

---

[7] The Tadaman (meaning 'solidarity') women's organization was not functioning during my stay in Kebkabiya due to the ban on all organizations other than those founded by the Islamist government.

With her narrative Sitt Ashia tried to legitimate her choices and her position both as a respected school director and as a single woman in the context of the current discourse on femininity. Her visibility and position as a headmistress meant she had to legitimate her single status while not denying or contesting the government's discourse on gender but rather to place herself within that discourse. She even constructed herself as a 'model' of her class although her single status seemed to defy the discourse. The question is, to what extent the negotiation of the discourse by Sitt Ashia and other 'mature' single female teachers meant that they took up a temporary liminal position or constructed a more permanent alternative identity in the border zone?

From Liminality to Border Zone: Avenues for Change?

In this chapter I have looked at the reflections and actions of working women, who in their negotiations of the discourse on gender, appeared to question and stretch, threaten and overcome, confirm and mould the boundaries between the elite class of female teachers and the low class of market women. The main markers of this difference, education and work, indeed proved to be also the main markers of the diversity within both classes. Illiterate market women were not just that. The compulsory education for girls resulted in a new generation of young market women who again were divided according to marital status, which influenced their attitude towards marketing and the future. However, in both cases their strategies in reflection of and with reference to the dominant discourse of gender, and its facilitators, the government officials, were similar. To keep aloof, in pretending not to know about the decrees concerning their demeanour. And to keep silent, not protesting, not even indirectly, to the actions of the same government officials who removed tea women, often their sisters, daughters, cousins or at least friends, from the market. And thus not to spoil their chances for a better future. This even was true for Zamzam. Although she had protested openly when she was removed from the market as a tea woman, she also did not want to jeopardize the possibility to explore new trading venues, for which stamps and permits from the government were needed. Single market women were not just in the border zone of their class but aspired a position in the class of the educated elite and therefore did not yet 'belong' in either: they were in a 'state of liminality'.

The chances for those young market women to become member of the educated elite are dim, but there are examples in their vicinity, even within their own families, of women like Sa'adiya who made it into a white-collar job. They served as a role model, which made some young girls, like Rana, quite determined to pursue education. If she makes it, she might be posted as a teacher in a town other than Kebkabiya and live in a boarding house for teachers, like Sitt Ashia, Fadjur, and more particularly like Karima.

The boarding house on the one hand gives all the single female teachers a comparable status as educated women and brides-to-be. This status, which is fragile and expected to change in the near future, will be marked by a change of locality. This is why the position of a single female teacher living in the boarding house is both liminal and contingent. A female teacher might get sent away due to 'misconduct' as we saw in the case of Karima. This is a device to safeguard the boarding house as a space of protection. Single female teachers are expected to marry and then move out automatically. That quite a few of the unmarried teachers were far into their thirties questions this assumption and thus the liminality of their in-between position.

The boarding house was not the only location, which defined the status and position of its frequenters: so did the market place. Not only were girls who threatened the already contested moral nature of the market place expelled. Maryoma, the single female teacher who traded on the market place was chastised precisely because she traded openly and in person on the public and 'strange' environment of the market. I experienced myself the change in status and respect this situadedness might trigger when I was once sitting behind a selling table talking to Arowa. She had returned from Khartoum, visiting her mother in Kebkabiya because of *Eed*. In Khartoum she held a high salaried position at one of the Ministries, but because of Ramadan she decided to take care of the stall of her elderly mother who then could take a rest. One of the single government officials who had always been very courteous to me, came up to us, and addressed us as '*chicks*', also in Sudanese Arabic a term for 'sexually enticing woman'. He went on asking us to come to his place that evening. Arowa and I were surprised and indignant at the same time. 'How dare he speak to us like that'! 'And', I wondered, 'why did he think we would accept his invitation? How could he think we could respect him after having been address in such a degrading way'?

The answer is both simple and complicated. *We* were sitting in the open, *we* thereby took the position of lower class market women, and in doing so *we* facilitated this way of addressing. Both the context, in which we were meeting, and the emphasis of the government discourse on market women, legitimated his behaviour. This means that by switching contexts, we switched position and status. So when sticking to one's location, and appropriate behaviour within that location, in dressing code and demeanour, a woman would be addressed accordingly.

In deciding to what extent these women indeed are in the border zone or just in limbo, the extent of their agency in the sense of the influence of their negotiations of the dominant discourse has to be established. The negotiations, as I indicated above, are not a goal in itself. In all cases they are to be seen as strategies to claim agency and to create space for pursuing their own interests: their well-being and that of their close ones. Agency in this case is thus not a self-evident given or a 'thing' in itself which women can or cannot reach at. Women try to construct their own agency, as persons who are members of their society and of different social groups, in being and becoming those members, in doing and acting as social beings surviving in the context which they share and in which they stand divided. They react or negate the decrees of the government while they differ in the ways they keep silent and talk; but they all relate to, reflect on and negotiate the dominant moral discourse and the structural boundaries it constructs as self-evident. All women, and men for that matter, are continuously engaged in defining en redefining their identities and the constructions of these multiple identities.

Each group of young educated women, whether market women or female teachers, seemed to constitute a diversion, or question mark as to the fixedness of the boundaries. Each group of the young generation of their class negotiated the boundary between themselves and the other class in different ways and from different localities. As long as the space of liminality for both is temporary, their position in the border zone is also intermediate and not structural: the women are therefore defined by the location in which they act out their identity, rather than 'having' a fixed identity.[8] In that case, the young working women in this border zone do not really pose a threat to the dominant discourse in itself. However, when these border zone positions become strategies

[8] See Nencel (1997) for the concept of 'gendered enclosures' to think through the situatedness of identity constructions.

for alternative positioning on a more permanent basis this might lead to a transformation of that discourse. The effect of these alternative positions depends also on the access to the discourse of which they now take up a border zone and the way these influence the relations of rule. The alternative positions of female traders and female teachers might create new role models and lead to a transformation of the image of their class positions and thus to the dominant discourse which allots these subject positions. At the same time these alternative positions might lead to their isolation from other members of their society and ultimately to either fame or failure within their class and might not challenge the boundaries as such.

From the perspective of the dominant discourse, however, the alternative positioning by educated elite women seems more threatening to its boundaries than those of female traders venturing into new types of trade. Their negotiations come from within the class, which seems to have most stakes in preserving the status quo: the government elite. Their relations to ruling makes their alternative perspective on femininity less easy to ignore as elite women working for the government are supposed to share and disseminate the elite moral discourse on gender, instead of challenging it from within.

However, I can not understand the force of this alternative positioning just by looking at the construction of femininities as I have done up till now, by focusing on the negotiations by working women with respect to the Islamist discourse on gender. Though I scrutinized the moral discourse by looking at the reflections of these women on that discourse, I have done so in terms of that same discourse. Taking femininity and women's strategies as my focal point I have contested and unravelled the stereotypes as put forward by the discourse, and the discursive strategies, images and subject-positions by working women which are related to these; but not the discourse itself. I took the boundaries of the discourse as point of departure by singling out femininity and leaving untouched the issue of masculinity. In fact I thereby 'stepped' into the dominant discourse on women and Islam as it is constructed both in the West and in the Sudan, unwillingly collaborating in leaving unaddressed a major silence. In order to deconstruct this silence I have to look for a subtext, for a hidden script, which seems to be related to the 'hidden' husband, or rather, husband-to-be. '*Cherchez l'homme*' will therefore be the goal of Chapter 7.

Epilogue—Sa'adiya Straddling the Border Zone

Although I enjoyed working with her and had come to regard her as a friend, I knew little of Sa'adiya's biography while we worked on those of others. I knew she had two daughters and her baby son to take care of, while her husband Jacub was only intermittently at home as he traded in other places. She was good-humored, with a quick mind and eagerness to participate, and her demeanor towards those whom we spoke with, elite or not, was always respectful. The young market women often singled her out as a role model. Interestingly, while as a teacher and a colleague she had a high status among her single and married colleagues, in the eyes of the single female teachers her position was symptomatic of the problems they believed a marriage might give them. As Sa'adiya virtually taped her biographic narrative herself, controlling the buttons on the tape-recorder often with, but sometimes without me around, I only realized when I was back home that she also belonged to the border zone. Despite the fact that during our talks Umm Khalthoum and Sa'adiya were of the opinion that their current lives were quite similar and Sa'adiya would point out the differences between herself as an educated woman and her non-educated relatives:

You know, Karin, they think that women in towns spend a lot of money. And when they come and see my furniture in the house they think that Jacub bought all these things. They never believe I bought these myself.

Only now I realize that she hardly reflected on her relationship with her husband Jacub, and if so, she would do that in positive terms, telling me that Jacub is good father and a friendly man. He took even care of their first-born baby while she attended a teaching course. But obviously he was not of much help in attaining an elite life-style. So when Sa'adiya continued on the subject of differences between educated and non-educated, she caught me by surprise when stating:

The educated woman, she knows how to obey the right words of her husband, if he is right. And where to guide him if he takes a wrong turn. So some men think that educated women do not obey their husbands, because they want a wife to obey orders. Whether it are right or wrong orders. Because an un-educated woman does not know what is right and what is wrong because she did not learn at school or a comparable place of education. So some men like to marry an educated and some an uneducated woman. Sometimes uneducated women stay at home to take care of the house and children and to receive his guests. They think that they are more taking care of their households.

Obeying your husband 'if he is right'? 'Guiding' your husband? 'Right and wrong orders'? 'Preference for uneducated women'? This really did not sound like anything the other female teachers had told me, neither in content nor in phrasing. Although Sa'adiya stated this in general terms, her reference to the relationship between husband and wife sounds like something that kept Sa'adiya personally occupied. Sa'adiya then told me that they had lived separately:

I have been living on my own for some time, you see, when Jacub was in Iraq. He went there because I hated him, after the birth of my second daughter. I told him: 'I don't want to stay with you because you drink, it is enough like this'. People from both our families came to talk to us…

This was in 1988 when Sa'adiya filed for a divorce in Al-Fasher:

And then the judge asked me: 'Why don't want to stay with him, this man, when you have children with him? We do not want a woman with children to be without a husband'. And I replied: 'He is drinking alcohol and he lost his money and he does not want to abstain from drinks'. And then he asked Jacub about his house, how it is furnished. 'Does it have a bathroom and toilet and a cooking place and a bedroom'? And he asked Jacub the names of the neighbours, to act as witnesses for this description of the house. Then the judge told Jacub to stop drinking because it is no use having a husband in jail. He told to me: 'Now I am speaking like your brother, and I will advise you like a friend. Before I apply the rules of the law, those laws do not forgive if someone is guilty. So it is better to go back to your house and to discuss the problem with your family, and his family. If you fail to solve it, you can come back to me'.

Although the issue went unresolved, Jacub left for Iraq and Sa'adiya went to live on the compound of her father with her half-sister Hauwa, the market woman we met earlier in this chapter. When Jacub returned in 1989, Sa'adiya went to live with him again, though he went on drinking. Sa'adiya however seems resigned to her fate of being married to him.

Although Sa'adiya does not articulate this in her narrative, the crux seems to be the difference in class, not just between her and her non-educated relatives, but even her husband. This is probably why she elaborates on the ruling of the judge who implicitly refers to this class difference when he questions Jacub for the way he has constructed and furnished their house, suggesting it should be up to elite standards. He then turns to Sa'adiya to speak to her as a 'brother', and advise her as a 'friend'. Rather than punishing the defendant for his alcohol abuse and neglect of his family, and grant the divorce, the judge warns a co-member of his own class not to get involved in a divorce case. Not only because it might 'harm the children', but it may damage Sa'adiya's status as well, and, by extension, the esteem of the elite class. As is clear from this incident, the class position of the complainant influences the ruling of the judge, in this case according to his idea of social standing and mores for an elite woman.

When we discussed this issue, Sa'adiya revealed that apart from taking care of her husband's task of furnishing the house according to elite standards, she also facilitated the education of Jacub's children by his first wife, her younger half-siblings, apart from her own children. When I asked her about being the second wife, she gave me a quite detailed account of the way her father had betrothed her to Jacub against her will, just as Umm Khalthoum's father had. Only after her marriage did she find out that Jacub was already married to a woman from his native village. This is yet another aspect of their marriage that Sa'adiya did not refer to as a good cause for 'proving' Jacub's misbehavior and her right to a divorce, while he is disrupting her life and reputation as a teacher. I realize that this is precisely the dilemma Sa'adiya faced when I asked her how she felt about her married life and to my surprise she answered:

I felt very good, because you are free, to do what you want, nobody is quarreling with you or making problems, or tells you what to do. It is very comfortable. You can decide what you want whether to visit friends or to invite them in your house.

Contrary to what I expected, that she would lament the *state* her marriage is in, she points out the positive sides of her *status* as a married woman. It might be that Sa'adiya wants to keep her problems quiet so her bad marriage will not damage her status as a female teacher. So far, none of her colleagues seemed to be aware of her problems. Like Umm Khalthoum, Sa'adiya must have felt that a divorce might reflect negatively on her status as an elite woman, as the judge clearly pointed out.

Sa'adiya chose a different solution to a problem that seems similar to that of Umm Khalthoum. At the same time she finds a solution to her predicament comparable to so many of the local women around her. By taking care of the tasks that should have been taken on by her husband, Sa'adiya in fact positions herself partly in the local discourse on gender, which stipulates that mothers are to quite literally take care of their children, also in the case where the husband is absent or unwilling to provide his share.

It is Sa'adiya's predicament that she, unlike her married colleagues, has to cope with the difference, the divide between educated and non-educated within her own household, with respect to her own husband, her own and his relatives, in her everyday life. Sa'adiya is thus continuously negotiating the thin line between her position as a member of the elite and as a member of a local Fur family. She is one of the first women in Kebkabiya who attained an elite status on her own account and not as a derivative status as daughter, sister or wife of a male elite member. Therefore, she feminized the acquisition of elite membership as an outsider. She has acquired this status through hard work and will continue to do so to keep that position. In the case of women like Sa'adiya this not only meant a change in taste or attitude, but a radical different perception of the self. Not only did girls like Sa'adiya learn new norms on behaviour, speech, lifestyle and dress code but she also experienced a completely different 'coming of age' than her female relatives. Attending secondary high school had prevented Sa'adiya from getting married at the same age as her mother, her aunts, and even some of her (half) sisters did, namely after her first menstruation. She and her contemporaries thus not only acquired a new lifestyle, but also a new life cycle, with an added age grade: adolescence.[9]

Sa'adiya shared with her educated colleagues a knowledge horizon and expectation of life which extended far beyond the physical aspects of that experience. The class of elite members consisted mostly of people who were unknown to the individual members such as Sa'adiya, and were therefore part of an imagined community. As we can read from Sa'adiya's answer when I asked her how she felt about her job:

Teaching is good because it is not only about money. It is also about acquiring 'ilm *and* ajr. *And I can learn more about other people and customs and make new friends. Like if non-educated people talk about Britain, they do not know exactly where it is or what. If you say you come from 'Holanda', they think 'London',*

[9] See Kerkhoff (1998) who analyzed a similar process among young women in colonial India.

because they heard about it on the radio, but they do not know what the difference is. I can know things about countries and people I have never seen myself. And also if I travel myself and I arrive somewhere where I do not know anyone, I can always make myself known to teachers who are living or working there and in they may treat you as a guest.

Sa'adiya's solution to the predicament she is in, with two classes 'on one pillow', is typical of the way she deals with her other non-elite relatives. Sa'adiya is taking care of it herself, doing it all on her own, keeping up appearances as both a class and an individual endeavor. Simultaneously, this freedom of decision-making and taking power elates her and makes her feel good about her married status, for it gives her the freedom to do as she wants and to invite who she likes. It allows her to be autonomous with regard to her family members and to live up to the standards and expectations of the newly acquired elite class.

This managing of boundaries between the two networks means Sa'adiya has to keep both groups apart in time and place as a routine daily practice. In this she differs from her married colleagues whose relatives do not live in Kebkabiya, like for example Sitt Khadija, which calls for a different attitude as well, as Sa'adiya articulates:

I always try to let people know each other. Teachers should know more about uneducated women. In their turn non-educated women can join teachers to hear about their problems and help each other so they can feel that they are the same, that teachers are not so different from them. But many women say that educated women look down upon others. So they said, 'Some of your colleagues are not like you, they are not good teachers'.

Sa'adiya might be located in the 'border zone' between the two classes and she resolves a possible ambivalence about her position by openly asserting the multiplicity of her identities and she constructs herself as an intermediary with stakes in both classes. However, Sa'adiya did not question the boundaries of the elite class as such, though in her daily life she regularly had to deal with its permeability. On the contrary, she preserved the idea of fixed boundaries. Therefore, she barely touched upon an aspect, which is crucial in maintaining this illusionary divide. Sa'adiya needed her female non-elite relatives, not only in order to be able to combine her job with her household cores, but also in order to cope with her husband and her home situation. When I asked her why she would still keep her relations with her female kin, she said:

Your colleagues, they will go, and they stay your friends, but you might not see them for a while or ever again. Your kin, ah, they will always be there to help you when you need them.

Although relatives are a nuisance to be kept apart from colleagues and one's assets, they can also be a source of help in times of need. Different from Umm Khalthoum and Sitt Khadija, she can make claims to the help of her female kin. How generalized this kind of reciprocity was, I learned at the end of my stay, when Sa'adiya's lodged her maternal aunt who wanted to trade some bags of grain for some weeks. In exchange Sa'adiya received seeds for herself to plant, with the help of some of her female relatives during the summer holidays, when no colleagues would be around. Despite her dependence on her relatives, Sa'adiya never left any doubt as to which class she felt she belonged. Not only in lifestyle and job, but also in the way she perceived herself as a social person, as part of a, partly imagined, community of people with the same ideas, hopes and goals: the female teachers. So if she straddled the divide between both classes, the stirrups are definitely at the side of the educated elite class.

CHAPTER 7

THE BURDEN OF BOUNDARIES: MASCULINITIES, FEMININITIES AND THE MORAL DISCOURSE

> Thousands of Sudanese have participated in mass marriages since their introduction by the government not long after the 1989 coup that brought President Omar Hassan El-Beshir to power. The move came at the behest of the National Islamic Front, which forms the backbone of the government. General El-Beshir himself officiates at most of the state-sponsored weddings, which he describes as an important step in the drive to increase the population of Africa's largest country: Sudan has an area of just over 2.5 million square kilometres for a population estimated of about 29 million.
>
> (Bol, 1996: 2)[1]

This quotation, taken from an article by the Sudanese journalist Nhial Bol (1996), indicates that the so-called 'marriage problem' was taken up as a national issue by the Islamist government.[2] One of the most conspicuous ways of stimulating single Sudanese to marry was by launching the so-called *zowag al-kora*[3] or 'mass-weddings'. Large numbers of couples were married at the same time during a ceremony organized and orchestrated by the government. From the perspective of the government, the bride price was one of the main reasons, which prohibited especially young professionals to get married since an educated woman required a high bride price. Thus the government tried to alleviate this problem by sponsoring the weddings: it donated part of the dowry (beds, furniture, pots and pans), and the bride price (up to 10.000 £S).

---

[1] This excerpt and others in this paragraph were presumably in Arabic. I quote them from an article by Bol (1996: 2) written in English (Nhial Bol "*Managing Their Lives for Them*", IPS, published on the Internet 20-9-1996—SudanList@emuv1.id/1.7f.—subject 'official marriages': accessed 2-9-1997.

[2] Parts of chapter 7 appeared as "On Globalization, Gender and the Nation-State. Muslim Masculinity and the Urban Middle-Class Family in Islamist Sudan", in: *The Gender Question in Globalization. Changing Perspectives and Practices*, edited by Tine Davids and Francien van Driel. Burlington USA: Ashgate Publishers. (2005): 159–179.

[3] Literally this means 'putting all the people in a bowl and marrying them' (cf. Hale 1997: 208).

In the case of high government officials, they were offered a plot of land to build a house on as well.[4]

The weddings were broadcast in order to advertise the government-subsidized marriages. As this proved insufficient to attract the desired number of couples, the possibilities to facilitate marriages were brought to the attention of young unmarried professionals working in the bureaucracy or (para-) statal organizations by circulars.[5] One such circular addressed employees of the Sudan broadcasting station. It opened with an encouragement by El-Tayeb Mustafa, the Director General:[6]

> Dear brothers, sisters and colleagues, on behalf of the [Sudan TV] trade union and board of directors, I call upon all staffers to make up their minds and get married… Those interested will apply within three months… with incentives for those who do so. They will be married en masse at a ceremony organized and financed by the institution. We would like to assure those who will join this blessed occasion, even by marrying for the second time, that they will receive considerable assistance that will help, Allah willing, in their future life…Allah has blessed marriage and in Islam marriage is considered the completion of the second half of the Muslim faith… The prophet said: 'The worst among Muslims, if any, are those yet unmarried'. Islam also calls on us to marry and have children in order to populate the earth with good citizens.

As is to be expected the advice to marry within the following three months is legitimated with reference to religious credos and *hadith*. In the media and religious addresses, marriage was cast as the duty of a good Muslim. In order to attain a society of 'good citizens', men and women who were single, needed to marry and procreate. The 'right' subject positions for women and men were thus to be wives and mothers, husbands and fathers.

---

[4] Hale (1997: 193) comes with a different perspective: that it was predominantly the poor who were targeted by these mass wedding ceremonies. I think the poor were those who might have made most use of it, but that the government was in particular addressing its 'own' employees. This will become clear when I discuss the article of Bol. See also Gruenbaum (1992: 29–32).

[5] As Umm Khalthoum indicated, an additional problem especially for highly educated women and men might be the fact that they are exposed on television since the mass-weddings are broadcast live. Most people I discussed the phenomenon with were therefore not surprised the project was not a success, since it would expose one's family not being able or prepared to pay for wedding expenses.

[6] It concerns comments on a circular of Sudan TV directed at the 170 unmarried employees of 204 of the Sudan broadcasting station. See for example the religious speeches party quoted in Chapter 1.

The question that arises however is why a government would want to invest in weddings while it already has huge financial problems as it is. Why focus on such a social issue, when it has to deal with a prolonged economic crisis, with problems of drought and desertification and a million-dollar per day war[7] at its hands, all stimulating massive migration to the capital?[8] Why is this problem prioritized and taken up with so much vigour, that the government almost forces marriage upon its single citizens of marriageable age? The similarity in the stipulated goal of marriage as stated by Omar Al-Bashir quoted by Bol and by El-Tayeb Mustafa is instructive: to bring forth children who can 'populate the earth with good (Muslim) citizens'. It refers to establishing the hegemony of Islam in the sense that *shari'a*, the 'right or good path', is the most appropriate way to establish the *umma*, the community of righteous believers. This was one of the main goals of the Islamist government with which they legitimated their policies and differentiated themselves from their political predecessors.[9] Apparently the government considered it a problem that too few people were married, which, consequently, formed an impediment to the efforts of this government to transform Sudanese society into the ideal Muslim society. Peculiar about the mass-weddings is that it was mainly professionals, especially those working at government institutions, who were addressed. Both the problem of marriage and the possibility of creating 'good citizens' were thus to be sought within the context of the working professional population, more particularly among professional *women*. Soon after the junta had gained power in 1989 it sent home women who held high positions within the government bureaucracy: on early retirement, special leave or by outright firing them.[10] The reason given, especially in the cases of young professional women was, that they should be wives and mothers within the confines of their houses (Hale 1997: 196–219). Being *good* mothers was implied. Therefore, even if the marriage problem was seen as a problem relating to both men and women, edu-

[7] For example Deng (1989), Lancaster (1990: 180). Copson (1994) states that this figure may be even higher as the debts at the end of the 1980s amounted to $12.1 billion plus $3 billion in arrears (19).

[8] See for example El-Shazali (1985, 1992), Simone (1994: 72).

[9] The relation to its political predecessors has been described in Chapter 1. See also Hale (1997: 185–227), Gruenbaum (1992: 29–32), Fluehr-Lobban (1990: 610–623).

[10] For example the KSOAP referred to in Chapter 1. However, it also refers to the government's annual appeal to women just after the month of Ramadan to dress more appropriately and veil more strictly in order to attain the righteous Islamic society (TV broadcast January 1999).

cated female employees were in this respect obviously singled out in this moral discourse on gender. The question remains: why?

In his article "Managing Their Lives for Them", Bol (1996: 2) concludes that the organized weddings were not very successful. First, most marriages seemed unstable and many had already failed. Second, because the intended groups were not responding.[11] Bol reports that in the case of Sudan TV about half of the employees applied for a wedding en masse: most of them drivers and other support staff of whom several had already married at least once. Another reason became apparent in interviews with several female employees of Sudan TV. According to Bol, the fear of getting fired was a convincing reason to marry. This was especially true for female journalists as "some 150 single women out of 200 unmarried employees at other state-run media houses indeed have been sent home in June of the same year (Bol 1996: 3)". Most interesting therefore were the reactions of some of the female employees Bol cites. For example Amal Abdel Rahman, a female journalist whose fiancé worked abroad, said: "The time given to us to get married is too short and I prefer to lose my job if that can solve the problem". Her self-assured statement that she would rather lose her job than marry contradicts the analysis of Bol that female employees opted for marriage out of fear. Amal Abdel Rahman did not even pretend she considered the option, which is remarkable given the fact that she had a fiancé, which meant that the prospect of marriage must have been on her mind for some time. She added: "We who are unmarried are being described as the most dangerous people in the society, but they don't specify what type of danger we represent".

She sounds indignant and in her statement she openly contested the idea that single people were dangerous. She thereby in fact challenged the legitimacy of the moral discourse of the government calling on the government to be clearer in its intentions. Amal's was not a rare case. Another female journalist who wanted to remain anonymous said: "I have no relations with any man so the deadline does not concern me. Let the TV director find me someone to marry instead of me looking

[11] The young male educated employees Bol interviewed denounced the call to marry by referring to personal, economical and social circumstances, such as a lack of finances, lodging or too short notice to be able to marry. One of the few positive reactions came from a blue-collar worker. He had already married twice and considered the mass-weddings an opportunity to marry a third time, commenting: "These young people, girls and boys alike, want to spoil this golden chance (1996: 2–3)".

for a man". The speaker does not sound meek or subdued either, on the contrary, she seems defiant, and she even called on her director to provide her with a husband. Thus she denied sole responsibility for being single. Her refusal to find herself a husband might be read in different ways. In the first place it is considered improper for a woman to 'hunt' for a man herself: this is something that 'traditionally' her guardian, mostly a close relative, is supposed to do. Secondly, although the speaker is anonymous, the way she phrased her answer shows she did not feel any inhibition to confess her difficulty in finding a man herself. In other words, she did not feel she exposed herself as being a 'bad' marriage candidate due to, for example, her behaviour, looks, or family background. She reflected on it as a general and shared problem, instead of an individual one, and something that not just concerned her family, but the society as a whole.

These were only a few reactions to the policy of forced marriages. I discussed the policy with colleagues working at the university and in the government service, and read reports from other parastatals. I concluded that there were many women not willing to marry en masse or in a hurry. Bol's report that around 200 women indeed were sent home, points in the same direction: these single educated women preferred to be fired than forcibly wed. This goes a long way to explain why the mass-weddings were not very successful: women did not want to be bullied into a marriage they did not want. The women who did not fit well into the dominant discourse displayed a remarkably self-assured attitude in resisting the same discourse that targeted them. Obviously, these female employees did not seem to fear that their unmarried status might have it's bearing on either their social position or their (self-) image.

The way these women referred to the problem of finding a marriage partner is reminiscent of the way women such as Sitt Ashia, Fadjur, Yasmin talked about the (im-) possibility of finding a suitable husband. As I pointed out in Chapter 7, the single female teachers in Kebkabiya would also talk about a future marriage in this vein: if and when the 'right' or 'good' husband would come along. These similarities among the single professional women in Kebkabiya and Khartoum in arguing and negotiating their position as respectable and admissible, points at a discursive strategy. The women justify their deviance of the dominant discourse by using that same dominant discourse: they refer to the 'missing' husband. So I have to look for the how and why of this 'missing' link: what is wrong with marriageable elite men?

In much of the literature on Islamism, it is mostly women who are focused upon. Hawley and Proudfoot (1994)[12] give one of the few theoretical reflections, which relates femininity to masculinity within fundamentalist discourses. The 'religious machismo', as they call it, requires a femininity, which constructs women as helpless:

> For the rhetoric of religious machismo to succeed, its proponents often find it very helpful to feel the presence of women who require defence. Often these are real women: mothers and wives... Such helpless women may also be symbolic: fundamentalists frequently depict territory, culture, and history that have been desecrated by the attacks of modernity as female (Hawley and Proudfoot 1994: 33).

Men can construct their manhood by proving they are capable of defending the moral order, if needed by using violence. The presence of women as objects to be defended is thereby an important part of the process of constructing masculinity. This view is interesting for it suggests a relationship between both gender constructions.[13] However, Hawley and Proudfoot then take this symbolic view as a description of reality, stating:

> These two kinds of women, the symbolic and the real, reinforce one another. Symbols of endangered womanhood can be more easily sustained if they are nourished in an environment where real women must depend on men to defend them (Hawley and Proudfoot 1994: 33).

However, this statement proposes that the symbolic construction of women forms in some circumstances an adequate description of and thus a transparent one-to-one relation with the ideas, actions, and decisions of real men and women in practice. This view is problematic since it first constructs men and women on a symbolic level and then both groups are supposed to act symbolically since it fits the discourse so neatly. The problem with this reasoning is that it conflates the symbolic with the real and reduces men and women to cultural dopes

---

[12] This is an introduction to an edited volume entitled 'Fundamentalism and Gender' which is one of the first in its kind. The fact that a volume on gender and fundamentalism as such has not come forward from feminist studies might precisely be the problematic usage of 'fundamentalism'. See Chapter 1; and for example Karam (1998), Nederveen-Pieterse (1994), Sayyid (1997).

[13] Recently the issue of masculinity has received more attention. See for example Badinter (1995); Berger et.al. (1995); Cornwall & Lindisfarne (1994); Epstein (1998); Harris (2000). For my discussion here I only refer to masculinity in relation to fundamentalisms in the plural. See also Van Santen en Willemse (1999).

and dupes, to objects instead of subjects.[14] However, it does suggest that at the centre of the Sudanese Islamist government's gender discourse is the construction of masculinity. Then, what is the relationship between the targeting of women in decrees related to the moral discourse and the construction of a masculine identity? Authors dealing with the symbolic construction of femininity in diverse contexts, apart from fundamentalism, are helpful in this respect.

In an article on ethnicity and nationalism, Anthias and Yuval-Davis (1992) differentiate between women as symbols, as boundary markers, and as reproducers of their group, as well as women as participants in conflicts. These diverse roles that women can have in relation to the construction of a group identity is therefore seen as related to the multiple identities of women both as objects and subjects of this process. Also the reverse is true:

> [N]ationality and citizenship, like race and ethnicity, are unstable categories and contested identities. They are all gendered identities and the construction of 'women', inside and outside their borders, are part of the processes of identity formation (Pettman 1996: 62, quoted in Wilford 1998: 16).

It is not clear however, what the exact nature is of the relation between men and women in these capacities in relation to the group they are thus member of and at the same time represent, symbolize, reproduce and defend. What is clear from these studies is that in order to understand the relation between men and women with respect to the dominant moral discourse my focus should be on the relation between the symbolic and social level in relation to the nation-state. I here also want to scrutinize the tenability of this imagery for the male elite members. So far, I have related to the educated elite men as a homogeneous group of educated, de-tribalised, and nationalized men who acquired their position and identity by attending schools and boarding houses and holding a white-collar job. This has set them apart from their non-elite peers and relatives 'back home', with clear, undisputed boundaries between the two. In the same way as I deconstructed the image of the educated woman as a bounded, homogenous and a-historical category, my aim here is to establish whether there are differences also *among* elite men. It might be that these 'differences-within' have had consequences

[14] It is unclear whether Hawley and Proudfoot agree with this view or mean simply to reproduce a supposed viewpoint of the male Islamists they are analysing. This in itself indicates the ease with which one can confuse the analysis with the analysed.

for the kind of masculinity and group identity they adhere to and the tenability of the boundaries between the classes. In other words, I will look at what constitutes a good 'Sudanese' Muslim man.

Dilemmas of the New Elite: Economic and Social Crises

As a district headquarters, Kebkabiya hosted educated men of different qualifications and grades, with varying degrees of experience, both in the bureaucratic structure and in the army. I knew that most of the low ranking officers came from Darfur, but once I knew the higher officers better, I realized to my surprise that almost all of them were also either from Darfur or Kordofan.

Although these officers were not posted near their hometowns, it is notable that most of them had ties to two of the most 'underdeveloped' areas of the Sudan, not counting the South. This is quite striking since one of the main principles of the government service is to post employees away from their homes in order to prevent nepotism.

One of the reasons was that, many government employees, especially the senior officers who have earned credit because of their service record, would try to be exempted from going to Darfur or Kordofan. Both states have a bad reputation among civil servants to such an extent, that the government pays a 'hardship allowance' to have employees accept a job there. Another, more recent reason is to be found in the attempt at implementing the so-called 'decentralization' policy, which was embarked upon in the 1970s under the Nimeiri regime.[15] The current junta has taken up this policy and although most of the decisions are still taken in Khartoum, the new federal states have to take care of most of the working of the bureaucracy at ground level.[16] This meant that each state collected its own taxes and would take care of populating the lower ranks of the government bureaucracy with available personnel. Therefore, it has become increasingly difficult to attract employees from other states. A major reason behind this is that the policy of transfers allows for refusing a post because of personal circumstances.

---

[15] See for example Hale (1997); Harir (1994a); Woodward (1990); Niblock (1987).

[16] During a short visit to Kebkabiya in 1995 people were complaining about the rise in taxes as the community itself now had to provide all 'free' services to government employees, such as housing and transportation apart from salaries, and the maintenance of government offices. None of the officers was able or willing to explain to me the exact terms of this policy.

These developments have resulted in a situation where those employees willing to be posted in these 'hardship' places are increasingly from the region itself. They were less negative about the area since they knew it well. They were therefore not only less resistant to being posted in the West, but they also felt more committed to try to attend to problems specific to the area, like famine, ethnic conflicts and general underdevelopment.

However, the commitment of these government officials to the problems with which one's own kin has to cope is problematic. Elite men still need to try to balance the demands on their resources. Another issue that has become evident under the current government is the accountability of government officers to their relatives with respect to the government decrees. The dilemma challenged those in the highest positions, as they were responsible for carrying out the government decrees. One of the officers told me he was afraid that his next assignment might be near his own hometown in Kordofan. He had been reluctant to remove tea women from the market in Kebkabiya district when the government called for this. He felt they were so destitute that he did not want to rob them of their livelihood: "These women remind me of my own mother, sister and aunt". He had been able to resist the policy, as it was not yet laid down in a Darfur State law at that stage (1992). However, he feared that he might not be able to do so after any future transfers, possibly nearer to home. Therefore, the officer decided to take study leave and to bide his time. Several other senior officers followed his example.

In addition, the dilemma of accountability with respect to kinship ties challenged in particular junior employees. Once after sunset during Ramadan, I met a young man whom I knew worked for the security. He was carrying a *kanoon*, a transferable stove on which women make their tea and coffee both at home and in the market. He hurried past me and I met him again at the door of the compound of Rana and Ighlas the two sisters who were selling vegetables at the market. They told me he was their maternal cousin. Due to the sudden arrival of a senior officer from Khartoum, he had received orders to remove all women from the lorry-parking place where they had started to cater again to travellers and lorry drivers because of Ramadan. As the decision was taken ad hoc, the security agent had not been able to warn his relative beforehand. So as soon as he received the order, he took his cousin's possessions to 'safety' before rounding up the other women and taking them to the police station.

So the fear for nepotism in the case of government officials who work in the vicinity of their relatives seemed to be justified: the interest of relatives comes before that of work. So why did these government employees not resist the transfer to their home area more fiercely? Why were these men not defending their own interest, defending their preference for living in nuclear households and at a distance to the demands of non-elite kin, with more vigour? Moreover, why did the government comply with an action that contested its own philosophy?

One of the main problems of the current elite was related to the economic crisis, which hit Sudan in the 1970s and 1980s.[17] If Sudan in the seventies was referred to as the 'breadbasket' of the Middle East, at the end of the 1970s its economy was dwindling.[18] The crisis also had its effect on government salaries and secondary labour facilities, as salaries did not keep pace with the inflation and many migrated abroad.[19] Those who stayed were forced to find additional means of income. Moreover, the Sudanese government was pressed by international lending organizations to reduce its overdeveloped civil service.

In short, the salaries especially of junior government employees and low rank teachers fell short of keeping up an elite life style. Towards the end of my second stay in 1992, this was the case in Kebkabiya. The salaries of teachers and government employees would not even be paid every month which meant teachers had to bridge one or two months with their savings or other sources of income.[20] Consequently, the dominant discourse on gender could also not be lived up to by those who took their identity from that discourse. In the Sudan of the 1990s, this has had its bearing on a whole generation of educated elite men and women and their gender identities. Men were not able to earn sufficient income to care for their families, which made it necessary for their wives to work, such as Umm Khalthoum. At the same time, another kind of feminization of the government service took place. In the last few decades, women increasingly replaced men, even at

---

[17] See Chapter 2. For example: Brown (1990a&b); Hale (1997); Wohlmut (1997); Woodward (1990); De Waal (1993) for assessments of this crisis.

[18] Both Nimeiri and several Arab countries used this label in the 1970s.

[19] See also Hale (1997: 197). As discussed in Chapter 6 this was one of the reasons why educated women got a chance to get a job within the government. I will return to this issue shortly.

[20] The government needed cash to pay for imports of food, luxury items, and arms, as well as for the salaries of employees living and working closer to the capital, of soldiers and officers in the army, and to keep up a war in the South.

higher positions. When at the Faculty of Medicine the intake of female students started to overtake the number of male students a discussion was initiated by, amongst others, NIF supporters whether a different entry system should be used to redress that 'imbalance' (Hale 1997: 198; El Hassan 2001: 347–364).

Consequently, elite women do not perform the 'right' role of women, as mothers and housewives at home, nor can men live up to their status as providers for the family. Practical solutions were found in exploiting local economic facilities. Several educated elite men posted in Kebkabiya tried to acquire plots of land at non-inhabited places along the *wadi* in order to try to cultivate irrigated crops.[21] Others started to trade or took in boarders. Relatives were given lodging whilst they were at school, or a plot of land the employee had acquired was subsequently rented out to relatives. Family members now proved more of an asset than an impediment to survival, because in return, most of the male employees regularly received gifts in kind, like grain and other edible and non-edible products. The gifts came mainly from non-educated family members who lived elsewhere in Darfur and Kordofan. In some cases junior administrators and other newly arrived employees even had to take recourse to the institution of the extended family in order to be able to start a family of their own at all.

The problem of economic sustainability is most urgent for the young, newly arrived staff members and those in the lower ranks. These employees have had their grades and connected to that their income redefined by the current government so that they always receive less than those who were already working for the government. At the same time, it is these young men who have to establish their own household yet, but who still have a strong relationship with those back home: whether educated or not. Because of the economic crisis, many employees, instead of keeping relatives away in order to maintain an elite lifestyle, now rely on their support. This has allowed them to overcome the government's cutting of the budget and postponing of the payment of their salaries, especially in 'far off' locations like Darfur. The distance to the central government prevents the access to the national representatives to call on for redressing this policy.[22] It even

[21] One of these places was called 'Mitkorro' after 'Monte Carlo', a radio station with one of the most listened to Arabic broadcasts in Sudan.

[22] Not only did the government withhold salaries for one or more months in a row, but also the value of the salaries did not keep pace with the devaluation of the Sudanese

seemed as if the Sudanese government capitalized on the relations between its employees and their rural relatives.

The choice by Sitt Ashia's suitor to marry his cousin can now be placed in perspective. The suitor would have wanted to keep his ties with his family since he needed them for his own upkeep and that of his newly wedded wife. By taking the marriage candidate of his family as a wife, the man ensured himself of their solidarity and economic support. Moreover, a wife who is his relative might have fewer objections to live among her family members when the need arose. For example, when his income would be insufficient to allow for an elite lifestyle or even to set up his own household. Another, more latent aspect is that it would make it possible for employees to go abroad to attend to a job on their own, leaving their wives and children in the care of their families for an unspecified period of time.

However, the question remains why women like Sitt Ashia, but also Fadjur and Yasmin, do not look for an educated husband within their own families? So far, I have taken the course suggested by the single employees themselves, that there is a lack of 'good' men in their surroundings, especially in towns like Kebkabiya. The same was suggested by the employees of Sudan TV interviewed by Bol (1996), while these women are all working in a social environment where most of the single male educated employees are to be found. Perhaps it is not the availability of men that is problematic, but the diverse perceptions of masculinity.

Deconstructing Elite Masculinity: The Issue of De- and Re-tribalisation

In order to understand the predicament of single female teachers, I must not only take a look at economic, political and social processes, but also at the effects of these on the construction of identities by the younger generation of educated males. Those educated elite men who left in the 1970s and 1980s to one of the oil countries or the West earned a much higher income than most could have ever earned in the Sudan. They consequently received a higher social status, although their absence meant they could not take care of most of their family responsibilities. The new generation of employees, which served the

Dinar (worth one tenth of the Sudanese Pound used previously) since the liberalization of the exchange rate in 1992.

government inside the Sudan therefore felt literally 'left behind' in economic, social, but also psychological terms. They took care of their family members under difficult circumstances, but there was no higher status to compensate for their lower salary. The situation caused discontent and frustration, especially among the growing numbers of low ranking employees of a younger generation. In addition, the situation has had its effects on the construction of masculinity.[23] It was, however, not the only cause of a split among the educated elite men.

The educated elite of government employees has its roots in the colonial period, when the British government trained Sudanese to become junior administrators. De-tribalization and acquiring a 'Sudanese' national identity went hand in hand with learning how to create a white-collar identity with an elite lifestyle and attitude (Doornbos 1986). This process would take time and energy and, as I have analyzed for girls in Chapter 5, the boarding house played an important role in this process.[24] In the 1970s under the Nimeiri regime,[25] the educated population and thus the number of potential elite members grew significantly when boys and girls, in towns and countryside, gained more access to education (cf. Woodward 1979, 1990). This plan proved too ambitious because it required more money to run these schools than was available.[26] In some cases, parents would pool labour and money to facilitate the schools and sometimes paid a bonus or even the whole salary to attract a teacher. In any case, Nimeiri's policy did result in more schools in the rural areas and in a larger number of children attending school than before.

Thus, the situation for the younger generation of educated males was similar to the situation of young female teachers. Unlike their predecessors, ambitious young men did not have to live in a boarding house as the schools were now in the vicinity of their homes. As a consequence they did not have the same exposure to the elite lifestyle and the process of de-tribalization as intensely as the former generation of students had.

---

[23] See Hawley and Proudfoot (1994); for a similar process in Egypt see: Jansen (1994); for Iran see Sanasarian (1992).

[24] See for a similar analysis of the importance of boarding houses for 'modernizing' pupils in Nigeria: Hannerz (1987: 546–559).

[25] See for example Woodward (1979) and (1990).

[26] Ustaz Breman, the Head of the Educational Department of the Kebkabiya District pointed out that until now several of the recently planned schools have not yet been established. Further, many officially registered schools in Darfur have insufficient means (tables, chairs, blackboard, books), buildings and even personnel to match the qualification of a 'school'.

Moreover, the proliferation of schools in rural areas and the attempts at decentralizing the government bureaucracy created possibilities for government officials to find employment closer to home. In addition, the shortage of teachers since the 1970s meant opportunities for school leavers who could start teaching as soon as they finished high school as we have seen for women like Sa'adiya and Maryoma.

Therefore, the posting of employees near their homes run parallel to a break down of the process of de-tribalization and 'Sudanization' at the boarding house of high schools in a larger town. The whole setting of education was 'ruralized' and this has had effects on the composition of the male elite and the construction of their class identity.

I was confronted with the blurred boundaries between the educated elite men and the local, 'tribal' men when I discussed the results of the first democratic elections held in seventeen years after Nimeiri was ousted in 1985. In Kebkabiya, the elections of 1986 had a profound influence on local power relations. Many locals, especially among the Tama, the descendants of Faqih Sinin, believed their political party, the UMMA would prove victorious in all of Darfur. Although the UMMA had a majority of votes nationally, in Kebkabiya and Kas district in Darfur the historical political opponent of the UMMA, the Democratic Union Party (DUP) won most of the votes. Both districts are bordering Jebel Marra and have a majority of Fur inhabitants.

Farrah, a teacher at the intermediary school for boys and who held positions in local committees and organizations, told me that the result of the elections devastated the Tama who are an ethnic majority only within the town of Kebkabiya. They had figured that if the UMMA won, the dominance of Tama residents in many of the public committees, market place, and on decision-making boards would continue.[27] So when the NIF toppled the democratic elected government in 1989, the Tama were ambivalent towards the new regime. The NIF was seen as a political opponent and enemy of the UMMA party, since the UMMA had led the national coalition government until the coup. However, locally the national military coup meant that the DUP, and thus the Fur, never got the chance to take effective political and social control

[27] Although the Fur were given administrative and political power in Kebkabiya District after the defeat of Ali Dinar in 1916, the Tama retained a strong control over local affairs. The town boasted two mosques. The smaller one was for the Tijaniyya to whom the *shartai* and most of the Fur in Kebkabiya adhered. The Tama dominated the biggest central mosque of the town, which had as a rule a Tama imam. At the market place and in local councils several Tama still have important positions.

in Kebkabiya. Subsequently, the strategy of some Tama was to become involved actively in local organizations founded by the NIF regime like the youth, women's, neighbourhood, or traders' committee (cf. Warburg). Indeed, Farrah stated that he participated in the NIF committees so the prominence of Tama in governmental committees would continue although he did not share the NIF's political conviction.[28]

What is interesting about this is the fact that Farrah articulated the conflict in political and ethnic terms. He used the old conflict between Faqih Sinin and the *shartai*, between Tama and Fur, to serve as a framework to interpret the results of the recent elections. The use of ethnic terms as a grid to understand and legitimate local power relations is even more remarkable because it comes from someone who belongs to the educated elite.[29] Moreover, under the current regime ethnicity was seen as a problem, which had to be erased. An Islamic society meant a community of Muslims, united by religion, not divided on ethnic or sectarian grounds, as Sudan had been in the past. A particular incident helped me realize how recent that past was in Darfur. Someone related to me an incident about a petition offered to the government in the democratic period '86-'89 by a group calling themselves the 'Arab Congregation'. The 'Arab'[30] group felt that the historical dominance of Fur in Darfur politics had been restored when the Regional Authority Act of 1980 resulted in the governorship of Ibrahim Draige, a Fur intellectual. Until that time:

> ...Most of the leaders of both the civil service and regimental forces were from riverain Sudan. The rulers, decision-makers, judges and, not least, the jailers were riverain Sudanese whom the Dar Furians generally regarded as alien to the region (Harir 1994b: 159).

---

[28] This is not as unusual as it seems since this has been a strategy during the sixteen years of forced participation in government orchestrated 'local' socialist organisations under the Nimeiri military regime (1969–1985). See for example Woodward (1990 & 1991); Hale (1997).

[29] Although referring to the past might be a 'safe' way to talk politics, as I argued in Chapter 1, to do so in ethnic terms is against the government policy and thus potentially dangerous.

[30] 'Arab' is a general reference for cattle and camel nomads, and in fact refers to numerous smaller 'Bedouin tribes' that wander the border area between Chad, Libya, Sudan and even Central Africa. They presented themselves during the peace negotiations as one 'tribe' in the so-called 'Arab Congregation' reflecting the political alliances forged during the years of ethnic conflict and cross boundary fights between Fur, Zaghawa and Arabs, as well as Chadian, Libyan, and Sudanese national forces (Harir 1994b: 165–166,175–178).

The installation of Draige meant that employees from Darfur had a chance to gain higher positions in the administration than they had before.[31] At the same time, it led to heightened ethnic sensitivity as the Fur local government was accused of favouritism in relation to the Fur-Arab conflict. The 'Arabs' claimed they feared that Draige's installation would re-establish the hegemony of the Fur in the area as it had been under the Fur Sultanate. What is interesting is that several members of the educated elite signed the petition, some of them in quite influential positions (Harir 1994b: 145–165).

The handing over of the petition came after a series of ethnicity-induced incidents[32] that were summarized under the labels of a conflict of the 'African Belt' against 'the Arab Belt'. Then in 1988, the National Council for the Salvation of Dar Fur was founded in Khartoum so that educated Dar Furians from diverse ethnic backgrounds could engage in finding a common solution to what Harir (1994b: 173) calls an 'a-traditional' ethnic conflict. The peace negotiations under Dr. Sese, the new governor of Darfur, resulted in an agreement between the parties on July 8, 1989, only nine days after the coup led by Omar Al-Bashir. At this point, the reconciliation speeches by both parties referred to their agreement as a 'gift' of to the new military government (Harir 1994b: 170–176)

The open assertion of tribal affiliation in these cases is a virtual negation of the core of elite identity, namely a national, Sudanese, de-tribalized identity. It seemed an indication of a process of re-tribalization in a democratic Sudan, though the military coup put an end to its crystallization. No one could then foresee that the same kind of ethnic rhetoric would become the mainstay of a war between the Sudanese government, its Islamist defectors who, together with the opposition from the South, allied itself with local ethnic groups. A war, which requires a more in-depth analysis than one can read in most of the media in order to understand its complexity, which I will attempt in Chapter 8.

---

[31] Harir quotes from an unpublished Ph.D. Thesis from A.A. Ibrahim (Sussex, 1985), which shows that in a survey of 1981 on senior civil servants, The Central, Northern and Khartoum Regions together held 39 %, while Darfur's share was 0. The same was true for the Department of Foreign Affairs with ambassadorial positions (Harir 1994b: 158–178).

[32] Harir refers amongst others to the Libya-Chad conflict, the fights over access to water and pasture, the different political parties and the government, which supported different ethnic groups and the establishment in 1963 of Soony and 1964 of the Red

What is clear for the purpose of my analysis of the issue of masculinity is, that the boundaries between elite and non-elite are more fragile and contingent than the elite would want to acknowledge. This has not only its bearing on the boundary between elite and non-elite classes, but also on the homogeneity of the elite class itself. In the eyes of the older generation of educated elite members and of government officials from Central Sudan, the assertion of an ethnic identity by new government employees in Darfur is due to the fact that they have had an insufficient and less profound training and are therefore to be considered not 'real' elite class members.

The Good Husband and the Construction of Elite Masculinity

That some members of the elite perceived this insufficient 'Sudanization' as problematic came to the fore during my first stay when Yasmin and I attended the temporary *shari'a* court cases presented to a 'touring' judge Omar Zayidi who visited Kebkabiya for one month in order to speak justice.[33] His assignment was to give judicial decisions in criminal cases. But he also took on some civilian cases, amongst them divorce cases. Because, as he stated: 'It is a difficult and lengthy trip for a woman and her two witnesses to travel to town'.[34] Yasmin and I attended some nineteen divorce cases filed for by local women. If I was surprised about the high number of local, even poor, women who applied for a divorce, I was even more surprised by Omar's rulings. For although he displayed a distant and non-committed attitude towards the women who appeared in his court his rulings were unequivocal

Flame organisations, which held a regional basis opposing *jellaba* dominance in Darfur (Harir 1994b: 152–161).

[33] Women can become judge in the different government courts to rule in both *shari'a* and criminal cases. In 1990 from the 150 registered judges, 40 were women who administer justice in any kind of cases (personal communication judge Zaayidi). This is interesting given the judicial obligation of two males against four female witnesses delivering testimony in court. This apparent paradox requires another line of analysis, which will not be pursued here.

[34] This was from October 15 until November 17, 1990. No payment is required to file for a divorce apart from the £S9 duty stamps. Since coming to power the Islamist government put more effort in having women filing for a divorce referred to official *shari'a* courts in one of the main towns of Darfur, instead of being judged by local leaders. Omar suggested he recommended appoint a *qadi-shari'a* in Kebkabiya in order to make the court permanently accessible to women.

and without exception in favour of the complainants.[35] He granted the divorces quite easily, almost too easy: in some cases he granted the divorce without even having heard the requisite two witnesses, relying on the testimony of the father of the defendant.[36] The applicant could pick up the divorce certificate by simply bringing in the two witnesses who would then confirm her story in writing at the clerk's desk.

What makes Omar's easy ruling so interesting is that Sa'adiya and Umm Khalthoum, as elite women, were both rebuked by two different judges in different towns and advised to try and reconcile for the sake of the children. Omar never gave such advice. When I afterwards asked why he approved of the divorces of these women, Omar answered:

You know, miss Catharina, it is quite common for women in Darfur to divorce and this is mainly due to the absence of their husbands. Drought and famine made these men travel to Gezeira, Khartoum, and abroad and nothing is heard from them again. Most of Darfur women are too patient; they wait much longer that the required six months to go to court.

Darfur women are the 'too patient' victims of their husbands' absence. What is interesting about this statement is, that this victim-perspective differs from the official speeches in which Darfur women themselves are condemned for their misconduct. Migrated men were in many cases the reason for women to want a divorce. Nevertheless, why would he grant them their divorces so easily? Omar's next reflection is illuminating:

These husbands, they do not respect their wives. These Darfur men, they are lazy. Especially a Fur man, he can easily marry four wives because he lets his wives work

[35] His rulings were so identical, that at the end of the second morning he even consulted Yasmin and me about his ruling, to 'test' what we had learned.

[36] About 24 cases were handled in the week during which we attended his court. Most cases were divorces filed by local women because of an absentee husband (*talaaq be ghiba*). However, there were also other cases: to pay for household expenses; to grant the final divorce after finishing the three months of waiting (*al-idda*) in which women who prove to be pregnant are obliged to stay with their husband so he can claim his child as his own; and women who wanted custody of the children. During the democratic regime, MP's in parliament decided per Personal Law clause which of the two law schools which are prevalent in the Sudan, Hanafi or Maliki, should be applied. The Maliki law is considered to be generally more harsh to women and most cases relating to divorce, custody of children and alimony are tried according to the, for divorced women considered milder, Hanafi law (personal communication *qadi* O.Z.).

for him while he is just sleeping on his angreb *[locally made wooden bed]. He has them work on the land and take care of the children, while he is doing nothing or even travels to towns to trade or to work and leaves his families behind.*

Looking closer at Omar's answer, it is clear that he is not so much addressing the situation of women, but the misdemeanour of their husbands. It is their 'lassitude' when at home and their 'irresponsible behaviour' when working elsewhere of which he disapproves. Omar's comment comes close to a more generally held prejudice offered by many educated men when they would discuss gender-relations in Darfur: that men are lazy and let their women work for them. Some would recite a saying: 'Fur women, they are cheaper than donkeys, but work harder'. They would even betray some envy. Saying that for them it would be much harder to marry more than one woman and thus gain respect since they had to provide for all of the wives and their families themselves.

By his ruling, then, Omar in fact positioned himself opposite Darfur husbands. In addition, he accused them without needing specific proof of any offence, condemning Darfur men in general, and Fur husbands in particular. It was clear that these men were by definition disqualified from being good husbands. Therefore, local women who came to complain at Omar's court were in his eyes in their right without doubt, although not all applicants were of the Fur tribe or had Fur husbands. Even when dealing with something as 'objective' as law, elite masculinity obviously was taken as the norm.

Initially I was puzzled. Omar clearly thought that the issue of the 'right masculinity' and thus of the right kind of fatherhood was so important, that he granted women their divorce so easily that it might have been questioned by his colleagues. Apparently not only he but also other government officials, and certainly those I met when they visited Kebkabiya, took Omar Zayidi's view on the good Muslim man to heart.[37]This attitude was also exemplified in the speeches delivered at the town square by the male speakers, as described in Chapter 1. Moreover, many of the visiting officials were of the opinion that even the educated men in Kebkabiya were not always working and living up to Islamic standards, due to their Darfur background. Omar clearly

---

[37] As the only foreigner present in Kebkabiya, I was often introduced to the visiting officials. Many of them would visit me more often if they were staying for more than a day, because, as they put it, they thought Kebkabiya to be so 'boring'.

felt the need to re-construct the boundary between the likes of him, the 'real' educated elite, and the non-elite, local men who do not know how to behave. It was not just education that demarcated this boundary or the position as government official or teacher in itself. The difference was connected to a combination of qualifications; place of birth related to 'job' location, generation, rank, and attitude, in the sense that 'one knows how to behave'. Omar thus acted upon a perceived difference between those he considered to be well-educated, living according to the right standards of 'educated elite-ness' and thus as proper husbands and fathers; and the, in his eyes, amorphous category of non-elite men. This category did not necessarily only refer to non-educated locals, but to 'badly' educated and insufficiently de-tribalized colleagues as well.

It appears that the Sudanese elite was less homogeneous and de-tribalized than they presented themselves to be, especially in small towns and remote areas like Kebkabiya. Because of economic circumstances and because of shallow socialization, particularly the younger generation seemed not to share all norms and values of the older generation or of their peers from Central Sudan. Moreover, every government inherits an already existing and functioning bureaucracy and political preferences and affiliations of employees do not necessarily match those of the government in power. Differences among educated elite men are thus based on a myriad of aspects, whether of an ethnic-local/Sudanese-national, rural/urban, and generational, political, economic or social nature. In addition, these differences have their bearing on the kind of masculinity and group identity to which these educated elite men adhere.

The heterogeneity of the elite class is a threat to the government's ruling apparatus itself. It thus constituted one of the main reasons for the government's investment in the moral discourse on gender, on the good Muslim man and woman. If the differences, the discontent about the economic and social situation of the employees, obtained the upper hand the younger generation of government employees might turn against that government. By directing the attention to an issue all men agreed on, namely the elite opinion on the correct gender roles, the current government tried to unify elite men at least on a symbolical level. For whatever the men's backgrounds, political affiliation, and actual position in the government, they were expected to agree on one issue: the 'correct' gender roles. Whatever differences men may have had, they would agree that their right role is that of providers and protectors of their families and guardians of their wives and daughters, in accordance with the elite view on gender relations.[38] By making this symbolic, moral order the mainstay of government policy; the attention is diverted from the more profound economic and political crises. The frustration especially of the younger generation of educated elite men is translated in terms of the problem of getting married. The emphasis on moral issues offers young educated men a meaningful identity of someone who is potentially in 'control', which gives men hope for a future.

The government's perspective on the ideal Muslim society thus hinged on the notion of the ideal Muslim man. This masculine Muslim identity was nowhere explicitly articulated: the more general notion of *quwama* was used for legitimizing the construction of gender relation, referring to: 'The one who is in charge of others' or 'who provides financial support' or 'who has guardianship'. In the context of Sudan this concept has come to imply male responsibility towards his family suggesting that a wife has to obey her husband in everything, except in those matters that contradict worshipping God (Al-Ahmadi 2003: 50–52). The Islamist government thereby had taken care of legitimizing this view with reference to the one identity all these males adhere to, that of the Muslim identity. This perspective held, moreover, the promise that once all women would be married and removed from the important positions within the government, men would also have in society the position of control and importance they felt should come with their (school) certificate.[39] Educated married men, moreover, were expected to be able to better protect and defend the social order as perceived by the Islamist government.

This construction therefore also explains the government's perspective of women as objects who serve to redeem an elite masculinity-in-crisis. The Sudanese masculinity was at stake as long as women were not acting according to the idea of the good Muslim woman. Women might have been symbolically constructed as boundary markers between the elite and the non-elite, and at the same time they also served as a means to overcome the differences among the educated elite men. However, it is still problematic, that this analysis has been

---

[38] See for a similar analysis of another kind of ruling elite, the Netherlands and British colonizers: Ann L. Stoler (1991).

[39] The expectation of young graduates to obtain a post in the government bureaucracy is a widespread phenomenon, or problem, and can be traced to the intentions of formal education by the colonial powers. See for example Moran (1990) for Liberia Jansen (1994) for Egypt, Niger-Thomas (2000) for Ghana.

concerned mainly with the symbolic aspect of masculinity in relation to femininity. Apart from the fact that many men might not adhere completely to this discourse, nor might see it as a solution to their problems, it is the educated women who are not prepared to play their part. They demand to be taken as subjects in their own right. Moreover, as long as women are visibly active in the public sphere, they constitute a threat to that same discourse. This brings up the question of what educated elite women themselves think about this discourse and how they act upon it? It directs me, again, back to Kebkabiya.

'A Sudanese Man Cannot Fail His Mother': Elite Women as Boundary Markers?

In Chapter 7 the issue raised by single female teachers of finding a suitable marriage candidate was related to the particularly high standards the prospective husband should live up to. Understanding, trust, respect, and freedom of movement were the qualifications used. Sitt Ashia was very clear on her wishes: to be able to work was one of the main preconditions to consider marriage at all. In this respect, the female teachers' hopes did not differ too much from those of the young market women. However, the masculinity-in-crisis did constitute a difference between both classes of single women.

As I indicated, in the period of Sitt Ashia's courtship Fadjur also had a suitor, who was an officer in the army. After some time, Fadjur broke off the relationship herself. When I asked her why, she was rather vague quoting in answer a saying: 'Sudanese men have two faces: one for outside the house and one for inside'. This refers to the unreliability of the promises men make before marriage when they want to make a good impression on their wife-to-be. A second saying: 'A Sudanese man cannot fail his mother' emphasizes the social value placed on the good relation between a man and his mother. In so doing, it gives the mother considerable power over her son and his choice of a bride. Fadjur later confided that she did not know her suitor well enough to know how much his promise to set up a place together was worth. 'And I do not want to live with my in-laws, I want my freedom. I want to work, to invite my friends, to act as I want', she kept on telling me, resonating the conviction of Sitt Ashia. She added: 'Just like you, Karin, don't you like it that Johan allows you to work and travel and you are not bothered with household chores or children'?

I realized that my feminist ideals together with Yasmin's might have influenced the discussions with both Ashia and Fadjur. However, the same litany was used repeatedly and single educated women I met elsewhere, even in Khartoum, would articulate their ambivalence about marriage in almost the same words and refer to the same reasons for their hesitation. Yasmin had a similar experience with a suitor who in the end married his mother's choice. Yasmin boldly claimed she would marry the first man who would come around to ask her hand. However, she added one condition: "As long as he leaves me to do what I want to do, and to travel and work when and where ever I want".

It is not just the ability to work, which the women cherish; but also the whole array of freedom of movement, choice of friends and activities, in other words their life-style that is at stake. In relation to the recent developments concerning the new generation of male members of the educated elite, we can understand their hesitations and premonitions better. If these young men who constitute the pool of possible future husbands still have to find their way into their careers and do not know what their future will look like, then there is a fair chance that these women will end up living with their husband's families, in particular when the man is a relative. It is the closeness of the young single men to their families that worries women like Fadjur, Yasmin, Sitt Ashia, not only as a practical problem, but as one of morality as well. They fear that, once married, they might fall back into that realm of family obligations and kinship morals. It is not just the fear that marriage might mean the end of their working life. It is also the possibility that the educated woman has to regress into kinship identities as not only wife or mother, but mainly as in-law, under the guidance and control of their, probably non-educated mother-in-law; a position of obedience and servitude that these women feel they have escaped because of their education. Such a marriage might mean an end to their relations with friends and colleagues, their freedom of movement and control over decisions making and taking processes concerning their own lives, in short, their autonomy.[40]

[40] Autonomy is to be distinguished from power as it refers to ability to decide independently on matters concerning the own destiny, body and life, having a sense of dignity and control over de direction of one's development (cf. Schrijvers 1985: 19, 233–237; Boesveld e.a. 1984): like these authors I maintain that it is a relational concept only feasible when considering persons as part of groups. My M.A. thesis was a study into the concept of autonomy with respect to the position of rural Fur women (Willemse 1990).

These female employees are the first generation of women who have what I have called a 'prolonged adolescence'.[41] Therefore, there are not many examples of how women can cope with both the moral discourse of the elite and the kin induced morality of relatives. The lack of role-models means that these young women are unsure about the extent to which marriage leads to a return to the 'heart(h)', in the sense of family, kin- and care relations, which might jeopardize their newly acquired female identity. In addition, examples of failed attempts, like Umm Khalthoum's, or problematic marriages, such as Sa'adiya's, abound. In short, these women would rather keep to the 'mind'. They prefer a life of work, colleagues and friends as their main focus. The generation of Sitt Ashia, Yasmin and Fadjur is one of pioneers of women who have acquired an elite status, like Sa'adiya, on their own terms and by their own merit. However, they are different from Sa'adiya because, by chance or 'planning' they have escaped early marriage and now dread having to make a step 'back'. Single female teachers want single educated men who are broadminded enough to let them have the life they attained by hard work and a bit of luck. This is what made Sitt Ashia emphasize the broadmindedness of her parents, and of her prospective husband: even her wish to find a man from among the *awlad ar-rif* was in her view related to broadmindedness. If not, if they have to take care of their lifestyle and status on their own while managing a household and non-elite relatives at the same time, like Sa'adiya is doing, they rather not marry. When Fadjur quoted the Sudanese saying 'A Sudanese man can not fail his mother', she in fact formulated her doubts about the possibility that her husband would be strong enough to stand up against his mother and his family in order to defend his wife's choices. In other words, she vented her acknowledgement of the double loyalty men have towards their mothers and wives.[42]

However, there were hardly any acknowledged and respected single professional women past their marriageable age. At least, they were not visible as such: there was no discourse on women that offered them different role models or subject positions which allowed for structural identities of mature women who were not married, nor of unmarried

[41] Kerkhoff (1998) gives a similar view referring to 'girlhood'.

[42] In fact, this phenomenon is not unique for Sudanese society: the double loyalty of men towards their mothers and their wives is prevalent in many Islamic societies. A phenomenon which also occurs in other than Muslim societies in many parts of Asia (see for example: Harris 2000; Schrijvers 1985, 1993; Den Uyl 1992).

mothers or lesbian couples.[43] In addition, there were no other possibilities by which they would gain social respect or a positive self-image. How could they cope with the government's urge to marry? What kind of future, what kind of social esteem could these women hope for if they were not in a position, nor in a hurry, to find a 'suitable' husband and thus might not find one at all?

Moral Motherhood: Elite Women Adjusting (to) the Discourse?

In the discourse of the government, it is not so much wifehood but the importance of motherhood that is emphasized. In contrast to marriage, the idea of motherhood appealed to all single female teachers. One of them even said in exasperation "I don't need a man, I need babies". She then wondered aloud how she could ever claim respect among the women she worked with, how could she go on teaching them about hygiene, child care and food preparation if she did not have children of her own? This refers to a common sense idea of womanhood in the Sudan, and certainly in Darfur: a woman is mature and respected only when she is a mother.

One day during Ramadan while Sitt Ashia was preparing a meal for breaking the fast, I recited to the female teachers of the boarding house the *hadith* quoted by Sitt Miriam during her speech: 'Heaven is under the feet of mothers', which proved to be central to the constructions of subject positions by Hajja and Umm Khalthoum. One of the teachers reacted by telling me a story about a man who asked Prophet Mohammed whom he should revere most if he had to choose. Then Mohammed answered: "First your mother, then your mother, then your mother, then your father". Another teacher gave me the same interpretation Umm Khalthoum gave me. Sitt Ashia who had been intent on cleaning lentils looked up when the discussion about the right interpretation was quietening down and addressed me:

Look at me, Karin. Do you see what I am doing? I am mothering all the time. I am mothering now, making a meal for you while I am fasting. I am taking care of my parents. I even take care of my younger sister and brother so they can go to school. So how would I not be a mother?

[43] See for example Jansen (1987) who shows how women who 'do not have a man' are placed outside society.

The teachers left and right from me start to push me in jest but Ashia has not finished yet:

I think all the explanations are pointing the same way; it means that mothers are the ones who save the Muslims. So if we teach the children of Kebkabiya, if they learn from us the right interpretation of the Holy Qur'an; *and how to pray and how to fast and the girls how to perform the* gusl;[44] *and to count and to read and write, and that London and Holanda are two different locations, then we are those meant with* Ummayaat, *motherhood. You have the mothers who give birth to children and feed their bodies and there are those who feed their minds. We all take care of children in our own way and we all get* ajr. *Where would Sudan be if we would not do that? Where would development be if we did not provide the basis?*

The way Sitt Ashia refers to motherhood is illuminating. In the first place she extends the function of motherhood to all women who are taking care of others, whether their own or other women's children. Since all women in the boarding house take turns to cook, clean, and sometimes even wash for each other, this she also considers to be 'mothering'. In addition teachers living at the boarding house also have the duty to watch over the cooks for the student's boarding houses and take care that the girls keep their lodgings and themselves clean and almost literally perform 'motherly' duties. Moreover, although relatives are not discussed, I learned from most of them that they supported siblings to get education or parents for their upkeep, which they saw as 'taking care' as well.

Sitt Ashia's second reference is even more insightful as she constructs a meaningful identity in the face of the pressure of the government to take up the role of motherhood. She and her colleagues are being mothers, in a specific way: if biological mothers give birth to children and feed them, the teachers take care of the children's mental development, raising them into a good Muslim generation of Sudanese. I refer to this as 'moral motherhood'.[45] Sitt Ashia thereby adjusts the reflections of the current Islamist regime on raising children and the need for

---

[44] *Gusl* refers to the ritual washing by women to purify themselves after menstruation, sex or giving birth.

[45] Azza Karam (1998) analyses a similar perspective on motherhood in the Egyptian context. This perspective on moral motherhood is neither new nor particular to Islamist discourses. Schrijvers (1985) elaborates particularly on this aspect when discussing the strengths of mothering, both individual and collective. See also Den Uyl (1992).

education to suit her own situation: she is not an Islamist, but she does take on their legitimisation for her own choices. When women who are closer to the current Islamist party articulated the same views on motherhood and work I realized that this view was more important than I had understood at first. It was an essential aspect of the way single female educated employees, also elsewhere in Northern Sudan, seemed to deal with the current moral discourse and their status.

Hale (1997) interviewed some of the women who have high positions in the NIF in Khartoum. About Hikmat Sid Ahmed, teacher and one of the two NIF representatives in the government Hale reports:

> Sid Ahmed stressed the idea that the Muslim woman is responsible for the education of the new generations... She expressed concern for those women who are gainfully employed... for their moral reputations, for their becoming coarse from hard work, and for whether they would have to neglect their children due to unsatisfactory childcare... Islamic childcare institutions would be constructed for working-class women whose abilities to raise their children in an 'Islamic way' were seen as limited by the NIF.

As women are among the most active organizers of the NIF,[46] their ideas have to be taken into account by the NIF government. Moreover, they have been instrumental in the period before the NIF came to power to influence the socialization of the youngest in nursery schools, which the NIF has been establishing for a number of years in mosques all over Sudan. The NIF has been active since the 1950s to infiltrate in other schools as well, especially via their female constituency of whom many are female teachers (Hale 1997: 208–214).[47]

These interviews with NIF women cannot be seen as informal chats as these women spoke from a high political position and were very aware that their words were recorded and thus public. NIF women would not want to jeopardize their male party members, but they obviously tried to adjust the discourse in favour of a female perspective. Interestingly, the discussion of these women, and of the educated women in the lower ranks of the extended network of the constituency who are mainly female teachers, had quite an impact on

[46] One of the reasons is that the NIF has many male supporters working outside the Sudan.

[47] Hale adds that the 'NIF pointed to this *public* activity of NIF women as its answer to the clichéd charge that should the party come to power it would send back women into the home (emphasis Hale, 217)'.

the policy of the Islamist government: in the end It adjusted its policy towards women and work.[48] It reduced the speed in which women were sent home and in some instances, this process was altogether halted (Hale 1997: 198–200; Al-Ahmadi 2003; Simone 1994: 66, 102) The junta announced that women would be allowed to work in those jobs that could be taken as an extension of their 'natural' task as mothers, notably teaching and nursing and some medical specializations. Strangely, obstetrics was blocked for women, although one would expect that this would be one of the specializations in which women and motherhood are closely related. The reason given was that this specialization required a female doctor to leave her house at all times while as a mother and a wife she was needed by her own family at home at least at night. The suggestion generally given by some female doctors is that the brain drain of the Sudan is continuing, especially of medical doctors. Obstetrics allows for blossoming private practices with a relatively high income and is one of the few specializations that keep male gynaecologists in the Sudan (Al-Ahmadi 2003; Hale 1997: 198).

In other words, the negotiation power of women, however small and marginal, has had its influence on the moral discourse of the government where it concerns the relation between women, work, and motherhood. Women are central to the moral discourse of the government not only in a symbolic way, but also as actors. Even women who are openly active as members of the NIF do not always support the government's view when it comes to the position of women. Hale (1997) quotes Wisal Al-Mahdi, the wife of Turabi, leader of the NIF, and the sister of the ousted premier Saddiq Al-Mahdi of the UMMA party:

> [Arab men] are against women, and that is why *we are much against them.* We know our rights; we have learned the *Qur'an* and *shari'a*; we know what *shari'a* gives us. We think that women *are better human beings* than they think… And *we are standing up for our sex*. We are working in the NIF *to praise women* and to make women have a better status and to tell the world that we are as equal to men and are as efficient as men and we are as educated as men and we are as good as men and as great as men (emphasis Hale 1997: 216).

[48] Karam (1998) detects the same stretching of the dominant discourse by women in Egypt. In her research the focus was on women in feminist organizations that claimed space to emancipate and construct their agency.

This quotation makes clear that these women create a difference between most Sudanese men whom they see as Arab men and Muslim men in general. Their membership of the NIF is thus legitimized since they claim they work to attain a better position for women in an ideal Islamic society. What is interesting is not so much whether Wisal Al-Mahdi is right in claiming this position, but rather that she is openly discussing the attitude of men towards women with reference to the Islam. As in the case of Sitt Ashia, Wisal Al-Mahdi is staying within the boundaries of the discourse, and at the same time claiming more space for women of her background, that is, educated women. See even seems to construct women as better Muslims than men who are confusing Muslim hood with their Arab identity.

Educated women are capable of entering a discussion with their male colleagues about the interpretations concerning the position of women because they are articulate and acknowledgeable about religious issues. This is due not only to the fact that educated women are educated and read the *Qur'an*. I have pointed out that this also might be the case with some of the younger market women. It is the fact that female employees are needed by their male colleagues, party members, relatives, and husbands and by the government. Both for practical matters like adding to the family income, as (prospective) wives and mothers their help in educating the next generation, but also as symbols: for giving flesh to the ideal Muslim Woman; as boundary markers of their class; as advertisement of the 'modern outlook' of the Islamist government etc. And, more importantly, they have access to knowledge and the speaking position on the basis of which they can discuss with men who make, disseminate or implement the government policy. They are 'included' and therefore more favourably positioned within the ruling relations than educated market women are. As such the educated women can make a difference to the effects of the moral discourse, however small and marginal.

In the Sudanese context it has become clear from the discussions among female employees that on the one hand they try to fit their position into the mould created by the Islamist moral discourse. And on the other, the government puts a lot of effort into suggesting that 'The Muslim Woman' exists, if the circumstances would only allow it. The government tries to facilitate this perfect Islamic community at a political level and to some extent on a social level by providing subsidies for weddings, veils, separated buscompartments et cetera. At the same time the openness of the reactions to the government policy by young women even vented in a public sphere, such as a journal, a book written by a foreign anthropologist indicate that these women consider their views on their alternative position to have validity and legitimacy.

Most elite men articulated their own and their female relatives' positions mainly in economic terms. Often they would point out to me that they 'allowed' their wives, daughters, or sisters to work because of the economic crisis. On some occasions men, like Yussuf and Omar in Chapter 2, would point out that the political signature of former governments was related to the economic downfall of Sudanese society and thus the main reason why men were not able to perform their duties as good Muslim men, as fathers and husbands. One of the other rare occasions that a man told me that women were to gain more from Islamization was when a young married government official told me that his wife was gaining more *ajr* than he could. She took care of his relatives who lived on their compound. He pointed out:

She is taking care of them, even while she is fasting. She cooks, she cleans, and she does not complain. And even when she teaches at school, she teaches the children the right Islam, the right conduct. She really stands to gain. Not me. I do not earn enough to provide a nice house for her, or to allow her to stay at home. And for me, no, there is no hope. There is no money, no jobs, and I smoke and play cards, just to kill the time, and it costs me my credit points.

Femininity and masculinity are thus closely related. Many educated elite men feel they are not able to live up to their role as husbands and fathers and they feel that Sudanese society has become worse and the proper order has to be restored. Educated elite women shared the economic hardships and the struggle to keep up a social standing as members of the elite. However, their evaluation of their position is ambivalent. Like Umm Khalthoum who pointed out that she started working because of economic need, but would not quit her job even if her husband would earn enough to sustain the family. Educated women also feel they have gained in the new situation, whether they are NIF supporters or not. By the opening up of economic positions they have gained (self-) esteem, economic and social status and decision-making influence in their households. They have acquired a new female identity established by their own doing: that of the female employee. It is a position, which they are not willing to let go easily. Even when the boundaries of female identity are defined more explicitly and seem more fixed, women feel they have autonomy to gain and a future to fight for. This is a position that is not unique for educated women in Sudan: it is a phenomenon, which is to be found in many other parts of Africa where rapid changes offer opportunities especially to women. Many men do not have much faith in the future and feel they only stand to lose.[49]

It is not so much the female identity, which is at stake, but an elite masculinity, which is in crisis.[50] It is in this context that I understand how seriously I should take the jesting of the single female teachers when they suggested that 'we should learn by heart those *sura*'s which defend our cases'. It exemplifies that the moral discourse is explicitly seen as negotiable and adjustable. In Chapter 1, one of the first sentences of the religious speech delivered by the second female speaker, Sitt Miriam, was: 'And the prophet Mohammed said that heaven is near the feet of women', instead of the habitual *mothers*. With hindsight, I think that the reference to 'women' instead of the usual 'mothers' or 'motherhood' is not a slip of the tongue or mistranslation. I think that this reference was strategic, even if unintended, in that it is an act of contesting a dominant interpretation. Thereby she was not only resisting the discourse but at the same time adjusting it as well.

[49] See for example Karam (1998); Moran (1990); Niger-Thomas (2000); Silberschmidt (1992: 237–253; 2001: 657–671).

[50] See Cornwall and Lindisfarne (1994: 11–47) who analyze masculinity as a derivative of femininity.

CHAPTER 8

BOUNDARIES CON/TEXT-ANALYSED: GENDER IDENTITIES AND RESISTANCE

On the evening before my departure from Kebkabiya in January 1996, Nura had organised a coffee-party at our compound as a farewell. As the evening wore on, the few men who had come to bid their farewell took their leave. Most women stayed until deep into the night. Umm Khalthoum and Sa'adiya were among the last who left. As I needed to tend to the remaining guests, Hajja told me she would accompany Sa'adiya and Umm Khalthoum some of the way, as is the custom. As I saw their silhouettes disappear in the moonless night, I could still hear some of their conversation. Umm Khalthoum asked Hajja if she could spare her some of her milk the following day. I could not hear the answer but I am sure Hajja promised to do so. Then I heard Hajja ask Sa'adiya if she might send some goods to her sister in Al-Fasher with Jacub's lorry. Sa'adiya replied that that would be fine, if Hajja allowed Sa'adiya to store some of the sacks of oranges at her compound which Sa'adiya intended to buy from the people coming from Jebel Marra on Saturday. Jacub, her husband could pick up all the goods on the next market day. I knew that Umm Khalthoum promised both Hajja and Sa'adiya to make them some *dilka*, the local scrub made of sorghum flour and local spices and oils, for which she is renowned.

At first, I considered these arrangements between Hajja, Umm Khalthoum and Sa'adiya as extraordinary. When I first arrived these women, who belonged to different classes, did not have the same relationship as they had when I left. I presumed that I had been a kind of intermediary to facilitate these contacts and I felt a little proud in having been instrumental in stretching the boundaries of the dominant discourse of the government elite. This discourse constructed the differences between these women in order for them to be seen as members of their proper classes.

Now, after having tried to understand the narratives of these women in their context, by reading and writing their texts against the grain, I am no longer so sure about my 'accomplishment'. After all, the contacts between the three women were not mine to set up, but in the end depended on the decisions and initiatives of the women themselves. I am more concerned with the implications of me considering the relation between Umm Khalthoum, Sa'adiya and Hajja as an anomaly. If I would go along with that view, I would conceptualise as fixed and stable the boundaries between educated elite women and market women. This would mean that I would go along with a difference between both classes as constructed by the government elite and legitimised by the dominant discourse. Yet, the analyses of the biographic narratives of Hajja, Umm Khalthoum and of the other market women and female teachers showed that constructions of subject-positions are closely related to the 'settings' in which they carry meaning, and that they are thus flexible and dynamic. In my analyses I have tried to move away from the rigid and circumscribed way the dominant moral discourse of the newly established Islamist Sudanese government allotted subject-positions to women, especially working women (Introduction, Chapters 1 and 2). By reading their biographic narratives against the grain, I wanted to discover the ways in which working women from different class backgrounds reflected on the discourse and further how they manoeuvred to position themselves in relation to that same discourse. The analyses of the narratives of Hajja and Umm Khalthoum (Chapters 3, 4, 5) and to some extent those of the other market women and female teachers (Chapter 6, 7) showed that all of the women were involved in a continuous process of construction and re-construction of their identities while reflecting on and positioning themselves within the dominant discourse. The subject positions offered by the Islamist dominant discourse were for all of these women the point of reference or of departure in these dynamic processes of self-reflections and representation.

In my analyses of these self-re/presentations, I have consistently referred to these constructions of self as 'subject-positions'. In my view, this term was most appropriate in these particular cases as it referred to the ways in which dominant and sub-dominant discourses offered possible positions for subjects to take on. Different discourses offer different subject positions and women as subjects may choose to take up these positions, or not. This does not mean that women are completely free in acting out certain subject positions rather than others. Dominant discourses allot subjects certain restricted, often stereotypical identities. However, the notion of subject position provides the possibility to refer to an active involvement of individuals who negotiate their positioning within those discourses. My usage of 'subject positions' therefore presumes the active participation of actors in processes of self-reflection on the practices and discourses in daily life. By using this term I refer to working women as agents of their own positioning while at the same time I give heed to the force of dominant discourses (Mills 1997: 77–102; Moore 1994: 4–5)

However, my research is positioned as well. Because of my focus on the ways women negotiate an Islamist discourse on morality and gender, the study field of 'Gender and Islam' formed an important context from which I analysed the narratives of working women in Kebkabiya. In Chapter 1, I pointed out that one of the major themes in feminist studies was the problematic of essentialist thinking when discussing gender identities in an Islamic society. Particularly in comparison to the West, the prejudiced image of Muslim women as subjugated, subservient and silenced victims of their male relatives stood out.[1] In this chapter I will reflect once more on the process of knowledge production, which took place in the 'world between [ourselves] myself and others' (Hastrup 1995: 117) this time from my perspective as a feminist scholar.[2]

The world 'in between' has been the starting point for all the descriptions and analyses in the dissertation, for my reflections on listening, reading, and writing against the grain (see Introduction). In Part One, my analysis of the speeches of a popular committee on the proper Muslim already hinted at the possibility of the existence of more than one image, which the Islamist discourse offered as a model for Muslim women. In Chapter 1, I looked into the way the dominant discourse was articulated in the speeches. This analysis indicated that location, education, class position and gender were put forward as the main axes of a differentiation between the educated elite, or white *tobe* women, and the amorphous local non-elite female population. My choosing to 'listen against the grain' to narratives of female teachers and market women was a direct consequence of the diverse differences which were

---

[1] Although in most academic studies on Islam and/or gender this view is considered as outdated, public debate on women and the veil as well as speeches of political leaders like Bush have given a new impetus to this view. See Chapter 1 in which I refer to a speech by Bush pointing out that in an 'archaeological' historical perspective there are parallels in the views on women and Islam among British colonial officers in Egypt at the beginning of the 19th century.

[2] *cf.* Okeley (1992: 1); Kloos (1988); Scholte (1974: 440); Schrijvers (1991, 1993); Davids and Willemse (1999). As for my inspiration of issues of women and resistance, see the literature mentioned in the introduction of Part Two.

constructed by the dominant discourse itself (see Chapter 2). In Part Two the biographic narratives of Umm Khalthoum and Hajja were central to understanding the way the differences were acted out, amplified or played down, in order to claim respectability and credibility as a good Muslim Woman by each woman. At the same time, these narratives gave access to an understanding of the diversity of the constructions of selves. The narratives proved to be negotiations of subject positions offered to working women, which both confirmed and questioned the suggested differences between market women like Hajja and female teachers like Umm Khalthoum.

In Part Three, I have taken another look at the narratives, not only of Hajja and Umm Khalthoum, but also of other members belonging to their classes who, by the dominant discourse, might be positioned in the 'border zone'. In this way I hoped to establish to what extent the moral discourse that allotted to women restrictive gender identities of wives and mothers, allowed for the construction of alternative subject positions. This led me to consider other aspects of differentiation among working women, like generation and education. These alternative positions to some extent crosscut the difference put forward as dominant by the moral discourse of the government: that between educated and non-educated working women. Education provided working women in both classes more social mobility than the dominant discourse would suggest. At the same time women who were positioned in either category of working women, however temporarily, differed considerably, especially in the way these women could, or could not, negotiate the terms of the discourse. That is why the educated women who were trading on the market opted for silence in relation to the power structure and dominant discourse. The educated women who were employed as white-collar workers could more easily choose verbal confrontation. In Chapter 7 I analysed the ways in which these negotiations and confrontations were related to the positioning of educated elite men within the dominant moral discourse of the government.

In this last chapter, I will reconsider the onion layers, which I have peeled off in the course of the book and cut across them. As I want to construct a 'grounded' notion of the relation between gender identity and Islam, I want to connect the narratives of the working women that I have represented above; the dominant discourse by the government on gender; and my own theoretical and methodological perceptions on gendered identities.

This re-reading of the narratives which here is meant to attain a grounding of my theoretical reflections is based on the same method that I have applied in reading all kinds of texts in the course of my research; a con/text-analysis. The introductions I gave at the beginning of each of the three Parts indicated where I have come from, theoretically and methodologically speaking. These introductions constituted the analytical 'map', which I used for navigating the narratives and contextualizing them while charting the construction of gendered identities by working women. This chapter is a kind of apotheosis of this journey and will reflect where the women and their narratives have taken me on an academic plane: it constitutes my narrative as anthropologist. I will thereby reconstruct my different, but related, contextualizations as represented in the previous chapters and articulate an analytical framework. The basis of this framework is formed by my consideration of biographic narratives as a performance of gender and power. Although the goals women had with these performances were, and are, of main importance, my own goal in re-reading the narratives here is to decide whether these narratives can be seen as resistance. In addition I will, in the Epilogue briefly reflect on the current 'war' in Darfur. Although there is no possibility here to give a complete and exhaustive analysis of this key-shift in the recent history of Darfur, I will look at the outburst of violence from the perspective of intersecting identities; the same perspective that I took in the analyses of the narratives of working women in Darfur

Auto/biographic Narratives

> The life history may be thought of as a process that blends together the consciousness of the investigator and the subject, perhaps to the point where it is not possible to disentangle them... If the investigator relies in a primary way on personal resources in understanding the subject of the life history as another person, then in some sense the life history may represent a personal portrait of the investigator as well. The portrait would take the form of a shadow biography, a negative image.
>
> — Gelya Frank quoted in Behar, 1993: 320

In portraying the narratives of the working women as I have done in the previous chapters, I must have been creating a 'shadow biography' as well. As an anthropologist I have not just represented the experiences of 'other' women in and by their narratives, I have thereby also constituted and produced my own 'experience' and myself in the texts:

> The 'I' or organizing subject in the text is the fictively created, unitary self which guarantees the authentic experience and thus the verisimilitude of the cultural representation the text contains. It is a magical trick and exceptionally difficult to pull off (Moore 1994: 118).

This shadow biography thus reflected my own preoccupations, which have become part of my reflections on the narratives of the working women whom I met in Kebkabiya. It is extremely difficult to get away from this 'magical trick' as it allows me to become, if fictive, still a unitary self as an anthropologist. I can only warn you that I will here turn the gaze to my own narrative, this time not so much to deconstruct, but in order to construct an analytical viewpoint; to tell my narrative as an anthropologist.

As I see it now, on that night in Kebkabiya my evaluation of the extraordinary nature of the relationship established by the three women was due to my own positioning within that same dominant discourse. I could see and hear women negotiate its boundaries, thereby not only stretching them but also transforming the discourse along the way. However, I could apparently not escape the dominant discourse since I was part of the context in which it carried meaning. In using the method of listening, reading and writing against the grain I have been alerted to the myriad readings to which these texts can give rise to. This means that, in terms of time and place, my readings and my representations of the narratives as well as my analyses in the foregoing chapters are as partial and context bound, as the narratives of women themselves were. I tried to understand my situatedness in the epilogues to the narratives of both Hajja and Umm Khalthoum and by deconstructing my contextualizations of the narratives in Part Three.

In feminist anthropological works, scholars think of biographic writing and writing autobiographically as closely related (Okely 1992: 1). Especially for anthropologists, like me, who often work with the biographic narratives of men or women who are themselves not able to write their autobiographies, the difference between the two genres becomes blurred.[3] My taping of biographic narratives means that I have not just represented, but also testified about someone else's auto-

---

[3] Increasingly anthropologists work with texts, like diaries, stories and autobiographies, written by people of the community they work in. See for example Caplan (1992); Mohanty (1991).

biography. At the same time my testifying has resulted in a process in which I gave a graph, an image, of the biographies of other women, which implicated my own. Autobiography here points at those aspects of the lives and narratives I shared with women like Hajja and Umm Khalthoum, and all the other women whom I have and have not portrayed in these pages.[4]

As I indicated at the beginning of Part Three, for me as a feminist scholar the attempt at finding alternative ways of dealing with texts, 'theirs' and 'mine', are not just a way of being creative, but it refers to a political stance in finding ways to better represent women and in the process to transform the academic discourse of which I am part. One of the ways in which anthropologists gain authority is by writing texts in which they present themselves as the specialists who know the truth about their 'people' (Marcus and Cushman 1982: 25–69; Nencel and Pels 1991: 9–19; Davids and Willemse 1999). In my endeavour to 'write against the grain', I attempted to present my analyses as open ended, multiple and depending on the context of 'reading against the grain'. This conscious attempt of me as an authoritative scholar at attaining a 'loss of control', an attempt that is never really successful, is related to a critical assessment of the power relations between the anthropologist's self and the others whose narratives have been represented here. This self-reflexive stance is articulate in the feminist adagio 'the personal is political' and its corollary in academic terms 'the personal is theoretical' (Okely 1992: 9; Schrijvers 1985: 225, 1993: 143–167).[5]

As I pointed out in the introduction to Part Two, an important means of breaking down the structures on which power differences are based, and which has become common practice in feminist studies, is to deconstruct binary oppositions such as researcher/researched, object/subject, knower/known, personal/political, emotions/ratio. Not only 'in the field', but in the academic world as well. When feminist scholars examined critically these taken-for-granted binary pairs, the authority of anthropologists and the gendered structures of thinking were problematised (Braidotti 1994: 146–213, 2001; 14–18; Moore 1994;

[4] Autobiography has a long tradition in the Islamic and Arab society, starting with the *Sira* of the prophet. In the setting of Kebkabiya his literary tradition was not part of the cultural repertoire. Badran refers to autobiography in the Arab world as an indigenous form, and she distinguishes 'interpretation of life', 'life story', and 'personal memoir' (Badran 1992). See also Booth (2001); Multi-Douglas (1991); Roded (1994, 1999). Thanks to Margot Badran for pointing this out to me.

[5] See also the introduction of Part Two.

Mohanty 1991: 1–51; Schrijvers 1991: 162–179). In my reading of the narratives I have deconstructed seemingly self-evident binary pairs of concepts as a method to uncover the way discourses work to establish certain power differences as 'normal'. One such binary opposition as constructed by the dominant discourse was the respected/disreputable working woman based on other dichotomies such as educated/non-educated, elite/non-elite, and more specifically, female teachers/market women. In Chapter 6, I deconstructed these seemingly self-evident categories by looking at differences amongst both classes of women.

In my analysis here, I represent my own auto/biographic narrative in order to claim a subject position as a feminist scholar in the context of feminist academic discourses. A conclusion formally brings to an end the process of knowledge production such as I have been describing along the way. This does of course not mean that the narratives on, by and for the working women in Kebkabiya have come to an end. Their negotiations of the dominant discourse are an ongoing process, in which their adjustments and reconsiderations of their subject positions and self-constructions are related to every shift and change in the contexts, or settings, of their daily lives. My reflections here therefore can be neither conclusive nor closing, neither definite nor definitive, and must be taken as the temporal, partial and contingent as the constructions in the narratives of the working women in Kebkabiya proved to be.

The Con/text as a Dynamic Process: From Gender Identity to Resistance

> The word *context* literally means to weave together, to twine, to connect. This interrelatedness creates the webs of meaning within which humans act. The individual is joined to the world through social groups, structural relations, and identities. However, these are not inflexible categories to which individuals can be reduced... Context is not a script. Rather, it is a dynamic process through which the individual simultaneously shapes and is shaped by her environment. Similarly, an analysis of context, which emphasises these dynamic processes, is an interpretive strategy, which is both diachronic and synchronic.
>
> — Personal Narratives Group 1989: 19, emphasis in original

In this quotation, the concept of context is described mainly in terms of relationships, as in social groups, structural relations, and identities. For me this perspective of context is attractive as it relates to the notion of 'settings' I proposed to use in the introduction to Part One. This perception of 'contexts' in fact connects my perception of 'relational agency' to 'relations of ruling' both important notions in order to understand how working women from different backgrounds relate to the dominant discourse. In Chapters 5, 6 and 7 the relational aspect in the self-constructions of market women and of female teachers appeared of utmost importance. The consideration of the relationships of both women in certain 'settings', both in their narratives and in their daily lives, enabled me to understand not only their respective positionings with respect to the relations of ruling, but also the silences and negations in their negotiations of the dominant discourse. The understanding of the dynamics of these processes of negotiation led me to considering agency in the 'world between' a text and its context.

The issue of relations has been paramount in the ways in which the differences between male and female auto/biographies have been evaluated, specifically with respect to gender and narratives. In the western tradition, the autobiographies of St. Augustine, Rousseau and J.S. Mill stand as important examples of a 'Great Man tradition that speaks of individual linear progress and power' (Okely 1992: 4; cf. Brodzki and Schenk 1988: 1).[6] Female auto/biographies are contrasted to this format for their cyclical, repetitive structure of daily routine and the reference to the self via others, by using 'us' and 'we', rather than an atomised and authoritative 'I' (Benhabib 1992; Mohanty 1992: 34–36; Okely 1992: 6). The danger in presenting these differences in autobiographies as based on a male/female distinction is that it might easily lead to an essentialist notion of knowledge constructions on the self. The relation is more complex as knowledge is partial, situated and thus embodied (Braidotti 1991: 219). However, as I pointed out with respect to the narratives of Hajja and Umm Khalthoum, women present themselves both as individuals and as members of collectives. These positions can alternate in one and the same narrative, and are to be understood in relation to the dominant discourse. Hajja claimed a shared subject position as a market woman, which had locally a low status, and individual achievement with respect to her position as a midwife, which allowed her to claim membership of the government elite. For Umm Khalthoum her fate as an almost-divorced woman was connected to a similar kind of positioning of her mother. She pointed at a shared

[6] Al-Ghazzali (d. 1111) and Usamah ibn Munqidh (d. 1188) are quoted as important examples in the Arab tradition (Ahmed 1988: 154).

subject position with respect to the decision taking power of her father and husband, in order to account for her bad marriage. Her reflection on her mother as a good and fortunate mother led Umm Khalthoum to also claim good motherhood, albeit on different grounds: as a working mother and a teacher by referring to her extraordinary position as headmistress of a crèche. These constructions of selves with respect to collective and individual gender identities are mutually related and reflect their positions as working women within the dominant discourse.

The foregoing chapters have in fact been an attempt at understanding processes of constructing gendered identities by women in the context of their daily lives. In conceptualizing these processes I need to take into account asymmetrical power relations. At the same time I wanted to get away from the suggestion of fixedness and stability that identities represent and gain an insight into the fluidity and multiplicity of constructions of self by women, in order to acknowledge that identities are 'always constructed through memory, fantasy, narrative and myth (Hall 1990: 225)', which makes identities inherently unstable (Silberstein 2000: 3).[7]

Biographic narrative proved to provide a good insight into the process of both 'fix and flux' in specific discursive contexts. The narratives offered not just a representation of the way gender and other identities intersected, but could also be perceived as a performance that in itself constructed and produced these identities while being narrated. In other words, biographic narratives produce and determine life (de Man 1979, in Josselson 1993: 19). Indeed, by telling our narratives, 'in the end we become the autobiographic narratives by which we "tell about" our lives (Bruner 1987: 15)'.

Fischer-Rosenthal (1995: 254–261) even suggests that we replace the static concept of identity by that of the more relational concept of biography. He envisages the biographic narrative as a social practice, a 'process by means of which individuals orient and produce themselves …' and 'master contingency…' (Fischer-Rosenthal 1995: 257).[8] Only a biographic narrative:

[7] For example Braidotti (1994: 31, 35–39, 2001: 15–16); Butler (1990: i–xi); Hall (1996: 1–17); Moore (1994: 1–7). See for definitions of gender and its problems the Introduction of Part One and Two.

[8] Other authors, like Bruner (1987); Deleuze and Guattari (1989); Silberstein (2000) also see this relation, but Fisher-Rosenthal is one of the few who suggests that identity

> ...seems to be able to encompass the complexity of one's self over time, including biographical transformations and contradictions...By telling who one is, one explains how one came to be that way... (Fischer-Rosenthal 1995: 257).

The temporal, relational and interactive nature of the biographic narrative, according to Fischer-Rosenthal (1995), makes it a concept better suited to capturing the flux and fluidity of constructions of self. In this respect, his view is comparable to that of De Lauretis (1984) who sees narrative as a fundamental way of making sense of the world, as 'the very work of narrativity is the engagement of the subject in certain ...positionalities of meaning and desire (196)'.

My method of con/text-analysis so far, focussed on the diverse contexts in which to read the narratives against the grain in order to understand the meaning constructed in the local setting of narrating. Here I shift to the academic setting, the context in which I place my narrative as text. In order to be able to consider the construction of gender identity in biographic narratives as a form of resistance I refer here to three perspectives on how the context shapes the narratives and its reading 'against the grain'. I call these the rhetorical, argumentative and strategic perspectives.

The 'rhetorical perspective' looks into the context in which and by which the working women I met in Kebkabiya formulated their reflections, or, as Billig (1991: 3–6) states, the 'context of opinion giving'. This is the physical context, the material and relational aspects of the location in which working women like Hajja and Umm Khalthoum narrated about their lives in a diachronic as well as a synchronic way. It was the location of my listening against the grain. Looking at these narrative processes from a rhetorical perspective I may be able to understand how the presence of people, including myself, and the institutional setting as part of the relations of ruling (Smith 1987: 13; 1990: 10–18), have had their bearing on the way both women formulated their views and experiences.

The 'argumentative perspective' refers to my endeavour to read 'against the grain' the narratives of Hajja and Umm Khalthoum in the context of the dominant moral discourse. I call it the argumentative perspective because all narratives negotiated and thus to some extent

---

construction is 'biographic work' and that the notion of the biographic narrative can thus replace the notion of identity. See also Holstein and Gubrium (2000).

argued with that discourse. This perspective leads to an understanding of how the diverse groups of working women took up different subject positions as offered by the dominant discourse, but never definite, completely or docilely. The process always entailed a critical consideration of that discourse. The diverse arguments used by each woman in negotiating their position in respect to the moral discourse are the focus in the argumentative perspective: 'The argument 'for' a position is always also an argument 'against' a counter position. Thus, the meaning of an 'opinion' is dependent upon the opinions that it is countering'. (Billig 1991: 17)

The 'strategic perspective' considers the goal of the way working women in Kebkabiya narrated their identities and argued with the dominant discourse. At the same time, this strategic perspective is part of my conviction as a feminist scholar that women are thinking and acting actors, that all women have agency. This strategic aspect in the narratives of Hajja and Umm Khalthoum appeared in the form of their claims to respectability and credibility as mothers and wives, with which they created room for being a working woman. This strategy was directed both at me, as their immediate audience, at the context in which they narrated and at the dominant discourse as exemplified in my analyses from a rhetorical and argumentative perspective. It is therefore from the strategic perspective that I may understand the extent to which these narratives of self constitute a form of resistance.

With respect to the local setting of Kebkabiya I referred to the differentiation of text and context in terms of intertextuality, intersectionality and intersubjectivity. These were analytical devices: in the context of my academic inquiry into the constructions of selves, of gendered identities and of strategies of resistance, the three perspectives I present here are analytical tools as well, and to some extent they even overlap. In no way should they be considered to reflect separate entities in real life.

The Rhetorical Perspective: 'I Narrate Therefore I Am'

> If narrative makes the world intelligible, it also makes ourselves intelligible.
>
> — Moore, 1994: 119

In reading the narratives of working women from a rhetorical perspective the past proved a relatively 'safe' way to reflect on their positions in the present, a present in which the dominant moral discourse so obviously targeted the female narrators.

In my analyses I looked at the way each woman talked about her self as part of her context. It thus appeared that the narrative structure of each woman differed and in this difference, the women reflected on their positioning in the context in which they lived their daily lives. Hajja mapped herself and her biographic narrative on to her immediate surroundings in order to claim ancestry of a once powerful elite and at the same time to assert her position as a midwife in the currently powerful government elite. Umm Khalthoum moved across the map between Omdurman and Zalingei in her quest to belong as a member of the new educated elite. This means that although for both women Kebkabiya was the shared setting of the prevailing ruling relations where they narrated about themselves and both constructed an elite identity, the rhetorical context in which each reflected on her life and constructed a self that belonged and gained credibility was quite different.

The immediate surroundings in which I taped both narratives constituted the physical surroundings which gave rise to marked spaces such as 'home', 'work place', 'street', 'public', 'private', 'known', 'strange'. These markings were only meaningful in relation to the positioning of the woman in this context and thus to her meaningful relationships with others. The differences between Hajja and Umm Khalthoum in marking their surroundings in a particular way was part of their situatedness; their different positions and positionings in a particular setting in both a discursive and physical sense. It was also mapped in relation to others who shared characteristics such as class, generation, belonging and perspectives on the future (cf. Moore 1994: 57). Therefore, it constituted the relational component of the rhetorical context. This means that although the way class intersected with gender and religion was of primary importance in how these women positioned themselves in their narratives, this was not necessarily done in the same way in every context. When Hajja narrated about her life with Zeinab, her co-wife, present, she did not elaborate on her position as a midwife, as she had done on earlier occasions. Apparently with Zeinab present, she did not feel the need to assert this part of her past; Hajja constructed herself at that moment on a experiential plane she shared with Zeinab, at that particular moment constructing her identity in relation to her co-wife. In this respect the context, in the sense of specific settings, was what shaped and directed the way a narrator articulated and formulated her or his texts.

The rhetorical context was apparent even in the way my relationship with each woman and her narrative was modelled on the most important relationships they held in their daily lives. Thus to Hajja, I became part of her compound, *naas* Hajja, to Umm Khalthoum I was a colleague-friend, like one of the other educated women with whom she socialised. By comparing the narratives of both women, not only their multiple subject positions came to the fore, but also the way each of them related to other persons in their surroundings, to those who made each of them a 'person'. Thus the rhetorical context in which the 'individual is joined to the world through social groups, structural relations, and identities' (*pace* PNG 1989: 19) also gives an idea of the landscape in and by which identities are constructed.

I therefore agree with Fischer-Rosenthal that the concept of biography captures the dynamics of the constructions of self better than the concept of identity does. However, I would not propose to completely do away with the concept of identity in favour of biography. This is not only because, as some of the discussants of Fischer-Rosenthal's proposition maintain, the concept of identity is widely used in current academic and popular debates (cf. Davis 1996: 7). As I stated in the introduction to Part Two, I think the concept of identity is important in order for subjects to experience a sense of self by attaining closure. For me the concept of identity is related to the argumentative perspective on the narratives.

The Argumentative Perspective on the Construction of Gender Identities

> To what extent do *regulatory practices* of gender formation and division constitute identity, the internal coherence of the subject, indeed, the self-identical status of the person? To what extent is "identity" a normative ideal rather than a descriptive feature of experience?
>
> — Butler 1990: 16, emphasis in original

In the intertextual reading that I undertook of the narratives of Hajja and Umm Khalthoum, the two *hadiths*, which were quoted in the speeches by the popular committee as I described in Chapter 1 appeared to be instrumental for both women in constructing their diverse identities. The *hadiths* articulated the two possible subject positions for women as put forward by the discourse and provided landmarks in the narratives of Hajja and Umm Khalthoum. However, each woman took up these positions in different ways and with different effects.

The *hadith* 'a woman's place is in her father's house, in her husband's house or in her grave' served as a point of reference for both women in their capacity as daughter and wife. Their narratives were similar with respect to the memories of the abundance of their youth and the subsequent decision by their fathers to marry them to men of their fathers' choice. Both women reflected on the decision with reference to the norms of being a good daughter in their time. However, Hajja was more resigned to her fate than Umm Khalthoum. Therefore, it may not be surprising that the last one is more resistant to this *hadith* by negating its implications: that her move from father's house to husband's house has brought her protection and well being.

At the same time, Umm Khalthoum claims good wifehood by trying to make her unwanted marriage work. First, because by selling her bracelets she provided the money they needed to keep their household going, next by working at the crèche. Hajja seems to take the implications of this *hadith* quite matter-of-factly, despite the reluctance of her father to 'hand her over' to the house of her husband. She uses the *hadith* in order to claim a good co/wifehood because she was a good, and non-jealous, caretaker of her husband's household.

The second *hadith*, 'heaven is under the feet of mothers', which was quoted more often than the first, referred to the virtue of motherhood. In the narratives, the emphasis now is reversed: Hajja plays down the positive implications of this *hadith* although she gave birth to two daughters late in life. Umm Khalthoum emphasises the effort she put into being a good mother for her children and possible future children-in-law, taking her mother as a role model. However, their position as working women is awkward in relation to these *hadith*s as the dominant discourse does not provide a legitimatisation of this subject position and is thus silenced:

> ...The cultural matrix through which gender identity has become intelligible requires that certain kinds of 'identities' cannot 'exist' ... Indeed, precisely because certain kinds of 'gender identities' fail to conform to those norms of cultural intelligibility, they appear only as developmental failures or logical impossibilities from within that domain (Butler 1990: 17).

In other words, the dominant discourse of the Islamist government defines the subject-positions open for 'a good Muslim woman'. The working woman as an identity 'cannot exist': its occurrence brought forward by the economic crisis, is a 'developmental failure' and as such the identity is constructed as transitory and temporary. From the perspective of the dominant discourse, the working woman constitutes an anomaly for a virtuous Muslim woman. The legitimate subject positions of mother and wife are constructed as fixed and self-evident and these constitute the boundaries of the subject-positions, which women can take up.

In both narratives this silenced, non-existent position of working woman is therefore tied to the subject positions that are offered by the discourse: of wife and/or mother. In Hajja's case, her role as a woman without a husband and therefore a single mother of daughters forces her to sell at the market. Thus her position as a mother has imposed the position of a working woman on her and this constitutes a good reason to play down both. Umm Khalthoum's narrative also has two positions. She links her position as a working woman firstly to her role as a good wife. Secondly, Umm Khaltoum relates it to Abbas' neglect of his role as a good husband-father and she thereby plays down her status as an 'almost ex-wife'. Her gaining an income particularly as a crèche mistress emphasised her ability to be a good mother as it allows her to raise, not only the children of others, but her own children as well: financially, socially and morally.

In both cases of intersectionality, the silence also implies space and location. It is not the importance of the identities of wife and mother which are contested or negated, but the implications of these legitimised identities in terms of the location in which women are expected to perform these: within the walls of their male guardians' compound. The work of both women takes them out of the house and therefore constitutes a visible deviation from the implications of the gender identities as put forward by the dominant discourse.[9]

So even when the reflections of both women on their work constitute 'counter-opinions' it cannot be presented in the form of an alternative gender identity since those which are constructed as self-evident, common sense, fixed and stable by the dominant discourse, do not allow for these. For working women, like Umm Khalthoum and Hajja, but also for the other market women and female teachers, the gender-identities put forward by the dominant discourse constituted stable and fixed points of reference against or with which they could position the diverse other aspects of their self-identities. This is not just a way to comply with demands of the dominant discourse. Nobody can easily present a self, which is constituted of continuously floating and fluid parts of that self. In order to cope with that contingency social subjects need an anchor for their diverse subject-positions and multiple identities (cf. Billig 1991: 17). These seemingly fixed identities thus constitute norms. Norms with which one cannot only claim credibility, respectability and visibility as a good Muslim woman, but also feel oneself to be a valuable member of society and, therefore, to be able to evaluate the conduct of others by the same standards.

This assessment brings me to connect the rhetorical and argumentative perspectives on subject positions of working women in Kebkabiya. The constructions of working women, their positioning in their narratives as subjects show an oscillation between reflecting on the 'fixed' and 'stable' gender identities while retaining the possibility of stretching the boundaries of these identities to suit one's own purpose, and one's alternative subject positions. These presumably 'fixed' identities are clearly articulated, and defined by and within the dominant discourse. At the same time they are performed and 'brought to life' in the ways in which women perform these identities in their daily lives. In this creative process fixedness is suggested while at the same time flux and flexibility is maintained.

---

[9] Azza Karam (1998) points out the same relation between motherhood and work outside the home as negotiated by what she calls Islamist feminists in Egypt and the related transformation of the private/public distinction (208–215;221–232).

Motherhood proved to be an identity, which was quite clearly defined by the dominant discourse. Simultaneously, this seemingly clearly defined concept of motherhood was referred to in diverse and divergent ways by working women with diverse backgrounds and different other identities, such as market women with children, unmarried female teachers, educated married mothers who worked full time. These alternative subject positions were related to sub-dominant moral discourses. For example, the way in which motherhood is perceived according to local gender norms. In this respect market women could define their work on the market as an extension of motherhood, of being a good mother and thus a virtuous Muslim woman. The alternative positioning could also be attained by referring to other aspects that were emphasised as virtuous by the dominant discourse, like acquiring or giving education. We saw Umm Khalthoum and also the unmarried female teachers at the boarding house connect aspects of hospitality and caring to the idea of being a good housewife, or to mothering other than only one's own children. At the same time the unmarried female teachers also connected motherhood and work in the positioning of themselves as 'moral mothers'. The common aspect was that all women used this concept of motherhood in order to claim credibility and respectability as proper Muslim women within a discourse in which they, particularly in their subject position as working women, did not really fit. In the process both the definition of motherhood and the dominant discourse that defined the identity were transformed.

The working of subject positions can therefore be compared to the way symbols unify persons with potentially diverse attitudes, ideas, and interests. The image of the ideal typical identity of the Muslim woman is impossible to live up to by any woman. The ideal is necessarily ambiguous in order to make it work for diverse groups of women who need to be unified under the same label of the good Muslim woman. It is precisely by contesting the homogeneity of the subject position allotted to women in the same 'category' that subverts that discourse.

I feel that this view facilitates an understanding of multiple identifications by women, even when they share in one and the same space and formal subject position. At the same time that it allows for opening up the closed analysis that I constructed in Part Two, it gives an insight into how women enact agency. I need a concept, which refers to the fixing and attempts at closure which is attained via the performance of subject identities as well as the flexibility and flux of the multiplicity of intersecting identities in negotiating these subject positions. In other words how to capture in an analytical concept the intertwining of intertextuality, intersectionality and intersubjectivity, which has both a discursive and a spatial/locational quality?

I refer to this relation between the rhetoric and argumentative perspectives of narratives as 'narrated identities'. Nencel (1997) uses the notion of 'gendered enclosures' in her study of women who prostitute in Lima, Peru, to refer both to the restricted and bounded spatial aspect of gender performances and the restricted and bounded self representations in these performances. She points out that these performances are in accordance with the meanings produced by those gendered enclosures (1997: 255–256). In this way she is able to give a dynamic and sensitive account of the bounded position and enclosed performances of women in economic and socially difficult circumstances. My concept of 'narrated identities' shows parallels with Nencel's perspective on gendered enclosures. In the case of working women in Kebkabiya, my emphasis was on the performances, verbal and non-verbal, which seem to be in accordance with and constrained by the meanings produced by dominant discourses in specific settings, or 'gendered enclosures'. At the same time, however, the working women proved to be constantly negotiating alternative subject positions. Thus I take the notion of 'narrated identities' to refer to this process of oscillation between fixed gender identities legitimated by the dominant discourse and the fluidity and multiplicity of acting out these identities in daily life. Both inhere in social and individual aspects, in a self-re/presentation and part of a relationship. As such, it comes close to the process of identification as put forward by De Lauretis (1984):

> Identification is a relation, part of the process of becoming a subject, and it involves the identification of oneself with something other than oneself, so that subjectivity is constituted through a series of such identifications (141).

In other words, identification is a process,[10] which makes both the discourse and the construction of subject positions part of the same dynamic process (Butler 1990: 57–62; Moore 1994: 53–63). However, the series of identifications which take place in the narration of identities by Hajja and Umm Khalthoum were not just different, their differences also pointed at different options open to them relative to their class

[10] Essed for example prefers identification as it suggests ongoing repositioning and thereby contingency of the constructions, which she finds especially fruitful in relation to policy and action (personal communication).

difference and thus to the status and power position of each woman and their positioning with respect to the relations of rule.

Thus, the government constructs an illusion of a general moral discourse on gender based on 'neutral' aspects of a shared culture in this case Islamic culture. The discourse becomes both a means and an end in acquiring and maintaining the power position of the ruling elite, of the status quo. This statement then raises the question to what extent this process of narrating identities also offers forms of resistance. As Moore (1994) states precisely in relation to this process of identification:

> The process of identification does not have to be complete and it can incorporate ...and very often does, a component of resistance or dissent (122).

The Strategic Perspective: Resistance, Defiance or Compliance?

> Looking for evidence of women's resistance only in articulated protests ... I ignored the possibility that their resistance was to be found precisely in their self-constructions.
>
> — Lynne Phillips quoted in Behar (1993: 268)

The strategic perspective is an aid in establishing the goal of the way in which working women in Kebkabiya narrated their identities. As a feminist scholar I am convinced that women have agency. This strategic aspect appeared in the narratives of Hajja and Umm Khalthoum as their claims to respectability and credibility as mothers and wives, with which they created room for being a working woman. This strategy was directed at me, as their immediate audience, as part of the context in which they narrated, as well as at the dominant discourse which they negotiated, as exemplified in my analyses of a rhetorical and argumentative perspective.

In Chapter 2, I posed the question as to whether we should read the alternative positioning of working women as defiance or resistance. The quotation from Lynne Phillips summarises neatly the problem of evaluating the narratives of the working women with respect to resistance. On the one hand, feminist scholars have been warned against recycling the stereotypes of Third World women as downgraded, silenced, lacking in initiative. This image emphasises domination and repression and caters for the image of women as victims, aspects that loom large in studies on women living in Muslim societies (see the Introduction). On the other hand, there is a risk of overcompensation: if I challenge the representation of Muslim women, I might ignore the restricting and potentially oppressive aspects of the dominant discourse. The result might be an image of women as heroines, which is as prejudiced and denigrating as the opposite: both views depart from the assumption that Islamic societies are intrinsically oppressive and dominating with respect to women. (Behar 1993: 269–273; Mohanty 1991 a & b; Moore 1994: 50).

I propose here that in order to understand the extent to which the narratives of market women and female teachers can be seen as resistance I have to look at them from a strategic perspective. From the rhetoric and argumentative perspectives, it appeared that gender is an aspect of the way people relate to other people and to the dominant discourses relevant in that physical space of narrating. This context-bound nature of the construction of selves makes narrated gender identities performative.[11]

This notion of performance is closely related to the work of Butler[12] who has written extensively on this aspect of performativity of gender identity:

> Consider gender, for instance, as a 'corporeal style', an 'act' as it were, which is both intentional and performative, where 'performative' suggests a dramatic and contingent construction of meaning (Butler 1990: 139).

Thereby the body may be a focus of performance of a gendered identity, but at the same time the:

> Gendered body has no ontological status apart from the various acts, which constitute its reality. Identities are an effect of discourses, not its basis, and the performative act is one that brings into being or enacts what it names. The subject is performatively constituted (Butler 1990: 136, see also Bell 1993: 19–27).

It is important to assert, however, that this performance is not voluntary:

> What is called gender identity is a performative accomplishment compelled by social sanction and taboo (Butler 1990: 270–271).

---

[11] In this respect I take it that a speech act is a social act and thus perfomative as well (Meijer 1996; Billig 1991; Fairclough 1987, 1991).

[12] For example: (1990); (1990 a and b); (1993); (1994); (1997).

Although Butler states that 'gender intersects with racial, class, ethnic, sexual and regional modalities' (1990a: 3), she ignores them throughout her analyses, which therefore seem to be focused mainly on the middle classes. The fact that Butler approaches the issue of strategy and resistance from a psychoanalytical perspective especially makes it difficult to use her viewpoints for understanding the resistance as a social-discursive act. I therefore turn to another anthropological work on gender and performance in an Islamic community.

In her anthropological research in an Islamic community in Tajikistan, Colette Harris also refers to Butler for her analysis (Harris 2000: 1–49; 235–250). Harris shares the perspective of post-colonial feminist and feminists of colour who criticize Butler's theories for being Eurocentric.[13]

Harris does refer to Butler, though, when studying 'control and subversion' of and by women living in an Islamic society in Tajikistan. A society which, just like the Sudan, is considered as marginal with respect to the 'core area' of Islam—the Middle East.[14] Harris states in respect to gender performances:

> It is inevitably related to the theatrical because it exists only in front of an audience. Moreover, variations on it are inevitable, indeed *demanded*, by the varied situations of lived experience (Harris 2000: 241, emphasis in original).

She employs in her analysis two notions which she relates to this view of the theatrical: the concept of 'gender masks' to refer to the outward appearance, and 'the use of gender performance for the intentional projection of an image' (2000: 27) which in her analysis is more important than the conviction of the performer, the internalisation of that gender identity (2000: 27–28; 242).

Harris' analysis is eloquent and interesting, giving in depth insight into the workings of identity constructions in Tajik daily life. Here it offers me a way to clarify the relation between resistance and the relations of ruling (Smith 1987: 3) that I proposed in Chapter 2 for understanding relational agency. In this respect I consider Harris' analysis problematic on two accounts. In the first place because of using a concept such as 'masks'. Even though Harris points out that the subordinate person is not pretending nor that a person might freely choose the

---

[13] See the introduction of Part Three for an elaboration of this critique.

[14] This is not related to the number of Muslims, but refers to a political, cultural and geographic centre-periphery relation.

identity one wishes to enact (2000: 27), it means that both the subject as well as the researcher would be able to distinguish between what is experienced as 'real' and what constitutes the mask in relation to gendered identities. Harris refers to this conscious act as 'as if' by subordinate persons. In relation to my own work it is problematic for me to suggest that women are hiding their 'real' selves behind a mask,[15] as the convictions and self-presentations of working women are so tied up in their negotiations of their subject positions within the dominant moral discourse.

A second problematic issue, is the fact that the subordination in the performances as Harris (2000) proposes is directed at powerful audiences, which permit subordinates:

> To subvert their gender performances, as long as this remains concealed and thus poses no overt threat to the dominant discourse. The result is that those in power rarely attempt to look behind the masks of the subordinated, although it is unclear whether this stems from their belief that the surface presentation is all that there is, or whether the very effort of subordinates' assuming the gender mask, an assumption that implies acknowledgement of the power of the dominant, generally suffices to satisfy them (2000: 242).

Here Harris seems to conflate the dominant discourse with those in power. Harris suggests that only subordinates would perform their identities in a subversive way, as if those in power were presenting their 'real' face completely in tune with the subject positions offered by the same dominant discourse. However, I think that narrated identities are performative for all subjects, which are positioned by the dominant discourse, albeit in different ways. I think that the dominant discourse allots people different positions of authority, but that it requires of all subjects to position themselves relative to that discourse and to other subjects: all subjects perform their identities and thereby construct a self.[16] And as the ideal typical images of the subject positions as put forward by the dominant discourse work in the same way as symbols, these constructions of self rarely conflate with the ideal typical identity.

---

[15] Butler formulates a similar kind of critique on Lacan's view of masquerade (1990a: 47–49).

[16] See with respect to Africa: Mbembe (1991: 4) who has a quite sombre view of this mutual relationship: '... the contradiction between overt acts and gestures in public and the covert responses made 'underground' ... has resulted in the mutual zombification of both the dominant and those whom they apparently dominate. This zombification meant that each robbed the other of their vitality and has left them both impotent...'

The differences in authority and relative power, as I pointed out in Chapter 2, construct a different positioning of groups of men and women towards the relations of ruling which refers to:

> A complex of organized practices, including government, law, business and financial management, professional organization, and educational institutions as well as discourses in texts that interpenetrate the multiple sites of power (Smith 1987: 3).

The dominant discourse is part of these relations of ruling, not a property of one group or the other. As I showed in the analyses of the narratives, the same gender identities are indeed used differently by different classes of working women, in relation to the self-re/presentations and claims on respectability and credibility in the light of the moral discourse. The importance of considering those in positions of power as positioned in a discourse as those who are seen as 'subordinates' lies in the fact that it allows consideration also of members of the powerful group able to induce change.

In Kebkabiya the different positioning of working women in relation to class and power effected a different evaluation of their conduct in the light of a dominant discourse, which claimed to refer to all Muslim women equally. Education in combination with a white-collar job, performed in a 'protected' and enclosed location, in combination with 'civilisation', or lifestyle, marked by a white *tobe* made all the difference in the way working women were positioned relative to the relations of ruling. It seemed that the closer one was related to those in positions of ruling, the more evident, and more articulate, the negotiations with the dominant discourse. In respect to the narratives of Hajja and Umm Khalthoum, this meant that Umm Khalthoum referred only to the dominant discourse in order to legitimate her current position, while Hajja and other market women, also related to a local, sub-dominant, discourse on gender relations when connecting motherhood and work as self-evident. Hajja thereby had to deal with both discourses as they were hierarchically related and her silence on motherhood might have been a result of the relative weight of either discourse in her claim for public respectability (cf. Moore 1994: 59).

The differences in argumentation by each woman as a member of her class also marked a difference in positioning with respect to the possibilities to resist that discourse. The construction of class difference based on education proved contingent in itself, but was never directly articulated as a proof of the fallacy of the construction itself. This means that the strategies of all the working women were directed at negotiating the dominant discourse, but never directed openly against it. Personal narratives are thus an occasion for the struggle for meaning and the control of interpretation as well as identity formation (Grele 1994: 1–17). Women, such as working women in Kebkabiya can therefore be seen to engage in a process of 'disidentification' which means that they 'map out ... new terrains' which allows them alternative and 'potentially more liberating ways' of constructing their identities (Mills 1999: 15).

It is in this respect, that resistance is to be found 'precisely in their self constructions' (Phillips, as quoted at the beginning of the paragraph). The dominant discourse of the government with its ideal typical construction of female gender identities is not the same reference point for the strategies of all classes of working women.[17] In Chapter 6, the commonalities and differences in negotiating the dominant discourse was evident from the way women were positioned in the 'border zone'. The commonalities of these 'non-fitting' women were clear not only by the ways in which married market women like Ashia, the sister of Sa'adiya, and Zamzam talked about the (lost) opportunities in their lives and in their work. It was also communicated by the silences in their reflections. Silences which were even more remarkable in the reflections and attitudes of some of the young unmarried market women, like Rhoda and Rana who had been to school and thus were knowledgeable about Islamic issues which they might have used to argue their cases. The silences drew attention to the fear of their loss of reputation by the young unmarried market women, which might mean the loss of chances to achieve social mobility by marriage or continued education. The same kind of fear of a loss of reputation was of major importance in the young unmarried female teachers' reactions to and reflections on gossiping and their silences on marriage and motherhood.

My deconstruction of the suggested homogeneity of the two classes of working women pointed at differences among working women of

[17] This aspect is referred to by Butler with the term 'iterability', a form of citationality, in this case the repeatability of an identity. Butler suggests that even by performing identities which seem to reenact dominant discourses; the fact that this takes place in different contexts produces different meanings that may undermine and subvert those same dominant discourses and produce change (See also chapter 2). My point is that this view makes it hard to articulate ways to understand the potential of alternative identity constructions to produce change.

one and the same class on the basis of age and education. In turn, this pointed to similarities in the negotiations by the younger generation of unmarried women in both classes of their subject positions as working women. My analysis of the new generation of working women brought out both the differences and commonalities in dreams and fantasies about the future, which influenced their strategic speaking or keeping silent. A common theme that was discussed among all unmarried young working women was the availability of the right husband and the right to work as unmarried and married woman, as mother and wife 'to-be'. Their fantasies and projections are not exorbitant out-of-the blue imaginations about a fictive *persona*, but concrete images of an ideal self within the bounds of the culturally imaginable. In their strategies to defend their interests it becomes apparent what different women want to strive for, what they want to attain in life.

Moore (1994) uses the idea of investment for this strategic positioning with respect to the dominant discourse. Investment refers to an emotional commitment and satisfaction as well as the expectation of material, social and economic benefits, which are the reward of taking up certain subject positions against others. Thus, investment is bound up with positions of power, as Moore (1994: 66)[18] puts it:

> This explains why concepts such as reputation are connected not just to self-representations and social evaluations and social evaluations of the self, but to the potential for power and agency, which a good reputation offers. The loss of reputation could mean a loss of livelihood, and the lack of good social standing can render individuals incapable of pursuing various strategies or courses of action. The term 'fantasy' is important here because it emphasizes the often affective and subconscious nature of the investment in various subject positions, and the social strategies necessary to maintain that investment.

Resistance is thus not directed at the terms of the discourse itself, for example the relevance of Islam, *shari'a* or the importance of wife and motherhood for the status of women. Rather, resistance is directed at the implications for those women who are not able or willing to take up the narrow subject positions: that it would make them bad Muslims, disrespectful and criminal at heart.[19] Therefore, the discourse is that

---

[18] Moore refers for the concept of investment to Holloway 1984: 238.

[19] Particularly with respect to the Islam there is among educated men and women in the Sudan an importance placed on 'inner' virtue as related to outside appearance. The strongest example is perhaps the criticism on the condemnation and subsequent price on the head of Rushdie by Ayatollah Khomeini. Those *Sunni* Muslims I discussed

'which is struggled for' in terms of who gets to define its terms and boundaries (Mills 1997: 16).

Resistance should therefore not be read only as an act 'against' something or someone, nor as a strategy only used by subordinate subjects. It should be read as resistance 'for': as a means to claim space for alternative subject positions while at the same time receiving public respect and approval. It refers to a strategy to attain the space for living one's life as one sees fit, and deciding about the course of one's future.[20] In this considering fantasy as the 'affective nature of investment' I feel Braidotti takes its effect a bit further, considering it a possible avenue for change:

> The positive aspect of this affectivity is that it mobilises people's desire and imagination, thus offering great opportunities for a process of transformation of identities (2001: 17).

The strategic perspective is thus a way to read narratives on the possibility of resistance by the alternative subject positions that are constructed in relation to the dominant discourse, by those women who are in the 'border zone'. To read the narratives on elements of resistance might point at possibilities of transformations of that same discourse because of negotiating alternative positions as legitimate.

It is interesting that the female teachers who were locally seen as having most direct access to the relations of ruling and who had a status which comes closest to the role model of the virtuous Muslim woman were the ones who most forcefully and openly defended their alternative positions as working unmarried women.

They made use of the fact that their position was taken to be transitory and temporary. In combination to their closeness to the relations of rule this obviously facilitated a strategy of resistance. Their strategy was to refer to subjects who seemed even more favourably positioned within the dominant discourse and the 'relations of ruling' it effected: the educated elite men. The single female teachers pointed at the absence of a prospective husband of the right standing and standard as a reason for

---

the issue with, both men and women in the Sudan and in Tanzania, considered this an 'un-Islamic' verdict, as this was something to be decided upon by Allah.

[20] These aspects are constitutive of the concept of autonomy as defined in the 1980s by Boesveld et al. (1986); Schrijvers (1985); Willemse (1991) The concept of autonomy indicates the capability of women of diverse structural positions to act and think according to their interests, to have power over their minds and bodies and the directions of change.

their prolonged liminal status. This in turn, removed the attention from other reasons these women might have had for not marrying, such as their resistance against giving up their status as working women and 'stepping back' into the realm of family relations and control. However, the critical assessments of their positionings were never directly addressed at the male subjects close to the relations of ruling themselves, but to their masculinity.

This brings me back to the issue of narrated identities that I put forward as a notion that refers to the process of oscillation between fluidity and closure, which women engage in when constructing identities. My construction of the strategic perspective must lead me to a related spatial notion that encompasses both 'gendered enclosures' and 'identifications'; both the tracing and mapping of identities; both by the narrators and the anthropologist: a combination, rather than opposition, of 'border zone' and 'home'. I find these aspects combined in the notion of 'belonging':

> What we cannot capture as a feature of subjectivity is the yearnings that people have to belong, and the ways these yearnings can be anchored to particular times and places, can change and can bring us into connection with very different groups of people, in a way that constitutes the singularity of our own subjectivity (Alsop et. al. 2003: 215).[21]

Belonging thus as a process escapes fixing, while the process itself is constituted as a means of finding closure. The challenge for anthropologists in dealing with this process is to engage in 'strategies of writing and of reading' as 'forms of cultural resistance (De Lauretis, 1984: 7)'. One of the strategies to use in practising this resistance is to write and read 'against the grain' (De Lauretis 1984: 7). This brings me full circle. It also brings me back to Kebkabiya.

Back to Kebkabiya: Coming to the End of This Journey

In re-reading the narratives I employed my three perspectives, the rhetorical, argumentative and strategic perspective. These have given me insight into the dynamics of and boundaries to the construction of identities, and the positioning of female teachers and market women in relation to the dominant discourse on the good Muslim of the current

[21] Their view is based on a discussion of the work of Probyn (1996) and Prosser (1999) who theorize the construction of identities by and in transsexual narratives.

Islamist regime in the Sudan. The rhetorical perspective gives an insight in the day-to-day negotiations and performances which women use in order to survive. These performances and positions are related to supposedly fixed gender identities that are presented as constituting the 'virtuous' Muslim woman. Considering these identities from an argumentative perspective, these appeared to be stretched to such an extent that diverse categories of women with different backgrounds and goals were able to relate to, and negotiate, the same images of mother- and wifehood. In my strategic perspective I pointed out that the goals of the self-presentations might be taken as acts of resistance without necessarily leading to overt protests or open criticism: silences can be taken to mark resistance in the same way as articulated protests are constituted as social acts.

The question to what extent these negotiations and resistances result in a transformation of the discourse, I cannot answer in a straightforward and definite way. In this respect the achievements of the educated elite women are most obvious. They have succeeded in negotiating the right to work by claiming moral motherhood. As I pointed out in Chapter 7, the jobs cut out for them by the government are defined as extensions of the role of mothers: predominantly nursing and teaching. At the same time, the majority of women are already working in these branches. The possibility to work was acknowledged by a male member of the Islamist party who told Hale (1997: 199):

> It is not that we forbid women to work. If she must work, then perhaps it is to the husband or to other male members of her family where we should look for any criticism. We only blame her if she goes to work as a frivolous act and does not behave appropriately in the workplace. For example, she must dress according to the respect she wants. We want to respect her (199).

Here again, the Islamist man addresses other men in their responsibilities towards their families: a proper Muslim man is a provider for his family. In my analysis of Muslim masculinity, I pointed out that in the constructions of Muslim manhood, elite ideas on masculinity are presented as 'Islamic'. The notion of the Muslim man is not only based on a class identity, however, it also carries ethnic overtones. Fur men, as I showed in Chapter 7, were considered to be irresponsible fathers and husbands because of their ethnic background, not because of proven acts of being bad fathers or husbands.

My consideration of the educated male elite members' subject positions in relation to the dominant discourse thus points at a silence, which is quite commonly shared by both classes of working women. None of the female teachers referred to ethnicity as a marker of identity. This silence was there among the market women as well, but in a different way. Even though market women and female teachers would, on request, state their ethnic background via their father's line, in the narratives there were peculiar silences and shifts with respect to this part of the women's identity constructions and subject positions. This came most clearly to the fore in relation to Hajja's narrative. Hajja's relationship to the renowned Faqih Sinin did not come up immediately, and could only be traced via her mother, or her eldest sister. Only when discussing the terms of kinship, did Hajja acknowledge her belonging to her father's line, but she did not elaborate on that. Crucial in this respect is her remark that her daughters do not belong to her own ethnic group, but to her husband's. This gives a clue as to why patrilineal ethnic identity is not important for the day-to-day lives of women, which centres on a 'belonging' to 'the hearth', i.e. their matrilineal kin. The female teachers I spoke with were even more reluctant to talk about their ethnic identity, as their status as female teacher made them a class of the 'elite'. Therefore, the women positioned themselves as 'Sudanese' rather than as members of a localised 'parochial' ethnic group. Interestingly, in the cases where ethnic affiliation did arise among the female teachers, it constituted an identity that went beyond being Sudanese. Umm Khalthoum emphasised in her narrative her mother's Egyptian ancestry, while in the case of Sitt Ashia, her *awlad ar-riif* background came up as significant to establish both broadmindedness and respect but above all a difference from Sudanese-ness.

With respect to denouncing ethnic identity the difference between 'Arab' men and Islamic values which Wisal Al-Mahdi, the wife of Al-Turabi, articulated is interesting. I quote again:

> [Arab men] are against women, and that is why we are much against them. We know our rights, we have learned the *shari'a*...We are working in the NIF to praise women and to make women have a better status, and to tell the world that we are as equal as men and are as efficient as men and we are as educated as men and we are as good as men and as great as men (Quoted in Hale 1997: 216)

On another occasion she added that Arab men 'think a woman's voice is like a woman's breast showing (quoted in Hale 1997: 226)'. Her assertion of a difference in an 'Arab' and a 'Muslim' male identity in relation to the equality of women is interesting as Al-Mahdi refers to ethnic identity, also among the Central Sudanese, as a male prerogative, while women are considered to adhere to a more pure, de-tribalised, Islam. She thus seems to argue for a national, Sudanese Muslim identity, which is basically female. I think the issue of masculinity as I have analysed it in Chapter 7 in relation to issues of nationalism and ethnicity may be less of a blind spot, or silence, than I figured, at least among women in high political positions like Wisal Al-Mahdi. However, it is not quite clear in what way this rhetoric indeed facilitates an alternative positioning of working women in relation to an Islamic moral discourse that creates space for a notion of 'belonging' that caters for the interests of women on a national level (cf. Karam 1996). In the meantime this issue of ethnic identity has become a major aspect in what has been called the 'ethnic conflict' in Darfur and to which I want to refer as the 'Darfur war'. Although it requires another book to do justice to the complexity of this war, in the Epilogue I will give an idea of how I perceive the conflict.

Epilogue—
The Darfur War, Gender, and the Contingency of Sudanese Citizenship

Since February 2003[22] Darfur has been the site of mounting violence, which has led the UN to describe the conflict as currently 'the world's worst humanitarian crisis'. The U.S. Congress even labelled the conflict 'genocide'. Diverse ethnic groups as well as the government were engaged in violence in the 1980s and 1990s. However, violence has reached a new dimension in the recent war, where racism has become the main legitimising discourse of the conflict.

In this short sketch I will try to understand the current 'crisis'[23] in Darfur from the perspective of gendered identities and the contingency of Sudanese citizenship. I feel hesitant to say anything definitive on the

[22] This was the date that a group calling themselves the 'Darfur Liberation Front' officially claimed the attack on Golo, the disctrict headquarters of Jebel Marra. Political as well as armed resistance against the government had been building for a longer period in Darfur, however. Flint and de Waal for example, refer to 21 July 2001 as an important date for the start of organized resistance, when 'rebels' attacked a police station in Golo (2005: 76). See also: http://en.wikipedia.org/wiki/Darfur_conflict: accessed 05–01–2006.

[23] I think that rather than a crisis, the conflict can be better termed a war. I put therefore quotation marks to indicate this problem. At the same time I want to retain the label conflict to indicate that it has a longer history than three years.

nature or sources of the current Darfur war. In the first place because as an anthropologist I base myself on what people in a certain location say and do. I have not been able to talk to people in Darfur since this war erupted in early 2000. I also find it hard to see the conflict in terms of an underlying all-overriding aspect or aspects, which could explain the crisis.

Here, I will attempt to look at the war from the perspective of the issue of intersecting identities. This is not to neglect economic, social, cultural, political, or other forms of marginalization of Darfur within the Sudanese nation state as important factors in the conflict. On the contrary, I think these are of major relevance for the scale and frequency of the violence.[24] At the same time since 'ethnicity', or even 'race', has become the major label with which the violence has been referred to, often in a context of exoticizing the conflict, I want to look at the problem from the perspective of identity construction.

In order to do this I will first give a brief outline of the war in Darfur. Next I will try and place the recent events in Darfur in the context of the project of the Sudanese nation state to construct a national Sudanese identity, by relating these to the way the Islamist government in Sudan has positioned the Darfur population since coming to power in 1989. I will argue that this positioning as well as the current war in Darfur fit into a pattern, which connects Muslim masculinity to the articulation of a Sudanese citizenship.

Some Background to the 'Darfur Crisis'

The war in Darfur has attracted ample media attention as well as international political concern. In general the current conflict has been cast as a conflict between 'Sudanese Arab nomads' and 'Black African farmers'. This dichotomy has been contested in both popular and academic publications. Particularly problematic in using ethnicity as shorthand for, if not the main denominator of the conflict is not only that it leads to an oversimplification of the causes of the current war.

---

[24] Some critical scholars, such as Ali Dinar, even state that the watershed that the war is thought to represent is exaggerated as violence, poverty, and the neglect by the government are symptomatic for Darfur. In this respect I agree with him. Here I will argue, however, that the way the violence has been legitimized does make a difference however (thanks to Ali Dinar for his critical remarks on a paper I presented at the 25th anniversary of the Sudan Studies Association, Bergen, Norway, 6–8 April 2006).

I think that if the ethnic labels, which are used in the Darfur war are not qualified, the users of these labels are complicit in the discourse the current Islamist government of Sudan uses to legitimize this civil war.

There are several arguments that allow for deconstructing the binary opposition, which seems so self-evidently to constitute the basis of the current conflict in Darfur. One of them is to point out that ethnic identity is not fixed, homogeneous or self-evident, but rather flexible, fluid and context bound. Another is to understand ethnicity as an aspect of the social, economic, political and cultural contexts in which it is put forward as an important marker of identity.[25] In this paper I will focus on the second strategy. I will therefore only briefly outline some of the arguments put forward to indicate the flexibility of ethnicity. The overview is scant and by no means an attempt to be exhaustive, nor is it meant to give a neat chronology of events.

The construction of the conflict as one of 'Arab Muslim nomads' against 'Black African farmers' glosses over the fact that the parties involved are all Muslims who are linked with each other by a history of exchange, intermarriage, and even lifestyle. Already in 1969 Haaland described how the shift from farming to nomadism by fortunate Fur farmers also meant a shift from a Fur to a Baggara identity: the so-called *Fur al-Baggara* as De Waal refers to them (1989: 50). Although the newcomer was not readily accepted as 'one of us' by the Baggara, the reason they gave Haaland for this was the lack of respect shown to visitors by not keeping to the cultural codes of hospitality (i.e. offering tea and food) and not the act of taking up nomadism in itself (Haaland 1972: 49–172; see also1969). The reverse was also true: whenever a person settled among sedentary farmers, the granting of land by the community leader meant that one could become part of that community within one generation (cf. De Waal 1989: 48–49). The relation between ethnic identity, location, livelihood, and land dates back to an even further removed past, when the Muslim sultanate was founded. Being 'Fur' meant that one lived within the boundaries of the Fur Sultanate ruled and protected by a Fur Sultan who, since the 17th century, adhered to Islam. A full subject of the sultanate therefore would also be a Muslim, and would accept the rights and duties, which came with

[25] Again, I consider identity not as a property of a person, but as performative and thus contingent, ambiguous and transformative (cf. Butler 1990a: 70–90; also Alsop et. al. 2003: 103).

belonging to a certain locality. An ethnic identity thus represented 'citizenship' (cf. De Waal 1989: 48).[26]

National and regional politics have been an important cause of the solidification of ethnic identities in the more recent past. Also the colonial government used ethnicity as a means to 'divide and rule' by literally dividing the former Fur sultanate into more or less fixed '*dars*', administrative areas under the control of appointed tribal leaders under the 'Native Administration' system set up in the 1920s. This division led to clearly demarcated 'homelands' related to fixed ethnic identities which was expressed in the names of these tribal areas, like 'Dar Zaghawa', while some of the nomadic Arab groups even did not receive a 'homeland' of their own, particularly in North-Darfur (see fold-out Sudan map 2, between pages 38 and 39). Although the tribal leaders never lost complete power, in 1994 the native administration council was 'reinvented' under the new Islamist military government in order to govern the area via local leaders 'on the cheap (De Waal 2004: 4)':[27] their re-established power over land-allocations directly led to renewed conflicts in the far west of Darfur (De Waal 2004; Flint and de Waal 2005: 12–13, 58–59; Harir 2004).

I do not want to suggest that ethnicity in the 17th century has remained unaltered in the last centuries; nor that there are strict analogies between 'being a Fur' in the period that the Fur Sultanate was founded, in the colonial era, and the experiences of those who consider themselves to be Fur by the end of the 20th century (cf. Johnson 2003: 4). On the contrary, ethnic identity can not be taken as an identity in and of itself as it has historically been intersected with other identifications such as religion, location, means of survival etc., shifting meaning in changing socio-economic and political contexts. My brief outline is meant to caution that one should be clear about the context in which ethnicity is given meaning and look for other important identities that intersect with ethnicity. As the late Claude Aké remarked 'ethnic groups do not exist',[28] referring to the fact that ethnicity only makes sense when analyzed as intersected with other social, economic,

[26] Those who did not want to acknowledge the Fur sultan, nor Islam as their religion were forced to move south, out of the sultanate; in due time some of them became 'Fertit'; see O'Fahey 1982.

[27] See Alex de Waal, "Counter-insurgency on the Cheap", *London Review of Books*, August 5, 2004, ⟨http://www.lrb.co.uk/v26/n15/waal01.html⟩.

[28] Professor Claude Aké stated this in an hour-long television interview in the series 'in my father's house' hosted by the anthropologist Anil Ramdas. He pointed out that

political and cultural identities. Considering a saying from the people of Dor in Northern Darfur, as quoted by Flint and De Waal: 'conflict defines origins (2005: 7)', I would maintain that it is the nature of the conflict that is of importance for understanding how ethnicity is articulated and validated as well as how these meanings were historically and locationally constructed (cf. Idris 2001: 57).

An important context is the ongoing desertification in the post-colonial era. Camel nomads and semi-nomadic groups who had been allotted 'dars' by the colonial government in the far north of Darfur, or none at all, suffered most from the deteriorating environmental conditions. In particular since the droughts of the 1970s and 1980s they would more frequently and earlier in the season come down from the desert in the North with their camels that trampled, ate, or otherwise destroyed the not yet harvested crops of the local farmers and threatened to deplete the local water resources.

In addition, recent politics have solidified ethnic identities even more. In 1981 Darfur was the last region to get a governor from the same area he was to rule under the 1972 Regional Autonomy Act. However, the installation of Ahmed Ibrahim Draige, a Fur, as governor turned out to be a bone of contention. Intellectuals claiming Arab descent organized themselves in the Arab Congregation. As a consequence raids by Arab *fursan* (knights) and Fur *malishat* (militia) were quite un-problematically cast as an ethnic conflict waged between the 'Arab belt' versus the 'African belt'. The Fur felt that the Arabs aimed at destroying their ancestral rights to the land, while Arabs claimed that Fur threatened to oust them under the slogan 'Darfur for the Fur'. The influx of high-tech weapons in the same period due to the war between Libya and Chad, the donations of arms by diverse political parties to their respective constituencies during and after the democratic elections, and the arming of militia by consecutive national governments has fuelled this conflict (cf. Flint and the Waal 2005; Harir 1994: 160–184).

In 2003 the Opposition Forces constituted by the SLM/A (the Sudan Liberation Movement/Army, formerly the Darfur Liberation Front, led by Abdel Wahid Mohammed Al-Nur) together with the Justice and Equality Movement (JEM, led by Khalil Ibrahim, a former member of the National Islamic Front) attacked government forces and instal-

---

it is theoretically problematic to think 'ethnic groups' or 'ethnic conflict' and that in situations where ethnic consciousness is called upon, issues of power and survival are at stake. See also his 'What is the problem with ethnicity in Africa'?

lations.[29] Though the SLM/A and JEM were not indigenous to Darfur they justified their cause by accusing the government of neglecting the huge economic problems in Darfur while doing nothing about the increasing insecurity and lawlessness related to the continuous influx of high-tech arms into the region. They thereby referred to a book handed out mainly in Khartoum in May 2000 entitled, *The Black Book: Imbalance of Power and Wealth in the Sudan* in which a group calling themselves 'The seekers of truth and justice', who would later found the JEM, had formulated their grievances about the socio-economic and political marginalization of Darfur (cf. Flint and de Waal 2005: 17–18).

Since members of the Fur and the Masalit, both predominantly sedentary farmers, and the Zaghawa, semi-nomads, have become involved in this rebel movement they have been cast collectively as 'Black African farmers', *black* suggesting the status of a slave and automatically of a non-Muslim. These so-called 'non-Muslims' have become opposed to the so-called Janjawiid, the other party in the conflict in Darfur, who are usually characterized as Muslim 'Arab' nomads. They are seen as the perpetrators of the violence enacted upon the sedentary population, supported by Sudanese soldiers and the Sudanese Air Force and provided with arms by the Sudanese government operating with total impunity.

Local Youth, Arms, and the Construction of a Social Self[30]

Originally, the government was caught by surprise. As it distrusted its own army which largely consisted of soldiers of Darfur origin, its response was to mount a campaign of aerial bombardment supporting ground attacks by an Arab militia. This militia, the Janjawiid, was recruited from local tribes and armed by the government.

The label Janjawiid, used to refer to the Arab nomadic militia, has been dissected into 'evil' (jaan) 'horsemen' (jawid), or even devils (jiin) riding horses carrying *jim*, Arabic for GM-3 rifles. However, prior to the recent conflict, the term was used more generally to refer to 'rabble', 'hordes', or 'outlaws', in particular in cases of banditry and camel theft

[29] The SLM / A is considered to be associated with the Fur and Masalit, while the JEM is associated with the Zaghawa of northern Darfur.

[30] Parts of this section appeared as "Darfur in War. The Politicisation of Ethnic Identities?" *ISIM Review* 15, Spring (2005): 14–15.

committed predominantly by young men.[31] It is this reference to young men that is crucial to my argument.

In the early 1990s, when I conducted anthropological research in Kebkabiya, a town that has been recently under heavy siege, conflicts over scarce resources such as land and water concerned predominantly Fur and Zaghawa groups that have now become allies in the Opposition Forces. The failure of traditional negotiation and peacekeeping mechanisms, such as tribal reconciliation conferences—the last large conference was held to settle a war between Fur and Arabs in 1989, but to no avail—proved to be not only due to the politicisation of ethnic identities or the unwillingness of the government to enforce the treaty. Of importance as well was the discontent within ethnic groups.

Young males increasingly contested the authority of tribal leaders, and elderly men in general. For example, during my stay in Kebkabiya in 1991, one of the Zaghawa representatives who had attended a reconciliation conference inside the town of Kebkabiya was ambushed when returning home. It turned out he was killed by youngsters of his own constituency as they felt their rights were thwarted and their needs neglected by the agreement he had signed.[32]

The general neglect of Darfur in national development plans left youngsters with few possibilities for establishing themselves as head of a family and thus of becoming a 'man' in socio-cultural terms. They had difficulties paying for the bride-price and wedding arrangements that mark maturity and social status. Even when they did marry, young nomads were hardly able to provide for their families as nomads. For their part, many young sedentary farmers had to migrate to towns for some extended period of time in order to earn the money necessary to raise a family. Moreover, despite the high expectations placed on education, educated young men, even when employed as white-collar workers, barely had the means and ability to provide for their families (Harir 1994: 170; Willemse 2005).

In most farming communities in Darfur, women are the main cultivators while single young men are often redundant. Formerly they would wander, sometimes from the age of eight, from one *Qur'an*ic

[31] Abdullahi Ali Ibrahim "Janjaweed: What's in a name", *Sudan Studies Association Newsletter* 24, 2 (2004):15; Flint and de Waal (2005: 38, 55). Also via personal communication with Ali bin Ali Dinar, November 2004, The Hague.

[32] Information from a talk with one of the Zaghawa negotiators present at this conference.

school to the next working for the *faqih*s, or engage in odd jobs in order to survive. In times of drought, young men would be the first to migrate out of the farmers' community in order to fend for themselves, followed by married men, while women, children and the elderly would only leave when cultivation was no longer possible: women were *de facto* 'keepers of the land' despite the fact that entitlement and landownership was a male affair (see also Barth 1972; Grawert 1992, 1998).

Among nomadic groups single young men were most important for herding camels. In times of drought only young men would tend to the smaller herds, leaving behind women, children, and the elderly in small temporary settlements near sedentary peoples. This process of settling by female nomads coupled with male out-migration among sedentary farmers has created communities that consist of predominantly female-headed households, of both sedentary and nomadic backgrounds. These engage with increasing frequency and scale in interethnic exchange, sharecropping and intermarriage. Although there are 'no true nomads in Darfur' as 'most of the people who are described as such are in fact semi-nomadic or transhumant (De Waal 1989: 50)' even the semi-nomadic lifestyle is increasingly difficult to maintain. The temporary nomadic settlements have become more permanent and, moreover, now host an increasing number of young male nomads, which might mean that the nomadic lifestyle has even become extinct. The result of this radical change is insecurity and anxiety among the settled nomadic communities. Moreover, in order to survive, the new settlers needed access to land, water, labour, money and knowledge, thus competing more directly over exactly the same resources that sedentary farmers used in these transition zones (cf. Flint and de Waal 2005: 46–48). These happened also to be the areas where most of the outbursts of violence have taken place.[33]

In these deteriorating conditions of deprivation and despair among nomadic and sedentary young men 'without a future', weapons form an easy and immediate satisfaction in the quest for respect, self-identity, and a sense of control. Due to the high presence of young disenfranchised men on both sides of the conflict, it has taken on an especially troubling gender dimension. Women are systematically verbally and physically abused, raped, mutilated, their relatives killed in front of their

[33] Even more remarkable is that there seems to be a pattern that the most violent killings have taken place between neighbouring communities, in other words, between those who knew each other (personal communication Human Rights Watch).

eyes, while young men of 'battle age' are targets for mass killings. This so-called 'gendercide'[34] is part of many recent so-called ethnic conflicts in Africa and elsewhere.[35]

The illusion of ethnic homogeneity of the Janjawiid has become part of the political-ideological project of those who cast themselves as the 'Arabs' in Darfur. Though it is not clear whether the Janjawiid were indeed as ethnically homogeneous as has been claimed, and there are even some indications that originally the militia included young men from diverse ethnic backgrounds, this ideology has become the mainstay of a regional discourse of ethnic and religious superiority.[36] However, even these 'Arabs' are composed of a diversity of groups with different backgrounds, like those formerly serving in the Sudanese Popular Defence Forces in Dar Masalit who, in turn, had been trained by the *Quwait al-Islam*, a militia under the control of the Northern Sudanese General Dabi in South Kordofan; recently migrated 'Arabs' from Chad and Libya; and Abbala and Baggara 'Arabs' from Darfur, who are constructed as the descendants of the Qureish, the ethnic group of Prophet Mohammed, and who migrated in the past from the Arabian Peninsula looking for 'new pastures'.[37] Musa Hilal, who is seen as one of the main new 'Arab' warlords directing the Janjawiid, claims he is waging a 'holy war' under the direction of the Sudanese government (cf. Flint and de Waal 2005: 33–65; Harir 1994: 161).

The strategy of turning Arab nomads into a militia is, however, not novel: it was applied by consecutive regimes in the civil war with southern Sudan. Both the democratic regime (1985–1989) under the leadership of Sadiq Al-Mahdi, and the current Islamist regime, armed Arab nomads from Kordofan and Darfur and turned them into so-

---

[34] Gendercide Watch (www.gendercide.org).

[35] In Darfur, where ethnic affiliation is traced patrilineally, intermarriage results in women begetting children of a different ethnic background than their own. This means that the involvement of women in ethnic politics differs from those of men who have a more unified ethnic identity. Even in ethnically more homogenous communities women and children of diverse ethnicities have in fact been caught similarly in the crossfire between rebels, government, and bandits.

[36] Despite the fact that Musa Hilal, the leader of the Janjawiid claims these consist of only Arabs and that 'Africans' were not allowed to become members (see for example Flint and de Waal 2005: 33–65), interviews with some 'defected' Janjawiid seem to contradict this statement.

[37] Interestingly, there are also Arab nomads who refused to join this 'Arab Gathering', or 'Congregation', for example the Bagarra Rizeigat under Saeed Mahmoud Ibrahim Musa Madibu (Flint and de Waal 2005: 122–125).

called *murahiliin* (Johnson 2003: 170). The recent deployment of similar counter-insurgency tactics in Darfur suggests that the conflict represents a 'southern Sudan speeded up' rather than a new 'Rwanda in slow motion'.[38] Although the Sudanese government denied allegations of supporting the Janjawiid militia—calling them 'thieves and gangsters'—the conflict in Darfur has thus become part of national politics and thereby it has been burdened with a new political meaning.[39]

Apart from fighting techniques and the application of a 'scorched-earth' policy, the ethnic rhetoric used to justify the violence also bears similarities with the war in the south. This suggests that the current religious-racial discourse of Islamic superiority used in the war in Darfur is part of an ongoing national 'project' of in- and exclusion. Moreover, although the Sudanese Arab government-elite from Central Sudan are affiliated to the Arab nomads in the current war in Darfur, the meaning of 'Arab' to denote each of this group carries different connotations of class and culture. The notion of 'Arab' that is used for the nomadic peoples in Darfur is used in the sense of Bedouin and indicates backwardness and marginality.[40] Alternatively, the educated Arab elite residing in the Nile Valley has constructed themselves as '*Awlad Arab*' and '*Awlad al-balad*', children (sons) of Arabs and inheritors of the land. They were instrumental in founding political Arab nationalism and claimed the Sudanese nation-state as theirs. By constructing Sudan both as Islamic and as Arab they excluded not only Southerners, but also other marginal groups of Muslims such as the Fur, the Beja, and the Nubians, respectively in the west, east and north of the country.

So, when the current military regime, backed by the Islamist National Islamic Front, took power in 1989 it proclaimed Darfur the 'least

---

[38] See for example John Ryle, "Disaster in Darfur", *The New York Review of Books*, 12 August 2004, 51, no. 13 (http://www.nybooks.com/articles/17326:) accessed 24-09-2005. See also Flint and de Waal 2005.

[39] Political resistance against the government, however, had been building for a longer period in Darfur. Flint and de Waal for example, refer to 21 July 2001 as an important date for the start of organized resistance (2005: 76). See also: http://en.wikipedia.org/wiki/Darfur_conflict: accessed 05-01-2006.

[40] The Arab nomadic groups that have come from Libya and Chad perceive this difference differently. They also claim ancestry with the Qoreish, the nomadic group of the Prophet Mohammed. They see themselves as the 'true custodians of Islam' and therefore entitled to rule Muslim lands. Adherents regard Sudan's riverain elite as 'half-caste' Nubian-Egyptians (Flint and de Waal 2005: 53) and thus not entitled to rule the Sudan. Historically, however, the riverain elite are at the center of political and socio-economic power and thus of notions of Sudanese citizenship. I will return to this issue later.

Islamized region after the South', this stigma concerned all Darfurians: nomads and sedentary farmers alike. This ethnicized Islamist discourse has been adjusted, or one could say 'refined' in the recent war in Darfur. I maintain that this discourse is part of a project of differentiation in order to construct an exclusive notion of 'Sudanese' Muslim citizenship, which is intersected with both ethnic and gender identities. Thereby the notion of multiple masculinities (Connell 1987: 183–190) in the sense of hegemonic or dominant and sub-dominant or alternative masculinities is important as this allows one to think difference among men, as well as women, from diverse social backgrounds, who have differential access to citizenship.[41] In order to place the current war in Darfur in this broader historical, national, context I will try to show that the war is related to the interplay between national identity, ethnicity and gender.

Contested Dominant Masculinity: The Case of Darfur

As I have argued in Chapters, 1, 2 and 7, when the Islamists took power in 1989 the government considered that the Sudan was not properly Islamized everywhere, it instigated what it called *al-mashru' al-hadari* or the 'Islamist Civilization Project' (Al-Ahmadi 2003: 28). I showed that in general the project focused on the conduct and appearance of women in public; both upper and middle class professional women and female street vendors were targeted specifically in the so-called street cleaning campaigns (Al-Ahmadi 2003: 50–52; Willemse f.c.). From chapter 1 and 2 it became clear that in the same period Darfur also constituted one of the targets of its re-Islamization offensive. The population of Darfur were cast as bad and thus lesser Muslims, as inferior and backward by the government. In speeches given by touring *ledgna sha'abia* or popular committees, some of which I analysed in the Introduction and in Chapter 1, Darfur men in particular were called upon to return to the right way, to control and teach their wives the right Islam, to take responsibility for their families and to become faithful members of the *umma*. As I pointed out in Chapter 1, despite the low status of Darfurians as Muslims, they were at that time considered Muslims who could be redeemed, their ways amended and their souls saved. Despite their

[41] See for example Connell (1995) Cornwall & Lindisfarne (1994); O'Neill and Hird (2001).

low status as Muslim, they were considered as Muslims who might be included into the community of righteous believers once they mended their conduct and became better ('proper') believers. Even though this might never have been a seriously inclusive project of the government, at that time Darfur was discursively constructed as part of the Muslim north, which only needed some re-Islamization in order to become included in the Sudanese Muslim nation state. This discourse of inferiority has changed since early 2000, when the war broke out in Darfur.

In the current discourse the Darfur population are cast not as fellow Muslim's whose ways must be redeemed, but as black non-Islamic enemies who, as non-Arabs, do not have a right to live on Muslim soil. This view is propagated by the Arab Gathering and condoned by the Sudanese government, which is, by extension, thus complicit in this rhetoric. The term black is not novel in Darfur: Fur and Masalati were cast as *zurug*,[42] black, even before the onset of the current conflict. However, this reference has now a different connotation related to national politics.

The 'Other' and the Construction of a Sudanese National Identity

In 1823 the Turkiyya established a mercantile economy in Central Sudan which replaced the Sultanic structure of the Funj Sultanate. The emergent urban administrative and mercantile class that had established itself in the Nile Valley in the preceding centuries, used a strict Islamic code of conduct, a specific lifestyle, and their position in the administration and trade as a means of distancing itself as *jellaba* from the local, tribal religious elite. (Kapteijns 1985: 66–67; Spaulding 1985: xviii–xix, 150, 178–198, 238).

When the Anglo-Egyptian Condominium came to power in the Sudan in 1899, the new colonial government made use of this powerful indigenous administrative class to rule the country for them. In the process formal education became part of the range of means with which the new urban administrative elite differentiated themselves from the amorphous 'non-elite other'. In the post-colonial era this formal edu-

[42] *Zurug* literally means 'blue'. The term *aswad* refers to the colour black. During my research *aswad* was only used for referring to non-Muslim slaves. It is therefore of importance to establish which terms are actually used in the war. So far I have no exact information on that.

cation coupled with a government position became the hallmark of the new ruling class, which referred to itself as Sudanese, thus claiming to represent a national identity without any ethnic differentiation. However, a citizenship open to all Sudanese subjects was never part of the nationalist project. The Riverain elite used its Nile Valley culture, with its specific history of Islamization and Arabization to legitimize their prerogative of political power, based on its superiority and privilege as '*Awlad al-Balad*', the legitimate sons of the land, and '*Awlad Arab*', sons of Arabs (Beck 1998: 267; Harir 1994: 27–33; Johnson 2003: 4–7). Thus Islam and its 'twin component, the Arab culture (Bob 1992: 125)' became the main aspects of a unifying national identity. This culture-cum-location-cum-class difference subsequently marked the difference between the 'Sudanese' and the 'other non-Sudanese' population. However, there is a paradox in incorporation education, being part of a process of inclusion, into the definition of the national elite based on a strategy of exclusion and this has caused cracks in the surface of the Sudanese national identity.

As I pointed out in Chapter 7, formal education proved to be one of the main avenues of upward mobility. I will here summarize some of the arguments I put forward in Chapter 7, in order to show how the construction of Darfur people as 'black non-Muslims', however implicit, by the Sudanese government, can be seen as part of the same project to focus on the conduct of women in order for the Sudanese government to construct a stable, exclusive, Sudanese Muslim citizenship.

Education created possibilities for upward mobility for men and women from the rural areas outside the Nile Valley. At first, predominantly young men migrated to the large towns in Central Sudan. There they would acquire, apart from formal education, also training into the culture of the Riverain elite: to perform a specific elite lifestyle, by means of language, dress codes, mores of hospitality etc.; in short a new code of conduct, of thinking, and of constructing themselves as a person. These new members of the educated elite thereby had to engage in a process of de-tribalization in order to attain this new status as 'Sudanese' nationals. This process of Sudanization was curbed by the liberal educational policy under Nimeiri in the 1970s as this policy has produced an enormous number of young 'insufficiently de-tribalized' men as they can now get an education closer to home with less training in the culture of the Nile Valley elite. In Chapter 7 it became clear that these young men came from the countryside with their diplomas with high hopes of obtaining a position in the government. Even if they did get a position, the wages were so low that these young men were not able to live up to ideal-typical notion of Muslim masculinity that the Islamist government they were to represent, had created: as head of the household taking care of his family with a particular lifestyle.

In addition, the economic crisis stimulated the new generation of elite members also to keep in contact with their family in local areas, even after they had entered the government service, in order to enhance the chances for survival. So the educated elite grew in numbers, but thereby lost control over its 'core culture' as it had to admit men and women as members who retained characteristics of 'other', non-elite, classes. This went against the construction of a Sudanese national identity that was expected in order to escape parochial identities.

In other words, recent processes of economic, social and cultural change led to a contestation of the dominant Sudanese identity and its middle class notion of the ideal family from within its own ranks. Though the national ruling elite had to construct boundaries to differentiate themselves from the 'non-elite' in order to safeguard its privileged position, it was this heterogeneity within the elite itself that posed the largest threat to the moral and political dominance of the government. Young middle class members of the administrative elite had not been 'properly Sudanized'.

One means of re-establishing ones' identity and boundary as an elite is to focus on women, as I analysed in Chapter 7:

> [N]ationality and citizenship, like race and ethnicity, are unstable categories and contested identities. They are all gendered identities and the construction of 'women', inside and outside their borders, are part of the processes of identity formation (Pettman 1996, quoted in Wilford 1998: 16).

In the Islamist state of Sudan women, indeed have become one of the markers of the boundaries of the Sudanese Muslims self. This boundary is important because notions of a national identity are necessarily ambiguous, vague and continuously changing as it has to incorporate many diverse peoples who have to believe the illusion they are all equal citizens within the same nation-state. The construction of a unifying national identity thus rests not so much on a common core, but needs a common 'other' against whom to define itself.

A national identity is related to a notion of a dominant masculinity: as this dominant masculinity has hardly got a well-defined core identity it also depends on the existence of the category of 'others' against which to construct its boundaries, as Donaldson points out:

> Through hegemonic masculinity most men benefit from having control of women; for a very few men, it delivers control of other men. To put it another way, the crucial difference between hegemonic masculinity and other masculinities is not the control of women, but the control of men and the representation of this as a 'universal social advancement', to paraphrase Gramsci (Donaldson 1993: 655, cited in Hooper 2001: 70).

Dominant masculinity as part of a national identity is derivative, relational and oppositional. In order to draw its boundaries it needs 'significant others': women and 'lesser' males who constitute the point of reference with which to construct a form of restrictive citizenship.

The Islamist Civilization project can be considered to be an attempt at constructing a modern Sudanese Muslim national identity related to the construction of a Sudanese hegemonic (or dominant) masculinity: a masculinity which formed part of the attempt at creating an exclusivist citizenship. In the case of the Sudan, the search for citizenship has therefore been marked by a process of securing the boundaries of the Sudanese national identity whereby ethnicity, and in its extreme form 'black non-Muslims', are constructed as the 'lesser males' and thus, apart from women, as the significant 'other'.[43]

So even though the Sudanese government denied direct involvement in the Darfur conflict and thus in its racist discourse, the timing of its occurrence does seem relevant: the notion of 'blacks' has shifted from a label by which to address the Sudanese in the South to those in Darfur. Even though the Fur and Masalit were called '*zurug*' before that time, in Darfur it came up as a an official discourse of 'non-Muslimhood' and the equivalent of a status as 'non-Sudanese' after the eruption of the current violence and the peace negotiations with the South in 2002. Thereby the position of 'significant other', and thus as non-citizens, shifted from the South to Darfur.[44]

The use of women and 'other lesser' males as markers of the boundaries of national elites is a recurrent theme, and not only in Islamic

---

[43] This is not to say that the Central Sudanese population is to 'blame' for racism. Rather, it has been part of the way national identity has been constructed and thus has become part of a discourse of power and privilege, which is related to the history of slavery. Central Sudan became a booming center of slave trade while ruling both the areas where the administrative elite resided and the slave-raiding areas. This past has become part of Sudan's national present.

[44] During my stay a difference was considered between '*zurug*', blue, to refer to local people who might even act as leaders, and '*aswad*', black, used for those considered '*abid*', slaves. I am not sure of the relevance of this difference in the current discourse of the Janjawiid, however.

societies. Masculinity does not necessarily refer to real men, but rather to features that a nation-state tries to use as a means to assert an image of respect and strength. The image of a strong nation-state is related to, for example, a large army, a winning sports team, a strong leader, or a severe national discourse on citizenship. Thereby some categories of men are, implicitly or explicitly, referred to as constituting the dominant masculine ideal, and others as its denial. In the case of the Sudanese nation state, this notion of 'other' has historically been cast in ethnic-religious terms. The war in Darfur can therefore indeed be seen as a 'southern Sudan' revisited. It is thereby important to note that 'black' does not refer to skin-colour in any determined way: the Central Sudanese elite as well as the Darfur population, both sedentary and nomadic peoples, consists of peoples with different shades of skin colour: thus it is very difficult to judge from the skin colour whether a person is an 'Arab' or an 'African'; a 'nomad', 'farmer', or a 'member of the riverain elite'. This is even evident when looking at those Sudanese who are members of parliament. The notion of 'black' seems to be, rather, a rhetorical device in a discursive struggle over political power and the legitimacy to rule.

Violence by the government seems to be the ultimate consequence of the search for means to mark the boundaries of an exclusionary form of citizenship such as is constructed in the Sudan. This is not to say that the application of violence by the Sudanese government in order to (re-) construct a national self is thereby made understandable, or justifiable, on the contrary. It does mean, however, that a more radical shift in thought and practice is needed for breaking with this past of constructing otherness by reference to the notion of 'black', in order to attain a more inclusive notion of citizenship. This is first and foremost a matter of balanced socio-economic, political and cultural development. However, I agree with Amir Idris when he states that:

> The legitimising function of the apparatus of truth in the Sudan is the official denial of race as a source of conflict. By abolishing racial otherness as a socially relevant frame of reference, the dominant discourse in the Sudan removed the critical issue of ethnic and racial hegemony and discrimination from the realm of legitimate debate... Contemporary scholars of Sudan's civil war thus need to seek an alternative discourse of history that can be used to understand the root causes of the tragedy (Idris 2001: 26–28 and 136).

An alternative discourse, I want to add that is inclusive, rather than exclusive, in terms of ethnicity, locality, gender, generation, marital status and so forth. I, we, as scholars of Sudan have to acknowledge the differences and diversity in local histories and trajectories of transformation, in order to be able to rewrite a common Sudanese national history as a means of finding alternative roads to change.

Postscript

In the meantime nation-states in the West have also been confronted with 'disenfranchised' young males. Although it requires more in-depth analysis to understand the current phenomena of male youths opting for certain forms of Islamic identity and practice I think a comparison of locations as diverse as Sudan and the Netherlands, as Africa and Europe, might point at some of the challenges that young men, and women, face in a rapidly changing, 'globalizing' world. That nation-states in the West need to engage in their own national projects of understanding the diversity of historical location of its citizens is a fact. The traditional orthodox notions of citizenship are no longer sufficient for catering for the huge diversity of nationals that nation states are representing.[45] *This, however, is a theme for future research.*

[45] See for example Ghorashi (2003: 163–169) "'Ayaan Hirsi Ali: Daring or Dogmatic?'

Debates on multiculturalism and emancipation in the Netherlands", who refers in this context to the 'dual discourse on citizenship' on 'real Dutch' and 'unwanted Dutch (2003: 166)'.

REFERENCES

Aalten, Anna. *Zakenvrouwen. Over de Grenzen van Vrouwelijkheid in Nederland sinds 1945*. Amsterdam: Sara/Van Gennep, 1991.

Abbashar, Jamal. "Funding Fundamentalism, Sudan", *Review of African Political Economy* 54 (1992): 24–41.

Abu-Lughod, Lila. "Local Contexts of Islamism in Popular Media", *ISIM paper 6*. Institute for the Study of Islam in the Modern World (ISIM). Leiden: Amsterdam University Press, 2006.

Abu-Lughod, Lila. "The Marriage of Feminism and Islamism in Egypt. Selective Repudiation as a Dynamic of Postcolonial Cultural Politics", in *Remaking Women. Feminism and Modernity in de Middle East*, edited by Lila Abu-Lughod. New Jersey: Princeton University Press. (1998a): 243–270.

Abu-Lughod, Lila. "Introduction. Feminist Longings and Post-Colonial Conditions", in *Remaking Women. Feminism and Modernity in the Middle East*, edited by Lila Abu-Lughod. New Jersey: Princeton University Press. (1998b): 3–33.

Abu-Lughod, Lila. *Writing Women's Worlds. Bedouin Stories*. Berkeley: University of California Press, 1993.

Abu-Lughod, Lila. "Zones of Theory in the Anthropology of the Arab World", *Annual Review of Anthropology* 18 (1989): 267–306.

Abu-Lughod, Lila. "Can there be a Feminist Ethnography?", *Women and Performance* 5, no.1 (1988): 7–27.

Adam, Farah Hassan, Mohammed El Tayeb El Amin, and Kamil Ibrahim Hassan. "Mechanized Agriculture in the Central Rain Lands of the Sudan", in *The Development Perspectives of the Democratic Republic of Sudan*, edited by P. Oesterdiekhoff and K. Wohlmuth. Muenchen: Weltforum. (1983): 54–80.

Adelberger, Jörg. *Vom Sultunat zur Republik. Veränderungen in der Sozialorganisation der Fur (Sudan)*. Ph.d. Dissertation at the Johann Wolfgang Goethe University, Frankfurt am Main, 1988.

Affendi, Abdelwahab El. *Turabi's Revolution. Islam and Power in Sudan*. London: Grey Seal, 1991.

Afshar, H., and M. Maynard (eds.). *The Dynamics of 'Race' and Gender. Some Feminist Interventions*. London: Taylor & Francis, 1994.

Afshar, Haleh (ed.). *Women in the Middle East. Perceptions, Realities and Struggles for Liberation*. Houndsmill: MacMillan, 1993.

Ahmadi, Hala, Abdel Magid, Al-. *Globalisations, Islamism and Gender. Women's Political Organisations in the Sudan*. Ph. d. Dissertation Catholic University of Nijmegen, 2003.

Ahmadi, Hala, Abdel Magid, Al-. *Patriarchal Islam, Secularist Discourse and Women's Subordination. Identity politics in Sudan*. Research Paper, M.A. Thesis. The Hague: Institute of Social Studies, 1994.

Ahmed A. Ahmed. "Foreign Investment in the Sudan. A Survey", *Sudan Notes and Records* 58 (1977): 135–141.

Ahmed, Leila. *Women and Gender in Islam. Historical Roots of a Modern Debate.* London: Yale University, 1992.

Ahmed, Leila. "Between two Worlds. The Formation of a Turn-of-the-Century Egyptian feminist", in *Life/lines. Theorizing Women's Autobiography*, edited by Bella Brodzki and Celeste Schenck. Ithaca and London: Cornell University Press. (1988):154–174.

Akbar S. Ahmed and Donnan Hastings. *Islam, Globalisation and Modernity*. London: Routledge, 1994.

Ake, Claude. "What is the Problem of Ethnicity in Africa?", *Transformation*, no.22, (1993):1–14.

Alsop, Rachel, Annette Fitzsimons and Kathleen Lennon (eds.). *Theorizing Gender*. Cambridge: Polity, 2003.

Altorki, Soraya. *Women in Saudi Arabia. Ideology and Behaviour Among the Elite*. New York: Columbia University Press, 1986.

Al-Tunisie, Muhammad. *Voyage au Darfour*, transl. A. Perron, Paris: Jomard, 1845.

Anderson, Benedict, *Imagined Communities. Reflections on the Origin. And spread of nationalism*. London: Verso, 1991 [1983].

Anthias, F. "New Hibridities, Old Concepts. The Limits of Culture", *Ethnic and Radical Studies* 24, no.4 (2001): 619–641.

Anthias, Floya and Nira Yuval-Davis. "Introduction", in *Woman-Nation-State*, edited by Nira Yuval-Davis and Floya Anthias. London: MacMillan. (1989).

Anzaldúa, G. and A. Keating (eds.). *This Bridge We Call Home. Radical Visions for Transformation*. New York: Routledge, 2002.

Anzaldúa, G. *Borderlands/La Frontera. The New Mestiza*. San Francisco: Aunt Lute, 1987.

Appadurai, Arjun. *The Social Life of Things. Commodities in Cultural Perspective*. Cambridge: Cambridge University Press, 1988.

Asad, Talal. *Genealogies of Religion. Discipline and Reasons of Power in Christianity and Islam*. Baltimore: The Johns Hopkins University Press, 1993.

Ashcroft, Bill, Gareht Griffiths and Helen Tiffin (eds.). *Post-Colonial Studies. The Key Concepts*. London: Routledge, 2000.

Badran, Margot. "Expressing Feminism and Nationalism in Autobiography. The Memoirs of an Egyptian Educator", in *De-Colonizing the Subject. The Politics of Gender in autobiography*, edited by Sidonie Smith and Julia Watson. Minneapolis: University of Minnesota Press. (1992).

Baffoun, Alya. 1994. "Feminism and Muslim Fundamentalism. The Tunesian and Algerian Case". *Africa Development* XIX, no.2 (1994): 5–20.

Bakri, Zeinab B. El- and Ruth M. Besha. *Women and Development in Eastern Africa. An Agenda for Research. Proceedings of the Workshop for Women and Development in Eastern Africa*. Held in Nazareth, Ethiopia, 1989.

Bakri, Zeinab B. El-, and Mohammed Kameir El-Watig. "Unequal Participation of Migrant Labour in Wage Employment", in *Population and Development Projects in Africa*, edited by John I. Clarke, Mustafa Khogali and Leszek A. Kosinski. Cambridge: Cambridge University Press. (1985): 53–67.

Bakri, Zeinab B. El-, and Tamadur Ahmed Khalid. *Women's Movements, Organisations and Strategies in an Historical Perspective with Special Reference to Colonial and Contemporary Societies*. Report. Sudan Final Report. In the series Women's Movements and Organisations in an Historical Perspective, Research Project 1983–1985, Women and Development, The Hague: ISS. (n.d.).

Bannaga, Mahmoud Y. "Family and Community Life in a Housing Estate. El-Sha'abiya, Khartoum North", in *Family Life in Sudan*, edited by Mohammed A. Mohammed-Salih and Margaret A. Mohammed-Salih. Graduate College Publication no.18. Khartoum: University of Khartoum. (1987).

Barad, Karen. "Posthumanist Performativity. Toward an Understanding of How Matter Comes to Matter", *Signs. Journal of Women in Culture and Society* 28 (2003): 801–831.

Barclay, Harold B. *Burri al- Lamaab. A Suburban Village in the Sudan*. New York: Cornell University Press, 1964.

Barnett, Tony and Abbas Abdelkarim (eds). *Sudan. State, Capital and Transformation*. London: Croom Helm, 1988.

Bartels, Edien. "Centrale Geloofsvoorstellingen", in *In Het Huis van de Islam*, edited by Henk Driessen. Nijmegen: SUN. (1997a): 107–124.

Bartels, Edien. "Plichten en de Rituele Praktijk", in *In Het Huis van de Islam*, edited by Henk Driessen. Nijmegen: SUN. (1997b): 25–140.

Barth, Fredrik. "Economic Spheres in Darfur", in *Themes in Economic Anthropology*, edited by Raymond Firth. London: Tavistock. (1970): 49–179.

Barth, Fredrik (ed.). *Ethnic Groups and Boundaries. The Social Organisation of Cultural Difference*. Bergen, Oslo: Universitetsforlaget, 1969.

Barth, Fredrik. *Human resources. Social and Cultural Features of the Jebel Marra Project Area*. FAO Report: Rome, 1967.

Barth, Fredrik. *The Fur of Jebel Marra, an Outline of Society*. Khartoum: Department of Anthropology of the University of Khartoum, 1964.

Baumann, Gerd and Andre Gingrich. *Grammars of Identity/Alterity. A Structural Approach*. New York and Oxford: Berghalm Books, 2004.

Bayart, Jean-Francois. *The State in Africa. The Politics of the Belly*. London: Longman, 1993.

Bayes, H. and Nayereh Tohidi. *Globalization, Gender and Religion. The Politics of Women's Rights in Catholic and Muslim Contexts*. New York: Palgrave, 2001.

Bayoumi, Ahmed. *The History of Sudan Health Services*. Nairobi: Kenya Literature Bureau, 1979.

Beasley, Ina. *Before the Wind Changed. People, Places and Education in the Sudan*, edited and annotated by Janet Starkey. Oxford: Oxford University Press, 1992.

Beaton, A.C. "A Grammar of the Fur Language", *Linguistic Monograph Series* 1, Khartoum: Khartoum University. (1968).

Beaton, A.C. "The Fur", *Sudan Notes and Records* 29 (1948): 1–39.

Beaton, A. "Youth Organisation Among the Fur", *Sudan Notes and Records* 24 (1941): 181–188.

Beaton, A. "Fur dance songs", *Sudan Notes and Records* 29 (1940): 305–329.

Beaton, A. "Fur Rain Cults and Ceremonies", *Sudan Notes and Records* 22 (1939): 186–203.

Beck, Kurt. "Tribesmen, Townsmen and the Struggle over a Proper Lifestyle in Northern Kordofan", in *Kordofan invaded. Periphal Incorporation and Social Transformation in Islamic Africa*, edited by Endre Stiansen and Michael Kevane. Leiden: Brill. (1998): 254–280.

Bedri, Balghis Y. "Food and Differential Roles in the Fetiehab Household" in: *The Sudanese Woman*, edited by Susan Kenyon. Oxford: Oxford University Press. (1987).

Behar, Ruth. "Introduction. Out of Exile", in *Women Writing Culture*, edited by Ruth Behar and Deborah Gordon. Berkeley, Los Angeles and London: University of California Press. (1995): 1–29.

Behar, Ruth. *Translated Woman. Crossing the Border with Esperanza's Story*. Boston: Beacon Press, 1993.

Behar, Ruth. Introduction Special Issue on Women Writing Culture. "Women Writing Culture. Another Telling of the Story of American Anthropology", *Critique of Anthropology* 13, no.4 (1993): 307–327.

Bell, Diane. "Introduction 1. The Context", in *Gendered Fields. Women, Men and Ethnography*, edited by Pat Caplan and Wazir Jahan Karim. New York and London: Routledge, 1993: 19–27.

Bendroth, Margareth L. *Fundamentalism and Gender, 1875 to the Present*. London: Yale University Press, 1993.

Benhabib, Seyla. *Situating the Self. Gender, Community and Postmodernism in Contemporary Ethics*. New York: Routledge, 1992.

Benyon, John. *Masculinities and Culture*. Buckingham and Philadelphia: Open University Press, 2002.

Berger, Maurice, Brian Wallis, and Simon Watson. *Constructing Masculinity*. New York and London: Routledge, 1995.

Bernal, Victoria. "Islam, Transnational Culture, and Modernity in Rural Sudan" in *Gendered Encounters. Challenging Cultural Boundaries and Social Hierarchies in Africa*, edited by Maria Grosz-Ngate and Omari H. Kokole. New York [etc]: Routledge. (1997): 131–151.

Bernal, Victoria. "Gender and the Remaking of Islamic "tradition" in a Sudanese Village", *Comparative Studies in Society and History* 36, no.1 (1994): 36–67.

Bernal, Victoria. "Gender, Culture and Capitalism in the Islamic Revival (Sudan)" *Working Paper* no. 160, African Studies Centre, Boston University, 1992.

Beshir, Mohamed Omer. *Educational Development in the Sudan 1898–1956*. Oxford: Clarendon Press, 1969.

Bertaux, D. and M. Kohli. "The Life Story Approach. A Continental View", *Annual Review of Sociology* 10 (1984): 215–237.

Billig, Michael. *Ideology and Opinions. Studies in Rhetoric al psychology*. London: Sage, 1991.

Billig, Michael. *Arguing and Thinking. A Rhetorical Approach to Social Psychology*. Cambridge: Cambridge University Press, 1987.

Billig, Michael. *Ideology and Social Psychology. Extremism, Moderation and Contradiction*. Oxford: Basil Blackwell, 1982.

Billig, Michael, Susan Condor, Derek Edwards, Mike Gane, David Middleton and Alan Radley. *Ideological Dilemmas. A Social Psychology of Everyday Thinking*. London: Sage, 1988.

Bob, Ali. "Islam, the State and Politics in the Sudan". *Northeast African Studies*, vol. 12, no.2–3, (1990), 201–219.

Boesveld, Mary, Claudine Helleman, Els Postel-Coster and Joke Schrijvers. *Naar Autonomie van Vrouwen. Onderzoek als Begeleiding van een Ontwikkelingsproces*. Leiden: Onderzoek en Dokumentatiecentrum Vrouwen en Ontwikkeling, 1984.

Boddy, Janice. *Wombs and Alien Spirits. Women, Men and the Zar Cult in Northern Sudan*. Wisconsin: University of Wisconsin Press, 1989.

Booth, Marilyn. *May Her Likes Be Multiplied. Biography and GenderPolitics in Egypt*. Berkeley: University of California Press, 2001.

Borland, Katherine. "'That's not what I said'. Interpretive Conflict in Oral Narrative Research", in: *Women's Words. The Feminist Practice of Oral History*, edited by Sherna Berger Gluck and Daphne Patai, London and New York: Routledge. (1991): 63–77.

Brah, A. *Cartographies of Diaspora. Contesting Identities*. London: Routedge. 1996.

Brah, A. "Difference, Diversity and Differentiation", in *"Race", Culture and Difference*, edited by J. Donald and A. Rattansi. London: Sage Publication. (1992): 126–145.

Braidotti, Rosi. *Metamorphoses. Towards a Materialist Theory of Becoming*. Cambridge: Polity. 2002.

Braidotti, Rosi. *Gender, Identity and Multiculturalism in Europe*, first Ursula Hirschmann Annual Lecture on 'Gender and Europe', Florence: European University Institute, 2001.

Braidotti, Rosi. "Sexual Difference Theory", in *A Companion to Feminist Philosophy*, edited by A. Jaggar and I.M. Young. Malden, Mass: Blackwell. (1998): 298–306.

Braidotti, Rosi. *Nomadic Subjects. Embodiment and Sexual Difference in Contemporary Feminist Theory*. New York: Columbia University Press, 1994.

Braidotti, Rosi. *Patterns of Dissonance. A Study of Woman in Contemporary Philosophy*. New York: Routledge, 1991.

Braidotti, Rosi and Judith Butler. "Feminism By Any Other Name", *Differences* 6 (1994): 27–61.

Brod, H. and M. Kaufmann (eds.). *Theorizing Masculinities*. Thousand Oaks, CA: Sage, 1994.

Brodzki, Bella and Celeste Schenck (eds.). *'Introduction' Life/Lines. Theorizing Women's Autobiography*. Ithaca and London: Cornell University Press. 1988: 154–174.

Brown, Richard. *Sudan's Debt Crisis. The Interplay Between International and Domestic Responses. 1978–1988*. Ph.D. Dissertation. University of Groningen, The Netherlands. Updated and published as *Public Debt and Private Wealth. Debt, Capital Flight and the IMF in Sudan*. Basingstoke. The Hague: Institute of Social Studies, 1990a.

Brown, Richard P.C. *Sudan's Other Economy. Migrants' Remittances, Capital Flight and Their Policy Implications*. ISS Working Paper, Sub-Series on Money and Finance and Development 31 The Hague: Institute of Social Studies, 1990b.

Bruner, J. "Life as Narrative", *Social Research* 54, no.1 (1987): 11–32.
Buitelaar, Marjo. *Fasting and Feasting in Morocco. An Ethnographic Study of the Month of Ramadan*. Proefschrift Nijmegen, 1991.
Burgat, Francois. *Face to Face with Political Islam*. London: I.B. Tauris, 2003 [i.e. 2002].
Butler, Judith. *Excitable Speech. A Politics of the Performative*. New York: Routledge, 1997.
Butler, Judith. "Melancholy Gender/Refused Identification", in *Constructing masculinity*, edited by Maurice Berger, Brian Wallis, and Simon Watson. New York and London: Routledge. (1995): 21–37.
Butler, Judith. "Against Proper Objects", *Differences*, 6 no.2 and 3 (1994): 1–27.
Butler, Judith. *Bodies that Matter. On the Discursive Limits of 'Sex'*. New York: Routledge. 1993.
Butler, Judith. *Gender Trouble. Feminism on the Subversion of Identity*. New York and London: Routledge, 1990a.
Butler, Judith. "Contingent foundations. Feminism and the Question of 'Post-modernism'", in *Feminists Theorize the Political*, edited by Judith Butler and Joan W. Scott. New York: Routledge. (1990b): 3–21; also in *Feminist Contentions. A Philosophical Exchange*, edited by S. Benhabib, J. Butler, D. Cornell and N. Fraser. London: Routledge. (1992): 35–54.
Butler, Judith. "Performative Acts and Gender Constitution. An Essay in Phenomenology and Feminist Theory", in *Performing Feminisms*, edited by S. Case. Baltimore: The John Hopkins University Press. (1990c): 270–282.
Callaway, Helen. "Ethnography and Experience. Gender Implications in Fieldwork and Texts", in *Anthropology and Autobiography*, edited by Judith Okely and Helen Callaway, London and New York. (1992): 29–50.
Caplan, Pat. "Introduction 2: The volume", in *Gendered fields. Women, Men and Ethnography*, edited by Diane Bell, Pat Caplan and Wazir Jahan Karim. New York and London: Routledge. (1993): 19–27.
Caplan, Pat. "Engendering Knowledge. The Politics of Ethnography", *Anthropology Today* 14, no.4 (1988): 8–12 & no.5 (1988): 14–17. (also published as "Engendering Knowledge", in *The Persons and Powers of Women*, edited by S. Ardener. Oxford: Berg Publishers. (1992): 65–87.
Caplan, Lionel. *Studies in Religious Fundamentalism*. New York: SUNY Press, 1987.
Certeau, Michel de. *The Practice of Everyday Life*. (Translated from French by Steven Rendall) Berkeley, CA: University of California Press, 1984.
Chouairi Youssef M. *Islamic Fundamentalism*. London: Twayne Publishers, 1990.
Chouliaraki, Lilie and Norman Fairclough. *Discourse in Late Modernity. Rethinking Critical Discourse Analysis*. Edinburgh: Edinburgh University Press, 2004.
Clark, Kate. "Is it Fundamentalist? Patterns in Islamism", *Women Against Fundamentalism*, 5 (1994): 10.
Clifford, James and George E. Marcus. *Writing Culture. The Poetics and Politics of Ethnography*. Berkeley [etc.]: University of California Press, 1986.
Cohen, Abner. *The Politics of Elite Culture. Explorations in the Dramaturgy of Power in a Modern African Society*. Berkeley: University of California Press, 1981.
Comaroff, Jean and John L. Comaroff. *Of Revelation and Revolution*, Volume II,

The dialectics of Modernity on a South African Frontier. Chicago: University of Chicago Press, 1997.
Connell, R.W. *Masculinities*. Cambridge: Polity Press, 1995.
Conrad, David C. and Barbara E. Frank-Conrad (editors). *Nyamakalaw of Mande*. Bloomington, Indianapolis: Indiana University Press, 1995.
Copson, Raymond W. *Africa's Wars and Prospects for Peace*. Armonk, New York: Sharpe, 1994.
Cornwall, Andrea and Nancy Lindisfarne. "Dislocating Masculinity. Gender, Power and Anthropology", in *Dislocating Masculinity. Comparative Ethnographies*, edited by A. Cornwall and N. Lindisfarne. London: Routledge. (1994): 11–47.
Couldry, Nick. *Inside Culture. Re-imaging the Method of Cultural Studies*. London: Sage Publications, 2000.
Coward, Rosalind and John Ellis. "The Critique of the Sign", in *Language and Materialism, Developments in Semiology and the Theory of the Subject*, edited by Rosalind Coward and John Ellis. Boston, London and Henley: Routledge & Kegan Paul. (1977): 122–159.
Craig, G.M. *The Agriculture of the Sudan*. Oxford: Oxford University Press, 1991.
Crang, Mike and Nigel Thrift. "Introduction", in *Thinking Space*, edited by Mike Crang and Nigel Thrift. Routledge: London and New York (2000): 1–30.
Cunnison, Ian. *Baggara Arabs. Power and the Lineage in a Sudanese Nomad Tribe*. Oxford: Clarendon Press, 1966.
Daly, M. *Modernization in the Sudan. Essays in Honor of Richard Hill*. New York: Lilian Barber Press, 1985.
Dareer, Asma, El-. *Woman Why Do You Weep? Circumcision and its Consequences*. London: Zed Press, 1982.
Davis, Kathy. 1996. "From Objectified Body to Embodied Subject. A biographical Approach to Cosmetic Surgery", in *Feminist Social Psychologies*, edited by Sue Wilkinson, Buckingham: Open University Press (1996): 104–118.
Davis, K. and H. Lutz. "Open Forum. Life in Theory—Three Feminist Thinkers on Transition(s)", *European Journal of Women's Studies* 7, no.3 (2000): 367–378.
Davids, Tine. *From Maria's to Macha's. Women in Mexican Politics*. Dissertation. (forthcoming).
Davids, Tine en Karin Willemse. "Inleiding Themanummer. In het Lichaam Gegrift. Feministische Antropologen op de Grens van Kennisoverdracht en Representatie", *Tijdschrift voor Genderstudies* 2, no.1 (1993): 3–14.
Deleuze, Gilles, and Félix Guattari. *A Thousand Plateaus. Capitalism and Schizophrenia*. Translated and edited by Brian Massumi. Minneapolis: University of Minnesota Press, 1989.
Deng, Francis M. *"Bonds of Silk". The Human Factor in the British Administration of Sudan*. East Lansing: Michigan State University Press, 1989.
Doornbos, Paul. "On Becoming Sudanese", in *Sudan. State, Capital and Transformation*, edited by Tony Barnett and Abbas Abdelkarim. London: Croom Helm. (1986).

Doornbos, Paul. "Trade in Two Border Towns. Beida and Foro Baranga (Darfur Province)", in *Trade and Traders in the Sudan*, edited by Leif O. Manger. Bergen: Bergen Occasional Papers in Social Anthropology, no. 32. (1984a).

Doornbos, Paul. "Regionalisation and the Quest for Revenue: Darfur Region", in *Perspectives on Development in the Sudan, Selected Papers from a Research Workshop in The Hague*, edited by P. van der Wel and M. Ahmed Abdel Gaffar. The Hague. (1984b).

Doornbos, Paul. "Some Aspects of Smuggling Between Chad and Sudan", *Discussion Paper* no. 33, Khartoum: Development Studies and Research Centre. (1983).

Duffield, M.R. "Fulani Mahdism and Revisionism in Sudan. 'Hijra' or Compromise with Colonialism Source", in *The Central Bilad al-Sudan. Tradition and Adaptation*, edited by Yusuf Fadl Hasan and P. Doornbos. Sudanese Library Series no.11, Khartoum: El-Taddamon P. Press Ltd. (1977): 283–305.

Epstein, Debby. "Marked Men. Whiteness and Masculinity", *Agenda* 37 (1998): 49–57.

Eriksen, Thomas Hylland. *Ethnicity and Nationalism. Anthropological Perspectives*. London: Pluto Press, 1993.

Esposito, James. *The Islamic Threat. Myth or Reality?* New York: Oxford University Press, 1992.

Essed, Philomena. *Understanding Everyday Racism. An Interdisciplinary Theory*. Newbury Park, CA: Sage, 1991.

Fairclough, Norman. *Media Discourse*. London: Arnold, 1995a.

Fairclough, Norman. *Critical Discourse Analysis. The Critical Study of Language*. London and New York: Longman, 1995b.

Fairclough, Norman. *Discourse and Social Change*. Cambridge: Polity Press, 1992.

Fairclough, Norman. *Language and Power*. London: Longman, 1989.

Fetterley Judith. *The Resistant Reader. A Feminist Approach to American Fiction*. Bloomington: Indiana University, 1978.

Fischer-Rosenthal, Wolfram. "The Problem with Identity. Biography as Solution to Some (Post-)Modernist Dilemmas", *Comenius* 15, no.3 (1995): 250–265. Also published in: *Newsletter Biography and Society*, Research Committee 38 (1996) 2–5.

Flax, Jane. "Postmodernism and Gender Relations in Feminist Theory", *Signs* 12, no.4 Summer (1987): 621–643.

Flint, Julie and Alex de Waal. *Darfur. A Short History of a Long War*. London: Zed Books, 2005.

Fluehr-Lobban, Carolyn, Richard Lobban and John Voll. *Historical Dictionary of the Sudan*. African Historical Dictionaries no. 53. London: The Scarecrow Press, Inc, 1992.

Fluehr-Lobban, Carolyn. "Islamization in Sudan. A Critical Assessment", *The Middle East Journal* 44, no.4 (1990): 610–623.

Foucault, Michel. "The Order of Discourse", in *Untying theTtext. A Poststructuralist Reader*, edited by Robert Young. London: RKP. (1981): 48–78.

Foucault, Michel. *Discipline and Punish. The Birth of a Prison*. New York: Vintage, 1979.

Foucault M. *The Archaeology of Knowledge*. Translated by Sheridan Smith. London: A.M. Tavistock, 1972.
Funck, Angelika von. *Fur, a Nilo-Saharan Language of the Sudan Republic. Phonology and Morphology*. Dissertation. Hamburg: Universität Hamburg, 1986.
Gelaleldin, M. el Awad. *Some Aspects of Sudanese Migration to the Oil-Producing Arab Countries*. DSRC Monograph Series no.24. Khartoum: University Press of Khartoum, 1985.
Gergen, Mary M. and Kenneth J. Gergen. "Narratives of the Gendered Body in Popular Autobiography", in *The Narrative Study of Lives*, edited by Ruthellen Josselson and Amia Lieblich (eds.) London: Sage Publications Ltd. (2003): 191–218.
Geschiere, Peter. "Historical Anthropology. Questions of Time, Method and Scale", *Interventions* 3, no.1 (2001): 31–39.
Ghorashi, Halleh. *Ways to Survive, Battles to Win. Iranian Women Exiles in the Netherlands and the United States*. New York: Nova Science Publishers, Inc, 2003a.
Ghorashi, Halleh. "Ayaan Hirsi Ali: Daring or Dogmatic? Debates on Multiculturalism and Emancipation in the Netherlands", *Focaal—European Journal of Anthropology*, 42 (2003b), 163–169.
Ghorashi, Halleh. *Ways to Survive, Battles to Win. Iranian Women Exiles in the Netherlands and the United States*. Ph.D. thesis, Nijmegen: KUN, 2001.
Gluck, Sherna Berger and Daphne Patai. *Women's Words. The Feminist Practice of Oral History*. New York and London: Routledge, 1991.
Grawert, Elke. *Making a Living in Rural Sudan. Production of Women, Labour Migration of Men, and Policies for Peasants' Needs*. Basingstoke: MacMillan, New York: St. Martin's Press, 1998.
Grawert, Elke. *Impacts of Male Out-Migration on Women. A Case Study of Kutum, Northern Darfur, Sudan*. Bremen: University of Bremen, 1992.
Gray, Leslie and Michael Kevane. "For Whom is the Rural Economy Resilient? Initial Effects of Drought in Western Sudan", *Development and Change* 24 (1993):159–176.
Grele, Ronald J. "History and the Languages of History in the Oral History Interview. Who Answers Whose Questions and Why?" in *Interactive Oral History Interviewing*, edited by E. McMahan and K. Lacey Rogers. (1994): 1–17.
Griffiths, V.L. *Teacher-Centred. Quality in Sudan Primary Education 1930–1970*. London: Longman, 1975.
Gruenbaum, Ellen. *The Islamist State and Sudanese women*, MERIP 22, no.6 (1992): 29–32.
Guha, Ranajit and Gayatri C. Spivak (eds). *Selected Subaltern Sstudies*. New York: Oxford University Press, 1988.
Guindi, Fadwa el-. *Veil. Modesty, Privacy and Resistance*. Oxford: Berg, 1999.
Haaland, Gunnar. "Social Organization and Ecological Pressure in Southern Darfur", in *Problems of Savannah Development. The Sudan Case*, edited by Gunnar Haaland. Bergen, Norway: Dept. of Social Anthropology, University of Bergen. (1982): 55–105.
Haaland, Gunnar. "Nomadisation as an Economic Career Among the Send-

entaries in the Sudan Savannah Belt", in *Essays in Sudan Ethnography*, edited by I. Cunnison and W. Jones. London: Hurst. (1972): 49–172.

Haaland, Gunnar. "Economic Determinants in Ethnic Processes", in *Ethnic Groups and Boundaries. The Social Organization of Culture Difference*, edited by Fredrik Barth. Oslo: Scandinavian University Press. (1969): 58–74.

Hale, Sondra. *Gender Politics in Sudan. Islamism, Socialism, and the State*. Boulder, Colorado: Westview Press, 1996.

Hale, Sondra. "Gender, Religious Identity and Political Mobilization in Sudan", in *Identity Politics and Women. Cultural Reassertions and Feminism in International Perspective*, edited by Valentine M. Moghadam. Boulder, Colo.: Westview Press. (1994): 125–146.

Hale, Sondra. "The Rise of Islam and Women of the National Islamic Front in Sudan", *Review of African Political Economy* 54 (1992): 27–41.

Hall, Stuart and Paul du Gay (eds.). *Questions of Cultural Identity*. London: Sage Publications, 1996a.

Hall, Stuart. "Who Needs Identity?", in *Questions of Cultural Identity*, edited by Stuart Hall and Paul du Gay. Thousand Oaks, California: Sage. (1996b): 1–17.

Hall, Stuart. "Cultural Identity and Diaspora", in *Identity, Community, Culture*, edited by J. Rutherford. London: Lawrence and Wishart. (1990): 222–237.

Haraway, Donna. "Gender for a Marxist dictionary. The sexual Politics of a Word", in *Symians, Cyborgs, and Women. The Reinvention of Nature*, edited by Donna Haraway. London: FAB. (1991).

Harding, Sandra. *Is Science Multi-Cultural? Postcolonialisms, Feminisms and Epistemologies*. Bloomington: Indiana University Press, 1998.

Harding, Sandra. *Whose Science, Whose Knowledge? Thinking from Women's Lives*. Milton Keynes: Open University Press, 1992.

Harding, Sandra. "Introduction. Is there a feminist method?" in: *Feminism and Methodology. Social Science Issues*, edited by Sandra Harding. Bloomington: Indiana University Press. (1987).

Harding, Sandra. *The Science Question in Feminism*. Ithaca and London: Cornell University Press, 1986.

Harir, Sharif. "Recycling the Past in the Sudan. An Overview of Political Decay", in *Short-Cut to Decay. The Case of the Sudan*, edited by Sharif Harir and Terje Tvedt. Uppsala: Nordiska Afrikainstitutet. (1994a): 10–68.

Harir, Sharif. "Arab Belt Versus 'African Bbelt' Ethno-Political Conflict in Dar Fur and the Regional Cultural Factors", in *Short-Cut to Decay. The Case of the Sudan*, edited by Sharif Harir and Terje Tvedt. Uppsala: Nordiska Afrikainstitutet. (1994b): 144–185.

Harir, Sharif, Kjell Hødnebø and Terje Tvedt. 1994. "A Chronology of the Sudan 1972–1992", in *Short-Cut to Decay. The case of the Sudan*, edited by Sharif Harir and Terje Tvedt. Uppsala: Nordiska Afrikainstitutet. (1994): 259–274.

Harir, Sharif and Terje Tvedt. *Shortcut to Decay. The Case of the Sudan*. Uppsala: Nordiska Afrikainstitutet, 1994.

Harris, Colette. *Control and Subversion. Gender, Islam and Socialism in Tajikistan*. Dissertation University of Amsterdam, 2000.

Harrison, Faye V. "Writing Against the Grain. Cultural Politics of Difference in the Work of Alice Walker", *Critique of Anthropology* 13, no.4 (1993): 307–327.
Harrison, Faye V. "Anthropology as an Agent of Transformation. Introductory Comments and Queries", in *Decolonizing Anthropology. Moving Further Toward an Anthropology for Liberation*, edited by Faye V. Harrison. Washington D.C.: American Anthropologist Association. (1991).
Hasan, Yusuf Fadl. "The Fur Sultanate and the Long Distance Caravan Trade, c. 1650–1850", in: *The Central Bilad al-Sudan; Tradition and Adaptation*, edited by Yusuf Fadl Hassan and Paul Doornbos. Khartoum: El Tamaddon Press (1977): 201–216.
Hasan, Yusuf Fadl and P. Doornbos. *The Central Bilad al-Sudan; Tradition and Adaptation.* Sudanese Library Series no.11, Khartoum: El-Taddamon P. Press Ltd., 1977.
Hassan, Idris Salim, El-. "The Local and the Global. Gendering Education in the Sudan", in *Globalization, Democracy and Development in Africa: Challenges and Prospects*, edited by Taye Assefa, Severine M. Rugumamu and Abdel Ghaffar M. Ahmed. Addis Ababa; OSSREA (2001): 347–364.
Hastrup, Kirsten. A Passage to Anthropology. Between Experience and Theory, London: Routledge, 1995.
Hawley, James Stratton and Wayne Proudfoot. "Introduction", in *Fundamentalism and Gender*, edited by James Hawley. New York: Oxford University Press. (1994): 1–44.
Hess, Amira. "I. Amira Hess". Poem quoted in Smadar Lavie, "Border Poets. Translating by dialogues". In *Women Writing Culture*, edited by Ruth Behar and Deborah Gordon. Berkeley, Los Angeles and London: University of California Press. (1995): 412.
Hoebink, Michel. "Thinking About Renewal in Islam. Towards a History of Islamic Ideas on Modernization and Secularization", *Arabica* 46, no.1 (1999): 29–62.
Holstein, James A. and Jaber F. Gubrium. *The Self We Live By. Narrative Identity in a Postmodern World.* New York and Oxford: Oxford University Press, 2000.
Holt, P.M. and M.W. Daly. *A History of the Sudan. From the Coming of Islam to the Present Day*. London and New York: Longman, 1988.
Holt, P.M. *The Mahdist State in the Sudan, 1881–1898. A Study of its Origins, Development and Overthrow.* Oxford: Clarendon Press, 1958.
Holy, Ladislav. *Kinship, Honour and Solidarity*. Manchester: Manchester University Press, 1989.
Holy, Ladislav. *Neighbours and Kinsmen. A Study of the Berti people of Darfur*. London: Hurst & Company, 1974.
hooks, bell. *Yearning. Race, Gender, and Cultural Politics*. Boston: South End Press, 1990.
hooks, bell. *Feminist theory. From Margin to Center*. Boston: South End Press, 1984.
hooks, bell. *Ain't I a Woman- Black Women and Feminism*. Boston: South End Press, 1981.
Hooper, C. *Manly States. Masculinities, International Relations, and Gender Politics.* New York: Columbia University Press, 2000.
Huizer, Gerrit. "Anthropology and Politics. From Naïvité toward Liberation?",

in *The Politics of Anthropology*, edited by G. Huizer and B. Mannheim. The Hague: Mouton. (1979): 3–41.

Hunter, James D. "Fundamentalism. An Introduction to a General Theory", in *Jewish Fundamentalism in Comparative Perspective. Religion, Ideology, and the Crisis of Modernity*, edited by Laurence Silberstein. New York: New York University Press. (1993): 27–40.

Ibrahim, Fouad, *Desertification in North Darfur*. Hamburg: Hamburger Geographisher Studien 35, 1980.

Ibrahim, Fouad, "The Role of Women Peasants in the Process of Desertification in Western Sudan", *Geo Journal* 6, no.1 (1982): 25–30.

Ibrahim, Hassan Ahmed. *Sayyid 'Abd al-Rahman al-Mahdi. A study of Neo-Mahdism in the Sudan, 1899–1956*. Leiden: Brill. 2004.

Ibrahim, Hassan Ahmed. "Imperialism and neo-Mahdism in the Sudan. A study of British Policy Towards Neo-Mahdism, 1924–1927", *The International Journal of African Historical Studies* 13, no.2 (1980): 214–239.

Ibrahim, Hassan Ahmed. "Mahdist Risings Against the Condominium Government in the Sudan, 1900–1927", *The International Journal of African Historical Studies* 12, no.3 (1979): 440–471.

Idris, Amir H. *Sudan's Civil War. Slavery, Race and Formational Identities*. (African studies 56), Lewiston, NY: Edwin Mellen Press, 2001.

Inowlocki, Lena. "Grandmothers, Mothers and Daughters. Intergenerational Transmission in Displaced Families in Three Jewish Communities", in *International Yearbook of Oral History and Life Stories II*, edited by D. Bertaux and P. Thompson. Oxford. (1993): 139–153.

Jansen, Willy. "The Economy of Religious Merit. Women and 'Ajr' in Algeria", *The Journal of North African Studies* 9 no.4 (2004): 1–17.

Jansen, Willy. "Mythen van het Fundament", *Tijdschrift voor Vrouwenstudies* 57, no.15 (1994): 79–97.

Jansen, Willy. "Ethnocentrism in the Study of Algerian women", in *Current Issues in Women's History*, edited by A. Angerman et al. London: Routledge. (1989).

Jansen, Willy. *Women without Men. Gender and Marginality in an Algerian Town*. Leiden: Brill, 1987.

Johnson, Douglas H. *The Root Causes of Sudan's Civil Wars*. Oxford: James Currey, 2003.

Joseph, Suad. *Gender and Citizenship in the Middle East*; with a foreword by Deniz Kandiyoti. Syracuse, New York: Syracuse University Press, 2000.

Joseph, Suad (ed.). *Intimate Selving in Arab families. Gender, Self and Identity*. Syracuse: Syracuse University Press, 1999.

Joseph, Suad. "Women and Politics in the Middle East", *MERIP Middle East Report* 16, no.1 (1986): 3–7.

Josselson, Ruthellen and Amia Lieblich (eds.). *Interpreting Experience. The Narrative Study of Lives*, vol. 3. Thousand Oaks, California: Sage, 1995.

Josselson, Ruthellen and Amia Lieblich (eds.). *The Narrative Study of Lives*, vol. 1. Thousand Oaks California: Sage, 1993.

Kabbani, Rana. *Europe's Myths of Orient. Devise and Rule*. London: Pandora Press, 1986.

Kandiyoti, Deniz. "Some Awkward Questions on Women and Modernity in Turkey", in *Remaking Women. Feminism and Modernity in de Middle East*, edited by Lila Abu-Lughod. New Jersey: Princeton University Press. (1998): 270–289.
Kandiyoti, Deniz. *Women, Islam and the State*. Basingstoke: Macmillan, 1991.
Kapteijns, Lidwien. *Mahdist Faith and Sudanic Tradition. The history of the Masalit Sultanate 1870–1930.*, Kegan Paul International Series. London: KPI, 1985a.
Kapteijns, Lidwien. "Mahdist Faith and the Legitimation of Popular Revolt in Western Sudan", *Africa* 55, no.4 (1985b): 390–399.
Kapteijns, Lidwien. "Islamic Rationales for the Changing Social Roles of Women in the Western Sudan", in *Modernization in the Sudan. Essays in Honor of Richard Hill*, edited by W. Daly. New York: Lilian Barber Press. (1985).
Kapteijns, Lidwien and Jay Spaulding. *After the Millennium. Diplomatic Correspondence from Wadai and Dar Fur on the Eve of Colonial Conquest, 1885–*. Michigan: East Lansing, 1988.
Karam, Azza M. *Women, Islamisms and the State. Contemporary Feminisms in Egypt*. London: MacMillan Press Ltd., 1998.
Kenyon, Susan. *Five Women of Sennar*. Oxford: Clarendon Press, 1991.
Kenyon, Susan. *The Sudanese Woman*. Oxford: Oxford University Press, 1987.
Kevane, Michael and Endre Stiansen. "Introduction. Kordofan Invaded", in *Kordofan Invaded. Peripheral Incorporation and Social Transformation in Islamic Africa*, edited by Endre Stiansen and Michael Kevane. Leiden: Brill. (1998): 1–45.
Khalid, Mansour. *The Government They Deserve. The Role of the Elite in Sudan's Political Evolution*. London: Kegan Paul, 1990.
Kloos, Peter. "No Knowledge Without a Knowing Subject", in *Studies in Qualitative Methodology*, edited by R.N. Burgess. London: JAI Press. (1988): 221–241.
Kloos, Peter. *Filosofie van de Antropologie*. Leiden: M. Nijhoff, 1987.
Landry, Donna and Gerald Maclean (eds.). *The Spivak Reader. Selected Works of Gayatri Chakravorty Spivak*. New York and London: Routledge. 1996.
Langness, L.L. and G. Frank. *Lives. An Anthropological Approach to Biography*. Navato, California: Chandler and Sharp, 1981.
Lampen, G.D. "History of Darfur", *Sudan Notes and Records* 31 (1950): 177–209.
Lancaster, Carol J. "The Horn of Africa", in *After the Wars. Reconstruction in Afghanistan, Indochina, Central America, Southern Africa, and the Horn of Africa*, edited by Anthony Lake. New Brunswick: Transactions Publishers (1990): 168–190.
La Rue, G.M. "Land and Social Stratification in the Dar Fur Region of the Sudan, 1785–1875: The Hakura System", in *The State and the Market. Studies in the Economic and Social History of the Third World*, edited by Clive Dewey. (1987): 24–44.
La Rue, G.M. "The Export Trade of Dar Fur, ca. 1785 to 1875", in *Figuring African Trade. Proceedings of the Symposium on the Quantification and Structure of the Iimport and Export and Long Distance Ttrade in Africa, 1800–1913, St. Augustin, 3–6 January (1983)*, edited by G. Liesegang, H. Pasch, and A. Jones. (1986): 635–668.

La Rue, G.M. "Hakuras in the Area Between al-Fashir, Kobbei and Kutum", *Paper* presented to the postgraduate seminar, History Department, University of Khartoum, 16 December 1980.
Lauretis, Teresa de. "Eccentric Subjects. Feminist Theory and Historical Consciousness", *Feminist Studies* 16, Spring (1990): 115–150.
Lauretis, Teresa de. *Technologies of Gender. Essays on Theory, Film and Fiction.* Bloomington: Indiana University Press, 1987.
Lauretis, Teresa de. *Feminist Studies/Critical Studies.* Bloomington: Indiana University Press, 1986.
Lauretis, Teresa de. "The Violence of Rhetoric. Considerations on Representation and Gender", *Semiotica* 54 (1985): 11–31.
Lauretis, Teresa de. *Alice Doesn't. Feminism, Semiotics, Cinema.* Bloomington: Indiana University Press, 1984.
Lawrence, Bruce B. *Defenders of God. The Fundamentalist Revolt Against the Modern Age.* San Francisco: Harper and Row, 1989.
Lazarus-Yafeh, Hava. 1993. "Contemporary Fundamentalism. Judaism, Christianity, Islam", in *Jewish Fundamentalism in Comparative Perspective. Religion, Ideology, and the Crisis of Modernity*, edited by Laurence Silberstein. New York: New York University Press. (1993).
Lazreq, Marnia. *The Eloquence of Silence. Algerian Women in Question.* London: Routledge, 1994.
Lazreq, Marnia. "Feminism and Difference. The Perils of Writing as a Woman in Algeria", *Feminist Studies* 14, no.1 (1988): 81–107.
Leydesdorff, Selma, Luisa Passerini and Paula Thompson. "Introduction", in *Gender and Memory*. Oxford University Press. (1996): 1–16.
Lorde, Audre. "The Masters Tools Will Never Dismantle the Master's House", in *Sister Outsider. Essays and Speeches by Audre Lorde*, edited by Audre Lorde. Freedom: The Crossing Press. (1984).
Lugones, Maria C. and Elizabeth V. Spelman. "Have We Got a Theory for You! Feminist Theory, Cultural Imperialism, and the Demand for 'The Woman's Voice'", *Women's Studies International Forum* 6, no.6 (1983): 593.
Lutz, Catharine A. and Lila Abu-Lughod (eds.). *Language and the Politics of Emotion.* Cambridge: Cambridge University Press, 1990.
Lutz, Helma. "Doeken des Aanstoots", in *Praten in het Donker. Multiculturalisme en Anti-Racisme in Feministisch Perspectief*, edited by Gloria Wekker and Rosi Braidotti. Kampen: Kok Agora. (1996).
Macleod, Arlene Elowe. *Accomodating Protest. Working Women, the New Veiling, and Change in Cairo.* New York: Columbia University Press, 1991.
Malik, Saadia Izzeldin Ali. *'Displaced' Women Speak. A Counter Discourse on the Drought 'Displaced' in Umdurman, Sudan.* Research Paper, M.A. thesis. The Hague: ISS, 1995.
Man, Paul de. "Autobiography as De-Facement", *Modern Language Notes* 94 (1979): 920.
Mann, Kristin. *Marriage, Status and Social Change Among the Educated Elite in Colonial Lagos.* Cambridge: Cambridge University Press, 1985.
Mansour, Khalid. *War and Peace in Sudan. A Tale of Two Countries.* London: Kegan Paul, 2003.

Marcus, George and Michael Fischer. *Anthropology as Cultural Critique. An Experimental Moment in the Social Sciences*. Chicago: Chicago University Press. 1986.
Martin E. Marty and R. Scott Appleby. *Fundamentalisms Observed*. Chicago: University of Chicago Press, 1991.
Martin, Adrienne. *Farming Systems in the Kebkabiya Area, North Darfur Province, Sudan. The Role and Potential of Small Scale Irrigated Gardening*. Unpublished study conducted for OXFAM, January–March 1985.
Mascia-Lees et. al. "The Postmodernist Turn in Anthropology. Cautions From a Feminist Perspective", *Signs* 15, no.1 (1989): 7–33.
Mbembe, Achille. *On the Postcolony*. Berkeley: University of California Press, 2001.
Mbembe, Achille. "Provisional Notes on the Postcolony", *Africa* 62, no.1 (1992): 3–37.
McClintock, Anne. *Imperial Leather. Race, Gender and Sexuality in the Colonial Contest*. New York and London: Routledge, 1995.
McNay, Lois. *Foucault and Feminism*. Oxford: Blackwell Publishers, 1992.
Meijer, Maaike. *In tekst Gevat. Inleiding tot een Kritiek van Representatie*. Amsterdam: Amsterdam University Press, 1996.
Meijer, Maaike and Jetty Schaap (eds.). *Historiography of Women's Cultural Traditions*. Dordrecht: Foris, 1987.
Mernissi, Fatima. *De Politieke Harem. Vrouwen en de Profeet*. Breda: De Geus, 1991.
Meyer, Gabriel. *War and Faith in Sudan*. Michigan and Cambridge: Wim B. Eerdmans Publishing co.: 2005.
Mies, Maria. "Towards a Methodology for Feminist Research", in *Theories of Women's Studies*, edited by Gloria Bowles and Renate Duelli Klein. London: Routledge & Kegan Paul. (1983): 117–140.
Mies, Maria. *The Lace Makers of Narsapur. Indian Housewives Produce for the World Market*. London: Zed Press, 1982.
Mills, Sara. *Discourse*. London and New York: Routledge, 1997.
Moghaddam, Valentine. *Gender and National Identity. Women and Politics in Muslim Societies*. London and Karachi: Zed Press and Oxford University Press, 1994.
Mohamed-Salih, Mohamed A. and Margaret A. Mohamed-Salih. *Family Life in Sudan*. Oxford: Oxford University Press, 1987.
Mohanty, Chandra Talpade. *Feminism Without Borders. Decolonizing Theory, Practicing Solidarity*. Durham: Duke University Press, 2003.
Mohanty, Chandra Talpade. "'Under Western Eyes Revisited'. Feminist Solidarity Through Anticapitalist Struggles", *SIGNS* 28, no.2 (2002): 499–535.
Mohanty, Chandra Talpade. "Cartographies of Struggle. Third World Women and the Politics of Feminism", in *Third World Women and the Politics of Feminism*, edited by Chandra Talpade Mohanty, Ann Russo and Lourdes Torres. Bloomington and Indianapolis: Indiana University Press. (1991): 1–47.
Moore, Henrietta. *A Passion for Difference. Essays in Anthropology and Gender*. Cambridge: Polity Press, 1994.
Moore, Henrietta. *Feminism and Anthropology*. Cambridge: Polity Press, 1988.
Moors, Annelies. *Women, Property and Islam. Palestinian Experiences 1920–1930*. Cambridge: Cambridge University Press, 1999.
Moors, Annelies. "Women and the Orient. A Note on Difference", in *Con-*

structing Knowledge. Authority and Critique in Social Science, edited by Lorraine Nencel and Peter Pels. London: Sage Publications. (1992).
Moraga, Cherrie, and Gloria Anzaldúa (eds.). *This Bridge Called my Back. Writings by Radical Women of Color*. Albany: Kitchen Table Press, 1981.
Moran, Mary. *Civilized Women. Gender and Prestige in Southeastern Liberia*. Ithaca: Cornell University Press, 1990.
Morée, Marjolein. "'*Mijn Kinderen Hebben er Niets van Gemerkt'. Buitenshuis Werkende Moeders Tussen 1950 en Nu*". Proefschrift Utrecht: Jan van Arkel, 1992.
Mosely, Ann Lesch. *The Sudan. Contested National Identities*. Bloomington and Indianapolis: Indiana University Press and Oxford: James Currey, 1998.
Multi-Douglas, Fedwa. *Woman's Body, Woman's Word. Gender and Discourse in Arabo-Islamic Writing*. Princeton: Princeton University Press, 1991.
Nederveen Pieterse, Jan. "Fundamentalism Discourses. Enemy Images", *Women Against Fundamentalism* 5, (1994): 2–6.
Nachtigal, G. *Sahara und Sudan*, vol. IV. 'Wadai and Darfur', London: Hurst, 1971. Translated by G.B. and H.J. Fischer, London.
Nageeb, Salma Ahmed. *New Spaces and Old Frontiers. Women, Social Space, and Islamization in Sudan*. Maryland and Oxford: Lexington Books. 2004.
McNay, Lois. *Foucault and Feminism*. Oxford: Blackwell Publishers, 1992.
Nencel, Lorraine. *Ethnography and Prostitution in Peru*. London and Virgina: Pluto Press. 2001.
Nencel, Lorraine. *Casting Identities, Gendered Enclosures. Women who Prostitute in Lima, Peru*. Amsterdam: Dissertation University of Amsterdam, 1997.
Nencel, Lorraine and Peter Pels (eds.). *Constructing Knowledge. Authority and Critique in Social Science*. London: Sage Publications Ltd, 1991.
Niger-Thomas Agbaw, Margaret. *"Buying Futures". The Upsurge of Female Entrepreneurship. Crossing the Formal and Informal Divide in Southwest Cameroon*. Research School of Asian, African and Amerindian Studies, University of Leiden, 2000.
Niblock, Tim. *Class and Power in Sudan. The Dynamics of Sudanese Politics, 1898–1985*. Hampshire: Macmillan Press, 1987.
O'Balance, Edgar. *Sudan, Civil War and Terrorism 1956–1999*. New York: St. Martin's Press, 2000.
O'Brien, Jay. "Cultural Concepts, Cultural Dynamics, and Class Formation in Sudan", Paper presented at the Africa Studies Association, December 1994.
O'Brien, Jay. "Ethnicity, National Identity and Social Conflict", in *Social Science and Conflict Resolution*, edited by A. Hurskainen and M. Mohammed Salih. Uppsala: Scandinavian Institute of African Studies. (1993).
O'Fahey, Rex Sean. *State and Society in Darfur*. London: Hurst & Company, 1980a.
O'Fahey, Rex Sean. "The Tunjur. A Central Sudanic Mystery", *Sudan Notes and Records* 61 (1980b): 47–60.
O'Fahey, Rex Sean and Jay Lloyd Spaulding. *Kingdoms of the Sudan*. London: Methuen, 1974.
O'Fahey, Rex Sean. "Religion and Trade in the Kayra Sultanate of Dar Fur", in *Sudan in Africa*, edited by Yusuf Fadl Hassan, Khartoum: Khartoum University Press. (1971): 87–97.

O'Fahey, Rex Sean and Muhammad Ibrahim Abu Salim. *The Writings of Eastern Sudanic Africa to c. 1900*. Leiden: Brill, 1994.
O'Fahey, Rex Sean, Muhammad Ibrahim Abu Salim. *Land in Dar Fur. Charters and Related Documents from the Dar Fur Sultanate*. Cambridge Cambridge University Press, 1983.
O'Neill, Norman and Jay O'Brien. *Economy and Class in Sudan*. Aldershot. Avebury, 1988.
Okely, Judith and Helen Callaway. *Anthropology and Autobiography*. London and New York: Routledge, 1992.
Okely, Judith. "Anthropology and Autobiography. Participatory Experience and Embodied Knowledge", in *Anthropology and Autobiography*, edited by Judith Okely and Helen Callaway, London and New York. (1992): 1–29.
Ong, Walter J. "Oral Remembering and Narrative Structures", in *Analyzing Discourse. Text and Talk*, edited by Deborah Tannen. Washington: Georgetown University Press. (1982): 12–25
Partha, Chatterjee. *The Nation and its Fragments. Colonial and Postcolonial Histories*. Princeton NJ: Princeton University Press, 1993.
Patai, Daphne. "U.S. Academics and Third World women. Is Ethical Research Possible?", in *Women's Words. The Feminist Practice of Oral History*, edited by Sherna Berger Gluck and Daphne Patai. New York and London: Routledge. (1991).
Personal Narratives Group. *Interpreting Women's Lives. Feminist Theory and Personal Narratives*. Bloomington and Indianapolis: Indiana University Press, 1989.
Piscitelli, A. "Love and Ambition. Gender, Memory and Stories from Brazilian Coffee Plantation Families", in *International Yearbook of Oral History and Life Stories IV, Gender and Memory*, edited by S. Leydesdorff, L. Passerini and P. Thompson. (1993): 139–153.
Potter, Jonathan and Margaret Wetherell. *Discourse and Social Psychology. Beyond Attitudes and Behaviour*. London: Sage, 1987.
Pratt, Mary Louise. *Imperial Eyes. Travel Writing and Transculturation*. London: Routledge, 1992.
Probyn, E. *Outside Belongings*. London and New York: Routledge, 1996.
Prosser, J.A. "Palinode on Photography and the Transsexual Real", *Autobiography Studies* 14 (1999): 1.
Prunier, Gérard. *Darfur. The Ambiguous Genocide*. Ithaca, New York: Cornell University Press. 2005.
Radin, Paul (editor and translator). *The Autobiography of a Winnebago Indian by Sam Blowsnake*. New York: Dover Publications, 1963.
Raven, Wim. "Ontstaan en Verbreiding", in *In het Huis van de Islam*, edited by Henk Driessen. Nijmegen: SUN. (1997): 31–58.
Ricoeur, Paul. *Oneself as Another*. Chicago and London: Chicago University Press, 1992.
Ricoeur, Paul. "Life in Quest of Narrative", in *On Paul Ricoeur. Narrative and Interpretation*, edited by David Wood. London and New York: Routledge. (1991).
Risseeuw, Carla and Rajni Palriwala. *Shifting Circles of Support*. Delhi: Sage, 1996.

Risseeuw, Carla. *The Fish Don't Talk About the Water. Gender Transformation, Power and Resistance Among Women in Sri Lanka.* Dehli: Manohar, 1991 (1988).

Risseeuw, Carla and Kamala Ganesh. *Negotiation and Social Space. A Gendered Analysis of Changing Kin and Security Networks in South Asia and Sub-Saharan Africa.* Delhi: Sage, 1988.

Robberts, Pepe and David Seddon. "Fundamentalism in Africa. Religion and Politics", *Review of African Political Economy*, 52 (1991): 3–8.

Roded, Ruth (ed.). *Women in Islam and the Middle East. A Reader.* London: I.B. Tauris, 1999.

Roded, Ruth. *Women in Islamic Biographical Collections. From Ibn Sa'd to Who's Who.* Boulder Colorado: Lienne Rienner, 1994.

Rosaldo; R. *Culture and Truth. The Remaking of Social Analysis.* Boston: Beacon Press, 1989.

Rosander, E.E. "Introduction", in *African Islam and Islam in Africa. Encounter between Sufis and Islamists*, edited by D. Westerlund and E.E. Rosander. London: Hurst & Company (1997).

Rose, Nikolas S. *Inventing Ourselves. Psychology, Power, and Personhood.* Cambridge and New York: Cambridge University Press, 1996.

Rünger, Mechthild. *Land Law and Land Use Control in Western Sudan. The Case of Southern Darfur.* London: Ithaca Press, 1987.

Ryle, John, "Disaster in Darfur", *The New York Review of Books*, 12 August 2004, 51, no. 13 (http://www.nybooks.com/articles/17326).

Sahgal, Gita and Nira Yuval-Davis. "The Uses of Fundamentalism. Response to Nederveen Pieterse", *Women Against Fundamentalism* 5 (1994): 7–9.

Sahgal, Gita and Nira Yuval-Davis. *Refusing Holy Orders. Women and Fundamentalism in Britain.* London: Virago Press, 1992.

Said, Edward W. *Covering Islam. How the Media and the Experts Determine How We See the Rest of the World.* New York: Pantheon Books, 1981.

Said, Edward W. *Orientalism.* New York: Penguin Books, 1978.

Salih, Sarah (ed.) with Judith Butler. *The Judith Butler Reader.* Oxford: Blackwell Publishing, 2005.

Sanasarian, Eliz. "The Politics of Gender and Development in the Islamic Republic of Iran", in *Women and Development the Middle East and North Africa*, edited by Joseph G. Jabbra and Nancy W. Jabbra. Leiden: Brill. (1992): 56–69.

Santen, José C.M. van. *They Leave Their Jars Behind. The Conversion of Mafa Women to Islam (North Cameroon).* Leiden: VENA Publications, University of Leiden, 1993.

Santen, José van and Karin Willemse. "The Issue of 'Islamic fundamentalisms', Masculinities and Femininities. A Joint Introduction", in *Transformations of Islam in Africa*, edited by Wim van Binsbergen, Anneke Breedveld and José van Santen. Leiden: Brill. (forthcoming).

Santen, José C.M. van and Karin Willemse. "Fundamentalismen. Discourses over Mannelijkheid en Vrouwelijkheid", Discussiestuk Lova Studiedag 28-5-1999. *Lova Tijdschrift* 20, no.1 (1999): 4–13.

Sayigh, Rosemary. "Roles and Functions of Arab women. A Reappraisal", *Arab Studies Quarterly* 3, no.3 (1981): 258–274.

Sayyid, Bobby. *A Fundamental Fear. Eurocentrism and the Emergence of Islamism.* London: Zed Books Ltd, 1997.
Sayyid, Bobby. "Sign O' times. Kaffirs and Infidels Fighting the Ninth Crusade", in *The Making of Political Identities*, edited by Ernesto Laclau. London: Verso. (1994).
Schneider, David. *A Critique of the Study of Kinship.* Ann Arbor: The University of Michigan Press, 1984.
Schrijvers, Joke. "Fighters, Victims and Survivors. Constructions of Ethnicity, Gender and Refugeeness among Tamils in Sri Lanka", *Journal of Refugee Studies* 12, no.3 (1999): 307–333.
Schrijvers, Joke. "Internal Refugees in Sri Lanka. The Interplay of Ethnicity and Gender". *The European Journal of Development Research* 9, no.2 (1997): 62–83.
Schrijvers, Joke. "Participation and Power. A Transformative Feminist Research Perspective", in: *Power and Participatory Development. Theory and Practice*, edited by Susan Wright and Nici Nelson. London: Intermediate technology Publications. (1995): 19–29.
Schrijvers, Joke. "Motherhood Experienced and Conceptualised. Changing Images in Sri Lanka and the Netherlands", in *Gendered Fields. Women, Men and Ethnography*, edited by Diane Bell, Pat Caplan and Wazir Jahan Karim. New York and London: Routledge. (1993): 143–157.
Schrijvers, Joke. *De Boodschap van het Vijfde Ontwikkelingsdecennium.* Inaugurele Rede, Utrecht: Van Arkel, 1992.
Schrijvers, Joke. "Dialectics of a Dialogical Ideal. Studying Down, Studying Sideways and Studying Up", in *Constructing Knowledge. Authority and Critique in Social Science*, edited by Lorraine Nencel and Peter Pels. London: Sage Publications. (1991).
Schrijvers, Joke. *Mothers for Life. Motherhood and Marginalization in the North Central Province of Sri Lanka.* Delft: Eburon, 1985.
Schrijvers, Joke. "Viricentrism and Anthropology", in *The Politics of Anthropology*, edited by G. Huizer and B. Mannheim. The Hague: Mouton. (1979): 97–117.
Scholte, Bob. "Towards a Reflexive and Critical Anthropology", in *Reinventing Anthropology*, edited by D. Hymes. New York: Vintage Books. (1974): 430–457.
Scott, James. *Everyday Forms of Peasant Resistance.* New Haven: Yale University Press, 1985.
Scott, Joan W. "The Evidence of Experience", *Critical Inquiry* 17, Summer (1991): 773–797.
Scott, Joan W. "Gender. A Useful Category of Analysis?", in *Gender and the Politics of History*, edited by J.W. Scott. New York: Columbia University Press. (1988).
Seuren, Germa. 1998. *Opvattingen over Moederschap en Werk. Een Onderzoek aan Ahfad University for Women in Sudan.* Scriptie Buitenlands Leeronderzoek CA/SNWS. Leiden: RUL, 1998. (n.p.)
Shahi, Ahmed Al-. 1990. "Response to Nimeiri's Policies. Some Observations on Social and Political Changes in Northern Sudan", in *Sudan, 1898–1989. The Unstable State*, edited by Peter Woodward. Boulder, CO: Lynne Rienner Publishers. (1990).

Shami, Sheteney. "Transnationalism and Refugee Studies. Rethinking forced Migration and Identity in the Middle East". *The Elizabeth Colson Lecture*, Refugee Studies Programme. Queen Elizabeth House, Oxford: Oxford University. 1995. (n.p.)

Shazali, Salah El-Din, El-. *Peripheral Urbanism and the Sudan. Explorations in the Political Economy of the Wage Labour Market in Greater Khartoum, 1900–1984*. Ph.D. Thesis, University of Hull, 1985.

Shostak, Marjorie. *Nisa. The Life and Words of a !Kung Woman*. New York: Vintage books, 1981. (also published by Suffolk: Penguin Books, 1983).

Silberschmidt, Margarethe. "Disempowerment of Men in Rural and Urban East Africa. Implications for Male Identity and Sexual Behaviour", *World Development* 29 no.4 (2001): 657–671.

Silberstein, Laurence, J. "Mapping, Not Tracing. Opening Reflection", in *Mapping Jewish Identities*, edited by Laurence J. Silberstein. New York: New York University Press. (2000): 1–36.

Silberstein, Laurence, J. (ed.). *Jewish Fundamentalism in Comparative Perspective. Religion, Ideology, and the Crisis of Modernity*. New York: New York University Press, 1993.

Silberstein, Laurence, J. 1993. "Religion, Ideology, Modernity. Theoretical Issues in the Study of Jewish Fundamentalism", in *Jewish Fundamentalism in Comparative Perspective. Religion, Ideology, and the Crisis of Modernity*, edited by Laurence Silberstein. New York: New York University Press. (1993).

Simone, T. Abdou Maliqalim. *In Whose Image? Political Islam and Urban Practices in Sudan*. Chicago and London: The University of Chicago Press, 1994.

Slot, Corry and Hamid Rushwan, *Female Circumcision in the Sudan. Prevalence, Complications, Attitudes and Change. A Report of a Study Conducted by the Faculty of Medicine, University of Khartoum, Sudan (1977–1982)*. Khartoum: University of Khartoum, Faculty of Medicine, 1983.

Smith, Dorothy. *The Conceptual Practices of Power. A Feminist Sociology of Knowledge*. Boston: Northeastern University Press, 1990a.

Smith, Dorothy. *Texts, Facts and Femininity. Exploring the Relations of Ruling*. London: Routledge, 1990b.

Smith, Dorothy. *The Everyday World as Problematic. A Feminist Sociology*. Boston: Northeastern University Press, 1987.

Smith, M.G. *Baba of Karo. A Woman of the Hausa*. New York: Philosophical Library, 1955.

Spaulding, Jay. *The Heroic Age in Sinnar*. Ethiopian Series Monograph no. 15, East Lansing: Michigan State University, 1985.

Spivak, Gayatri C. "Three Women's Texts and Critique of Imperialism", in *The Postcolonial Studies Reader*, edited by Bill Ashcroft, Gareth Griffiths, and Helen Tiffin. Routledge: London. (1995): 269–273.

Spivak, Gayatri C. *The Postcolonial Critic. Interviews, Strategies, Dialogues*. Sarah Harasym (ed.). Routledge: London, 1988a.

Spivak, Gayatri C. "Can the Subaltern Speak?", in *Marxism and the Interpretation of Culture*, edited by C. Nelson and L. Grossberg. Basingstoke: Macmillan Education. (1988b): 271–313.

Stacey, Judith. "Can There be a Feminist Ethnology?", in *Women's Words. The Feminist Practice of Oral History*, edited by Sherna Berger Gluck and Daphne Patai. New York and London: Routledge. (1991).

Stiansen, Endre and Michael Kevane (eds.). *Kordofan Invaded. Peripheral Incorporation and Social Transformation in Islamic Africa*. Leiden: Brill, 1998.

Stoler, Ann. "Carnal Knowledge and Imperial Power. Gender, Race, and Morality in Colonial Asia", in *Gender at the Crossroads of Knowledge. Feminist Anthropology the Postmodern Era*, edited by Micaela di Leonardo. Berkely: University of California Press. (1991).

Taheri, Amir. *The Spirit of Allah. Khomeini and the Islamic Revolution*. Maryland: Adler & Adler Publishers Inc., 1985 (appendix 2, 317–320).

Tamari, Tal. "The Development of Caste Systems in West Africa", The Journal of African History 32, no.2 (1991): 221–250.

Theobald, A.B. *'Ali Dinar. Last Sultan of Darfur, 1898–1916*. London: Longmans, Green and Co, 1965.

Theobald, A.B. "Darfur and its Neighbours Under Sultan Ali Dinar 1898–1916", *Sudan Notes and Records* 40 (1959): 113–120.

Thesiger, Wilfred. *The Life of My Choice*. London: Collins, 1987.

Tohidi, Nayereh and Jane H. Bayes, "Women Redefining Modernity and Religion in the Globalized Context", in *Globalization, Gender and Religion. The Politics of Women's Rights in Catholic and Muslim Contexts*, edited by Nayereh Tohidi and Jane H. Bayes. New York: Palgrave. (2001): 17–61.

Torsvik, Bente. *Receiving Gifts of Allah. The Establishment of a Modern Midwifery Service in the Sudan 1920–1937*. Bergen, 1983 (n.p.).

Trinh, Minh-ha, Thi. *Framer Framed*. New York: Routledge, 1992.

Trinh, Minh-ha, Thi. *Women, Native, Other. Writing Postcoloniality and Feminism*. Bloomington: Indiana University Press, 1989.

Tubiana, Marie-Jose and Joseph Tubiana. *The Zaghawa from an Ecological Perspective. Foodgathering, the Pastoral System, Tradition and Development of the Zaghawa of the Sudan and the Chad*. Rotterdam: Balkema, 1977.

Tucker, Judith E. (ed.). *Arab Women. Old Boundaries, New Frontiers*. Bloomington and Indianapolis: Indiana University Press, 1993.

Tully, Dennis. *Culture and Context in Sudan. The Process of Market Incorporation in Dar Masalit*. New York: State University of New York Press, 1988.

Umbadda, Siddig and Abdul-Jalil, Musa Adam. *Problems and Prospects of Horticulture in a Subsistence Economy. Wadi Kutum (Sudan)* The Hague: ISS, 1984.

Uyl, Marion den. *Onzichtbare Muren. Over het Verinnerlijken van Seksuele Grenzen. Een Onderzoek in een Dorp in Zuid-India*. Utrecht: Jan van Arkel, 1992.

Villareal, M. *Wielding and Yielding. Power, Subordination and Gender Identity in the Context of a Mexican Development Project*. Ph. D. dissertation Wageningen: U.R, 1994.

Voll, J.O. 1983. "The Evolution of Islamic Fundamentalism in Twentieth-Century Sudan", in *Islam, Nationalism, and Radicalism in Egypt and Sudan*, edited by G.R. Warburg and U.M. Kupferschmidt. New York: Praeger Publishers. (1983): 113–142.

Vries, Hent de. *Religion and Violence. Philosophical Perspectives from Kant to Derrida*. Baltimore, Md.: John Hopkins University Press, 2002.

Vries, Hent de and Samuel Weber (eds.). *Violence, Identity, and Self-Determination.* Stanford, CA: Stanford University Press, 1997.

Waal, Alexander de. *Islamism and its Enemies in the Horn of Africa.* London: Hurst & Company, 2004.

Waal, Alexander de. "Sudan. Searching for the Origins of Absolutism and Decay", Review article, *Development and Change* 24, (1993): 177–202.

Waal, Alexander de. *Famine That Kills, Darfur, Sudan, 1984–1985.* Oxford: Clarendon Press, 1989.

Warburg, Gabriel. *Islam, Sectarianism and Politics in the Sudan since the Mahdiyya.* London: Hurst, 2003.

Warburg, Gabriel. *Islam, Nationalism and Communism in a Traditional Society. The Case of Sudan.* London: Cass, 1978.

Watson, Helen, 1994. "Women and the Veil. Personal Responses to Global Processes", in *Islam, Globalisation and Modernity*, edited by S. Ahmed Akbar and Donnan Hastings. London: Routledge. (1994).

Wekker, Gloria. "Praten in het Donker. Reflecties op de Praktijk van het Weten in Nederlandse Vrouwenstudies", in *Praten in het Donker. Multiculturalisme en Anti-Racisme in een Feministisch Perspectief*, edited by Gloria Wekker and Rosi Braidotti. Kampen: Kok Agora. (1996a): 1–14.

Wekker, Gloria. "Praten in het Donker", in: *Praten in het Donker. Multiculturalisme en Anti-Racisime in Feministisch Perspectief*, edited by Gloria Wekker and Rosi Braidotti. Kampen: Kok Agora (1996b): 57–88.

Werbner, Richard (ed.). *Memory and the Post-Colony. African Anthropology and the Critique of Power.* London: Zed Books, 1998.

Werbner, Richard and Terence Ranger (eds.). *Postcolonial Identities in Africa.* London: Zed Books, 1996.

Weekes, Richard (ed.). *Muslim peoples. A World Ethnographic Survey.* London: Aldwych Press, 1984.

Weiss, Anita M. "Challenges for Muslim Women in a Post-Modern World", in *Islam, Globalisation and Modernity*, edited by S. Ahmed Akbar and Donnan Hastings. London: Routledge. (1994).

Wel, Paul van der and Abdel Ghaffar Mohamed Ahmed (eds.). *Perspectives on Development in the Sudan.* Selected Papers from a Research Workshop in The Hague. The Hague: Institute of Social Studies, July 1984.

Westerlund, D. and E.E. Rosander. *African Islam and Islam in Africa. Encounter Between Sufis and Islamists.* London: Hurst & Company, 1997.

White, H. "The Value of Narrativity in the Representation of Reality", in *On Narrative*, edited by W.J.T. Mitchell. Chicago & London: University of Chicago Press. (1981): 1–23.

Wilford, Rick. "Women, Ethnicity and Nationalism. Surveying the Ground", in *Women, Ethnicity and Nationalism. The Politics of Transition*, edited by Rick Wilford and Robert L. Miller. London and New York: Routledge. (1998).

Willemse, Karin. "'In My Father's House'. Gender, Islam and the Construction of a Gendered Public Sphere in Darfur", Sudan. *Journal for Islamic Studies* Special Issue: 'Islam and African Muslim Publics', vol. 27, (f.c. 2007): 72–113

Willemse, Karin. "Structures of Violence in Darfur. Interview Jan Pronk", *ISIM Review*, Spring (2007): 58–59.

Willemse, Karin. "'A Room of One's Own'. Single Female Teachers Negotiating Alternative Gender Roles", *Northeast African Studies Journal*, Special Issue 'Women in the Horn of Africa' VIII, no.3 (2006). Back issue 2001: 99–128.

Willemse, Karin. "On Globalization, Gender and the Nation-State. Muslim Masculinity and the Urban Middle-Class Family in Islamist Sudan", in *The Gender Question in Globalization. Changing Perspectives and Practices*, edited by Tine Davids and Francien van Driel. Burlington USA: Ashgate Publishers. (2005a): 159–179.

Willemse, Karin. "From Modern Myths to Global Encounters. Ph.D. Students Journeying with Peter Geschiere", in *From Modern Myths to Global Encounters. Belonging and Dynamics of Change in Post-Colonial Africa.* A Liber Discipilorum in honour of Peter Geschiere, edited by Anke van der Kwaak, Rachel Spronk and Karin Willemse. Leiden: CNWS-Publications. (2005b): 31–37.

Willemse, Karin. "Darfur in War. The Politicisation of Ethnic Identities?" *ISIM Review* 15, Spring (2005c): 14–15.

Willemse, Karin. "The Burden of Boundaries. The Construction of Masculinities", in *Transformations of Islam in Africa*, edited by Wim van Binsbergen, Anneke Breedveld, & José van Santen. Leiden: Brill. (forthcoming).

Willemse, Karin, with Nawal H. Osman and Catrien Bijleveld. "'One from the heart'. Family and Friends in Al-Halla, West-Sudan", in *Negotiation and Social Space. A Gendered Analysis of Changing Kin and Security Networks in South Asia and Sub-Saharan Africa*, edited by Carla Risseeuw and Kamala Ganesh. New Delhi: Sage. (1998).

Willemse, Karin. *Werken Maakt Sterk. Een Antroplogische Studie naar de Mate van Autonomie van Fur-Vrouwen in Jebel Marra, West-Soedan.* Leiden: VENA Publications, University of Leiden, 1990.

Willemse, Karin and Anke van der Kwaak, "*Karama* and *Ducayn*: Foreigners, Food and Gender in Sudan and Somalia", in *From Modern Myths to Global Encounters. Belonging and Dynamics of Change in Post-Colonial Africa.* A Liber Discipilorum in honour of Peter Geschiere, edited by Anke van der Kwaak, Rachel Spronk and Karin Willemse. Leiden: CNWS-Publications. (2005): 182–200.

Wohlmuth, Karl. "Alternative Economic Strategies for the Sudan", in: *Short-Cut to Decay. The Case of the Sudan*, edited by Sharif Harir and Terje Tvedt. Uppsala: Nordiska Afrikainstitutet. (1994): 204–247.

Woodward, Peter. "Constitutional Framework for Peace and Stability", in *Short-Cut to Decay. The Case of the Sudan*, edited by Sharif Harir and Terje Tvedt. Uppsala: Nordiska Afrikainstitutet (1994): 248–258.

Woodward, Peter (ed.). *Sudan after Nimeiri.* Centre for Near and Middle Eastern Studies. (SOAS) London: Routledge, 1991.

Woodward, Peter. *Sudan, 1898–1989. The Unstable State.* Boulder, CO: Lynne Rienner Publishers, 1990.

Woodward, Peter. "Islam, Radicalism, and Nationalism in Sudanese Politics Before Independence", in *Islam, Nationalism, and Radicalism in Egypt and Sudan*, edited by G.R. Warburg and U.M. Kupferschmidt. New York: Praeger Publishers. (1983): 97–110.

Woodward, Peter. *Condominium and Sudanese Nationalism.* London: Rex Collings, 1979.
Yegenoglu, Meyda. *Colonial Fantasies. Towards a Feminist Reading of Orientalism.* Cambridge: Cambridge University Press, 1998.
Zarkov, Dubravka. *From "Media War" to "Ethnic War". The Female Body and the Production of Ethnicity in former Yugoslavia (1986–1994).* Ph.d. Dissertation, Nijmegen: Catholic University of Nijmegen, 1999.
Zur, Judith. "Remembering and Forgetting. Guatemalan War Widows' Forbidden Memories", in *Trauma and Life Stories. International Perspectives,* edited by Kim Lacy Rogers and Selma Leydesdorff with Graham Dawson. London and New York: Routledge. (1999).

Internet sources

Bol, Nhial. "Managing Their Lives for Them", *IPS,* (published on the Internet 20-9-1996; SudanList@emuv1.1d/1.7f—subject 'offical marriages'): accessed 2-9-1997.
Darfur Conflict (http://en.wikipedia.org/wiki/Darfur_conflict): accessed 05-01-2006.
'President, Mrs. Bush mark progress in global women's human rights. Remarks by the First Lady and the President on efforts to globally promote women's human rights' (The East Room, March 12, 2004, 2,34 p.m.–3.08 p.m. EST;) (http:/www.whitehouse.gov/news/releases/2004/03/20040312-5.html): accessed 24-09-2005.
Ryle, John, "Disaster in Darfur", *The New York Review of Books,* 12 August 2004, 51, no. 13 (http://www.nybooks.com/articles/17326): accessed 24-09-2005.
Viner, Katharine. "Feminism as Imperialism. George Bush is Not the First Empire-Builder to Wage War in the Name of Women", *The Guardian* (UK), Saturday, September 21 (2002) (http://www.commondreams.org/views02/0923-07.htm): accessed 24-10-2005.
Waal, Alexander de. "Counter-insurgency on the cheap" *London Review of Books* 26, no.15 (2004), August 5, (2004), (http://www.lrb.co.uk/v26/n15/waal01.html): accessed 6-10-2004.

Sudan Maps

Sudan Map 1: Sudan (Political), 2000: retrieved from the "Perry-Castañeda Library Map Collection" of the University of Texas at Austin (http://www.lib.utexas.edu/maps/africa/sudan poloo.pdf, source: U.S. Intelligence Agency): accessed 17-09-2007.
Sudan Map 2: Sudan (Tribes) 1961 [1949]. Source: Sudan Survey Department Khartoum (Map collection Sudan, Africa Studies Centre, Leiden University)
Sudan Map 3: Sudan (Political, in Arabic) 1961 [1952]. Source: Sudan Survey Department Khartoum (Map collection Sudan, Africa Studies Centre)

ANNEX I

TABLES WITH SOME RESULTS FROM THE SURVEY IN KEBKABIYA TOWN 1991

Table 1. *Distribution of age*

15–20	3.4 %
21–25	11.2 %
26–30	16.5 %
31–35	10.7 %
36–40	6.3 %
41–45	3.4 %
46–50	7.3 %
>50	8.7 %

N = 139

source: survey Willemse and Osman. 1991
The total number of inhabitants was about 10.000 to 15.000 in 1991. This figure is highly unreliable due to in- and outmigration which is not registered. For the state of Darfur no reliable figures are available either. About one milion people is often quoted as an approximate.

Table 2. *Birthplace of migrants to Kebkabiya during drought periods*

Kebkabiya and vicinity	41.6 %
Al-Fasher district*	20.8 %
Darfur	20.9 %
Dar Sabah**	4.2 %
Southern Sudan***	12.5 %

N = 24

* Al-Fasher is the capital of North Darfur
** Central and East Sudan
*** Women whose husbands serve in the army

source: survey Willemse and Osman 1991

Table 3. *Arrival in Kebkabiya*

before independence	26 %
before Nimeiri (1969)	20 %
1970–1977	19 %
1978–1983	14 %
during the drought of '84–'85	12 %
Recently	9 %

N = 109

source: survey Willemse and Osman 1991

Table 4. *Marriage patterns: ethnic background husband and father**

ethnic background husband	*ethnic background father*						
	Fur	*Arab*	*Jellaba*	*Zaghawa*	*Tama*	*Tunjur*	*Other*
Fur	19.2 %	–	–	–	.7 %	.7 %	.7 %
Arab&Bagarra	1.3 %	9.3 %	.7 %	1.3 %	.7 %	–	.7 %
Jellaba Howara	–	–	1.3 %	–	–	–	1.3 %
Zaghawa	–	–	.7 %	17.2 %	.7 %	–	–
Tama	.7 %	2.0 %	–	.7 %	15.9 %	1.3 %	.7 %
Tunjur	.7 %	.7 %	1.3 %	–	–	6.0 %	–
Other	2.0 %	1.3 %	–	.7 %	2.0 %	–	7.9 %

N = 151

*As people are indicated with the ethnic group of the father the background of the mother is not given here. However, about the same percentages were found for background of husband and mothet. This might indicate an even higher endogamic marriage pattern for former generations.

source: survey Willemse and Osman 1991

Table 5. *Female headed households*

	husband in the household	*husband not in the household*
Married	61 %	13 %
divorced	–	10 %
widowed	–	16 %
unmarried	–	1 %

N = 132

source: survey Willemse and Osman 1991

Table 6. *Land: ownership * and average size owned*

	ownership	*average size*
land owned by woman	79 %	3.8 feddan
land owned by husband	16 %	3.9 feddan
land owned by son**	2 %	2.5 feddan
land shared with relative	4 %	4.3 feddan***

N = 113

* 'ownership' means usufruct rights, not private property.
** daughters were not mentioned
*** 1 feddan = 0.4 hectare approx.

source: survey Willemse and Osman 1991

Table 7. *Work on the land*

land worked on by woman	71 %
land worked on by husband	15 %
land worked on by children	3 %
land worked on by relatives	5 %
land worked on by the family and labourers	5 %

N = 59

source: survey Willemse and Osman 1991

Table 8. *Education by age*

	15–20*	21–25	26–30	31–35	36–40	41–45	46–50	>50
none	1 %	7 %	7 %	10 %	9 %	2 %	5 %	8 %
Khalwa	1 %	1 %	3 %	–	1 %	3 %	6 %	4 %
part of primary school	–	1 %	3 %	4 %	4 %	–	–	–
Primary school	1 %	2 %	7 %	1 %	1 %	–	–	–
intermediate	1 %	2 %	3 %	1 %	–	–	–	–
secondary	–	–	–	–	1 %	–	–	–

N = 135

*in this cohort persons are still school going and might go on to higher levels of education

source: survey Willemse and Osman 1991

INDEX

WOMEN AND GENDER THE MIDDLE EAST AND THE ISLAMIC WORLD

ISSN 1570-7628

1. Sadiqi, F. *Women, Gender and Language in Morocco*. 2003.
   ISBN 90 04 12853 0
2. Jawad, H. and Benn, T. *Muslim Women in the United Kingdom and Beyond*: Experiences and Images. 2003.
   ISBN 90 04 12581 7
3. Droeber, J. *Dreaming of Change: Young Middle-Class Women and Social Transformation in Jordan*. 2005.
   ISBN 90 04 14634 2
4. Torab, A. *Performing Islam*. Gender and Ritual in Iran. 2006.
   ISBN-10: 90 04 15295 4, ISBN-13: 978 90 04 15295 3
5. Willemse, K. *One Foot in Heaven*. Narratives on Gender and Islam in Darfur, West-Sudan. 2007. ISBN 978 90 04 15011 9